T0391780

THE OXFORD HANDBOOK OF

TWENTIETH-CENTURY AMERICAN LITERATURE

THE OXFORD HANDBOOK OF

TWENTIETH-CENTURY AMERICAN LITERATURE

Edited by
LESLIE BOW *and* RUSS CASTRONOVO

OXFORD
UNIVERSITY PRESS

OXFORD
UNIVERSITY PRESS

Great Clarendon Street, Oxford, OX2 6DP,
United Kingdom

Oxford University Press is a department of the University of Oxford.
It furthers the University's objective of excellence in research, scholarship,
and education by publishing worldwide. Oxford is a registered trade mark of
Oxford University Press in the UK and in certain other countries

© The several contributors 2022

The moral rights of the authors have been asserted

First Edition published in 2022

Impression: 1

All rights reserved. No part of this publication may be reproduced, stored in
a retrieval system, or transmitted, in any form or by any means, without the
prior permission in writing of Oxford University Press, or as expressly permitted
by law, by licence or under terms agreed with the appropriate reprographics
rights organization. Enquiries concerning reproduction outside the scope of the
above should be sent to the Rights Department, Oxford University Press, at the
address above

You must not circulate this work in any other form
and you must impose this same condition on any acquirer

Published in the United States of America by Oxford University Press
198 Madison Avenue, New York, NY 10016, United States of America

British Library Cataloguing in Publication Data

Data available

Library of Congress Control Number: 2022935317

ISBN 978–0–19–882403–9

DOI: 10.1093/oxfordhb/9780198824039.001.0001

Printed and bound by
CPI Group (UK) Ltd, Croydon, CR0 4YY

Links to third party websites are provided by Oxford in good faith and
for information only. Oxford disclaims any responsibility for the materials
contained in any third party website referenced in this work.

List of Contents

List of Figures ix
List of Contributors xi
List of Abbreviations xv

Introduction: Structures, Movements, Attachments, Imaginaries 1
LESLIE BOW AND RUSS CASTRONOVO

PART 1 STRUCTURES

1. The Book of Love is Long and Boring: Reading Aloud, Care Work, and Children's Literature 15
ELIZABETH FREEMAN

2. Colonization to Climate Change: American Literature and a Planet on Fire 40
JOHN LEVI BARNARD

3. Nuclear Poetry: Cultural Containment and Translational Leakage in Robert Lowell's *For the Union Dead* 59
SIMON VAN SCHALKWYK

4. Precarious Forms: Reading Labor in and beyond the Neoliberal Novel 78
JOSEPH B. ENTIN

5. Asian Americans in the Novel of Late Capitalism: Samuel R. Delany's *The Mad Man* and Kevin Kwan's *Crazy Rich Asians* 98
CYNTHIA WU

PART 2 MOVEMENTS

6. The Hidden Voice: Indigenous Experience and Authenticity in Twentieth-Century American Literature 115
SEAN TEUTON

7. "Jumpin' with Symphony Sid": Post-1945 American Literature and Radio 135
   Lisa Hollenbach

8. Faulkner at the Speed of History 153
   Mark Goble

9. Twentieth-Century Western Man of Color: Richard Wright, Race, and Rootlessness 171
   Yogita Goyal

10. "Warm with Tipsy Embraces": Allen Ginsberg, the US–China Writers' Conferences, and Queer Internationalism 189
    Harilaos Stecopoulos

PART 3 ATTACHMENTS

11. *The Last Puritan* in Shanghai: The Faded Romance of China Trade Finance and the Queerly Transnational Melancholy of Emily Hahn's Wartime Opium Smoking 209
    Kendall Johnson

12. Modernism's Cares: Reading For and With 246
    Rachel Adams

13. Black Literary History and the Problem of Identification in Ishmael Reed's *Mumbo Jumbo* 264
    Aida Levy-Hussen

14. Andrea Lee's Europe: Race, Interracial Desire, and Transnationalism 281
    Melissa Daniels-Rauterkus

15. Where Border Meets Narrative, Where Body Meets Word: The Animality of Border Subjectivity 299
    Bernadine Hernández

PART 4 IMAGINARIES

16. Of Canons and Cabinets: Indigenous Bodies, Epistemological Spectacle, and an Unusual Indian in the Cupboard 321
    Becca Gercken

17. The Liberal Imagination Revisited: Saul Bellow, Ralph Ellison, and
    the Crisis of Democracy   337
    JOHANNES VOELZ

18. Constructing Whiteness: Faulkner, Ferber, and the American Racial
    Imagination   356
    HEIDI KIM

19. Unidentified Flying Objects: Conceptualism, Interpretation, and
    Adrian Piper   380
    RACHEL JANE CARROLL

20. Cultural Memory Studies and the *Beloved* Paradigm: From
    Rememory to Abolition in the Afterlives of Slavery   398
    MICHAEL ROTHBERG

Index   417

List of Figures

Figure 1.1	Sound table for letters A–L from Johan Amos Comenius, *Orbis Pictus* (1887 [1685]), Facsimile Reproduction (Whitefish, Montana: Kessinger Publishing), p. 3. Public domain.	21
Figure 1.2	The Voom from Dr Seuss (Theodor Geisel), *The Cat in the Hat Comes Back* (New York: Random House, 1958), pp. 58–59	31
Figure 1.3	From Dr Seuss (Theodor Geisel), *On Beyond Zebra!* (New York: Random House, 1958). Unpaginated	32
Figure 1.4	From Dr Seuss (Theodor Geisel), *On Beyond Zebra!* (New York: Random House, 1958). Unpaginated	33
Figure 1.5	"Waz" from http://www.iheartspeech.com/2013/07/skill-focus-writing-create-your-own.html. Photo by Lauren Barnett, courtesy of Lauren Barnett.	34
Figure 1.6	"Paxter Wanwi" from http://www.iheartspeech.com/2013/07/skill-focus-writing-create-your-own.html. Photo by Lauren Barnett, courtesy of Lauren Barnett.	35
Figure 8.1	Still from *What Price Hollywood?* (George Cukor, RKO Pictures, 1932)	156
Figure 8.2	Eadweard Muybridge from *The Horse in Motion* (1878). Library of Congress Prints and Photographs Division Washington, D.C.	164
Figure 11.1	"Russell Sturgis" from a painting by George Richmond. From *Some Merchants and Sea Captains of Old Boston* (1918), p. viii 'One of the best-known merchants of his time. He was partner of Russell & Sturgis and of Russell, Sturgis & Co.; of Russell & Co., after the consolidation of the two latter firms. He was later partner and, finally, head of Baring Brothers of London.	212
Figure 11.2	Book cover with Hahn's Chinese name, "Sha Mei-Lee" or 項美麗 (Xiàng Měi-lì).	233

List of Contributors

Rachel Adams, Columbia University. Rachel Adams is Professor of English and Comparative Literature and Provost's Senior Faculty Teaching Scholar at Columbia University where she teaches 20th and 21st century American literature. She is the author of three books: *Raising Henry: A Memoir of Motherhood, Disability, and Discovery*; *Continental Divides: Remapping the Cultures of North America*; and *Sideshow U.S.A.: Freaks and the American Cultural Imagination*. The chapter in this collection comes from her current book project on dependency, care, and narrative, which was recognized by a 2019-2020 Guggenheim Fellowship.

John Levi Barnard, University of Illinois, Urbana-Champaign. John Levi Barnard is Associate Professor of English and Comparative Literature and faculty affiliate with the Institute for Sustainability, Energy, and Environment at the University of Illinois, Urbana-Champaign. He is the author of *Empire of Ruin: Black Classicism and American Imperial Culture* (Oxford, 2018). His work on the ecological ramifications of US empire has appeared in *American Literature*, *American Quarterly*, and *Resilience: A Journal of the Environmental Humanities*.

Leslie Bow, University of Wisconsin-Madison. Leslie Bow is Vilas Distinguished Achievement Professor of English and Asian American Studies and Draheim Professor of English at the University of Wisconsin-Madison. She is the author of the award-winning *'Partly Colored': Asian Americans and Racial Anomaly in the Segregated South* (New York University Press, 2010); *Betrayal and Other Acts of Subversion: Feminism, Sexual Politics, Asian American Women's Literature* (Princeton University Press, 2001); and *Racist Love: Asian Abstraction and the Pleasures of Fantasy* (Duke University Press, 2022).

Rachel Jane Carroll, University of Illinois, Urbana-Champaign. Rachel Jane Carroll is an ACLS Emerging Voices Fellow and Humanities Postdoctoral Fellow at the University of Illinois, Urbana-Champaign. Her work can be found in *Social Text*, *Criticism: A Quarterly for Literature and the Arts*, *ASAP/J*, and the *Los Angeles Review of Books*. Her book, *Reading for Pleasure: Race and Aesthetics in American Experimentalism*, is forthcoming with New York University Press.

Russ Castronovo, University of Wisconsin-Madison. Russ Castronovo is Tom Paine Professor of English and Dorothy Draheim Professor of American Studies at the University of Wisconsin–Madison. He is author of four books: *Fathering the Nation: American Genealogies of Slavery and Freedom* (University of California Press, 1995); *Necro Citizenship: Death, Eroticism, and the Public Sphere* in the Nineteenth-Century United States (Duke University Press, 2001); *Beautiful Democracy: Aesthetics and Anarchy in a Global Era* (University of Chicago Press, 2007); and *Propaganda 1776: Secrets, Leaks, and Revolutionary Communications in Early America* (Oxford University Press, 2014).

Melissa Daniels-Rauterkus, University of Southern California. Melissa Daniels-Rauterkus is Associate Professor of English at the University of Southern California. She is the author of *Afro-Realisms and the Romances of Race: Rethinking Blackness in the African American Novel* (Louisiana State University Press, 2020), which won the SAMLA Studies Book Award and received Honorable Mention for the William Sanders Scarborough Prize from the MLA. She is currently at work on a monograph about Black expatriate women and interracial desire.

Joseph B. Entin, Brooklyn College, CUNY. Joseph B. Entin is Professor of English and American Studies at Brooklyn College, City University of New York. He is the author of *Sensational Modernism: Experimental Fiction and Photography in Thirties America* (2007), and co-editor of three other books: *Teaching American Studies: The State of the Classroom as State of the Field* (2021) with Elizabeth Duclos-Orsello and Rebecca Hill; *Remaking Reality: U.S. Documentary Culture after 1945* (2018) with Sara Blair and Franny Nudelman; and *Controversies in the Classroom: A Radical Teacher Reader* with Robert Rosen and Leonard Vogt (2008). His forthcoming book is, *Living Labor: Fiction, Film, and Precarious Work*, examines contemporary narratives of work and struggle in the context of global economic restructuring, transnational migration, and labor precarity.

Elizabeth Freeman, University of California, Davis. Elizabeth Freeman is Professor of English at the University of California, Davis. She has written three books published by Duke University Press: *The Wedding Complex* (2002), *Time Binds* (2010), and *Beside You in Time* (2019). She was editor of *GLQ* from 2011-2017 and her most recent book-length publication is *Crip Temporalities*, a special issue of *South Atlantic Quarterly* co-edited with Ellen Samuels.

Becca Gercken, University of Minnesota-Morris. Becca Gercken is a Morse Distinguished Teaching Associate Professor of English and American Indian Studies at the University of Minnesota-Morris. She is the co-editor of *Gambling on Authenticity: Gaming, the Noble Savage, and the Not-So-New Indian* (Michigan State University Press, 2017) as well numerous scholarly articles and book chapters. She is currently at work on a monograph about historical and contemporary American Indian ledger narratives.

Mark Goble, University of California, Berkeley. Mark Goble is Associate Professor of English at the University of California, Berkeley. He is the author of *Beautiful Circuits: Modernism and the Mediated Life* (Columbia University Press, 2010), and is currently at work on a book project entitled *Downtime: The Twentieth Century in Slow Motion*. His essays have appeared *ELH, MLQ, ELN, American Literature,* and in volumes on Alfred Hitchcock, Henry James, global modernism, and time and American literature. He also is a contributor to the *Los Angeles Review of Books*.

Yogita Goyal, University of California, Los Angeles. Yogita Goyal is Professor of African American Studies and English at University of California, Los Angeles and editor of the journal, *Contemporary Literature*. Her most recent book, *Runaway Genres: The Global Afterlives of Slavery* (NYU Press, 2019), received the René Wellek Prize from ACLA, the Perkins prize from the International Society for the Study of Narrative, and Honorable Mention for the James Russell Lowell Prize from MLA. The past president of Association for the Study of the Arts of the Present, she is the author of *Romance, Diaspora, and Black Atlantic Literature* (2010), editor of the *Cambridge Companion to Transnational American Literature* (2017), and the *Cambridge Companion to Contemporary African American Literature* (2022).

Bernadine Hernández, University of New Mexico. Bernadine Hernández is Assistant Professor of American Literary History at the University of New Mexico. She specializes in transnational feminism and the sexual economies of the US-Mexico borderlands, American literary and empire studies, border and migration history and theory, and Chicana/Latina literature. Her forthcoming book with UNC press is *Border Bodies: Racialized Sexuality, Sexual Capital, and Violence in the Nineteenth Century Borderlands*.

Lisa Hollenbach, Oklahoma State University. Lisa Hollenbach is an Assistant Professor of English at Oklahoma State University. Her work on post-1945 U.S. poetry and sound culture has been published in *American Literature, Modernism/modernity Print Plus,* and the *Chicago Review*. She is currently writing a book about American poetry and the FM revolution.

Kendall Johnson, University of Hong Kong. Kendall Johnson is Professor of American Literature at the University of Hong Kong where he researches material print culture in transnational and global historical frames of race, national, religion, and culture. He is the author of *The New Middle Kingdom: China and the Early American Romance of Free Trade* (Johns Hopkins University Press, 2017) and *Henry James and the Visual* (Cambridge University Press, 2007). He is the editor of *Narratives of Free Trade: The Commercial Cultures of Early US-China Relations* (HKU Press, 2012) and, with Yuan Shu and Otto Heim, a contributing co-editor of *Oceanic Archives, Indigenous Epistemologies, and Transpacific American Studies* (HKU Press, 2019). His work has appeared in *Modern Fiction Studies, American Literary History, American Literature, American Quarterly, Literature & History*.

Heidi Kim, University of North Carolina at Chapel Hill. Heidi Kim is Professor in the Department of English and Comparative Literature at University of North Carolina at Chapel Hill and Director of the Asian American Center. Her publications include *Illegal Immigrants/Model Minorities: The Cold War of Chinese American Narrative* (Temple UP, 2021), *Invisible Subjects: Asian America in Postwar Literature* (Oxford UP, 2016), and *Taken from the Paradise Isle: The Hoshida Family Story* (UP Colorado, 2015). Her current project is entitled *Beyond Reparations*.

Aida Levy-Hussen, University of Michigan. Aida Levy-Hussen is Associate Professor of English at the University of Michigan and the author of *How to Read African American Literature: Post-Civil Rights Fiction and the Task of Interpretation* (NYU, 2016). Her teaching and research foreground modern and contemporary African American literature, histories and theories of academic field formation, and memory studies and psychoanalysis.

Michael Rothberg, University of California, Los Angeles. Michael Rothberg is the 1939 Society Samuel Goetz Chair in Holocaust Studies and Professor of English and Comparative Literature at the University of California, Los Angeles. His latest book is *The Implicated Subject: Beyond Victims and Perpetrators* (2019), published by Stanford University Press in their "Cultural Memory in the Present" series. Previous books include *Multidirectional Memory: Remembering the Holocaust in the Age of Decolonization* (2009), *Traumatic Realism: The Demands of Holocaust Representation* (2000), and, co-edited with Neil Levi, *The Holocaust: Theoretical Readings* (2003).

Harilaos Stecopoulos, University of Iowa. Harilaos Stecopoulos is Associate Professor of English at the University of Iowa where he teaches US literature and creative writing. He is the author of *Reconstructing the World: Southern Fictions and U.S. Imperialisms, 1898-1976* (Cornell University Press, 2008). His new monograph is tentatively titled *Telling America's Story to the World: Literature, Internationalism, Cultural Diplomacy*.

Sean Teuton, University of Arkansas. Sean Teuton is Professor of English and Director of Indigenous Studies at the University of Arkansas, and the author of *Red Land, Red Power: Grounding Knowledge in the American Indian Novel* (Duke University Press, 2008) and *Native American Literature: A Very Short Introduction* (Oxford University Press, 2018). He is a citizen of the Cherokee Nation.

Simon van Schalkwyk, University of the Witwatersrand. Simon van Schalkwyk is a lecturer in the English department at the University of the Witwatersrand. He also serves as the academic editor for the *Johannesburg Review of Books*. His research focuses on American and World Literature with an emphasis on poetry, travel, and transnational modernism.

Johannes Voelz, University of Frankfurt. Johannes Voelz is Heisenberg Professor of American Studies, Democracy, and Aesthetics at Goethe University Frankfurt, Germany. He is the author of *Transcendental Resistance: The New Americanists and Emerson's Challenge* (UP New England, 2010), and *The Poetics of Insecurity: American Fiction and the Uses of Threat* (Cambridge UP, 2018). He is currently working on two book projects, one on the aesthetics of populism, the other on the transformation of privacy in contemporary American literature.

Cynthia Wu, Indiana University. Cynthia Wu is Professor of Gender Studies and Asian American Studies and Director of the Program in Race, Migration, and Indigeneity at Indiana University. She is the author of *Chang and Eng Reconnected: The Original Siamese Twins in American Culture* (Temple, 2012) and *Sticky Rice: A Politics of Intraracial Desire* (Temple, 2018).

List of Abbreviations

ARCO	Atlantic Richfield Company
AWC	Art Works Coalition
BIA	Bureau of Indian Affairs
#BLM	#Black Lives Matter
CCF	Congress of Cultural Freedom
CIA	Central Intelligence Agency
CIO	Congress of Industrial Organizations
CWA	Chinese Writers' Association
EIC	East India Company
MAD	Mutually Assured Destruction
NAACP	National Association for the Advancement of Colored People
NASA	National Aeronautics and Space Administration
NOAA	National Oceanic and Atmospheric Administration
PRC	People's Republic of China
UCLA	University of California, Los Angeles
UCRI	University of California Research Institute
UN	United Nations
USIA	United States Information Agency

INTRODUCTION
Structures, Movements, Attachments, Imaginaries

LESLIE BOW AND RUSS CASTRONOVO

DIVERSITY is the American brand. The poet William Carlos Williams famously turned this maxim inside out, distorting it in a poem that begins, "The pure products of America/go crazy." The fact that the subject at the center of Williams's ode is a mixed-raced woman named "Elsie" suggests how the ideological parameters of American diversity are borne more acutely and traumatically by some than by others. For Max Horkheimer and Theodor Adorno, writing as German-Jewish emigrés from Nazi Germany, these "products" would be the commodities of consumer capitalism, which, in all their shining and dazzling array, find unity under the homogenizing sameness of the American marketplace. Since then, the revival of rhetoric around the idea of an American "homeland" would combine with liberal multiculturalism, especially in its corporate and neoliberal forms, to emphasize diversity as a national brand that gives the United States a competitive economic, social, and even moral edge over other nations. This volume sits astride the tensions of diversity and unity, fragmentation and coherence, as they are expressed in national as well as global contexts.

The Oxford Handbook of Twentieth-Century American Literature is designed around an impossibility: that of representing the diversity of the texts and methodologies that comprise—as well as trouble—the field. Rather than attempt a compilation of 100 years' worth of novels, poetry, autobiography, and other forms of narration and writing that would provide an illusory notion of coverage or representation, this volume seeks to foreground the interstitial, the fissures, the "in-between" spaces within established histories, canons, genres, and ideologies. We suggest that the "in-between" represents a rich and productive site of literary inquiry, one that makes visible the multiple oppositions that structure and inspire literary and critical imaginaries. In challenging North/South, Black/white, urban/rural, national/transnational, high-culture/popular-culture, Indigenous/settler, or citizen/noncitizen binaries, for example, this anthology engages any number of continuums clustered around both realities and fantasies of difference. Highlighting these intersecting continuums—whether socio-political, generic, or identity-based—simultaneously maps and displaces, assembles and disassembles, locates and makes strange the body of texts and approaches that both constitute and defamiliarize the field of twentieth-century American literature.

The Oxford Handbook of Twentieth-Century American Literature testifies to the startling variety of content, approaches, and visions of US literature over the past 100 years. It registers pluralism at the level of form and genre as well: in addition to engaging established literary genres and canonical texts that readers might expect, it also devotes critical attention to film, performance art, children's books, memoir, and literary and cultural theory. These forms of expression might be taken, in part, as the equivalent of the sociological diversity that exists in conflict with demands for national coherence. These tensions over representation animate multiple questions: can one discern an aesthetic equivalent to the political principle of *e pluribus unum* in which the centripetal forces of canonization and liberal pluralism organize this diversity into a singular tradition? If the twentieth century was indeed "the American Century" as Henry Luce proposed, how does the nation's literature reflect this grandiose, inflated, and quintessentially American sentiment? And who exactly is left out, subsumed, or crushed on the pathway to fulfilling it? If the twentieth century has been partitioned into the Lost Generation, the counterculture, baby-boomers, the nuclear generation, and Gen X, it is surely the case that the nation's literature also reflects a far less coherent, less grandiose story. Ironically, the very idea of American exceptionalism has become exceptional.

The standard response to such tensions has been to map the literary landscape with respect to formal, stylistic, temporal, and geographic markers. Naturalism, realism, modernism, and postmodernism are among the most recognizable points on this mapping. But so too are the Harlem Renaissance of the 1920s and 1930s or the Chicago Renaissance of the 1940s. Likewise, the power of the Southern gothic links William Faulkner to Toni Morrison, while genres such as "the Western," despite its deformation by the inclusion of Indigenous and feminist writing, illustrate how any number of regionalisms retain their explanatory sway. Other approaches fall back on formal omnibus categories such as "the American novel" or seek to account for the continuing force of a literary technique such as irony or pastiche. Whether the nation's literature takes shape as American tragedy or as American pastoral, as titles of novels by Theodore Dreiser and Philip Roth might suggest, perspectives on the field also rely on genre as a means of representing the literary history of the United States across the twentieth century.

Yet these modes of charting have been exploded by the emergence of new methods of literary classification following social movements of the 1960s and 1970s: Asian American, American Indian, Latinx, and gay and lesbian literature turned the concept of a single American canon on its head. Identity-based creative categories became indistinguishable from the critical methods that they inspired: disability studies, postcolonial discourse, and ecofeminism, to name a few, emerged as modes of analytic thinking indistinguishable from, and no longer tethered to, their original archives. As these methods called for new objects of study and prioritized social justice concerns, the white male canon and its fascination with adventure became upended. Jack London and Ernest Hemingway now share space with Alison Bechdel and Louise Erdrich. To preview an example from John Levi Barnard's chapter, London's and Hemingway's stories might now be productively reinterpreted from the perspective of anthropogenic climate change. Or, to invoke Heidi Kim's chapter in this volume, a modernist innovator such as William Faulkner cedes space to a popular novelist such as Edna Ferber. By turning a critical eye on matters of representation, identity, and authority, new methods and the new canons that they helped to engender shattered projections of national unity along with the fetishized political boundaries that they once relied upon. With that displacement, the very ways of seeing that marked the national literary enterprise in all its mythic, youthful, aggressive, and often tone-deaf muscularity were rendered suspect. Could literature reflect "the American Experience" if one no longer existed?

Near the end of the twentieth century, notions of what constitutes "American" and "literature" have undergone radical challenge and revision. Among critics, the very term "American literature" has ceded to "US literature," signaling a self-critical and self-conscious orientation in the field while imparting a modicum of geographic modesty and expanding objects of study beyond national borders. The scope of "American" has widened to include hemispheric, diasporic, and archipelagic texts or has collapsed into the "postnational" under global capitalism. And yet each of these moves is haunted by the aggrandizing gesture to claim terrain as "American"—including the literary terrain, a tendency that José Martí sought to accent differently by writing about "Nuestra América." In this volume, "literature" variously encompasses lyrics, spoken-word poetry, historiographic accounts, biography, mass-market fiction, and other popular culture texts and is widely recognized to be in conversation with film, performance art, radio, and other sonic and visual forms. Thus, even as this anthology's approach necessarily recognizes the indispensability of "American literature," it places both these terms under contestation.

In this regard, then, the chapters gathered here do not establish a singular field so much as they register the ongoing shocks and shifts to its putatively organizing principles. Not to be confused with a rejection of the category *tout court*, the interstitial approaches suggested in this volume instead at once expand, revise, reposition, interrogate, and seek new combinations among the texts that contour the field of twentieth-century American literature. One obvious sign of this critical energy is manifested by the fact that several contributions overflow temporal borders by extending their mediations to twenty-first-century transnational identities, social justice movements such as #Black Lives Matter, and the context of neoliberal capital. In Bernadine Hernández's chapter in this volume, literal borders assume new and expanded urgency in the context of the human/animal divide, while in Rachel Adams's chapter, "care work" provides a new lens for interpreting the modernist canon. At a broader level, then, the task is to understand not what twentieth-century American literature means but rather what it means to read, study, and teach twentieth-century American literature in the twenty-first century.

Familiar ways of organizing literature around schools, movements, traditions, and styles that gave ascendancy to temporal, spatial, and generic considerations take new form as they enmesh with emerging approaches. Comparative racialization, affect theory, queer theory, transnational studies and glocalism, new materialisms, and performance studies, to mention only a few critical orientations of the past twenty-five years, supply a rich and varied toolkit for placing twentieth-century American literature into conversation with twenty-first-century critical concerns. That said, multidisciplinary and varied approaches should strive to do something other than produce an already recognizable map that highlights a "representative" queer text or one exemplary reading of race and ethnicity—as if each were marked with a starred state capital that stands out on the map of national literature. The image of federalism here is apt in more ways than one: the logic of identifying and implicitly celebrating a representative text or reading echoes the logic of state-sanctioned pluralism that emphasizes individual points of diversity as exceptional while keeping them few in number and isolated from one another. What fails to come into view is a potential for intersectional perspectives that cross and combine the neat demarcations of chronology, national boundary, or genre. As Michael Rothberg asks in the pages that follow, "How does *Beloved* time travel?" Virtually any engagement with US literature requires critical modes that are attuned to what Lisa Gitelman calls the "always already new" of media forms such as telephones, radio, film, and the internet (Gitelman 2006). When it comes to race and ethnicity, experimental novels and overnight successes, as Cynthia Wu demonstrates, are typically singled out for their innovations and breakthroughs. But how does a focus on singularities disconnect literary criticism from practices and institutions that put literature into circulation within the flows of migration, global inequities, and histories of traumatic violence? In short, these questions challenge the implicit and inadvertent federalism of literary historical approaches whose focus on the diversity of race, class, region, sexuality, and language sets up a singular example whose significance is to reaffirm a stable overarching unity. This volume instead represents an effort toward something else: an opening up of future directions toward twentieth-century American literature that not only questions each of its core components (the chronological of "twentieth-century"; the national of "American"; the aesthetical of "literature") but also strives to combine methods, texts, and genres in ways that do not necessarily reassemble into a static whole. In this volume, we seek to register what is happening—as opposed to what has happened—in the field of US literary criticism.

To that end, the chapters gathered in this volume frequently assess the scope and scale of analysis that they employ even as they remain devoted to examining specific works of literature. With contributors writing from North America, Asia, Europe, and Africa, the handbook also situates US literature within the context of global criticism. The chapters do not demonstrate a fidelity to established forms of literary classification but instead operate within interstitial space of new as well as established epistemologies. As editors, we have tasked our contributors with explaining, reflecting on, and, when possible, problematizing the stakes of the methods they use. In terms of the recent interdisciplinary focus on care studies, how might a critic read care-fully? How might readers use novels to chart a pathway from Cold War liberalism to expose the ways in which the tenets of neoliberalism have become second nature? How does one read poetry in a nuclear age or the novel at the advent of the eco-crisis? How can the student or critic begin to say something new about a text like Toni Morrison's *Beloved*, which has garnered close to 20,000 scholarly entries? In grappling with these and other related questions, this volume is devoted not only to specific works of twentieth-century literature but also to the methods and approaches that variously enable, elicit, and even interrogate the field and its contours. The result, we hope, is a collection that provides models for undertaking literary critical analysis where matters of canon, authority, and storytelling are themselves in flux. In place of static models for assessing literary tradition, the chapters compiled here insist upon the fluid, destabilizing possibilities of the in-between.

In order to mine the tension between diversity and coherence that animates the field of twentieth-century American literature, we have shaped the volume into four parts: (1) Structures, (2) Movements, (3) Attachments, and (4) Imaginaries. Overlapping but also in balance with one another, these categories are designed to represent the interplay of social energies, material conditions, and formal features that define a century of innovation. By pushing both across and beyond traditional means of grouping and defining creative literary endeavors, these categories blur and blend into one another, demonstrating neither an assemblage nor intersectionality's Venn diagram but instead constellations and unexpected connections.

STRUCTURES

Institutions provide structure, as do political boundaries. For that matter, rubrics, canons, disciplines, and identity categories likewise organize, make legible, and construct "the real." No matter how stable, structures always imply their opposite, whether as unbounded popular energies that trouble governmental structures or the chaos of natural systems that pay no regard for human intentions or planning. Boundaries limit as well as enable. Transcending existing rubrics of literary classification, the chapters in this section are invested in identifying—as well as destabilizing—linguistic, rhetorical, social, economic, and political structures that construct twentieth-century American literature. At the same time, however, the authors in this section remain attentive to the literary structure and formal features provided by categories such as the novel and the affordances of verse. In the process, they pose questions about the forms and structures that we so often take for granted. How do neoliberalism and other emanations of late capitalism change how novels seek to represent the real? How do the very linguistic structures through which adults and children name and apprehend the world create the nearly ubiquitous social identification known as "the reader"?

In a wry and unorthodox examination of the elementary processes through which children learn—and resist—reading, Elizabeth Freeman reveals how the innocent pleasures of story time and reading aloud can also lead to behaviors of nightly opposition. Situating how-to-read books and parenting manuals in a theoretical matrix that draws equally on readers of reading in such unlikely pairings as Dr Seuss and Friedrich Kittler, Freeman explores how the wonders of reading are redolent with scenes of coercion and recalcitrance. Her chapter is an ideal start for a volume that as whole intends to throw into question the basic literary forms, pedagogical rituals, and critical practices through which "American" worlds are constructed. Equally as capacious as Freeman's take on reading, John Levi Barnard's chapter examines how the destructive forces of industrialization, capitalism, and colonialism unleashed climatological changes whose shocks Jack London and Upton Sinclair registered in their naturalist fiction. Barnard's ecocritical approach zeroes in on everyday commodities and then zooms out to assess the everyday conditions that bind individuals to colonial capitalism. Moving from the Chicago stockyards to the goldfields of the Yukon, this chapter provides readers with a model about how focusing on material objects can serve as the building block for interpretations in the environmental humanities. Global thermonuclear war, of course, presents the quintessential threat to any notion of the environment or the humanities, to say nothing of its capacity to annihilate the worlds that human beings have made. And yet, that constant threat became tolerable but necessary to maintaining the ideological structures of the Cold War containment culture. In his analysis of Robert Lowell's poetry, especially *For the Union Dead*, Simon Van Schalkwyk describes how Lowell's experiments with cultural translation and transnational borrowings might be read as "leaky forms" that withstand the logic of containment. Formal considerations also drive Joseph B. Entin's analysis of how novels by Tomás Rivera, Jamaica Kincaid, and Jesmyn Ward do battle with the structures of neoliberalism. In looking at migrant workers, drug addicts, incarcerated persons, and domestic workers whose lives have become disposable under a system that maximizes private profit, these writers turn to what Entin calls "precarious forms" in an effort to represent the possibilities of solidarity that have been pushed to the margins of social life. But late capitalism, according to Cynthia Wu, is also a capacious form in which money, leisure, and access hold out the false promise of transcending or escaping structures of racialization. In pairing Samuel Delany and Kevin Kwan, Wu examines Asian and Asian American transnational subjects whose hyperbolic displays of wealth, sexuality, and racial stereotypes offer exaggerated representations of the real in an era of exaggerated capitalism.

In all, the contributors in this section chart a conflicted double movement: on the one hand, these first five chapters examine how structures rooted in industrialization, globalization, racial categories, and even language itself influence and encircle literary production; on the other, they consider how literary forms and structures associated with narrative and poetry have the potential to defamiliarize the accepted coordinates of social life and identity.

MOVEMENTS

In traditional historical terms, movements usefully describe works that have similar aesthetic tendencies, consistent ideological outlooks, or are located in roughly the same place and time. Literary movements allow critics to arrange writers and their works into categories that emphasize this relatedness: the Southern Agrarians, the Beats, the Black Mountain poets, maximalists and minimalists. Some of these movements are self-proclaimed (e.g. imagism), while others are more the product of critical consensus (e.g. postmodernism and now into the twenty-first-century post-postmodernism). Movements can be expressly political such as literature that is allied with the Civil Rights movement, the Black Arts movement, or the American Indian movement. In addition to movements organized around the possibilities of racial solidarity, the Women's movement, ACT UP, and the Disability Rights movement spawned a proliferation of newly visible constituencies on the US political landscape. More recently, as Yogita Goyal demonstrates in her contribution, twentieth-century American literature can be placed into productive conversation with twenty-first-century protests and activism associated with #Black Lives Matter. In all, literature has been essential to social movements, whether by expressing the concerns of communities and collectives or by foregrounding views that challenge the biopolitical consensus for managing populations at the end of the twentieth century. With these multiple understandings of "movements," we intend to signal how this keyword in our rubric registers the mobility, flexibility, and border crossing that is inherent to twentieth-century American literature.

As convenient and handy as these markers are, they nonetheless can create dead-end discussions about fit and placement, especially markers that uncritically presume notions of authenticity accessed through prevailing historiography. "Movement," after all, defines part of an antiquated American mythos: the pioneer democracy of westward migration, according to the frontier thesis that Frederick Jackson Turner proposed at the cusp of the twentieth century, fostered social mobility, hardy individualism, and national advancement. But as Sean Teuton shows, the mixture of the mythic, speculative, and official notions of history that circulate through Native American literature requires careful attention to the back-and-forth between essentialist and constructed notions of Indigenous identity. For Teuton, then, fixedness is the enemy of nuanced understandings of Native American literature: authors such as N. Scott Momaday, Leslie Marmon Silko, and John Milton Oskison destabilize the authority of historical evidence by turning to the dynamic aspects of oral tradition, memory, and Indigenous belief. Equally problematic are the chronological brackets that confine writers within the span of a particular literary movement. Is the designation the "Golden Age of Radio" adequate for comprehending the vibrant sonic landscapes of jazz broadcasting that animated the techniques of racial listening practiced by Amiri Baraka and his Beat contemporaries? Lisa Hollenbach's work instead argues for a more capacious understanding of how radio, even after it was eclipsed by the advent of television, continued to resonate as a powerful media form for changing the intelligible frequencies of race in America. Spanning the Civil Rights movement and the Nuyorican poetry movement, her chapter focuses on "listening as a way of tuning in to overlapping discourses about race, media, music, and writing that generate diffusive interferences" between music and poetry.

Hollenbach's focus on radio demonstrates that movement often happens across mediascapes, and Mark Goble extends this insight with a richly textured reading of how visual culture, particularly film, both accelerates and slows the speed at which history unfolds in William Faulkner's novels about the South, racial violence, and memory. As Faulkner grappled with racial modernity in *Light in August* and other

Yoknapatawpha novels, he delved into the "optical unconscious," a phrase from Walter Benjamin that Goble employs, in an effort to slow the pace of and reflect on multiple scales of change from the social to the environmental and from the aesthetic to the historical. Movement becomes "rootlessness" in Yogita Goyal's chapter on African American writers who reached beyond the nation's borders in an effort to articulate Black civil rights as human rights. In a chapter that moves from Richard Wright's *Native Son* to *The Color Curtain*, Goyal suggests how the dislocations and global settings of twentieth-century Black internationalism can contribute to contemporary anti-racist struggles. Transnational movement acquired a queer poetic sensibility in Allen Ginsberg's cross-cultural exchanges with Chinese scholars and writers. Starting with the idea of propaganda as a mode of communication that is designed to spread a state ideology, Harilaos Stecopoulos considers how cultural diplomacy literally becomes embodied in Ginsberg's poetry, especially in its engagement with Walt Whitman and classic Chinese poetry. As a unit, these five chapters collectively attest to the importance of collective struggle as an inspiration for creativity and a vehicle for change.

Attachments

Reading is an act of intimacy. If the image of the solitary writer is a cliché, the motivation underlying literary production and dissemination is, as Elizabeth Freeman reminds us in Chapter 1, connection. Literature, it is said, provides the illusion of emotional intimacy. Nevertheless, in this section, "attachments" gestures beyond this form of individual connection to encompass a multitude of affiliations and community forms, both normative and queered. We claim kinship with those who share our religion, belief system, racial-ethnic identity, labor niche, and even the disciplining state institutions that name, stigmatize, or oppress us. We bond with animals, the natural landscape, machines, and things. We forge connections through patriotism, sexual passion, social media. The most obvious attachments are feelings of national identification that would suture American literature to some notion of Americanness almost out of reflex. But obvious does not mean predominant: while often steeped in triumphalism, attachments to the nation form also generate feelings of humiliation, abjection, and resentment, especially for racial and sexual minorities. As in political theorist Wendy Brown's notion of "wounded attachments" (1995: 52), literature offers the possibility of recognition that is at best ambivalent, often demanding political subordination while leaving open the question of how subjects "might perform such a subversion" of normative categories of identity (55). Above all, an attachment often "manifests an intelligence beyond rational calculation," as Lauren Berlant suggests (2011: 2), in order to explain why people cathect to affective registers of risk, threat, and disempowerment that endanger the boundaries of the sovereign self. Literature constitutes both the source of conflicted senses of belonging and identification and an opportunity for confronting and reworking the ways in which subjects connect to the fetishized objects of desire, longing, or degradation.

Kendall Johnson conveys attachment through the pangs of opium addiction as a vehicle for opening up a trans-Pacific horizon to think about the needs and desires created by global finance capital. Turning to novels by George Santayana and Emily Hahn about the China trade, Johnson examines how queer forms of the romance become wrapped up with opium smoking, itself a metaphor for the needs and desires that are alternately primed and left unfulfilled by the ideology of free trade imperialism. The needs, requirements, and affordances of the body, as Rachel Adams argues, are everywhere but seldom acknowledged in modernist literature. Her chapter, "Modernism's Cares: Reading For and With," draws on Gertrude Stein and William Faulkner to outline the interpretative steps and critical moves for centering relations of care that are wrapped up with dependency, vulnerability, intimacy, and mothering. If Adams's capacious view provides a new angle on American modernism, then Aida Levy-Hussen's take on racial identifications, especially those rooted in notions of authenticity, offers a newly calibrated lens on the paradoxes of the Black literary tradition. Using Ishmael Reed's *Mumbo Jumbo* as something of a field guide, Levy-Hussen re-examines the complex interplay between Black aesthetics and white appropriation in the Harlem Renaissance and beyond.

Attachments, of course, can also take shape as romantic or sexual entanglements. For Melissa Daniels-Rauterkus, this possibility manifests in the work of Andrea Lee, whose novel, *Sarah Phillips*, presents attachment as a matter of dividedness, an experience of the "in-between" that combines interracial desire with transnational movements. Those border crossings form the center of Bernadine Hernández's exploration of traditional Chicanx border narratives with a twist: Gloria Anzaldúa's concept of *mestizaje* takes a radical turn. Her chapter, "Where Border Meets Narrative, Where Body Meets Word: The Animality of Border Subjectivity," situates the body as a site for interrogating the connections between race and animality through the performance art of Naomi Rincón Gallardo, Xandra Ibarra, and Rafael Esparza.

Overinvestment in a desired object can be read in a variety of modes and emotional valences: as pathological, as romantic, as self-obliterating. The contributors in this section render feelings of attachment as a conduit for unveiling larger political and social structures. To echo Raymond Carver, this is indeed what our contributors talk about when they talk about love, using "attachment" as a means of analyzing what—and who—we value.

Imaginaries

Leveraged against history, fiction is often devalued and dismissed as in, "It's *only* fiction." But literature is valued precisely for its other-worldliness, its ability to imagine what is not yet or what is unthinkable. If the nation indeed represents an "imagined community" (Benedict Anderson), literature has long been situated as its voice. An expansive sense of the imaginary does not pit genres such as realism, naturalism, or memoir against mythic history, science fiction, or comics. Rather, it suggests the deeply political projects of envisioning both truth and difference, projects that can be both progressive and self-serving. At stake for the authors in this section is not the distinction between the fictive and the real but understanding how the power of the imaginary has been harnessed across the expanse of the twentieth century; the chapters in this section, "Imaginaries," evoke the horizons of social possibility.

In "Of Canons and Cabinets: Indigenous Bodies, Epistemological Spectacle, and an Unusual Indian in the Cupboard," Becca Gercken poses a question about the correspondence between representation and social effects, citing Craig Womack's query about the role that Native American literature might play in contributing to belief in the "vanishing Indian" by "allowing Native people to be fictional but not real" (1999: 11). Through the native spectacle popularized by the fantastical trope of the "Indian in the Cupboard," the childhood imagination of a tiny Indigenous friend, her contribution to this volume raises issues surrounding literary canon formation and its suspect preference for specific American Indian texts, bodies, and means of narrating them.

The political valence of the imagination was famously claimed by Lionel Trilling as an essential attribute of liberalism. While it might be easy to dismiss this heritage, Johannes Voelz provides a forceful reminder that authoritarian illiberalism is on the rise, making Trilling's "the liberal imagination," especially as it was deployed and reworked in different ways by Saul Bellow and Ralph Ellison. In their hands, the American novel provides a powerful resource for liberal democracy. Yet, as Voelz contends, any notion of democracy, then as now, must confront its psychic investments in whiteness. Heidi Kim extends this argument with her chapter, "Constructing Whiteness: Faulkner, Ferber, and the American Racial Imagination," which sets up a comparative analysis of two authors with very different positions with respect to the literary establishment and popular culture. Her focus on their depiction of economic exploitation during the Great Depression and the Second World War registers how attachments to white identity were beset with anxieties surrounding social mobility during the Cold War era. While novels figure prominently in these investigations of whiteness, Rachel Jane Carroll turns to the textual and performance art of Adrian Piper in order to think about the relationship between aesthetic abstraction and race. Her chapter, "Unidentified Flying Objects: Conceptualism, Interpretation, and Adrian Piper," opens out onto a wider consideration of conceptual art to examine the linkages between Black radicalism and conceptualism and the constitutive role that language plays in imagining the self as racialized object.

Michael Rothberg provides an apt conclusion for this section and the volume as a whole by revealing how American literature—his case study is Toni Morrison's *Beloved*—refuses a single temporal moment. Engaging the field of cultural memory studies, he examines how this twentieth-century novel about the nineteenth century accrues new contexts and meanings in the twenty-first. His work demonstrates how *Beloved* becomes a "multidirectional" text, a contention that we would apply to our rendering of the literary field as a whole. Rothberg's engagement has significance for all the texts engaged in this volume: as important as their situation in context is the imagination of their continuing afterlives.

Our organization of US literature in the twentieth century here deliberately eschews rubrics based on chronology, region, form, schools, or identity categories. In *Structures, Movements, Attachments*, and *Imaginaries*, we seek new forms of literary critical engagement that are not simply thematic or descriptive but highlight potent means of critical intervention, at once political and abstract, historical and collective, transformatively affective, and conceptual yet impactful. That interstitial space illuminates the ways in which US literary studies are changing, and will continue to change, for twenty-first-century readers and critics.

References

Berlant, Lauren. 2011. *Cruel Optimism* (Durham, NC: Duke University Press).
Brown, Wendy. 1995. *States of Injury: Power and Freedom in Late Modernity* (Princeton, NJ: Princeton University Press).
Gitelman, Lisa. 2006. *Always Already New: Media, History, and the Data of Culture* (Cambridge, MA: MIT Press).
Womack, Craig S. 1999. *Red on Red: Native American Literary Separatism* (Minneapolis, MN: University of Minnesota Press).

PART 1
STRUCTURES

CHAPTER 1

THE BOOK OF LOVE IS LONG AND BORING

Reading Aloud, Care Work, and Children's Literature

ELIZABETH FREEMAN

> The book of love has music in it
> In fact that's where music comes from
> Some of it is just transcendental
> Some of it is just really dumb.
>
> Stephin Merritt (1999), "The Book of Love"

> The mother's job is to surround objects with the sounds of her voice, so that everything in the world adverts to her authority.
>
> Patricia Crain (2000). *The Story of A: The Alphabeticization of America from* The New England Primer *to* The Scarlet Letter

HERE'S a confession: my child, who is a teenager at the time of this writing, doesn't like to read. I did everything an early twenty-first-century, middle-class parent was supposed to do. I read to him at bedtime while he was in the womb and every night thereafter until he declared it too babyish in third grade. I took him to the library, got him a library card, and signed him up for summer readathons. I subscribed to a monthly tote bag of picture books published by small independent presses, books filled with rich illustrations and lush language. I bought him any book he asked for. I bought him many he didn't. His response to my precious over-attention was not the overjoyed entry into the world of children's literature that I had assumed was his destiny but a stony rejection of the printed page. I tell this story (a story about how and why we read stories) to focus on adult reading—not the hermeneutic act of literary interpretation but the seemingly non-hermeneutic, or even anti-hermeneutic, act of transmitting texts literally, of performing them (Penteado 2019: 87).[1] My son's obstinacy, I can see now, suggests that he recognized and refused something about why adults read aloud to children: though we think of it as an act of care, it is also designed to inculcate a "love" of literature. This affection, as Richard Brodhead (1993) has argued about nineteenth-century sentimentality, subjects the child to a disciplinary apparatus far more effective than punishment.

A few more details clarify the specifically textual aspect of this discipline. My child refused to read the little primers I bought him (the "Bob Books," which parents of my era will remember) because they were boring and plotless, with literally flat characters who were geometric shapes and spoke in monosyllables (Maslen 2006). More puzzlingly, he disdained Beginner Books and Early Readers, either as read-alouds or as books to read on his own, suggesting that he understood and snubbed the pedagogical function of these books. He preferred that I read complex, engaging stories to him: fair enough. But then, even after attaining reading fluency, he would not pick up books of his own accord if they had more than a few lines of print per page, seemingly because he found large blocks of text unwieldy and alienating and loved pictures so much—graphic novels have, significantly, been the exception to his refusal to read, suggesting that, at least in some cases, the visual may be less a tool of discipline than the aural and oral. He finally ended our bedtime story ritual because he did not like the competition between the pace of my reading and his quick apprehension of the words on the page and because pictures, apparently a medium for imaginative play, had disappeared from the more complex books I was reading to him. Eventually, he hardly read at all, and we ended up in huge fights where I said things I am ashamed of now, things like "People who do not read grow up to be stupid." What I really heard from the critical voice in my own head was, "Mothers whose children do not love to read are failures."

Reading aloud, then, is such a vital aspect of child rearing that not to do it is tantamount to negligence—or to do it and not see the tangible results in a child's attachment to their parent, to story time, and eventually to all of literature, constitutes defeat. It is no longer enough, if it ever was, to teach your child the ABCs and simple phonics in preparation for kindergarten or to tell your children long and rambling made-up bedtime stories as a way of bonding with them. The two imperatives have been joined. Parents, especially mothers, are supposed to inculcate both fluency in and a love for reading, an enjoyment that will solidify and reflect back the attachment between parent and child and eventually compete with the twenty-first-century addictions fostered by video games and social media. The read-aloud bedtime story, in particular, has become the *sine qua non* of good parenting. Books such as *The Read Aloud Handbook* (Trelease 1982), *The Book Whisperer* (Miller 2009), and *The Read-Aloud Family* (Mackenzie 2018) have been wildly popular, with *The Read Aloud Handbook* in its eighth edition at the time of this writing. These books appear alongside mass media articles with titles like "The Brainy

---

[1] "Surface reading, by stating on a literal level what the text states on a literal level, is transcendentally impossible, for any type of literality about literality would only be so if the text restated what the text literally states" (Penteado 2019: 87).

Benefits of Bedtime Stories" (Oklahoma's Glenpool Fire Department Dads 2005), or which tell parents things like "[t]he bedtime story is the best way to end the child's day and lead them into a night of wonderful rest" ("Stories to Grow By"). Taken together, these materials suggest that reading to children is vital to their emotional and intellectual development as well as to their physical health.

Read-alouds, especially at bedtime, are thus both a dispensation and a manifestation of care. But like many forms of care, reading aloud to children involves coercion: most obviously, the sense of obligation foisted upon parents, usually mothers, to do it no matter how exhausted they are. My own child's rejection of reading also hints that the recipients of such care might also be or feel coerced into becoming readers themselves. Finally, Robin Bernstein (2020) has recently explored the dynamic between adult coercion and children's agency as it plays out through the genre of the "going-to-bed" book that explicitly enjoins children to go to sleep. In this essay and her book *Racial Innocence* (2011), Bernstein argues that children's books are "scriptive things," inviting not only juvenile obedience but also revision and resistance. In this chapter, I will focus on the adult act of reading children's books in general, but especially alphabet books and beginning phonics readers, to children who may transform and/or contest what they hear. For "script" itself names not only a set of instructions for action and dialogue, as it does in Bernstein's work, but also written letters, or graphemes. Inert, squiggly pictures until they are transformed into spoken phonemes, syllables, and whole words, graphemes invite and even demand performance, particularly when they are presented to children through books read out loud by their care givers. The verbal acts solicited and coerced by reading aloud are in turn complicated by the parental voice and body and also by pictures. As this chapter will demonstrate, the case of Dr Seuss is key to understanding this complexity. Letters, sound, body, and images, I claim, are sometimes competing and sometimes conjoined vectors for coerced caring labor on the part of adults reading to children, coerced receipt of caring labor on the part of children being read to, and resistance to this form of care on the part of both actors.

The Coerced Reader

The function of, and anxiety around, shared reading between parent and child has a history. In the United States, family-based instruction goes back to at least 1642, when the Massachusetts colony passed the Massachusetts School Law mandating that all children should be taught to read by parents or masters—both of whom were presumed to be male (Eberling 1999: 225). The influence of Locke's 1693 *Some Thoughts Concerning Education* was also profound, according to historians (Fliegelman 1982: 5). The latter treatise was addressed primarily to fathers of sons and enjoined them to approach reading instruction as play or reward, recommended illustrated Aesop's fables and the tales of Reynard the Fox, and suggested that parents invent playthings, most famously dice, to surreptitiously teach reading (Locke 1693: 183–187). Books intended to be read at bedtime emerged with Louise Chandler Moulton's 1873 compilation *Bedtime Stories* (Bernstein 2020: 880). By the 1920s, concerns with the quality and quantity of children's sleep began to regularly appear in periodicals, which advocated a calm, predictable bedtime routine for children, including the reading of stories that were not too stimulating (Stearns et al. 1996: 351, 349). During the same era, a heightened emphasis on marital sex, privacy, and adult recreation also meant that children were banished from much of adult evening life, and the middle-class ritual of family read-aloud time had dwindled to the bedtime story (359). Thus, reading to children increasingly combined parental responsibilities for routine, sleep enhancement, and what we now call quality time. In the contemporary moment, when parents have very little time to spend with children after dinner and homework, bedtime stories are also a vital part of what sociologists call "choreographies of emotion" and "emotion socialization" (Costa 2012: 118). More than just inducing sleep, read-alouds are supposed to enhance children's emotional self-regulation and bonds with parents.

The multiple functions accorded to reading aloud today, and to bedtime reading in particular, explain the sudden, viral popularity of a children's book for adults, initially released as a PDF, called *Go the Fuck to Sleep* (Mansbach 2011). This little book tapped into the genre of soporific kid lit while perfectly capturing adult exhaustion with the nightly reading imperative. One part of *Go the Fuck to Sleep* is typical bedtime fare, listing the animals who cozy up for the night in the style of Mem Fox's *Time for Bed* (1997): in a loosely anapestic meter, Mansbach's cats "nestle close to their kittens," lambs "have lain down with the sheep," and on and on through whales, eagles, field mice, frogs, lions, tigers, sparrows, and even "the giant pangolins of Madagascar."[2] As in such famous bedtime books as Margaret Wise Brown's *Goodnight, Moon* (2007 [1947]), the environment also closes up shop: whereas the room portrayed in *Goodnight Moon* is progressively dimmed in the visual space of the book and quieted through the repetition of "hush," in *Go the Fuck to Sleep,* windows "darken," the wind "whispers," seeds "slumber," and flowers "doze." But reflecting the contemporary adult desire for child-free recreational evening time, the other half of each verse of *Go the Fuck to Sleep* portrays and mimics the adult reader's mounting frustration with a child who will not settle down: "I'll read you one very last book," pleads the parent, who goes on to declare that "I know you're not thirsty. That's bullshit;" "It's been thirty-eight minutes already;" "Hell no, you can't go to the bathroom;" "A hot crimson rage fills my heart, love;" and "Fuck your stuffed bear, I'm not getting you shit;" crescendo-ing with "My life is a failure, I'm a terrible parent." These two parts of each verse are capped with variations on the title phrase, such as "Lie the fuck down, darling, and sleep;" "Jesus Christ, what the fuck? Go to sleep;" and "Come on, shut the fuck up and sleep." The exhausted narrator nods off, wakes up to find out that the child has indeed fallen asleep, and settles down to a movie and popcorn with another adult, at which point the microwave beeps and, "Oh shit. Goddamn it. You've gotta be kidding. Come on, go the fuck back to sleep."

---

[2] *Go the Fuck to Sleep* is unpaginated.

The narrator of *Go the Fuck to Sleep* is portrayed by the illustrator as male. This may be because the author is male, or it may be because the image of a mother dropping f-bombs on her toddler would seriously disrupt the ideal of American motherhood. It may also reflect a nostalgic nod to the colonial era when fathers were in charge of household religious instruction.[3] Historically, though, reading aloud solidified as a sign of good *mothering*. Pre-revolutionary "dame schools" certainly situated women as teachers of early reading (Wyman 1995). But it is the turn of the eighteenth to the nineteenth century that seems to mark the maternalization of reading and—most importantly for the purpose of this chapter—the definitive fusion of reading aloud with the nurture of children. In *Discourse Networks 1800/1900*, Friedrich Kittler claims that "[t]he mother as primary instructor is, quite literally, an invention of 1800 .... Around 1800 [in Europe] a new type of book began to appear, one that delegated to mothers first the physical and mental education of their children, then their alphabetization" (Kittler 1990: 26–27).[4]

In the English language, something of this shift seems to have appeared almost a century earlier in British conduct books for women like *The Ladies Library*, which argued that "The Principle Care of the *Mother* [is] to Educate her Children Well" (Berkeley 1714: 134, quoted in Arizpe and Styles 2006: 7). By the mid-1740s, leisured English mothers, most famously Jane Johnson, were hand-making instructional reading materials for their children (see Arizpe and Styles 2006). The preface to Rousseau's famous educational treatise *Emile* notes that the work "was begun to gratify a good mother who knows how to think" (Rousseau 1979 [1762]: 33). And pre-1800 English works that address mothers in particular include *The Mother's Gift: Or, a Present for All Little Children Who Are Good* (1769); *Illustrations of Maxims and Principles of Education, in the Second Book of Rousseau's Emile* (Williams 1783); and *An Address to Mothers, Under the Following Heads: Maternal Authority. Domestic Attention. Diligence and Activity. Oconomy. Simplicity. Objects of Female Pursuits. Knowledge, Virtue, and Religion* (1784). On the other side of the Atlantic, the American text *The Mother's Gift* (1787) was part of the project of "republican motherhood" or the early national era's shift in women's roles from household manufacture to the education of young citizens (see Kerber 1976), a transformation that does seem to have delegated reading instruction primarily to mothers. The American women's rights advocate Judith Sargent Murray, in "On the Domestic Education of Children," clarifies the role of literature for the republican mother: "she is anxiously studious to awaken, or to *create*, the finer feelings of the soul. To this end she hath ever at hand a number of well chosen tales, calculated to promote the interests of virtue, to excite commiseration, and suited to their tender years" (Murray 1790: 276). We can see here not only what Brodhead (1993) has called the antebellum era's "disciplinary intimacy" or discipline through ostensibly warm emotional closeness but also the extension of this project to and through story time, as indeed

---

[3] Robin Bernstein, in conversation.
[4] Kittler's primary evidence for this historical shift is a list of German and Italian mothers' manuals.

Brodhead acknowledges when he describes reading "as the nurture-centered home's chief pastime, gathering point, and instrument of domestic instruction" (1993: 45).

This broader context of a maternalized European–American culture supports Kittler's claim that education, especially reading instruction, became increasingly correlated with mothers—whether or not 1800 is the crucial turning point. But what precisely is Kittler's "alphabetization" of children, beyond mere instruction, and how does it relate to care? This term seems to denote a disciplinary process antithetical to contemporary post-structuralist thought: not the teaching of the ABC to children as unruly graphemes, as letters whose names (ay, bee, see) bear an arbitrary relation to the shapes on the page, but instead the incitement to take in and reproduce their sounds (ah, buh, kuh/suh), as if these sounds were onomatopoeia or the guttural sounds of animals—"alphabetization," in short, is phonics. In fact, Patricia Crain's magisterial history of alphabet instruction, based in large part on Kittler's analysis, describes a 1658 alphabet by the father of modern education, the Czech bishop Johann Amos Comenius, in which each letter is illustrated with the animal whose sound it imitates (see Figure 1.1).

In the Comenius alphabet (1887 [1658]), for letter A the crow says, "ah ah ah," for letter B the lamb says "buh buh buh," for letter C the grasshopper says "ck ck ck," and so on. Whatever fantastic menagerie the pictures here call forth is brought to order by the sequencing of the alphabet and by the reduction of the animal to its sonic performance. And though modern children no longer learn that animals utter the phonemes of their native language, when they learn the alphabet sounds they also tend to learn, in parallel, the sounds that animals make: if a dog says "woof woof," it makes sense that the letter B says "buh," and that "buh" would feel—like a bark—sensuously or mimetically rather than conventionally linked to that letter. Animal noises, of course, are onomatopoeic: they mean nothing more than what they are. A dog's bark can be misinterpreted as aggressive by humans or other dogs when it is excited, but the bark is not subject to semiosis, to poetic combinations with other sounds that reveal obsolete or emergent meanings.[5]

Furthermore, the primary purpose of animal noises is not to transmit thought but to feel auditory enjoyment in noise, to echolocate, and to create or foster relationality. Beyond functions such as echolocation, animal noises communicate sensuously to humans and to other animals. They imitate (think of the repertoire of parrots); they transmit sensations such as safety (think of the purring of cats); they connect creatures to one another in relations of care, reproduction, or warning (think of the gentle bleating of mother sheep to their lambs, the mating calls of birds, or the alarmed shrieking of monkeys to one another and at a perceived enemy). Thus, it is not coincidence that a

---

[5] This paragraph owes something to the provocative essay by Walter Benjamin, "On the Mimetic Faculty" (1978 [1955]), in which Benjamin argues that words are not completely arbitrary but maintain a "nonsensuous similarity" to the things they designate, an imitative element that only appears in semiosis. Benjamin traces a movement from patterned objects like the stars or dances, to runes and hieroglyphs, to language whose mimetic elements are only revealed in poiesis.

FIGURE 1.1 Sound table for letters A–L from Johan Amos Comenius, *Orbis Pictus* (1887 [1685]), Facsimile Reproduction (Whitefish, Montana: Kessinger Publishing), p. 3. Public domain.

primal scene in which children learn the sounds that both animals and letters make is the parental lap. For sound conjoins living beings on a visceral level, one that feels non-arbitrary: the parental voice saying "woof woof" imitates the sounds that bind creatures to one another, and in doing so, binds the child to the parent. Phonic instruction, as the Comenius alphabet reveals, is very close to this.

That this scene of inculcation is generally the *maternal* lap, suggests Kittler, makes the woman seem to be the source of a restored wholeness even after the child's entry into a supposedly alienated and alienating language. Kittler argues that reading aloud—figured in the eighteenth century as a project toward children's "understanding" rather than of instilling the memorization of texts, and then as play, and eventually, we might add, as quality time—naturalizes writing into and as speech, unmaking *écriture*:

> The whole of primary education circa 1800, however, attempted the impossible proof for which the writer Carl Phillip Moritz was known, namely, 'that letters are not arbitrary, but grounded in human nature and native to all the distinct regions of inner consciousness.' In a first phase at the turn of the century, this naturalization of the alphabet was mediated by supplementary sensory stimuli. In a second and decisive phase, all arbitrariness disappeared in an inner sense called the Mother's voice.
>
> (Kittler 1990: 29)

In Kittler's analysis, the apotheosis of reading as maternal care keeps the arbitrary at bay: for the child, the mother reunites sound and referent, resensualizes meaning, and reconstitutes a seemingly lost mimetic element between phoneme and grapheme (see Benjamin 1978 [1955]).

In brief, sometime during the eighteenth century, reading aloud seemed to conjure the Kristevian "semiotic" and invoke a pre-Oedipal union between the mother's body and the child's (Kristeva 1980). This oral stage was, as Kittler indicates, originally literally so. At least one Enlightenment educational reformer, Johann Bernhard Basedow, advocated the use of alphabet letter cookies (Smith 1965: 7), and indeed, this method of instruction goes back at least to Erasmus's 1530 treatise *De Recta Pronuntiatione* (Crain 2000: 19). Turning this gustatory scene into metaphor for the relegation of reading instruction to mothers and to the read-aloud, Kittler describes a "culinary orality" (Kittler 1990: 30). This metaphor suggests that reading aloud was remade as care akin to breastfeeding. This, in turn, is confirmed by the emergence of what Crain calls "swallow alphabets" in the mid-eighteenth century: in these alphabets, "A" is "apple pie," but thereafter "B bit it," "C cut it," etc. (Crain 2000: 85). In the swallow alphabet, the written letter, as the agent of each sentence, initially seems to consume and subsume sound in the unruly way that poststructuralists and visual theorists celebrate—but the forceful single-syllable verbs that begin with the letter-sound ultimately emphasize the triumph of the sonic element over the graphic.

We might therefore see swallow alphabets as the most disciplinary of all reading primers. For Kittler also reminds us that "the simple letter is the cliff against which hermeneutics can be dashed" insofar as letters have "no meaning" (28). Thus, though sound would at first glance seem to be a less representational and therefore more anti-hermeneutical medium than writing, Kittler's analysis situates aural delivery and reception of the printed text—beginning with phonics—on the side of a disciplinary hermeneutics that leashes sound to meaning, and by implication, situates silent reading on the side of anti-hermeneutic play with language. To put it differently, signifiers that mean what they are--the sounds of animals, onomatopoeia, the phonemes of a language—allow, under the regime of phonics, for no interpretive leeway whatsoever.

One claim that might follow from this is that during the eighteenth century, mothers took symbolic charge of ensuring an anti-hermeneutic fealty to sound. Another is that the anti-hermeneutic activity constituted by reading aloud solidified the authority of mothers, producing what Heather Love, in other contexts, has jokingly termed the "hegemommy."⁶ Either way, in the context of a new emphasis on phonics imparted by women, reading aloud to children became a process, at least as Kittler describes it, of inoculating against a threateningly *discontinuous* relationship between sound and sense, mother and Other. This fusion of the sonic and the body of the (female) reader-aloud *as against the graphic* was, and still is, particularly true in relation to picture books read to children: for example, Alberto Manguel, in his history of reading practices in the West, describes the difference between his preliterate perusal of picture books, in which he could tell any story at all using the images, and being read to as a kind of hostage situation, in which he gave up possession of the book and became "nothing but hearing" (Manguel 1996: 109). Sound, then, not only stabilizes a heterogendered mother–child dyad but also overtakes pictures, a process that young Manguel (and perhaps my son) found coercive.⁷

THE COERCED LISTENER

As anyone who has raised a child knows, the young control very few aspects of their upbringing, but elimination, eating, and sleeping are the sites at which parental control and children's capacities to exert a force of their own meet one another. One might add to this listening. Through Kittler's metaphors, Manguel's reminiscences, and the popularity of *Go the Fuck to Sleep*, we can see that reading aloud is, like all forms of caretaking, not only nurturant but also a vector of unequal power: perhaps as an attempt to leash the child to the maternal body or perhaps simply as a demand for an anti-hermeneutic fealty, for getting the child to understand through alphabetization, or phonics, that consonants and animals can "say," or "mean," only one (or sometimes two) sound(s). Kittler's analysis allows us to conceive of a child's resistance to reading in two ways. If children resist silent, solo reading, then perhaps they resist, in a way we don't traditionally associate with children, the play of the signifier. If they resist being read to instead, or as well, or if they prefer pictures to stories, perhaps they resist a certain maternal engulfment or even a certain implantation of sensory, sonic data. Vis à vis the implantation of sonic data, it is useful to remember that the acquisition of a "mother tongue" is achieved through synaptic pruning, which eventually eliminates the sounds of other languages.

---

⁶ Heather Love, in conversation. If I understand the joke right, Love means this term to designate feminist mentors who do not recognize themselves as the agents of institutional discipline and yet wield it heavily.

⁷ The role of reading aloud in the disciplinary project of inculcating children into hetero-gendered subjectivities is further solidified by the practice of adults giving characters "voices," usually those that the reader deems appropriate in terms of gender, among other qualities. Thanks to Juana María Rodríguez for this observation, in conversation.

We tend to assume that pleasurable play is the primary way that children resist discipline, even when we know that so much of children's play is deadly serious, rehearses adult disciplinary regimes, and frequently involves children disciplining one another while playing. But what if children perform resistance with other senses than pleasure, in other modes besides the play that poststructuralism generally values? I'm thinking here of the link between phonemes and the animal sounds that indicate *fear,* such as warning screams, squawks, growls and barks. In fact, my son had a moment of opposing shared reading that might illustrate how children resist alphabetization by mobilizing fear. At the age of about two, he became afraid of the letter Y. In his alphabet book, we would get to the page that said, "Y is for yo-yo" and he would shriek in alarm, so we took to skipping that page and just going from X to Z. The letter Y was also the first one he recognized outside of books, in the world, when we passed our local Safeway, with its bright red sign in all capital letters. In his car seat, he would cover her eyes and scream, "Y! Nooooooo! No Y! Don't like Y!" as we drove by. This was an utter mystery to me. Was it existential angst? Did "Y" sound like "Why," a question he asked incessantly—did he want to be in charge of all the questions or did he fear the answers? Was the shape of the letter, arms upraised like the Village People in the song "YMCA," signifying an unwanted embrace? Was Y the primal sign of the mother's forbidden crotch? Was it the sound of "Yeh" that I had been patiently trying to leash to this simple shape that frightened him (though "Yes," a word he loved, also began with this sound, so that didn't make sense)?

I finally figured it out when I went to his preschool and saw the scary picture book *Abiyoyo* (Seeger 1986), which the preschool teachers often read aloud to the children. Abiyoyo, an enormous monster who terrorizes a village, is illustrated by Michael Hays as a hulking, shaggy, shadowy presence looming over tiny fleeing humans. My son thought that the page in his alphabet book declaring that "Y is for yo-yo" had something to do with Abiyoyo. He unleashed that phoneme from the visual image of the toy that would make the sign both less arbitrary and more comforting, for a yo-yo is a *fort-da* toy that comes back, alleviating fear of the parental leave-taking that inevitably follows a bedtime story. And he leashed it to a frightening image of his own choosing, one that arguably suggests the parent's power to threaten or even to kill their child. My son also disconnected sound from my soothing maternal body and attached it to that of a masculine giant, scrambling the gender relations that Kittler's analysis insists upon. In my child's mind, the shape of the letter, the read-aloud sound "Yeh," and the book that linked that sound to the last two syllables of Abiyoyo's name *were* the monster. Or perhaps *we* were the monsters, the female preschool teachers and I, for insisting that he hear this sound and associate it with a more soothing object, the yo-yo that stages return.[8] Maybe my child understood that loss could be total and terrifying. Maybe, like those of us who read to him, he resisted the arbitrariness of the written sign, but unlike his adult

---

[8] Another popular read-aloud book of that era was *Owl Babies* (Waddell 2002), in which anxious fledglings learn that Mommy Owl always comes back in the morning with food for them.

readers, he also resisted phoneticization. Perhaps he displaced sound onto a visual plane with more interpretive freedom, or perhaps he merely wrestled the letter into a hermeneutic of his own, whereby Y = "Yeh" = an animal-sound warning of an impending violence that the mother's voice could not abate.

At the very least, as my son recognized, the sound "Yeh," like all the alphabetic sounds we adults teach our children at bedtime, might indeed be the monster who runs children out of their happy daytime villages and into a space they fear, where nightmares are as likely as visions of sugar plums and parents might *not* protect their children or return to them. Thus, the power of *Go the Fuck to Sleep* isn't just about an exasperated tone that contradicts its soothing imagery and meter, even if this particular book is not meant for adults to actually read aloud to children. This satirical book also knows something about reading aloud to children as a supposed offering of care. It knows that we read to children to get them to do things: register the sounds of their native language, decode letters, bond with us, learn valuable moral lessons, or just be quiet, lie still, go to sleep—as Bernstein reminds us in a formulation her own essay eventually contests, *Go the Fuck to Sleep* "expose[s] the going-to-bed book, a central and intensified exemplar for children's literature most broadly, as a noninnocent deployment of top-down power" (Bernstein 2020: 885).[9] For my purposes, what *Go the Fuck to Sleep* lays bare, what my son's resistance to the letter Y in attaching a phoneme to a monster who kills, rather than a yoyo that comes back, and in insisting that his parents skip the letter Y to assuage his fear, is that care is a form of violence, a coercion *demanded in exchange for protection*. To put it in psychoanalytic terms, the enigmatic signifier, as Jean Laplanche calls the unconscious and inscrutable messages sent unknowingly by adult caretakers to their charges in the course of care—here the alphabet itself—contains secrets both seductive and cruel.[10]

If reading aloud to children is the paradigm of sending them messages that exceed their (and possibly our) understanding, of what might the violence of the enigmatic, alphabetic signifier consist? Glossing Kittler, Crain (2000: 130) writes that the bedtime

---

[9] Bernstein is concerned, as I am here, with what children *do* with "scriptive" objects like children's books. Bernstein takes *Go the Fuck to Sleep* and its curse-cleansed rewrite intended for children, *Seriously, Just Go to Sleep* (Mansbach 2012), as paradigmatic examples of books that invite children to take an adult perspective on the difficulties of the bedtime routine, thereby creating a space in between adulthood and childhood and establishing children as *akin* to adults rather than their constructed polar opposite. This is a convincing intervention on the general tendency of children's literature, as a field, to assume that children are powerless in scenes of discipline: for Bernstein, the very existence of going-to-bed books exposes the frustrated limitation of adult power over children's bodies. But in her model, children assume power or muddle the adult–child divide by incorporating adult perspectives, particularly the discipline of bedtime, as she suggests happens in the picture book *Bedtime for Frances* (Hoban 1960), whereas in mine they route sound elsewhere.

[10] In Laplanche's work, the enigmatic signifier consists of the message that the adult unconsciously transmits to the child during the process of care, the contents of which are often sexual but which the child is too immature to metabolize, and which he or she grows up responding to belatedly and unconsciously. This is Laplanche's rewriting of Freud's more literal scene of primal seduction, which Freud abandoned in favor of the theory of infantile sexuality. See Laplanche 1989.

kiss actually cloaks reading's disciplinary operation, to which both mothers and children are subject:

> [The mother] "prints" (imprints, enstamps, impresses) representations on the child's memory; her voice and her actions, fully internalized, echo within the child's mind; and her present is in order—static, consistent, and exactly repeatable—owing to the management of her "self-." The metonymic condensing of these operations to a mother's kiss, lips, tongue, and voice blurs their origins.

Here, maternal self-regulation (or rather, the mother's acquiescence to a regulative order) is a conduit to the regulation of children, and, as in Brodhead's scene of disciplinary intimacy, the lush orality of reading and kissing are a ruse for the confining orality of phonics. But in her book *Making Out* (2019), Kathryn Bond Stockton takes a more pleasurably perverse view. Stockton clarifies the extent to which reading—not specifically reading aloud to others but reading in general—is a matter of penetration, a seduction of the child. Crucially, she asks: "How should children regard ... the force of words put onto them?" (26). She begins with the metaphor of reading as kissing, fusing the orality of the two just as Crain does. But as Stockton's book goes on, reading becomes more and more erotic: it is "getting in" someone using no genitals (8); it is a way for words to "pierce the body's envelope" (12); it is an exchange of fluids like gay barebacking (55); it is, finally, like being penetrated by a dildo, which, for the bedtime parental reader-aloud, I know, I know ... you yourself may want to stop reading here. And while it may be that Stockton's literalization of the enigmatic signifier is precisely an *adult* decoding of something barred to the child, might this penetration also be what children unknowingly resist when they resist reading (might it also be what college students resist when they fear being triggered by a text or brainwashed by its bad politics)? Another way to put this: in light of Stockton's analysis, *Go the Fuck to Sleep* exposes reading aloud, and the caretaking represented by that act, as a form of both pedophilic seduction and parental brutality. The book reveals not only the literalness of "Fuck you" but also the "Fuck me" of reading-as-caretaking—both the parent's wish to penetrate the child and the masochistic subject-position of the parent-who-must read.[11]

At the same time, though, adults reading aloud to children often leave out more than they put in. Sometimes, this is just about being tired or not wanting to bore the child, as in William Goldman's *The Princess Bride* (1974), where the fictional father-reader skips the long historical digressions in the book he reads to his son. Sometimes, as my skipping over the letter Y in my child's alphabet book suggests, the adult wishes the child not to experience something worse than boredom, and this is a different form of power. What the enigmatic signifier cannot signify in the moment of its transmission matters as much as the surface messages that the child simply cannot interpret. The literary critic Peter Hunt thus acknowledges that not only do adult readers-aloud (and not just authors) determine what is appropriate for the child to hear, as indeed is true of every communicative

---

[11] Thanks to Nat Hurley for the observation about masochism and for a clarifying conversation about the enigmatic signifier.

act between human beings, but also that this power to manipulate what children are exposed to "carries a much stronger freight of sexual anxiety than any other: it is no less than potential violation" (Hunt 2011: 45). But while Kittler, Crain, Stockton, and Manguel focus on inculcation, Hunt explores the act of excision: his example is parents' choice not to name or describe the Caterpillar's hookah in *Alice's Adventures in Wonderland*, either because the word *hookah* is too difficult or out of a wish not to glorify smoking or drugs. Though these acts tend to have as their justification sparing the child from discomfort, excision and abridgement are as powerful as seduction, implantation, or premature exposure. A message withheld or barred is as powerful as an uninterpretable message sent because a letter—even the letter Y—always eventually arrives, through the very long processes of relationality and sexuality, at its destination.

Thus, the "alphabetization" of children through phonics might also be thought of not just as seduction back into or towards the mother's body but as a violent kind of excision, a castration of the child's own body and desires: when we insist that "Yeh" emerges from "yoyo" but not "Abiyoyo," when we withhold the monstrous image of Abiyoyo from the alphabet book, we insist that the sound of the letter Y *cannot* mean whatever perversity the child conjures up for it. And yet children do conjure. I'm reminded of my own fear of the word "wump," an onomatopoeic nonsense word I encountered in *Peanuts* comics when I was five or six, supposedly signifying only the sound made by Charlie Brown kicking a football or landing on his back after missing the kick. I said the word over and over to myself. It felt menacing for reasons I could not articulate even to myself, and I had nightmares of being followed around by the word "wump," written in the distinctive comic san serif font in which it appears in *Peanuts*, its bouncing movement set to a repetitive rhythm like the opening of *Jaws*. Wump wump wump wump, wump wump wump wump. In reading aloud, in leashing sounds to words and then insisting that words correspond with pictures, perhaps we are closing these potential thrills down, the way that the narrator of *Go the Fuck to Sleep* wants to close down the exciting world of being awake for his offspring. Yet this form of excision may foreclose on a referent or a sensation that, to the child, is a lifeline—even if that sensation is unpleasant and has nothing to do with Mommy. My child, for example, found himself in Abiyoyo rather than in the anodyne pictures of his alphabet book, for he eventually declared, at the age of seven, that his gender was "werewolf."

Nonsensibilities

Given all this, the world of children's nonsense literature—literature in which words like *wump* feature regularly—would seem to be profoundly liberating.[12] It's tempting to

---

[12] See, e.g. Eugene Field's 1885 not-for-children political ditty "Song of the Mugwump," Dr Seuss's "seven-hump Wump" in *One Fish, Two Fish, Red Fish, Blue Fish* (1960: n.p.), and Bill Peet's *The Wump World* (1970).

claim for this genre, of whom Edward Lear is generally counted as the English-language father, the potential to liberate sound from sense. But nonsense is, in T. S. Eliot's words, not a complete absence of sense but a "parody of sense" (Eliot 1960 [1942], quoted in Barton 2015). In parodying the patterns of English phonetics, morphemics, syntax, and genre, nonsense also teaches these things: nonsense literature harnesses the enticing *possibility* of chaos to alphabetization as well as to syllabification, spelling, grammar, and so on but actually organizes and solidifies these aspects of language. The word "wump," for example, is recognizable as nonsense precisely because its sequence of sounds follow the rules of English phonology, in a way that "mpwu" is not ("mpwu" is something like not-sense, in English). "Wump" teaches children, among other things, that the "mp" sound can end a word or a syllable but cannot begin one. It alerts them to other common-sense words that follow this rule: bump, clump, dump, frump, hump, jump, lump, pump, rump, stump, sump (I will not say Trump). It also teaches them that a vowel must precede or follow two blended consonant sounds unless that blend ends with one of the two phonemes that are liquid in English, "r" and "l," such that "schlump" is recognizable as a word to English speakers but "brnump" is not. Let us call the phonetic rules intimated by nonsense "nonsensibilities," a term with which I mean to suggest the competencies with sound that are inculcated by sonic play.

The case of Dr Seuss's nonsense literature is especially illustrative of the way nonsense, phonemic and beyond—appears to flout sense but actually teaches it. As is well known to historians of children's literature, Theodor Geisel, a.k.a. "Dr Seuss," was inspired to write *The Cat in the Hat* (1957) by a 1954 article in *Life Magazine* written by John Hersey, which examines the supposed failure of reading instruction in the United States (this article preceded, by one year, Rudolph Flesch's more famous, pro-phonics *Why Johnny Can't Read*). Hersey's article lists a multitude of reasons why American children of the 1950s read so badly, only passingly mentioning instructional materials. But his essay is illustrated with a contrasting two-page spread headlined "Pallid Primers" on the left-hand side, below which appear pages from the *Fun With Dick and Jane* series. "In the classroom," the caption to these pictures reads, "Boys and girls are confronted with books that have insipid illustrations depicting the slicked-up lives of other children…. All feature abnormally courteous, unnaturally clean boys and girls" (Hersey 1954: 136). On the right hand side, the headline "Stores' Jaunty Juveniles" appears above pictures from Alice and Martin Provensen's *The Animal Fair*, Jean de Brunhoff's *Babar*, and Ludwig Bemelmans's *Madeline's Rescue*. The caption below reads, "In bookstores anyone can buy brighter, livelier books featuring strange and wonderful animals and children who behave naturally, i.e., sometimes misbehave" (137). Flesch would go on to champion phonics over sight words (the latter, "Look-Say," was later renamed "whole word instruction"), but the Hersey illustrations, if not the article as a whole, present a clear contrast between textbooks and trade books, focusing on content and, especially, illustration as a counterpoint to alphabetization. In the small part of the article where Hersey does discuss instructional materials, he asks, "Why should [readers] not have pictures that widen rather than narrow the associative richness children give to the words they illustrate—drawings like those of the wonderfully imaginative geniuses among children's illustrators, Tenniel, Howard Pyle, 'Dr. Seuss,' Walt Disney?" (Hersey 1954: 148). This analysis champions the graphic as the site of hermeneutic free-play, something for which Seuss is generally credited.

A well-known children's author by 1954, Seuss had already published a dozen illustrated nonsense books with no overt pedagogical mission, from *And to Think That I Saw It On Mulberry Street* (1937) to *Horton Hears a Who* (1954). According to the literary critic Louis Menand (2002), in 1955 William Spaulding, the education editor at Houghton Mifflin, read Hersey's article and Flesch's *Why Johnny Can't Read*. Hoping for a book he could sell to schools, Spaulding made a list of 660 first-grade-reading-level words compiled by experts and asked Seuss to write a book with them. Seuss chose 199 of the words, added 21 of his own, and composed and illustrated a story in loose anapestic dimeter: the result was *The Cat in the Hat*, whose nonsensibilities teach, among other things, the differences between short and long vowels and voiced and unvoiced consonants. Furthermore, though Seuss's comic-book-like, zany illustrations seem to open up the picture plane to multiple association in the ways Hersey asks for, *The Cat in the Hat's* illustrations, like those in *Fun With Dick and Jane*, actually established a one-to-one correspondence between the objects portrayed and those named in the text (Macdonald 1988: 116) in ways very different from his earlier books, which were rich with excessive pictorial detail for its own sake and with visual puns.

The publication history of *The Cat in the Hat* bears out its legacy as a tool for teachers rather than simply a ludic pleasure: Random House got the rights to the trade edition, and eventually to the textbook edition, and began to copy Spaulding's model of giving commissioned authors lists of words from primers (Menand 2002). And thus, in 1958, was born Beginner Books: the strange, the wonderful, the misbehaving, and the pictorial now all served the project of phonic reading instruction, especially insofar as these books were intended to be adult read-alouds that eased children into silently reading them alone and into a more general love of reading. Combined with the historical changes that had already shifted reading-aloud time to the evening, Beginner Books hooked bedtime into phonics.

Critics love to celebrate the anarchy of *The Cat in the Hat* (see, e.g. Shortsleeve 2012), as if nonsense liberates not only sound but also plot. Two children, left at home alone by their mother, pine at the window for her until a cat shows up and disorders the entire house, stacking things into wobbly towers and words into staccato rhymes. But notably, just as the cat's machine ultimately cleans up the glorious mess he makes, Seuss's most famous book, a graded reader from its inception, actually represents the containment of semiosis by the machine of phonics. And in a sense, *The Cat in the Hat's* commitment to phonics also brings back the children's mother, who returns after order is restored. She reappears not as Kittler's imaginary sensuous maternal body that naturalizes the relationship between sound and sense but as a disembodied and colorless leg, wearing a neatly tied shoe, peeking through the door as she returns: her physical plenitude is excised. In the end, the story resutures both the child protagonists and its juvenile audience to the maternal by asking, in its last line, "What would YOU do if your mother asked YOU?" In other words, the child-reader is enjoined to hear, in their mind, the mother's querying voice.

Seuss's 1958 sequel, *The Cat in the Hat Comes Back*, makes the disciplinary work of Kittlerian alphabetization—phonics—even more obvious. In this story, the cat reappears at the door, eating a pink-frosted cake and eventually leaving a pink ring in the children's bathtub, a stain that spreads uncontrollably onto everything the cat wipes it with. Unable to eradicate the stain, the cat lifts his hat to reveal his minions, twenty-six miniature cats in ever-diminishing sizes, named alphabetically from Little Cat A to Little Cat Z. Just as the written alphabet threatens to undo meaning and hermeneutics, these baby alphabet-cats spread the pink stain (which Menand [2002] reads as a figure not merely for semiosis but specifically for queerness and Communism) until the whole snowy yard is pink. Only another unspecified technology, the Voom, can suck up the pink and restore order, clearing the snowy sidewalk, putting the cats back into the hat, and allowing the Big Cat to recite the alphabet in proper order as he leaves: the last words of the book are "X, Y, and Z." Notably, there is no turn to the mother or the child-audience in the end, as there is in the original *Cat in the Hat*, only to the alphabet. But here is what Menand misses in his otherwise astute reading of the story as a brief against semiosis: notably, "Voom" is an onomatopoeic sound of the very sort that Kittler associates with the maternal disciplinary work of reading aloud to children. Never pictured except as a word, "Voom" is not a machine or a substance but mere sound: "Now don't ask me what Voom is./I never will know" (Seuss 1958: 59). "Voom," arresting semiosis in the name of phonics, is the antithesis of my son's disorderly, terrifying "Yeh." And like the readers-aloud who held Alberto Manguel hostage, it literally sucks up pictures into sound, for the cats and children disappear as the Voom does its work (see Figure 1.2).

The Voom, in turn, is a cleaning technology modified from an earlier Seuss book, *On Beyond Zebra!* (1955), which preceded *The Cat in the Hat* and may go missing from the story of how Seuss's nonsense literature was arrogated into the project of reading instruction because it was not initially solicited by a textbook publisher and did not become part of the Beginner Books series. *On Beyond Zebra!* presents "two brothers called Vrooms/Who, strangely enough, are built sort of like brooms."[13] The brothers, stuck on a world near the sun, are terminally bored, "[a]nd so, to kill time, just for something to do/ Each one of these fellows takes turns with the other/ In sweeping the dust off his world with his brother." Yet the Vrooms don't have the last word or act in *On Beyond Zebra!*, nor does this book end with Z. Instead, its conceit is that there are twenty letters after Z, for spelling special words: "*My* alphabet," says the narrator to his small friend Cornelius, "starts where *your* alphabet ends." What might a fantasy alphabet contribute to or resist about the discipline of alphabetization, and more broadly, what is its relation to the coercive care of reading aloud?

The narrator of *On Beyond Zebra* introduces his new alphabet to his younger friend Cornelius, who begins the story by reciting the usual animal abecedary: "The A is for Ape. And the B is for Bear./ The C is for Camel. The H is for Hare." This is what Crain (2000: 91) calls an "alphabet array," which offers an encyclopedic ordering of the

---

[13] *On Beyond Zebra!* is unpaginated.

FIGURE 1.2 The Voom from Dr Seuss (Theodor Geisel), *The Cat in the Hat Comes Back* (New York: Random House, 1958), pp. 58–59

world through objects whose arbitrariness is reduced by their sequencing according to the alphabet—however arbitrary that sequence actually is. This might initially be seen as a reduction of the free play of both the sonic, through phonics, and the graphic element, through reducing the picture's possibilities to the single function of illustrating sound. But according to Crain, the alphabet array endows the letter with meaning through the figure of synecdoche: that which is part of "Ape," the letter A, stands in for ("is for") it, such that "Ape" is the prop of, the syntax of, the extension of, or what Crain calls the "legs" of A (96). In the alphabetic bestiary that Cornelius recites, then, we can see the alphabet as a kind of hybrid interspecies monster, with Ape the legs of A, Bear the legs of B, and Camel the legs of C. Perhaps the Ape-A, then, is not a reduction of the pictorial but the same kind of monster as Abiyoyo or the "Wump" that chased me around in my dreams: in *On Beyond Zebra*, sound leashes the arbitrary letter to a threatening fullness of meaning that is, in this exchange between a male narrator and a younger male pedagogue organized around animals, irreducible to the mother–child relation.

And perhaps this scene of instruction, more perverse than it initially looks and then growing even wilder, is what it means to go "beyond" the Zebra who traditionally terminates alphabet arrays. For the narrator goes this bestiary one better. Having declared that *his* alphabet begins where Cornelius's ends, the narrator presents his friend with an extension of the alphabet and a corresponding series of creatures that are, this time, entirely fictional and overtly hybrid. This new alphabet consists of a series

FIGURE 1.3 From Dr Seuss (Theodor Geisel), *On Beyond Zebra!* (New York: Random House, 1958). Unpaginated

of combined letters such as "YUZZ," a kind of Y with a lightning-bolt tale shaped like two Zs, (see Figure 1.3), which the narrator says is used "to spell Yuzz-a-ma-Tuzz." All of the letters, it turns out, are calligraphic portmanteaus of two or more letters and signify fantastic crossbreeds of animals. A large W perched on a lower-case M is "WUM" for "Wumbus," a "high-spouting whale" with human-like legs. A U sitting on the same M is "UM" for "Umbus," a cow with ninety-eight udders. These letters and their corresponding sounds follow what Ferreiro and Teberosky (1982) call the "syllabic hypothesis," offering one alphabetic symbol per syllable rather than one per phoneme: it is not that "Y" is for "Yuzz" but that "Yuzz" is for "Yuzzmatuzz."[14] Here, the synecdochal quality of the alphabet array is both preserved and canceled out: preserved because "Yuzz" is part of "Yuzz-a-ma-tuzz," the way A is part of "Ape," but canceled out because the Y and Z require the speaker to articulate another sound, the short "U," that the letter-shape does not actually contain. Arguably, "Yuzz" also reveals that letters only imperfectly stand for even phonemes because B may indicate "buh" but the extra vowel sound produced with that plosive is not "in" the letter B: most phonemes are impossible to produce purely. In other words, Seuss's alphabet reveals play even in the anti-hermeneutic work of phonics.

---

[14] The exception is "Fuddle," the only two-syllable "letter."

As this Seussian alphabet progresses, even its initial link between sound and conventional alphabetic characters sometimes loosens: SNEE hides part of its lower-case "N"; the "U" in QUAN is barely visible as such; THNAD's lower-case "D" is open at the side and has an odd little tail; ITCH consists of an upper-case "I" and a cross with curled arms that could combine a "T" and an "H" but has a random bend in its smaller vertical line. Many of the letters look unletter-like, with the vaguely humanoid form of HI! perhaps the culminating example.

In short, some of the letters in *On Beyond Zebra!* are more pictorial than alphabetic, suggesting a graphic "takeover." At the same time, it's also notable that "Vroo," the letter that attaches to the "Vrooms" who phonetically clean up the mess of semiosis, looks vaguely uterine: the disciplinary alphabetizing mother lurks even in this anti-alphabet.

On Beyond Zebra's final page is an elaborate scarlet monogram containing seven or eight letters connected by swooping lines, some letters with coils and tassels at their ends. Its unnecessary curls and swoops tilt it away from pure monogram and into pictogram. In typical Seuss fashion, the narrator asks, "... what do YOU think we should call this one, anyhow?" (see Figure 1.4). Even as this does not recapitulate *The Cat in the Hat*'s demand that children answer their mother's question, here, in a typical read-aloud book, would be the typical place for the "mother's" return, as the reader solicited the child's answers. However, aligning with, if not quite caused by, the book's marginalization of mothers, *On Beyond Zebra*'s final letter, we might say, breaks the sound barrier: it simply refuses to be read aloud. It is conceivably a portmanteau of at least A, B, C, E, F, G, J, and Y, and a child who has recognized the alphabet characters embedded in Seussian script might well offer up a name for it like "Gab-Jec-Fy," placing vowel sounds between consonants as the narrator has done for sounds like "Yuzz." Or, in light of synecdochal qualities of both the alphabet array and the Seussian one, a child might add syllables to the end of the letter "sound" and speculate that Seuss's final letter "stands for" a creature called "Gab-jec-fy-o-floog" or some such thing.

FIGURE 1.4 From Dr Seuss (Theodor Geisel), *On Beyond Zebra!* (New York: Random House, 1958). Unpaginated.

In fact, one mother, speech language pathologist Lauren Barnett, has created an exercise for children that prompts just such speculation. After reading her toddler daughter *On Beyond Zebra* several times, Barnett asked the child to invent a letter and name the creature it spells. On Barnett's website (2013), she shows an example of this exercise done by her daughter and also by her husband, who, she tells her readers, "got in on this activity." The letter Barnett's husband's invented follows the Seussian program exactly: the husband's letter "Waz," a W perched atop a triangle that sits in the middle of two mirror-facing Zs, is used to spell "Waz-Mataz" (see Figure 1.5).

But Barnett's daughter's response to the exercise absolutely refuses the logic of phonics and syllabics. "So," writes Barnett on her blog, "her letter is the 'Paxter Wanwi' and it will help her spell the creature 'Naninona.'" Presumably because this child is a pre-alphabetic toddler and has not yet developed certain fine motor skills, the "letter" Paxter

FIGURE 1.5 "Waz" from http://www.iheartspeech.com/2013/07/skill-focus-writing-create-your-own.html. Photo by Lauren Barnett, courtesy of Lauren Barnett.

Wanwi consists of three disconnected shapes: a check mark at lower left, a staggering V that looks like a graph line at lower left, and what looks like a lower-case "f" floating on top (see Figure 1.6). As a portmanteau letter, Paxter Wanwi violates the Seussian imperative that its major parts should be recognizable alphabet letters. It also refuses Seuss's monogrammatic cursive, in which all the parts are connected. But the most charming aspect of the letter's lack of adherence to alphabetization is on the level of sound: no shape corresponding to any of the sounds in "Paxter Wanwi" appears on the page. Nor do any of the sounds in "Paxter Wanwi" reappear in "Naninona." Nor do any of the sounds in "Naninona" show up as letters within this child's portmanteau letter.

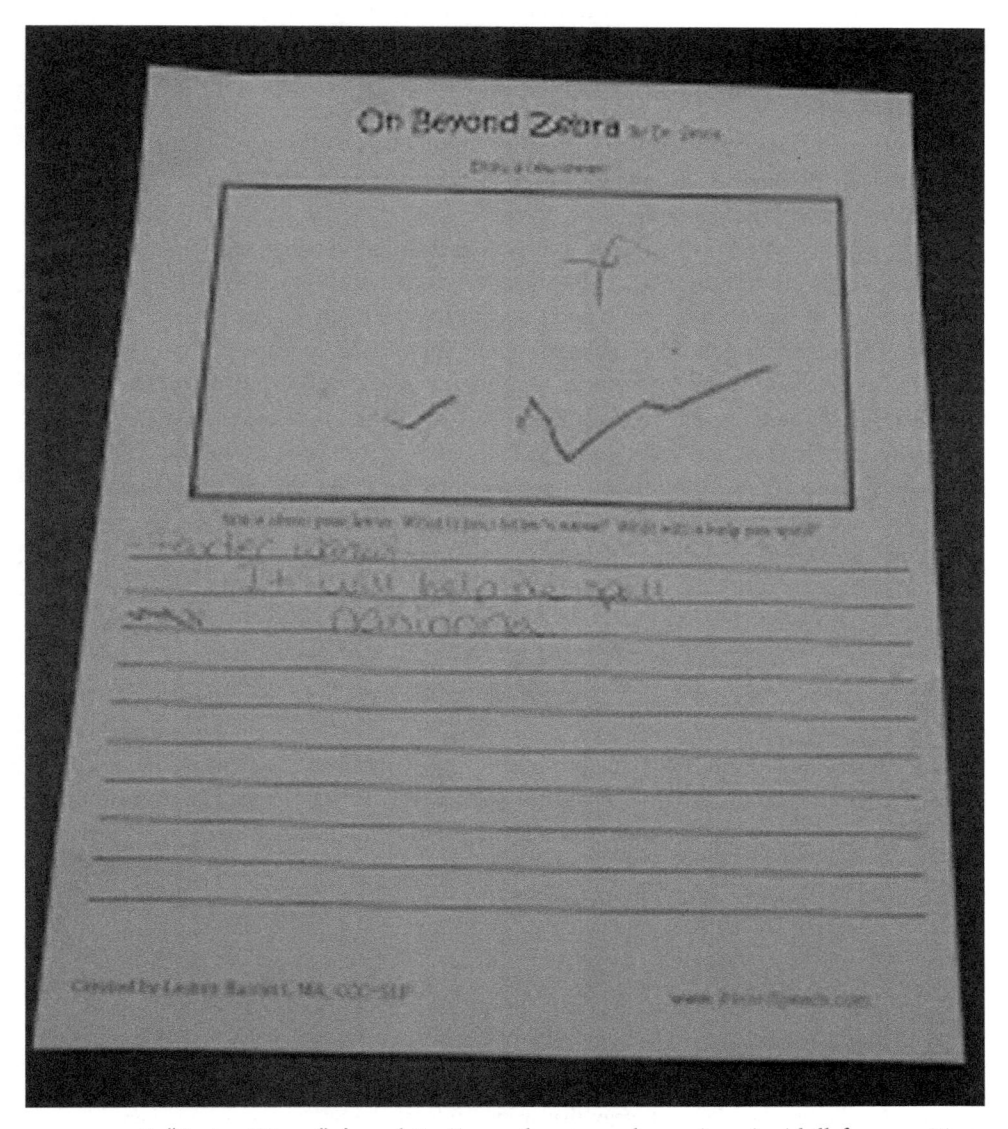

FIGURE 1.6 "Paxter Wanwi" from http://www.iheartspeech.com/2013/07/skill-focus-writing-create-your-own.html. Photo by Lauren Barnett, courtesy of Lauren Barnett.

What Barnett's daughter has done, it seems to me, is refuse the alphabetization of the maternal, or the maternalization of the alphabet, though Barnett confirms that her daughter loves books. This child's wedging apart of the parts of the portmanteau letter into letter-like figures but not precisely letters, her seemingly arbitrary naming of the letter with something that sounds like a human name and has no relation to the marks on the page—as indeed letter-sounds actually have no relation to graphic marks—seems at first to be an intervention into and on the level of writing. But by telling her mother what the marks "will help her spell" or *sound like,* this child literally rescripts alphabetization and, in this sense, reworks the scene of reading aloud.

The mother's reaction is also somewhat resistant to her socially ascribed role as the child's source of plenitude and meaning. She describes the child's response to the exercise, and then says, "Interesting, right? Well, maybe not so much …." Barnett's website shows her to be a creative, resourceful, and attentive mother, although this feigned disinterest in and detachment from the child lightheartedly fissures the tight bond of attachment that shared reading is supposed to reflect and produce. Barnett rescues the situation, finishing that sentence with the assurance that "… the act of being creative and putting new thoughts down on paper is a great skill that will lead to better things in the future." This prediction reflects the status of shared reading and writing as forms of disciplinary investment in the child and their future, the form that care currently ideally takes in American households.[15] Barnett's daughter will likely learn phonemes, in part through her encounter with the many Dr Seuss books that Barnett describes reading with her. But if she doesn't love reading, doesn't perform a love of reading as evidence of her mother's love of her, will that be failure? Or will it be a movement toward other sources of pleasure and plenitude, ones less apprehensible through the heterofocal, gender-bifocal lens of American domesticity? Perhaps Barnett's daughter and my son will meet someday through an alphabet of their own.

Acknowledgements

I thank Robin Bernstein for sharing her unpublished manuscript, "You Do It!" with me and for commenting on the first draft of this chapter and Nat Hurley for commenting on the first draft as well. I am also grateful to Bethany Qualls for research assistance, to Jess Krzeminski and Timothy Walker for help with images, to Juana María Rodríguez for a helpful suggestion toward a longer version of this chapter, to Lauren Barnett for

---

[15] Annette Lareau (2003) provides empirical evidence that middle- and upper-middle-class parents concertedly cultivate their children's skills, including and especially literacy, as opposed to letting children develop on their own terms, as poorer families do. While I question her characterization of poorer families as choosing a strategy that may simply be the result of economic hardship, her assessment of wealthier parents' strategies strikes me as apt.

generous correspondence and for sharing photos, and to Candace Moore for sustaining intellectual conversations with me throughout the time I wrote this.

References

An Address to Mothers, Under the Following Heads: Maternal Authority. Domestic Attention. Diligence AND Activity. Oconomy. Simplicity. Objects of Female Pursuits. Knowledge, Virtue, and Religion. 1784. (Oxford: Sold by Messrs. Fletcher and Son; also Merril, at Cambridge; Debrett, Egerton, Kearsley, Bew, and Swell, in London; and Tesseyman, at York).

Arizpe, Evelyn and Morag Styles, with Shirley Brice Heath. 2006. *Reading Lessons from the Eighteenth Century: Mothers, Children, and Texts* (Shenstone: Pied Piper Publishing).

Barnett, Lauren. 2013. "Skill Focus-Writing: Create Your Own Letter with *On Beyond Zebra*," *iHeartSpeech.com*, July 19, www.iheartspeech.com/2013/07/skill-focus-writing-create-your-own.html, accessed February 18, 2022.

Barton, Anna. 2015. "Nonsense Literature," *Oxford Bibliographies*. DOI: 10.1093/OBO/9780199846719-0099.

Benjamin, Walter. 1978 [1955]. "On the Mimetic Faculty," in Peter Demetz, ed., *Reflections*, trans. Edmond Jephcott (New York: Schocken Books), 333–338.

Bernstein, Robin. 2011. *Racial Innocence: Performing American Childhood from Slavery to Civil Rights* (New York: New York University Press).

Bernstein, Robin. 2020. "'You Do It!': Going-to-Bed Books and the Scripts of Children's Literature," *PMLA* 135.5: 877–894.

Brodhead, Richard. 1993. *Cultures of Letters: Scenes of Reading and Writing in Nineteenth-Century America* (Chicago, IL: University of Chicago Press).

Brown, Margaret Wise. 2007 [1947]. *Goodnight, Moon* (New York: HarperFestival).

Comenius, Johann Amos. 1887 [1658]. *The Orbis Pictus of John Amos Comenius*, facsimile reprint edn, 1942 (Whitefish, MT: Kessinger Publishing).

Costa, Rosalina Pisco. 2012. "Choreographies of Emotion: Sociological Stories Behind Bedtime, Fairy Tales, and Children's Books," *Global Studies of Childhood* 2.2: 117–128.

Crain, Patricia. 2000. *The Story of A: The Alphabetization of America from* The New England Primer *to* The Scarlet Letter (Stanford, CA: Stanford University Press).

Eberling, Eric R. 1999. "Massachusetts Education Laws of 1642, 1647, and 1648, in Richard J. Altenbaugh, ed., *Historical Dictionary of American Education* (Westport, CT: Greenwood Press), 225–26.

Eliot, T.S. 1969 [1942]. *The Music of Poetry: The Third W. P. Ker Memorial Lecture Delivered in the University of Glasgow, 24 February 1942* (Fulcroft, PA: Fulcroft Press).

Ferreiro, E. and Teberosky, A. 1982. *Literacy before Schooling* (Exeter, NH: Heinemann).

Field, Eugene. 1901 [1885]. "Song of the Mugwump," in Martin Roswell Field, ed., *The Writings in Prose and Verse of Eugene Field*, Vol. XII (New York: C. Scribner's Sons), 37–38.

Flesch, Rudolph. 1955. *Why Johnny Can't Read: and What You Can Do About It.* (New York: Harper & Brothers).

Fliegelman, Jay. 1982. *Prodigals and Pilgrims: The American Revolution against Patriarchal Authority, 1750–1800* (New York: Cambridge University Press).

Fox, Mem. 1997. *Time for Bed* (New York: Harcourt Brace).

Goldman, William. 1974. *The Princess Bride: S. Morgenstern's Classic Tale of True Love and High Adventure. The "Good Parts" Version, Abridged* (New York: Ballantine Books).

Hersey, John. 1954. "Why Do Students Bog Down on First R: A Local Committee Sheds Light on a National Problem: Reading," *Life* (May 24): 136–150.

Hoban, Russell. 1960. *Bedtime for Frances* (New York: HarperTrophy).

Hunt, Peter. 2011. "The Fundamentals of Children's Literature Criticism: *Alice's Adventures in Wonderland* and *Through the Looking Glass*," in Julia Mickenberg and Lynne Vallone, eds, *The Oxford Handbook of Children's Literature* (New York: Oxford University Press), 35–51.

Kerber, Linda K. 1976. "The Republican Mother: Women and the Enlightenment—an American Perspective," *American Quarterly* 28.2: 187–205.

Kittler, Friedrich. 1990. "The Mother's Mouth," in *Discourse Networks 1800/1900*, trans Michael Metteer, with Chris Cullens (Stanford, CA: Stanford University Press), 25-69.

Kristeva, Julia. 1980. *Desire in Language: A Semiotic Approach to Literature and Art* (New York: Columbia University Press).

Laplanche, Jean. 1989. *New Foundations for Psychoanalysis*, trans. David Macey (Oxford and Cambridge, MA: Basil Blackwell).

Lareau, Annette. 2003. *Unequal Childhoods: Class, Race, and Family Life* (Berkeley, CA: University of California Press).

Locke, John. 1693. *Some Thoughts Concerning Education* (London: A. and J. Churchill).

Macdonald, Ruth K. 1988. *Dr. Seuss* (Boston, MA: Twayne Publishers).

Mackenzie, Sarah. 2018. *The Read-Aloud Family: Making Meaningful and Lasting Connections With Your Kids* (Grand Rapids, MI: Zondervan).

Manguel, Alberto. 1996. *A History of Reading* (New York: Penguin Books).

Mansbach, Adam. 2011. *Go the Fuck to Sleep* (Brooklyn, NY: Akashic Books).

Mansbach, Adam. 2012. *Seriously, Just Go to Sleep* (Brooklyn, NY: Akashic Books).

Maslen, Bobby Lynn. 2006. *Bob Books, Set One: Beginning Readers* (New York: Scholastic).

Menand, Louis. 2002. "Cat People: What Dr. Seuss Really Taught Us." *The New Yorker*, 23 December. Online at https://www.newyorker.com/magazine/2002/12/23/cat-people, accessed March 5, 2022.

Merritt, Stephin. "The Book of Love." The Magnetic Fields, *69 Love Songs*. Merge Records, compact disc. Originally released in 1999.

Miller, Donalyn. 2009. *The Book Whisperer: Awakening the Inner Reader in Every Child* (Hoboken, NJ: Jossey-Bass).

Moulton, Louise Chandler. 1873. *Bedtime Stories* (Boston, MA: Roberts Brothers).

Murray, Judith Sargent ("Constantia"). 1790. "On the Domestic Education of Children," *Massachusetts Magazine* 2.5: 275–277.

The Mother's Gift: Or, a Present for All Little Children who are Good. Embellished with Cuts. 1769. (London: Carnan and Newbery).

The Mother's Gift. 1787. (Worcester, MA: Isaiah Thomas).

Oklahoma's Glenpool Fire Department Dads. 2005. "The Brainy Benefits of Bedtime Stories," *Parents Magazine*, October 5, www.parents.com/fun/entertainment/books/the-brainy-benefits-of-bedtime-stories/, accessed February 18, 2022.

Peet, Bill. 1970. *The Wump World* (Boston, MA: Houghton Mifflin Harcourt).

Penteado, Bruno. 2019. "Against Surface Reading: Just Literality and the Politics of Reading," *Mosaic* 52.3: 85–100.

Rousseau, Jean-Jacques. 1979 [1762]. *Emile, or on Education*, trans. Allan Bloom (New York: Basic Books).

Seeger, Pete. 1986. *Abiyoyo* (New York: Simon and Schuster Children's Publishing).

Seuss, Dr (Theodor Geisel). 1955. *On Beyond Zebra* (New York: Random House).

Seuss, Dr (Theodor Geisel). 1957. *The Cat in the Hat* (New York: Random House).
Seuss, Dr (Theodor Geisel). 1958. *The Cat in the Hat Comes Back* (New York: Random House).
Seuss, Dr (Theodor Geisel). 1960. *One Fish, Two Fish, Red Fish, Blue Fish* (New York: Random House).
Shortsleeve, Kevin. 2012. "The Cat in the Hippie: Dr. Seuss, Nonsense, the Carnivalesque, and the Sixties Rebel," in Julia Mickenberg and Lynne Vallone, eds, *The Oxford Handbook of Children's Literature* (New York: Oxford University Press). DOI: 10.1093/oxfordhb/9780195379785.013.0010.
Smith, Nila Banton. 1965. *American Reading Instruction: Its Development and Its Significance in Gaining a Perspective on Current Practices in Reading* (Newark, DE: International Reading Association).
Stearns, Peter, Perrin Rowland, and Lori Gianella. 1996. "Children's Sleep: Sketching Historical Change," *Journal of Social History* 30.2: 345–366.
Steele, Richard (Berkeley, George, Bishop of Cloyne). 1714. *The Ladies Library. Written By a Lady. Published by Mr. Steele* (London: Jacob Tonson).
Stockton, Kathryn Bond. 2019. *Avidly Reads: Making Out* (New York: New York University Press).
"Stories to Grow By." 2020. www.storiestogrowby.org/bedtime-stories-kids-free/, accessed February 18, 2022.
Trelease, Jim. 1982. *The Read-Aloud Handbook* (New York: Penguin).
Utley, Matthew. 2017. "How to Tell a Bedtime Story that Puts Children to Sleep," *Fatherly.com*, December 27, www.fatherly.com/parenting/how-to-tell-bedtime-story-makes-children-sleep/, accessed February 18, 2022.
Waddell, Martin. 2002. *Owl Babies*, reprint (Somerville, MA: Candlewick Press).
Williams, David. 1783. *Illustrations of Maxims and Principles of Education, in the Second Book of Rousseau's Emile. In Four Letters to the Mother of a Young Family, Disposed to Adopt Them: But Embarrassed by Difficulties in the Execution, and Particularly by the Objections and Prejudices of her Friends* (London: J. Dodsley, Pall-Mall, and R. Baldwin).
Wyman, Andrea. 1995. "The Earliest Early Childhood Teachers: Women Teachers of America's Dame Schools," *Young Children* 50.2: 29–32.

CHAPTER 2

COLONIZATION TO CLIMATE CHANGE

American Literature and a Planet on Fire

JOHN LEVI BARNARD

When gold was discovered in the Yukon Territory in 1896, atmospheric carbon dioxide levels were already higher than they had been in all of recorded human history. That same year, the Swedish scientist Svante Arrhenius published his paper "On the Influence of Carbonic Acid in the Air upon the Temperature of the Ground," in which he accurately described what would come to be known as the greenhouse effect, through which increasing carbon dioxide and other gases trap solar energy and raise the temperature of the earth (Arrhenius 1896). By the time Jack London's iconic story "To Build a Fire"—in which a nameless prospector freezes to death in the Yukon—was republished in the collection *Lost Face* in 1910, carbon dioxide had tipped over 300 parts-per-million, a threshold never crossed in the 800,000 years for which we have records in polar ice cores.[1] This carbon dioxide was already driving global warming as London was writing, yet the three years encompassing the publication of "To Build a Fire"—first in *The Century Magazine* (1908) and later in *Lost Face*—were anomalously cold. In fact, these were the coldest years of the twentieth century, marking a low point that humans will likely never see again, as global temperature has been rising—as Arrhenius rightly predicted—ever since.[2]

---

[1] For carbon dioxide by year since 1850, see the "Datasets and Images" produced by the National Aeronautics and Space Administration's (NASA's) Goddard Center for Space Studies, https://data.giss.nasa.gov/modelforce/ghgases/Fig1A.ext.txt, accessed February 10, 2022. For carbon dioxide over 800,000 years, see Lindsey (2020).

[2] For average global temperatures, see NASA's "Vital Signs of the Planet," https://climate.nasa.gov/vital-signs/global-temperature/, accessed February 10, 2022.

Just over 100 years later, carbon dioxide passed the threshold of 400 parts-per-million.[3] Over the first two decades of the twenty-first century, global average temperatures hit new records almost every year, and the news has become increasingly saturated with stories and images of a planet literally on fire, with landscapes burning from the arctic to the Amazon.[4] These fires offer compelling evidence for Jesse Oak Taylor's theorization of the "Anthropocene as a planetary condition defined by combustion," and I have opened with these atmospheric and ecological facts and figures surrounding London's "To Build a Fire" as a way of moving that story out of its usual contexts of the "gold rush" and American literary naturalism and into the more expansive frameworks the idea of the Anthropocene invokes (Taylor 2017). While the Anthropocene concept has been useful in drawing attention to the severity of human-generated ecological crises like global warming and mass extinction, scholars working across the fields of postcolonial studies, Indigenous studies, critical geography, and the environmental humanities have noted how it subsumes radical differences of economic and geopolitical power under the universalizing sign of the "human," problematically obscuring the differential responsibility for creating those crises and the differential exposure to their accelerating impacts between the rich world and the poor. Following the lead of many of these scholars, among them Heather Davis, Zoe Todd, Kyle Powys Whyte, and Kathryn Yusoff, who have worked to decolonize or even dispense with the Anthropocene concept altogether, in this chapter I consider the crises of the Anthropocene not as the impacts of the human as a species but as the ramifications of what Walter Mignolo has described as a specifically "Western" modernity underpinned by a logic of "coloniality."[5]

As Mignolo explains it, coloniality is the "constitutive and darker side" of a modernity typically described in terms of enlightenment and progress (Mignolo 2011: 2). Coloniality expresses itself through a series of divisions that inscribe hierarchies of race, gender, and species, all of which are rooted in the fundamental division—articulated in the seventeenth century by thinkers such as Francis Bacon and René Descartes—between culture and nature, the human and the nonhuman world.[6] These hierarchical divisions structure the "colonial matrix of power," which has enabled and justified centuries of territorial conquest and capital accumulation through what Whyte calls "industrial settler campaigns" (Mignolo 2011: 16; Whyte 2017a). Most damaging among these "campaigns" have been "large-scale mineral and fossil fuel extraction" and "sweeping, landscape-transforming regimes of commodity agriculture," which have developed into a petroleum energy regime and an industrial food system that

---

[3] For carbon dioxide levels (January 2022), see https://climate.nasa.gov/vital-signs/carbon-dioxide/, accessed February 10, 2022.

[4] On record temperatures, see the National Oceanic and Atmospheric Administration (NOAA) website, updated January 29, 2021, www.ncei.noaa.gov/news/projected-ranks, accessed February 10, 2022.

[5] On the Anthropocene, see Davis and Todd (2017), Whyte (2017), and Yusoff (2019). On coloniality, see Mignolo (2011).

[6] On Bacon and Descartes, see Mignolo (2011: 11–12) and Patel and Moore (2017: 52–53).

together have profoundly shaped American life and culture and radically disrupted the atmospheric and ecosystemic orders upon which human life itself is dependent (Whyte 2017b: 208). Viewed not merely as "industrial" but specifically *colonial* phenomena, these regimes of petroleum fuel and industrial food appear as part and parcel of what Davis and Todd describe as an uninterrupted and ever-intensifying "seismic shockwave of colonial earth-rending," which, unsurprisingly, has led to planetary-scale catastrophes that will reverberate for thousands, if not millions, of years into the future (Davis and Todd 2017: 774).

By tracing the origins of twenty-first-century ecological crises back beyond more recent periods of industrialization and globalization to the beginnings of colonization, while describing their impacts in terms of seismic processes and geological time, scholars like Whyte, Davis, and Todd all aim to highlight the interrelated but disparate scales—both spatial and temporal—on which those crises unfold. Literary texts can be especially effective at capturing these disparate scales, registering the embeddedness of the human individual within both historical trajectories and planetary systems. Though it is known for the austerity of its setting and style, London's "To Build a Fire" exemplifies literature's ability to depict these relations between the individual, the historical, and the planetary. London's protagonist is a man alone on "the tip of the planet," subjected to the forces of nature and the "cold of space," but he is also a creature very much of his own time, place, and culture, shaped and motivated by the economic and geopolitical forces of human history (London 1910a: 80). Those historical forces are behind not only the markets for gold and other resources the man hopes to extract but also the agricultural and industrial systems that produce the supplies—like the bacon in his sandwich and the tobacco in his pipe—that sustain him along the way. If the story's cosmic vision encourages readers to "meditate," as London puts it, on "man's place in the universe," the things the man carries and consumes insistently return that meditation to the confluence of historical structures and contemporary circumstances that motivated and enabled this particular man's journey to this particular region of the natural world in the first place.

In what follows here, I take London's story as a starting point for the elaboration of an ecocritical method, one that attends to such quotidian things and habits of consumption as they have appeared across an array of American literary and cultural productions over the long twentieth century. I focus in particular on consumable commodities like meat, tobacco, and petroleum, tracing them back to their points of origin—not only through space to distant sites of industrial production but also through time to the longer colonial histories from which American industrialization emerged—as a way of drawing out what Lawrence Buell has called the "environmental unconscious" of these various works and of modern American culture more broadly. Buell explains that literary texts engage this unconscious—which is really a "chronic unawareness" of the ways human experience is profoundly imbricated with nonhuman life, organic and inorganic material, and the forces of "nature"—through "a certain bringing to awareness by exposure" (Buell 2001: 26). As my readings here will suggest, "exposing" the environmental unconscious often means merely attending to the materiality and provenance of what is hiding in plain sight. Scholars like Stephanie LeMenager and Allison Carruth have shown how consumable commodities—things like the gas in the car in Vladimir Nabokov's *Lolita* or the chocolate bars in Toni Morrison's *Tar Baby*—serve to reflect not only the technologies and cultures of production and consumption that mark the respective moments of the novels' composition but also the longer history of colonial capitalism in which those commodities and the novels themselves are implicated.[7] In the case of "To Build a Fire," such attention to what might seem like evocative but extraneous things can help us apprehend the story's indebtedness not only to the gold rush as a historical event but also to the systems of industrial production and colonial expropriation that made the rush possible in the first place.

By attending to both the colonizing nature of the rush—which laid the groundwork for further extractive enterprises in the region—and the industrial systems that enabled it, we can see London's story as a powerful crystallization not only of the state of US empire and industrial capitalism at the turn of the twentieth century but also of the underlying logic and material ramifications of coloniality itself. This encapsulation of coloniality is evident not only in the story's superficial narrative of a contest between "man" and "nature" but also more specifically in the way that deceptively simple narrative fits within the larger history of colonial capitalism's unfolding, over the course of centuries, through the entire "web of life" (Moore 2015). Though in its broad strokes it is indeed a story of a frozen landscape resistant to "the man" and his attempts to master it with fire, if we linger over its seemingly unessential elements—the sandwich he has for lunch, the tobacco he incessantly chews—and consider those elements in relation to the broader networks of industrial production and the longer history of colonialization, what emerges is a story of a planet already engulfed in the flames (and the carbon emissions) of industrialization, a world defined, as Taylor says, by combustion. And applied more broadly, as I show here with a range of literary texts and other works, from pop art and beat poetry to apocalyptic fiction and film, such attention to material things reveals the deep implication of modern American life, from its food culture to its literary forms, in the intersecting contexts with which I began: five hundred years of colonial conquest, expropriation, extraction, industrialization; and the planetary systems the crises of the twenty-first century compel us to consider.

Yukon Gold, Chicago Pork

Marx observed that it was "the discovery of gold and silver in America" that "signalised the rosy dawn of the era of capitalist production" (Marx 2019: 823). London's prospector fits right into the history of gold extraction and speculation that discovery inaugurated,

---

[7] On cars and oil in novels like *Lolita* and *On the Road*, see LeMenager (2014). On sugar and chocolate in *Tar Baby*, see Carruth (2013: 90–116).

and London's story fits into a tradition of American gold rush narratives extending from Mark Twain's *Roughing It* (1872) to John Huston's *Treasure of the Sierra Madre* (1948) and David Milch's HBO cable television series *Deadwood* (2004–2006). Yet from the earliest days of colonization to the latest stage of late capitalism, gold has been only one resource among many within a broadly extractive economy—from the cod fisheries of New England and the whaling grounds of the Pacific to the northern Alberta tar sands and the lithium deposits on the Andean plateau.[8]

In light of the scope and diversity of that economy, it is worth noting that while gold lures London's Yukon prospectors, the occasion for "To Build a Fire" stems from a distinct yet related scheme of extraction. "The man" has separated from his friends and turned away from the main trail not in order to unearth some undiscovered claim but "to take a look at the possibilities of getting out logs in the spring from the islands in the Yukon" (London 1910a: 66). As Taylor has said about the Anthropocene, the gold rush—like London's aptly titled story—was entirely dependent on combustion. The title refers most specifically to the fire the man ultimately fails to build to stay alive, but the fires of the gold rush and an accelerating industrial economy are burning everywhere in the background. Most notable in its absence is the fire the man imagines at the camp, where "the boys" would be waiting for him "and a hot supper would be ready" (London 1910a: 66). But the most demanding fires in the Yukon at the time would have been underground in the claims themselves. All through the winter, miners would set fires in holes they had dug in order to thaw the frozen earth in which the gold was embedded. This burning and thawing required massive inputs of cord wood, which was extracted largely from the banks and islands of the Yukon and its tributaries.[9] In the spring and summer, these same woods would fire the boilers on the steamers that ferried miners and supplies up and down the Yukon, ships "loaded down," as London would put it in the story "Flush of Gold," with "Klondike dust and nuggets" and various other forms of "freight and baggage" (London 1910b: 146–147). As the historian Kathryn Morse has observed, in order to "produce gold" prospectors "consumed whole ecosystems"; deforestation—the man's active pursuit in London's story—was among the most notable manifestations of this consumption (Morse 2003: 91).

Deforesting the Yukon in order to deliberately thaw the permafrost seems almost a farcical anticipation of the ecological catastrophe that would unfold over the twentieth century and beyond, but it is also a perfect encapsulation of the colonial orientation toward the nonhuman world that Mignolo and others have identified. As Mignolo describes it, this orientation developed first through the creation of an idea of "nature" as distinct from and subordinate to the "human" and the subsequent transformation of "nature" into "natural resources" (Mignolo 2011: 10–13). In Sylvia Wynter's terms, coloniality figures the world as *propter nos homines* (for us humans), while at the same

---

[8] On cod and whales in American history and literature, see Barnard (2017). On the Alberta tar sands as a "Neo-liberal Klondike," see Urquhart (2019). On lithium extraction in South America, see Arboleda (2020: 75–76).

[9] On thawing and deforestation, see Morse (2003: 94–100).

time restricting the category of the human to the "ethnoclass" of white Euro-American colonizing "man" (Wynter 2003: 260, 280). London's "man" exemplifies this raced and gendered human exceptionalism as well as the general attitude toward the non-human world that accompanies it. Disregarding even the wisdom of the "old-timer," who advises no one to go alone in the Yukon when the temperature drops to under fifty below zero, the man ventures out armed only with his whiteness, his maleness, and his humanness to buffer him against what the narrator calls the "cold of space" that strikes the "unprotected tip of the planet" (London 1910a: 80–81).

In contrast to the humility inherent in the narrator's planetary perspective, the man says to himself that "any man who was a man could travel alone" (London 1910a: 81–82). But despite this claim to self-reliance, the man is never alone; he relies on a massive yet largely invisible labor force and productive apparatus that transforms natural resources into the various things he carries that allow him to survive. That labor force also includes his actual, living traveling companion: "a big native husky, the proper wolf-dog ... without any visible or temperamental difference from its brother, the wild wolf" (London 1910a: 67). Though the narrator here emphasizes the dog's "wildness," this serves only to highlight the fact of its domestication. Though not pulling a sled on the day of the story, the dog is nonetheless the "toil-slave" of the man, a working relationship in this case dedicated specifically to the extraction of gold and other resources. Such animals figure prominently throughout London's Klondike fiction, from the dogs in *The Call of the Wild* to the horses that lie dead all along the Chilcoot Trail in the story "Trust," their rotting bodies filling the air with "stray and awful odors" that remind the men of the tally of animal lives sacrificed "in the rush for gold" (London 1910c: 48).

If the terrain and climate of the Yukon demanded the use of animal power, animal food was equally integral both to survival on that extractive frontier and to an increasingly industrialized American economy. Though miners would sometimes eat their dogs if supplies ran low (one of London's characters recalls eating "eleven dogs" one winter when other food was scarce), pork was the meat that predominated in the Yukon (London 1910b: 139). In this regard, the man's bacon sandwich is as vital as the other more conspicuously "environmental" details—the logs, the weather—to understanding the story's positioning within the ecologies of empire and capital. While pig raising and pork eating had been central to settler-colonial American life from the beginning, by the turn of the twentieth century the production and transportation of commodity meats had reached a scale and efficiency that was previously unimaginable. Industrial pork production began in Cincinnati in the decades prior to the Civil War, but by the 1890s, Chicago had become what Carl Sandburg would rightly call the "Hog Butcher for the World" (Sandberg 1914).[10] In his novel *The Jungle* (1906), Upton Sinclair described Chicago's meatpacking industry as "a thing as tremendous as the universe," a "marvelous machine" that turned "some eight or ten million live creatures into food every year" (Sinclair 1906: 37, 38, 47). The historian Dominic Pacyga echoes Sinclair in describing

---

[10] On the growth of Chicago meatpacking, see Cronon (1991: 207–259) and Pacyga (2015).

that machinery as both an industrial horror and a "spectacle of the modern," drawing not only laborers but also tourists who flocked by the thousands to witness the spectacle for themselves (Pacyga 2015: 22). Meatpacking companies like Swift and Armour capitalized on this interest by offering tours of the stockyards and slaughterhouses. These tours, along with the accompanying literature and souvenir postcards the companies distributed, all worked to advance and normalize for bourgeois consumers the idea of industrial animal production as modern, progressive, and desirable, despite the obvious violence and environmental hazard involved in that industrialization.[11]

As Nicole Shukin has argued, the meatpacking tours and corporate promotional materials accomplished this normalization by emphasizing the distance and distinction between the human tourist and the slaughtered animals (Shukin 2009: 95–100). *The Jungle* resists this physical and figurative separation, dwelling instead on the individuality and lived experience of the animals and the workers who kill and dismember them, considering them together as sacrificial cogs in the "slaughtering-machine" (Sinclair 1906: 41). Sinclair makes this affiliation between human and nonhuman most viscerally explicit in his depiction of the rendering operations of the Durham packing house, where the "alchemists" of meat processing turned every last remnant of animal flesh into some marketable commodity, and human workers occasionally "fell into the vats," where they might be "overlooked for days, till all but the bones of them had gone out to the world as Durham's Pure Leaf Lard!" (Sinclair 1906: 114–117).

If this scene literalizes the dehumanization, reducing the man to processed meat, Sinclair elsewhere depicts the dehumanizing nature of slaughterhouse labor through a reflection on its brutality, focalized through the experience of a group of newly arrived immigrants—about to become workers themselves—who take a slaughterhouse tour. Entering the Durham packing plant, Jurgis Rudkus (Sinclair's Lithuanian protagonist) realizes that this was where the innumerable products that "pestered him"—from "advertising signs ... that defaced the landscape," from "staring advertisements in the newspapers and magazines," and in the "silly little jingles that he could not get out his mind"—were actually made. These products range from "Brown's Imperial Hams and Bacon" to the "Pure Leaf Lard" and "Peerless Fertilizer," and the violence of their production belies the appealing aesthetic of the advertisements (Sinclair 1906: 39). To the new arrivals, this mechanized violence is astonishing, and the slitting of throats, the sawing of bones, and the scooping and scraping of carcasses, along with the "squeals, grunts, and wails of agony" of the dying hogs were "too much for some of the visitors—the men would look at each other, laughing nervously, and the women would stand with hands clenched, and the blood rushing to their faces, and the tears starting in their eyes." By contrast to these affective responses, the workers on the kill floor and throughout the packing house had no response at all: "Neither squeals of hogs nor tears of visitors made any difference to them" (Sinclair 1906: 40). Completely assimilated to the "slaughtering-machine," these human laborers no longer even register the "relentless,

---

[11] On slaughterhouse tours and promotional materials, see Pacyga (2015: 9–27).

remorseless" brutality that constitutes their employment and characterizes the industry itself (Sinclair 1906: 41).

Sinclair describes that industry as "porkmaking by machinery, porkmaking by applied mathematics," an enterprise controlled entirely by a logic of efficiency (Sinclair 1906: 40). And in the name of that efficiency, industrial animal food production—from Sinclair's day to our own—has relentlessly externalized and deliberately concealed its actual costs in terms of animal cruelty, labor exploitation, and environmental hazard.[12] Sinclair described these accumulated costs as something like a "horrible crime committed in a dungeon, all unseen and unheeded, buried out of sight and memory" (Sinclair 1906: 41). In this regard, his novel looks forward to a number of literary, journalistic, and scholarly engagements with the ethics and ecological impacts of industrial animal production, from Isaac Bashevis Singer's "The Slaughterer" (1967) and Ruth Ozeki's *My Year of Meats* (1998) to Eric Schlosser's *Fast Food Nation* (2001) and Timothy Pachirat's *Every Twelve Seconds* (2011). These texts all contribute to exposing what the animal industry would conceal, the true costs of what Raj Patel and Jason Moore identify as the "cheap food" that has fueled—along with "cheap energy" sources from wood to coal to petroleum—the accumulation of capital through ongoing processes of resource extraction and industrial production (Patel and Moore 2017). These costs lie hidden not only in the labor exploitation and animal cruelty that Sinclair identified but also in the environmental injustices of waste lagoons and toxic run-off and the planetary threats—driven by deforestation, habitat destruction, and greenhouse gas emissions—of climate change and mass extinction.

But if the Chicago stockyards, slaughterhouses, and meatpacking plants were a "spectacle of the modern," laying the groundwork for the industrial system that would accelerate and proliferate around the world over the long twentieth century, that modernity is inextricable from the longer history of empire and capital since at least the arrival of Columbus in the Caribbean. Chicago achieved its status as hog butcher to the world only after 400 years of multispecies Euro-American invasion, and the urbanization of the landscape and the industrialization of the food system could be seen—as Whyte has said of the various crises of the "Anthropocene"—not as novel phenomena but as "intensifications" of a continuous process of colonization that has been ecologically catastrophic from the beginning. Colonization has always involved not only white human invaders but also a whole array of invasive nonhuman species, from the deadly pathogens that swept through Indigenous populations across the long sixteenth century to the millions of cows, pigs, and other livestock that would constitute a colonial animal economy that would radically transform ecosystems throughout the Americas. Virginia DeJohn Anderson calls these livestock animals the "creatures of empire" and such creatures contributed to major geopolitical and ecological disruption wherever they arrived (DeJohn Anderson 2004). From the seventeenth century onwards, pigs

---

[12] On labor exploitation and animal cruelty in the meat industry, see Pachirat (2011). On environmental impacts, see Machovina et al. (2015) and Charles et al. (2018).

proved to be what J. L. Anderson calls "valuable allies" to Anglo-European settlers in North America, ravaging Indigenous food systems from clam beds to corn fields and committing "repeated trespasses" on Indigenous land that precipitated or exacerbated larger conflicts over territory, sovereignty, and land use, conflicts that would expand over the ensuing centuries into the "seismic shockwave" of settler-colonial expropriation and transformation (Anderson 2019: 11–16; Davis and Todd 2017: 774).

CANNED MEATS AT THE END OF THE WORLD

By the time of the gold rush of the 1890s, that wave had resulted in a continental US empire and a system of industrial animal production that would shape the physical landscape and the food culture of the United States and increasingly the world. In Sinclair's account at the dawn of the twentieth century, the Chicago plants were transforming millions of animal bodies into prime cuts and processed meats "destined to be eaten in all the four corners of civilization" (Sinclair 1906: 46). Those destinations included the extractive frontier of the Yukon, as Kathryn Morse has detailed, where miners relied on mass-produced foods that "came across great distances from the agricultural empires of North America" (Morse 2003: 139). Most common among these foods was bacon, and it is unsurprising that the man's lunch in "To Build a Fire" consists only of a pair of "biscuits, each cut open and sopped in bacon grease, and each inclosing a generous slice of fried bacon" (London 1910a: 67). The typical miner, as the writer and illustrator Tappan Adney recounted in *The Klondike Stampede* (1900), budgeted 150 pounds of bacon for a single year, and the " 'three B's,' bread, beans, and bacon," made up the staples of "Alaska fare" (Adney 1900: 22, 335). While beans were often carried dry into the Yukon Territory, they also took the form of "pork and beans," canned and distributed by companies like the Indianapolis-based Van Camp's. As Morse observes, not only were canned and other "mass produced foods" central to prospectors' subsistence but also they were "bringing a revolution to the American diet" in general (Morse 2003: 143). While military campaigns—beginning with the US Civil War and accelerating through the First and Second World Wars—would be significant factors in the rapid growth of the canned and processed food industry, these foods were increasingly incorporated into everyday habits of consumption to such an extent that by the 1950s and 60s they could be subjected to the ironic treatment of beat poets and pop artists, from Allen Ginsberg's "brilliant stacks of cans" in "A Supermarket in California" to Andy Warhol's iconic cans of Campbell's Soup (Ginsberg 2006: 144).[13]

If Warhol's cans evoked the homogenization of consumer culture in general and industrial food in particular, Campbell's soup was also, as the art historian John Curley has

---

[13] On the relation between US military campaigns and food cultures and technologies, see de Salcedo (2015).

observed, the quintessential "comfort food of the cold war" (Curley 2017). As Ginsberg was telling America to "Go fuck yourself with your atom bomb," Americans stocked their bomb shelters with cans of soup and pork and beans (Ginsberg 2006: 154). As corporate advertising and civil defense pamphlets would demonstrate, these cans came to serve the somewhat uneasily twinned desires for domestic comfort and sheer survival.[14] More recently, these desires have animated what we might see as two related genres of Anthropocene writing: the postapocalyptic novel and the "prepper" manual for surviving the apocalypse. As Julie Languille writes in the introduction to *Prepper's Food Storage: 101 Easy Steps to Affordably Stock a Life-Saving Supply of Food* (2013), the prepper manual can be a "helpful resource" for "preparing your family for a variety of challenging circumstances" (Languille 2013: 1). Among the 101 clearly delineated sections of Languille's book, all of which are geared toward helping the reader "sleep better knowing you are prepared," at least 10 are dedicated specifically to canned foods, from salmon and tuna to a wide array of fruits, vegetables, and meats, from "Spam" and "Vienna Sausage" to "Canned Beef, Canned Ham, and Canned Chicken" (Languille 2013: 1, 247). The table of contents reads like the shopping list for the preppers who stocked the bunker that serves as a temporary sanctuary in Cormac McCarthy's postapocalyptic novel, *The Road* (2006). Like London's focus on "the man" in "To Build a Fire," McCarthy's novel follows a pair of nameless white people ("the man" and "the boy") trying to survive in what has become an uninhabitable world. After walking for weeks across an American landscape scorched by some apocalyptic event, pushing their few belongings in a shopping cart, the man and boy survey the contents of the bunker as the "richness of a vanished world": "Crate upon crate of canned goods," from "canned hams" and "corned beef" to peaches, pears, and apricots (McCarthy 2006: 138, 139). With all these products on hand, the man and boy experience a temporary return to normative American domesticity, eating meat and potatoes and even saying grace, as the boy insists on thanking the absent preppers "for all this food and stuff," and hoping they're "safe in heaven with God" (McCarthy 2006: 146).

During their respite in the bunker, the man and boy feast on ham and eggs and baked beans—we learn earlier that the boy's favorite is "pork and beans"—and for dessert they especially relish the canned fruits. In fact, their first meal underground consists entirely of fruit: first pears, then peaches, and when the fruit was done "they licked the spoons and tipped the bowls and drank the rich sweet syrup" (McCarthy 2006: 76, 141). McCarthy's novel is threaded through with extended allusions to Ernest Hemingway's collection *In Our Time* (1925), most obviously in the man's recurring memories of trout fishing, in which the fish—like the canned foods—are metonyms for the "vanished world." But the meals in the bunker in *The Road* have a particular resonance with a striking scene of consumption in the final story of Hemingway's collection, "Big Two-Hearted River"—a story in which both trout fishing and canned pork and beans are critical elements. The story opens with Nick Adams setting out through a forest ravaged

---

[14] On canned food in bunkers, see Henrikson (1997: 204, 208) and Pruitt (2020).

by fire on his way to fish an upper Michigan river he remembers from his childhood. For Nick, who has returned from the war afflicted with trauma that is to some extent reflected in the burned-out landscape, his dinner of canned food seems to serve the dual purposes of solace and survival. "I've got a right to eat this kind of stuff if I'm willing to carry it," he announces, before emptying "a can of pork and beans" into his frying pan; and like the man and the boy in *The Road*, Nick savors his dessert of "a small can of apricots," drinking the "syrup of the apricots, carefully at first to keep from spilling, then meditatively, sucking the apricots down" (Hemingway 1996: 139, 141). The meal satisfies Nick's hunger in a way he had never been able to during the war, and the pleasure he takes in the satiation recalls the pleasure the man in "To Build a Fire" anticipates in the "warm supper" awaiting him at the camp with the boys, while providing an antecedent to that of the man and the boy in the bunker in *The Road*.

These scenes of refuge in the comfort of canned food are critical to the broader thematics of both Hemingway's story and McCarthy's novel, which are fundamentally about traumatized white masculinity and white male attempts to reclaim or recuperate a past world that has "vanished." These attempts are forms of what Renato Rosaldo has called "imperialist nostalgia," through which imperial subjects manifest a longing for the world as it was before they themselves transformed or destroyed it (Rosaldo 1989). As these men try to recover from catastrophes largely generated by the culture, economy, and geopolitics of the white-colonial world order of which they are representative (in one case the "Great War," in the other most likely nuclear Armageddon), it is worth noting that the cans of beans and fruit are artifacts of a system deeply implicated in the "shockwave of colonial earth-rending" that has unfolded in the Americas and around the world over the past 500 years. These foods are products of the "industrial settler campaigns" Whyte has described, regimes of extraction and production that have disrupted and reordered ecosystems from the North American prairies to the Amazon rainforest, while at the same time driving global warming and mass extinction (Whyte 2017b: 208). And though fossil fuel extraction and the "petroleum culture" it facilitates have been the primary concerns of both scholars and political activists concerned with these planetary threats, the industrial animal food system—which makes the man's lunch in "To Build a Fire" as much as it stocks the bunker in *The Road*—is an equally egregious offender, contributing significantly to climate change through greenhouse gas emissions and constituting the single largest driver of species extinctions worldwide.[15]

Neither London, nor Hemingway, nor McCarthy has much to say about these impacts, and I do not mean to suggest that the mere presence of a bacon sandwich or a canned ham in a text should lead us to read that text as a polemic on the ethics, economics, or ecological ramifications of industrial food. But we might approach these stories as LeMenager approaches *Lolita* and *On the Road* with regard to petroleum. Those novels are not "about" oil in any explicit way, but oil is the condition of their

---

[15] On "petroleum culture," see LeMenager (2014); on meat impacts, see Machovina, et al. (2015).

possibility, both in terms of what happens in the narratives and with regard to the aesthetics of the road novel more broadly. While LeMenager's reading of these novels demystifies the "mystified ecological unconscious of modern car culture" in particular, the larger impact of her work has been to illuminate the ways that oil shapes and animates every aspect of modern life (LeMenager 2014: 80). "Modern" people in general and "most especially modern Americans" are "living within oil, breathing it and registering it with our senses," and in a world structured by petroleum in such a totalizing way, LeMenager shows how almost all culture—manifested in everything from films and books to highway rest stops and national parks—is "petroleum culture" (LeMenager 2014: 6). Given petroleum's centrality to modern life, Graeme Macdonald has argued that "*every* modern novel" is "to some extent an oil novel," and we could say something similar about the industrial food system, which has itself become deeply imbricated with the petroleum-industrial complex (Macdonald 2012: 7). While some novels—like Sinclair's *The Jungle* (1906), Ozeki's *My Year of Meats* (1998), and Helena María Viramontes's *Under the Feet of Jesus* (1995)—make it the focus of their attention, that food system constitutes a feature of the ecological unconscious of both modern life and modern literature that is as pervasive and impactful as petroleum. Even Kerouac's road trippers are as dependent on cans of pork and beans and hamburgers cheap enough to buy with their "last food dollar" as they are on fuel cheap enough to keep them on the road (Kerouac 1976: 116). If we can say that every novel in the age of petroleum culture is to some extent an oil novel, we might also say that in an age of factory farms and mechanized slaughter—the infrastructures and processes of what Patel and Moore call "cheap food"—every story is to some extent an industrial food story as well.

As Patel and Moore have argued, the modern world order—which, like Mignolo, they trace to the early European voyages of extraction, enslavement, and colonization—depends as much on cheap food to sustain and reproduce human workers as it does on cheap energy to fuel the machines they operate. And that cheap food sustained the miners at the extractive frontier just as it did the wage laborers in the slaughterhouses of Chicago where it was produced. So while the events of "To Build a Fire" may seem far removed from those of *The Jungle*, none of what takes place in London's story is possible without what takes place in Sinclair's. London's own foray into the Yukon, and thus his story and indeed his entire career, were all contingent as much on the availability of bacon as they were on the presence of gold. As Morse observes, foods like the "canned Cudahy roast" and "Van Camp's pork and beans" constituted the "essential capital of the gold rush," and those foods in turn "contained a small fraction of the millions of dollars in capital invested over decades in the land, factories, and railroads which made the consumption of canned meat possible" (Morse 2003: 142). But what remains missing, even in Morse's careful accounting of the capital investment and labor power embedded in a can of pork and beans, are the centuries of expropriation of Indigenous land and the "rending and disruption of lifeways and life-worlds" that have characterized colonial-capitalist development from the outset, that "rosy dawn" Marx traced to the arrival of Europeans in what they would call the "New World" (Davis and Todd 2017: 774).

Fossils of the Future

If "To Build a Fire" should be understood as part of the long trajectory of empire and capital that precedes and facilitates the gold rush, the story also looks forward to the development of Alaska and the northland as an "extractive zone" over the long twentieth century.[16] Both London's "man" and "the boys" he's going to meet are part of a continuous process of white invasion, building on the settler-colonial and extractive projects of the prior three centuries and extending them forward in ways that would both transform the landscape of the North and lay the groundwork for ongoing ecological disruption across the twentieth century and beyond. To put it in Patel and Moore's terms, the man's objectives—getting out logs, digging for gold—are part of the broader imposition of "capitalism's ecology" on the territory (Patel and Moore 2017: 22). Within that ecology, the logs the man hopes to extract would not only thaw the permafrost and fuel the steamers on the Yukon but also would build the towns, rail lines, and other infrastructures that would be the gold rush's more lasting economic and ecological legacy. In an article that appeared in *The American Monthly Review of Reviews* in 1900, London himself noted that the real beneficiaries of the gold rush were not the prospectors—who all told spent ten times as much as they extracted in gold—but those who had invested in the infrastructure of further extraction and expanded commerce (Morse 2003: 194). Over the three short years of the rush itself, such investment had "placed hundreds of steamers on the Yukon, opened the navigation of its upper reaches ... put tramways around the unnavigable Box Cañon and White Horse Rapids, and built a railroad from salt water at Skaguay ... to the head of steamboat traffic on Lake Bennett." While this transportation network grew up in response to the demand generated by the rush, its real benefit, as London predicted, lay in the future. As London imagined it, "the importation of ... machinery" would "cheapen many enterprises and render many others possible," while "easy traveling and quick communication between it and the world and between its parts" would facilitate the "true development" of the region (London 1900: 73).

That development largely meant the expansion of extractive enterprises, and by the time Henry W. Clark's *History of Alaska* appeared in 1930, mining interests had "diversified enough to guarantee a healthy permanent industry" (Clark 1930: 162).[17] This diversity included, by Clark's account, "silver, tin, quicksilver, marble, lead, cinnabar, platinum, cement and numerous other minerals" as well as commercial fishing and canning and hunting whales and other marine mammals—but most important to the already accelerating processes of global industrialization and global warming were fossil fuels (Clark 1930: 160; Willis 2010: 11). Clark noted that coal had been "a known deposit in

---

[16] Macarena Barris-Gomez defines the "extractive zone" as a region "mark[ed] out ... in order to reduce life to capitalist resource conversion" (2017: xvi).

[17] For more on extractive projects in Alaska, see Willis (2010).

Alaska from the earliest times," with the first mine being "worked" by Russians in order to power their own extractive "voyages into the Arctic," and production had accelerated along with the general development of the region, especially along the rail lines (Clark 1930: 160). But if coal fired Alaskan development in the first few decades of the twentieth century, the future lay in the oil fields. Deposits in southern Alaska produced modest amounts of oil beginning in the 1920s, but everything would change in 1968, when an exploratory team from the Atlantic Richfield Company (ARCO) struck oil at Prudhoe Bay (Clark 1930: 163; Willis 2010: 113–114). Alaska's North Slope would prove to be the largest oil field in the United States, and before long major oil companies—including Arco, BP, and Exxon—were churning out up to two million barrels a day.

That oil would travel southward 800 miles through the Trans-Alaska Pipeline to a terminal at the port of Valdez, where a steady stream of supertankers carried it off to refineries in California. Among these tankers was the town's namesake, the *Exxon Valdez*, which on March 24, 1989 ran aground on Bligh Reef, releasing millions of gallons of oil into Prince William Sound in what would be—until the explosion of BP's *Deepwater Horizon* drilling rig just over twenty-one years later in the Gulf of Mexico— the worst oil spill in US history (Naske and Slotnik 2011: 488). The oil spread across the sound and over 1,000 miles of shoreline, contaminating ecosystems and killing hundreds of thousands of shore birds and marine mammals and untold numbers of fish. Images of the spill, especially those of animals dead or drowning in oil, would be seared into the US environmental imagination, and the ship itself would become a metonym for the kind of ecological catastrophe that inevitably attends the business of extraction.[18] But in an age of climate change driven by fossil fuel combustion, it is worth thinking about not only the local catastrophe the *Valdez* unleashed in Prince William Sound but also the planetary emergency to which the ship contributed. Massive as it was, the *Valdez* was one small cog in the global machinery of petroleum production and consumption; and massive as the spill was, a full accounting of the ship's impact would include not only the oil it spilled but also the oil it successfully delivered. Considered in this regard, the *Valdez* becomes an icon not merely of spectacular environmental disaster but of the banal, quotidian operation of petroleum culture itself.

The director Kevin Reynolds actually figures the *Valdez* in this way in his 1995 film *Waterworld*, in which the tanker serves literally as the life raft for petroleum culture in a world drowned by the global warming which that culture had produced. In the film's rather unlikely scenario, the seas have evidently risen by thousands of feet such that "dry land" is as elusive as Atlantis, while somehow a rogue nation of pirates called "the smokers" has survived by living on the *Exxon Valdez*. The smokers apparently live on nothing but a stash of cigarettes, whiskey, and a Spam-like product called "Smeat," and they draw on the slowly diminishing oil in the ship's hold to fuel their fleet of jet skis, fan boats, and sea planes, which they use to raid other floating human colonies for resources while pursuing the ultimate goal of discovering dry land. Leaving aside the

---

[18] On the *Valdez* spill, see Keeble (1999). On images of animals, see LeMenager (2014: 35–36).

preposterousness of all of this, the film does advance something of a coherent ecocritical vision—less through the conditions of the drowned world than through the residue of the culture that drowned it. The name "smokers" refers first of all to the pirates' cigarette habit, but it is an apt descriptor for their culture as a whole. That culture is dominated by what Stacy Alaimo has called a "carbon-heavy masculinity," and the film consists of scene after scene of smokers indiscriminately machine-gunning from their various petroleum-powered vehicles (Alaimo 2016: 91–108). While the smokers' habits of violence and consumption are exaggerated, to be sure, they are nonetheless reflective of American cultures of individual automobility and imperial militarism that have predominated across the long twentieth century.

Waterworld's exaggerated depiction of these cultures reaches its apogee in a scene of thousands of smokers gathered on the deck of the *Valdez* drinking a frenzied toast to "St. Joe" Hazelwood, the captain in command of the tanker when it ran aground in Alaska. If such depictions may seem a little blunt, a scene in Margaret Brown's 2014 documentary *The Great Invisible* perhaps reveals how on the nose they really are. In Brown's film, which traces the social, economic, and ecological ramifications of the *Deepwater Horizon* explosion, a group of oil executives—gathered together for the annual petroleum producers conference in Houston—participate in an extended and unrepentant exercise in self-caricature as they smoke cigars, drink whiskey, and reminisce about the "golden age" of oil extraction when everyone got rich and "had Texas longhorns on their Cadillac." If the longhorns and Cadillacs perfectly encapsulate the overlaid histories of petroleum culture and animal production, the oilmen's cigars—like the smokers' cigarettes—are equally implicated in the rise of colonial capitalism in North America from the first plantations in Virginia to the ascendancy of big tobacco across what Allan Brandt calls the "Cigarette Century" (Brandt 2007). The scenes of smoking, drinking, and oil consumption in both *Waterworld* and *The Great Invisible* evoke not only the long and interrelated histories of these commodities and resources but also the notion that the modern American relationship to oil—like the smokers' to whiskey and cigarettes—constitutes a form of addiction about which the nation has been in collective denial. As Naomi Oreskes and Erik Conway have shown, that posture of denial has been fueled by the industries themselves, which for decades deliberately disseminated misinformation to the public regarding the addictive nature and lethal effects of their own products (Oreskes and Conway 2010). Though tobacco and climate denialism are to some extent particular phenomena of late capitalism, we might say that denial is a central feature of the whole ideology of exceptionalism that has underpinned Anglo-US imperialism and extractivism from the beginning: denial as disavowal of settler-colonial expropriation; of enslavement and exploitation of labor; of ecological limitations to economic ambition; and of the externalized costs of an industrial economy and petroleum culture that are measurable now in rising carbon dioxide concentrations, rising temperatures, and rising tides.

We can see that denial at work in the man in London's story, both in his rejection of the wisdom of the "old-timer," who advises him never to travel alone, and in his failure to register the true "significances" of the "tremendous cold" that threatens him (London

1910a: 64–65). As the narrator suggests, that cold might have led the man "to meditate upon his frailty as a creature of temperature" and even to consider the larger question of his "place in the universe," but for him it is merely an obstacle to be overcome on the way to his objectives (London 1910a: 65). His frailty will only become clear to him when it is too late, as he senses the "freezing extending" from his extremities to the rest of his body (London 1910a: 95). But that slow freezing is prefigured for readers not only in the narrator's ironic and ominous warnings but also in the material substance of the frozen tobacco juice that encases the man's beard as he incessantly chews and spits. The narrator calls this "a muzzle of ice," which freezes the man's mouth almost entirely shut such that he can neither speak nor eat without building a fire to thaw it out—but the man accepts this "appendage" as "the penalty all tobacco-chewers paid in that country" (London 1910a: 69).

The payment of such debilitating penalties is perhaps a hallmark of addiction, and, like the association of oil and tobacco in *Waterworld*, the "amber" color of the "ice-muzzle" might suggest an association between tobacco and gold (London 1910a: 70). But if these agricultural and mineral resources hearken back to Marx's "rosy dawn" of primitive accumulation, signalizing the man's participation in a long and ongoing story of colonial extractivism in the "New World," that "amber beard" also gestures toward the more expansive framework of geological time. In describing the ice beard as amber (a fossilized resin the color of gold, in which insects and other creatures are often found suspended), London foreshadows not only the man's death by freezing but also his potential status as a fossil of the future. Yet while this projection of the man as both corpse and fossil might indicate the "frailty" of what the narrator calls "man" in general, the fact that the agent of fossilization is not merely the ice and cold but also the tobacco he chews reminds us that this man is not some universalizing figure for the human species but rather a particular creature embedded in, and emblematic of, the particular structures and processes that constitute the colonial matrix of power.

By extension, reading with an eye to those particulars might help us to resist the surprisingly persistent impulse to read London's stories—and the larger tradition that includes Hemingway and McCarthy—in terms of universalizing abstractions like "man" and "nature." These abstractions are even replicated in the opposition implied by terms like ecocriticism and "environmental humanities." As Mignolo has argued, the idea of the environment or "nature" as a thing that could be separated or extracted from the concerns of humans or the humanities is fundamental to coloniality, and the distinction "has been consolidated and persists" "in the hegemonic domain of scholarship" (Mignolo 2011: 10–11). Within the field of literary studies, the historical construction of the "environment" is often as obscure as the "natural" provenance of the commodities and cultural artifacts hiding in plain sight throughout the literature of modernity. My readings here, which dwell at length on commodities and the supply chains and infrastructures that produce and deliver them, thus aim less to expand a discrete canon of environmentally focused stories than to suggest that all stories are susceptible to this kind of environmental analysis—not in the sense that they explicitly foreground "human" impacts on the "natural" world but insofar as they depict the ways colonial capitalism threads itself through the earth system and the web of life to produce the world as we know it.

Literary texts and films like the ones I have considered here make this interweaving of human history and nonhuman systems especially legible. This legibility arises in my readings through attention to particular commodities in individual works, but it is enhanced and intensified by the cumulative effect of drawing these works into a new constellation. By considering an array of texts across various genres and over the historical sweep of the long twentieth century, this cumulative mode of literary historiography and analysis can help us track the emergence and entrenchment of the patterns of production, consumption, accumulation, and waste that have come to both characterize modern American life and produce a planetary ecological emergency. It is within these patterns and the histories of their development that I have tried to situate both the things "the man" carries—the "cheap" consumables that fuel his extractive labor—and the reason he carries them: the demand for resources and capital that motivated individual prospectors and the gold rush as a whole. And I have read that rush as what Whyte would call a single "episode" in a colonial enterprise that began with the arrival of Columbus and has now pushed atmospheric carbon dioxide to a level not seen since the Pliocene Epoch, when seas were fifty feet higher and forests stretched across the arctic (Whyte 2017a: 155; Anon 2022). By situating the story in this way, within the context of the larger enterprise that both led the man to the Yukon and has brought about the convergent geological-scale crises of the twenty-first century, we might read the man's frozen and even *fossilized* body not as an image of the extinction of the human but as evidence of the unsustainability of the colonial-capitalist project and the white supremacist and human exceptionalist idea of "man" that has always underpinned and enabled it.

References

Adney, Tappan. 1900. *The Klondike Stampede* (New York: Harper & Brothers).
Alaimo, Stacy. 2016. *Exposed: Environmental Politics and Pleasures in Posthuman Times* (Minneapolis, MN: University of Minnesota Press).
Anderson, J. L. 2019. *Capitalist Pigs: Pigs, Pork, and Power in America* (Morgantown, WV: West Virginia University Press).
Anderson, Virginia DeJohn. 2004. Creatures of Empire: How Domestic Animals Transformed America (New York: Oxford University Press).
Anon, "CO2 Levels Hit Highest Levels in 3 Million Years," May 19, 2019, YaleEnvironment360, https://e360.yale.edu/digest/co2-concentrations-hit-highest-levels-in-3-million-years, accessed February 10, 2022.
Arboleda, Martín. 2020. *Planetary Mine: Territories of Extraction under Late Capitalism* (London: Verso).
Arrhenius, Svante. 1896. "On the Influence of Carbonic Acid in the Air upon the Temperature of the Ground," *The London, Edinburgh, and Dublin Philosophical Magazine and Journal of Science* April: 237–276.

Barnard, John Levi. 2017. "The Cod and the Whale: Melville in the Time of Extinction," *American Literature* 89.4: 851–879.

Barris-Gomez, Macarena. 2017. *The Extractive Zone: Social Ecologies and Decolonial Perspectives* (Durham, NC: Duke University Press).

Brandt, Allan M. 2007. *The Cigarette Century: The Rise, Fall, and Deadly Persistence of the Product that Defined America* (New York: Basic Books).

Buell, Lawrence. 2001. *Writing for an Endangered World: Literature, Culture, and Environment in the U.S. and Beyond* (Cambridge, MA: Harvard University Press).

Carruth, Allison. 2013. *Global Appetites: American Power and the Literature of Food* (Cambridge: Cambridge University Press).

Charles, H., Godfray, J., Aveyard, Paul et al. 2018. "Meat Consumption, Health, and the Environment," *Science* 361, 243.

Clark, Henry W. 1930. *The History of Alaska* (New York: Macmillan).

Cronon, William. 1991. *Nature's Metropolis: Chicago and the Great West* (New York: Norton).

Curley, John J. 2017. "Andy Warhol's Comfort Food for the Apocalypse," OUP Blog, August 22, https://blog.oup.com/2017/08/andy-warhol-nuclear-apocalypse/, accessed February 10, 2022.

Davis, Heather and Zoe Todd. 2017. "On the Importance of a Date, or Decolonizing the Anthropocene," *ACME: An International Journal for Critical Geographies* 16.4: 761–780.

de Salcedo, Anastacia Marx. 2015. *Combat-Ready Kitchen: How the U.S. Military Shapes the Way You Eat* (New York: Current).

Ginsberg, Allen. 2006. *Collected Poems, 1947–1997* (New York: HarperCollins).

Helena María Viramontes, *Under the Feet of Jesus* (New York: Penguin, 1995).

Hemingway, Ernest. 1996. *In Our Time* (New York: Scribner).

Henrikson, Margot A. 1997. *Dr. Strangelove's America: Society and Culture in the Atomic Age* (Berkeley and Los Angeles, CA: University of California Press).

Keeble, John. 1999. *Out of the Channel: The Exxon Valdez Oil Spill in Prince William Sound* (Cheney, WA: Eastern Washington University Press).

Kerouac, Jack. 1976. *On the Road* (New York: Penguin).

Languille, Julie. 2013. *Prepper's Food Storage: 101 Easy Steps to Affordably Stock a Life-Saving Supply of Food* (Berkeley, CA: Ulysses Press).

LeMenager, Stephanie. 2014. *Living Oil: Petroleum Culture in the American Century* (New York: Oxford University Press).

Lindsey, Rebecca. 2020. "Climate Change: Atmospheric Carbon Dioxide", National Oceanic and Atmospheric Administration (NOAA), updated October 7, 2021, www.climate.gov/news-features/understanding-climate/climate-change-atmospheric-carbon-dioxide, accessed February 10, 2022.

London, Jack. 1900. "Economics of the Klondike," *The American Monthly Review of Reviews* 21.1 (January): 73.

London, Jack. 1910a. "To Build a Fire," in *Lost Face* (New York: Macmillan), 80.

London, Jack. 1910b. "Flush of Gold," in *Lost Face* (New York: Macmillan), 146–147.

London, Jack. 1910c. "Trust," in *Lost Face* (New York: Macmillan), 48.

Macdonald, Graeme. 2012. "Oil and World Literature," *American Book Review* 33.3: 7.

Machovina, Brian, Kenneth J. Feeley, William J. Ripple. 2015. "Biodiversity Conservation: The Key Is Reducing Meat Consumption," *Science of the Total Environment* 536: 419–431.

Marx, Karl. 2019. *Capital: Volume One*, trans. Samuel Moore and Edward Aveling (Mineola, NY: Dover).

McCarthy, Cormac. 2006. *The Road* (New York: Vintage).
Mignolo, Walter. 2011. *The Darker Side of Western Modernity: Global Futures, Decolonial Options* (Durham, NC: Duke University Press).
Moore, Jason. 2015. *Capitalism in the Web of Life: Ecology and the Accumulation of Capital* (London: Verso).
Morse, Kathryn. 2003. *The Nature of Gold: An Environmental History of the Klondike Gold Rush* (Seattle: University of Washington Press).
Naske, Claus-M. and Herman E. Slotnik. 2011. *Alaska: A History* (Norman, OK: University of Oklahoma Press).
Oreskes, Naomi and Erik Conway. 2010. *Merchants of Doubt: How a Handful of Scientists Obscured the Truth on Issues from Tobacco Smoke to Global Warming* (New York: Bloomsbury).
Ozeki, Ruth. 1998. *My Year of Meats* (New York: Penguin).
Pachirat, Timothy. 2011. *Every Twelve Seconds: Industrialized Slaughter and the Politics of Sight* (New Haven, CT: Yale University Press).
Pacyga, Dominic. 2015. *Slaughterhouse: Chicago's Union Stock Yard and the World It Made* (Chicago, IL: University of Chicago Press).
Patel, Raj and Jason W. Moore. 2017. *A History of the World in Seven Cheap Things: A Guide to Capitalism, Nature, and the Future of the Planet* (Berkeley and Los Angeles, CA: University of California Press).
Pruitt, Sarah. 2020. "At Cold War Nuclear Fallout Shelters, These Foods Were Stocked for Survival," "History Stories", February 26, www.history.com/news/cold-war-fallout-shelter-survival-rations-food, accessed February 10, 2022.
Rosaldo, Renato. 1989. "Imperialist Nostalgia," *Representations* 26: 107–122.
Sandburg, Carl. 1914. "Chicago," *Poetry: A Magazine of Verse* 3.6 (March, 191–192).
Schlosser, Eric. *Fast Food Nation* (New York: HarperCollins).
Shukin, Nicole. 2009. *Animal Capital: Rendering Life in Biopolitical Times* (Minneapolis, MN: University of Minnesota Press).
Sinclair, Upton. 1906. *The Jungle* (New York: Grosset & Dunlap).
Singer, Isaac Bashevis. 1967. "The Slaughterer," trans. Mirra Ginsberg, *The New Yorker*, November 25: 60–65.
Taylor, Jesse Oak. 2017. "While the World Burns: Joseph Conrad and the Delayed Decoding of Catastrophe," *19: Interdisciplinary Studies in the Long Nineteenth Century* 25. DOI: 10.16995/ntn.798.
Urquhart, Ian Thomas. 2019. *Costly Fix: Power, Politics, and Nature in the Tar Sands* (Toronto: University of Toronto Press).
Whyte, Kyle Powys. 2017a. "Indigenous Climate Change Studies: Indigenizing Futures, Decolonizing the Anthropocene," *English Language Notes* 55.1–2: 153–154.
Whyte, Kyle Powys. 2017b. "Our Ancestors' Dystopia Now: Indigenous Conservation and the Anthropocene," in Ursula Heise, Jon Christensen, and Michelle Niemann, eds, *The Routledge Companion to the Environmental Humanities* (London: Routledge), 208.
Willis, Roxanne. 2010. *Alaska's Place in the West: From the Last Frontier to the Last Great Wilderness* (Lawrence, KS: University Press of Kansas).
Wynter, Sylvia. 2003. "Unsettling the Coloniality of Being/Power/Truth/Freedom: Towards the Human, after Man, Its Overrepresentation—an Argument," *CR: The New Centennial Review* 3.3: 260, 280.
Yusoff, Kathryn. 2019. *A Billion Black Anthropocenes or None* (Minneapolis, MN: University of Minnesota Press).

CHAPTER 3

NUCLEAR POETRY

Cultural Containment and Translational Leakage in Robert Lowell's For the Union Dead

SIMON VAN SCHALKWYK

Introduction

THE immediate prospect of nuclear annihilation on a global scale exerted immense and productive pressure upon mid-twentieth-century American poetry. As a significant body of critical responses to "nuclear poetry" suggests, however, these cultural productions are frequently confined to expressions of poetic protest—justifiable (if reductive) objections to the deleterious effects of the nuclear upon everyday life, strident (yet potentially didactic) calls for nuclear decommissioning, or to an evasive "turning away" from the nuclear.[1] If such approaches establish the relatively clear contours of what has come to be known as "nuclear criticism," Jacques Derrida's foundational suggestion that the nuclear question remains a "fabulously textual" phenomenon continues to haunt the field. For Derrida, "the nuclear age […] is constructed by the fable, on the basis of an event that has never happened (except in fantasy, and that is not nothing at all)" (Derrida 1984: 23). From this vantage point, he adds, "to the extent that, for the moment, a nuclear war has not taken place […] one can only talk and write about it" (1984: 26). Were it to occur in the full force of its potentially global destructive power, in other words, nuclear cataclysm would leave no one to think or write about it and nothing about which to think or write. At the same time, however, it is precisely because nuclear apocalypse is always deferred that it can be thought or written about.

Literature and poetry, to use a Jamesonian coinage, thus emerge as allegorical or representational shorthands for nuclear anxieties that can only ever occupy the frustratingly numinous realm of fantasy (Jameson 1991: 38). In this way, perhaps, the nuclear

---

[1] See, e.g. Kaladjian (1999), Klein (2000), Brickey (2009), Milne (2017), and Keown (2018).

question's fabulously textual deferral is arguably answered by either explicit portrayals of atomic anxiety or by potentially paranoid readings elevating seemingly innocuous mid-twentieth-century American poetic images and allusions to the apocalyptic specter of the nuclear. Sylvia Plath's mushrooms, for example, emerge as both ironically delicate and furtive iterations of either a nuclear explosion's atomic cloud, threatening to "inherit the earth," or suspicious foreign bodies, akin to the double agents furtively encroaching upon, and fueling, the Cold War paranoia of mid-century America's domestic sphere (Plath 1981: 140). By contrast, John Berryman's description in his *Dream Songs* of Henry Pussycat's "radioactive [...] pal" who has "the night sweats & the day sweats" invokes a more explicit, if fantastical, nuclear subject, irradiated by the toxic residue of nuclear technology and Cold War nuclear anxieties produced by the prospect of Mutually Assured Destruction (MAD) (Berryman 1969: 55).

Alongside nuclear allegories such as these, however, it may also be useful to link the nuclear (or anxieties about the nuclear) to its production of institutional and ideological systems of power. Forecasts of apocalyptic nuclear futures may be understood as instances of "premediation" that is not only preoccupied with "predicting and controlling the future attendant upon the increased risk and consequences of industrial accidents in modernity," as Richard Grusin argues, but which also informs the securitization, control, and immunization of the present against paradoxically numinous future risks.[2] Containment—as policy and ideology—was one manifestation of the securitizing logic associated with nuclear risk. As Alan Nadel explains, containment described a series of processes by which "insecurity was absorbed by internal security, internationalism by global strategy, apocalypse and utopia by a Christian theological mandate, and xenophobia by the fear of the Other-by courtship, the activity in which Otherness is the necessary supplement to seduction" (Nadel 1995: 14).

A similarly domesticating logic informs Richard Gray's understanding of mid-twentieth-century American poetry. For Gray, Cold War anxieties spurred by a rapidly escalating nuclear arms race and the very real prospect of global catastrophe that it entailed were contained by what Irving Howe has elsewhere described as a more general culture of conformity (Howe 2014: 3–25). By this account, mid-twentieth-century American poets strove to defuse Cold War nuclear "anxiety by channeling it into socially established and accepted structures" (Gray 1976: 216). As Nadel continues to add, however, containment was also characterized by a "repressed duality" that it struggles to conceal and which troubles the singular or "straight" story that it hopes to tell about the American mid-century (Nadel 1995: xi, 34). This duality directs us toward what Tim Melley has more recently described as those "metaphorically 'leaky' forms of identity"—and, I would add, poetic forms—incommensurable with containment's primary, conformist, and domesticating demands (Melley 2012: 23).

---

[2] As Grusin suggests, premediation is preoccupied with "predicting and controlling the future attendant upon the increased risks and consequences of industrial accidents in modernity" (Grusin 2004: 38n).

Attending to the dualistic logic of containment and, more crucially, the "leakage" it implies, this chapter re-reads the most nuclear of all of Robert Lowell's works: *For the Union Dead*. This volume, notable for its self-contained insularity and hermeticism (further indices of the domesticating logic of containment), initially appears to represent a conformist and conservative expression of anxieties associated with the nuclear age.[3] Yet the collection also relies on little-mentioned compositional methods of revisionary rewriting—translation, imitation, and cultural translation—that Stephen James has identified as central to Lowell's compositional procedures.[4] These "leaky" modes of poetic rewriting, I suggest, are indicative of containment's duality, foregrounding intertextual and transnational porosities that complicate containment's attempt to straighten out, insulate, or domesticate the nuclear story. Reading *For the Union Dead* as a symptomatic manifestation of containment's "leaky" opposite; in other words, I hope to suggest that Lowell's poetic expressions of nuclear anxiety exceed the immediate and nationally circumscribed localities of Cold War's America's various crises of nuclear brinkmanship and that it produces a poetics that does far more than agitate against or turn away from the nuclear question. Rather, nuclear anxiety seen through the lens of containment and translational leakage reveals the parameters of the nuclear to be implicated in much wider spectrums of mid-twentieth-century American political anxiety and commitment, expanding the purview of Lowell's seemingly personal and domestic American concerns to transnational and potentially global political and poetic proportions.

For the Union Dead: Revision, Translation, and the Movement of Survival

Lowell gave a public reading of "For the Union Dead" at the Boston Arts Festival in June, 1960 (Lowell 2003; hereafter *CP*), introducing the poem with the declaration, "We've emerged from the monumental age" (Hart 1995: 144). Noting that the Boston Arts Festival was located in close proximity to Boston's Shaw memorial, a bas-relief by Augustus Saint-Gaudens depicting Colonel Robert Gould Shaw and the 54th regiment of the Massachusetts Volunteer Infantry, "the first black regiment recruited in the North" during the Civil War, Michael Thurston measures Lowell's declaration against

---

[3] Stephen Yenser, Steven Gould Axelrod, and Vereen Bell respectively describe the collection as a movement from either self-enclosed hermeticism to "renewed concern with the objective and the historical world," from "isolation to hoped for connection," or else utterly "remote from the common ground shared by the reader" (Yenser 1975: 237; Axelrod 1978:132; Bell 1983: 73).

[4] As James suggests, Lowell's compulsive acts of revision play out across translational and imitative modes of composition (James 1996; 2004; 2005).

the precarious circumstances attending the poem's immediate performative occasion. The Shaw memorial, as Thurston explains, had undergone architectural stabilization as Boston underwent a large-scale, government-funded, yet ultimately symbolic, project of urban renewal designed to create "a 'New Boston' from the wreckage of what historian Thomas O'Connor has called 'the ethnic ascendancy' " (Thurston 2000: 97).

These details capably frame "For the Union Dead" as a poem that sets public expressions of memorialization against the "Boom" of mid-twentieth-century modernization, historical genealogies of America's racial legacy, and contemporaneous eruptions of racial dissent. Yet the poem also sets these respective contexts in relation to more unusual temporal and spatial scales, presenting the renewal of Boston's historic Beacon Hill district as a series of ecological, epochal, and geological disasters: the South Boston Aquarium stands in a desertified "Sahara of snow"; steam shovels are "yellow dinosaur[s]"; and Beacon Hill's Massachusetts Statehouse, along with Saint-Gaudens' Robert Gould Shaw Memorial, are shaken by the tremors of urban renewal's "earthquake" (*CP*, 376). In this way, the Shaw monument and the Statehouse (and, by metonymical extension, the State itself) together represent anachronistic and potentially disposable monuments occupying an increasingly precarious public sphere. For Lowell, the "savage servility" of Boston's age of renewal is comparable to the late Cretaceous and, like that era, riskily poised on the brink of extinction. By setting his own contemporary moment against the vaster timescales of the geological calendar, in other words, Lowell's juxtaposition participates in the satirical deflation and diminution of the inflated excesses of his era. Yet even these timescales are rendered insignificant by Lowell's premonition of a post-apocalyptic nuclear future. Prompted by an advert depicting a Mosler Safe that has survived the atomic bombing of Hiroshima, and noting that there are "no statues for the last war" on Boylston Street, Lowell laments the further extinction of historical and public memory while hinting at its supersession by a financial era unethically driven to exploit images of historical suffering for commercial gain (*CP*, 376).

Lowell's image of Hiroshima's nuclear ruin "boiling" over a Mosler Safe casts a long, recursive shadow across "For the Union Dead." On the one hand, it recalls the poem's opening, where Lowell's seemingly oxymoronic depiction of the Boston Aquarium standing in its "Sahara of snow" now seems less of a contradiction in terms than a perfectly logical analogy for nuclear winter—the hypothetical climatic cooling instigated by firestorms produced by global thermonuclear war. On the other hand, the image returns to inform the almost cartoonish concluding portrayal of Colonel Shaw "riding on his bubble" as he "waits/for the blessèd break" (*CP*, 378). Inviting suggestive associations between "bubble" and nuclear mushroom cloud, Lowell's Shaw now appears as a Civil War counterpart to Slim Pickens's Major Kong riding an atomic bomb to thermonuclear death at the end of *Doctor Strangelove* (1964), Stanley Kubrick's satirical take on the hyperbolic absurdity of the Cold War arms race, and the absurdly tautological madness of MAD.[5] In these overlapping ways, "For the Union Dead" simultaneously

---

[5] William G. Simon acknowledges a broader critical investment in reading *Dr Strangelove* as a "comic satire about the conditions and potential consequences of the continuously escalating nuclear arms race

acknowledges the architectural instability of its immediate occasion, the escalation of racial tensions attending the Civil Rights movement brought into sharper focus by debates concerning non-violent forms of protest initiated by the Greensboro sit-ins on the one hand and the more confrontational forms of social disruption practiced by Civil Rights activists such as Robert F. Williams on the other,[6] and mounting Cold War anxieties precipitated by the Bay of Pigs and the Berlin Crisis of 1961.

Lowell's conflation of various types of extinction—mnemonic, racial, and genocidal—is tellingly informed and enveloped by nuclear anxiety. In this way, "For the Union Dead" announces a totalizing impulse that anticipates Derrida's suspicion that "the scope or dimension of an absolute nuclear catastrophe that would irreversibly destroy the entire archive and all symbolic capacity, would destroy the 'movement of survival,' what I call '*survivance*,' at the very heart of life" (Derrida 1984: 28). Though initially associated with his reflections on the nuclear, it is intriguing to note that Derrida, in an essay titled "Des Tours de Babel" (1985), proceeds to associate this "movement of survival" with questions pertaining to the field of translation. In this essay, the meaning of survival depends on the translational potentialities of the term *survie*, which, as Derrida's translator Joseph F. Graham explains, "means both 'survival' as well as 'afterlife'; its use in the text also brings out the subliminal sense of more life and more than life" (1985: 206). Following Walter Benjamin, Derrida understands of translation as something more than the "*representative* or *reproductive*" image or copy of an original (180). Rather, as Ángeles Carreres explains, the survival indicated by translation is better understood as a form of "Überleben [which] refers to both life after death and an excess of life" rather than to *Fortleben*, that is, the "continuation of life that takes place in life and not beyond it" (Carreres 2008: 177). Translation, like the postapocalyptic aftermath following nuclear cataclysm, exists in curiously contiguous rather than fluidly continuous relation to that which has come before.

With this in mind, I now wish to suggest that Lowell's investment in revisionary forms of rewriting and imitative methods of translation in *For the Union Dead* are indicative of Derrida's understanding of "survival." Lowell's translations and imitations, in other words, are forms of "kinship" or "alliance" emerging but also departing from lived originals or finished sources.[7] In this way, I understand them as instances of poetic "survival" attempting to sustain the play of traces—*différance*—when the "absolute referent" of the nuclear threatens literature with "the absolute effacement of all possible

---

between the United States and the USSR within the Cold War political assumptions of the early 1960s," while George W. Linden argues that "the film plays on our repressions and our basic anxiety of total nuclear annihilation" (Simon 2003: 215; Linden 1977: 66).

[6] For an account of the difference between the Greensboro quartet and Robert F. Williams, see Tyson (1998: 563).

[7] As Derrida speculates, the "contract of translation" is closer to an "enigmatic connection, an affinity" or "a kinship [that is like] an alliance" (Derrida 1985: 186). Lowell's own musing on the act of imitation frequently appeal to terms such as "life" and "originals" to describe his own translations and "finished" to refer to source materials. It is worth noting that he described the poems collected in *For the Union Dead* as "plated, far from conversation, metaphysical"(*CP*, 269).

trace" (Derrida 1984: 28). It is against this conceptual background of "finished" monumentality and translational afterlife that Lowell's epigraph to "For the Union Dead," an imitative mistranslation of the dedication inscribed on Saint-Gaudens' monument, begs to be understood. The original inscription, *Omnia relinquit sevare rem publicam* ("He leaves all behind to protect the state") tends to reserve praise for Shaw, the regiment's white leader, and to nominate him as the heroic individual worthy of remembrance at the relative expense of the Union forces' African American troops. By amending the epigraph to *Relinquunt Omnia Sevare Rem Publicam* ("*They* leave all behind to protect the state" (my italics)), Lowell deploys revisionary forms of rewriting in tacit conjunction with translation to re-inscribe the monument toward a more racial reading of American history and invites the public to do the same.

Yet what does it mean to revise a monumental inscription in this way and at a time of public renewal, racial dissent, and against the looming specter of nuclear crisis that threatens such monumentality with erasure? On the one hand, Lowell's revision anticipates, and hopes to address, Judith Butler's observations about "how certain forms of grief become nationally recognized and amplified, whereas other losses become unthinkable and ungrievable" (Butler 2004: xiv). By revising the monument's dedication to include both Shaw and his African American infantry, Lowell anticipates, and hopes to correct, what Butler calls "the erasure from public representations of the names, images, and narratives" of African American soldiers who, though monumentalized, remain excluded from the Latin inscription which originally honored only Shaw's commitments (xiv). In this way, his revision attempts to allocate honor and, more crucially, grievability to subjects formerly excluded from conceptions of the human.

Read against the background of racially motivated forms of public disturbance coalescing around the Civil Rights movement, however, Lowell's desire for ethnic inclusivity seems both pertinent and problematic.[8] On the one hand, his translation posits the implicit incorporation of African American experience into the broader context of the largely Western-European traditions of the classical cultural imperium.[9] The soldiers, initially excluded from the Latin epigraph, are therefore not inscribed within a broader image of American history according to which national bonds are traditionally linked to a transatlantic Western-European tradition with classical status and authority. Excluded from the Latin inscription, they are denied entry into the symbolic domain of language, public life, and national memory such that their figurative depiction alongside Shaw only offers them an imaginary gesture of inclusivity, a false image of the unity and plenitude of the public body. The African American members of the regiment, in other

---

[8] Similar questions regarding the efficacy of white allyship arguably inform more recent expressions of African American agency coalescing around the #Black Lives Matter (#BLM) movement.

[9] At this point, Jacques Lacan's suggestion that subject formation depends largely on the degree to which accession into language [*langage*] is accomplished is worth bearing in mind. Despite Slavoj Zizek's suggestion that Lacan's insight essentially means that "I am what I am through signifiers that represent me, signifiers constitute my symbolic order," it is clear, as my argument regarding the status of the Union soldiers' accession to monumental status suggests, that there are orders of accession that remain incomplete or partial (Zizek 2007: 112n).

words, are only available to the public gaze as a monumental image, and this image is relegated to a supplementary status confined within the bounds of domestic American politics and history in relation to the Latinized epigraph. Lowell's translation arguably acts as a racially idealized corrective to such exclusions. Yet his attempt to "translate" the regiment into the classical Western-European imperium remains problematic in relation to more strident demands for non-Westernized or unmediated forms of African American agency. From this vantage point, Lowell's desire for ethnic inclusivity runs counter to the desires of those who, at the time, were agitating for non-Western (and non-white) forms of political and aesthetic self-determination (Fine 1971: 374).

As an ethical ideal, Lowell's racially inclusive gesture, however admirable it may be, thus runs counter to the desires of those committed to forms of self-determination epitomized by Black Power, a movement that, as Stokely Carmichael would later demand, needed to "smash everything Western civilization has created."[10] At the same time, however, "For the Union Dead" tacitly stages the difficulties associated with any attempt to translate cultural and racial others into the ambit of histories from which they have traditionally been excluded. For example, Lowell later suggests that it is precisely the fact that the African American soldiers have been excluded from complete accession into monumental status that liberates them for continued "life."[11] Recalling that "William James could almost hear their bronzed impressions breathe," Lowell renders the Union soldiers more lifelike, and indeed more human, than Shaw, who is reduced to mechanical functionality creatureliness and Puritanical austerity (Lowell compares Shaw to a compass needle; an angry, vigilant wren; a gentle yet taut greyhound; adding that he winces at pleasure and suffocates for privacy.) In this way, Lowell calls into question the worth of the Union soldiers' accession to a monumental status that appears to do little more than etiolate and disfigure Shaw's historically significant heroism. For Lowell, in other words, monumental forms of public memorialization may in fact serve to intensify rather than to assuage distorted, superficial, or entirely amnesic responses to history. Lowell thus suggests that the exclusion of the African American soldiers have been excluded from complete accession into monumental status that secures their potential "afterlife"—to survive beyond their monumentally "finished" status. At a moment when all monuments seem threatened by local forms of "renewal" or the specter of global nuclear destruction, Lowell here seems to be calling

---

[10] Stokely Carmichael, quoted in US Government (1967: 320). Though it was published in 1964, many of the poems in *For the Union Dead* appear to track events in Lowell's personal and public life occurring over the previous four or five years. In this respect, it is worth suggesting that Lowell wrote many of the poems in the collection while Robert F. Williams, the Nation of Islam, and Malcolm X's commitments to forms of self-determination were taking place and as Amiri Baraka's Black Arts movement emerged as the aesthetic complement to Black Power's political interventions.

[11] My subsequent analysis is indebted to, while departing from, Michael Thurston's more optimistic argument that Lowell's conferral of "breath" upon the "unnamed and publicly unremembered" African American soldiers serves to render them "more human than their leaders' graven images" (Thurston 2000: 101, 102).

into question (while tacitly calling for alternative modes of) public memorialization, commemoration, and memory.

Lowell proceeds to develop his complication of public forms of memorialization as the poem progresses. Reasserting the implicit idea that breath and life lay with those who have not been memorialized for public consumption, Lowell notes that Shaw's father resisted his son's monumentalization and that he preferred to see Shaw's body interred, alongside his African American troops, in "the ditch" (*CP*, 377). For Michael Thurston and Henry Hart, Lowell's "ditch" acts as a metonym for the "postmodern atrocity" of Cold War nuclear anxiety.[12] Yet given the racial unrest of Lowell's immediate context, it is also worth remembering that Claude McKay, widely regarded as one of the founders of the Harlem Renaissance, referred to "The Ditch"—the popular name of the multiracial *quartier* in Marseilles, France, where many of the artists associated with the "New Negro" movement lived during the 1920s and 1930s—in his novel, *Banjo* (Cooper 1987: 255). In this way, the racial differences between Shaw and his troops recalls an earlier iteration of racial integration that stands as an alternative to contemporary expressions of racial separatism even as the image signals the burial of this ideal. Racial animosities are dissolved, if not entirely resolved, by death. Reading Lowell through McKay thus sets a far-flung multiracial genealogical pretext against America's domestic history of racial subjugation simultaneously indicating Shaw's hope that racial animosity will dissolve into a multicultural future while offering tragic confirmation of Cold War America's tragic failure to answer this hope with anything other than a deathly resolution to racial crises.

The fate of Shaw and his platoon, moreover, stands in uneasy relation to Lowell's personal engagement with contemporary racial tensions as he finds himself crouching in front of his television screen to watch the faces of African American students rise into view like "balloons" (*CP*, 377). Initially, this image appears to anchor Lowell's domestically distant encounter with the racially explosive contexts informing the Civil Rights movement and the Greensboro sit-ins. Screened off from any immediate involvement, as Henry Hart observes, Lowell's encounter with the emergent politics of the Civil Rights and Black Power movements is mediated by a technologically informed "postmodern sublime" that "mimes a nuclear explosion by 'subliming' or 'blowing up' everything into a spectacular spectacle of gray dots [...] thin filmic images" available for popular consumption rather than genuine political solidarity (Hart 1995: 44). Yet, this image is not simply an objective correlative for the postmodern ethical etiolation of new media. Rather, it emerges as a device that performs a mediating function, drawing together and linking in the manner of nuclear fission's chain-reaction, "For the Union Dead's" preoccupation with incompatible scales of violence. That the children's faces are compared to "balloons," for instance, links them to both the troubling specter of

---

[12] Cf. Thurston (2000: 99) and Hart (1995). For Thurston, "the ditch" represents the "postmodern atrocity" of nuclear annihilation, and "For the Union Dead" consequently enacts a "brutal mathematics" linking the violence of the American Civil War to civilian populations by making "modern warfare 'total.'"

Shaw's nuclear "bubble" at the poem's end and to the air bubbles rising from the noses of the fish depicted at the start of the poem when Lowell recalls his childhood visit to the South Boston Aquarium. Lowell's recollection of how his hand "tingled to burst" these bubbles anticipates the shaky foundations of the similarly "tingling" Statehouse while informing the central image of the mushroom cloud suggested by the commercial photograph of Hiroshima and the Mosler safe and the final image of Shaw riding his own thermonuclear bubble to breaking point. In this way, anxieties about potentially violent racial encounters are again paradoxically elevated to national and international scales of concern and rendered insignificant in relation to the terrifying prospect of global nuclear death.

If Lowell evokes the potential, and potentially totalizing, violence of the encounter between self and other, however, it is worth noting that he defuses that prospect with a series of images foregrounding mis-identification rather than direct engagement. That he *crouches* to his television set, for instance, stands in direct contrast to the image of faces that *rise* like balloons—they are bound to miss each other. And, despite the troubling suggestion that Lowell's childish desire to burst the air bubbles rising from the noses of the fish in the Boston Aquarium might inform his later characterization of faces as balloons similarly available for bursting, it is worth noting that this desire, along with the violence that it implies, appears to be dispelled as quickly as it is evoked: Lowell's hand "draws back," a movement simultaneously charged with, and resistant to, violent action.

Lowell, in other words, repeatedly acknowledges his own disturbing identification with, and capacity for, savagery. The similarities between the child who presses a snail-like nose to the aquarium's glass, for instance, invites the suggestion that Lowell once identified closely with the "dark downward vegetating kingdom / of the fish and reptile" (*CP*, 376). For Lowell, sympathetic identification is haunted by the potential for violence. Yet, if he retains a degree of longing to identify with all that is dark and downward, he avoids their dubious comforts even as he resists the (no less dubious) claims of the present moment. In this way, Lowell strives to circumvent the apparent ideal of absolute immanence or identification which, as we have seen, remains invested with sublime, potentially violent and explosive power, by staging uneasy (mis-)alliances between self and other.

Inheriting the Globe

Lowell's ambivalent and ambiguous attempt to grapple with the twinned and curiously related specters of racial and nuclear cataclysm in "For the Union Dead" proceeds from his revisionary rewriting (or imitative translation) of the Saint-Gaudens inscription. As we have seen, the poem narrows the gap between also draws anxieties about the broader prospect of nuclear annihilation on a global scale and those pertaining to questions of cultural difference, assimilation, and even extirpation, informing Lowell's understanding of the racial antagonisms of his particular mid-twentieth-century American context. A similar gesture, whereby the desire for cross-cultural correspondence is counterbalanced by an avowal of cultural difference and an anxiety regarding cultural destruction, underscores Lowell's attempts to read the world in terms of the home. As the following excerpt from Lowell's March 1962 letter to Edmund Wilson suggests, he drew upon the metaphors irradiated with nuclear anxiety in "For the Union Dead"—the icy "encrustations" enveloping the South Boston aquarium in its "Sahara of snow"—so as to distinguish or to disambiguate the "crust" of his own "culture" from his experience of Caribbean culture:

> I'm just back from Puerto Rico [he writes], sunned and shaken—partly by the country, all the sun and water all the creeping Puerto Rican life, which is all around us here on the West Side, but which is revealed there in greater purity perhaps, that creeping life that will survive the crust of our culture—or will it?
>
> (Hamilton 2007: 405)

Lowell's exotic and potentially pejorative description of Puerto Rican otherness admittedly relies on Orientalizing binaries in order to establish a differential relationship between self and other: "the crust of *our* culture" [my italics] recalls the possessive limits of the pronoun originally attributed to Shaw in the Saint-Gaudens inscription and is set in exclusionary contrast to a troublingly racist portrayal of "creeping Puerto Rican life." Though familiar to Lowell due to his personal experience of West Side New York, this "life" is "revealed ... in greater purity" in Puerto Rico, where it is naturalized by virtue of its association with "sun and water" but also as an unincorporated US territory, set in curiously strategic relation to the US mainland at a time of intensifying Cold War conflict in the Caribbean.

If the metaphors in Lowell's letter draw allusively upon his engagement with otherness in "For the Union Dead," they return in revised and allusive ways to inform another of *For the Union Dead*'s poems, "July in Washington." In this poem, much like Colonel Shaw, "green" monuments of South American freedom fighters "ride" above a landscape of "breeding vegetation," the "prongs and spearheads of some equatorial / backland that will inherit the globe" (*CP*, 366). As these lines suggest, Lowell retains the vegetal metaphors evident in his letters, but he also subjects them to chiasmatic transposition and alteration. By replacing the word "creeping" with the adjective "breeding," for instance, he lends the original vegetal metaphor a creaturely dimension that imbues his earlier allusion to elemental nature with an organic and racially distasteful aura in ways that recall his preoccupation with the pejoratively primitive or prehistoric "dark downward and vegetating kingdom / of the fish and reptile" of "For the Union Dead." Lowell thus overlays or translates his domestically American experience of racial difference associated with his mediated encounter with Black consciousness and Black Power with forms of racial otherness initially located in Puerto Rico's unincorporated US territory. In this way, he betrays an ideological alignment with the widespread Cold War American assumption that, as Charles Venator-Santiago has argued, "black Americans and Puerto Ricans were more likely to achieve racial justice when their interests converged with those of white elites" (Venator-Santiago 2012: 423).

If "white Americans have invoked narratives of interest convergence to selectively address the claims raised by black Americans and Puerto Ricans," Lowell proceeds to expand his own poetic narrative to include a more general evocation of "South America" (424). "July in Washington" thus establishes a differential binary between self and other: "culture," represented by a local monument found in Washington, is deemed to be under threat from the nondescript denizens of "some equatorial backland" who, by virtue of their metonymic association with "breeding vegetation" and "prongs and spearheads," represent primal, primitive, sexualized "nature." In plain terms, it is hard not to escape the suspicion that Lowell is here registering his anxiety that the "crust of our culture"—of white, Western culture that is—threatens to be overcome or extirpated by an encroaching (creeping) and multiplying (breeding) racial otherness.

Like "For the Union Dead," "July in Washington" suggests that Lowell's appeal to forms of revisionary rewriting brings to light a repressed transnational archive emerging from Cold War anxieties about the nuclear and the supposed encroachment of Communism that reveals containment policy to be as much about the protection of the US domestic sphere as about the linkages between its racial assumptions and its strategic, potentially neo-imperial, forms of Cold War expansionism.[13] This is all the more apparent if the broader context of the poem's compositional history is taken into account. "July in Washington" had originally appeared in Allan Nevins's *Lincoln and the Gettysburg Address* in 1964 under the title, "Washington" (*CP*, 932, 1158n). In that version, the image presently under discussion offered no indication of Lowell's experiences in South America; Lowell simply states that "The circles are held by green statues, tough as weeds" (*CP*, 932). Lowell's later description of the Washington statues as "South American / liberators" broadens the scope of his interest in the domestic politics of race relations in "For the Union Dead" to transnational, if not entirely global, proportions.

By conflating a monument found in Washington with the image of a South American liberator, Lowell nevertheless offers a wry and subtle commentary on the question of freedom, democracy, and national sovereignty within the dubious political context of the Cold War. The kinship that Lowell sees between South American liberators and the memory of the United States' liberation movements represented by the monumental "crusts" of American statuary and "culture" indicates his acknowledgement of sub rosa political imperatives whereby the heroic liberator may be little more than an imperialist proxy. One thinks, for instance, of US participation in the overthrow of reforming governments—such as those of Guatemala in 1954 and Chile in 1973—because of their communist leanings. President Dwight D. Eisenhower and John F. Kennedy's respective interventions in Cuban politics following Fidel Castro's successful uprising against Fulgencio Batista's regime reflects a similar attempt to meddle in foreign affairs in order to secure US interests. In this context, Lowell's

---

[13] As Ediberto Román notes, "Puerto Rico became even more strategically significant during the second half of this century with the emerging power of the Soviet Union and Fidel Castro's revolution in Cuba" (Román 1997: 1150).

lines might recall the Bay of Pigs Crisis of 1961, the culmination of Kennedy's disastrous attempt to support a factional uprising against Castro-led Cuba. US intervention in international affairs, like Lowell's poetic interventions spurred by his imitative revisions of foreign poems, public monuments, and his own work, suggests a complicity with the other that serves to undermine potentially clear-cut differences between self and other, home and world.

CAESAR OF ARGENTINA

Lowell's revisionary procedures gain a more properly translational edge when they are read in relation to his journey to South America in the winter of 1962 in his capacity as cultural ambassador for the Congress for Cultural Freedom (CCF), a fact that appears to confirm his affiliation with Western cultural and political institutions during the Cold War.[14] Established in 1950 for the purpose of promoting "cultural exchange" between foreign nations across the globe, the CCF's links to the US State Department and the Central Intelligence Agency (CIA) during the Cold War were eventually exposed in the journal *Agenda* in 1967. As the centerpiece of a covert campaign initiated by the US government, the CCF operated

> a sophisticated, substantially endowed cultural front in the West, *for* the West, in the name of freedom of expression. Defining the Cold War as a "battle for men's minds" it stockpiled books, conferences, seminars, art exhibitions, concerts, awards.
>
> (Saunders 1999: 1–2)

Lowell's translations, similarly "stockpiled" in his recently published Bollingen award-winning collection *Imitations* (1962), arguably form a further dimension of this "cultural front," particularly when they are regarded alongside his potential as cultural "Cold Warrior." As Peter Robinson has suggested, for example, Lowell's free-wheeling, libertarian method of imitative translation implies that "the freedoms that Lowell claims may be thought [...] to oppose the restrictions upon what writers may be allowed to do, or not do, by Warsaw Pact states" (Robinson 2010: 35).

Lowell's participation in the Conference, however, raises questions about the efficacy of his collusion, however inadvertent, with Cold War cultural institutions. According to reports, he dispensed with the medication that he had been taking to control his manic depression upon his arrival in South America and suffered yet another of his chronic attacks of "mania." During a reception at the presidential palace in Buenos Aires, Lowell reportedly downed several double martinis, insulted a military general who would

---

[14] For an account of Lowell's participation in the Congress for Cultural Freedom see Hamilton (1982: 299–309).

soon become Argentina's next interim president (probably UCRI's José María Guido), declared himself "Caesar of Argentina" and delivered a speech in which he extolled the virtues of Adolf Hitler before stripping naked and mounting an equestrian statue in one of the city's main squares. Lowell indulged in similarly erratic behavior for several days before finally being wrestled to the floor by medical orderlies, dosed with Thorazine, and sent home.

While accounts of Lowell's breakdown in Argentina do acknowledge time he spent with writers such as Jorge Luis Borges and Rafael Alberti, they usually linger on the more scandalous dimensions of these meetings at the expense of their potential impact upon his poetry. This oversight is particularly apparent with respect to his encounter with Alberti, the leftist Spanish poet who was living in exile in Argentina at that time. Commentaries devoted to this encounter routinely mention Lowell's arm-wrestling contests with Alberti, adding that Alberti and his "stoutly left-wing friends" attempted to protect Lowell from what they suspected to be a CIA attempt to kidnap him (Hamilton 1982: 302).[15]

Lowell's contests with Alberti, and Alberti's misguided attempts at guardianship, encapsulate the kind of macho brinkmanship, exhibitions of strength, and paranoia characteristic of Cold War politics. A similar pressure may be detected in Lowell's terse acknowledgment of Alberti in the note preceding *For the Union Dead*. "The Lesson," he admits in passing, "picks up a phrase or two from Rafael Alberti" (*CP*, 319), though as Robinson suggestively points out, Lowell may well have borrowed "rather more" (Strand 2002: 129, 154). Yet by neglecting to reveal the extent of Lowell's borrowings and by eschewing further engagement with how he has reworked this material, Robinson participates in a broader critical tendency to overlook the translational and transnational significance of Lowell's work. Such unwillingness occludes a notable current of interest in Hispanic and Latin American poetry in the United States and across the globe since the early 1940s. It is therefore worth recalling that a significant portion of Alberti's work in English translations by Beatrice Poske, Elizabeth du Gué Trapier, Jessie Wendell, and Alice McVan had been in circulation since the Hispanic Society of America's publication of *Translations from Hispanic Poets* (1938: 167–175). As a poet, former graduate of Kenyon College, and contributor to the *Kenyon Review*, Lowell would also probably have been aware of Lloyd Mallan's frequent contributions to the field of Spanish and Spanish American poetry in journals such as *Poetry: A Magazine of Verse* and the *Kenyon Review*.

Mallan's translation of Alberti in an issue of *Transformation Four* had been accompanied by an introductory essay notable for its remarks about translation (Mallan c.1946). In a comparison between Alberti and Federico García Lorca, Mallan prioritizes the latter as "the most Spanish of all modern Spanish poets" whose "best […] most intense […] work […] is almost completely lost in translation" (176–177). By contrast, he perceives Alberti's work as being "not only accessible emotionally to all non-Spaniards,

---

[15] For an account of Lowell's encounter with Alberti see Hamilton (1982: 300–301).

but at the same time [...] offers new techniques, new forms of expression and an originality that might be incorporated to advantage in the poetic expressions of other languages" (176–177). Lorca and Alberti, therefore, were very much the focus of a broader institutional interest in Hispanic poetry centered on questions of translation and transnationalism, both in the United States and across the globe, during the postwar years.

Drawing close to and departing from the source poem, Lowell's translation mimics the similarly paradoxical play of camaraderie and rivalry underpinning his encounter with Alberti, while also echoing the well-known idea of *traduttore, traditore*—the Cold War translator as traitor. Though the greater part of "The Lesson" is derived from Alberti's *Retornos del amor los vividos paisajes*,[16] a poem in which questions of loss, memory, and repetition or return are reflected in a series of modal shifts, Mark Strand's recent translation of Alberti's work suggests that Lowell's poem is in fact a combination of this poem and "They have Gone" (Robinson 2010: 55). The image of the leaf that dominates both of these poems, along with Alberti's meditation on themes of loss, memory, and nostalgia, all recur in Lowell's "The Lesson." Lowell's translational borrowings, therefore, appear to capitalize on the sense of loss and nostalgia central to Alberti's work. Beginning with a skeptical attitude toward the finality of loss ("We believe, my love, that those landscapes have remained asleep or dead within ourselves at the age and time when we inhabited them"), Alberti then turns his attention to the immediate details of lived experience grounded in the present tense ("And so, my love, you wake up to-day at my side among the currant bushes and hidden strawberries, protected by the firm heart of the woods") (Cohen 1956: 412). Concluding with an optimistic appeal to the subjunctive mode ("be happy, leaf, for ever; may you never know autumn"), his poetic speaker strives to redeem loss via a nostalgic invocation for the continuance or repetition of lived experience into the present moment and futurity (412).

If Lowell follows Alberti's skepticism about the consignment of experience to the past when he admits that "All that landscape, one likes to think it died / or slept with us, that we ourselves died / or slept in the age and second of our habitation," his attitude to this past, and to its continuance into the present and future, is less optimistic (*CP*, 332). Instead, as Lowell's reflections on "the same" footprint or boat suggests, past landscapes recur, repetitively, in the present moment (*CP*, 332). Lowell, in other words, laments the survival (or continuation, *Fortleben*) into the present and future of past disappointments. This emphasis on sameness is a particularly intriguing aspect of Lowell's imitation, where repetition may be understood as textual performances of personal and political seizure and dread expressed as deadening alliterative and assonantal sonic equivalences (the "the *l*ight *l*ights"; books "*l*ie in the *l*ibrary"; "the bar*berry berry*" [my italics]) (*CP*, 332). Given the heightened nuclear tensions of his particular Cold War moment, we may therefore understand Lowell's pessimism and Alberti's optimism as

---

[16] I refer to "Memories of landscapes that are alive", J.M. Cohen's prose translation of Alberti's *Retornos del amor en los vividos paisajes* (Cohen 1956: 412).

complementary responses to a present caught in the Cold War's autumnal interregnum paradoxically haunted by the apocalyptic future prospect of a nuclear winter. Reading these lines for their nuclear significance therefore invites the suggestion that Lowell is here hoping to deploy repetition and sameness as a stay against the apocalyptic prospect of a nuclear future's inevitable arrival.

A similar example of the critical occlusion of translational and transnational modes of signification informs "Returning," a poem that, as Jonathan Raban and Katherine Wallingford have both observed, addresses themes of homecoming and nostalgia. For Raban, "Returning" juxtaposes a "frizzled landscape, with memories of greener times" (Raban 1977: 173), while Wallingford, in turn, situates the poem alongside a series of others in *For the Union Dead* in which "the remembered past is superior to the present" (Wallingford 1999: 131). She points out that the unfavorable image of the present offered by the poem is a result of the speaker's inability to resist comparing the present with the distortions of idealized memory or nostalgia. Yet, Raban and Wallingford both overlook the fact that Lowell's poem began as an imitation of Giuseppe Ungaretti's *Penultima stagione*, a poem whose title anticipates a final crisis and which, as Frederic L. Jones has suggested, is imbued with a typically "autumnal" reflection on the waning of a youthfully exuberant poetics devoted to the thrilling immediacy of sensuous experience (145–146). Raban and Wallingford tend to foreclose further inquiry into how Lowell's dealings with memory and nostalgia may have been shaped by their relationship to a foreign counterpart. In doing so, they occlude the ways in which imitative modes of translation to might link the inward-looking themes of memory and homecoming—and the larger claims about mid-century American poetry's domestication and containment—to a more expansively transnational matrix of poetic symbolism.

Lowell's imitation of Ungaretti foregrounds an intertextual openness by engaging with sources at odds with the presumably private, insular, and domestic dimensions of the rhetoric of cultural containment. More suggestively, "Returning" re-writes the Italian poet's work (as he had also done with Alberti) as forming part of a transnational response to the nuclear question—a figurative attempt, as I suggest above, to arrest temporal progression in ways comparable to the Doomsday Clock which, at the time of the Cuban Missile Crisis and therefore roughly contemporaneous with Lowell's writing, stood still at seven minutes to midnight (Hendershot 2003: 132). To this end, it is worth bearing in mind that on the reverse side of the sheet of paper containing an early draft of "Returning," Lowell had transcribed a dream that reflected his anxiety about the prospect of nuclear genocide on a global scale:

> World has ended, or wasted suffered a disaster. Two groups, one American (?) which I head, the other Russian, headed by Khrushchev, much bigger and physically stronger than in life […] Struggle to survive, in second part of dream, the corner has been turned, stench receding, also barrenness, very fond and intimate with K […] I rely on K. as a weight to test myself against, as someone to talk to, somehow in the end as my guide.
>
> (Hart 1995: 70)

Lowell's dream emerges from a keen awareness of the stakes involved in the standoff between the United States and the Soviet Union in the Cuban Missile Crisis of 1961 and presents a terrifying dystopian vision of a post-nuclear future. Cast in the role of John F. Kennedy, Lowell hopes to reduce the sublimely global scales of the political confrontation of the Cuban Missile Crisis to a physical contest between himself and the more powerful Soviet leader Khrushchev. This contest, however, is progressively invested with a dimension of personal intimacy, reliance, and mentorship—a surprising alternative to the official narrative of the frigid, unyielding nature of US–Soviet relations during the Cold War.

"Returning" does not appear to address Lowell's dream, or even his anxiety about the Cuban Missile Crisis, directly. Nevertheless, the specter of nuclear anxieties, whether as affect or as the bright afterimage of an atomic explosion, haunts Lowell's description of "those nervous waters" in which he finds his "exhaustion, the light of the world" and the post-apocalyptic landscape where "Nothing is deader than this small town main street, / Where the venerable elm sickens, and hardens" (*CP*, 347).

As with his modification of Alberti's treatment of nostalgia, Lowell again recognizes and resists the illusions of memory and nostalgia when he acknowledges that the past was always "somewhat overshaded" (*CP*, 347). For Lowell, nostalgic evocations of the past are dangerously seductive rather than comforting, and he remains distinctly unsettled by memory's capacity to allow the sickly, tar-hardened elm that he encounters upon his return home to give shelter by growing more and more "green" (*CP*, 347). "Greenness" here does not simply convey fructifying connotations but chimes rather more ominously with Lowell's earlier reference to the anxiety-inducing "green go-light" of a world held to ransom by those with access to nuclear codes and, finally, to the post-apocalyptic wasteland where "barked elms" are plainly presented as withered "sticks along the street" (*CP*, 348). Lowell's interest in questions pertaining to homecoming and memory at a time when heightened Cold War tensions threatened to culminate in global genocide thus recalls Theodore Adorno's suggestion that nostalgia is determined by a "fear of gaping meaninglessness."[17] At the same time, the transnational and transcultural sweep implicit to the mode of imitation challenges any attempt to reduce it to the totalizing discourse of domestic containment prompted by Cold War and nuclear anxiety.

Conclusion

By attending to the shadowy revisionist and translational archive haunting Lowell's presumably "finished" or "monumental" poetic canon, I have attempted to perform readings that seek to undo the totalizing or absolutist logic underpinning the

---

[17] Adorno, quoted in Bewes (2002: 168).

apocalyptic specter of the nuclear question as it pertains to the containment, via the assimilationist principles of "cultural diversity" on the one hand and transnational American expansion on the other. Far from Robinson's charge that Lowell's imitations are involved in "colonizing another person's occasion for a display of incompatible mannerisms,"[18] Lowell's translations invite us to attend to both the translational and transnational leakages subtending containment culture's domesticating imperatives. They also introduce into otherwise settled texts notes of ambivalence and ambiguity attesting to containment's invisible duality.

Re-reading Lowell's work with an eye to these porosities and dualities thus invites an understanding of Lowell's work that hews closely to Amy Kaplan's (2002) conceptualization of "the anarchy of empire": "the breakdown or defiance of the monolithic system of order that empire aspires to impose on the world, an order reliant on clear divisions between metropolis and colony, colonizer and colonised, national and international spaces, the domestic and the foreign" (12). By consistently foregrounding the porosity of the boundary between national and global interests, home and world, the personal and the political, the anarchic dimensions of Lowell's work present a challenge to the totalizing imperatives of the nuclear.

References

Axelrod, S. G. 1978. *Robert Lowell: Life and Art* (Princeton, NJ: Princeton University Press).
Bell, Vereen M. 1983. *Robert Lowell: Nihilist as Hero* (Cambridge, MA: Harvard University Press).
Berryman, John. 1969. *The Dream Songs* (New York: Farrar, Straus and Giroux).
Bewes, Timothy. 2002. "An Anatomy of Nostalgia," *The New Left Review*, 14 (March-April): 167–172.
Brickey, Russell. 2009. "Turning Away from the Blast: Forms of Nuclear Poetry," *War, Literature and the Arts* 23.1 (February 21), www.wlajournal.com/wlaarchive/23_1-2/brickey.pdf, accessed February 15, 2022.
Butler, Judith. 2004. *Precarious Life: The Powers of Mourning and Violence* (London: Verso).
Carreres, Ángeles. 2008. "The Scene of Babel," *Translation Studies* 1.2: 167–181.
Cohen, JM, ed. 1956. *The Penguin Book of Spanish Verse* (Harmondsworth: Penguin).
Cooper, Wayne F. 1987. *Claude McKay: Rebel Sojourner in the Harlem Renaissance, a Biography* (Baton Rouge, LA: Louisiana State University Press).
Derrida, Jacques. 1984. "No Apocalypse, Not Now (Full Speed Ahead, Seven Missiles, Seven Missives)," *Diacritics* 14.2 (Summer): 20–31.
Derrida, Jacques. 1985. "Des Tours de Babel," translated by Joseph F. Graham in *Difference in Translation* (Ithaca, NY and London: Cornell University Press), 165–207.
Fine, Elsa Honig. 1971. "Mainstream, Blackstream, and the Black Arts Movement," *Art Journal* 30.4 (Summer): 374–375.
Gray, Richard. 1976. *American Poetry of the Twentieth-Century* (Cambridge, New York: Cambridge University Press).

---

[18] Robinson, quoted in Reynolds (2011: 67).

Grusin, Richard. 2004. "Premediation," *Criticism* 46.1 (December): 17–39.
Hamilton, Ian. 1982. *Robert Lowell: A Biography* (New York: Random House).
Hamilton, Saskia, ed. 2007. *The Letters of Robert Lowell* (New York: Farrar, Straus and Giroux).
Hart, Henry. 1995. *Robert Lowell and the Sublime* (Syracuse, NY: Syracuse University Press).
Hendershot, Cyndi. 2003. *Anti-Communism and Popular Culture in Mid-Century America* (Jefferson, NC and London: Mcfarland & Co.).
Hispanic Society of America. 1938. *Translations from Hispanic Poets* (New York: Hispanic Society of America) https://catalogue.nla.gov.au/Record/990781.
Howe, Irving. 2014. "This Age of Conformity," in Nina Howe, ed., *A Voice Still Heard: Selected Essays of Irving Howe* (New Haven, CT and London: Yale University Press) 3–25.
James, Stephen. 1996. "Revision as Redress? Robert Lowell's Manuscripts," *Essays in Criticism* 46: 28–51.
James, Stephen. 2004. "On Second Thoughts," *Essays in Criticism* 54: 196–204.
James, Stephen. 2005. "Energy and Enervation: The Poetry of Robert Lowell," *Cambridge Quarterly* 34: 109–129.
Jameson, Fredric. 1991. *Postmodernism, or, the Cultural Logic of Late Capitalism* (London: Verso).
Kaladjian, Walter. 1999. "Nuclear Criticism," *Contemporary Literature* 2.2 (Summer): 311–318.
Kaplan, Amy. 2002. *The Anarchy of Empire in the Making of US Culture* (Cambridge, MA: Harvard University Press).
Keown, Michelle. 2018. "Waves of Destruction: Nuclear Imperialism and Antinuclear Protest in the Indigenous Literatures of the Pacific," *Journal of Postcolonial Writing*, 54.5: 585–600.
Klein, Richard. 2000. "The Future of Nuclear Criticism," *Yale French Studies* 97: 78–102.
Linden, George W. 1977. "'Dr. Strangelove' and Erotic Displacement," *Journal of Aesthetic Education*, 11.1 (January): 63–83.
Lowell, Robert. 2003. *Collected Poems*, ed. Frank Bidart and David Gewanter, with the editorial assistance of DeSales Harrison (London: Faber and Faber).
Mallan, Lloyd. *c.*1946. "Rafael Alberti," in Stefan Schimanski and Henry Treece, eds, *Transformation Four* (London: Lindsay Drummond), 175–185.
Melley, Tim. 2012. *The Covert Sphere: Secrecy, Fiction, and the National Security State* (Ithaca, NY: Cornell University Press).
Milne, Drew. 2017. "Poetry After Hiroshima?: Notes on Nuclear Implicature," *Angelaki* 22.3: 87–102.
Nadel, Alan. 1995. *Containment Culture: American Narratives, Postmodernism, and the Atomic Age* (Durham, NC and London: Duke University Press).
Plath, Sylvia. 1981. *Collected Poems* (London: Faber & Faber).
Raban, Jonathan, ed. 1977. *Robert Lowell's Poems: A Selection* (London: Faber and Faber).
Reynolds, Matthew. 2011. *The Poetry of Translation: From Chaucer & Petrarch to Homer & Logue* (Oxford: Oxford University Press).
Robinson, Peter. 2010. *Poetry and Translation: The Art of the Impossible* (Liverpool: Liverpool University Press).
Román, Ediberto. 1997. "Empire Forgotten: The United States's Colonization of Puerto Rico," *Villanova Law Review* 42: 1119–1211.
Saunders, Francis Stoner. 1999. *The Cultural Cold War: The CIA and the World of Arts and Letters* (New York: New York Press).

Simon, William G. 2003. "Dr. Strangelove or: the Apparatus of Nuclear Warfare," in Richard Allen and Malcolm Turvey, eds, *Camera Obscura, Camera Lucida: Essays in Honor of Annette Michelson* (Amsterdam: Amsterdam University Press), 215–230.

Strand, Mark. 2002. *Looking for Poetry: Poems by Carlos Drummond de Andrade ad Rafael Alberti and Songs from the Quechua* (New York: Alfred A Knopf).

Thurston, Michael. 2000. "Robert Lowell's Monumental Vision: History, Form, and the Cultural Work of Postwar American Lyric," *American Literary History* 12.1–2 (Spring-Summer): 79–112.

Tyson, Timothy B. 1998. "Robert F. Williams, 'Black Power,' and the Roots of African American Freedom Struggle," *Journal of American History* 85.2 (September): 540–570.

US Government. 1967. *Hearings: Riots, Civil, and Criminal Disorders* (Washington, DC: US Government Printing Office), https://play.google.com/books/reader?id=wbA3AAAAIAAJ&hl=en&pg=GBS.PP8, accessed February 15, 2022.

Venator-Santiago, Charles. 2012. "Cold War Civil Rights: The Puerto Rican Dimension," *California Western International Law Journal* 42.2: 423-435.

Venuti, Lawrence. 2000. "Translation, Community, Utopia," in Lawrence Venuti, ed., *The Translation Studies Reader* (London: Routledge), 468–488.

Wallingford, Katherine. 1999. "A Poetry of Memory: For the Union Dead," in Steven Gould Axelrod, ed., *The Critical Response to Robert Lowell* (London: Greenwood Press), 128–133.

Yenser, Stephen. 1975. *Circle to Circle: The Poetry of Robert Lowell* (Berkeley and Los Angeles, CA and London: University of California Press).

Zizek, Slavoj. 2007. *How to Read Lacan* (New York: W.W. Norton & Co.).

CHAPTER 4

PRECARIOUS FORMS
Reading Labor in and beyond the Neoliberal Novel

JOSEPH B. ENTIN

THIS chapter makes the case for reading contemporary US literature through figures and forms of precarious labor. Precarious labor typically refers to the expanding array of unstable, flexible, nonguaranteed work arrangements, from seasonal and temporary employment to part-time, free-lance, and piecework to independent contracting and so-called self-employment. Critics have contended that precarity denotes not only the undermining of labor security but also what Andrew Ross calls a "new experiential norm" under neoliberalism, which I want to discuss here with reference to a short essay, "The Essence of Neoliberalism," published in 1998 by French sociologist Pierre Bourdieu (Ross 1998: 9).[1] Bourdieu argues that neoliberalism is a theory of a "pure and perfect order" founded on the putative rationality of free markets and competitive individualism (Bourdieu 1998). While neoliberalism may be a theory, Bourdieu asserts that it is also "an immense political project" that is attempting, through economic and social policies promoting financial deregulation, capital mobility, and the privatization of public goods and services, to bring about the conditions under which that theory can be realized. At its heart, this project aims for what Bourdieu describes as "*the methodical destruction of collectives.*" Through the dismantling of collective structures, from the welfare state to labor unions, neoliberalism works to produce an individualistic, "Darwinian world" marked by the struggle of "all against all at all levels of the hierarchy" that renders everyone's "situation precarious." "The ultimate foundation of this entire economic order placed under the sign of freedom," Bourdieu continues, is "the structural violence of unemployment, the insecurity of job tenure and the menace of layoff that it implies." In other words, the production of neoliberal "freedom" entails a coordinated assault on the economic stability and political leverage that organized labor, primarily in

---

[1] See also Neilson and Rossiter (2008) and Berlant (2011).

the Global North, had been able to achieve during the twentieth century. And indeed, in the United States, as neoliberal policies and ideas have taken hold, precarity has spread and labor's power has declined: working-class wages have stagnated; union membership has plummeted from a high of over 30 per cent in the 1950s to less than 10 per cent today; and organized labor's collective militancy, as measured by the number of strikes, has dropped sharply—from an average of 288 major job actions per year in the 1970s to fewer than 13 per year since 2010.[2]

In what follows, I contend that reading contemporary US literature via labor precarity—a condition at the heart of the neoliberal world order—paradoxically contradicts neoliberalism's prevailing ethos in at least two ways: first, by directing attention to dynamics of solidarity, which are precisely what Bourdieu contends that neoliberalism, as a project devoted to the "destruction of collectives," aims to abolish; and second, by steering us beyond the middle-class frame of most neoliberal literature to the struggles of the working (and nonworking) poor and consequently to more expansive material and literary histories of precarity, which have been integral to capitalism since its inception and always structured by race and empire as well as labor. I begin with a paradigmatic novel about the neoliberal condition, Dave Eggers's *A Hologram for the King* (2012), which recounts the unraveling of white, male, professional life in the face of globalization, corporate downsizing, and white-collar precarity. In *Hologram*, precarity precipitates an inward-looking narrative of middle-class anxiety and anomie, although that story is ruptured in one particularly disorienting scene, which stages an encounter with figures of global subaltern labor that opens otherwise occluded questions about the lines of commonality that precarity can make room to consider. Focusing on labor precarity in *Hologram* thus takes us to the very edge of—and allows us to peer past—the individualistic paradigm that marks the book's narrative and ideological structure.

As a dialogic counterpoint to *Hologram*'s focus on professional-managerial interiority and aesthetic irony, I then examine three novels—Tomás Rivera's *... y no se lo tragó la tierra / ... And the Earth Did Not Devour Him* (1971), Jamaica Kincaid's *Lucy* (1990), and Jesmyn Ward's *Sing, Unburied, Sing* (2017)—that narrate forms of precarity and structural vulnerability linked to diverse modes of low- and no-wage labor, from agriculture to care work to prison labor. While *Hologram* suggests that precarious labor has intensified since the rise of neoliberal economic policies and post-Fordist forms of production, the narratives by Rivera, Kincaid, and Ward insist that the economic, social, and political insecurity of migrant, Chicanx, and Black workers has been a foundational condition under the long arc of racial capitalism's uneven developments. Neoliberalism's much-discussed precarity may have been a shock to workers, who, over the course of the twentieth century, had come to expect stable employment and adequate compensation, but for most working people, especially racialized workers at the

---

[2] On the decline in job actions, see Greenhouse, who also notes that, at present, nearly 50 million Americans work for less than $15 per hour: Greenhouse (2019: 11, 13).

bottom of the economic hierarchy, precarity has long been the norm, not the exception. Looking at labor precarity in contemporary literature, including in a neoliberal novel like *Hologram*, directs our gaze beyond neoliberalism as an historic, literary, and ideological horizon.

In reading these novels, I focus not only on the heterogenous figures of labor contingency but also on the precarious forms these writers adopt to lend aesthetic shape to conditions of economic, legal, and social uncertainty as well as to the nascent possibilities of solidarity that typically hover just beyond full articulation as opaque, but still palpable, contradictions to the privatized individualism that otherwise pervades neoliberal literary culture. While *Hologram* represents an example of what Jeffrey Williams, in his overview of neoliberal fiction, calls "resigned realism," the scene of radical labor precarity on which I focus is surreal, almost allegorical, at odds with the tone and fabric of the book more generally. Rather than resignation, the novels by Rivera, Kincaid, and Ward represent innovative aesthetic attempts to render both crisis and possibility, structural violence and cultural emergence, isolation and connection: in Rivera's *Earth*, experiments in voice to narrate a tenuous migrant "peoplehood" in the midst of dispersion, transit, and hardship; in Kincaid's *Lucy*, a paratactic style to express fraught modes of interpersonal feminist alliance in the context of immigrant estrangement, colonial history, and American anti-Blackness; in Ward's *Sing*, shifting narrative perspectives and gothic conventions to underscore both the variability and continuity of racial terror and unorthodox modes of collective being, seeing, and remembering. In these works, solidarity itself appears as a precarious form—a tentative, fragile process, frequently a matter of imagination or speculation visible only through the contours of its absence.

My claim that precarity provokes a contemplation of collectivity draws on particular ideas about labor as a social and aesthetic form. Under capitalism, workers find themselves caught between the antinomies of what Marx termed competition and association. Precarious labor conjures up the neoliberal landscape of competition, where workers seem more than ever to be on their own, competing for a limited set of economic opportunities, "companies of one" navigating "the gig economy" without the security provided by industrial unions, steady labor, or a robust welfare state. Yet however precarious or atomized, labor is also inherently cooperative; even when one labors alone, that labor draws on, and contributes to, knowledge and materials created by others. Philosopher Jason Read notes that while capital aims "to reduce the social dimension of labor to a purely market relation" and to underscore the divisions and differences among and between workers, labor as a category, activity, and figure also evokes an opposing tendency "to transform the implicit shared cooperative and social dimension of labor into solidarity" (Read 2017). The vectors of connection and cooperation between workers are, of course, cross-cut by the fragmentation of work, the division of labor, the continual production of a surplus population *without* work, and the heterogeneity of an increasingly global work force. As capital expands, labor multiplies, becoming more heterogeneous, "more diverse, more internally differentiated," as Marx put it in the *Grundrisse* (1973: 408). Over the past sixty years, as capital has become more flexible and mobile, as borders and partitions have proliferated, and as the capitalist workforce has become ever larger and more diverse, solidarity has become more fluid and harder to imagine. And yet, even in a novel like *Hologram*, which centers a protagonist who has absorbed neoliberalism's ethos of entrepreneurial individualism, the encounter between differentially positioned figures of precarious labor raises the specter—if only briefly—of collective economic and political relation. *Earth*, *Lucy*, and *Sing*, novels that frame precarity beyond the confines of neoliberalism and beyond the middle-class perspectives that dominate most neoliberal fiction, offer more robust and imaginative, if still incomplete and fleeting, visions of collective interconnection.

"People Were Done Manufacturing on American Soil"

Eggers's *A Hologram for the King* recounts the travails of Alan Clay, a fifty-four-year-old former bicycle salesman, corporate manager, and now consultant, who is leading a team of young engineers to pitch a holographic videoconferencing system to the King of Saudi Arabia. Published during the extended recession that followed the crash of 2008, the novel offers Alan's tale as a meditation on globalization, downsizing, and white-collar precarity, thereby joining an emerging constellation of literary texts that address the neoliberal condition.[3] As Alan and his team wait for weeks on end in a tent in the uncompleted King Abdullah Economic City for the monarch to appear, we learn through flashbacks that Alan's father worked as a foreman in a unionized shoe factory and retired with a full pension. While his father enjoyed the benefits of the corporate-labor compromise available to many white, blue-collar workers during the vaunted mid-twentieth-century era of American prosperity, Alan's career, which unfolded in the decades during which neoliberal globalization emerged, has followed a notably different arc. Alan sold Schwinn bicycles before moving into management and helping the company migrate its manufacturing overseas. From there, he "bounced around between a dozen or so other stints, consulting, helping companies compete through ruthless efficiency, robots, lean manufacturing, that kind of thing. And yet, year by year, there was less work for a guy like him. People were done manufacturing on American soil" (Eggers 2012: 13). Now, divorced, deep in debt, and unable to pay his daughter's next college tuition bill, he finds himself "nearly broke, virtually unemployed, the proprietor of a one-man consulting firm run out of his home office" (Eggers 2012: 4).

Through Alan's story, *Hologram* provides a textured account of the unraveling of white middle-class economic and emotional life across the late twentieth and early twenty-first centuries as new forms of flexible accumulation and multinational, "lean production" eroded the Fordist arrangements that had made possible stable employment, robust

---

[3] See, for starters, Huehls and Smith (2017), Williams (2013), and Michaels (2009).

wages, and secure retirement for men like Alan's father.[4] As an example of neoliberal literature, then, Eggers's novel directs readers' attention to the ways in which structural economic forces, including corporate downsizing, offshoring, and the growing contingency of white-collar work, shape the contours of professional-managerial subjectivity. Formally, the novel is written from a mildly ironic, close third-person perspective, which places readers in intimate proximity to Alan's thoughts but always with a measure of critical distance. We may feel for him, but we also grasp how his bullheaded, masculinist desire for control and authority makes him ill-suited for the rapidly shifting, globally interdependent society he inhabits.

Alan's incapacity to read the world around him comes strikingly to the fore in a bizarre scene that occurs as he walks into an unfinished tower in King Abdullah Economic City to look at one of the many empty apartments for sale. On his way up, he hears voices and opens the fire door from the stairwell, where he finds "a large raw space full of men, some in their underclothes, some in red jumpsuits, all yelling. It looked like pictures he'd seen of prison gyms converted to dormitories. There were fifty bunks," but "all the men were gathered in the center of the room, barking, pushing" (Eggers 2012: 206–207). Alan realizes the men are "Malaysian, Pakistani, Filipino" (207) workers imported to build the city. Two of the workers appear to be scuffling over a cell phone, and when the group notices Alan, they gesture to him, which he interprets as a request to mediate the dispute. As Alan tries to intervene, one worker grabs the phone and bolts; other workers surround Alan, "yelling in his face" (209). Alan runs; a few workers chase him, but he eventually makes his way up two flights to his destination: the one finished floor in the building.

In a story organized around signs that Alan fails to read, this tumultuous scene is another moment that he cannot parse. To him, it is a brief, unsettling interlude that erupts—as the workers themselves do—out of nowhere and makes little sense, and the novel gives readers no other way to comprehend it. Indeed, the scene is an interruption in multiple senses. First, its chaotic, frenzied quality—the emphasis on shouting and shoving—and the shadowy nature of the amassed workers, who appear as a globalized image of what Jacob Riis termed the "Other Half," provide a shock that clearly unsettles Alan's sense of safety and control. Perhaps, the scene proposes, there is an obscured world of intense, desperate work and struggle behind the realm of gleaming glass surfaces and immaterial production that Alan inhabits. Further, in its disruptive singularity, the scene prompts an intriguing question: what is the relation between Alan's own sense of impotence and precarity and the radical precarity of these hyper-exploited migrant workers? The incident may provoke this question, but it does not provide an answer or elaborate the terms of the social and economic relations that it raises. Neither Alan nor, it seems, the novel itself can grasp the scene as a missed moment of potential solidarity, in which these men from profoundly different economic locations might

---

[4] The literature on the demise of Fordist, welfare-state capitalism is vast, but on "flexible accumulation," see Harvey (1989); on "lean production," see Moody (1997).

for a moment see their structural vulnerability echoed back to them across a social and cultural chasm. In this instance, dynamics of commonality and difference come into explosive contact, and the result is a profound failure of linguistic, cultural, political translation: even as Alan and the workers are thrown together, they cannot find a common language to speak. The chaotic intrusion of these workers into the text gives us a fleeting reminder that there is a much larger narrative of economic precarity that has been displaced or suppressed by Alan's story of contingency, which is organized around his solipsistic failure to discern a wider world, or other people, beyond the narrow confines of his own concerns, desires, and preoccupations. To tell the story of these workers, who appear to Alan as a threatening, brown horde, would be to turn *Hologram* upside down and would require a literary form less beholden to an individualistic, ironic, aesthetic frame.[5]

Critics have argued that *Hologram* forms part of a new line of fiction—the neoliberal novel—geared to the newly precarious era of capital mobility and market fundamentalism.[6] Recent commentary on neoliberalism and literature has exposed the alignment (and occasional dis-alignment) of much contemporary fiction, memoir, and poetry with the deep ideological structures of market-based, austerity thinking. Mitchum Huehls and Rachel Greenwald Smith posit that neoliberalism develops across four phases (economic, political, sociocultural, and ontological), gradually coming to appear "natural, universal and true" (Huehls and Smith 2017: 8). "Culture absorbs and diffuses neoliberalism's bottom-line values," they write, which eventually become "normative common sense" (Huehls and Smith 2017: 8). Although compelling, these claims tend to overinflate the ubiquity of neoliberalism's influence and thus obscure the zones of literary culture and production that lie beyond or that actively complicate, or offer alternatives to, neoliberal ideology as a form of class struggle. However multifaceted, neoliberalism is not a totalizing atmosphere, not the "air we breathe," but a contested, contradictory, and partial, if certainly very powerful, formation (Robbins 2019). As I have suggested, *Hologram* itself, while for the most part affirming neoliberalism's ethos of possessive individualism, offers possibilities, however transient, for thinking and seeing otherwise. In the remainder of this chapter, I turn to three contemporary novels that narrate modes of labor precarity largely outside the terms set by neoliberal hegemony and the neoliberal novel.

"THE PEOPLE WERE BECOMING PEOPLE"

If *Hologram*'s close, third-person form keeps us tied to a single (and notably self-centered) perspective, Tomás Rivera's *... y no se lo tragó la tierra / ... And the Earth Did*

---

[5] On the politics of individualism in neoliberal literature, especially memoir, see Worden (2017).
[6] See, for starters, Huehls and Smith (2017), Williams (2013), and Michaels (2009).

Not Devour Him represents an experiment in collective narration. *Earth* is a compilation of short fragments and vignettes about migrant farmworkers, loosely but not exclusively narrated from the point of view of a young boy over the course of a single year during the early 1950s. The novel was originally published in Spanish, then translated (initially by Herminio Ríos and more recently by Evangelina Vigil-Piñón) into English and is now published in a dual-language format.

Written in what one critic calls "a brutal and concise style," the book's fourteen vignettes narrate a litany of hardships that migrant farmworkers endure, ranging from quotidian indignities, such as being refused a haircut by the local barber, to prejudicial assaults (a "gringo" classmate "make[s] a gesture with his finger" and attacks the narrator in the school bathroom), to violent traumas, such as the death of two young children in a fire while their parents are laboring in the fields and the death of sixteen spinach pickers, recounted in a vignette of merely six sentences, when the truck taking them home after work is hit by a drunken driver and bursts into flames.[7] As these last two vignettes suggest, the highly precarious, often explicitly discriminatory and punitive, conditions of racialized migrant labor provide a baseline for the characters' narratives. The very first story in the book, "The Children Couldn't Wait," depicts the viciously oppressive conditions of migrant agricultural work. The tale chronicles several days in April that were "so hot that the bucket of water the boss brought [the workers] was not enough" (Rivera 1987: 86). But the boss "didn't much like the idea of their losing time going to drink water because they weren't on contract, but by the hour" (86). The children in the fields, however, grow thirsty, and when a young boy heads for water, the boss decides to scare him by firing his rifle. Inadvertently, he shoots the child in the head, and the boy's small body "just stayed in the water like a dirty rag and the water began to turn bloody ..." (87). The story thus renders the disposability of migrants and the authoritarian power of the boss—who is found not-guilty when tried for the boy's death in court—not only over the terms and conditions of labor but also over the workers' very lives.

The formal structure of the book, which is divided into fourteen diptychs, each composed of two short vignettes, one prefatory and one slightly longer, refuses synthesis and resolution, underscoring a tension between disconnection and unity, fracture and resonance. The twelve middle diptychs echo the number of months in a year, with the first and last pairings standing as introductory and concluding texts. The shape of the year gives the book a rounded, natural form, but the short pieces and diptych structure foreground gaps and separation. It is hard, even impossible, to locate the time or location of many of the tales and difficult to construct continuities of character or setting between the segments, some of which are only three and four sentences long, mere fragments of memory or story. There is no comprehensive narrative through-line or plot, and many of the characters are unnamed and appear only once. The individual

---

[7] The initial quotation is from Sánchez Prado (2016); the remaining quotations are from Rivera (1987: 103, 93, 129, 120). Additional citations parenthetically in the body of my text.

vignettes within the diptychs themselves don't often seem to bear any relation to one another, which further extends the sense of disorientation that pervades the text. Yet there are elements of continuity: the young boy whose point of view and whose dreams loosely organize the book; the emphasis on oral stories; the thematic threads of harm, loss, family, and spirituality that course through the volume.

The book's aesthetics of displacement, which confound strict chronological order and linear plot progression, echo the focus on disruptive migratory transit, labor instability, and mutable collectivity at the heart of the text. These are stories about migrants following the harvest, moving from location to location; the shape and pace of the book is choppy and quick, as readers are abruptly shuttled from scene to scene, much as roving laborers proceed from farm to farm. Additionally, the formal dynamics of isolation and connection are grounded in an emergent politics of labor and ethnic solidarity that were crucial to the context of the book's creation and to the stories within it. Rivera, who had himself labored in the fields in the 1940s and 1950s, wrote *Earth* during a moment of burgeoning activism in the Chicanx community, including the United Farm Workers' Delano grape strike and boycott and the 1968 student walk-outs and 1969 adoption of the Plan Spiritual de Atzlán at the Chicano Youth Conference in Denver. Historian John Hyman has argued that the crucial strategic challenge confronting working-class movements is "how to mobilize maximum solidarity from a socially defined constituency which has no essential unity in the sphere of consciousness, but on the contrary a series of particularistic loyalties and preferences and a widely differing experience in everyday life, a mosaic of individual histories"; any effort to achieve collective unity "begins with this dialectic—the contradictory and dynamic intersection of unifying and fragmenting tendencies."[8] It is precisely this problematic—the contradictory intersection of unifying and fragmenting tendencies in the construction of solidarity—that Rivera's book takes up, both in its form and in its content.

These dynamics of migration and labor, fragmentation and unity, are rendered most powerfully in one of the longer vignettes, "When We Arrive," which appears near the end of the book. The chapter recounts the interior thoughts of several braceros, traveling from Texas to the Midwest, when the truck they are riding in breaks down at 4 o'clock in the morning.[9] The story is composed of fourteen anonymous internal monologues, like thought bubbles, each a paragraph long. Written in Faulknerian-like streams-of-consciousness, each monologue embodies a singular perspective, voice, and concerns, ranging from physical discomforts and frustrations ("Fuckin' life, this goddamn fuckin' life!... This is the last time I go through this, standing all the way like a goddamn animal" [144]) to economic and existential anxieties ("With the money Mr. Thompson loaned me we have enough to buy food for at least two months... Just hope we don't get in too much debt" [143]) to aspirations ("If things go well this year, maybe we'll buy a car so we won't have to travel this way, like cattle" [143]) to plaintive concerns and expressions

---

[8] Hyman quoted in Moody (1997: 145).
[9] The Bracero program facilitated the importation of contract laborers from Mexico in US agriculture from 1942 to 1964. See, among many other sources, Ngai (2004: ch. 4).

of sympathy ("When we get there I'm gonna see about getting a good bed for my vieja. Her kidneys are really bothering her a lot nowadays" [145]). These are intimate, interior thoughts, but readers are positioned to hear them all, to see moments of overlap and resonance, to discern the way individual fears and hopes are echoed in the minds of others on the same truck. Out of isolation emerge gossamer filaments of connection which the aesthetic structure of the story—individual monologues side-by-side in constellation—enables us to grasp.

At the conclusion of the vignette, dawn arrives, "gradually reaffirm[ing] the presence of objects." The final two sentences read: "And the people were becoming people. They began getting out of the trailer and they huddled around and commenced to talk about what they were going to do when they arrived" (146). Working-class, migrant "peoplehood" begins to materialize as private hopes and trepidations are shared in a fragile dialogue and "individual experience is gradually replaced by conditional solidarity with others who also suffer an inarticulated victimization," in the words of critic Ramón Saldívar (1990: 88). However, unity, like arrival itself, is deferred ("When we arrive, when we arrive, the real truth is.... [w]e never arrive" [145]), much as the chapter's voices are held in suspension rather than merged. The chapter, like *Earth* more generally, centers on liminal states: between night and day, pain and hope, history and futurity, individuality and collectivity. Solidarity—a sense of collective belonging that is grounded in and across material conditions—is a never-finished process of stitching together "this to this, that to that, all with all" (152), as the young narrator explains on the book's final page, to create a shared sense of "peoplehood." Like the perpetual cycle of arrival and departure that governs the migrant farmworkers' circulatory existence, this process is ongoing, without definitive end. In the final vignette, the narrator has a vision of unity: "I would like to see all of the people together. And then, if I had great big arms, I could embrace them all.... But that, only in a dream" (151). Solidarity is an unrealized—perhaps even impossible—figure, a utopian dream that can be imagined and spoken, but may remain forever just out of reach.

"The Mantle of a Servant"

If *Earth* engages possibilities of migrant community formation through experiments in narrative fracture and resonance, Jamaica Kincaid's *Lucy* confronts dialectics of interpersonal disconnection and entanglement, detachment and intimacy through the first-person chronicle of a nineteen-year-old Antiguan woman who comes to an unnamed US city much like New York to work as an *au pair* for a wealthy couple, Mariah and Lewis, and their four children. The story takes the shape of a *bildungsroman*, an echo in particular of *Jane Eyre*, a young domestic who, like Lucy, comes into her own as an artist, although Kincaid's novel conspicuously refuses marriage as a form of narrative resolution and ends on a resolutely uncertain note. On its face, Lucy's story largely follows an upward swing as she moves from colony to metropole, from a room in another family's apartment to a Woolfian "room of her own," from a feeling of being possessed by others to a sense of self-possession. The heart of her story is her sexual awakening, which Lucy recounts in memories of her first fantasies and erotic encounters in Antigua to her affairs with three Americans, Hugh, Roland, and Paul. But the putatively progressive arc of assimilation and uplift is troubled by several elements, including the persistence of class, racial, and colonial structures; Lucy's seething anger about how those structures obstruct her self-realization; and the recursive presence of memory flashbacks, which regularly pull the narrative into the past even as it progresses forward.

In *Lucy*, Mariah represents the emblematic figure of neoliberal angst—the well-off white liberal whose life unravels over the course of the novel. But *Lucy* is not centered on Mariah: rather, it directs our attention to an immigrant domestic worker whose physical and affective labor upholds the lifestyles of the wealthy white folks for whom neoliberal precarity comes as such an unsettling surprise. Lucy's position as an *au pair* is a form of women's care work that hovers, uncertainly, between formal and informal labor. Such care work is part of what Barbara Ehrenreich and Arlie Hochschild call "the female underside of globalization, whereby millions of [women] from poor countries in the south migrate to do the 'women's work' of the north—work that affluent women are no longer able or willing to do" (Ehrenreich and Hochschild 2003: 3). The result has been a "feminization of migration," as over half the world's illegal and legal migrants are believed to be women—a sharp turn from mid-twentieth-century patterns of migration from the Global South that were dominated by men.

The novel depicts Lucy's job as an *au pair* as a decisively contradictory position, in which the ambiguities of feminized reproductive labor, the uncertainties of precarious work, and the racialized dimensions of colonial power all converge.[10] At one level, Lucy is welcomed into the family, treated warmly by Mariah, and enjoys the children. Yet the text never lets the uneven power dynamics of Lucy's position slip from view. "I was a woman from the fringes of the world," Lucy reflects, "and when I left home I had wrapped around my shoulders the mantle of a servant" (Kincaid 1990: 95). In the family's sprawling apartment, Lucy is housed in "the maid's room," which she notes is "like a box—a box in which cargo traveling a long way should be shipped" (7). The reference to this young Black woman from the Caribbean imagining herself as "cargo" shipped in a "box" to the United States of course raises the specter of the Middle Passage, reminding readers that Lucy's current position is shaped by a long history of slavery and racial capitalism. "But I was not cargo," she insists, "I was not even the maid" (7).

The family does in fact have a maid, but she and Lucy, while potential allies as the family's two domestic workers, fail to connect as the maid "had let me know right away, on meeting me, that she did not like me" (9). Other fleeting moments of potential, but undeveloped labor-based affiliation flash across the text. In the dining car on the train to

---

[10] Bruce Robbins writes superbly on this: "As a transnational figure, the literary *au pair* stands in for global capitalism's systematic destabilization of local class divisions, which is by no means the effacing of those divisions. This is perhaps how to understand the *au pair*'s distinctive class indeterminacy": Robbins (1999: 109).

Mariah's childhood home in the Midwest, Lucy realizes that "[t]he other people sitting down to dinner all looked like Mariah's relatives; the people waiting on them all looked mine" (32). When she meets the caretaker of Mariah's family house, a Swedish immigrant, Lucy thinks, "I wanted to say to him, 'Do you not hate the way she says your name, as if she owns you?'" (34). These glimmers of possible common cause are traces of undeveloped solidarities, moments when Lucy glimpses the grounds of incipient but unrealized connection that are visible ultimately only through their absence.

Lucy's domestic labor brings her into complex relation with Mariah, who is at once Lucy's employer, surrogate mother, and confidante. On the one hand, their relationship is structured by substantial disparities of wealth, position, and race, which are compounded by the fact that Mariah is largely unaware of her privilege and the way that privilege shapes even her intimate interactions with Lucy. When Mariah boasts that she is good at fishing because "I have Indian blood" (39), Lucy "could swear she says it as if she were announcing her possession of a trophy. How do you get to be the sort of victor who can claim the vanquished also?" (40–41). While Lucy loves the children she cares for and is encouraged to feel like one of the family, she also "began to feel like a dog on a leash, a long leash but a leash all the same" (110). Lucy's growing awareness of the structuring force of class privilege can be seen in the connection she observes between table manners and cultural power. "I had just begin to notice," she observes, "that people who knew the correct way to do things such as hold a teacup, put food on a fork and bring it to their mouths without making a mess on the front of their dress—they were the people responsible for the most misery, the people least likely to end up insane or paupers" (99) It is worth noting that, while the novel's focus on mother–daughter dynamics and sexual awakening lends it a largely psychoanalytic tilt, the use in this passage of "misery" and "pauper" seems to echo Marx's description of the proletariat as a class of "virtual paupers," always a short step away from destitution, and his "immiseration" thesis, which suggests that as capital consolidates, misery for workers spreads. In these passages, the novel suggests that Mariah and Lucy's relationship, however reciprocal, is never entirely free from the dynamics of employer–employee relations compounded by discrepancies of racial and colonial power.[11]

At odds with the novel's understated style, Lucy is a figure of strong desires who does not fear being disruptive. She is especially resentful of the demands placed on her to adhere to traditional gender roles. While Mariah, with her blond hair and blue eyes, appears angelic and "smells pleasant," Lucy, who claims irreverently that her name is short for Lucifer (152), "wanted to have a powerful odor and would not care if it gave offense" (27). In fact, Lucy bristles with "rage" (6), "anger" (19), "hatred" (20), "fury" (56). In large measure, her anger reflects the resentments she holds against her mother, whom Lucy feels sought to constrict her sense of possibility by bending it towards submissive, gendered expectations, including "a sense of duty to my parents; obedience to

---

[11] The of roots of colonialism and colonial labor in Lucy's family are visible in part via the history of her paternal grandfather, who was a member of the West Indian work force employed by the United States to build the Panama Canal (125).

the law and worship of convention" (133). But Lucy's simmering rage is also a response to the structural forces of colonial power that have shaped her life, both as a young person in Antigua and in the United States. When Mariah takes Lucy to see daffodils, a flower Lucy had never before seen in person, but which she had experienced through being made to memorize Wordsworth's "I Wandered Lonely as Cloud" as part of her education at "Queen Victoria Girl's School" (18), Lucy notes: "I wanted to kill them. I wished I had an enormous scythe" (29). For Lucy, who is here figured as an anticolonial avenging angel of death, the flowers conjure up not an image of bucolic peace or universal beauty but rather what she calls "a scene of conquered and conquests" (30), which she finds infuriating.

Yet the book also suggests that Mariah's fondness for Lucy and their sense of connection are genuine. When Mariah asserts, early in the book, that she loves Lucy, the narrator states, "I believed her" (27). Mariah sometimes overpays Lucy, takes her to museums and encourages her love of the arts, ensures that she has contraception. Lucy admits that, "I had grown to love her so" (46), that Mariah "was like a mother to me, a good mother" (110), and "was the kindest person I had ever known" (72). Mariah and Lucy's relationship is thus structured by insistent imbalances of class and race but is also a point of connection and reciprocal comfort.[12] Lucy insists that she "shall always like to be with the people who stand apart" (98), but the novel emphasizes that she is in fact entangled with others, especially women, in relations of friendship and mutual support—although those relations remain fraught, never free of friction. The gender solidarity that Lucy and Mariah share, however uneasily, is echoed in Lucy's relationship with Peggy, whom she meets through another *au pair*. Peggy and Lucy become friends, drift apart, then finally rent an apartment together, although Lucy continues to find several of Peggy's habits grating. "Peggy and I were not alike," Lucy explains, "but that is what we liked about each other" (61). Social, racial, and interpersonal differences are not resolved but in fact are imagined—counterintuitively—as grounds of mutuality.

The novel ends with Lucy in her own apartment, a job in the art world, and a newfound sense of autonomy. She has left the *au pair* work behind and is now making her way without the overweening guidance of her mother or Mariah. Yet the text continually troubles the narratives of upward mobility and assimilation that it also in some large measure follows, questioning the security of what Lucy has achieved, and indeed the upward mobility narrative itself, as she notes the threat of financial precarity that looms. "I could do whatever I wanted now, as long as I could pay for it. 'As long as I could pay for it.' That phrase soon became the tail that wagged my dog" (146).

Gayatri Spivak, among others, has argued that *Lucy* is paratactic, structured by what Brent Edwards describes as "the lack of conjunction, the absence of connection" (Edwards 2003). The novel's cool, detached tone and its emphasis on Lucy's desire to break with her mother, on her persistent sense of isolation, and on the interpersonal and

---

[12] Susan Fraiman notes: "In Kincaid's depiction ... the relation between these two women (Mariah and Lucy) is imbued with a complexity that goes beyond the mutual comprehension and serves to trouble a simple opposition between conquered and conquering": Fraiman (2017: 140).

structural barriers that racial–colonial–capitalist ideologies and histories generate—all these elements create a resounding sense of disconnection. "I would never be part of [the world she sees from her window]," Lucy reflects near the novel's conclusion, "never penetrate to the inside, never be taken in" (154). The text foregrounds separation, discontinuity, and discrepancy as legacies and ongoing effects of racial domination and colonialism and of the fury those interlocking dynamics generate in persons, like Lucy, who are subject to their force. Yet, *Lucy* is also about interpersonal bonds, however fraught and conflicted, about the prospects of affiliation, indeed about solidarity in the face of continual tension and asymmetrical economic and social power. As a diasporic text, *Lucy* is about scattering and rupture, about the ambivalent longing for home in the context of elective departure.[13] As a labor text, *Lucy* is about the ways in which the intimate relations of domestic care work, inflected by the ongoing histories of colonial power, produce highly fraught forms of social connection. Shaped by the novel's autobiographical mode and its paratactic style, these nascent bonds do not generate forms of collective belonging or common cause that solidarity typically implies but nonetheless constitute precarious lineaments of reciprocity that looking through the lens of labor helps us to see, even as they remain largely evanescent.

A "Black-Knuckled Multitude"

If *Lucy* narrates the persistence of colonial dynamics within modern, metropolitan, middle-class liberalism, Jesmyn Ward's second National Book Award-winning novel, *Sing, Unburied, Sing*, underscores the haunting power of racial terror as an enduring form of precarity that organizes the labor and life chances of the Black working class. *Sing* narrates a road trip taken by a drug-addicted Black mother, Leonie, her thirteen-year-old son Jojo, and her six-year-old daughter Kayla to retrieve the children's white father, Michael, who has been released after serving a sentence in the Mississippi State Penitentiary, also known as Parchman Farm, for drug dealing. Against this narrative backdrop, the novel, written with echoes of Homer, William Faulkner, and Toni Morrison, also recounts the stories that Leonie's father, Pop, tells JoJo about his own term in Parchman decades before and of two ghosts who haunt the family. Written in the wake of Trayvon Martin's 2013 murder by vigilante George Zimmerman, Michael Brown's 2014 murder by police officer Darren Wilson in Ferguson, Missouri and the ensuing uprising and protests, and the deaths of so many other Black people at the hands of the police before and since, *Sing* can rightfully be considered a #BlackLivesMatter (#BLM) novel. Ward's novel expands the historical context of the #BLM movement through the use of oral stories, memories, and ghosts to recall the historical continuities

---

[13] Suzanne Rozak writes: "Despite its often bleak perspective, *Lucy* is a quintessentially diasporic text in that it embraces ambiguity, resisting one-dimensional cultural narratives that extol the virtues of home in counterpoint to the struggles of a new place": Rozak (2017).

between slavery, Jim Crow, and contemporary racial violence, including mass incarceration as a form of anti-Black control, discipline, and death.

In addition to being a novel about the long history of racial terror, *Sing* is also a book about labor—in particular, about the absence of secure labor in the context of the organized economic abandonment of Black Southern communities and about forced labor and the violence of state-sanctioned exploitation and extraction. Precarity in Ward's novel refers not only to the relative unavailability of work but also, and even more directly, to the precariousness of Black life itself under conditions of forced penal labor, which recalls and extends the slave labor regime and stands as a metonym for racial capitalism more generally.

The novel opens on a scene in which death and birth converge: it is JoJo's thirteenth birthday and Pop slaughters a goat. The description of Pop's treatment of the animal—before gutting it, he "ties a rope around its head like a noose"—foregrounds the stories of lynching that pervade the novel: of Given, who is shot by a white man without any provocation; of Blue, who is skinned and burned alive; in the stories that Ritchie recounts to JoJo, including a memory of playing with siblings in the woods and finding "what had once been a man, hanging from a tree" (Ward 2017: 2, 189). This thread of racialized violence and death is tied to matters of labor when, a few pages after slaughtering the goat, Pop tells JoJo that, when he was fifteen, a group of white men whom Pop's half-brother had fought at a local bar "*tied both of us and took us up the road. You boys is going to learn what it means to work ... You boys is going to Parchman*" (Ward 2017: 19; original italics). Here, white supremacist violence is expressed as a demand for Black incarceration to perform forced labor at the Mississippi State Penitentiary, built on the site of a former slave plantation, Parchman Farm, where inmates—overwhelmingly Black—are routinely made to work in the fields without pay.[14]

As this abduction suggests, Ward's novel underscores the continuity between racialized chattel slavery and Parchman. The prison guards, Pop tells Jojo, "*come from a long line of men bred to treat you like a plowing horse, like a hunting dog ... from a long line of overseers*" (22, original italics). Pop's description of working in the prison's fields likewise recalls the history of Black bondage in the United States: "*That was our whole world: the long line. Men strung out across the fields, the trusty shooters stalking the edge, the driver on his mule, the caller yelling to the sun, throwing his working song out*" (69, original italics). Under these conditions, where prisoners live and work in one of fifteen discrete "camps" (21), existence is stripped to a form of bare life, and labor becomes a mode of intensified extraction organized to produce Black death. As Pop explains, carceral labor was less punishment for crimes than "*murder. Mass murder*" (73). Here, labor precarity refers not to the uncertainty of work—indeed, there is no getting out of the compulsive work routine—but rather to the *precarity of life itself* under this punitive system of racialized labor violence. In Parchman, which the novel proffers as a paradigm

---

[14] In 2020, "Black Mississippians account for 70% of Parchman's incarcerated population, while making up 37% of the state's population": Innocence (2020).

for Black labor more generally, precarity means working under conditions of disposability, in which labor is a form of social death (removed from civil society) and, quite often, literal death (forced to work under conditions that routinely, predictably kill the laborers).

The labor landscape in the novel beyond Parchman is structured largely by lack and uncertainty. Leonie works sporadically at a backwoods bar with her white friend Misty, who lives in a FEMA trailer she acquired after Hurricane Katrina. The two of them are addicted to drugs and also work as drug mules on their road trip—labor that is not only hazardous (when they are pulled over by a police officer, Leonie swallows a bag of meth) but also feeds their habit rather than providing steady income. Michael is in prison for drug-related offences, and his and Leonie's habit eventually undermines their family as the couple effectively abandons JoJo and Kayla at the end of the novel. Michael had previously worked as a welder on the *Deepwater Horizon*, which exploded into flames in 2010; the trauma of the experience, and his inability to find another welding job anywhere along the Gulf Coast, precipitate his drug addiction (93). So even ostensibly stable labor proves to be hazardous—for the workers and also for the environment. One other form of regular labor the novel acknowledges is unpaid reproductive labor, which JoJo performs with such care for Kayla and which appears fleetingly in an image, near the end, of Mam's hands: "Her knuckles bear all the scars: slipped knives, broken dishes, pounds of laundry" (214). Even here, as in almost every other depiction of work in the novel, labor is bound up with damage, injury, and harm. In *Sing*, work is less about the making of the world than its unmaking, less an extension of vital energies than the undoing of human vitality. In other words, what makes work precarious in this novel is its intimate imbrication with politically imposed, premature death.

Ward's novel is, appropriately enough, given its emphasis on the prevalence of death, a ghost story. Ghosts, Mam tells Jojo, are generated "when the dying's bad. Violent," leaving behind a spirit that "wanders, wanting peace" (256). The two ghosts who emerge as characters in the novel, Given and Ritchie, are both victims of white racial terror. Given is shot by Michael's cousin after Given bests him in a hunting contest. Michael's father, a former sheriff, reprimands his nephew for murdering Given, insisting, "*This ain't the old days*" (49–50), but when the court declares Given's death a hunting accident and his killer only serves three years in prison, the novel suggests that, when it comes to the arbitrariness of white power over Black death, the present looks quite a lot like "the old days." Ritchie was incarcerated at Parchman at the age of twelve, after being convicted of stealing food to feed his nine younger siblings. On the farm, he is whipped, abused, and overworked to the edge of death. He is finally killed by Pop, in what the older man, who was Ritchie's lone friend and mentor at Parchman, sees as an act of mercy to prevent Ritchie from being lynched by a white mob.

Racial violence thus produces ghosts who haunt the present, reminding us that the history of white supremacist terror cannot be relegated to the past. Ritchie insists that he has lessons for JoJo about "home," "love," and "time" (183–4). The latter Ritchie describes as "a vast ocean," in which "everything is happening at once"; significantly, he calls Parchman "past, present, and future all at once" (186). Parchman figuratively and literally consumes Ritchie's life, and the novel suggests that the racialized violence Parchman embodies and inflicts is, in fact, "past, present, and future" for many Black people in the United States.

In the final pages, JoJo follows Ritchie's ghost to a stand of trees behind the house, where he sees that the branches are full of other ghosts who "speak with their eyes," articulating their stories of abuse and violent death—suffocations, hangings, shootings, beatings, gougings, and more. JoJo stands there looking up "until the forest is a Black-knuckled multitude" (283). This striking figure of "the Black-knuckled multitude" crystallizes the novel's braiding together of work and death. The ghosts JoJo sees are unable to rest easy because they met violent ends; the reference to the hand ("knuckle") and the use of the word "multitude," a term associated in critical theory and to some extent in popular discourse with Michael Hardt and Antonio Negri's revisionist theory of the global working class, suggest that that these restless ghosts are also in some important measure figures of labor.[15] Here and elsewhere, Ward's novel, and the harrowing story of carceral labor and violent death at its heart, suggests that Black workers are constituted *through* violence, through exposure to the threat or reality of premature death. That threat of death, and its corresponding violent realities, have been used to render Black life precarious and disposable and also to extract energy, labor power, and life itself which propel capital accumulation.

Sing is thus not only a story of what Marx calls living labor or "labor as subjectivity" but also a story of *dead labor*—that is, labor under the persistent threat of premature, arbitrary death (Marx 1973: 272).[16] In this context, *precarity* is a term not only of political economy but also of biopolitical subjectivity, referring not just to the uncertainty of labor but also to the socially enforced insecurity of life itself. Echoing other narratives of Black labor, from Wright's *Native Son* to Morrison's *The Bluest Eye*, *Sing* suggests that Black life is targeted for destruction and death but that Black labor has also been crucial to capitalist development. In *Sing*, Black labor represents a *precarity of another kind*—a precarity beyond precarity, which Saidiya Hartman describes as "the precarious life of the ex-slave, a condition defined by the vulnerability to premature death and to gratuitous acts of violence" (Hartman 2008). Black labor has been essential, but Black persons, especially Black workers, have also been marked for death, considered fungible, as flesh that can be violated, discarded, destroyed at will. Racial capitalism is thus also necrocapitalism, which actively produces the social, civic, and physical death of populations which are targeted for incarceration, hyper-exploitation, and abandonment.

---

[15] Hardt and Negri describe the multitude as the collective singularities of all those who labor under capitalism, "an open and expansive concept" that "gives the concept of the proletariat its fullest definition": Hardt and Negri (2004: 107).

[16] James Tyner argues that "one's exposure to death is ... conditioned by one's position in capitalism. Stated differently, the relations between labor and capital necessarily inform the relations between life and death": Tyner (2019: x). On racism as "the state-sanctioned and/or extra-legal production and exploitation of group-differentiated vulnerability to premature death," see Gilmore (2006: 28).

Yet the figure of the "black-knuckled multitude" is also an incipient image of collectivity, of emergent solidarity. Each ghost has a discrete, individual story, but these stories run together, as they do in this stream-of-consciousness passage:

He raped me and suffocated me until I died I put my hands up and he shot me eight times she locked me in the shed and starved me to death while I listened to my babies playing with her in the yard they came in my cell in the middle of the night and they hung me....

(282, original italics)

The tension between singularity and commonality is echoed in the very structure of the novel itself, which might be considered an aesthetic incarnation of precarious collectivity: a narration that is divided into multiple, at times contradictory, voices and perspectives (including one narrator who speaks from the dead) but that together compose a larger, if unresolved and ununified, whole.[17]

Forms and Figures of Precarious Labor

My claim here is not that *Earth*, *Lucy*, and *Sing* are, or are not, working-class novels. In fact, these three texts, which focus on modes of precarious work (farm, domestic, and carceral labor) that fall outside traditional wage labor trouble the presumption that there is a unified or singular working class, certainly not one that is rooted in industrial labor, as the prevailing image of the twentieth-century proletariat implied. Rather, these three novels conjure up the originary meaning of the term "proletariat," the Roman *proles*, those "without reserves."[18] In that sense, these texts could be read as proletarian

---

[17] Sheri-Marie Harrison writes, "In its resolution, *Sing, Unburied, Sing* does not offer safe passage home for the ghosts of the past who have suffered racial violence across centuries. In this way, Ward's new Black Gothic does not offer correctives or hope for a brighter future, nor does it exorcise the ghosts from past brutality. It instead lays bare the realities of our time and their roots in systems that depend on the criminalization and disenfranchisement of black people."
Harrison (2018)

[18] For an expansion of the concept of the proletariat beyond wage laborers, including the unemployed, see Denning (2010). On "proletariat," see Tim Kreiner:

At its root, proletarian is a Roman legal term. It refers to those with nothing to lose but their children, or *proles*.... Historically, moreover, *proletariat* gathered together—however rudely, and with no shortage of internal divisions too numerous to enumerate here—all those *both shackled by and excluded from* the wage relation. A proletarian is not a wage-laborer per se. The proletariat encompasses all those for whom the fate of more or less miserable and immiserated wage-labor is the only available dream [my emphasis].
Kreiner (2017)

novels, given that the proletarian literary tradition itself is organized as much around precarity and the absence of work as it is around work itself, and certainly industrial work. While these novels were not written under the sign of proletarian literature, they do—whether intentionally or not—allude to and draw from that tradition, which itself is more variegated than is often presumed.[19]

In the final three novels discussed above (and in *Hologram* as well, we noted), precarious labor serves as an aesthetic figure that invokes tensions between conflict and connection, heterogeneity and commonality that have long been at the heart of the politics of solidarity. Because precarity occurs across such a wide field of labor arrangements, it is not a class or the basis for an identity along class lines; rather, as critic Franco Barchesi contends provocatively, "the commonality that practically defines precarity as a concept can only be the result of experimentations and encounters" (Barchesi 197). "Experimentations and encounters" are indeed what these novels stage. The scene where Alan confronts the construction workers in *Hologram* is one such experiment: it bursts into the novel as a disorienting flash—a dramatic encounter that emerges as a moment of failed linguistic and social translation. Together, these novels suggest that precarity is thus an increasingly common, if highly varied, form of structural vulnerability that has the potential to underscore shared social and political conditions. It is a material and affective state that can direct attention to collective circumstances. More broadly, US literature about labor is often less interested in detailed depictions of work as an activity than in the social relations that work generates, especially the possibilities of collective affiliation and belonging. As a literary critical method, looking at labor brings into relief dynamics of antagonism and alliance, singularity and collectivity as elements of both content and literary form. Reading for and through labor thus opens up literature and literary criticism in and beyond neoliberalism—by directing our attention to questions of exploitation and issues of common belonging that much neoliberal literature tends to efface or ignore.

At the level of literary form, Rivera, Kincaid, and Ward bring heterogeneous voices and perspectives into association without eliding discontinuities. Yet the three novels respond to different social and political moments and movements. *Earth*, written in the context of the Chicanx Civil Rights movement and the United Farm Workers' public struggle for labor unity, and *Sing*, written in the context of the emerging #Black Lives Matter movement, both adopt collective, ensemble forms in which diverse narrators share common literary space. *Lucy*, about an isolated immigrant working in a highly privatized domestic setting and written before the more recent outgrowth in domestic worker organizing, adopts a more individualized, first-person form. Yet it, too, consistently, if discreetly, raises the prospect of social connection across and along lines of gender, race, nation, and class.

---

[19] On the capaciousness of the proletarian literary tradition, see Denning (1996); on proletarian fiction as a literature of precarity, see Entin (2018).

The articulations of solidarity in the novels by Rivera, Kincaid, and Ward—whether primarily a matter of interpersonal alliance, in *Lucy*, or framed in broader collective terms, in *Earth* and *Sing*—are decidedly tentative and provisional (and in *Hologram*, I argued, solidarity is visible only as the faintest trace of a missed opportunity, a kind of spectral figure, perhaps not unlike the hologram itself). Yet these texts also contain figures of potentially revolutionary transformation—from the vision of an emergent, "people"-in-formation in *Earth*, to the scythe-wielding anticolonial avenger in *Lucy*, to the "black-knuckled multitude" in *Sing*. These images are themselves precarious, distant, undeveloped, speculative, but they have a rhetorical and imaginative force that attention to labor helps us to discern. In these novels, precarity emerges both as a thematic focus and a formal matter that approximates the always unfinished quest for solidarity. If neoliberalism is, in some measure, embodied in Margaret Thatcher's famous dictum that, "There is no such thing as society. There are individual men and women and there are families," then figures of precarious labor can open the door to narratives and motifs of complex social connection, radical transformation, and collective possibility that contemporary society, and contemporary literary production, are largely organized to obscure.

References

Barchesi, Franco. 2015. "Precarity as Capture: A Conceptual Reconstruction and Critique of the Worker-Slave Analogy," in P. Khalil Saucier and Tryon P. Woods, eds., *On Marronage: Ethical Confrontations with Anti-Blackness* (Trenton, NJ: Africa World Press).

Berlant, Lauren. 2011. *Cruel Optimism* (Durham, NC: Duke University Press).

Bourdieu, Pierre. 1998. "The Essence of Neoliberalism," *Le Monde diplomatique*, December, https://mondediplo.com/1998/12/08bourdieu, accessed February 11, 2022.

Denning, Michael. 1996. *The Cultural Front: The Laboring of Twentieth-Century American Culture* (New York: Verso).

Denning, Michael. 2010. 'Wageless Life,' *New Left Review* 66: 79–97.

Edwards, Brent. 2003. "Selvedge Salvage," *Cultural Studies* 17.1: 31.

Eggers, Dave. 2012. *A Hologram for the King* (San Francisco, CA: McSweeney's Books).

Ehrenreich, Barbara and Arlie Hochschild, eds. 2003. *Global Woman: Nannies, Maids, and Sex Workers in the New Economy* (New York: Metropolitan Books).

Entin, Joseph. 2018. "The Working Class," in Ichiro Takayoshi, ed., *American Literature in Transition: The 1930s* (Cambridge: Cambridge University Press), 56–74.

Fraiman, Susan. 2017. *Extreme Domesticity: A View from the Margins* (New York: Columbia University Press).

Gilmore, Ruth Wilson. 2006. *Golden Gulag: Prisons, Surplus, Crisis, and Opposition in Globalizing California* (Berkeley, CA: University of California Press).

Greenhouse, Steven. 2019. *Beaten Down, Worked Up: The Past, Present, and Future of American Labor* (New York: Alfred A. Knopf).

Hardt, Michael and Antonio Negri. 2004. *Multitude: War and Democracy in the Age of Empire* (New York: Penguin).

Harrison, Sheri-Marie. 2018. "New Black Gothic," June 23, https://lareviewofbooks.org/article/new-black-gothic, accessed February 11, 2022.

Hartman, Saidiya. 2008. "Venus in Two Acts," *Small Axe* 26 (June): 1–14.

Harvey, David. 1989. *The Condition of Postmodernity: An Enquiry into the Origins of Cultural Change* (London: Blackwell).
Huehls, Mitchum and Rachel Greenwald Smith, eds. 2017. *Neoliberalism and Contemporary Literary Culture* (Baltimore, MD: Johns Hopkins University Press).
Innocence Project. 2020. "The Lasting Legacy of Parchman Farm, the Prison Modeled after a Slave Plantation," May 29, www.innocenceproject.org/parchman-farm-prison-mississippi-history, accessed February 11, 2022.
Kincaid, Jamaica. 1990. *Lucy* (New York: Farrar, Straus and Giroux).
Kreiner, Tim. 2017. "The Fate of the Fast against the Slow," *Viewpoint Magazine*, June 1, www.viewpointmag.com/2017/06/01/the-fate-of-the-fast-against-the-slow, accessed February 11, 2022.
Marx, Karl. 1973. *The Grundrisse* (London: Penguin).
Michaels, Walter Benn. 2009. "Going Boom," *Bookforum*, February/March, www.bookforum.com/print/1505/the-economic-collapse-points-up-how-little-our-literary-world-has-to-say-about-social-inequality-3274, accessed February 11, 2022.
Moody, Kim. 1997. *Workers in A Lean World* (New York: Verso).
Neilson, Brett and Ned Rossiter. 2008. "Precarity as a Political Concept, Or, Fordism as Exception," *Theory, Culture & Society* 25.7–8 (December): 51–72.
Ngai, Mae. 2004. *Impossible Subjects: Illegal Aliens and the Making of Modern America* (Princeton, NJ: Princeton University Press).
Sánchez Prado, Ignacio M. 2016. "Discovering Mexican Literature of the United States: Reading Chicano Narrative of Yesterday and Today," *The Common Reader*, December 5, commonreader.wustl.edu/c/discovering-mexican-literature-united-states/, accessed February 11, 2022.
Read, Jason. 2017. "Work and Precarity," in Imre Szeman, Sarah Blacker, and Justin Sully, eds, *A Companion to Critical and Cultural Theory* (London: John Wiley & Sons Ltd), 275.
Rivera, Tomas. 1987. *… y no se lo tragó la tierra / … And the Earth Did Not Devour Him* (Houston, TX: Arte Público Press).
Robbins, Bruce. 1999. *Feeling Global: Internationalism in Distress* (New York: New York University Press).
Robbins, Bruce. 2019. "Everything is Not Neoliberalism," *American Literary History* 31.4 (Winter): 840–849.
Rozak, Suzanne. 2017. "Blurring Boundaries: Women's Work and Artistic Production in Jamaica Kincaid's *Lucy* and Cristina García's *Dreaming in Cuban*," *Lit: Literature Interpretation Theory* 28.4: 275-95.
Saldívar, Ramón. 1990. *Chicano Narrative: Dialectics of Difference* (Madison, WI: University of Wisconsin Press).
Tyner, James. 2019. *Dead Labor: Towards a Political Economy of Premature Death* (Minneapolis, Min: University of Minnesota Press).
Ward, Jesmyn. 2017. *Sing, Unburied, Sing* (New York: Scribner).
Williams, Jeffrey. 2013. "The Plutocratic Imagination," *Dissent Magazine*, Winter, www.dissentmagazine.org/article/the-plutocratic-imagination, accessed February 11, 2022.
Worden, Daniel. 2017. "The Memoir in the Age of Neoliberal Individualism," in Mitchum Huehls and Rachel Greenwald Smith, eds, *Neoliberalism and Contemporary Literary Culture* (Baltimore, MD: Johns Hopkins University Press), 160–177.

CHAPTER 5

ASIAN AMERICANS IN THE NOVEL OF LATE CAPITALISM

Samuel R. Delany's The Mad Man *and Kevin Kwan's* Crazy Rich Asians

CYNTHIA WU

THE latter half of the twentieth century inaugurated a shift in the economic status of Asian Americans. Although US immigration policies, residential segregation, and laws restricting citizenship, property ownership, marriage, and other facets of life had targeted people of Asian descent in the past, social changes during this period appeared to suggest that Asian Americans were no longer impacted by discrimination. The descendants of working-class Asian immigrants who had arrived in the United States in the late 1800s and early 1900s experienced upward mobility after the Second World War, some of it due to the benefits of the G.I. Bill. Although redlining, the practice of denying mortgages in neighborhoods deemed unfavorable by the US federal government, stymied the economic growth of African Americans and Latinxs, Asian Americans encountered fewer barriers entering the suburban middle classes. The McCarran–Walter Act in 1952 lifted restrictions that prevented immigrants of Asian descent from obtaining naturalized citizenship. The Hart–Celler Act in 1965 abolished quotas on national origin in immigration. The United States recruited upper-middle-class professionals from abroad to fill niches in its economy. Many of these workers were from East and South Asia. Meanwhile, Asian nations in the decades following the Second World War shifted to speculative capital from their prior reliance on production-based industries in order to jockey for position in the global economy. The mainstream US press published columns in the 1960s that extoled the virtues of Asian Americans—trumpeting their work ethic, law abidance, and willingness to assimilate. These articles also served up thinly veiled condemnations of African Americans for their organized protest.[1] This divide-and-conquer tactic, which attempted to drive

---

[1] One of the best known among these examples is "Success Story of One Minority Group in U.S.," *U.S. News and World Report*, December 26, 1966.

a wedge among populations of color, gave rise to the "model minority myth," a belief that Asian Americans' securing of middle-class status came from inherent cultural traits. In the popularization of this myth, the structural conditions of selective post-1965 immigration from East and South Asia and the uneven allocation of resources that disenfranchised African Americans and Latinxs receded from view.

By "late capitalism" in this chapter's title, I refer to an economic structure that is post-industrial—one where labor is decreasingly empowered and financial speculation is increasingly enabled. This structure is supported by federal policies that ease the movement of raw materials and commodities across national borders even as they restrict the passage of the working-classes from the Global South and other areas who harvest and/or manufacture these items. Meanwhile, the agents of financial speculation, the upper classes whose capital is desired and courted, have their movements across borders expedited. These social changes are associated with the Reagan-era policies of the 1980s, a decade that further solidified the Asian American model minority myth. Literary portrayals of Asian Americans at the end of the twentieth century and the beginning of the twenty-first tend to situate them at the juncture of multiple discourses, aligning them with capital, be it economic or other types readily associated with it. These fictional worlds depict societies where racialization ostensibly disappears in the face of socio-economic class. The increasing wealth gap in the United States and elsewhere in the world reveals bifurcations that do not fall neatly along racial lines. At the same time, these model minority characters continue to bear the traces of their racialization even in narratives that are set in a seemingly post-racial world.

Perhaps best known for work on the link between structural conditions and aesthetics is Fredric Jameson. According to Jameson, postmodernism signals a break from earlier artistic forms in several ways: its foregrounding of fragmentation and synchronicity, its blurring of the lines between high and popular culture, and its dissolution of the humanist subject, among other things. These stylistic elements of contemporary architecture, painting, literature, film, and other creative expression disorient the viewers or readers, creating a disconnect between the human body's capacities for perception and a world generated by the alienating effects of multinational capital.[2] To Jameson's list of aesthetic features marked by late capitalism, I would add excess and exaggeration. In fictional narratives about Asian American or Asian transnationally mobile model minorities, excess and surplus convey privileged social location. Asian American and Asian transnational subject successes index a more-than-enoughness that is magnified to extremes. The structural forces that allow the economic flourishing of some Asian Americans or Asian transnational subjects may be opaque in these representations. However, these material conditions then get refracted stylistically through the exaggerated, over-the-top prose used to describe these characters.

---

[2] Yet Jameson carefully refrains from an analysis that regards the aesthetic forces of late capitalism as totalizing. They, like everything else, contain within themselves the seeds for their own undoing. A key example is the disorienting layout of the Bonaventura Hotel in Los Angeles. It actually makes access to the retail stores inside difficult and, therefore, it thwarts the interests of capitalism (Jameson 1991: 83).

This chapter examines two texts, Samuel R. Delany's *The Mad Man* (1994) and Kevin Kwan's *Crazy Rich Asians* (2013), in order to show how Asian American and Asian transnational model minority characters function in novels of late capitalism. The exaggeration in these novels—be it of the hagiographic praises of a dead philosopher in *The Mad Man* or of Singapore's unbridled consumerism in *Crazy Rich Asians*—are ways of making sense of the widening chasms between the poor, the middle classes, and the rich at the turn of the twenty-first century. These novels portray hyperbolic scenarios whereby Asian Americans appear larger-than-life in their excesses of intellectual or economic capital. However, they never entirely escape their racialization as people of color and/or colonial subjects. Delany and Kwan portray the ostentatiousness that surrounds Asian American characters with tongue firmly in cheek, signaling to readers the necessity of challenging the model minority myth. At the same time, the conditions that separate the owning and middle classes from the working classes and the poor become opaque. The crackdown on New York City's homeless population during the HIV/AIDS crisis and the presence of Asian guest workers in the homes of the ultra-rich in Singapore form a backdrop against which Delany's and Kwan's privileged Asian American characters are made legible. The casting of the most intellectually respected and economically affluent characters into high relief by contrasting them with the most precarious members of society (who are usually of color) may allude to a post-racial world where only capital matters. However, these Asian American characters continue to carry the traces of their material histories, even when the storylines in which they appear seem to erase them.

***

Samuel Delany's *The Mad Man* features an African American protagonist, John Marr, a graduate student in philosophy at a fictional university in New York. A white professor, Irving Mossman, has taken John under his wing. John feels genuine passion for his course of study, but he also finds the codes and conventions of academia demoralizing. He understands that Irving's interest in mentoring him is crucial to his professional development, but Irving's attention is also paternalistic in ways that reveal his inadvertent racism. John and Irving fashion a collaborative research project on the late Timothy Hasler, a fictional Korean American philosopher who, in his brief career, which ended just short of his PhD's completion, produced highly regarded, game-changing scholarship. Hasler's life had ended by murder outside a gay bar seventeen years before the narrative present. For John, the unsolved crime adds another element of mystery to an already ambitious research project. Throughout the storyline, John's life merges with Hasler's as the former retraces the steps of the latter while learning as much as possible about his subject. John also indulges in the same sexual adventures that Hasler kept hidden from the academic world and develops romantic and friendship bonds with the city's underclasses, a multiracial group of homeless men.

The Mad Man, published in 1994, is set in the 1980s. Delany's novel materializes in the second decade of the HIV/AIDS epidemic, which had then reached horrific proportions because of the Reagan Administration's inattention and, later, mismanagement. John, the first-person narrator, opens the novel by declaring: "I do not have AIDS. I am surprised that I do not" (Delany 1994: 5).[3] *The Mad Man* locates itself in the temporal milieu of the HIV crisis, its necropolitical demonization of homeless people, and the changes to New York City's urban landscape that attempted to eradicate the city's most vulnerable populations. The novel functions as a fictional precursor to the polemic offered in Delany's nonfictional *Times Square Red, Times Square Blue*, published five years later. The latter argues that New York's revitalization of its famed Times Square neighborhood during the 1990s divested many same-sex desiring homeless men of a once-vibrant community. The forced closing of porn theaters, adult video stores, and peep shows allowed "family-friendly" venues and other forms of class-privileged commerce to take root and decimated a neighborhood where the city's residents had once communed across racial, religious, and class lines (Delany 1999: 91–92). These processes of gentrification went hand in hand with the economic changes in the 1980s I discussed earlier.

In the midst of these late capitalist events, *The Mad Man*'s African American protagonist draws inspiration from its dead Korean American philosopher in negotiating the strictures of white, middle-class heterosexual propriety in academia while maintaining a satisfying personal life that runs counter to its values. The key players in this story are not on equal footing in the profession, regardless of what an early scene might suggest. Irving, John's advisor, frames a triptych of photographs featuring himself and his mentee alongside Hasler to symbolize their intellectual linkages, and he self-congratulatorily marvels at the multicultural array. Far from signaling the subjects' equivalence, however, the triptych exposes the differences among them. The alterity of John's social location exposes him to more scrutiny than his white, heterosexual mentor. As Archie Lavelle Porter argues about *The Mad Man*, Delany's novel "challenges us to think about the necessity of a black queer intellectual practice, for it is the black homosexual who has so often borne the brunt of this normality [policing], both within and outside of the black community" (Porter 2014: 187). The research that John conducts on Hasler, which is situated in a discipline notorious for its lack of racial diversity and its hostility toward women, may seem to validate the social privileges he would sooner reject. However, John's pursuit of the rarefied knowledge of the academy actually leads him to a dissident sexual knowledge. The latter disrupts the former's stubborn normativities and provides John with a source of comfort, pleasure, and community.

The criticism on *The Mad Man* has not yet explored the implications of Hasler's racialization as Asian American, nor has it located his ethnic designation within late-twentieth-century structural changes taking place at the time of the novel's publication. Hasler's racialization is significant insofar as his model minority status functions as a point of measured identification for the novel's African American protagonist. If Hasler can be celebrated for his intellectual achievements while maintaining life experiences that offend the academy's bourgeois sensibilities, John reasons that perhaps the scholarly

---

[3] All further references to the text will be cited by page number.

profession may have space for him as well. Yet Hasler's nonwhiteness is often elided in ways that are convenient for his admirers, something impossible for John in the context of US society's stubborn anti-Blackness, even if that erasure of Asian racialization occurs only within certain limits.

Hasler's racial identity is most salient during moments that show the contingency of the regard the field of philosophy holds for his work. Most readers of *The Mad Man* may be struck by the detailed, lengthy depictions of John's sexual encounters, many of which span multiple pages of prose and feature stigmatized practices such as piss drinking and shit and snot eating. Delany himself had anticipated the notability of these passages such that he included a disclaimer disavowing their basis in fact. The preface claims that the novel is meant to be "take[n] wholly as a pornotopic fantasy: a set of people, incidents, places, and relations among them that have never happened and could never happen for any number of surely self-evident reasons" (ix). However, the equally embellished style that illustrates Hasler's professional achievements goes unmentioned by Delany, as do the exorbitant praises his fellow philosophers sing for him:

> Besides his sixteen refereed articles, Hasler was a book on the rhetoric of Blaise Pascal, Friedrich Nietzsche, and Charles Sanders Peirce, published the year of Hasler's father's death, 1967, by an alternative philosophical press ... a book that looked at the semiotic aspects of all three philosophers, and that could be looked at in turn as an interesting contribution to what would eventually be called "the New Nietzsche." (Hasler had apparently *read*—in German—those thousand pages of lecture notes Heidegger had left on the bad-boy of German philosophy, published in four volumes at Pfullingen in 1961. And he'd done some serious searching in *The Hidden God*.) Hasler was also seven elegant review articles on two interesting and five wholly inconsequential new works of philosophy....
>
> And (my favorite) Hasler was six published (and, we discovered, two fragmentary and unpublished) science fiction stories that, against titanic intergalactic backgrounds to dwarf *Star Trek*, *Star Wars*, and *Dune*, turned on some of the finer mathematics that informed his articles on the philosophy of natural languages....
>
> But, finally, ultimately, Timothy Hasler was his own shocking death: The prodigy who'd entered graduate school at 18 was still working on his thesis eleven years later at twenty-nine. Back in New York from Breaker's Point, in the autumn of 1973, the twenty-nine-year-old Korean-American philosophy graduate was stabbed to death in, or just behind, a bar ...
>
> But even as far as two years before Hasler's death, Irving M. had told me, he'd already noticed several prominent philosophers referring to "Hasler structures" and, sometimes, even to "Hasler grammars." And in the half dozen years after, the number of references to those structures and grammars had only grown.
>
> (9–10)

I cite the above passage at length and, even then, in drastically excerpted form to show how ebulliently Delany's prose portrays Hasler's productivity and reception. These professional achievements tap into notions of the Asian American model minority. Yet the depiction is so exaggerated that it suggests caricature. The passages describing

Hasler's professional output mirror those in the novel that depict sexual activity. The "pornotopic fantasy" to which Delany refers when describing the sex scenes might apply here, too, given how normative academic cultures celebrate the career excesses among their most highly vaunted. But then we could also use Delany's disclaimer to describe Hasler's professional track record. It "never happened and could never happen for any number of surely self-evident reasons" (ix), especially when we consider that Hasler also tutored students for several hours daily, hosted orgies at his apartment that lasted entire weekends, and—at times—maintained a dyadically partnered long-term relationship, which is also a significant time commitment. (One wonders, "Does this guy sleep?") Note, also, in the above passage the conveyance of Hasler's superhuman productivity and the lore surrounding his demise with the past tense of the verb "to be." The renowned philosopher did not "write" his intellectual or creative works. He *was* those things. Likewise, the stories about how he died became him. He *was* those speculations.

However, there are limits to how solidly Hasler can occupy this celebrated status. Once Irving learns the particulars about Hasler's personal life, he withdraws from the collaborative research project he and John had agreed to carry out—Irving writing Hasler's biography and John writing an analysis of his scholarship. Irving is not bothered by the fact of Hasler's gayness. He sidesteps the charge of homophobia by locating his displeasure not with Hasler's identity but with his actions. Irving claims an inability to continue with the collaboration because of "the *kind* of gay man he was .... 'He was an obnoxious little chink with an unbelievably nasty sex life'" (40–41). Hasler chose to align himself with the transient world of the poor and the sexually non-normative rather than maintain a respectably and exclusively homonormative existence in line with the academy's middle-class ideals. By calling Hasler the racial slur "chink" in the context of denouncing his sexual activities, Irving reveals how intertwined the regulatory systems of race and sexuality are, especially once someone chooses the wrong side of the line drawn between propriety and disrepute.

The model minority myth upholds late capitalism because it makes the racialized disparities it both relies on and reproduces invisible. The phenomenon of socioeconomically stable Asians in the United States is often explained through a culturalist perception of "Asian values" that prioritize hard work, resilience, and rule-following—not an exposure of the conditions that have selectively generated Asian immigration and shuttled immigrants into specific labor needs. Curiously, Hasler's embeddedness in these late-twentieth-century structures is illegible. He was not the child of immigrant grocers who arrived in the United States after the Korean War. This archetype most readily comes to mind when considering Korean Americans as an ethnic group, especially in the year *The Mad Man* was published, 1994.

Delany's novel is notable for its thematization of an identification an African American man develops with a Korean American one. This ethno-racial pairing would, at the time of the novel's setting and publication, conjure a specific type of Black–Korean relationality in many US cities. In the 1980s and 1990s, tensions between African Americans and Korean Americans in the form of uneven customer–shopkeeper dynamics gained high visibility. Boycotts of several Korean-owned stores, organized by

Black community leaders in Brooklyn, began in 1990 after customers had been accused of theft and, in some cases, physically assaulted by owners. Known as the Red Apple Boycott, after the name of one of the stores, it lasted a year-and-a-half. The much more highly profiled Los Angeles Rebellion occurred in 1992, after convenience store owner Soon Ja Du shot and killed teenager Latasha Harlins and received no jail time for a conviction of involuntary manslaughter. The mainstream media simplified these events as a matter of Black–Korean conflict. This was a mischaracterization that, as Claire Jean Kim contends, obscured the operations of racial capital, which unevenly sustains populations of color (Kim 2000). Small business ownership in areas rejected by white entrepreneurs was one of the few economic niches open to Koreans arriving in the United States after the Korean War. The readiness with which US banks were willing to fund Korean-owned stores in Black neighborhoods while denying the same to locals points to a historically sedimented practice of using nonwhite and/or immigrant labor to subjugate African Americans economically. The supports for Korean immigrant entrepreneurship also assuaged US guilt for its instigation of a proxy war with the Soviet Union on Korean soil. These practices allowed Korean immigrants to secure middle-class status through channels difficult for African Americans to tap because of discriminatory lending from banks.

The only mention of shopkeeping in *The Mad Man* merely highlights the gulf between Hasler and his co-ethnics engaged in that line of work. One day, John muses to himself during a stroll:

> I walked down past the Korean vegetable place where we got our beer. It was ironic: When Hasler lived here, when Hasler had walked the avenue of a July night, there'd be none of this summer revelry, nor, then, would anyone have imagined his Korean countrymen would one day dominate this aspect of the city's commerce . . . .
>
> (411)

Instead, Hasler's social location is unintelligible in Delany's narration of his genealogy. His paternal grandfather was an Englishman who was working as an engineer in Korea when he married a local woman and fathered children with her. Later, he brought his family to the United States before the Second World War, whereupon a son married another Korean American, a woman who had arrived in the country shortly before the Korean War. The two became Hasler's parents. These instances of migration across two generations disrupt the master narrative of the Korean American presence in New York City, which carries the baggage of a political economy that pits communities of color against each other. Neither of Hasler's parents lived through the decimation of their homeland in the Korean War. They did not arrive with a suffering that needed to be repaired. Their pasts do not prompt a Cold War liberal guilt that casts the Korean asylum seeker as what Josephine Park calls a "friendly"—that is, a racialized ally-turned-immigrant who is always tainted by their proximity to an enemy (Park 2016). In effect, the anomaly of Hasler's family history makes him embody even more so than usual what Leslie Bow calls the "difference without grievance" (Bow 2016: 69) that Asian Americans (especially those in the academy) signify. Hasler is domesticated through his distance from other Korean Americans and their messy entanglements in racial capitalism and the fight against communism. His complex and exceptional family history obscures his racial difference even if only in limited ways.

John's research on Hasler takes a back seat once he becomes more invested in solving his murder. Through establishing contacts and trusted relationships with New York City's impoverished, he finds out that Hasler died while trying to defend a homeless lover, Mad Man Mike, from a knife attack at a hustler bar. The regular clientele and sex workers at The Pit interact according to a logic aligned with sanctioned forms of capital, despite the underground nature of their economy. Both parties understand the exchange of money for sexual services as the bedrock of the community's cohesion. Neither wants to disrupt the equilibrium between those who are able to pay and those who are willing to provide. The same bartender who was working seventeen years ago on the night of Hasler's murder explains it to John: "You see ... this place is a lot of older men who think the only way they can get anything worth having sexually is to pay for it. And the kids who come here are all kids who want to get paid—need to get paid" (313). Mad Man Mike, however, was a young newcomer who was sexually indiscriminate and egalitarian in his desires. He regarded all men, the young and the old, the beautiful and the homely, equally attractive. He pursued them all. "[T]he thing that makes this whole place possible," the bartender continues, "is a belief that sex—the kind of sex that gets sold here—is scarce. Because it's scarce, it's valuable. And because it's valuable, it goes for good prices.... So what happens if one of these guys comes in and starts hanging out here, huh?" (313–314), he asks John rhetorically. The stabbing was the outcome of the sex workers protecting their financial interests.

Although Mad Man Mike is portrayed in ways that racialize him as white, the fact that he depressed the regulars' earnings at The Pit and the fact that an Asian American died defending him reference historical anxieties about the relationship between Asian bodies and capital. Much of the hostility directed at Asian immigrants during the nineteenth century stemmed from their willingness to work for lower wages than whites, thereby cheapening their labor. The way Mad Man Mike functioned at The Pit, however, was different from that of the "coolies" of the past. He was not an underpaid worker undercutting the prices of the established young men at the bar. Rather, he disrupted a place of commerce by replacing their paid services with uncommodified sex, freely and ludically circulated in the context of leisure. Yet the hint of monetary exchange still remained in these sex games. As John learns in his own relationships with Mad Man Mike and his associates, the use of pennies to buy one another for sexual services is part of the role playing of client–prostitute scenes in this circle of friends. Unlike the payment between johns and sex workers at The Pit, however, "value disappears due to the lack of a category of abstract equivalence through which both sexual practices can be subsumed and value can be expressed and measured," as Christian Ravela argues. The penny changes hands. However, it "only enables the exchange of bodies rather than measures their value" (Ravela 2016). Building on Ravela's analysis, I concur that the penny fails to cheapen the bodies that make themselves available for sex through its exchange during role play, and I want to add that it also renders them priceless. The members of the underclasses are elevated to a state of infinite value through their abundance instead of the supply–demand dynamic of scarcity the bartender describes.

When we consider how the unhoused and the transient in *The Mad Man* become priceless not despite their dearth of capital but *because* of it, we can recognize the martyr's death accorded to Hasler at the novel's end. As someone endowed with an excess of intellectual capital, to an extent that its depiction can only be read as hyperbole, Hasler opted out of the logic of economic capital in his choice to consort with and defend New York City's itinerant classes. However, we must not conceive of Hasler's relationships with Mad Man Mike and other men of similar means as one of paternalism or charity. As Michael Buchner and Simon Dickel claim in their reading of Delany's novel: "This is not a situation in which the intellectual lectures the homeless person, but one in which the homeless person's reflections on life constitute an original contribution even to philosophical discourse" (Buchner and Dickel 2015). The organic knowledge issuing from economically oppressed lived experiences is just as, or even more, valuable than the knowledge of the academy. The conversations John holds with his lovers are portrayed with a straightforward verisimilitude in Delany's prose. Even the sometimes unsettling dialogue that accompanies their sexual role playing, where racial and other types of slurs are impishly used, does not require a suspension of disbelief. These passages are markedly different from those depicting Hasler's adoration by the academy, which are overt instances of exaggeration.

***

If *The Mad Man* is set during the very beginning of an era we now understand to be late capitalism, *Crazy Rich Asians* immerses itself squarely in the economic extremes that have already overtaken life under these conditions. The first book in Kevin Kwan's chick-lit trilogy, *Crazy Rich Asians* portrays the relationship between Chinese American Rachel Chu and Singaporean Nick Young, who are both professors at New York University. Nick invites Rachel to his home one summer so she can meet his parents and accompany him to his best friend's wedding, for which he is serving as best man. Unbeknownst to Rachel, who was raised in a single-parent, middle-class home, Nick hails from a family that is part of the global economic elite. The disconnect between Rachel's ordinary, but still privileged, upbringing—her mother is a realtor—and Nick's old money lineage reveals itself soon after the couple arrives in Singapore. Upon meeting Rachel, Nick's friends and family become disdainful, believing that Nick should stop associating with someone below his economic station. They cast aspersions on Rachel's intentions, believing her to be a gold digger. Their attempts to drive a wedge between the couple fail, however. In a conclusion befitting the novel's romantic comedy conventions, Nick chooses his relationship over the expectations imposed by high society. Rachel and Nick reaffirm their bond and remain together.

The Mad Man may posit the university as a world of stuffy propriety from which its misfits find solace through befriending New York City's unhoused. However, in *Crazy Rich Asians*, Kwan portrays academia as a sanctuary from the pretenses of the "crazy rich." Both Rachel and Nick are assistant professors, Rachel in Economics and Nick in History. They begin dating after a colleague introduces them. Although Nick had been mum about his upper-class origins early in their relationship, the trip back home for his best friend's wedding forces the couple to confront their class differences. The groom, Colin Khoo, one of the novel's sympathetic characters, alerts Nick to how uncomfortable Rachel may feel at a party scheduled at Nick's grandmother's opulent house the day of the couple's arrival: "It's just that the two of you have been living this idyllic fantasy, this 'simple young lovers in Greenwich Village' life. Up until now, you've been struggling to get tenure. Don't you think she's in for a shock tonight?" (Kwan 2013: 147).[4] Colin's prediction comes true. Rachel attends the party and feels out of place. The morning afterwards, she muses to herself:

> It was as if she had stumbled into a secret chamber and discovered that her boyfriend had been living a double life. The ordinary life they shared as two young college professors in New York bore no resemblance to the life of imperial splendor that Nick seemed to lead here, and Rachel didn't know how to reconcile the two.
> (213)

Delany's John Marr was never misguided enough to bring any of his lovers to a department party, but one can imagine the same awkwardness that may have resulted had they been convinced to accompany him.

Readers of *Crazy Rich Asians* who are employed in academia tend to poke fun at the likelihood of two untenured professors taking the entire summer off from research to engage in months of partying overseas.[5] Also, the "simple" and "ordinary" life Kwan visualizes professors living—improbably removed from the adherence to credentialing, rank, and pedigree rampant in Nick's social and familial worlds—exists only as a foil for the excesses of Singapore's upper classes. Lengthy passages of *Crazy Rich Asians* read as paeans to consumerism. However, their exaggerated details prompt the reader to take them firmly tongue in cheek. For instance, during a scene where Eddie, cousin to Nick, seethes with jealousy at a minor character's more monied upbringing and conspicuous display of wealth, the narration shifts to Eddie's own holdings:

> Edison and [his wife] Fiona lived in the duplex penthouse of Triumph Towers, one of the most sought-after buildings high on Victoria Peak (five bedrooms, six baths, more than four thousand square feet, not including the eight-hundred-square-foot terrace), where they employed two Filipino and two Mainland Chinese maids....
>
> In the parking garage of their building, they owned five parking spots (valued at two hundred and fifty thousand each), where their fleet consisted of a Bentley Continental GT (Eddie's weekday car), an Aston Martin Vanquish (Eddie's weekend

---

[4] All further references to the text will be cited by page number.
[5] The filmic adaptation of *Crazy Rich Asians* makes a small change in this regard. Rachel and Nick's visit to Singapore takes place over spring break. This change was likely made *not* to render it more faithful to reality but to condense the plot into a more manageable time span for a feature-length movie.

car), a Volvo S40 (Fiona's car), a Mercedes S550 (the family car), and a Porsche Cayenne (the family sport-utility vehicle). At Aberdeen Marina, there was his sixty-four-foot yacht, Kaiser. Then there was the holiday condo in Whistler, British Columbia....

Eddie was a member of the Chinese Athletic Association, the Hong Kong Golf Club, the China Club, the Hong Kong Club, the Cricket Club, the Dynasty Club, the American Club, the Jockey Club, the Royal Hong Kong Yacht Club, and too many private dining clubs to recount. Like most upper-crust Hong Kongers, Eddie also possessed what was perhaps the ultimate membership card—Canadian Permanent Resident Cards for his entire family (a safe haven in case the powers that be in Beijing ever pulled a *Tiananmen* again). He collected watches, and now possessed more than seventy timepieces from the most esteemed watchmakers (all Swiss, of course, except for a few vintage Cartiers), which he installed in a custom-designed bird's eye maple display in his private dressing room....

(79–81)

Kwan's hyperbolic listing of Eddie's material possessions echoes the style of Delany's portrayal of Timothy Hasler's research productivity. Again, I cite at length, even as I drastically excerpt the passage, to provide an adequate example of the author's narration when portraying excess. In both Kwan's and Delany's novels, passages that describe a variety of abundances—whether pertaining to professional capital, sexual activity, consumerist accumulation, or elective transnational mobility—take up vastly more space on the page than is necessary to advance the plot. For Kwan and Delany, the surfeit of narration is performative. It does what it means. The language used to convey the lavishness is itself lavish.

Kwan's intended reader is not meant to identify with Eddie. (This is where Kwan's and Delany's rhetorical commitments depart from each other. Delany *does* want to elicit a meaningful connection between the reader and the practitioners of non-normative sex in his novels, even as his portrayal of Hasler's professional capital is larger than life.) The exaggerated depiction of Eddie's material possessions sets the narration up for an unsympathetic characterization of his own assessment of this inventory. Eddie dolefully thinks of himself as lacking in comparison to others higher up the chain. Kwan's strategy of listing objects to instill abject marveling at their excesses then inverts itself by naming all that Eddie does not own:

> Despite this embarrassment of riches, Eddie felt extremely deprived compared to most of his friends. He didn't have a house on the Peak. He didn't have his own plane. He didn't have a full-time crew for his yacht, which was much too small to host more than ten guests for brunch comfortably. He didn't have any Rothkos or Pollocks or the other dead American artists one was required to hang on the wall in order to be considered truly rich these days.

(81)

The passage does not invite the intended reader to nod along with Eddie and affirm his resentment. Rather, it signals that he is out of touch.

Crazy Rich Asians may be notable as both a novel and its filmic adaptation, which has garnered mainstream popularity in the United States despite its almost exclusively Asian cast. These texts mark a rare moment in the world of commercial publishing and Hollywood film, industries notable for their white racial homogeneity. Some might claim, convincingly, that this success actually stems from the novel's and the film's Asian and Asian American portrayals, given the mainstream's exoticizing tendencies. However, we also need to pay attention to the class and, sometimes, interethnic discrepancies *among* Asian characters in these texts. To be sure, Rachel and Nick's class differences are thematized in the plot. Yet the cultural divides between the couple seem inconsequential when compared to others. Eddie and Fiona's staff includes Filipina and mainland Chinese domestics, women whose subjectivity is never broached because they are deemed unimportant. Additional references to Asian guest workers are peppered throughout the novel. In the movie, nonspeaking extras in maid uniform hover silently in the background or tend to the characters' meals and high-end shopping purchases. Turban-clad South Asian armed guards in colonial-style uniforms greet visitors to secluded estates. Global investors like Eddie may game the processes that nation states set for regulating migrants' passage across their borders—hence, Eddie's ability to move his family to Canada at a moment's notice. As Aihwa Ong argues, this leverage is part and parcel of a structure that has incentivized Asian transnational subjects' yoking of capitalist accumulation to global mobility (Ong 1999). However, the working-class subjects in *Crazy Rich Asians*, whose domestic labor props up the capital of individuals like Eddie, have their cross-border movements spurred very differently. Because of colonial and neocolonial pressures, they have little choice but to leave home and separate themselves from family in search of an income equal to only the tiniest percentage their employers enjoy. Furthermore, those employers exert control over the terms on which they may remain in their host country, as Rhacel Salazar Parreñas's research uncovers (2001). In sum, as Aimee Bahng (following Lauren Berlant) asserts, Singapore's increasing reliance on guest workers means that "its flexible accumulation trades on the cruelly optimistic drive toward a good life and the promise of an Asian futurity that will never arrive for the vast majority of the workers who sustain the wealth of the few" (Bahng 2018: 145). These workers' movements and actions are not facilitated through capital but demanded by it.

Given the vast gulf in resources within racial categories, the fictional world of *Crazy Rich Asians* may seem to suggest that the here and now of late capitalism is one that has eliminated the usefulness of race as a category. The exploiters of labor and the providers of it, alike, are found among Asians rather than across racial lines. However, as Grace Kyungwon Hong soundly argues, the novel's post-racial landscape is illusory. A case in point is the opening scene, which takes place years before the narrative present. Nick, as a young child, arrives with his mother Eleanor, an aunt, and two cousins at an exclusive hotel in London. Despite having a reservation, they are snubbed by the desk attendant, who insists they must be mistaken. Following a tense interchange, Nick's aunt makes a phone call, after which it is revealed that she has just purchased the hotel. She fires the attendant on the spot, and the family emerges triumphant in this instance of discrimination. As Hong notes, however, this scene is evidence that "the narrative of Asian capital's ascendance cannot quite evade the specter of racism and colonialism" (Hong 2018). To Hong's analysis, I would add that this flashback functions in much the same way as Delany's disclaimer about the fictional nature of the sex scenes before the story proper in *The Mad Man*. The scenes that follow, *Crazy Rich Asians* implicitly warns its readers, are strictly imaginative. They have never happened. They never could happen. The reasons should surely be self-evident. The fantasy of overcoming the fact of racial difference, using whatever capital at your disposal, is just that. The extensive resources these characters possess, be it financial or intellectual, never completely erase race.

***

That being said, I close with a meditation on how professed claims of fiction in both Delany's and Kwan's preambles read when the authors divulge that the exaggeration and hyperbole they employ as literary devices do, in fact, have their basis in lived experience. Darieck Scott points out that Delany had disclosed in an interview that the scenes in *The Mad Man* are not that far removed from his own sexual history. Scott, instead of dismissing Delany's disclaimer as disingenuous, proposes another way of taking the highly embellished depictions of sex in the novel. "[W]e ought not to lose sight of the *possibility* of actually practicing what *The Mad Man* describes; we should not, simply because this is a work of fantasy, be seduced to cushion our discomfort with the relieving reminder that these perhaps-disturbing representations are 'not real.'" (Scott 2010: 209). Particularly when referencing the sexual acts, practices, and fantasies associated with marginalized populations, the refusal to acknowledge that these incidents "*could happen*" (Scott 2010: 209) is a refusal to lend credence and visibility to stigmatized inclinations linked with racial and sexual difference. However, returning this discussion to my earlier assertion that what is most unrealistic in *The Mad Man* is not the sex but Hasler's curriculum vitae and the field of philosophy's unbridled (if conditional) adulation of it, I contend that Delany's ultimate claim about the authenticity of certain aspects of his novel only render other parts ever more fantastical. The caveat conveyed to potential Asian American academics wistfully eyeing Hasler's success: your results may vary.

Kwan has also attested to the reality of the extravagances depicted in *Crazy Rich Asians*. In an interview, he revealed himself as a native informant hailing from Singaporean high society. The portrayals of rampant consumerism and clannish family drama, he insisted, are all true to life. To the average reader, the lengthy scenes that illustrate these excesses in *Crazy Rich Asians* may appear as caricature, but Kwan expressed frustration about the revisions he was forced to make because of pre-publication feedback:

> I actually had to tone it down! ... [M]y editor was like, *No one will believe this.* And I would say, *But this really happened,* and she'd reply, *It doesn't matter. You're going to lose readers because it's going to seem so unreal that people would spend this much money, or do something this excessive.* So those parts were changed.
>
> (Christensen 2013)

If the characterizations of wealth in the novel are not so much tongue-in-cheek exaggerations as they are subdued illustrations of Kwan's eyewitness accounts, then the opening scene depicting the Young family's inability to escape racism completely through the mobilization of class privilege takes on even greater urgency.

Yet this privilege is held over the heads of Asians who fail to measure up in the socioeconomic hierarchy. Even more, the policing of the line between the upper classes and the middle classes occurs intraracially. One of the most recognizable lines from the filmic adaptation of *Crazy Rich Asians* is "You will never be enough," spoken by Eleanor (portrayed by Michelle Yeoh) to Rachel (portrayed by Constance Wu). Eleanor, the formidable matriarch of the Young family, had confided in Rachel that she also came from humble origins and struggled to gain acceptance from her unwelcoming in-laws. This disclosure shows her to be a more sympathetic character than initially perceived. Eleanor remains persistently aware, even after decades of marriage, that her lineage prevents her from fully belonging among the Youngs. Hence, the declaration of never being enough comes from a place of personal experience. She speaks about herself as well as about Rachel. This reveal, however, does not soften her intentions as the keeper of the family gate who attempts to prevent Rachel from entering. I want to repurpose this iconic line as the screenplay's implicit warning to the global Asian economic elite, who seemingly have unlimited material resources. So long as you continue to uphold and reproduce the structures of imperialism and racial capitalism, your own difference will ensure ... you will never be enough.

References

Bahng, Aimee. 2018. *Migrant Futures: Decolonizing Speculation in Financial Times* (Durham, NC: Duke University Press).

Bow, Leslie. 2016. "Difference without Grievance: Asian Americans as the Almost Minority," in Patricia A. Matthew, ed., *Written/Unwritten: Diversity and the Hidden Truths of Tenure* (Chapel Hill, NC: University of North Carolina Press), 69.

Buchner, Michael and Simon Dickel. 2015. "An Affinity for the Lumpen: Depictions of Homelessness in Delany's Bread & Wine and The Mad Man," *African American Review* 48.3 (Fall): 300.

Christensen, Lauren. 2013. "Crazy Rich Asians Author Kevin Kwan on the Lavish Culture of Asia's Upper Crust: 'The Reality Is Simply Unbelievable,'" *Vanity Fair*, June 11, https://www.vanityfair.com/culture/2013/06/crazy-rich-asians-kevin-kwan-asia-upper-crust. Accessed March 6, 2022.

Delany, Samuel R. 1994. *The Mad Man* (Rutherford, NJ: Voyant Publishing).

Delany, Samuel R. 1999. *Times Square Red, Times Square Blue* (New York: New York University Press).

Hong, Grace Kyungwon. 2018. "Speculative Surplus: Asian American Racialization and the Neoliberal Shift," *Social Text* 36.2 (June): 119.

Jameson, Fredric. 1991. *Postmodernism, or the Cultural Logic of Late Capitalism* (Durham, NC: Duke University Press).

Kim, Claire Jean. 2000. *Bitter Fruit: The Politics of Black–Korean Conflict in New York City* (New Haven, CT: Yale University Press).

Kwan, Kevin. 2013. *Crazy Rich Asians* (New York: Anchor).

Ong, Aihwa. 1999. *Flexible Citizenship: The Cultural Logics of Transnationality* (Durham, NC: Duke University Press).

Park, Josephine Nock-Hee. 2016. *Cold War Friendships: Korea, Vietnam, and Asian American Literature* (New York: Oxford University Press).

Parreñas, Rhacel Salazar. 2001. *Servants of Globalization: Migration and Domestic Work* (Stanford, CA: Stanford University Press).

Porter, Archie Lavelle. 2014. "The Over-Education of the Negro: Academic Novels, Higher Education, and the Black Intellectual," PhD dissertation, Graduate Center of the City University of New York.

Ravela, Christian. 2016. "'Turning Out' Possessive Individualism: Freedom and Belonging in Samuel R. Delany's The Mad Man," *Modern Fiction Studies* 62.1 (Spring): 102.

Scott, Darieck. 2010. *Extravagant Abjection: Blackness, Power, and Sexuality in the African American Imagination* (New York: New York University Press).

PART 2
MOVEMENTS

CHAPTER 6

THE HIDDEN VOICE

Indigenous Experience and Authenticity in Twentieth-Century American Literature

SEAN TEUTON

In *House Made of Dawn* (1989 [1968]), Kiowa writer N. Scott Momaday strands us in 1950s Los Angeles, where Indigenous people from afar struggle to survive. Readers feel the pain of the novel's protagonist Abel, a Second World War veteran who suffers in exile from his New Mexico Pueblo people. Those Native Americans who do make a home in the city immerse themselves in memory and recitation of their ancient earth and ancestors. To recall those lands and people, the survivors arrange weekly meetings from, of all places, the basement of an office supply warehouse. It is a fitting venue as they are the objects of governmental paperwork to send Indians from reservations to cities. "Rev. J. B. B. Tosamah, Pastor & Priest of the Sun" oversees the "Holiness Pan-Indian Rescue Mission." In the "cold and dreary" cellar, Tosamah appears from behind threadbare curtains, "big, lithe as a cat, narrow-eyed" and, with the "voice of a great dog," begins his sermon in recalling his Kiowa homeland and people:

> To look upon that landscape in the early morning, with the sun at your back, is to lose the sense of proportion. Your imagination comes to life, and this, you think, is where Creation was begun.
> I returned to Rainy Mountain in July. My grandmother had died in the spring, and I wanted to be at her grave....
> Her name was Aho, and she belonged to the last culture to evolve in North America. Her forebears came down from the high north country nearly three centuries ago. The earliest evidence of their existence places them close to the source of the Yellowstone River in western Montana. They were a mountain people, a mysterious tribe of hunters whose language has never been classified in any major group. In the late seventeenth century they began a long migration to the south and east. It was a journey toward the dawn, and it led to a golden age.... According to their origin myth, they entered the world through a hollow log. From one point of view

their migration was the fruit of an old prophecy, for indeed they emerged from a sunless world.

I could see that. I followed their ancient way to my grandmother's grave. Though she lived out her long life in the shadow of Rainy Mountain the immense landscape of the continental interior—all of its seasons and its sounds—lay like memory in her blood.

Momaday (1989 [1968]: 127–129)

The small congregation nods its assent and, at least for the moment, recalls and returns to ancestral lands and peoples. Tosamah's sermon is mythic in the truest sense. It hearkens to an ancient, "mysterious" time of the Kiowas' "creation" and charts a journey over sacred geography and across time that destines by "prophecy" the people's eventual greatness on their arrival at Rainy Mountain. While the vast and colorful Southwestern landscapes of *House Made of Dawn* transfix readers, it is the urban "The Priest of the Sun" part of the novel that displays true genius. For Momaday could create no greater contrast than between the gritty streets of Los Angeles and the timeless land imagined by the priest as a "memory in the blood," and yet Tosamah's visionary account prevails. Indeed, like his grandmother, Tosamah need not physically visit his ancestral land or past to know it intimately. Instead, the Kiowa pastor seems to draw on a mystical, unlearned connection to his people's memory that arrives in his mind fully intact and immutable.

In offering a different path to history, Momaday is revered by Native American readers. For such readers often have been denied access to an Indigenous past. Indeed, while Europeans and Americans robbed Indigenous peoples of their ancestral lands, they also imperiled their cultures, their languages, and so their histories. The Kiowa author and other Native writers thus draw on a traditional view of knowledge, history, and time that relies more on Indigenous notions of narration and cultural memory than on Western ideas of historical fact and evidence. In the face of this tension, Momaday and other such Native writers invite Indigenous readers and others to imagine a self that embodies an ancient, mythic essence to reclaim a stolen past, even at the expense of the mainstream's hallowed sources of knowledge such as research and historical evidence. That embodiment as it intersects, moreover, with Black and Brown peoples, complicates racial authenticity and so liberates a more complex Native epistemology. In what follows, I describe this Indigenous historiography, trouble its use, and apply it to uncover the hidden Indigenous voices in the conquest narratives of American literature. In the end, that writing and reading practice displays a contradiction that many Indigenous moderns both acknowledge and embrace.

Momaday's invocation of this Indigenous epistemology as "memory in the blood" has drawn criticism for relying on a notion of a racialized "essence" to connect with the past. He passionately writes his people's history in this manner in a number of works, such as in his memoir *The Names* (1976), in which he embodies and reconstructs the memory of his family: "Mammedaty was my grandfather, whom I never knew. Yet he came to be imagined posthumously in the going on of the blood, having invested the shadow of his presence in an object or a word, in his name above all. He enters into my dreams; he persists in his name" (26). In his physical description and "The Way to Rainy Mountain" sermon in *House Made of Dawn*, Tosamah is unmistakably a direct embodiment of the author. In fact, the narrative of home appears verbatim a year later in Momaday's *The Way to Rainy Mountain* (1976 [1969]). In this mixed-genre work, however, Momaday explains his project to recover a relationship with his ancient lands and ancestors, a project that includes not only mythic longing but also rigorous genealogical and ethnographic research. While numerous Native American and other non-white writers draw on this "blood" memory to reclaim a stolen history and land and to resist domination, one might accept its practical use, if not its exercise of traditional, non-Western historiography.

Though perhaps one of the most breathtaking and memorable narratives in all of Indigenous literature, Momaday's tribal history is not unique in its purpose to ground Native Americans. Indeed, his project exemplifies a pattern in twentieth-century Native literature, from novel to poetry to memoir, that does not appear in earlier decades, which were more focused on non-fiction. With Native nations under more modern threats—less war than bureaucracy, poverty, hunger, or displacement—twentieth-century Indigenous authors seek to imagine and recover the past and land, if only in the mind. Of course, the historical novel presents an ideal genre for this venture, and many Native writers seek it out for their own restorations of earth and life. In *Fools Crow* (1986), Gros Ventre and Blackfeet writer James Welch returns us to 1871 Montana when the Pikuni people witness the bison extermination, a plague, a massacre, and the end of their traditional life. While often mournful in its recollection, the novel asks Native people to protect "a happiness that sleeps with sadness" (390). Carefully researched and gently offered, the novel accomplishes a historical reckoning and even healing of Indigenous and white readers alike. From that paragon of the Native American historical novel, such other Native novels as Anishinaabe author Louise Erdrich's *Tracks* (1988) direct us to the devastating consequences of the 1887 General Allotment Act to divide and sell communally owned Indigenous land. In an early twentieth-century Chippewa town in North Dakota, characters suffer land theft, disease, and famine and learn to survive through each other's forgiveness and humor. Choctaw writer Louis Owens's *Bone Game* (1994) plumbs California history to deliver a Native American professor haunted by the Santa Cruz mission's abuse of the Ohlone people. These Indigenous historical novels grow from Western ways of knowledge—that is, research—and assemble histories and landscapes that can educate and heal us.

Other Native writers, however, conduct tribal history projects more similar to those of Momaday than to those of Welch. At times historical facts are less available, and authors must dare to imagine ancestors' lives and lands to keep them from falling away in silence. This more imaginative approach perhaps inspires Creek poet Joy Harjo who, in *A Map to the Next World* (2000), seeks a deep history of Muscogee thriving, where "Fresh courage glimmers from planets. / And lights the map printed with the blood of history, a map you will have to know by your intention, by the language of suns" (20). The poet offers an Indigenous futurity that expands the frame of memory to include the celestial world and makes available the "writing" of lost voices of conquest, reminding us that "your skin is the map" (102). Elsewhere, Native authors like Leslie Marmon Silko, who is Laguna, enlist ancient time to find oral literary models for contemporary feminism. In *Storyteller* (1981), the past and present collapse: "You should understand / the way it was / back then, / because it is the same / even now" (94). In a brief poetic narrative, the ancient voice places a modern Laguna woman in a mythic landscape, where women chose their husbands and lives freely. Such authors employ this Indigenous history to confront colonialism and deny their disinheritance: "The white man does not understand the Indian for the reason that he does not understand America.... But in the Indian the spirit of the land is still vested...." (248), writes Sioux autobiographer Luther Standing Bear in *Land of the Spotted Eagle* (1978 [1933]).

Whatever their approach, twentieth-century Native American writers often seek to reconstruct a past unavailable or forgotten, suppressed, or destroyed by their conquerors. Such authors seek these "hidden voices" to reclaim a history and thus a nation and a purpose. While some Indigenous history writers seek unmediated, metaphysical knowledge, others confront the highly mediated narratives of conquest and the colonial past. In this chapter, I illustrate some of the many subdued utterances found in Indigenous and American literature to argue for their liberation. Such expressions might call for our recognition as we search in unfamiliar historical locales, as we read and listen in the ways Dakota historian Philip Deloria recommends in *Indians in Unexpected Places* to find a corrective to our assumptions, where "broad cultural expectations are both the products and the tools of domination and ... are an inheritance that haunts each and every one of us" (2004: 4). At times, the search for suppressed Indigenous voices challenges Western conventions for historical evidence. Scholars such as Arnold Krupat, whose book chapter inspires this chapter, question what some have described as the West's "fetishism" of history and instead seek to understand Native accounts through historical facts but also historical "truths" (2002: 53). From this more Indigenous view, narrative serves a community seeking to organize the past, placing an event to properly order the world. Overlooking this more mythic sense of history risks missing some of the story and perhaps denies what Wai Chee Dimock has called "deep time." Deep time, says Dimock, offers a more "planetary" scope for the human story and so necessarily includes oral histories that impinge on our graphic worlds (2006: 3–4). Immersed in that broader, more inclusive conception, twentieth-century Native American writers openly speculate regarding historical facts received second hand or even through media devoid of words—visual arts, gestures, impressions. Such imaginative acts connect today's Indigenous people to ancestors and other Native voices of the pre-contact or colonial past in the manner Osage scholar Robert Warrior describes as "synchronicity" (2005: 38–43).

In order to clarify the risks and rewards of the mythic search for hidden voices in "blood memory," this chapter turns to that other means of historiography, the written account. In reading earlier European accounts, for example, one discovers an Indigenous world otherwise unavailable. Some such narratives of travel and exploration, witness and interview have been questioned for their mediation of "authentic" Native voices. I argue that we must speculate on, and even accept, their mediation if we are to revive, authorize, and share the lives of Native Americans found within. Most importantly, in relentlessly redirecting the twentieth century back to the Indigenous past, we exercise a methodology of decolonization. From there, I turn to race, the hidden voice of our times, in which I search for earlier unacknowledged Black or Brown voices in Indigenous narratives and call for their utterance in the twentieth century. The intent of this exploration is to complicate, liberate, and connect some of the many Indigenous faces and gestures, voices and writings that make up the shared literary world we call "America." We must seek such connection, I argue, if we are ever to grow as scholars and readers.

Memory in the Blood

In 1989, N. Scott Momaday received a fellowship at the School of American Research, during which he completed the project "In the Presence of the Sun: A Gathering of Shields." It was a series of sixteen painted shields. Each expresses a story from the Kiowa oral tradition and, grouped in four sets of the Kiowa sacred number four, each offers its viewer an object for meditation over sixteen days "in the presence of the sun"—and while fasting on days four, eight, twelve, and sixteen. That he dares to reproduce a Plains traditional art form, as though he and it exist impervious to the passing of time, might itself invite charges of essentialism, and indeed critics have repeatedly rebuked Momaday for his purported essentialism regarding Indigenous identity and especially for his use of the term "blood memory." But anyone familiar with his fiction can see that his Native characters do not instinctively know their ancestral history but instead labor to recover identity and culture. They struggle painfully to know their homeland. In the end, Momaday's view of the Native American world is not essentialist but constructed. His essays on art, however, and his visual art itself unavoidably express unmediated Indigenous knowledge. His stated purpose for the shields project is clearly essentialist and in fact is identical to his aesthetic theory repeated elsewhere. I will return to that aesthetic in a moment. For now, I would like to clarify the desires for and dangers of an essentialist account of Native land and experience.

For many Native Americans in the 1970s, to be Indian was to be essentialist. Back then, Native scholars like Paula Gunn Allen celebrated an essentialist view of American Indian cultural geography. She begins:

> We are the land. To the best of my understanding, that is the fundamental idea embedded in Native American life and culture in the Southwest. More than remembered, the Earth is the mind of the people as we are the mind of the earth. The land is not really the place (separate from ourselves) where we act out the drama of our isolated destinies. It is not a means of survival, a setting for our affairs, a resource on which we draw in order to keep our own act functioning. It is not the ever-present "Other" which supplies us with a sense of "I." It is rather a part of our being, dynamic, significant, real.
>
> (1979: 191)

Allen explains the Native attachment to the land as a mathematical equivalence rather than a mere affinity. In these terms, tribal people and the land are interchangeable, homogeneous components of an organic whole. The distinction of Indigenous people from the land is an illusion because Native people, Allen explains, are inseparable from the land. Allen accounts for the relationship of Native Americans to homelands in rather mystified terms that cannot be questioned. We, in fact, must accept her claim on terms of religious belief. Like faith in a deity, a strictly spiritual explanation of Indigeneity can either be accepted as truth or dismissed as superstition, but it cannot be examined. For this reason, Westerners have largely departed from ontology in philosophy, leaving the study of religion to theologians. In considering non-physical explanations of land relationships, scholars working within a European tradition that rejects metaphysical knowledge are likely to tolerate but not to seriously consider such explanations.

The most prevalent use of essentialism, however, has to do with genetics as a source of encoded tribal knowledge of ancestral lands. Your blood, it says, leads you back to your land and people. Momaday is not the only writer who invokes his Indian blood to claim himself. The very pulse of Native American literature seems to rely on plasma. On this "blood memory," Momaday writes: "The land, *this* land, is secure in the Native American's racial memory" (1997: 39). Also consider Paula Gunn Allen: "There is a permanent wilderness in the blood of an Indian, a wilderness that will endure as long as the grass grows, the wind blows, the rivers flow, and one Indian woman remains alive" (1992: 183). Or Simon Ortiz: "Don't fret. / Warriors will keep alive in the blood" (1981: 33). And Leslie Marmon Silko: "Maybe the dawn woke the instinct in the dim memory of the blood when horses had been as wild as deer and at sunrise went into the trees and thickets to hide" (1977: 182–183). Here is James Welch: "The answer had come to me as if by instinct, sitting on the pump platform, watching [his grandfather's] silent laughter, as though it was his blood in my veins that had told me" (1974: 160). Gerald Vizenor: "The elders ruled that we were tricksters in a wicked world, in a world of dead voices, poisoned by the wordies who would never hear their stories in the blood" (1992: 46). Since even the skeptic Vizenor invokes blood memory, we might question the essentialist intent of Native writers. After all, such other non-Native minority writers as African American poet Langston Hughes writes: "I've known rivers: / I've known rivers ancient as the world and older than the flow of human blood / in human veins" (1994: 23).

To Indigenous writers with essentialist leanings, biology not only determines whether one is a Native person but also how one develops socially and morally as well as geographically. In Native Studies, critics object not only to the clearly racialist entanglements of such theories of biological essence, metaphorical or otherwise, but also to the analysis of Native American place-making these views preclude. From the essentialist view, the relationship to lands can be neither examined, questioned, nor improved, for it is believed to be given in advance, timeless and unchanging. Perhaps underlying this critique of the unmediated identification with land is the worry among theorists that strong attachments to lands contribute to a destructive form of nationalism, in which the idea of homeland relies on the absolute conception of territory as the destined extension of a people.

After all, since invasion Europeans have justified their very presence on Native lands on essentialist footing, from the Puritans' idea of the preordained City on the Hill, to the metaphysics of manifest destiny in the nineteenth century. Some argue that because they potentially also serve empire, we should temper essentialist explanations of the human place in North American land with a more self-examining, and thus politically enabling, theory of Native dwelling. Employing what scholars call a "realist" theory of Indigenous place, Native Americans critically construct, evaluate, and improve their relationship with the land through and for tribal identity (Teuton 2008: 46–51). Linguistic anthropologist Keith Basso asserts that "place-making is a form of cultural activity" (1996: 7). In this profoundly social sense, selfhood becomes continuous with what we call "homeland" over time.

Despite the political power of claims to a self-evident Indigeneity, belonging to ancestral places is also a social process of identification with lands. This vital relationship is maintained in the oral tradition, the medium through which tribal peoples recall the significant past events on the land, the interpretation of which often functions as a moral theory for the present. In this way, sacred sites signify not only because ancient cultural events transpired there but also because stories of those places continue to guide behavior and sustain culture. The cultural construction that is sense of place demands work of the imagination, as one recalls how a tribal event took place and interprets the story to answer today's ethical questions, a process Basso calls "world-building" (5).

As the vehicle for Native sense of place, the oral tradition can only exist as a flexible collection of stories. It is nothing less than the corpus of communal knowledge through which group members introduce and evaluate, accept or reject, replace or refine ideas for their ability to order the world. Managing this open-ended hermeneutic, storytelling cultures offer new, revised accounts of events tied to places and thus maintain a center of historical and moral value. Regulated through the normative lens of oral tradition, Indigenous attachments to land are continually shaped yet stable. Leslie Marmon Silko explains how her Laguna people

> depended upon collective memory through successive generations to maintain and transmit an entire culture, a worldview complete with proven strategies for survival. The oral narrative, or story, became the medium through which the complex of Pueblo knowledge and belief was maintained. Whatever the event or the subject, the ancient people perceived the world and themselves within that world as part of an ancient, continuous story composed of innumerable bundles of other stories.... The myth, the web of memories and ideas that create an identity, is part of oneself. This sense of identity was intimately linked with the surrounding terrain, to the landscape that has often played a significant role in a story or in the outcome of a conflict.
>
> (1996: 30–31, 43)

The oral tradition acts as a communal tool for the open interpretation of tribal knowledge to attach Native Americans to places—and, like good art, it may even transport Indigenous people home, if only in the mind. Thus, while this act is excitingly metaphysical it is also socially mediated, describing a contradiction that Native moderns both accept and employ.

Through this oral traditional relationship with the earth, one knows one's homeland by recalling some of the countless stories that took place on that land's specific topographical features: in the hollows, on the peaks, at the banks of streams, within the whirlpools. Indigenous people maintain their social world by pointing to significant places and recalling (often word-for-word) the legendary and historical events held in the tribal imagination. Storytellers are the elected keepers of a group's oral tradition for they are especially adept at reconstructing a narrative world where stories reduce the distance between the individual and the community, between the community of today and of ancient times. Barry Lopez explains this function as the creation of an "interior landscape": the imagined response to the story-laden landscape, the internalized place world of the mind (1984: 51). The storyteller fulfills their responsibility by realigning tribal members' interior landscapes with the geography on which they daily interact. Most important, Native people value story to convey and sustain a moral universe and preserve a cultural identity. Indigeneity has thus always been constructed through and through.

But while Indigenous relationships to land are, at least in part, a culturally mediated process, the status of Indigenous experience might prove unavoidably essentialist. Nonetheless, the legitimacy of experience rests at the heart of Native American culture. Despite differing Native views, tribal experience proves vital to any Indigenous social movement or artistic production. Momaday legitimates Native experience and literature through mysticism. For instance, in one essay he recalls the evening he finished writing his second work, *The Way to Rainy Mountain* (1969):

> I went back over the final paragraphs. My eyes fell upon Ko-sahn. All at once, absolutely, I had the sense of magic of words and of names. Ko-sahn, I said. And I said it again, KO-SAHN. Then it was that that ancient, one eyed woman stepped out of the language and stood before me on the page.
>
> "Yes, grandson," she said. "What is it? What do you want?"
>
> "I was just now writing about you," I replied. "I thought—forgive me—I thought that perhaps you were... That you had..."
>
> "No," she said. "You have imagined me well, and so I am. You see, I have existence, whole being, in your imagination. It is but one kind of being, to be sure, but it is perhaps the best of all kinds. If I am not here in this room, grandson, then surely neither are you."
>
> (1997: 44)

Scholars have written much about Momaday's notion of the Indigenous imagination. It is not to be confused with fantasy but rather is the capacity to bring a world from nothing into existence and so is not unlike the purpose of the oral tradition described above. In other words, he did actually see his ancestor in the flesh on his page. Momaday's experience, however, arrives thoroughly intact, a "whole being" free from all forms of mediation or interpretation. In fact, that is the beauty of such uncorrupted—pure—visions.

In a sense, he acts as do other artists who, throughout history, have found their inspirations from the religious or metaphysical world. Most exciting, Momaday imagines the dreamer dreamed: "If I am not in this room then surely neither are you." In other words, we ourselves exist only through our imaginations. Art imagines us. This collapse between the viewer and the object of art is, in fact, at the center of Momaday's aesthetics. It too, however, could be considered essentialist.

The indispensability of Indigenous experience is only matched by its disregard in the majority culture. In Western philosophy, the rise of Cartesianism enabled thinkers to isolate human experience for they knew that with experience lay the point of inquiry into knowledge of the world. This isolation began with the eschewing of non-physical forms of experience, those viewed to be extremely mediated and thus non-verifiable, such as dreams, visions, and revelations. Phenomenologists such as Edmund Husserl clarified the interpretation of human experience but also restricted vital phenomena from their inquiries. Today, literary theory bears this legacy and still relies on this model of experiential foundationalism to contend with experience; personal experience must be self-evident and unambiguous to engender reliable knowledge. For better or worse, dominant literary scholarship rarely even considers the non-physical forms of experience in its critique of experience. To Western eyes, tribal forms of experience such as dreams, visions, and ceremonial, athletic—and certainly narcotic—revelations cannot possibly produce reliable knowledge. And yet these have been fundamental to Indigenous lives.

Considered unmediated and thus extraordinarily powerful art and religious experience are nearly indistinguishable. Today, we distrust the prophets but still celebrate the artists, even though both often rely on an essential experience. This engagement with essentialism in Indigenous artistic inspiration finally brings us back to Momaday's gathering of shields. He explains that the shields, which in practical terms are armor, are ultimately medicine and not only for the defense of the warrior. Like art itself, the shield works a kind of magic on its viewers by imagining those who behold it. "The shield is a mask," he writes.

> The mask is an appearance that discloses reality beyond appearance. Like other masks, it bespeaks sacred mystery. The shield is what you see, believes the Plains warrior. It reflects your own reality, as does mine, he says. It reveals to you the essence of your self. It charms you, frightens you, disarms you, renders you helpless. You behold my shield, and you are transfixed and transformed, perhaps inspired beyond your imagining. Nothing will ever be the same again, for you have entered into the presence of my power. Oh, my enemy! Behold my shield!
>
> The shield is involved in story. The shield is its own story. When the shield is made visible it means: Here is the story. Enter into it and be created. The story tells of your real being.
>
> (1997: 74)

Through Momaday's essentialism we are given Native American art. We are invited to merge with and be transformed by it but, as fallible yet conscious humans, we also assert control in social mediation, existing somewhere within that tension.

Despite the mystical power of the visual, it is not the only avenue to free voices or reclaim histories. As twentieth-century Native American writers search the record to produce historical novels and poetry to liberate hidden Indigenous voices, so can readers pursue earlier works by white visitors who represent Native Americans. By plumbing and rebirthing the Indigenous past, we better understand but also decolonize the Native twentieth century. Because we define Native American literature as literature by and about Native people, in doing so, we necessarily blur the lines between Indigenous literature and American literature, between Native past and Native present. Readers might declare such accounts unreliable, at best well meaning but highly meditated, at worst deliberately racist. I argue, however, that not to do so is to allow Indigenous voices to remain hidden.

The Past Present

Some such voices might be muted by a twentieth-century mainstream that bears a colonial history intent on "disappearing" Indians. From its very beginning, Native American literature has presented Indigenous voices that readers must extract—by reading Native gestures, by imagining histories, by accepting translations—from within the colonial narratives that make them disappear. While the authenticity of their authorship, words, accounts, publication—as well as the mediation of Indigenous voices—remains a viable critical issue, I argue that the inclusion of colonial narratives in our literary understanding of America is worth the risk.

Christopher Columbus returned to America in October 1493 not with 3 ships but 17 and not with around 89 deckhands and sailors but with 12,000 to 15,000 criminals and mercenaries. His new show of force was met on the beach by a small formal procession, with a royal Arawak woman at its head. Her name was Anacaona, meaning "Golden Flower." The Admiral was disappointed to find that the first colony in the New World, dubbed La Navidad, had been destroyed. The army found eleven of the thirty-six "Christians" near the charred ruins of the fort with grass growing through their skeletons. Columbus questioned members of the nearby village and, through an interpreter working with a royal named Caonabo, learned that the Spanish men had "taken three or four women apiece" and so the village men had killed all of the Christians "out of jealousy." Careful readers look behind the Admiral's words to surmise that the La Navidad men repeatedly abducted and raped the Arawak women, and the Arawak men came to their rescue. But other accounts place not Caonabo but his wife, Anacaona, at the center of the resistance. Not only a brave leader of overthrows, Anacaona is said also to be the tribal historian, artist, singer, dancer, and poet. Of course, these many offices were probably combined in a single performance, in an "areíto," a ceremonial song and dance to honor the heroism of ancestors. In her sole remaining areito, Anacaona exhorts: "Aia, bombaia, bombe / Lamma samana quana / Aia, bombaia, bombe / Lamma samana quana," a chant variously translated as "We swear to destroy the whites and all they possess, let us die rather than fail to keep that vow" (Pettinger 2012: 87). Fearing another uprising on the island, Governor Nicolás de Ovando ordered suspected leaders to be rounded up and executed, and so Anacaona was hanged in 1503. In her small, remnant voice, Anacaona speaks for the countless Indigenous women tortured, raped, and murdered by Columbus and his men. To stop this cruelty, Hispanola's women organized and fought their abusers. Yet, the most enduring abuse is perhaps the suppression and silence of women's Indigenous voices in the Admiral's narrative. We hear only of the purchase of women at the age of nine or ten (271), who are "accommodating" (233) and "so shameless they might have been whores" (297). In our greatest challenge in Indigenous literary studies, we answer the ethical demand to imagine, reconstruct, and liberate such buried and deliberately misrepresented voices.

In other moments, Columbus's Indians "speak" without utterance, in expressions as subtle as simple gestures. On this same second voyage to the New World, in May 1494, the Admiral led his ships into a channel on an island off the coast of Cuba. The sailors were amazed to find a canoe before them with Arawaks fishing. Assuming the Indians would scream and flee, and as usual prepared to fire upon them, the soldiers instead paused in wonder as the "Indian fisherman ... remained calm and unperturbed, motionlessly awaiting the boat's approach, and when it came close they signed to it to wait a little until they had finished their fishing" (174). In perhaps an ordinary, if not universal, raising of the hand, the Arawak men stopped a fleet of warships but even asserted their sovereignty and territory in the face of the Admiral of the Ocean Sea. Tying leashes to remoras, sending them down, and retrieving their bounty of fish, the Arawak men displayed a bizarre genius before the Christians.

In one of the earliest published statements by an Indigenous person, indeed in all of American literature, Powhatan, chief of his confederacy, gives a speech to Captain John Smith, leader of the Jamestown colony. The chief, in control of hundreds of miles of land and 32 tribes, allowed 105 Englishmen to establish a colony in Virginia in 1607. The colony traded with the confederacy for food, but shortages made Powhatan suspend trade, and in 1609 Captain Smith confronted Powhatan with threats. The chief's reply is only about a page in length, but his words continue to move us: "Why should you take by force that from us which you can have by love? Why should you destroy us, who have provided you with food? What can you get by war?" (Powhatan 2000: 4). The calm, even gentle repeated questions shame the Captain and later Americans for their betrayals, invoking our shared humanity and calling on our better angels who choose love over war. John Smith recorded Powhatan's speech in his account of the colony, but it also appeared later in Samuel Drake's popular, if inaccurate, volume on Native Americans, *Biography and History of the Indians of North America, from Its First Discovery* (1851), which is my source for the above quotation. By the twentieth century, however, scholars came to question the speech's authenticity. Every other fall, around Thanksgiving, I share Powhatan's words with my students. I am sure to state the speech's possible fraudulence, yet its veracity does not seem to matter. Perhaps, like my students, and like many Indigenous people, I am not willing to surrender Powhatan and his potential words of humanity, respect, and peace, all in the name of authenticity. After all, we do know there was a Powhatan, and we know he interacted with John Smith. However, we do not know the chief's exact words for they are a translation. Despite claims that they may be corrupt, Native American writers often allow such historical Indigenous words, gestures, translatable utterances, and translated speech to inform their modern visions of land, literature, and life.

Other encounters allow later writers to tell a more complete story of America. Though Thomas Jefferson held an ugly notion of race, he at times held to his Enlightenment principles on universal human rationality when it came to Indigenous people, declaring the Indian "in body and mind equal to the white man" (June 7, 1785). He envisioned the "amalgamation" of Native Americans with European Americans and ominously announced to various Native nations "your blood will run in our veins" (December 21, 1808). In *Notes on the State of Virginia* (Jefferson 1999 [1785]), Jefferson seeks to understand the ancient burial mounds and earthworks found throughout eastern North America. In approaching his subject, he immediately breaks from others who have called these Indigenous architectural forms "monuments":

> I know of no such thing existing as an Indian monument: for I would not honour with that name arrow points, stone hatchets, stone pipes, and half-shapen images. Of labour on the large scale, I think there is no remain as respectable as would be a common ditch for the draining of lands.
>
> (103–104)

Knowing of an Indian mound in his "neighborhood," the obviously monumental nature of which eludes him, the founder decides to examine its contents. Digging into an earthwork "of spheroidical form, of about 40 feet diameter at the base, and ... about twelve feet altitude" (104) he "first dug superficially in several parts of it, and came to collections of human bones...." (105). On describing the bones and their anatomy in the dispassionate voice of a scientist, he remarks:

> The sculls were so tender, that they generally fell to pieces on being touched.... There were some teeth which were judged to be smaller than those of an adult; a scull, which, on a slight view, appeared to be that of an infant.... a rib, and a fragment of the under-jaw of a person about half grown; another rib of an infant; and part of the jaw of a child, which had not yet cut its teeth. This last furnishing the most decisive proof of the burial of children here.
>
> (105)

Even as Jefferson inadvertently proves the grandeur of Native American earthworks, he overlooks the reasons one might find an Indigenous children's cemetery in his neighborhood. It might be that these were the victims of an epidemic, when disease took the lives of the old and young Native people. Most curious, however, is the strange muted tenderness the statesman uses to handle the children's skulls, which crumble and float away in his very hands. Perhaps he is driven by a grotesque desire for intimacy with Native Americans, through which he might discover a means of belonging to this land. A man of his times, Jefferson desecrated Indigenous burials as his ancestors had, a common event in America until a 1990 act of Congress made it illegal. Today, readers worry that the lost Native children will never speak but instead wind up in a museum, their voices silenced. Jefferson, however, continues his account of the Indian mounds:

> But on whatever occasion they may have been made, they are of considerable notoriety among the Indians; for a party passing, about thirty years ago, through the part of the country where this barrow is, went through the woods directly to it, without any instructions or enquiry, and having staid about it some time, with expression which were construed to be those of sorrow, they returned to the high road, which they had left about half a dozen miles to pay this visit, and pursued their journey.
>
> (106)

In this solemn gesture that reaches across cultures, Jefferson is implicitly rebuked for his refusal to honor Indigenous monuments. Moreover, we find that the Native American children are not forgotten and even express their lives from beyond the grave. In Thomas Jefferson's blindness toward Native American signifying forms, he was not unique but indeed the rule in the voluminous accounts of Native Americans throughout the colonization of North America. However, despite colonists' troubling mediation in representations, which range from benign cultural baggage to overt racism, where readers seek to see them, Native people nonetheless "bleed" through the page. Such readers look behind Columbus's misogyny and Jefferson's disavowal to see the hidden Indigenous voices that allow twentieth-century writers to perform the ethnographic research through which they in part imagine memories in the blood.

While we might work to allow the above Native American voices to speak, we should continue to challenge the hidden Indigenous voices scrutinized and dismissed as fraudulent. For years, scholars and the public were convinced the famous Sauk and Fox Black Hawk's autobiography, *Life of Black Hawk* (1834) was inaccurate, if not fabricated by a white recorder wishing to make a dime off the old chief. Black Hawk defends his people's land with a command of *"reason"* (36). He offers their own understanding of property to contradict American definitions, arguing that "we have a right to use it, in determining what is right or wrong." He continues:

> My reason teaches me that land cannot be sold. The Great Spirit gave it to his children to live upon, and cultivate as far as is necessary for their subsistence; and so long as they occupy and cultivate it, they have the right to the soil—but if they voluntarily leave it, then any other people have the right to settle upon it. Nothing can be sold but such things as can be carried away.
>
> (42)

In relying on "reason" to present his claim, Black Hawk challenges the prevailing conclusions about Indians' incapacity to think or govern; in fact, he couples reason with governance in his narrative. Happily, Black Hawk's defiant words are now found to be legitimate, even though another Native autobiography did not appear for nearly a century. Other earlier Indigenous writers, even those who speak and write in English, have been questioned for their veracity. Readers have doubted the authenticity of Potawatomie writer Simon Pokagon's *Queen of the Woods* (2011 [1899]). At the 1893 World's Columbian Exposition in Chicago, where historian Frederick Jackson Turner famously announced the American frontier closed, Pokagon publicly stated: "In behalf of my people, the American Indians, I hereby declare to you, the pale-faced race that has usurped our lands and homes, that we have no spirit to celebrate with you" (1893, 211). Into the twentieth century, American readers still questioned the veracity of some Indigenous writers. Some suggested that it was not the Dakota physician Charles Eastman who wrote his many published narratives, books such as *From the Deep Woods to Civilization* (2003 [1916]) in which he details "the savagery of civilization," but his white wife Elaine Goodale.

Though spanning the generations, the above Native figures share a few traits in their voices or actions. They defy the prevailing assumption among earlier American settlers that Indigenous people were savage: brutally violent, devoid of emotion, and incapable of reason, learning, or history. In fact, these writers display the exact opposite: a rejection of violence, an expression of emotion, an appeal to reason, and a possession of history. When we decry the mediation of translators, amanuenses, and recorders of Indigenous voices, we set a standard of truth impossible to achieve. Those who question the authenticity of Native literature might argue that scholars and readers need to determine whether a Native American actually said or wrote such words, but it is difficult to deny that such scrutiny—often proven unfounded—conveniently silences Indigenous voices. One could even argue that, as a right of sovereignty, that determination ultimately resides with Native nations.

This skepticism or outright demand for authenticity in Indigenous speakers and writers in American literature grows from a deeper concern for the authentic Native American, the culturally pure and timeless "real Indian": that Indigenous person looking and living as did his pre-contact ancestors. While impossible to produce, the real Indian pairs with the "fake Indian" or the "play" Indian in a nation that has been "playing Indian" since its founding. From the Boston Tea Party to the Mountain Meadows Massacre, from fraternal orders to sports mascots, youth organizations to summer camps, Americans have been dressing up as Indians and inventing Indian ceremonies for centuries. We perhaps pair the impossibly real Indian with the fake Indian, a racial attitude that leads readers to question and determine the authenticity of Indigenous writings and authorship. Still today, readers and scholars feel a sense of duty to determine the cultural depth of a Native American author—whether he or she grew up "on the reservation," for instance—but also the purity of a writer's race, sometimes deeming an Indigenous author "part" Native American. "Which part?" asks Thomas Builds-the-Fire in Spokane and Coeur d'Alene Sherman Alexie's *Reservation Blues* (82). Twentieth-century Native writers reject blood quantum as a criterion for this racial authenticity and instead argue the power of an intersectional Native identity that includes not only white but also Brown and Black voices. Of course, the rights of sovereignty ask Native nations themselves to determine their peoplehood.

In our calls of cultural corruption and demand for authenticity, readers might have erased, silenced, or marginalized historical Indigenous voices in twentieth-century literature, performing another act of colonization. Inheriting this perspective still today, literary scholars both in American literature and Native American literature allow this silencing to continue but often in more subtle ways than by policing counterfeits and frauds. Before Native people learned to speak and write in European languages, their words were translated and recorded. Scholars intent on studying these early, translated texts face critiques from those who insist one cannot and should not work with a manuscript in translation. Furthermore, some of those texts written in Indigenous languages often cannot be read, for no speakers survive. On another front, Indigenous expressions—sometimes just a gesture—remain forgotten or disregarded in some of the earliest travel accounts into the nineteenth century. In those texts, Europeans usually "authorize" the presence of Indigenous people offered therein. Ultimately, readers and scholars must work to listen to the many suppressed, or at least unacknowledged, Indigenous expressions in American literature.

LIBERATING BLACK AND BROWN VOICES

In October 1804, the Lewis and Clark expedition had made its way to the Mandan and Arikara towns on the Missouri River, in present-day North Dakota, and was preparing for a winter stay. The crew included twenty-two men and three sergeants. In addition, William Clark brought his slave, York. The man is described as big, strong, and dark, and in his mid-thirties, like Clark. In fact, the two had been companions all their lives, York's father having been the slave of Clark's father (Ambrose 1996: 180). The Arikara community had never seen an African American man, and one warrior asked that York sleep with his wife so to gain his power, as the man guarded the entrance to his lodge. In their journals, Lewis describes York as "the big Medison" (Ronda 1984: 63). In a generation, the American West saw other Black men trade, marry with, and lead Indigenous nations, such as did Jim Beckwourth, a freed slave from Virginia who, as a young man, went west as a trapper. He lived with the Crows for years, marrying a chief's daughter, becoming a war chief, and leading their dog clan. The fur trader narrated his story that became *The Life and Adventures of James P. Beckwourth* (1965 [1856]). Perhaps not surprisingly, readers doubted the veracity of Beckwourth's account. Indeed, many have long questioned the authorship and truthfulness of African American testimony, as is the case with slave narratives.

Black people and Indigenous people, however, share more than a doubting readership intent on "authentic" narratives. As York was surely valued differently for his race in Indian Country than in the states, the Crows might not have seen race in the same manner. Indeed, in one story, a chief recognized in Beckwourth a lost son, and so adopted Beckwourth. This cultural pattern would fit with the widespread Native American custom behind the captivity narrative. Perhaps also like some works in the genre, Beckwourth became Crow, as well as enjoying greater freedom in an Indigenous community than in the antebellum American South. In such narratives of African Americans journeying west and discovering belonging in America, readers imagine a world of greater racial equality. At the risk of sounding utopian, accounts of Indigenous and Black melding in the West offer a glimpse of American ideals on which the United States was founded. Tragically, some twentieth-century Native American writers have largely forgotten this fascinating interaction among peoples. Others have not. In his poetry, Sherman Alexie links the struggles of African Americans and Native Americans. In *The Summer of Black Widows* (1996), he offers the poem "Capital Punishment," in which the narrator imagines an "Indian killer" to be executed: "I once heard a story / about a black man who was electrocuted / in that chair and lived to tell about it / before the court decided to sit him back down / an hour later and kill him all over again" (87). The image of horrific torture demands our witnessing and action. In another poem included in the volume, "Prayer Animals," the narrator declares America an indigenous space, only here it is clearly an African one:

> Do not try to convince me the United States is anything other than / savannah. / Weeds burst through the sidewalk. / …. The newspaper explains about the food chain. / …. I am the gazelle in braids and powwow jeans. / Sometime before sunset, I scan the horizon, then bend my head to / the stream…. My only question: Will the hunter use the rifle or his teeth?
>
> (Alexie 1996: 84)

In his subtle genius, the poet allies with African Americans in an urban space where poverty, hunger, and violence turn people into prey. The predators announce their right to kill and eat—exploit—these communities as the natural process of inequality in the "food chain." In this phrase alone, Alexie metaphorically invokes animal rights and Indigenous lands but also human hunger, predation, and bondage in a manner that joins Red and Black voices in struggles.

Such Native authors certainly link arms with African American and Latinx people in the name of colonial resistance, but here I argue Indigenous writers do so also in pursuit of better knowledge. In embracing and offering a more intersectional identity, authors defy dominant demands for Native racial authenticity as well as present a different, more complex understanding of corporeal knowledge and its alternative histories. Indeed, in risking to expand the very ownership of Indigeneity they, ironically, join the hemisphere in decolonization. And, again, in irony, this practice begins in the city. Despite its strain, the urban space brings together African American and Native, as well as Latinx people. In Pomo writer Greg Sarris's *Grand Avenue* (1994), for instance, Black and Brown people live in a converted army barracks in Santa Rosa, California. Their dwelling is a fitting reminder that they are "at war" with the powerful, or that they are the already defeated objects of the government. The impoverished families share their resources as well as their stories, as tangled histories disclose, to become Sarris's woven basket of group connection. Perhaps more than any other Indigenous writer, Leslie Marmon Silko imagines connection among Black, Brown, and Native communities. The ties, however, are abraded by colonial forces that dehumanize the peoples who survive in homeless camps in a riverbed in Gallup, in *Ceremony* (1977). The protagonist Tayo suffers rejection from his Native community in part because of his mixed-race appearance. His hateful Aunt Velma speculates on the race of Tayo's father. Whether he was Black, Brown, or white, Auntie views Tayo as an outsider because his father does not share her race. When Tayo finally visits a mixed-race healer, Tayo discovers the truth of his identity. The Navajo medicine practitioner Betonie relates a story of his own Hispanic mother and helps Tayo resist demands for racial purity, even embracing the strength of multiple heritage.

Only recently has a colonial border divided America's Indigenous people, and twentieth-century Native writers cross and deny that border to embrace a more hemispheric vision of belonging, dispossession, and resurgence. To do so, some Indigenous writers lead us to the distant archaeological past, when a thousand years ago ancient Pueblo people rejected superstition and embraced science, as in Salish anthropologist D'Arcy McNickle's *Runner in the Sun* (1987 [1954]). The boy Salt travels to Mexico in search of maize to end his people's drought and their isolation from a greater hemispheric Indigenous world. In *The Singing Bird* (2007 [c.1930]) Cherokee writer John Milton Oskison departs for Mexico to safeguard tribal literacy and national sovereignty by imagining the life and writings of Sequoyah, the famous inventor of the Cherokee written language. In so doing, Oskison gives Cherokees and Indigenous readers the opportunity once again to possess a history and agency to overturn the dominant American story of Indian racial decline. At first reading, the novel could be dismissed as a straightforward portrayal of the Dwight mission to the Western Cherokees in the 1820s. But by chapter four, in steps the fascinating character of Sequoyah. While the mission becomes a plot device to report on Sequoyah's efforts, those efforts represent historical truths. In 1843, Sequoyah actually departed in search of the Lost Cherokees in Mexico, where he died and was buried in a cave. In the novel, however, Oskison speculates that Sequoyah hopes to find in Mexico the "sacred symbols" that record ancient Cherokee history. Here, the fictional missionary Dan Wear writes about Sequoyah's deepening scholarly immersion:

> I guessed that it was a history of his people, and that he could not complete it without the material he hoped to find in Mexico. This is pure speculation, but I believe it has to do with the theft, long ago, of certain sacred symbols of the Cherokees. I recalled what an old chief once told me, that after their loss there was unrest and spiritual discontent amongst the people. Perhaps Sequoyah believes these sacred symbols are somewhere in Mexico, and that he may be able to recover them. I have felt that a reunion in peace of all the tribes dominates him. It is believable that he hopes to restore the faith of the Cherokees in their old god.
>
> (2007 [c.1930])

Again, Oskison writes factually. Ethnologist James Mooney actually records the myth of the Lost Cherokees, who had, in some distant primordial past, left the homeland, either west or south, and gradually lost touch. And he also documents an oral account of an Ark of Covenant—a wooden box wrapped in furs—in which Cherokees kept their sacred symbols. One day, this ark was stolen and the Cherokees soon weakened in collective spirit. Most compelling, however, Oskison, like Sequoyah, looks to Mexico for the origin and recovery of a lost Cherokee history and concomitant sovereignty. For as Sequoyah knew, that sovereignty is best protected in a sacred text that unites a people with their ancient land and charts its destiny.

Oskison's novel offers a more Indigenous form of historiography to challenge Western history and politicized geographic divisions by including oral traditions. Oskison draws on Cherokee oral history offered in writings of anthropologists, traders, and travelers, and even develops what Timothy Powell and Melinda Mullikin call his "spiraling history" in which "old and new combine to form a future society deeply rooted in ... the precolonial past" (xxxv). *The Singing Bird* might model this alternative methodology herein described. In the telling passage above, the author himself—through the guise of the missionary—engages in "pure speculation" about his tribe, against the limits of Western history, to better connect Cherokees with their past, each other, and a shared future. However, in so doing, Native writers also immerse themselves in what scholars call the "transnational imaginary," that space where, they say, "political allegiances are undone and imagined communities reshaped" (Saldívar 2006: 59). Such wanderings across geography and time might well discover a Black Atlantic for the Americas that traces and recovers the many departures and arrivals that unite and distinguish the greater Indigenous hemisphere.

This pattern of documenting and speculating to demand histories bursts forth in the twentieth century with Leslie Marmon Silko's *Almanac of the Dead* (1992). Silko absorbs prophecy itself to imagine a hemispheric resistance that includes Native American, Black, and Latinx peoples, in which African American Vietnam War veterans such as Clinton educate us about Black Indians and pre-colonial African spiritual survival. The novel also draws its force from Indigenous women in cities like Tucson and others over the hemispheric map. There, it overturns our romantic assumptions that Brown women are bountiful, yielding caregivers by beginning with a scene of elder sisters Leche and Zeta cooking up not nourishing food but illegal drugs in their kitchen: "The old woman stands at the stove stirring the simmering brown liquid with great concentration. Occasionally Zeta smiles as she stares into the big blue enamel pot. She glances up through the rising veil of steam at the young blond woman pouring pills from brown plastic prescription vials" (19). In its unprecedented hemispheric scope that combines actual historical events with Indigenous prophecy, *Almanac of the Dead* performs the very process of historical recovery this chapter describes. The sisters above just desire their stolen land returned, but El Feo, a Mayan Marxist visionary, believes we are swirled into a foreordained juggernaut of change: "El Feo daydreamed about the days of the past—sensuous daydreams of Mother Earth who loved all her children, all living beings. Those past times were not lost. The days, the months, and years were living beings who roamed the starry universe until they came around again" (313). Silko's seer and his view of Indigenous time now coheres as an expression of traditional culture but also as a modern means of historical recovery. While Native American writers understand the risks of holding this non-Western approach to knowledge, they also feel the calling to reclaim stolen histories, to liberate lost voices buried in colonial accounts. They reject the insidious operation of textual and racial authenticity and seek to embody a complex multiple identity and history, unfolding in intersection and contradiction. In the necessity to liberate the "hidden voice," readers and scholars alike imagine a richer, more ethical—and empowered—future for the Indigenous in twentieth-century American literature.

References

Alexie, Sherman. 1995. *Reservation Blues* (New York: Warner).
Alexie, Sherman. 1996. *The Summer of the Black Widows* (Brooklyn, NY: Hanging Loose).
Allen, Paula Gunn. 1979. "Iyani: It Goes This Way," in Geary Hobson, ed., *The Remembered Earth: An Anthology of Contemporary Native American Literature* (Albuquerque, NM: University of New Mexico Press), 191–193.
Allen, Paula Gunn. 1992. *The Sacred Hoop: Recovering the Feminine in American Indian Traditions* (Boston, MA: Beacon).
Ambrose, Stephen E. 1996. *Undaunted Courage: Meriwether Lewis, Thomas Jefferson, and the Opening of the American West* (New York: Touchstone).
Basso, Keith. 1996. *Wisdom Sits in Places: Landscape and Language Among Western Apache* (Albuquerque, NM: University of New Mexico Press).
Beckwourth, James. 1965 [1856]. *The Life and Adventures of James P. Beckwourth* (Minneapolis, MN: Ross and Haines).
Columbus, Christopher. 1969. *The Four Voyages*, ed. and trans. J. M. Cohen (New York: Penguin).
Deloria, Philip J. 2004. *Indians in Unexpected Places* (Lawrence, KS: University of Kansas Press).
Dimock, Wai Chee. 2006. *Through Other Continents: American Literature Across Deep Time* (Princeton, NJ: Princeton University Press).
Drake, Samuel G. 1851. *Biography and History of the Indians of North America, from Its First Discovery*, 11th ed. (Boston: Sanborn, Carter, and Bazin).
Eastman, Charles. 2003 [1916]. *From the Deep Woods to Civilization* (Mineola, NY: Dover).
Erdrich, Louise. 1988. *Tracks* (New York: Henry Holt).
Gilroy, Paul. 1993. *The Black Atlantic: Modernity and Double-Consciousness* (Cambridge, MA: Harvard University Press).
Harjo, Joy. 2000. *A Map to the Next World* (New York: Norton).
Hughes, Langston. 1994. "The Negro Speaks in Rivers," in Arnold Rampersad, ed., *The Collected Poems of Langston Hughes* (New York: Vintage), 23.
Jefferson, Thomas. 1999 [1785]. *Notes on the State of Virginia*, ed. Frank Shuffelton (New York: Penguin).
Krupat, Arnold. 2002. *Red Matters: Native American Studies* (Philadelphia, PA: University of Pennsylvania Press).

Lopez, Barry. 1984. "Story at Anaktuvuk Pass," *Harpers* 269.1615: 49–51.
McNickle, D'Arcy. 1987 [1954]. *Runner in the Sun* (Albuquerque, NM: University of New Mexico Press).
Momaday, N. Scott. 1976 [1969]. *The Way to Rainy Mountain*. (Albuquerque, NM: University of New Mexico Press).
Momaday, N. Scott. 1976. *The Names: A Memoir* (Tucson, AZ: University of Arizona Press).
Momaday, N. Scott. 1989 [1968]. *House Made of Dawn* (New York: Perrenial).
Momaday, N. Scott. 1992. *In the Presence of the Sun* (New York: St Martin's Press).
Momaday, N. Scott. 1997. *The Man Made of Words: Essays, Stories, Passages* (New York: St Martin's Press).
Ortiz, Simon J. 1981. *From Sand Creek* (Tucson, AZ: University of Arizona Press).
Oskison, John Milton. 2007 [c.1930]. *The Singing Bird* (Norman, OK: University of Oklahoma Press).
Owens, Louis. 1994. *Bone Game* (Norman, OK: University of Oklahoma).
Pettinger, Alasdair. 2012. "'Eh! Eh! Bomba, Hen! Hen!': Making Sense of a Vodou Chant," in Diana Paton, Alasdair Pettinger, and Maarit Forde, eds, *Obeah and Other Powers: The Politics of Caribbean Religion and Healing* (Durham, NC: Duke University Press), 81–102.
Pokagon, Simon. 1997 [1893]. *The Red Man's Rebuke by Chief Pokagon (Pattawattamie Chief). The Red Man's Greeting*, reprint in Cheryl Walker, ed., *Indian Nation: Native American Literature and Nineteenth-Century Nationalisms* (Durham, NC: Duke University Press), 211.
Pokagon, Simon. 2011 [1899]. *Queen of the Woods* (East Lansing, MI: Michigan State Press).
Powell, Timothy B. and Melinda Smith Mullikin. 2007. "Introduction," *The Singing Bird* (Norman, OK: University of Oklahoma Press), xix–xlvii.
Powhatan. 2000. "Why Should You Destroy Us, Who Have Provided You with Food?," in Bob Blaisdell, ed., *Great Speeches by Native Americans* (Mineola, NY: Dover), 4.
Ronda, James P. 1984. *Lewis and Clark among the Indians* (Lincoln, NE: University of Nebraska Press).
Saldívar, Ramón. 2006. *The Borderlands of Culture: Américo Paredes and the Transnational Imaginary* (Durham, NC: Duke University Press).
Sarris, Greg. 1994. *Grand Avenue* (New York: Hyperion).
Silko, Leslie Marmon. 1977. *Ceremony* (New York: Penguin).
Silko, Leslie Marmon. 1981. *Storyteller* (New York: Seaver).
Silko, Leslie Marmon. 1992. *Almanac of the Dead* (New York: Penguin).
Silko, Leslie Marmon. 1996. "Interior and Exterior Landscapes: The Pueblo Migration Stories," in *Yellow Woman and a Beauty of the Spirit: Essays on Native American Life Today* (New York: Simon and Schuster), 25–47.
Standing Bear, Luther. 1978 [1933]. *Land of the Spotted Eagle* (Lincoln, NE: University of Nebraska Press).
Teuton, Sean. 2008. *Red Land, Red Power: Grounding Knowledge in the American Indian Novel* (Durham, NC: Duke University Press).
Vizenor, Gerald. 1992. *Dead Voices: Natural Agonies in the New World* (Norman, OK: University of Oklahoma Press).
Warrior, Robert. 2005. *The People and the Word: Reading Native Nonfiction* (Minneapolis, MN: University of Minnesota Press).
Welch, James. 1974. *Winter in the Blood* (New York: Penguin).
Welch, James. 1986. *Fools Crow* (New York: Penguin).

CHAPTER 7

"JUMPIN' WITH SYMPHONY SID"

Post-1945 American Literature and Radio

LISA HOLLENBACH

How does one listen to radio after the death of radio?

By title alone, Amiri Baraka's poem "In Memory of Radio" (1961) casts radio into the past, evoking a sentimental nostalgia for the sunset-tinted "golden age" of 1930s and 1940s network radio. In the poem, this nostalgia is a generational feeling, associated with those who, like Baraka (and, he names, Jack Kerouac), spent their childhoods around the family radio set, internalizing the auditory imaginaries of serial dramas like the *Lone Ranger, Gangbusters, Green Hornet,* and *The Shadow*. But if radio has seemingly become obsolete with the onset of the televisual age, that only makes its hauntology all the more apprehensible: its invisible voices, echoing beyond all sense of source; its powers of possession and mass hypnosis; its pervasive whiteness diffusing into the ether. For the African American listener, Baraka suggests, a nostalgic "Love" for radio will always be ambivalent, haunted by its "evil" inverse: "Turn it backwards/see, see what I mean? / An evol word" (Baraka [Jones] 1961: 12). The "evol" pun, which must be seen as well as heard, marks the poem's phono-graphic revolution around an absent presence in the archive of American radio that resonates as a kind of interference to disrupt the temporal, generational, and racial logics of cultural transmission. The poet thus imagines while doubting that the "white noise"[1] of his childhood harbors a submerged and subversive Blackness, as "invisible" as the crime-fighting radio hero The Shadow: "What was it he used to say (after the transformation, when he was safe / & invisible & the

---

[1] "I transformed the radio in my transmutating mind so it told brown tales somehow. (Yet you understand the term brainwash and must acknowledge certain brain damage. Yet I claim the transduction of certain impulses, so that the output was not just white noise, but a heroic grimace when I smile that contains absolute desire for the destruction of evil.)" (Baraka 1997: 61–62).

unbelievers couldn't throw stones?) 'Heh, heh, heh, / Who knows what evil lurks in the hearts of men? The Shadow knows'" (Baraka [Jones] 1961: 12–13).

In this poem, Baraka thus performs while critiquing the powerful "maudlin nostalgia" for golden age radio that continues to frame it as an age of (media) innocence by imbuing it with what he elsewhere describes as his "envious blues feeling."[2] Yet, the retrospective tone of "In Memory of Radio" and Baraka's other radio-themed poems of the late 1950s and early 1960s could appear, as they did to Lorenzo Thomas, somewhat out of tune with "the new aural environment" (Thomas 1978: 60).[3] After all, the post-Second World War decades did not witness the death of radio so much as the sweeping transformation of its economics, technology, content, aesthetics, and audience. Think Top 40 pop music formats, fast-talking disc jockeys, and portable transistor radios; think early FM radio and the arrival of an FM underground; think local and regional broadcasters arising in the vacuum left by the major networks when they pivoted to TV. The remaking of the radio industry also involved the emergence of Black radio, as a wave of African American disc jockeys and the first "Black-appeal" radio stations for African American consumer markets came onto AM frequencies in the late 1940s, contesting and remapping radio's color line after decades of activism by African American listeners, performers, and writers against the industry's discriminatory practices and racist representations (Barlow 1999). By the early 1960s, the radio soundscape in the United States had changed dramatically, and Baraka would contribute to it, appearing frequently on and occasionally producing programs for independent and Black radio stations throughout his career.[4]

This chapter is about how Baraka and his Beat contemporaries responded to the postwar transformation of American radio, and in particular to the heightened role radio played in disseminating and defining Black music, by variously reconceptualizing the means and ends of radio listening. I focus on the period from the late 1940s to the early 1960s as an interstitial period in American media, literary, and social history, during which time a powerful national imaginary—the image of a national listening public—was dissolved, exposing and enabling alternative, even resistant ways of consuming auditory media that dovetailed with the Civil Rights movement's to end legal segregation.[5]

Literature was an important discursive arena for redefining radio and its racial politics in this period, in part because of the history of mutual influence that had shaped

---

[2] "Look for You Yesterday, Here You Come Today" (Baraka [Jones] 1961: 17, 15).

[3] In Thomas's view, the "new radio environment" of the 1950s—"a world of Alan Freed's rock 'n' roll muzak with 'News On The Hour' interruptions"—was better represented in the 1960s poetry of Umbra poet David Henderson (1978: 59).

[4] Baraka's experiences in radio include his many appearances on the Pacifica Radio network (including as host of a freeform music program on Pacifica station WBAI–New York in the early 1980s) and his role producing the *Black NewArk Radio* program for Newark radio station WNJR in the 1970s.

[5] On US network radio's construction of an "imagined community" of listeners in the 1920s and 1930s, see Hilmes (1997) and Loviglio (2005).

both modernist literature and broadcasting in the earlier twentieth century.[6] As Tom McEnaney has argued, "in the radio age, writing, in particular, became a practice of listening: a specific audile technique that sought to influence radio listening practices in turn" (McEnaney 2017: 6). Whether or not writers could still be said to be living in "the radio age" after 1950, however, was—and still is—considered very much in doubt. The popularization of television, of course, represented the primary challenge to the hegemony of radio, but for many the sense of an end of an era was also due to the falling-off of literary radio genres like serial dramas and broadcast poetry as prerecorded popular music became the primary content through which the commercial radio industry maintained its profitability. Indeed, widespread laments about the cultural decline of US radio after 1950 often express a sense of *literary* decline. This is in part what Baraka's "In Memory of Radio" appears to record: an (ambivalent) lament for the vanishing audio worlds of the network era that allows the poet to reclaim poetry as the privileged form for the renewal of auditory imaginaries. Yet, even as radio began to sound less literary, writers continued to engage with what they heard over the airwaves—albeit in ways that were often critical of mainstream radio culture and generative for emerging alternative radio forms and countercultures.

I am interested, then, in how we might read post-war literature for the different "audile techniques" and counter-techniques that emerged out of writers' diverse engagements with the new sounds of post-"golden age" radio, including the rhythm and blues and bebop jazz beginning to be heard on Black radio stations and spun by late-night disc jockeys. Jonathan Sterne defines *audile technique* as "a set of practices of listening that were articulated to science, reason, and instrumentality and that encouraged the coding and rationalization of what was heard" within discourses of Western modernity from the nineteenth century onwards (Sterne 2003: 23). In the post-Second World War United States, the proliferation of new sound technologies and discourses—from "hi-fi" stereo to audiotape to underground FM radio—intensified audile techniques that had been developing for more than a century to isolate hearing as a sense, privatize and individualize listening, commodify sound, and articulate certain sounds and aural practices to racialized and gendered bodies. But the cultural and technological uncertainty of the period also proved generative for critiques of these forms of listening and alternative aural practices to emerge. And because the intersection of audile technique, sound technologies, and racial formations of Blackness as well as Black cultural production is, as Alexander Weheliye has argued, central to the formations of Western modernity, post-war literature's engagement with radio is a particularly interesting site for exploring the contradictions and complexities of what Weheliye terms "sonic Afro-modernity" (Weheliye 2005).

In what follows, I examine literary representations of radio listening that center on one of the most iconic figures of 1950s American radio—the disc jockey—to show how

---

[6] Since the mid-1990s, there has been a growth of scholarship about the intersections of literature and radio, much of it focused on early twentieth-century and mid-century modernisms. See, to cite just a few examples, Campbell (2006), Cohen et al. (2009), Feldman et al. (2014), and Whittington (2014).

the jazz aesthetic of post-war experimental literature is also a radio aesthetic. Tracing the influence of the legendary jazz radio deejay "Symphony Sid" Torin on Jack Kerouac, Allen Ginsberg, Amiri Baraka, and other post-war writers, I show how specific audile techniques and counter-techniques—such as ambient listening—that mediated the Beat reception of jazz as a source of innovation and resistance to bourgeois conformism are critically reworked and subverted in Baraka's early poetry and prose. Baraka has long been recognized for his groundbreaking contributions to jazz criticism, but more recently there has been a turn to recognize him as a theorist and critic of media (Fouché 2006; Harrison 2014; Punday 2006). In this spirit, this chapter builds toward a broader examination of Baraka's early writings about jazz and about radio to trace Baraka's development of a critical listening practice that hinges on the reversible flows of "love" and "evol" in Black cultural production's engagement with sound media and twentieth-century discourses of Western modernity.

I opened with "In Memory of Radio" to foreground the ways in which once-dominant narratives about the death of radio have obscured ongoing and specific histories of relation between literature and radio after 1945. But I am also interested in how Baraka's poem models an approach to the radio archive that is at once creative and critical, critical and affective, surface and submerged, and historically specific and temporally out-of-joint. What might literary criticism learn from the aural attunements of twentieth-century literature? What methodologies, what critical aural techniques, might we adopt to better understand the complexly mediated relationship between literary and sound culture? In this chapter, I work toward a practice of radiophonic reading as I listen figuratively for what is (or might be) sounded in the background of a text and as I read for the ways that listening (and not only sound) is, and is not, transmitted through inscriptive technologies. In other words, I listen to writers listening as a way of tuning in to overlapping discourses about race, media, music, and writing that generate diffusive interferences at "the lower frequencies" of twentieth-century American literature (Ellison 1980 [1952]: 581).

Ambient Listening: Broadcast Jazz and Beat Literature

The 1950s is enshrined in American popular memory as the decade when teens gained control of the radio dial.[7] It is the decade when rock 'n' roll, the Top 40 countdown, and the disc jockey as cultural tastemaker and celebrity personality were born. The origins of 'fifties rock radio lie, however, in the growth of "Black-appeal" radio stations and formats beginning in the late 1940s that appealed directly to African

---

[7] Susan J. Douglas, for example, titles her chapter on 1950s radio, "The Kids Take Over: Transistors, DJs, and Rock 'n' Roll" (Douglas 2004: 219–255).

American consumer markets, though they remained overwhelmingly white-owned. As Baraka himself observed in *Blues People*, "By the forties, after the war had completely wiped out the remaining 'race' record categories, the radio became the biggest disseminator of blues music" (Baraka [Jones] 1999 [1963]: 169). In the immediate post-war period, Baraka argues, "[r]hythm & blues was still an *exclusive* music," in that it exclusively addressed and was responsive to an African American audience. It is the non-exclusivity of radio signals, however, that makes radio central to the well-known story of how rhythm and blues music "crossed over" into white youth markets in the 1950s. As a segment of young, urban white listeners began to tune in to "Black-appeal" radio stations and disc jockey programs broadcasting rhythm and blues music, they opened a new chapter in the long history of "love and theft" that would come to be heard not only in the musical appropriation of white rock 'n' roll performers but also in the racial ventriloquy of white disc jockeys like Alan Freed (Lott 1993). According to radio scholar Susan Douglas, the symbolic crossings of the color line in 1950s radio within the context of the burgeoning Civil Rights movement made radio, even more than television or print media, "*the* media outlet where cultural and industrial battles over how much influence black culture was going to have on white culture were staged and fought" (Douglas 2004: 222).[8]

As a result, commercial radio in the 1950s was imbued with a subversive aura in the popular American imaginary, as a white-dominated media sphere conjured images of a new generation of rebellious, oversexed, drug-addled, race-mixing teens hooked to their cheap transistor radios. Or, as a 1961 *Time* magazine article mockingly dubbed them, "bleatniks."[9] Linked to the sensationalized image of the beatnik, then, was the transistor radio, with its ceaseless blare of popular music, DJ chatter, station jingles, and ads. Restless sounds for a restless generation—especially as the technology of the transistor radio also made car radios more ubiquitous:

> We were suddenly driving along the blue waters of the Gulf, and at the same time a momentous mad thing began on the radio; it was the Chicken Jazz'n Gumbo disk-jockey show from New Orleans, all mad jazz records, colored records, with the disk jockey saying, "Don't worry 'bout *nothing!*"
>
> (Kerouac 2003 [1957]: 140)

It's true that in Jack Kerouac's Beat classic, in Beat literature in general, "[t]he radio was always on" (2003 [1957]: 249). And as Kerouac and other Beat writers channeled the new sounds of post-war radio, and especially Black radio, into their work, they

---

[8] These battles culminated in the radio payola scandal of 1959–1960, which many media scholars see as motivated by the racist backlash to rock 'n' roll. The scandal ruined the careers of several high-profile deejays, including Freed, and generally allowed industry management and consultants to reseize control over increasingly preformatted playlists. But the scandal also, as Barlow notes, "had the unintended effect of curtailing ... racial ventriloquy on the nation's airwaves" (Barlow 1999: 193).

[9] "The Bleatniks," *Time*, August 11, 1961, 48, quoted in Douglas (2004: 226).

also modeled ways of listening to radio as a form of countercultural rebellion and self-fashioning. Take, for example, the many literary representations of Neal Cassady, radio junkie, "blasting the dashboard with original bop," as Allen Ginsberg imagines him in the early road poem "The Green Automobile" (Ginsberg 1988: 83). In Kerouac's *On the Road*, the Cassady character Dean Moriarty listens to radio like it's a physical performance: twisting the dial, drumming the dashboard, shouting over booming brass, conversing with a sports announcer's play-by-play. Dean's consumption of radio falls outside the familiar binary of passive and active listening; it is continuous and disjunctive, distracted and enthralled, private and social, and violent and tender, all at once. When they hit on a jazz station, Dean acts as a mediator between the music and his acolytes, instructing Sal Paradise and others how to subjectively internalize what they hear: "'listen will you to this old tenorman blow his top'—he shot up the radio volume till the car shuddered—'and listen to him till the story and put down true relaxation and knowledge'" (Kerouac 2003 [1957]: 135). Kerouac may have wished he was "a jazz poet, / blowing a long blues in an afternoon jam / session," but the hero of his fiction appears more like a disc jockey, the Benzedrine speed yet seductive intimacy of Dean's talk cutting from one thought, one moment, one bop record to the next, hell, even "[h]is laugh was ... exactly like the laugh of a radio maniac, only faster" (Kerouac 1990 [1959]; 2003 [1957]: 114).

Exactly like, perhaps, the New York disc jockey and jazz promoter Symphony Sid, whose late-night program "with all the latest bop" comes into signal range near the end of *On the Road* (Kerouac 2003 [1957]: 247). Kerouac's interest in bebop can partly be traced to the influence of Symphony Sid, who was one of the first radio deejays to bring musicians like Dizzy Gillespie, Coleman Hawkins, Thelonious Monk, and Charlie Parker onto the airwaves.[10] Sidney Tarnopol, aka Sid Torin, aka "Symphony Sid," was born in 1909 to Jewish immigrant parents from Russia and Romania and got his start in radio in the 1930s on Bronx station WBNX, playing "race records" rarely heard on the radio at the time and gaining an African American listenership. In the 1940s, Torin moved to a late-night slot on New Jersey station WHOM and later to the ABC flagship station WJZ, where he spun bop records and hosted live shows from iconic clubs like the Royal Roost and Birdland. While jazz in the form of swing and big band music by predominantly white ensembles had long been standard radio fare, Symphony Sid's radio show was one of few in network radio to broadcast the new jazz and promote it as Black music. Like many white and Jewish jazz musicians and disc jockeys at the time, Symphony Sid also appropriated hipster slang and vocal styles racialized as Black, though he occasionally included Yiddishisms as part of his distinctive deejay patter too. Listeners and musicians who appeared on the program sometimes balked at Sid's announcing style, but they could not deny his cultural impact; by 1950, the show was

---

[10] Jim Burns highlights the importance of radio alongside records, clubs, and music criticism in fostering Kerouac's interest in jazz in Burns (2018).

broadcasting in over thirty states, "ma[king] Symphony Sid a household name among jazz aficionados nationwide" (Barlow 1999: 158).

This was certainly true for the proto-Beat scene in New York that circled around Kerouac, Cassady, and Ginsberg; as Ginsberg later put it, "the whole atmosphere from 1940 on was permeated with be-bop and (DJ), Symphony Sid" (Ginsberg 2019: 182). This "atmosphere" is captured in a series of acetate disc recordings that Ginsberg, Kerouac, John Clellon Holmes, and others made c.1949–1951 on an early home recording machine at Holmes's apartment. On one of these recordings, an excerpt from which was digitally remastered in the mid-1990s for Ginsberg's compilation CD *Holy Soul Jelly Roll*, Ginsberg reads the early poem "A Mad Gleam" while broadcast jazz from Symphony Sid's program can just be heard faintly in the background (Ginsberg 1994: track 2). In the CD liner notes to this track, Ginsberg explains, "Symphony Sid was background in Holmes' early recordings.... The radio was on when he turned on his tape machine. It wasn't a deliberate attempt to put poetry and jazz together. Jazz was all around anyway, it was part of the ambient sound" (1994). We can hear this recording as documenting, then, not an early example of a Beat poet performing with jazz accompaniment but Ginsberg engaged in the everyday practice of ambient or distracted listening. Once seen by the radio industry as a problem that audiences had to be educated out of (in other words, as the opposite of audile technique), ambient listening was increasingly cultivated as a norm in the post-war era as a way of keeping listeners tuned in to hours of block programming (Russo 2010: 14). For the Beats, the ambient listening facilitated by radio and modeled by early disc jockeys allowed jazz to take on the aspect of a mood or "atmosphere" whose cultural influence could be felt to be as unconscious and vital as breathing, as structural to experimental writing as the technology of inscription itself.

In other recordings, however, the radio does occasionally come into the foreground, with Kerouac in particular drawing a direct connection between what he was hearing on the radio and his own compositional experiments. Phil Ford, who details his experience of listening to Holmes's archival recordings, notes several moments when Kerouac "hums a riff along with the radio," sings choruses over a broadcast of Dizzy Gillespie's "Hot House," or performs "vocal improvisations" inspired by Symphony Sid broadcasts of white jazz pianist Lennie Tristano (Ford 2013: 96, 99, 100). Ginsberg recalled that during one of their recording sessions, Kerouac "imitate[d] Symphony Sid's tone of voice as a professional announcer, announcing his latest novel or his latest vision," adding that the deejay "had a professional bebop hippie tone of voice that enters into Kerouac's prose"—a "tone of voice," as I have already noted, constructed through racial ventriloquy (Ginsberg 2017: 35). Kerouac's "spontaneous bop prosody" can thus be understood as a compositional practice derived from listening not only to jazz but also to *broadcast* jazz: an "audile technique," moreover, that ultimately reproduced the hegemony of elite white male practices of listening or what Jennifer Stoever terms "the listening ear" (2016).

Ginsberg, for all his distracted listening, might have been more attuned to Symphony Sid's specifically Jewish identification with Black culture. Charles Hersch argues that

Symphony Sid, like many Jews in the jazz industry, sought to construct a "hybrid identity" in his radio persona that would link his identification with Black culture to his own sense of exclusion from white bourgeois society and desire to resist the post-war pressures on Jewish Americans to assimilate (Hersch 2013: 277). It seems to me important to emphasize, however, that Symphony Sid's appropriation of a Black idiom on his radio show—particularly as it participated in the codification of racial ventriloquy as an announcing style in 1950s youth radio—was also conditioned by an ideology that understands racial identity as essentialized for those racialized as Black and constructed and mutable for those with proximity to (a deracinated) whiteness. This is not to deny the fact that Symphony Sid used his radio platform to promote Black musicians and educate his audience not only about bebop but also about Afro-diasporic music more broadly, and in so doing resisted the segregationist logics of the music and radio industries while acting as "a cultural intermediary between white and black culture" (276). Indeed, the complexities of Symphony Sid's legacy—including for post-1945 American literature, as I am tracking here—reflect in many ways the contradictions of "love and theft" at this moment in US history.

Amiri Baraka and "the Sounds"

The Beats were not the only writers to listen to Symphony Sid, however. The disc jockey show, which lasted in various forms into the 1970s, is also frequently cited as an influence by Black and Latinx writers—not to mention jazz musicians, such as Lester Young, whose "Jumpin' with Symphony Sid" became the program's theme song. Sonia Sanchez, for example, who moved to Harlem in 1943, describes herself as "growing up on 'Symphony Sid' " along with a panoply of other musical influences that would inform her own jazz poetics (Sanchez 1990: 157). Kwame Ture remembers listening to Symphony Sid and the Black disc jockey Douglas "Jocko" Henderson every night as a teenager in the Bronx on an old shortwave radio, noting that he "listened carefully and learned a lot" from Symphony Sid in particular, who "was erudite and commented in interesting ways on the music" (Carmichael 2003: 96, 98). And Victor Hernández Cruz, who hadn't yet been born when Ginsberg and Kerouac first starting bopping to Sid's records, used to tune in as a teenager in the 1960s to the Afro-Cuban jazz and Latin music that the deejay promoted later in his career, contributing to the multilingual, multicultural sonic mix of the Lower East Side that would foster Cruz's bilingual poetics and the Nuyorican poetry movement. "Ah, to be fifteen and Latin in Manhattan," he writes, "walking around the Avenue D housing projects with a portable transistor radio listening to the Symphony Sid show" (Cruz 1997: 112).

Amiri Baraka listened to Sid, too, first picking the show up in Newark as a college student home on summer breaks from Howard University. In the autobiographical novella *6 Persons*, Baraka recalls those hot, restless nights, when he and a friend would drive around, and "[s]ometimes we'd sit in the car and listen to Symphony Sid play the sounds.

The sounds. Our true religion. The true mask of hipness."[11] That the features of this "mask" of hip Black masculinity derived from both the "true" "sounds" of bebop and the mediumship and racial ventriloquy of a Jewish deejay on a nationally syndicated radio show was not lost on Baraka. But the ventriloquy was more complicated than it might seem; like (and unlike) Kerouac, Baraka depicts himself as an imitator of Symphony Sid's "funny" radio voice: "And we roamed all over, stretching into the darkness, imitating Symphone Sid, and *Esquire*, and Colored School, and White School, being the actual Quixote of college evenings, looking for the rituals."[12] "Symphone Sid," with the second syllable of the abbreviated moniker pointedly accented, joins the list of white and middle-class African American influences (from the nominally integrated "White School" Baraka attended as a high schooler, to the men's magazine *Esquire*, to the assimilationist, in Baraka's view, "Colored School" of Howard University) that the young men—would-be heroes of their own road narrative—signify on as they cruise around the streets of Black Newark. Looking back, Baraka depicts these youthful imitations, however parodic, as driving the young men in the wrong direction, "slowly and fastly toward the white-out" where a Du Boisian "veil of colorless fog descends, envelopes us in it, laughing" (Baraka 2000: 268, 269). Radio is often represented in Baraka's work as one of the principal vehicles of double consciousness (cue The Shadow's haunting laugh), but here it produces a double ventriloquism, in which the young Black listener imitates a Jewish radio announcer ventriloquizing Blackness to express his own sense of class rebellion—a rebellion that will eventually lead Baraka, in his own autobiographical retellings, to the interracial, bohemian arts scene of downtown New York. "You cannot say what you wd be without slavery," Baraka writes in *6 Persons*, addressing his younger self, "Readied for the white-out age 18, sitting by the curb listening to Symphony Sid" (267).

At times, Baraka's writing about radio, including these passages from *6 Persons* and early poems like "In Memory of Radio," appear to critique radio's capacity to encroach on the autonomy of the listener and the autonomy of literature. In the "Thieves" chapter of *The System of Dante's Hell*, for example, the sudden interjection of the sentence, "You're listening to the Symphony Sid Program," seemingly spoken by a character, "Donald," but without explanation or quotation marks to signal when this "broadcast" ends, indicates that the writer's voice is not wholly his own.[13] Justin St Clair, in a study of the "radiophonic anxiety" of postmodern American fiction, argues that radio's relationship to its

---

[11] *6 Persons* (Baraka 2000: 264). Baraka narrates a similar scene in *The Autobiography of LeRoi Jones*:

> Me and a dude named Joe Brown would sit on the stoop outside the parties after passing through looking at the babes. We'd sit outside ... or sit in the car with the door open.... We'd be out there listening to Symphony Sid and talking shit, passing comments on the women that went in and out and the dudes too.
>
> (Baraka 1997: 126)

[12] *6 Persons* (Baraka 2000: 264).
[13] LeRoi Jones, *The System of Dante's Hell* (Baraka 2000: 66).

audience has often operated through a ventriloquist logic in which programs simulate audience participation by speaking for their listeners, who in turn come to adopt those opinions as their own so that they are, in a sense, "bespoken" by the medium (St Clair 2013: 47, 57). Referring to actual radio ventriloquists like Edgar Bergen, St Clair suggests that the counterintuitive success of these performances, which would seemingly rely on the visual illusion, had to do with the ways they dramatized, in the dummy's comical one-upmanship of his human counterpart, "the process by which members of a radio audience are made to feel autonomous by the very medium engaged in appropriating their autonomy" (57). In St Clair's view, radio ventriloquism as a literary trope therefore tends to expose writers' concern about the threat that radio supposedly poses to both the individual autonomy of the listener and the autonomy of literature as a cultural form.

Baraka's critique of radio in his poetry and prose (and his understanding of artistic autonomy) is more specific, though, than St Clair's diagnosis of postmodern American fiction's "radiophonic anxiety" would suggest because of his awareness of the indirect and contradictory ways that Black listeners have been "bespoken" by radio. After all, prior to the Second World War, the industry rarely considered African Americans to be an important part of the radio audience and therefore did not ventriloquize them as members of that audience, even as it did ventriloquize minstrel stereotypes. The breaking of radio's color line by African American radio announcers and disc jockeys changed this, but the racial ventriloquy heard on jazz and rock programs helmed by white and Jewish deejays, while of a different kind than the racist caricatures that preceded them, still mobilized aural constructions of Blackness in order to bespeak a predominantly white audience—albeit one in rebellion against the dominant culture. As a gateway and gatekeeper to the new jazz, Symphony Sid thus figures repeatedly in Baraka's work as another example of the poet's love for radio turning back on itself into an "evol" that drives his heroic, spiritual quest for a Black(er) art.

But the music still comes in, Charlie Parker and Dizzy Gillespie and Thelonious Monk still come in, and what will "the sounds" communicate to the teenage LeRoi Jones, parked curbside in front of some party, learning to listen? In their live broadcasts from Birdland, Parker and Symphony Sid played a kind of two-man show, with Parker occasionally slipping in subtle insults to mock the "hip" deejay (Hersch 2013: 275). But this was no ventriloquist act; what Parker communicated, what bebop in general would come to communicate for Baraka, is the autonomy of Black music, which does not mean that it exists outside the contexts of its making and reception. As many scholars have observed, Baraka's music criticism of the 1960s works toward a theory of Black music as a response to the historical, sociological, and technological particulars of Black experience in America, while at the same time driven by a continually renewed aesthetic impulse toward abstraction that repels its containment and appropriation by white dominant culture. In *Blues People*, Baraka terms this anti-assimilationist strain "the blues continuum," which Nathaniel Mackey explicates as signifying in Baraka's work "[a] black *position*, one of outsidedness or of alienation and resistance" that functions as "a kind of 'unmoved mover' at the root of black America's transformations" (Mackey 1978: 360). But this theory of "black music as ... willful dissociation from mainstream American culture" is also, as Mackey rightly notes, "very much a Beat interpretation of black music" that Baraka developed in dialogue with writers like Kerouac and Ginsberg and, I would add, in relation to cultural sources like Symphony Sid's radio show (362, 361).

In a 1961 essay on "The Jazz Avant-Garde," for example, Baraka paraphrases Robert Creeley's famous dictum on projective verse as "[f]orm can never be more than an extension of content," in order to advance his own theory of how formal innovation in jazz revitalizes its "roots" through the fusion or non-separation of form and "ideas," "technique," and "emotion."[14] Arguing that bebop, like the blues, has become a roots music for a new generation of jazz musicians, Baraka writes:

> They sit autonomous. Blues and bebop are *musics*. They are understandable, emotionally, as they sit: without the barest discussion of their origins. And the reason I think for this is that they *are* origins, themselves. Blues is a beginning. Bebop, a beginning.
>
> (Baraka [Jones] 1970: 72)

Origins without the quest for origins: this is what makes bebop and the blues autonomous for Baraka and also what enables each new generation of jazz innovators to formally innovate in relation to them as a resounding of "the blues continuum."

But Baraka is equally concerned with how "the blues continuum" can be *heard*, which is to say that his music criticism offers a theory and history of Black music and also a theory and practice, a *poiesis*, of listening that derives from the specific auditory experiences and critical frameworks that Black audiences bring to sound media culture. A subtle distinction, perhaps, but in my view an important one. Before returning our attention to the trope of radio in Baraka's poetry, then, I want to briefly consider one of his other, slightly later essays on jazz to show how this poetics of listening emerges in relation to his thinking about how the artistic autonomy of jazz is realized in and through (to borrow St Clair's phrasing) "the very medium engaged in appropriating [its] autonomy."

In an essay penned as liner notes for John Coltrane's 1964 album *Coltrane Live at Birdland*, Baraka begins with the suggestion that the title, if read literally, presents a paradox that "can be rendered 'symbolic' and more directly meaningful" in relation to a central contradiction about the United States: "that despite its essentially vile profile, so much beauty continues to exist" (Baraka [Jones] 1970: 63). He goes on to explain:

> To me Birdland is a place no man should wander into unarmed, especially not an artist, and that is what John Coltrane is. But, too, Birdland is only America in microcosm, and we know how high the mortality rate is for artists in this instant tomb. Yet, the title tells us that John Coltrane is there *live*. In this tiny America where the most delirious happiness can only be caused by the dollar, a man continues to make

---

[14] "The Jazz Avant-Garde" (Baraka [Jones] (1970: 71, 72).

daring reference to some other kind of thought. Impossible? Listen to "I Want to Talk about You."

"Coltrane Live at Birdland" (Baraka [Jones] 1970: 63–64)

The title *Coltrane Live at Birdland* thus opens up in Baraka's reading onto an aporia that deconstructs the relationship between "live" and recorded sound, and life and death, for the Black artist. For Baraka, Coltrane's achievement is that he in fact finds a way to "live at Birdland," to escape the "instant tomb" of social death by making—musically—"daring reference to some other kind of thought": the thought of a Black world that Baraka will later describe as "another place. A place where Black People live."[15] Coltrane's music, moreover, transforms both the live and recorded contexts of its making and reception. "Coltrane apparently doesn't need an ivory tower," Baraka writes; "It does not seem to matter to him (nor should it) that hovering in the background are people and artifacts that have no more to do with his music than silence."[16] The LP album that will further objectify the already commercial event of Coltrane's performance at Birdland into the commodity form of the recording is one such "artifact." But the autonomy of Coltrane's art, Baraka tells us, will continue to renew itself in phonographic replay—and it will do so in part because it contains as a trace within itself an equally impossible experience of listening.

Partway through the liner notes, Baraka reveals that he was one of the people "hovering in the background" at Birdland on the evening of Coltrane's performance, which means that he, too, was an artist who "wander[ed] unarmed" into this "America in microcosm" only to experience the destruction of its evil, or the transmutation this time of "evol" back into love. In the following passage, Baraka remarkably insists that the record somehow inscribes not only Coltrane's music but also Baraka's own listening, though it's more accurate to say that what gets inscribed is the rupture of that listening ear, the rupture of a certain kind of aural technique that would reduce the music to mere technical prowess and the critic to a distanced observer rather than emotionally engaged participant:

> to hear a man destroy all of it, completely, like Sodom, with just the first few notes from his horn, your "critical" sense can be erased completely, and that experience can place you somewhere a long way off from anything ugly. Still, what was of musical value that I heard that night does remain, and the emotions ... some of them completely new ... that I experience at each "objective" rehearing of this music are as valuable as anything else I know about. And all of this *is* on this record[.] [ellipses in original].

"Coltrane Live at Birdland" (Baraka [Jones] 1970: 65)

---

[15] "The Changing Same (R&B and New Black Music)," (Baraka [Jones] 1970: 186).
[16] "Coltrane Live at Birdland" (ibid 64).

It's not that the LP record somehow restores the aura of live performance; as Baraka makes clear elsewhere in the essay, the album's studio-recorded tracks inspire similar listening experiences for him as the ones he originally heard live. It's that the record creates the possibility for "'objective' rehearing"—a phrase that itself reclaims the term "objective" from its usual, academic sense to describe a mode of technologized listening that recovers, in each instance, the "completely new" that is Black performance. If, following Fred Moten, we understand "enslavement—and the resistance to enslavement ... [as] the performative essence of blackness (or, perhaps less controversially, the essence of black performance)," then the poetics of listening that Baraka develops in his early jazz criticism might be understood as a counter-audile technique that itself performs the "resistance of the object," or the performative "fact that objects can and do resist" (Moten 2003: 16, 1). Like the ellipses in Baraka's description quoted above, this radical experience of aural possibility inscribes itself on the record not as sound but as cut, trace, groove, interference.

What, then, does this phonographic "objective rehearing" have to do with radio—or Symphony Sid for that matter, who, if Coltrane's recording session had happened a decade earlier, we might have found ensconced in a broadcasting booth in the back of the club? In my reading, the radical listening practices that Baraka developed as a jazz critic were also informed by his lifelong love of radio and the subversive and *submerged* modes of listening that had enabled him as a young listener to transmute the "white noise" of popular American culture into Black auditory imaginaries. I'd like to conclude, then, by turning (and turning back) to one of the lesser-known radio poems from Baraka's first book, *Preface to a Twenty Volume Suicide Note* . . . . .: a poem titled, simply, "Symphony Sid."

"Symphony Sid"

Unlike other poems in *Preface* that directly address the poet's complex attachment to radio, there is little beyond the title of Baraka's poem "Symphony Sid" to suggest that this is a poem about radio. Instead, the proper name "Symphony Sid" seems at first to function simply as a metonym for the modern jazz that the radio show helped to popularize nationally, as if the concerns over radio ventriloquism or the distortion of Black culture by white mainstream media expressed in Baraka's other works that allude to the disc jockey show were not at issue in this poem. Indeed, one could read the poem "Symphony Sid" as building toward a scene of ambient listening, in which jazz transmitted via the radio sets the mood for (or rather casts a shadow over) the two lovers revealed in the final lines of the poem as "[a] man, a woman / shaking the night apart" (Baraka [Jones] 1961: 36). While the music that accompanies the lovers is never specified, its ambient effects and affects are rendered throughout the poem in synesthetic images that appeal predominantly to vision, smell, touch, and taste rather than hearing, as in these lines from the middle of the poem: "music, black shadow / from highest wild / fingers placing evening / beneath our tongues." This atmosphere is further conveyed through the heavily enjambed, short lines and terse lyric mode of the poem, which intensify its expressive feeling through a hesitant, disrupted breath. These formal qualities reflect the influence of Robert Creeley on Baraka's early poetry, but if we recall that Creeley's approach to the line was influenced by jazz, and Charlie Parker specifically, we might also rehear in this poem the jazz behind projective verse.

At the beginning of the poem, however, we find the broadcast music positioned as neither ambient background nor attention-grabbing foreground but rather *underground*. Like the protagonist in Ralph Ellison's *Invisible Man*, who, listening while high to Louis Armstrong on his "radio-phonograph," "discover[s] a new analytical way of listening to music" that enables him to "slip into the breaks and look around" and find that *"beneath the swiftness of the hot tempo there was a slower tempo and a cave,"* the speaker in Baraka's poem leads the reader on a similar Dantean descent (Ellison 1980 [1952]: 8, 9).[17] The opening lines begin with the instruction to "First / take the first / thing. Blue" (Baraka [Jones] 1961: 36). Echoing his claim in "The Jazz Avant-Garde" that "Blues and bebop ... are origins" and "a beginning" in and of themselves, Baraka's use of the singular noun, "Blue," also implies that "the first / thing" the music communicates is the complex emotional signification of *feeling* and *being* blue, à la Louis Armstrong's "What did I do to be so black and blue?" on perpetual and simultaneous replay in the invisible man's "underworld of sound" (Ellison 1980 [1952]: 12).[18] But while Ellison figures this submerged listening as a metaphorical descent into the grooves of an LP record, Baraka opens an unexpected vertical dimension in listening to the continuous waves of sound transmitting from the radio so that ambience becomes not just surface or surround but depth and underground. As the poem continues, the blue note opens a vertical space and time-outside-of-time: a mythic landscape that rises first as a (phallic) "mountain" before descending into a (vaginal) "dark hall at / the bottom." There, "the shapes / a shadow" quicken in the darkened form of the lovers "without / hardness, or that / ugly smell / of blackening flesh," a description that evokes, while claiming to have escaped, the grotesque imagery of lynching (Baraka [Jones] 1961: 36).

This is no arrival at a natal origin, not even an arrival at an originary trauma. Instead, I read these lines in connection to Fred Moten's assertion that "Black art neither sutures nor is sutured to trauma" but "is, rather, a perpetual cutting, a constancy of expansive and unfolding rupture and wound" that is, moreover, enveloped and involved in a "diffusion" of violence that for Moten marks an aporia (Moten 2017: ix, xi). As Moten writes (in dialogue with Saidiya Hartman), "Jazz does does not disappear the problem; it *is* the problem, and will not disappear. It is, moreover, the problem's diffusion" in which what is "[a]t stake is an ambience that is both more and less than atmospheric" (Moten 2017: xii, xi). In my reading of Baraka's poem, the evocation of the unspeakable violence of lynching as an image simultaneously sounded and silenced within the jazz music broadcast on Symphony

---

[17] Italics in original.
[18] "The Jazz Avant-Garde" (Baraka [Jones] 1970: 72).

Sid's radio show cuts the lines that come before and after so that the musical ambience that surrounds the lovers—"[a] man, a woman," perhaps now "LeRoi" and "Hettie"—flows into the insidious, pervasive racial terror that looms over their interracial marriage and their reproductive future.[19] In the poem's final lines, the speaker seeks to pull off his vanishing act: "Forget / my fingers," he writes as he fades, like his childhood radio hero The Shadow, into the poisonous ether.

But before we take the escape of lyric closure, can we descend further into the hall of the mountain? Let's imagine that the strange radio transcription that this poem performs secretly inscribes a specific song that Symphony Sid might have played on his radio show circa 1960 and that the Joneses, in one of the downtown Manhattan apartments where they hosted poets, jazz musicians, and friends nearly every night, might have heard if they could get the signal to come in.[20] The images in Baraka's poem of "a dark hall" in a "mountain" has always surfaced in my auditory memory the tune to Edvard Grieg's "In the Hall of the Mountain King," and in 1960, Duke Ellington and His Orchestra recorded a jazz arrangement of this song—and four other movements from Grieg's *Peer Gynt Suites I & II*—for the album *Swinging Suites by Edward E. and Edward G* (Duke Ellington and His Orchestra 1960a). It is conceivable that the record would have been played by Symphony Sid on his radio show; it certainly would have been known by Baraka, who saw Ellington as one of the prime movers of the "blues continuum" in jazz.[21] Ellington, who composed the arrangement to "In the Hall of the Mountain King," supposedly did so "while strolling around the halls of the Chateau Marmont Hotel on Hollywood's Sunset Strip"—one of the few prominent Hollywood hotels to permit African American guests, of which Ellington was one of the first in 1959.[22] Ellington's swinging rendition of Peer's dangerous adventure in the court of the troll mountain king could thus be heard as a subversive commentary on the Black musician's journey across the color line into the underground of rich white Hollywood.

Interestingly, Ellington also cited a few bars from "In the Hall of the Mountain King" in another recording from 1960: an adaptation of the jazz standard "Lullaby of Birdland." The song was originally composed in 1952 by the British jazz pianist George Sheering for Birdland owner Morris Levy, who wanted a promotional theme for the club that

---

[19] Though Baraka represents an archetypal "man" and "woman" in this poem, several other poems in *Preface* directly address Hettie Jones and the pregnancy and birth of the Joneses' first child.

[20] In *How I Became Hettie Jones*, Hettie Jones quotes from a 1961 letter she wrote to Helene Dorn: "It's midnight and I think I've finally caught Symphony Sid, although this radio is prone to stick on less desirable stations" (Jones 1990: 142).

[21] A further level of descent: as musicologist Anna Celenza has persuasively shown, Ellington and his longtime collaborator Billy Strayhorn's adaptations of the *Peer Gynt Suites* were motivated less by their investment in Grieg's music or the European classical canon than they were by their engagement with American adaptations of Henrik Ibsen's original play *Peer Gynt* by Owen Dodson and Paul Green, both of which radically revised the play to comment on US racial politics (Celenza 2011). Dodson, who incorporated African American folklore and music into his 1947 adaptation, *Bayou Legend*, was the theater director at Howard University during the time when Baraka was a student there.

[22] Irving Townsend, quoted in Celenza (2011).

would broadcast "every hour, on the hour" on Symphony Sid's nightly live program.[23] Symphony Sid had long since left his booth at Birdland by 1960, but one imagines that the deejay could hardly have resisted putting an Ellington version of one of his signature theme songs on the air—a version that included a playful trolling from "highest wild / fingers" linking the iconic jazz club to the demonic court of the mountain king.

I am far into the realm of speculation here, and in the end, I'm not concerned with whether or not I can prove that Baraka's poem "Symphony Sid" was inspired by a particular radio broadcast or actually contains a submerged allusion to Duke Ellington. What I am interested in is the relationship between the title and the poem itself, which bears some analogy in my reading to the relationship between the disc jockey program and the jazz music it broadcasts. If the poem seems at first to bypass the medium for the message, the radio for the music, and finally both radio and music to disseminate an ambient "blues feeling," the title "Symphony Sid" nonetheless remains the only proper noun, the only specific reference at all in the poem. In its own way, the title is as "symbolically" meaningful as *Coltrane Live at Birdland* because it represents the structure of commodification against which, but also in and out of which, the Black artist, the Black poet, "continues to make daring reference to some other kind of thought"—the thought of *love*.[24] In this early, melancholic poem, it is perhaps not yet a thought that could be sounded fully by Baraka nor, for that matter, by American radio, which in the ensuing decades would see increasing centralization, formatization, deregulation, and exploitation of artistic labor as part of the rise of a new era of network hegemony dominated by multinational media conglomerates. But one could still tune in to the "lower frequencies," where an invisible voice might be heard broadcasting an "SOS," calling a new world into being: "calling all black people, come in, black people, come / on in" (Ellison 1980 [1956]: 581; Baraka [Jones] 1969: 115).

I suggested earlier that the Beat enthusiasm for bebop as a source of anti-authoritarian rebellion was shaped in part by, and contributed to, the transformation of ambient listening into audile technique in post-war radio, as disc jockey programs like Symphony Sid's gave jazz the appearance of being ubiquitous, pervasive, "in the air," so to speak. For Baraka, however, it was jazz musicians' ability to transmute the toxicity of anti-Blackness in the American air and airwaves into something Black people can breathe that called for not only new practices of listening but also the critique of audile technique as such as an instrument of Western modernity (Mackey 2018). The dynamic of "love and theft" that affectively structured white countercultural appropriations of Black culture thus finds, in my view, its deconstruction and subversion in Baraka's writing of love and/as/against "evol" as a radical poetics of and possibility for Black reception. The death of radio portended in the post-war years did not, of course, come to pass, and the dynamic history of American literature's relationship to radio culture continues to change and renew itself into our present moment, more than a century after radio's early development as

---

[23] "Lullaby of Birdland" (Duke Ellington and His Orchestra 1960b: track 10); Shearing (2004: 137). Celenza notes the citation of "In the Hall of the Mountain King" in this recording (Celenza 2011).

[24] "Coltrane Live at Birdland" (Baraka [Jones] 1970: 64).

a mass broadcasting service. Yet, I am interested in what it might mean to still imagine, after Baraka, the death of radio as symbolic of the destruction of a particular kind of American evil that diffuses its suffocating whiteness across the capitalist mediascape. What afterlives might arise from such residual fantasies? How will they sound?

REFERENCES

Baraka, Amiri [LeRoi Jones]. 1961. *Preface to a Twenty Volume Suicide Note....* (New York: Totem Press/Corinth Books).
Baraka, Amiri [LeRoi Jones]. 1969. "SOS," in *Black Magic: Poetry 1961–1967* (Indianapolis, IN and New York: Bobbs-Merrill), 115.
Baraka, Amiri [LeRoi Jones]. 1970. *Black Music* (New York: W. Morrow).
Baraka, Amiri. 1997. *The Autobiography of LeRoi Jones* (Chicago, IL: Lawrence Hill Books).
Baraka, Amiri [LeRoi Jones]. 1999 [1963]. *Blues People: Negro Music in White America* (New York: HarperPerennial).
Baraka, Amiri. 2000. *The Fiction of LeRoi Jones/Amiri Baraka* (Chicago, IL: Lawrence Hill Books).
Barlow, William. 1999. *Voice Over: The Making of Black Radio* (Philadelphia, PA: Temple University Press).
Burns, Jim. 2018. "Jack Kerouac's Jazz Scene," in Simon Warner and Jim Sampas, eds, *Kerouac on Record: A Literary Soundtrack* (London: Bloomsbury Academic), 19–30.
Campbell, Timothy C. 2006. *Wireless Writing in the Age of Marconi* (Minneapolis, MN: University of Minnesota Press).
Carmichael, Stokely [with Ekwueme Michael Thelwell]. 2003. *Ready for Revolution: The Life and Struggle of Stokely Carmichael (Kwame Ture)* (New York: Simon and Schuster).
Celenza, Anna. 2011. "Duke Ellington, Billy Strayhorn, and the Adventures of *Peer Gynt* in America," *Music and Politics* 5.2. DOI: 10.3998/mp.9460447.0005.205.
Cohen, Debra Rae, Michael Coyle, and Jane Lewty, eds. 2009. *Broadcasting Modernism* (Gainesville, FL: University Press of Florida).
Cruz, Victor Hernández. 1997. *Panoramas* (Minneapolis, MN: Coffee House Press).
Douglas, Susan J. 2004. *Listening In: Radio and the American Imagination* (Minneapolis, MN: University of Minnesota Press).
Duke Ellington and His Orchestra. 1960a. *Swinging Suites by Edward E. and Edward G.* (New York: Columbia Records).
Duke Ellington and His Orchestra. 1960b. *Piano in the Background* (New York: Columbia Records).
Ellison, Ralph. 1980 [1952]. *Invisible Man* (New York: Vintage).
Feldman, Matthew, Henry Mead, and Erik Tonning, eds. 2014. *Broadcasting in the Modernist Era* (London: Bloomsbury).
Ford, Phil. 2013. *Dig: Sound and Music in Hip Culture* (New York: Oxford University Press).
Fouché, Rayvon. 2006. "Say It Loud, I'm Black and I'm Proud: African Americans, American Artifactual Culture, and Black Vernacular Technological Creativity," *American Quarterly* 58.3: 639–661.
Ginsberg, Allen. 1988. "The Green Automobile," in *Collected Poems: 1947–1980* (New York: Harper Perennial), 83.
Ginsberg, Allen. 1994. "A Mad Gleam," track 2 of *Holy Soul Jelly Roll: Poems and Songs, 1949–1993*, vol. 1 (Rhino), audio CD.

Ginsberg, Allen. 2017. *The Best Minds of My Generation: A Literary History of the Beats*, ed. Bill Morgan (New York: Grove Press).

Ginsberg, Allen. 2019. "Allen Ginsberg Interview," conducted by Harvey Kubernik, 1996, in David Stephen Calonne, ed., *Conversations with Allen Ginsberg* (Jackson, MS: University Press of Mississippi), 170–186.

Harrison, K. C. 2014. "LeRoi Jones's Radio and the Literary 'Break' from Ellison to Burroughs," *African American Review* 47.2–3: 357–374.

Hersch, Charles. 2013. "'Every Time I Try to Play Black, It Comes Out Sounding Jewish': Jewish Jazz Musicians and Racial Identity," *American Jewish History* 97.3: 259–282.

Hilmes, Michele. 1997. *Radio Voices: American Broadcasting, 1922–1952* (Minneapolis, MN: University of Minnesota Press).

Jones, Hettie. 1990. *How I Became Hettie Jones* (New York: Penguin).

Kerouac, Jack. 1990 [1959]. "Note," in *Mexico City Blues* (New York: Grove Press).

Kerouac, Jack. 2003 [1957]. *On the Road* (New York: Penguin).

Lott, Eric. 1993. *Love and Theft: Blackface Minstrelsy and the American Working Class* (New York: Oxford University Press).

Loviglio, Jason. 2005. *Radio's Intimate Public: Network Broadcasting and Mass-Mediated Democracy* (Minneapolis, MN: University of Minnesota Press).

Mackey, Nathaniel. 1978. "The Changing Same: Black Music in the Poetry of Amiri Baraka," *boundary 2* 6.2: 355–386.

Mackey, Nathaniel. 2018. "Breath and Precarity: The Inaugural Robert Creeley Lecture in Poetry and Poetics," in Myung Mi Kim and Cristanne Miller, eds, *Poetics and Precarity* (Albany, NY: State University of New York Press), 1–30.

McEnaney, Tom. 2017. *Acoustic Properties: Radio, Narrative, and the New Neighborhood of the Americas* (Evanston, IL: Northwestern University Press).

Moten, Fred. 2003. *In the Break: The Aesthetics of the Black Radical Tradition* (Minneapolis, MN: University of Minnesota Press).

Moten, Fred. 2017. *Black and Blur* (Durham, NC: Duke University Press).

Punday, Daniel. 2006. "The Black Arts Movement and the Genealogy of Multimedia," *New Literary History* 37.4: 777–794.

Russo, Alexander. 2010. *Points on the Dial: Golden Age Radio beyond the Networks* (Durham, NC: Duke University Press).

Sanchez, Sonia. 1990. "Sonia Sanchez: The Will and the Spirit," in D. H. Melhem, ed., *Heroism in the New Black Poetry: Introductions and Interviews* (Lexington, KY: University Press of Kentucky), 133–180.

Shearing, George [with Alyn Shipton]. 2004. *Lullaby of Birdland: The Autobiography of George Shearing* (New York: Continuum).

St Clair, Justin. 2013. *Sound and Aural Media in Postmodern Literature: Novel Listening* (New York: Routledge).

Sterne, Jonathan. 2003. *The Audible Past: Cultural Origins of Sound Reproduction* (Durham, NC: Duke University Press).

Stoever, Jennifer. 2016. *The Sonic Color Line: Race and the Cultural Politics of Listening* (New York: NYU Press).

Thomas, Lorenzo. 1978. "The Shadow World: New York's Umbra Workshop and Origins of the Black Arts Movement," *Callaloo* 4: 53–72.

Weheliye, Alexander G. 2005. *Phonographies: Grooves in Sonic Afro-Modernity* (Durham, NC: Duke University Press).

Whittington, Ian. 2014. "Radio Studies and 20th-Century Literature: Ethics, Aesthetics, and Remediation," *Literature Compass* 11.9: 634–648.

CHAPTER 8

FAULKNER AT THE SPEED OF HISTORY

MARK GOBLE

Over the past forty years, critics have made William Faulkner's career as a screenwriter increasingly essential to our understanding of both his most significant fictions and of his larger place in the twentieth-century literature of the United States. From the relatively circumscribed account we get in Bruce Kawin's *Faulkner and Film* (1977)—which assessed Faulkner's scripts and various Hollywood projects in light of his modernist commitments to montage and formal experimentation—to recent books that situate Faulkner in much more complex and varied media ecologies, it is now the case that the period that he himself dismissed as largely wasted labor in another culture industry gives us ample reason to keep returning to his writings even as many of their central arguments and stylistic preoccupations feel more dated, if not actually anachronistic.[1] At this point, it seems safe to say that there has been a decisive turn to media in Faulkner studies—as technologies of representation and communication, as emblems of modernity, as an intellectual and material environment—and that it has already lasted longer than a prior critical moment that at best begrudged his time in Hollywood as an interlude or a distraction. Critics no longer bemoan the fact that Faulkner turned to film when faced with commercial pressures during the years of his most extraordinary productivity nor blame Hollywood for the declining powers on display in later novels. We no more take Faulkner at his bitter word when we encounter his complaints about the film industry than we accept the brooding melancholy of his views on race as a political horizon worth chasing into another century of white gradualism, or worse. At least in respect to Faulkner's own engagement with cinematic techniques and institution, history has moved far more quickly than it ever seems to in his fiction where, as Watson

---

[1] I am thinking in particular of Lurie (2004), Murphet (2017), Gleeson-White (2015), and Watson (2019). Two recent essay collections also feature a range of vital work exploring Faulkner's writings in light of film and other media technologies: Lurie and Abadie (2014) and Murphet and Solomon (2015). All these writers have helped form the ideas in this chapter in crucial ways.

writes, if we "picture a scene from the work of William Faulkner ... odds are that what comes to mind will be something slow" (Watson 2019: 100). I think that this impression is right, and it tells us much about Faulkner's most representative temporalities, especially those of the actions and events that punctuate his narratives and those of the grinding, seemingly interminable histories of race and capital that his characters and readers must alike endure. Paradoxically, though, we will realize that nothing may go faster in Faulkner's fiction than what we witness happening in slow motion.

I confess that, in one sense, I am asking a question about Faulkner and his writing that is hardly new: "What Price Hollywood?" Some will hear in this admittedly grandiloquent formulation a more specific invocation of George Cukor's 1932 film that offered the terms of this exchange as a cautionary tale for any man in the movie business of a certain age (middle) and tolerance for alcohol (high). Starring Lowell Sherman as "Maximillan Carey," a veteran director who almost entirely by accident discovers a new star in Constance Bennett's "Mary Evans" on the awkward morning after a night of chaste, though very drunken, excess, *What Price Hollywood?* was released just weeks after Faulkner arrived to work at MGM. The story of a fading filmmaker whose descent into irrelevance and addiction leads to his suicide even as a younger actress flourishes without him, *What Price Hollywood?* was a commercial wash in 1932 but then eventually became the prototype for 1937's *A Star is Born*, which was close enough to the original that RKO sued David O. Selznick for plagiarizing the earlier flop that he had co-produced. From the Janet Gaynor and Fredric March version (in 1937) to that of Judy Garland and James Mason (which Cukor himself directed in 1954), Barbra Streisand and Kris Kristofferson (1976), and Bradley Cooper and Lady Gaga (2018), the basic outline of the story has remained stupendously adaptable and there is no reason to rehearse it here. All these later films, however, turn on a romance between older man and younger "star" that in Cukor's original, with its script by legendary screenwriter and journalist Adela Rogers St Johns, is instead a somewhat clunky, half-Platonic love quadrangle of Max, Mary, her estranged husband Lonny, and her burgeoning career. My interest in *What Price Hollywood?*, though, has little to do with the lore that it eventually inspires nor with the convenient parallels we can find scattered across Faulkner's biography and legend, from his affair with Meta Wilde to his masterfully distorted incarnation as "W. P. Mayhew" in *Barton Fink* (1991). At one level, the acknowledgement that Faulkner was, in fact, a "Hollywood" writer reflects the critical consensus that whatever the "price" that Faulkner may have felt the movie industry extracted, his standing as a novelist obviously won out, and his proximity to the world of the mass media has weirdly helped maintain his status and authority. But on another level, which, as we will see, applies some of the methods of media archaeology to Faulkner, this chapter explores a far smaller network of connections between cinematic form and Faulkner's writing. In *Light in August*, the novel that he published in the midst of his first months at MGM, we will see that Faulkner turns to film not just as a visual language that can move like history itself: at varying speeds, at different scales, in multiple directions. Film represents a new medium for Faulkner that, perversely enough, lets him conceive his present as more deeply patterned by older pasts and unseen acts of racial violence. What Faulkner shows us cinematically is nothing that Hollywood could have put on screen in the 1930s, which is perhaps why he is particularly drawn to slow motion as a special effect. Its appearance in *Light in August* goes fast, but as we might expect for Faulkner, even the briefest moment can take almost forever, finally, to figure out. So, no time to lose.

Very near the end of *What Price Hollywood?*, many viewers in 1932 would have seen something at the movies that they had never seen before: the use of slow motion in a major-studio feature film of the sound era. The entire sequence surrounding Max's death offers a catalog of cutting-edge effects for the period, and while Cukor is not especially remembered for his spectacular visual style as a director, there is no mistaking the sheer amount of technique here put on display. Waking up at Mary's mansion after another bender leads to jail, Max finds himself alone to take a hard look in a mirror—a moment of overdetermined "reflection" on his past that is underscored when he pushes aside a framed picture on Mary's guest-room table showing him as he looked at the height of his career. He has already inadvertently discovered a gun kept in another fancy table—for no apparent reason save dramatic convenience—while hoping to find some matches to light his cigarette, which he lets drop from his mouth. The remaining fifty seconds or so he has to live will unfold entirely with special effects. Dissolves and double-exposures let us see him as he once appeared on set, professional and dapper even as his face constricts into a close-up of regret and shame. More images from Max's past waver in a sort of dreamy superimposition that we immediately recognize as Hollywood code for flashback—used for the first time in a major American film just a year before in Rouben Mamoulian's *City Streets*. The bars of a jail cell fade into the image at a rakish Dutch angle that turns into a pan across the bars before fading into an abstract vortex that will haunt the screen as we follow Max's steps back to the drawer and to the gun, which he then puts up to his chest in a tight shot that fills the frame with hand and weapon. With the sound of the gun firing, Max's life flashes before our eyes in a frantic montage—thirteen shots in only thirty-four frames—that was the work of Llyod Knechtel and, more intriguingly, Serbian avant-gardist Slavko Vorkapich, who was about to become one of Hollywood's most prominent special effects designers of the 1930s and early 1940s. Vorkapich had been interested in modernist visual culture since the late 1910s and, in 1928, had co-directed with Robert Florey the surprisingly successful experimental film *The Life and Death of 9413: A Hollywood Extra* (1928). But the dizzying montage he makes for *What Price Hollywood?* is truly star material, with no shot staying on the screen for more than six frames. There are two blank frames at the traumatic start and finish that pass by invisibly in real time. One image of Max and Mary appears at first to be an expressionist blur before coming into focus and then vanishing in a less than an eighth of a second. Two other shots are profoundly overexposed to the point of looking like printed negatives, though, of course, for viewers at the theater they wouldn't have looked like much at all since little of this visual excess would have registered on screen in this second or so of Soviet montage amidst Hollywood melodrama at its ripest. But there would have been no missing the slow motion of Max's dying fall (Figure 8.1), which we witness from a slightly lowered perspective that lets his body descend towards us and then out-of-frame for almost five seconds (122 frames at a standard 24 fps). It is

FIGURE 8.1 Still from *What Price Hollywood?* (George Cukor, RKO Pictures, 1932)

a remarkably affecting performance from Carey even without the pyrotechnics Cukor and Vorkapich unleash, and the total power of the scene is at once radical in its modernism and classical in its utter legibility—never mind how few would have experienced anything like it at the movies before.

I have indulged the ornate formalism and slow motion of *What Price Hollywood?* for several reasons but, for now, would like to single out just one. We know from Kawin— who takes his dates from Joseph Blotner's biography—that Faulkner arrived at MGM on May 7, 1932 and that the manuscript of *Light in August* was largely finished by the time he went to work on the first treatments and screenplays he would write in Hollywood (Kawin 1977: 70).[2] Cukor's film premiered on June 2, 1932. But Faulkner, as Blotner, of course, painstakingly details, did not settle on final changes to the galley proofs to the novel until early August, meaning that it is at least possible that Faulkner could have witnessed Max's death before publishing the novel that just coincidentally features his first explicit reference to the special effect that I will shortly track painstakingly myself: "It—the horse and the rider—had a strange, dreamy effect, like a moving picture in slow motion as it galloped steady and flagging up the street and toward the old corner where he used to wait, less urgent perhaps but not less eager, and more young" (Faulkner

---

[2] See also Blotner (1984: 304–310).

1990a: 210).³ The "rider" is Joe Christmas, and he is on his way to his last meeting with Bobbie, the waitress he falls for on one of his early trips to town with his adoptive and abusive father, McEachern. When he arrives, two white men will beat him for being Black, and so for the crime of miscegenation, though no one at this point in the novel, neither character nor reader, can know his race. Even Joe's assailants observe the indeterminacy of his identity, noting that, though they think they're hitting a Black man, *"He don't look like one"* (219). That we also can't know what "moving picture in slow motion" Faulkner might be mentioning is, by comparison, a trivial ambiguity. But I want to say it also marks a historical vanishing point of sorts, a primal scene of media where Faulkner invokes a cinematic form that he has seen before but will not name or address directly. This is also quite possibly the first mention of slow motion in the history of American literature. Yet, as we saw with Max's death scene in *What Price Hollywood?*, this fleeting moment of "slow motion" feels originary and familiar at the same time, conventional and maybe even formulaic, despite the fact that Faulkner might represent a ground zero for a metaphor that we take as a cliché. I am not saying it isn't, which is precisely why it might tell us something about the experiences of speed and slowness across the twentieth-century cultural landscape that Faulkner himself helps to define.

I have both a very narrow and an impossibly broad interest in Faulkner's reference to slow motion in *Light in August*. Or put differently, there are some questions I can put to rest quite quickly and others that I would still leave lingering even if I had world enough and time.

What examples of cinematic slow motion could Faulkner have seen by the summer of 1932? In a terrifically illuminating essay on Faulkner "mediated time," Mark Steven argues that Faulkner's rampant use of hypotaxis—not just in the famously distended run-on sentences of *Absalom, Absalom!* (1936) or "The Bear" from *Go Down, Moses* (1942), but visible too in more syntactically straightforward moments of narrative action or description in the fourth section *The Sound and the Fury* (1929)—reflects the "determining correlation of modernist aesthetics with the regulation of time under capitalism," which he situates alongside Mary Ann Doane's crucial work on how early film captured, in this same period, everyday modern life as an ongoing dialectic of sheer contingency (violence, shock, ecstasy) and rationalism (discipline, productivity, exchange) (Steven 2015: 199).⁴ In tracing these various homologies between Faulkner and film, Steven powerfully demonstrates how literary critics drawing on the protocols and sensibilities of media studies have changed our views of Faulkner's dominant stylistic and thematic preoccupations; like other critics of Faulkner and film, Steven proves

---

³ According to Blotner, Faulkner was working on the galleys for *Light in August* in the period immediately following his father's death on August 7, 1932. Correspondence from these weeks also shows that Faulkner was continuing to write various drafts and treatments for MGM and returned to the studio in early October after spending the summer in Mississippi. This means that the final text of the novel was established over weeks and months that marked an especially intense engagement with film (Blotner 1984: 308–309).

⁴ See also Doane (2002).

that Faulkner was always already cinematic, as the saying goes. To put this in Faulkner's own equally portentous theoretical idiom from *Light in August*, we might say that his cinematic "thought" went faster than his "seeing" movies, either up close as a screenwriter in Hollywood or from the distance of a Southern spectator in Mississippi or New Orleans, or for more limited periods, as an aspiring cosmopolitan in New York or Paris (214). The point is not that Faulkner wrote "in imitation of the technological medium," but rather that his "mode of production ... articulates the media ecology as a whole" (200). And as Kawin was insisting in the 1970s, Faulkner "is the most cinematic of novelists," which means it should come as no surprise that "such techniques as montage, freeze-frame, slow motion, and visual metaphor abound in his fiction" (5). Thinking about literature and media in terms of an "ecology"—a figure first proposed by McLuhan in the early sixties—allows us to explore sensoriums and cultural systems instead of individuals and their influences. Thus, I am posing a question that is redolent of the very biographical methodologies that the Faulkner critics from which I have learned so much have moved beyond, not only to get past the considerable cult of his authority but also to indicate the ubiquity of modern media and the natural shape, so to speak, of their character as technologies that "determine our situation," to invoke a first principle of Friedrich Kittler's (1999: xxxix). I am also posing a question I can't answer since Faulkner does not allude to any films by title nor to any film-makers by name in *Light in August* (or elsewhere either, for the most part). Following Kawin, we can call Faulkner "cinematic" or suggest, as Steven does, that the "new temporalities" he constructed in his prose were analogs to "commonplace techniques such as slow motion or 'time-stretching.'" It might be interesting to know what films influenced Faulkner in particular, but more details about his influences and biography—of which his fans and readers have a lot already—might also circumscribe our thinking about media and (and in) Faulkner's novels. The question isn't so much what slow motion Faulkner could have seen by 1932 but rather why slow motion mattered to him in *Light in August* as he was contending with different histories of racial modernity and their velocities, slow, fast, and otherwise.

Still, thinking about slow motion from our present—on the other side of its proliferation in the late 'sixties and its pervasiveness in contemporary visual culture—makes it hard to remember that it was not quite so commonplace as critics and film historians assume. For us, slow motion is undoubtedly the least special effect, so familiar and pedestrian that we barely see it unless it is again rendered spectacular in *The Matrix Trilogy* (1999–2003) or *Inception* (2010); or else aestheticized beyond its generic use in high-art action films like Wong Kar-wai's *The Grandmaster* (2013) or Hou Hsiao-Hsien's *The Assassin* (2015); or so overdone that it becomes a tic for *auteurs* as tonally distinct (though linked by gender, race, and generation) as Michael Bay, Zach Snyder, and Wes Anderson. That there are literally thousands of films featuring slow motion from the early 1970s to the present—with action films and other mainstream narrative genres representing the vast majority of examples in both US and global cinema—should not obscure the fact that there are no more than thirty or so instances of slow motion as we would recognize it now across the history of narrative cinema before 1968. Reckoning with art cinema and the *avant garde* would change little here in terms of numbers, and while things would certainly look different if we were considering the vast and largely forgotten output of sports newsreels, documentary footage, and scientific film as well, the status of slow motion as a decidedly minor and vanishingly rare effect in narrative cinema for most of the medium's twentieth-century history becomes only more striking when seen in the context of its uneven distribution across the visual field. Textual evidence of changes in the typescript and galley proofs for *Light in August* provide no reason to conclude that Faulkner dramatically revised the cinematic symbolism in the book after his arrival in Hollywood. Whatever "moving picture in slow motion" Faulkner saw before the novel's publication was likely not a movie or feature at all, but rather a short of some kind or one of the sports newsreels employing slow motion to record and accentuate the physical action of boxing, horse racing, or tennis—newsreels we know existed as early as the 1920s.

This also means that "slow motion" in *Light in August* is not necessarily a nod toward "modernism" in any narrow sense of the term. Rene Clair's *Entr'acte* (1924) is one of three films employing slow motion that Siegfried Kracauer mentions in his *Theory of Film* (1960), where it is generally disparaged as an aspect of experimental or fantastic cinema that the spectator soon "recognizes … as tricks pure and simple and disparages them accordingly" (Kracauer 1997 [1960]: 88). Faulkner was in Paris just a few months after *Entr'acte* debuted, but the film was conceived and originally shown to punctuate the first and second parts of a single ballet performance and it circulated afterwards in circles which, putting it mildly, were not Faulkner's. Jean Epstein's *Fall of the House of Usher* (1928) is a technically dazzling exploration of the gothic, and its dramatic use of slow motion to materialize the increasingly disordered temporality of its protagonists would make it richly evocative as a counterpart to Faulkner's many returns to "haunted houses" and accursed bloodlines in his major fictions, *Light in August* chief among them. But it is vanishingly unlikely that he saw it, and this goes for Dziga Vertov's *Man with a Movie Camera* (1929) as well, another iconic work of modernism featuring slow motion. By the late 'thirties, Faulkner will conspicuously name-drop Sergei Eisenstein in *If I Forget Thee, Jerusalem* (1939), describing "a scene like something out of an Eisenstein Dante," but for all formal innovations and visual imagery that "Eisenstein" might be conjuring here, slow motion is one that does not figure in his films at all (Faulkner 1995 [1939]: 157). The only theatrical release before 1932 in the United States that included slow motion is a classic of sorts, but not exactly celebrated for any *avant garde* ambitions: Raoul Walsh's silent, swashbuckling epic *The Thief of Bagdad* appeared in 1924; it starred Douglas Fairbanks in the title role and, in a flashy underwater sequence, he fights a giant spider in slow motion. As perhaps the first use of slow motion in a film with designs on the mass audience, the resplendently generic *The Thief of Bagdad* could be regarded as the most "contemporary" of any of these examples since it best predicts how Hollywood will come to use slow motion in later action extravaganzas, again, literally by the thousand, where it operates as a "tamed attraction," to borrow one of Tom Gunning's signature terms for any number of aggressively self-conscious aestheticizations of display that must be displaced and contained for narrative cinema to develop in the early decades of the twentieth century (Gunning 1986). And if any of these films ever played in Oxford, Mississippi, it was this one.⁵

This sort of historical spadework brings us closer to understanding how slow motion would have signified for Faulkner in the early 'thirties: on the one hand, we see in retrospect that it already distinguished a style of modernist cinema whose reach in the United States was limited and hard to specify; on the other hand, there is a just single Hollywood example along with a largely anonymous and all but unrecoverable archive of shorts and newsreels where slow motion revealed the "optical unconscious," in Benjamin's famous phrasing, of kinetic action at speeds too great for human beings to process (Benjamin 2008: 37).⁶ We know even less about how much early film would have appeared as slow motion as an accident or within the ample margins for technological error in the years before frame rates were standardized at 24 per second (fps) over the course of the twentieth century; or before motorized cameras became widely available after 1912, which would have reduced the amount of accidental "overcranking" by camera operators whose bodies were themselves the essential mechanism for producing cinematic time—slow or fast. This is one of the reasons why, as Doane has crucially argued, film lent *"representability"* to both the cognitive vagaries of human temporal perception and the various regimes of modernity that depended on new technologies for storing, rationalizing, and commodifying time (Doane 2002: 25). For while there are some very early shorts that were purposefully shot at faster frame rates so that they would project at slower speeds, such as the Edison "Serpentine Dance" from 1894, which is also hand-tinted for added spectacle, in the hand-cranked era it is theoretically possible that half of all films would have looked like they were at least slowed down a little, with the other half accelerated at various degrees of perceptibility.

And it is back to this earliest epoch of the moving image—primitive and archaic even in 1932—that Faulkner returns us to in *Light in August*, where slow motion might technically align the novel's narrative style to the latest in special effects but only to shroud its cinematic form in a pervasive sense that we can never really know whether the history we are living through is moving fast or slow.

Light in August is a novel almost preposterously committed to pushing at the very limits of narrative speed. While critics and readers have long debated how best to map the formal and thematic connections between its multi-plotted parts and intersecting trajectories of character and symbolism, we could also reckon with the novel as an

---

⁵ The history of slow motion in early cinema remains somewhat murky and, given the loss of so many films from before the era of the major studios, it is impossible to offer a complete account of slow motion's use in this period. Many shorts and newsreels employed slow motion for sports highlights throughout the 1920s and 1930s, and catalogs of educational films highlight slow motion nature and science documentaries from these decades as well. But in fiction films produced by major studios, slow motion remained vanishingly rare in Faulkner's lifetime. Besides *The Thief of Bagdad*, there is a very subtle use of slow motion in Erich Von Stroheim's *The Merry Widow* (1925, MGM), but it is relatively fleeting—and the film was not nearly as successful at the box office, making it even less likely for Faulkner to have seen it during its theatrical release.

⁶ Originally written in 1935–1936; first published posthumously.

experiment in rhythms, temporalities, and durations. The novel's constantly shifting sense of primary focalization—from Lena Grove to Byron Bunch to Joe Christmas to Joanna Burden to Gail Hightower and back to Bunch and Lena—makes it particularly difficult to think about the events and incidents that constitute its timeline, or, in language I'm taking from Gérard Genette, "the concurrence between diegetic sequence and narrative sequence" in this flamboyantly asynchronous and anisochronous text (Genette 1980: 87). None of the novel's stories feel like they are taking place at the same time—even though they are and do at last converge in Jefferson where Lena gives birth and Joe is lynched—and there is little regularity to how the novel goes through its paces in terms of staging conversation, delivering information, or constructing character. Much the same, of course, could be said of Faulkner's manipulations of narrative time in such early masterpieces as *The Sound and the Fury* (1929), *As I Lay Dying* (1930), and *Absalom, Absalom!* (1936), and even *Sanctuary* (1931), his infamous so-called "potboiler," is often a bewildering mix of pauses and ellipses, to again invoke Genette, and is structured, like practically all his major fictions over the course of his career, around effects of analepsis (flashback) and prolepsis (flash-forward), drawing now on Mark Currie's more recent work in narratology (Currie 2007: 33–39). If, as Currie insists, "teleological retrospect" is a defining feature of narrative as such, Faulkner's somewhat late command over this temporality in *The Sound and the Fury*—he had, after all, written three novels already—effectively inaugurates his emergence as a significant figure in American and, eventually, world literature.

But *Light in August* is not just longer than any novel Faulkner had previously published but it also encompasses more time within its diegetic scope. There are traumas looming everywhere in the Compson family's history as we get glimpses of it in *The Sound and the Fury*, and Addie Bundren's devasting backstory—voiced posthumously in her section of the text—informs and recalibrates our understanding of her family's slow pilgrimage to bury her in Jefferson. When the circumstances of Joe's birth are finally revealed in Chapter 16, the momentum of the novel's plots are stopped for many pages, but the logic of the analepsis is immediately resolved when Chapter 17 cuts abruptly to the news that Lena has delivered her own miraculously conceived son, whose father may be "Brown" (Joe Brown) but is not distinguished by the ambiguous Blackness that surrounds Joe Christmas and gets him killed. Given that the events of the novel's present take place in late 1932, in the near future of the period of its composition, this extends the timeline of its story or *fabula* to the 1890s (Shklovskiĭ 1991). With the telling of Hightower's family history in Chapter 20, we are pushed back into the past another generation so that we can see how his own hesitancy to save Christmas from Percy Grimm strangely rehearses his own father's twisted allegiance to the Confederacy despite his father's antipathy to slavery itself. That the Civil War is still unfolding for Faulkner characters in the 1930s is manifestly unsurprising. The story of Joanna Burden's family—related in a long flashback in Chapter 10—locates the earliest events in the novel's chronology squarely in the antebellum period, with Calvin Bundren's wayward abolitionism, along with his son's Mexican wife, crudely prefiguring Joanna's political and sexual deviations from what is demanded of white women in the South. In a novel that turns on two brutal crimes of racial passion in 1932, it is worth remembering that the oldest murder that we read of in the text—when Joanna's grandfather kills a man "in an argument over slavery"—probably occurs sometime very late in the 1840s.

If we take this expanded timeline seriously as part of the story Faulkner tells in *Light in August*, the novel's interest in slow motion takes on a differently historical character. This isn't to say that an explicit reference to slow motion in 1932 would not have felt entirely contemporary nor that, for many readers, the reference would have evoked anything besides the media aesthetic of modern cinematic technology and style. The larger scene itself, however, summons up a stranger network of afterimages and visual echoes that are unanticipated and anachronistic, which perhaps is only fitting for a moment trying to capture every detail of Joe's frantic retardation:

> Though the horse was still going through the motion of galloping, it was not moving much faster than a man could walk. The stick too rose and fell with the same spent and terrific slowness, the youth on the horse's back leaning forward as if he did not know that the horse had flagged, or as though to left forward and onward the failing east whose slow hooves rang with a measured hollow sound through the empty and moondappled street. It—the horse and the rider—had a strange, dreamy effect, like a moving picture in slow motion as it galloped steady and flagging up the street and toward the old corner where he used to wait, less urgent perhaps but not less eager, and more young.
>
> The horse was not even trotting now, on stiff legs, its breathing deep and labored and rasping, each breath a groan. The stick still fell; as the progress of the horse slowed, the speed of the stick increased in exact ratio. But the horse slowed, sheering in to the curb. Joe pulled at its head, beating it, but it slowed into the curb and stopped, shadowdappled, its head down, trembling, its breathing almost like a human voice. Yet still the rider leaned forward in the arrested saddle, in the attitude of terrific speed, beating the horse across the rump with the stick. Save for the rise and fall of the stick and the groaning respirations of the animal, they might have been an equestrian statue strayed from its pedestal and come to rest in an attitude of ultimate exhaustion in a quiet and empty street splotched and dappled by moonshadows.
>
> (Faulkner 1990a: 210)

This passage does many things, including beautifully confirm the "media romance" that Murphet sees at work in Faulkner's major fiction, which, he argues, is never more "splotched" with the trappings of decadence and melodrama than when it actually is contending with the technologies of modern life (Murphet 2017: 15–23). For all the aura Faulkner is trying to squeeze out (or in?) here, the prose is also strikingly mechanical and programmatic. The way that the "moondappled street" is then "shadowdappled" and finally "dappled by moonshadows" feels like elegant variation produced by charmless algorithm. The horse is "flagging" because it "had flagged"; "slow" because it had "slowed." These repetitions are the opposite of artful, and we might wonder whether Faulkner himself is merely "going through the motion[s]" save for the exquisite shifts in tone and temporality that track through the sentences. This goes beyond, I think, the manipulations of narrative time that Steven powerfully explores in Faulkner's use of "hypotaxis" (Steven 2015: 205). For the densely suggestive grammar and heady symbolism here not only captures the sweep of Joe's short life so far in a distended moment of trauma that predicts its future course but also projects it onto a history of media forms, some fleetingly cinematic and some far more, well, concrete. It is telling—and scathingly ironic—that Faulkner has us picture Joe, for even a second, as a kind of Confederate monument ("an equestrian statue"). His eventual lynching, after all, is the real historical re-enactment of white power in the novel, while this image of an anachronistic statue—Oxford, Mississippi's monument was erected in 1907—invokes a form of "old media" that is as hallucinatory and virtual as any work of cinema. Joe thus arrives exhausted at "the old corner where he used to wait" when he was "more young," as if these mere split seconds on horseback have already aged him into the suffering, violent figure he will become. In this most sadomasochistic of novels, this is a moment where the abuse that Joe is delivering exists so obviously as just an instance of a much larger economy of pain that spans his childhood, adolescence, and adulthood; that lashes out at the white women whom he attacks when they do not believe he's Black; and that explodes in the exorbitant punishment of his body by the lynch mob who definitely believes he's Black enough. There are some lighter moments in *Light in August*—I'm thinking of the "who's on first" schtick of Lena getting sent to Byron Bu*n*ch when she is looking for Lucas Burch, who is living as *Joe* Brown with *Joe* Christmas—but not much that happens to Joe himself is even slightly funny, and most of what he does to others is as bleak. Which is why this wildly comic set-up isn't played for laughs, even though it is suggestive of exactly the sort of joke that silent film actor Buster Keaton, say, made so frequently from mistimed affects and various means of locomotion. If slow motion is often said to aestheticize motion as such (a somewhat tautological proposition since cinematic motion is an idealization and illusion in the first place), we do at least see here what this might mean in literary terms since every gesture in these paragraphs aims at a kind of semantic thickening of sense and sound that, when it stops at last, amounts to a lot of time spent beating an almost dead horse.

At the risk of extending an already "labored" reading of a scene that signifies duration so meticulously, it is worth pointing out that Faulkner doesn't seem to have Keaton in mind here (unlike moments of deadpan action in *As I Lay Dying*) nor any of the modernist landmarks of slow motion from the 1920s that he likely hadn't seen. If there is any cinematic intertext for the slow motion we see in *Light in August*, it is not a film like *What Price Hollywood?* or, from Paramount later in 1932, Mamoulian's *Love Me Tonight*, which even features some horses floating in slow motion—a "strange, dreamy effect" that looks a lot like the famous procession scene in Clair's *Entr'acte* but with Maurice Chevalier instead employing it to woo Jeanette MacDonald. But, as I said before, the timing isn't right for us to see these films as influences on Faulkner, though the coincidence would give this chapter a real Hollywood ending I could prove otherwise. There is, I think, another motion picture haunting this allusion to slow motion—again, arguably the first in US fiction—and it is not to one of the latest features Faulkner might have come across in Hollywood but rather to the most archaic of their ancestors: Eadweard Muybridge's 1878 photographic sequence of "The Horse in Motion," which he adapted for the presentations of his zoopraxiscope as early as 1879 (Figure 8.2). The resemblance is only circumstantial, but compelling, with Joe frozen in the "motion of galloping" on a horse that barely walks. His "attitude of terrific speed" is simultaneously ludicrous and monumental, and though Joe is never going to find himself immortalized on any "equestrian statue" in a Mississippi town in 1910 or so, it is the case—however harrowing and grisly—that his own violently stilled body will prove a public spectacle when he is lynched and mutilated by Percy Grimm. Joe's body will eventually be made into a monument to white supremacy but not in the nostalgic form of a Confederate statue that can obscure its shallow provenance as a Jim Crow instrument of power in the ponderousness of granite, bronze, or marble. Joe dies in a frenzy of impossibly overburdened images that must bear more symbolism and time than they can sustain even as they become indelible. "The pent black blood seemed to rush like a released breath," Faulkner writes, "It seemed to rush out of his pale body like the rush of sparks from a rising rocket; upon the black blast the man seemed to rise soaring into their memories forever" (1990a: 465). The violence itself is mercifully brief considering the lengths to which we know Faulkner can protract things when he feels like it. But in the last seconds of Joe's short and brutal life, we get more metaphor and euphemism than photorealist precision. We should be glad that this is something Faulkner tells and doesn't show.

I have been pursuing a single reference in *Light in August* to understand better what alluding to "a moving picture in slow motion" might have meant to Faulkner and his readers in 1932. Though the aesthetic of slow motion has a suggestive provenance in

FIGURE 8.2 Eadweard Muybridge from *The Horse in Motion* (1878). Library of Congress Prints and Photographs Division Washington, D.C.

the modernist *avant garde*, and was emerging, very slowly indeed, as a special effect in Hollywood, its first explicit appearance in his fiction seems less a gesture of presentism or contemporaneity and more a phantasmatic excavation of the cinematic past at its most primordial, a gesture, in other words, of what we would now call media archaeology. Most closely associated with European figures such as Wolfgang Ernst, Siegfried Zielinski, Jussi Parikka, and Erkki Huhtamo but encompassing work by John Durham Peters and Jonathan Sterne as well, media archaeology argues against the implicitly progressive temporalities that shape traditional histories of technology—innovation begetting innovation, accelerating to a future of abundance or apocalypse or both—and seeks to discover instead the sedimented layers of alternative and obsolete technologies, and our experiences of them, that also shape the present and its potential futures.[7] Zielinski proposes that we pay closer attention to the "deep time of the media," which spans back to at least the early Renaissance in his critical formulations, if not further to the ancient Mediterranean, East Asian, and Islamic worlds. As an appropriation of timescales from geology and evolutionary science, even this expanded field of media history would leave us in the shallows of deep time, and so Parikka suggests that we think harder about the relays between the extraction of natural resources and the media we make from them over the millennia as "metals and chemicals get deterritorialized from their strata and reterritorialized in machines that define our technical media culture" (Parikka 2015: 35). We could, for example, trace the history of film in *Light in August* in even slower motion by starting with the ruins of the lumber industry that Lena notices on her magnificently slow walk to Jefferson in the opening chapter of the novel. Though barely older than she is, much of the machinery already seems like relics from a lost world and economy: "gaunt, staring, motionless wheels rising from mounds of brick rubble and ragged weeds with a quality profoundly astonishing" (Faulkner 1990a: 4). The speed of northern Mississippi's deforestation over the turn of the twentieth century means that the slow processes of decay have become a symbol for the accelerating turnover times of fixed capital itself. And the vanishing ancestral forests that Lena is too young to have known—but which form the racial masculinity of some boys and men in Faulkner's fiction—have perhaps provided some infinitesimal fraction of the cellulose that goes into the film stock that materially makes slow motion visible as a media aesthetic of modernism's epoch. I admit that this is dubious and far too literal as an experiment in media ecology. But, at the very least, it might help us grasp some of the more measured and imperceptible cycles of modernity that his novels track. Slow motion is at once an index to Faulkner's growing awareness of what "contemporary" film was in 1932 and also an historical icon of a modern world that doesn't go quite as fast as we might think. Both the invention of cinema and the failure of Reconstruction, to put it plainly, predate Faulkner by a couple decades. Muybridge's breakthroughs in motion photography are older than William Clark Falkner's creaky melodrama *The White Rose of Memphis* (1881), which would remain the most celebrated literary output of the Fa(u)

---

[7] See, e.g. Ernst (2016), Zielinski (2006), and Sterne (2012).

lkner family until after the Second World War. It turns out the past of media isn't even past either.

Media archaeology might only bring a metaphorical sense of deep time and its unfathomably slow velocities to our present, but even this is worth embracing as a corrective to the assumption that modernity—as enshrined in modernist iconographies of speed and acceleration—goes only and forever fast. "Temporalization and acceleration," notes Reinhart Koselleck, "constitute the temporal framework that will probably have to be applied to all concepts of modern social history" (Koselleck 2002: 121). Koselleck is observing changes at the highest levels of abstraction but still is giving voice to a commonplace about the period that spans the the various timelines of Faulkner's fiction—and, of course, our own lives in the twenty-first century. The modernity that has been experienced since "the advent of technology and industry" is, as Koselleck elsewhere writes, a "now temporality" that absorbs and transvalues different ways of thinking about the past into a more rationalized view that "the acceleration of time is a human task" (Koselleck 2002: 121; 2004: 13) Since the Enlightenment, in his particular version of a story that has taken many forms before, the "denaturalization of historical temporalities" patterns the rise of capitalism and the disenchantment of a lifeworld where seemingly everything that happens is the product of "coefficients of motion and acceleration" that are calculable in the "minimal temporalities" that define societies that are "increasingly technical in nature" (Koselleck 2004: 96, 103). I am drawing mostly on the work of Koselleck, but we could find similar claims that the "modern"—whatever it also is, whenever it may have started—is axiomatically bound to speed, velocity, and acceleration across the social textures of everyday life, the economic imperatives of capitalism, and the aesthetic articulations of modernism as a network of stylistic features. This is not to overlook a growing body of criticism and social theory devoted to forms of slowness that might be genuinely more resistant and politically useful than the many popular "slow" movements (slow food, slow fashion, slow sex) whose blindnesses about, and capitulations to, the larger systems that push speed upon us—even when things seem stuck or paused—have been well documented.[8] What we need, as Sarah Sharma notes, are more searching accounts of "differential time" and to the "micropolitics of temporal coordination and social control between multiple temporalities"; otherwise, she fears that "subject of value in the critique of speed ends up being the same subject who will confirm speedup most readily as *the* reality," which on the ground means a narrow focus on the dilemmas facing Western consumers trying to maximize their precious time amidst the escalating options that their class and racial privileges make possible (Sharma 2014: 7).

Closer to the contours of modernity in Faulkner, it is increasingly clear that many of the formal innovations he pursued in representing time and temporality with such dazzling complexity display the mix of intimacy and ignorance he brought to his

---

[8] For more on politics and aesthetics of contemporary "slow" movements, see Koepnick (2014), Rosa and Wagner (2019), Rosa (2013).

depictions of Black life "in the wake," to borrow from Christina Sharpe (2016). Sharpe's meditations on racial being are too rich to summarize in full, but she calls attention to the radically disparate temporalities to which Black subjects were exposed by New World slavery and its ongoing afterlife. At one extreme, the brutal contingencies of Black existence outside the bounds of legal personhood meant that white acts of violence could come with startling speed and shocking suddenness; but, as Sharpe argues, this historical accumulation of death also makes Black writers and artists especially attuned to the longer timelines that are shaped by the almost invisible remains of slavery, both material and psychic. In a brilliant reading of NourbeSe Philip's *Zong!*, Sharpe suggests that ultimately it might be impossible to outlive a past that—when measured in the aeons over which the very chemical substance of the ocean will contain traces of Black bodies—has a "residence time of 260 million years" (Sharpe 2016: 41). This is a historical process far too slow for human beings meaningfully to observe, despite the fact it is one we put in motion.

"Faulkner has laid hold of a frozen speed at the very heart of things," writes Jean-Paul Sartre, "he is grazed by congealed spurts that wane and dwindle without moving" (1955: 81) It would be an overstatement to say that Faulkner's monumental reputation as a novelist proceeds from Sartre's famous reflections on his capacity to comprehend slow motion. But it is still true that many of Faulkner's best critics remain intensely focused on what Sartre termed his "metaphysics of time," which, as we have seen, must necessarily address questions concerning technology, race, and economics too. Sartre's eminence rubs off on Faulkner and speeds his belated rise to global prominence, despite the fact that Sartre doesn't really know what time (it) is. As Sartre admits, "I like his art, but I do not believe in his metaphysics" (Sartre 1955: 84). For me, the image of "congealed spurts" is enough to tip Sartre's hand, given the altogether phobic fluid dynamics that bring his magnum opus, *Being and Nothingness* (1943), to an awkward, gooey end. Sartre hates slime: "its fluidity exists in slow motion"; "it is the agony of water"; it is like "a retarded annihilation"; it is "foundationless," "*degraded*," and embodies how "the invisible suction of the past" assists in the "slow dissolution" of consciousness at the very moment it projects itself into a world of action (Sartre 1956: 776–779). Slow motion is neither a cinematic form nor a way of figuring the "micropolitics" or "multiple temporalities" we live in now. For Sartre, and at times in Faulkner, slow motion signifies a goopy mess of abject qualities and identities. We need only think about Quentin Compson in *The Sound and Fury*, deep in the "*hogwallow the mud yellowed up to [his] waist*," or obsessing over the "liquid putrefaction" of semen, blood, and shit to see how Faulkner might have inspired and reinforced Sartre's disgust about this particular slow-motion materiality (Faulkner 1990b: 128, 136). Or, if you have the stomach for it, recall the entire tube of toothpaste Joe eats as a child—"the pink worm coil smooth and cool and slow"—which he then vomits onto the orphanage dietitian whose sexual encounter he witnesses as an unknowing voyeur (122). Faulkner makes us wait for the fully bodily eruption. Joe is trapped, "motionless now, utterly contemplative, he seemed to stoop above himself like a chemist in his laboratory, waiting" (122). On the other side of these eternal microseconds, a critical transformation will have taken place, with Joe immediately declared a "little n--- bastard" (emphasis mine, 122). This experiment in slow-motion horror takes almost no time to produce results yet could just as easily be said to run for the duration of Joe's life.

But I don't want to give Sartre's wretched view of Faulkner in slow motion the last word on what we might learn about the ways his fiction explores how time exists as mediated by technologies, subjectivities, and race. At almost the very moment Sartre was wallowing in the turgid viscosity of a past that flows too slowly toward the future, Fernand Braudel was preparing the materials that would become *The Mediterranean and the Mediterranean World in the Age of Philip II* (first published in 1949 as *La Méditerranée à l'Epoque de Philippe II*). This book would popularize the *Annales* school of history and introduce the concept of the *longue durée* as a fundamental unit of analysis and thought that functions "on the basis of an infrastructure," obscured at every instant by "all the thousands of explosions of historical time [that] can be understood on the basis of these depths, this semistillness" (Braudel 1980: 33). It is tempting to get swept up (or is it down?) in Braudel's rhapsodies about the *longue durée* and more appealing to think that history is always moving, even when it feels like muck and mire. There are also limits to the usefulness of the *longue durée* as a conceptual frame and reasons to worry whenever it gets invoked in images of redemptive suffering or consolation. That said, Braudel helps us see Faulkner's preoccupation with slow motion—figural, literal, and cinematic—not as an aesthetic or romanticization of timelessness as an ideal but rather as an effect of "differential time" and the modernity that produces it. Unlike Sartre, for whom Faulkner emblematizes the slimy revulsions of "motionless movement" ("*de movement immobile*"), we might look instead to Braudel's commitment to "a history in slow motion" ("*une historie au ralenti*"), which borrows its language directly from the world of film, at least in part, to help remind us that our image of the past is an experience of temporality and chronology at every turn (Braudel 1992: 1). Faulkner's last reference to slow motion occurs in his second-to-last novel, 1959's *The Mansion*, and it offers his version of this history lesson in the less bracing, but no less difficult, language of his late phase. As V. K. Ratliff thinks about how long it might take Linda Kohl (*née* Snopes) to work her vengeance on her father, Flem, through the interminable machinations of her much older cousin Mink, he realizes that even when Flem's cold predation and capitalist ferocity have seemed permanent and unyielding, things he cannot see are moving toward a different end, "slowed down by the camera trick but still motion, still a moment, irrevocable" (Faulkner 1994: 855). The sentiment is broader and, for some readers, less convincing than Faulkner's earlier fiction, when his narratives felt more, in a word, fluid and moved more easily from registers of abstract historical reflection and intricate descriptions of distended action. But from another angle, in a longer view, perhaps, the relentless consistency of Faulkner's project appears enduringly remarkable in novel after novel, detailing, as he writes in *Go Down, Moses,* both the "slow amortization" and "specific tragedy" of racial capitalism (Faulkner 1990c: 254). This is much that Faulkner couldn't and wouldn't see about this history and good reason to wish he personally would have been willing to go faster. But we must also be ready to look hard at what slowed him down.

References

Benjamin, Walter. 2008. "The Work of Art in the Age of Its Technological Reproducibility [Second Version]," in Michael W. Jennings, Brigid Doherty, and Thomas Y. Levin, eds, *The Work of Art in the Age of Its Technological Reproducibility, and Other Writings on Media*, trans. Edmund Jephcott, Rodney Livingstone et al. (Cambridge, MA: The Belknap Press of Harvard University).

Blotner, Joseph. 1984. *Faulkner: A Biography*. One-Volume ed., 1st edn (Random House).

Braudel, Fernand. 1980. *On History*, trans. Sarah Matthews (Chicago, IL: University of Chicago Press).

Braudel, Fernand. 1992. *The Mediterranean and the Mediterranean World in the Age of Philip II*, trans. Siân Reynolds (New York: HarperCollins).

Currie, Mark. 2007. *About Time: Narrative, Fiction and the Philosophy of Time* (Edinburgh: Edinburgh University Press).

Doane, Mary Ann. 2002. *The Emergence of Cinematic Time: Modernity, Contingency, the Archive* (Cambridge, MA: Harvard University Press).

Ernst, Wolfgang. 2016. *Chronopoetics: The Temporal Being and Operativity of Technological Media*, trans. Anthony Enns (London: Rowan & Littlefield International).

Faulkner, William. 1990a. *Light in August* (New York: Vintage Books).

Faulkner, William. 1990b. *The Sound and the Fury* (New York: Vintage Books).

Faulkner, William. 1990c. *Go Down, Moses* (New York: Vintage Books).

Faulkner, William. 1994. *Snopes: The Hamlet, The Town, The Mansion* (New York: The Modern Library).

Faulkner, William. 1995 [1939]. *The Wild Palms [If I Forgett Thee, Jerusalem]* (New York: Vintage Books).

Genette, Gérard. 1980. *Narrative Discourse: An Essay in Method*, trans. Jane E. Lewin (Ithaca, NY: Cornell University Press).

Gleeson-White, Sarah. 2015. "Faulkner Goes to Hollywood," in John T. Matthews, ed., *William Faulkner in Context* (New York: Cambridge University Press), 194–203.

Gleeson-White, Sarah. 2017. *William Faulkner at Twentieth Century-Fox: The Annotated Screenplays* (Oxford: Oxford University Press).

Gunning, Tom. 1986. "The Cinema of Attractions: Early Film, Its Spectator, and the Avant-Garde," *Wide Angle* 8:3–4: 63–70.

Kawin, Bruce F. 1977. *Faulkner and Film* (New York: Frederick Ungar Publishing Co.).

Kittler, F. A. 1999. *Gramophone, Film, Typewriter* (Stanford, CA: Stanford University Press).

Koepnick, Lutz P. 2014. *On Slowness: Toward an Aesthetic of the Contemporary* (New York: Columbia University Press).

Koselleck, Reinhart. 2002. *The Practice of Conceptual History*, trans. Todd Samuel Presner et al. (Stanford, CA: Stanford University Press).

Koselleck, Reinhart. 2004. *Futures Past: On the Semantics of Historical Time*, trans. Keith Tribe (New York: Columbia University Press).

Koselleck, Reinhart. 2018. *Sediments of Time: On Possible Histories*, trans. Sean Franzel and Stefan-Ludwig Hommann (Stanford, CA: Stanford University Press).

Kracauer, Siegfried. 1997 [1960]. *Theory of Film: The Redemption of Physical Reality* (Princeton, NJ: Princeton University Press).

Lurie, Peter. 2004. *Vision's Immanence: Faulkner, Film, and the Popular Imagination* (Baltimore, MD: Johns Hopkins University Press).

Lurie, Peter and A. J Abadie. 2014. *Faulkner and Film* (Jackson, MS: University Press of Mississippi).

Murphet, Julian and Stefan Solomon, eds. 2015. *William Faulkner in the Media Ecology* (Baton Rouge, LA: Louisiana State University Press).

Murphet, Julian. 2017. *Faulkner's Media Romance* (New York: Oxford University Press).

Parikka, Jussi. 2015. *A Geology of Media* (Minneapolis, MN: University of Minnesota Press).

Rosa, Hartmut. 2013. *Social Acceleration: A New Theory of Modernity*, trans. Jonathan Trejo-Mathys (New York: Columbia University Press).

Rosa, Hartmut and James C. Wagner. 2019. *Resonance, A Sociology of Our Relationship to the World*, English edn (Cambridge: Polity Press).

Sartre, Jean-Paul. 1955. "'On the Sound and the Fury': Time in the Work of Faulkner," in *Literary and Philosophical Essays*, trans. Annette Michelson (London: Rider).

Sartre, Jean-Paul. 1956. *Being and Nothingness: A Phenomenological Essay on Ontology*, trans. Hazel E. Barnes (New York: Washington Square Press).

Sharma, Sarah. 2014. *In the Meantime: Temporality and Cultural Politics* (Durham, NC: Duke University Press).

Sharpe, Christina. 2016. *In the Wake: On Blackness and Being* (Durham, NC: Duke University Press).

Shklovskiĭ, Viktor. 1991. "Art as Device," in *Theory of Prose*, trans. Benjamin Sher, Russian Literature Series (Elmwood Park, IL: Dalkey Archive Press), 2–14.

Sterne, Jonathan. 2012. *MP3: The Meaning of a Format* (Durham, NC: Duke University Press).

Steven, Mark. 2015. "William Faulkner's Mediated Time: Capitalism, Cinema, Syntax," in Julian Murphet and Stefan Solomon, eds. *William Faulkner in the Media Ecology* (Baton Rouge, LA: Louisiana State University Press), 195–216.

Watson, Jay. 2019. *William Faulkner and the Faces of Modernity*, 1st edn (Oxford: Oxford University Press).

Zielinski, Siegfried. 2006. *Deep Time of the Media: Toward an Archaeology of Hearing and Seeing by Technical Means* (Cambridge, MA: MIT Press).

CHAPTER 9

TWENTIETH-CENTURY WESTERN MAN OF COLOR
Richard Wright, Race, and Rootlessness

YOGITA GOYAL

In June 2020, George Floyd's family appealed to the United Nations Human Rights Council to set up an international probe investigating the killing of unarmed Black people in the United States. Philonise Floyd, brother of the man whose recorded death at the hands of a police officer kneeling on his neck for more than eight minutes on May 25th sparked an uprising against police violence and pervasive racist discrimination, made a powerful appeal to the United Nations (UN):

> You watched my brother die. That could have been me. I am my brother's keeper. You in the United Nations are your brothers' and sisters' keepers in America, and you have the power to help us get justice for my brother George Floyd. I am asking you to help him. I am asking you to help me. I am asking you to help us. Black people in America.
>
> (Dickinson 2020)

Here, Floyd invokes a biblical antecedent to appeal to the UN—a clear acknowledgement that the nation has failed to protect its citizens. That the Council's African Group of nations called for this Urgent Debate on racism, in the name of "recurring violations of human rights against people of African heritage" further underscores the limits of the nation state as a container for political subjectivities but also points to the complicated nature of race across the Black diaspora. For Floyd, his brother's killing testified to the unfitness of US democracy and required outside intervention. The UN committee asked the United States to accede to the principles outlined in the International Convention on the Elimination of All Forms of Racial Discrimination, which the nation had ratified in 1994. Along similar lines, in 2014, Michael Brown's parents had testified before the United Nations Committee against Torture in Geneva, marking the same need for racial justice from an entity outside the nation state but alas all too powerless to curb the excesses of the world's only superpower. While the twenty-first century has brought global awareness of the enormity of anti-Black racism and pervasive white supremacy in the United States, we still lack a full accounting of the long history across the twentieth century of volatile moments of racial crisis that could only be understood by reaching across the nation's borders to an elsewhere.

Such testimonies recall most vividly Malcolm X's famous distinction between a focus on civil rights and the demand for a more capacious and unyielding conception of human rights in "The Ballot or the Bullet," a speech delivered on April 3, 1964 in Cleveland, Ohio. Civil rights encapsulate the goals of justice and equal rights, rolling back segregation, providing equal opportunity, voting rights, and ending discrimination in education, housing, and employment to make possible full inclusion of the Black citizen within the national polity. In contrast, human rights directly challenge US exceptionalism, entangling the question of racial discrimination with the systemic forces of colonialism, capitalism, and communism. Malcolm X's forceful rejection of any notion of asking for inclusion—"I don't see any American dream; I see an American nightmare," he thunders—evinces a sophisticated understanding of what globalizing the demand for racial justice can do in terms of expanding collectivities and reframing provincialism. Malcolm X argues that being beholden to civil rights continues the project of "asking Uncle Sam to treat you right," whereas "human rights are something you were born with. Human rights are your God-given rights. Human rights are the rights that are recognized by all nations of this earth. And any time any one violates your human rights, you can take them to the world court." Here, Malcolm X invokes inalienable rights as a birthright, divinely sanctioned, and certified by a world community of nations. This is why he counsels

> Expand the civil-rights struggle to the level of human rights. Take it into the United Nations, where our African brothers can throw their weight on our side, where our Asian brothers can throw their weight on our side, where our Latin-American brothers can throw their weight on our side, and where 800 million Chinamen are sitting there waiting to throw their weight on our side.
>
> (Malcolm X 1965)

Daring to imagine that what we now call the Global South would come to the aid of African Americans, Malcolm X also suggests that the definition of who is a minority and who is a majority changes when we alter our scope of vision. His notion of human rights is thus firmly tied to the articulation of Third World solidarities, which, he hopes, may provide alternatives to imperial and racial domination.

The idea of "800 million Chinamen" coming to the aid of battling US minorities might seem whimsical or far-fetched today, precisely because the subsequent trajectory of the twentieth century led to very different outcomes following the global ferment of the 1960s. Civil rights achievements gathered force in the United States even as the always limited power of the UN to enforce any meaningful change was whittled down over the decades as the Cold War simmered and the destinies of the decolonized nations continued to be tied to First World agendas. And since the end of the Cold War, it remains difficult to imagine any kind of Third World counterweight to seemingly unchallenged US hegemony in world affairs. Returning to such prior efforts to expand the question of justice for African Americans in a global frame allows us to connect the full demand for human rights—including economic rights—with a darker world arrayed in solidarity against colonial and capitalist power. W.E.B. Du Bois imagined precisely this coalition in his 1928 novel, *Dark Princess*, prefiguring the later Afro–Asian solidarities to come (Du Bois 1995). To do so is neither to ask for nostalgia nor to beckon to utopian longings but to assess more clearly the paths not taken, the intertwined histories that have been forgotten, and help make visible possible alternatives to current impasses.

In this chapter, taking Richard Wright as my case study, I hope to show how centering questions of locality and movement stretches and reshapes conventional understandings of the African American literary canon, reframing the relation between race and global politics. I focus on *The Color Curtain: A Report on the Bandung Conference* (1956) to draw out a method of reading for transnationalism as a widening of our critical horizons about race, transnational geopolitics, and their relation to political possibility. Why was the decolonization of Africa and Asia such a galvanizing moment for African Americans in the middle of the twentieth century and how might we now assess the complicated relations between anti-colonial nationalism and anti-racist struggles in the United States? Because racialization takes place within and across national boundaries, exploring events like the historic 1955 Bandung conference from Wright's perspective further allows for a consideration of multiply affiliated subjectivities and potential alliances of subordinated populations outside the frame of the nation state. It also enables a fuller look at Wright's changing conceptions of race as he reckons with the impact of colonialism and decolonization in Africa and Asia, formulating a new humanism based on a foundation of rootlessness for all. I first show how Wright's assessment of the promise of Bandung yields necessary lessons for global anti-racist struggles today. I then consider how his unflinching commitment to Western modernity limits his ability to forge true Third World alliances even as he needs the detour through Asia and Africa to understand his own location in the West. Finally, I return to Wright's *Native Son* in light of *The Color Curtain* and close with some speculations on what his notions of race and rootlessness might contribute to our current political moment.

Assembling such critical histories of Wright's rootlessness is especially crucial because efforts to internationalize the struggle against anti-Black racism in the United States punctuate the twentieth century, bookended by the failure of Reconstruction at the dawn of the century and the tragic revelation of the incomplete progress of full inclusion and civic equality signaled by Hurricane Katrina. The famous image of Milvertha Hendricks, an elderly Black woman displaced by Hurricane Katrina wrapped in the American flag, crystallizes the tragic irony of African American struggles to achieve full citizenship in the post-segregation era. Notwithstanding common national narratives of public memory, the history of civil rights achievements demonstrates not the inevitable march of progress but the jagged grooves of history—the uncertain march forward, the retreat, the regrouping, the repetition of the demand for full humanity. To more fully fathom the weight of Floyd's appeal to the UN (as well as its likely impossibility) and what it says about the past, present, and future of racial citizenship in the United States, it is necessary to recall the history of such efforts to shift from the national frame of civil rights to the global context of human rights. Doing so also requires not simply highlighting obscured moments of global connection but reflecting on how a transnational rather than a domestic arena elucidates the varied alliances, cross-fertilizations, and solidarities too often dismissed as fanciful or feeble. Remembering these fuller histories of Black internationalism accentuates how the very notions of freedom, equality, and human rights were constituted via detours through (presumably) alien contexts. Because Black political aspirations have always overflowed the boundaries of the nation, the history of Black internationalism remains a vital resource for American literary study, not least because most of the highly cherished writers in the tradition—from Frederick Douglass to Zora Neale Hurston, Langston Hughes to Alice Walker, Amiri Baraka to Suzan-Lori Parks—have funneled their aesthetic and intellectual concerns through explorations of home and belonging, migration and displacement. Black citizenship has been made and unmade numerous times since the Fourteenth Amendment and remains an unfulfilled dream.

To understand moments of crisis when domestic failure can only be repaired by turning to the global, we may, for instance, call on Sutton Griggs's impassioned despair in *Imperium in Imperio* (1899) anticipating Marcus Garvey's militant Black nationalism, dreaming of race wars and planning insurrections against the US government as Griggs grappled with the dying embers of hope during the nadir of African American history (Griggs 1969). We might trace the history of Liberia as a nation, from its founding amid a strange array of desires at once about colonization and fear of Black rebellion, and consider George Schuyler's *Slaves Today: A Story of Liberia* (1931) warning about Americo–Liberian colonization of the natives rather than an instantiation of Black self-determination (Schuyler 1931). We could further pinpoint the promise aroused by Kwame Nkrumah's rise to power in independent Ghana, serving as a beacon to African American hopes for their own emancipation. In accounts as varied as Richard Wright's *Black Power* (1954), Maya Angelou's *All God's Children Need Traveling Shoes* (1986), Eslanda Goode Robeson's *African Journey* (1945), and Era Bell Thompson's *Africa: Land of My Fathers* (1954), we could trace the vivid contradictions of diasporic longing and nationalist romance. And perhaps, above all, we could turn to the magisterial presence of W.E.B. Du Bois, who interwove the history and destiny of Black folk in America with the masses of darker people across the world in such works as *Darkwater* (1920), *Dusk of Dawn* (1940), and *The World and Africa* (1947). The Spanish Civil War, the invasion of Ethiopia, and the transformative upheavals wrought by the Second World War all became flashpoints for an interrogation of the meaning of freedom and tested the limits of territoriality as a container for Black political collectivities.[1] And the intellectual

---

[1] Foundational studies of Black internationalism in this era include Baldwin (2002), Meriwether (2002), Plummer (1996), and Young (2006).

contours of such writers as James Baldwin, Audre Lorde, Claude McKay, Paul Robeson, Caryl Phillips, Paule Marshall, and Edwidge Danticat are unthinkable without a consideration of their varied transnational wanderings and imagined geographies. Yet the most canonizing documents of American literary history refuse to reckon with the true scope and power of such internationalism or to illuminate the questions at the center of the canon through such global horizons. Richard Wright's prodigious output of fiction and non-fiction after his "voluntary exile" from Jim Crow America, for instance, continues to be regarded as somehow less authentic and less valuable than his works set in Mississippi and Chicago, routinely taught in high schools and colleges across the nation. While Irving Howe rightly resorted to hyperbole describing the explosive impact of *Native Son* (the day it was published, American culture changed forever), many of Wright's books from the 1950s—*Black Power: A Record of Reactions in a Land of Pathos* (1954), *The Color Curtain: A Report on the Bandung Conference* (1956), *White Man, Listen!* (1957), and *Pagan Spain* (1957)—remained out of print until recently and only rarely make an appearance in the American classroom. In other words, even as arguing for the value of Wright's internationalism is not novel today, a deep reckoning with the specificity of his concerns still remains missing.

In a 1950 letter to the first Prime Minister of independent India, Jawaharlal Nehru, Wright outlined his growing realization of the entwined fate of minorities such as himself and the populations of decolonizing African and Asian nations. Wright maintained that

> the changing physical structure of the world as well as the historical development of modern society demand that the peoples of the world become aware of their common identity and interests. The situation of oppressed people the world over is universally the same and their solidarity is essential, not only in opposing oppression but also in fighting for human progress.
>
> (Fabre 1993: 387)

As Wright's biographer Michel Fabre notes, racism in the Jim Crow American South had become increasingly linked in some complicated way for Wright to the "problem of freedom in the Western world, the problem of Africa and Asia" (Fabre 1993: 364). In going to attend the Bandung Conference in 1955, the historic occasion where twenty-nine African and Asian nations representing two-thirds of the world's population met to discuss their affinities and common goals in a polarized world, Wright was testing the value of his theories about modernity and tradition, race and religion, and groping toward a new conception of humanism distinct from national, ethnic, or racial anchors.

While the idea of decline in creative power and racial authenticity in Wright's travel writings has formed a critical consensus since the 1950s, two recent arguments defending the value of these later writings seek to reverse such longstanding laments about his departure from the United States. For Paul Gilroy and Cedric Robinson, such assessments fall short of recognizing the value of Wright's later writings, which in fact help broaden our understanding of the larger intellectual tradition of African American letters. Gilroy thus annexes Wright to an "anti-essentialist conception of racial identity" embodied by Black Atlantic roaming intellectuals, who search for meaning outside of racialist and nationalist confines (Gilroy 1993: 149). Focusing on *The Outsider, The Long Dream*, and *Eight Men*, Gilroy draws out Wright's relation to Europe to rescue him from the charge of abandoning the Black and Southern American vernacular. Instead, Gilroy calls attention to the "double vision" Wright develops as an expatriate, shifting from a "literary realism defined by race" to "a metaphysics of modernity" hostile to "racial particularity" (Gilroy 1993: 161, 164). While such a rethinking of Wright's later writings usefully develops an appreciation of Wright's philosophical concerns, in sidestepping his African and Asian writings about decolonization, Gilroy misses a chance to fully grapple with Wright's efforts to interweave American Blackness with the fate of decolonizing nations, downplaying as well Wright's ongoing fascination with the power of anti-colonial nationalism.

Robinson offers a different understanding of Wright's later years, situating him as the apotheosis of the Black radical tradition. Emphasizing the attacks on Wright during this period from American leftists, liberals, and government agents, Robinson underscores the risks faced when criticizing US foreign policy in the Third World. Reading Wright's novels as social theory, Robinson explores the efforts to theorize African Americans as world proletariat and reads *The Outsider* as a critique of messianic narratives of Christianity and Western Marxism. Despite the official departure from the Communist Party, Robinson argues for Wright's long-lasting interest in class as an analytic for understanding revolutionary potential across the globe (Robinson 2000).

Drawing from both these compelling re-readings but focusing squarely on Wright's relationship to the Third World (rather than to Western Marxism and Europe, as Gilroy and Robinson do), I want to situate *The Color Curtain* (1956) at the center of Wright's exploration of race and revolution at the historical conjuncture of the end of empire and the devastation of the Second World War.[2] Of course, such critical judgments are inevitably about what a Black writer is allowed to say and do, both then and now, and the critical discomfort with watching a "Black Boy," a "Native Son" transform himself into a voluntary exile and global rootless intellectual, speaking as a self-styled "Twentieth Century Western Man of Color" (Wright 2008). It is worth recalling that Wright was the first African American writer who was a major figure in world literature, routinely referred to as the most famous Black writer in the world during his travels in Africa, Spain, Asia, Central and South America. Born in Mississippi in 1908, his journey from the Deep South to the South Side of Chicago, to Paris after the Second World War, and his coming of age during the Depression and subsequent involvement with the Communist Party all prepared him for his ensuing Third Worldism. His Parisian sojourn brought him into frequent contact with Pan-African thinkers (via his contributions to Alioune Diop's journal *Présence Africaine*, for example) as he developed his ideas about the meaning of

---

[2] This historical conjuncture is also, of course, the moment when conceptions of human rights begin to be codified, mostly from the experience of Jewish refugees fleeing Nazi Germany.

race in dialogue with such diaspora intellectuals as Aimé Césaire and Leopold Senghor. Famously describing himself as an outsider and a rootless man at a historical moment when these rubrics did not have the currency they now hold, Wright's life and work prefigure the central conundrums of the twentieth century, from country to city, from the domestic to the global, while exploring the competing pulls of cosmopolitanism and communism and seeking a way around the draconian surveillance of the US state even in exile.

A quick reading of *The Color Curtain* actually bears out the common notion of a drop-off in Wright's artistic and political vision. There is more than enough evidence of a closed mind, prone to adjusting events and conversations to pre-conceived theses about race and religion. The book reveals the limits of the self-styled American observer, the man of the West, seeking to measure the limits of his identification with Asians and Africans from the Third World. But I want to suggest that the book is exemplary for us to determine the limits and possibilities of transnational literary method precisely because it captures so many contradictions about race and coloniality and the ways in which the two do not map on to each other seamlessly. Wright's account gives us a window into American empire described by a racial minority—an uneven mix of hegemony and privilege, persecution and vulnerability, the stunted vision of imperial eyes and the unrelenting hope for a decolonial utopia. As Robinson urges, it also enjoins upon us the need to read outside structures of identification or individual racial injury and instead with an eye to Wright's analysis of racism as part of the same world system that created colonialism and was dividing the world into blocs for the Cold War to come.

To do so, Wright was searching for a method, actively giving it creative shape without pre-existing models, inventing new styles of writing—the genres of Black Atlantic travel writing, postcolonial ethnography, or cosmopolitan flânerie—all of which gain currency long after Wright's experiments with them. How we read *The Color Curtain* now thus tells us something about the American century, the search for dominance in the wake of European empires, and US efforts to manage the circulation of race in a global frame. The Second World War had exposed the irony and incoherence of fighting fascism abroad while maintaining Jim Crow at home, and the United States could no longer afford to gloss over such contradictions in an era when self-determination and racial justice were being adopted as goals by the worldwide community of nations. Further, what we now remember and forget about Bandung and the promise of Third Worldism, the tradition of Black internationalism, and solidarities that are not subsumed by nation states will ultimately determine our ability to imagine alternatives to the dispiriting present. And while recovering the memory of these forgotten alliances is key, even more useful is to reckon with efforts like Wright's that do not issue a straightforward appeal to solidarity but propose more searching explorations of the meaning of race and place, rights and belonging.

If there was such a thing as an archive of Bandung literature, *The Color Curtain* would occupy pride of place in that canon. Wright offers a serious engagement with Bandung, where his misreadings are ultimately as illuminating as his insights. He opens the book with a deceptively casual moment—reading the evening newspaper's account of the coming Bandung conference, which electrifies him, as a "kind of judgment upon that Western world" which had dominated the "despised, the insulted, the hurt, the dispossessed" of the human race (Wright 2008: 12). He decides at once that this meeting was about the power of the forces of race and religion and that he must attend: "I represented no government, but I wanted to go anyhow" (14). "The hot, muddy faraway places filled with people yelling for freedom" could then come into less blurry shape and form as he channeled his experience with the "burden of race consciousness" and of "class consciousness" (15) to understand and communicate their hopes and dreams.

If this opening promises a somewhat straightforward account of the events at the conference and its historic import, Wright immediately deviates and spends almost the first half of the account on his preoccupations before he even reaches Indonesia. The bulk of the long first chapter (almost half the book), "Bandung: Beyond Left and Right," takes up Wright's self-drafted questionnaire about Asia. "Since I had resolved to go to Bandung, the problem of getting to know *the Asian personality* had been with me day and night" (20, emphasis added), he confesses. But as an amateur ethnographer, Wright's questions are far more wide-ranging and less essentialist than this grandiose statement suggests, covering attitudes toward education, marriage, language, generational conflict, the death penalty, geography, religion, liberation movements, racial beliefs, war, aid, contact with the West, approaches to nationalism and globalism, industrialization, world culture, the meaning of the Left and the Right, and the future of democracy. His informants include an Indonesian-born Dutch journalist, a Eurasian of Irish Catholic and Indian Muslim descent, a Westernized Asian, Mr X, whom Wright dubs "the H.L. Mencken of Indonesia" (53), a "full-blooded Indonesian in his twenties" (55), and a young Pakistani journalist. These subjects reveal suitably complex and fascinating responses to Wright's questions. But disconcertingly, Wright seems to have made up his mind already. Two stances structure his responses to the questionnaire—and indeed to the conference as a whole—and that they seemingly contradict each other is key. First, Wright seeks to define "the Asian personality" and translate it to the West. Just as *Black Power* is framed by Wright's opening preface and closing letter to Nkrumah (whose ear he could not quite access in his travels), there remains something voyeuristic about Wright's insistence that he is going to unlock the secret to the Asian personality, to the souls of these leaders and intellectuals speaking for the masses of the world. The reason he can serve as a translator, he tells us, is because he is one of them, as an "American Negro" (15). And this belief forms the second stance throughout the book—Wright's deep conviction that he is one of them, one with them, and can thus speak for them. *The Color Curtain* thus enacts a delicate and occasionally frustrating dance—Wright asserts kinship as "colored;" recognizes his difference as fundamentally Western; commits to the decolonization of the world; wonders how the West will respond to real needs and fears a communist or fascist revolution; finds common ground with decolonized peoples as similarly deracinated from tradition and ancestry; establishes difference by mouthing platitudes about wily Asian leaders and religious masses stuck in immemorial ways of life. And it is this mélange, this array of passions and ideas, I want to suggest, that we need to return to because it tells us something not just about Wright—his ideas of race and nation, his conception of the relation between the legacy of colonialism and slavery, and his incipient formulation of the Global South as a political force—but also about the encounter (neither peaceful nor smooth) between conceptions of race forged via the US experience and those shaped elsewhere across the globe. This line of analysis allows us to more fully assess whether Jim Crow in the US South may speak meaningfully to segregation and discrimination—what Frantz Fanon memorably termed the "Manichean" structure of the colony—across the Global South (Fanon 1967: 41).

To better understand the historical moment of *The Color Curtain* in relation to the long history of Black internationalism, it is further helpful to recall Penny Von Eschen's historicization of African American relations to anti-colonialism in *Race against Empire* (Von Eschen 1997). Von Eschen shows that in the 1940s, spurred by leftist internationalism and the efforts of such committed intellectuals as Du Bois, Robeson, Alphaeus Hunton, and Max Yergan to theorize African Americans as part of the darker races globally, there was a moment when African Americans understood their struggle as akin to anti-colonialism—they saw themselves not just as a national minority but also in alliance with a global majority. This kinship was not largely symbolic or cultural but in fact a very substantial element understood of the same political struggle against racism, colonialism, and capitalism, and the interlocking effects of these forces. African Americans saw racial oppression as rooted in the imperialist expansion of Europe, which scattered people of African descent in the New World and colonized them on the continent. Unlike later moments, such as the more well-known Black Power identification with the Third World, African American activists, intellectuals, and journalists argued that decolonization movements in Africa and Asia were structurally linked to the struggle against domestic racism, thus enabling a critique of the very idea of America. But with the onset of the Cold War, increased surveillance, and anti-Communist repression, this sense of kinship declined as liberal leaders of the National Association for the Advancement of Colored People (NAACP) forged the dominant civil rights argument and chose to highlight racism as a blot on an otherwise morally great nation—the last bastion and rightful champion of freedom in the world, misrecognizing the shift from British to American empire that Du Bois and Robeson warned against. They also shifted their focus to domestic political and civil rights rather than international ones. Carol Anderson further limns this pivotal moment in *Eyes Off the Prize*, tracing the brief decade from 1944 to 1955 when the question of human rights, prompted by the horror of the Holocaust, was at the center of the anti-racist agenda for the NAACP. Only the language of human rights, as articulated by the United Nations, had the power to signal a true universalism, addressing not just political and legal forms of discrimination but social and economic rights as well (Anderson 2003). While race was at the center of African American identities, communities, and solidarities in this era, it was understood as a shaping force of modernity's instruments—transatlantic slavery, racial capitalism, and colonial exploitation.

In the 1950s, race and racism came to be understood not only as aberrations from the norm of US democracy and as domestic, internal issues but also were located internally—as psychological problems to be overcome rather than rooted in structures of slavery and colonialism. Von Eschen reveals how racism was thus rewritten as an ahistorical evil during the Cold War. Because of analogies with Nazism, racism ceased to be located in US history specifically and was also delinked from its constitution in colonial and imperial history. Racism was thus relocated in specific places and times—the US South, apartheid South Africa, Nazi Germany, which all good liberals could be against. The rewriting of race in popular African American discourse after the Second World War thus moved away from "a sophisticated analysis rooted in history and toward psychological and social psychological research on race relations" (Von Eschen 1997: 155). In the 1940s, racism was located in the history of slavery and colonialism. The 1950s flipped the script, and now slavery and colonialism were explained as caused by racism and colorism.

As we learn more about the extent of the US government's efforts to control Wright's words and movements, even in exile, we can thereby also learn to read for the hints of a US imperial policy that disavows its name. While Du Bois and Robeson could not attend Bandung because their passports had been revoked in an era of anti-Communist purges, Adam Clayton Powell Jr had requested that the State Department send a team of observers, though the organizing nations of Bandung had pointedly not invited the United States, the Soviet Union, or other Western powers. Although he was denied, Powell insisted on attending and spoke as a defender of American policies at home and abroad. Wright's three-week trip was funded by the Congress for Cultural Freedom with the understanding that Wright would produce several written accounts of the conference while avoiding any explicit acknowledgement that Wright was not a freelance writer. Subsequent research has proved that the Congress was backed by the Central Intelligence Agency (CIA) and was thus part of the Cold War era's persistent attempts to control the image of the United States at home and abroad. While Bandung certainly represents the apotheosis of Afro–Asian solidarity, it also serves as a prism for viewing a relatively unstudied moment in the American century, where the United States sought to side-step an alliance of African and Asian nations in the very moment that it assumed the historical role of the new imperial power, stepping into the vacuum created by the decline of European empires and the decimation of the Second World War. The African American press, as Von Eschen notes, reported on the conference with great interest and enthusiasm, eager to adopt the possibility of non-alignment from Soviet communism and Western capitalism, celebrating the meeting "as a turning point in world history and potentially the most important event of the twentieth century" and as "a clear challenge to white supremacy [as a] gathering of the world's yellow, brown, and black races" (Von Eschen 1997: 168).

In doing so, the Black press was tapping into what is now often termed the Afro–Asian analogy (Ho and Bill 2008). Inspired by the historic meeting of Bandung, Afro–Asian scholarship looks before and after Bandung to excavate encounters and alliances among communities across Asia and Africa. The story of anti-colonial thought and decolonization often pinpoints Bandung, which has come to acquire a legendary quality, imbued with misty-eyed nostalgia for a time when the rest of the world came together to look for an alternative to Western hegemony and racial and imperial power. It is important, as recent reassessments of Bandung have urged, to avoid such nostalgia and assess in a clear-headed fashion the limits, potential, and symbolic meaning of the conference and the internationalist desires it evoked (Lee 2010). This means reactivating the conceptual and theoretical possibilities for the study of race and postcolonialism offered by Bandung rather than recreating it as a lost utopian moment. No seamless Afro–Asian coalition can afford to overlook wedges between various minoritized populations or de-emphasize those moments of real division that do not support such a vision or those practices (social, cultural, aesthetic) that do not translate or transplant easily. The story is, especially as Wright constructs it, as much about fracture, as it is about connection. Stuart Hall has influentially cautioned against "extrapolating a common universal structure to racism" since "it is only as the different racisms are historically specified—in their difference—that they can be properly understood" (Hall 1980). Reading Wright in Indonesia thus also requires unraveling the varying meanings of race as they emerge in his many conversations with Asians and Africans. For Wright, "Bandung was a decisive moment in the consciousness of 65 per cent of the human race, and that moment meant: HOW SHALL THE HUMAN RACE BE ORGANIZED? The decisions or lack of them flowing from Bandung will condition the totality of human life on this earth" (Wright 1994: 207–208).

While one strain of *The Color Curtain* sensitively probes the limits and potentialities of Afro–Asian and Third Worldist alliance, another remains caught up with exposing the secrets of the inscrutable Asian soul, irreducibly opposed to what the West symbolizes. In trying to find the key to the Asian soul, as Wright navigates the binaries of Black/white, North/South, left/right, United States/Europe, he finds them subsumed under the larger one of East/West. A somewhat static sense of the immutability of this difference between East and West leads Wright to identify an Asian "instinct toward hierarchy" and "a hunger for a strong leadership, for authority" (73). As soon as he meets someone at the conference who seems poised or thoughtful, he immediately ascribes a Western sensibility to them. He views Nehru, for instance, as an allegory for India— "part East, part West" (165). He collapses the various forces at play—Nehru's ploy for Asian leadership, Chou En-lai's negotiation of communism, the conflicting desires of Russia and the United States, the lingering legacy of the European colonial powers— into the preconceived swirl of race and religion. While he appreciates the ready confidence he receives from every Asian he interviews, as a fellow "colored" person he also realizes his gulf from his interlocutors, concluding that "many Asians hated the West with an absoluteness that no American Negro could ever muster" (25). This difference occurs because while African Americans have specific grievances, for Wright they also fully share "a normal Western outlook" (26). In contrast, Asians have simultaneously been deprived of their own culture and denied access to Western culture, so they feel a double sense of deracination.

In this way, Wright seems to have reached some conclusions even before he arrives in Indonesia that race and religion ("two of the most powerful and irrational forces in human nature" [140]) are at the heart of the question. No matter what he hears (of the rights of Palestine, for instance), he concludes that religious sentiment is the reason rather than a political question of refugee rights. For Wright, "the moment I left the dry, impersonal, abstract world of the West, I encountered at once: religion" (77). Similarly, any sign of cultural identity—a skull cap or a beard—speaks of religion. And religion for Wright connotes the end of discourse: "There is nothing that can be said when one faces men in whom there is a total mobilization of all the irrational forces of the human personality to a point of organized militancy" (80). No wonder that though Wright recalls all the people he meets seething with revenge and hatred of the West, many of them have subsequently disavowed such an account, suggesting that, in a long line of Western travelers, Wright was seeing what he wanted to see. Mochtar Lubis, one of Wright's Indonesian interlocutors, for example, complained that Wright had been looking at the Bandung conference through "colored glasses," allowing his racial preconceptions to shape everything he saw. For Lubis, Wright was projecting his own obsession with race and color on to Indonesians instead of grasping a "true and balanced picture of the intellectual situation in Indonesia" (Roberts and Foulcher 2016: 9–10).[3]

Despite such blind spots, Wright's account remains powerful in its ability to represent the existential void created by colonial violence. One of his most perceptive moments occurs when he gets hold of a booklet designed to teach the Indonesian language to Dutch visitors and officials. All the words are commands, with no examples of any civil conversation. Wright concludes, "Whether the author knew it or not, he was writing a book to instruct an army of invaders how to demean, intimidate, and break the spirit of an enemy people in a conquered, occupied country" (180). It is in such insights that Wright approaches the revelations made vivid in Fanon's account of colonial rule and racist depersonalization in *The Wretched of the Earth*. Like Fanon, Wright is interested in the distortions to the psyche produced by the structural violence of racism and colonialism. So, when he diagnoses his Eurasian subject with neurosis, we could see it as akin to Fanon's theories of the nervous condition produced by colonial rule—a historical outcome that indicts the system rather than a psychological failing that demeans the individual.

To understand Wright's contradictory assertions, it is necessary to turn back to his US writings. Just as *Black Power* was obsessed with revealing the truths of the African personality and *The Color Curtain* of the Asian personality, in explaining the genesis of *Native Son*'s Bigger Thomas, Wright had noted his desire to explicate the type that Bigger represented—in Mississippi or in Chicago. Wright's own gradual realization that Bigger wasn't only Black but could also be white (e.g. Russian or German) constituted "the pivot of [his] life; it altered the complexion of [his] existence." We should thus understand Wright's later global explorations as an extension and an intensification of his domestic writings rather than as a radical departure. "How Bigger Was Born" already sounds the

---

[3] The archival evidence in this book belies Wright's claims in several ways. For example, Wright notes that "in many respects the Javanese countryside reminded me of Africa; ... there were those same bare-breasted young women with somber-colored cloths—sarongs—rolled and tucked about their waists" (129). As Roberts and Foulcher point out, it's unlikely that this would have happened in a mostly Muslim Java.

notes we hear in *The Color Curtain* and *White Man, Listen*, as Wright describes his time in Chicago and with the labor movement: "I began to feel far-flung kinships, and sense, with fright and abashment, the possibilities of *alliances* between the American Negro and other people possessing a kindred consciousness" (Wright 1987: 441).

So when Wright muses that the many Bigger Thomases he had met growing up express the larger desires of African Americans (the desire for their own flag and country, or an appreciation, however complex, for Japanese aggression in China, or for the aggressive actions of a Hitler or Mussolini), we must understand this not as an assessment of the latent potential for fascism among the Black population but Wright's core belief—at home and abroad—that modernity itself created this hunger and found no way to sate it. The extent of estrangement from settled values—of religion, of place, of spirit and soul—and the rampant inequality and consumerism of the culture created a void which couldn't be filled by anything other than fantasies of violence. He realizes that the "deep sense of exclusion" that characterized the experience of modernity across the world "transcended national and racial boundaries" (Wright 1987: 443). Accordingly, Wright finds that the same void births Bigger Thomas in Indonesia and in Ghana, and indeed, in Spain. In *The Color Curtain*, the Pakistani journalist he interviews is bitter and "as dark as a Negro" (65), for whom racism and imperialism are the same. Wright wonders, "if he were restless, how much more would be the illiterate millions when cast into the void?" (70). In *Native Son*, Wright had created a figure, Bigger Thomas, who was the "product of a dislocated society; he [was] a dispossessed and disinherited man" (446). For Wright, this made Bigger also a "figure who would hold within him the prophecy of our future" (447). Wright allegorizes Bigger in relation to his own sense of homelessness and alienation:

> Bigger was attracted and repelled by the American scene. He was an American, because he was a native son; but he was also a Negro nationalist in a vague sense because he was not allowed to live as an American. Such was his way of life and mine; neither Bigger nor I resided fully in either camp.
>
> (450–451)

It is these contradictions of living as an African American—neither allowed to be an American, nor still connected to Africa—that shape Wright's responses to the Third World.

The Color Curtain testifies both to the urgent need to connect race to coloniality and to the difficulty of making that connection and translating one historical experience into another. Wright at times expands the purview of each and at other times deflects the question of differences, or struggles with misrecognitions. Brent Hayes Edwards has called such moments of failed translations a form of *décalage*, necessary delays or gaps that are actually constitutive of the practice of diaspora (Edwards 2001). But thinking about *The Color Curtain* and the Bandung moment requires more than an acknowledgement of difference; it entails reckoning with ideological disagreement and differences in political vision. That is to say, we can certainly understand Wright's complex and conflicted responses to the people he meets in Ghana or Indonesia as evidence of his deeply felt sense of kinship with the rest of the world, which highlights the extent of his alienation from his native land. But because he ends both his Africa book and his Asia book with essentially an endorsement of dictatorial method to modernize the masses of these lands and hurtle them into the twentieth century, it is difficult to square the valence of these anti-democratic ideas with his anti-racist philosophies, especially with the hindsight of postcolonial authoritarian rule in the late twentieth century.

Even as Wright's insights about the ideological and interpersonal clashes at Bandung help illuminate the historical record, we simply cannot ignore the fact that many of Wright's non-fiction books of the 1950s end with an advocacy of suspending democratic norms in favor of autocratic rule for the good of the people. His firm belief in a "secular and rational base of thought and feeling" (219) is unquestionable. It comes from his ongoing naturalist inclination to see everything as a force of history rather than individual or collective pathology. Yet this tendency casts some doubt on his self-fashioning as eloquent spokesperson for the decolonizing masses if he cannot imagine them capable of self-government and democratic opportunity. I should note that many scholars have defended Wright's approach as a reflection of his commitment to the modernizing project, especially in relation to *Black Power*.[4] But I think instead of rationalizing Wright's approach, it is more generative to understand it as part of his larger belief in the violence of tradition.

Wright clarifies his ideas in his address to the Conference of Negro-African Writers and Artists in Paris in 1956. Speaking in a highly charged atmosphere, Wright delivers a polemic about the benefits of colonialism that explains his advocacy of rootlessness as the source of a new humanist imagination. He argues that colonialism actually liberated Africa and Asia, albeit unwittingly so, because it destroyed their stultifying traditions, freeing them from their irrational past. Colonialism thus left behind "a procession of shattered cultures, disintegrated societies, and a writhing sweep of more aggressive, irrational religion than the world has known for centuries" (Wright 2008: 655). Colonialist "plundering" ironically provided the "conditions for the possible rise of rational societies for the greater majority of mankind" (722). This is why Wright dedicates *White Man, Listen* to "the Westernized and tragic elite of Asia, Africa, and the West Indies—the lonely outsiders who exist precariously on the clifflike margins of many cultures … who … seek desperately for a home for their hearts: a home which, if found, could be a home for the hearts of all men" (633). For Wright, these elite outsiders were like him—neither fully of the West nor free from it, and therefore had the objectivity to assess the needs of their worlds ruthlessly. As he says of himself, "historical forces more powerful than I am have shaped me as a Westerner" (701). And yet, this recognition

---

[4] See, for instance, Diawara (1998), who concludes that Wright was for Africa; Gaines (2006), who places Wright's concluding letter to Kwame Nkrumah against a larger backdrop of Black expatriate writing; and Rasberry (2016), who reads it as part of the longer discussion of race and totalitarianism. Mark Christian Thompson (2007) further limns the valence of twentieth-century totalitarian thought in *Black Fascisms: African American Literature and Culture between the Wars*.

does not mean embracing the West's faults; rather, Wright claims that his "point of view is a Western one, but a Western one that conflicts at several vital points with the present, dominant outlook of the West" (712). Rejecting the racial and religious code of Mississippi freed him in the same way that the elite Third World leaders arrived at Bandung only after having been forced to learn to distance themselves from their own debased cultures and learning to speak like Westerners. In fact, for Wright, the true heritage of the West—"man stripped of the past and free for the future"—is now most fully embodied by the Asian and African elite—"an elite that is more Western, in most cases, than the West." It is Wright's potent belief in the ability of these elites to extend "the spirit of the Enlightenment and the Reformation" to all of humanity that explains his counsel to give them unchecked, even quasi-dictatorial power to reform their broken societies (722).

Wright's dual investment in Western norms and Asian and African elite adoption of these norms frame his frequent declarations in his 1950s writings—often unreciprocated—of a common homelessness, a shared void among African Americans, Asians, and Africans. He seeks to make this commonality the source of a potentially transformed future, searching for South–South affinities born out of a common condition of disinheritedness and deterritorialization. As he had confessed to Ralph Ellison some years earlier, some of this deracination came from his departure from Communism: "After I broke with the Communist Party, I had nowhere else to go" (Ellison 1986: 198). He had also asserted his freedom to write *Native Son* without fear of the white gaze, or the Black bourgeois expectations of positive representation, or any diktats of the Communist Party as a question of his inalienable human rights. The same existential void he had identified in the United States he finds across the world. Speaking of his most famous literary creation, Bigger Thomas, Wright had said:

> The civilization which had given birth to Bigger contained no spiritual sustenance, had created no culture which could hold and claim his allegiance and faith, had sensitized him and left him stranded, a free agent to roam the streets of our cities, a hot and whirling vortex of undisciplined and unchannelized impulses.
>
> (Wright 1987: 445)

It is these ideas of the void, of racist depersonalization, and of the violence of the breaking of tradition that help explain one of the most confounding aspects of Wright's travel writings. Of course, it must also be said that he extends the secular rational outlook he values to the elite of Asia and Africa but not to the populations they seek to govern. And here too, we find parallels to the debates in the United States surrounding *Native Son*, where Zora Neale Hurston and others sought to draw a distinction between Wright's literary creation—Bigger Thomas, fated to run out a racist script of criminality and violence—and Wright himself—celebrated writer and intellectual.

To be sure, Wright does exhibit some self-reflexivity about the value of Westernization. In *Black Power*, for example, when he drives to a small fishing community in a taxicab, he suggests to an African electrician that he invent a machine to pound fufu. When his family responds with ridicule, Wright proceeds to question his own assumptions rather than suggest that this shows their backwardness:

> And suddenly I was self-conscious; I began to question myself, *my* assumptions. I was assuming that these people had to be pulled out of this life, out of these conditions of poverty, had to become literate and eventually industrialized. But why? Was not the desire for that mostly on *my* part rather than *theirs*? I was literate, Western, disinherited, and industrialized and I felt each day the pain and anxiety of it. Why then must I advocate the dragging of these people into my trap?
>
> (Wright 1995: 165)

Recognizing that an unthinking call to modernize Africa might only exacerbate things further, Wright cautions that "the pathos of Africa would be doubled if, out of her dark past, her people were plunged into a dark future, a future that smacked of Chicago or Detroit" (Wright 1995: 251). Such moments of self-doubt further obscure a clear view of his political assessments of decolonizing nations.

Wright establishes difference *and* articulates kinship with the people of the former colonies so rapidly across these books that it is difficult to extract the conceptual terms that dictate his relation. His own imbrication within the West—as place, as concept—only seems to come into view fully by detouring through Africa and Asia. In doing so, he takes us beyond the important achievements of his canonical works like *Black Boy* and *Native Son*. There, he tells an important story about the American century—in terms of form, race, autobiography, the creation of Black masculine identity, and forces of naturalism and region. But we miss out, I would submit, on something else unless we turn to something like *The Color Curtain*. There, Wright is uncertain, out of his depth, constrained by his funding sources as much as he is confounded by the alien worlds he encounters. Urgently groping for explanations, he announces kinships that seem neither fully reciprocated nor warranted. The book thus allows us to highlight a different literary tradition—the American abroad, jettisoning provincialism, learning to see anew outside the blinkered vision of imperial eyes. To be able to see a great American writer in this vulnerable avatar is important since the collective psychological dimension of US empire has never invited navel gazing. This unheroic Wright is also the Wright who insists on his Westernness, on his rationality, and seeks to make it so for everyone he meets—the gifts of enlightenment, as he saw them, made accessible to the teeming masses who baffle him and from whom he remains distant. But he does know enough to insist that how Bandung was born had something to do with how Bigger was born and that the futures of the racialized populations within and without the United States would continue to be articulated together. Wright thus also serves as herald of the moment when African American popular culture will assume unprecedented global reach, shaping conversations about race and difference across varied landscapes. Writing of African American literature in 1957, Wright declares that "during the past twenty-five years the great majority of the human race has undergone experiences comparable to those which Negroes in America have undergone for three centuries." All these people across the world want to know about the Black experience, he predicts: "they want our testimony since we live here amidst the greatest pretense of democracy on earth." And he concludes with a flourish: "So, the voice that America rejected is finding a home at last, a home such as was never dreamed of" (Wright 2008: 769). This vision of African American "freedom dreams" finding a home in the revolutionary Third World is one that we must hold on to even as we learn to examine more fully the connections and disjunctures between race and coloniality (Kelley 2002).

Returning to Wright in the era of the Black Lives Matter movement may seem immediately obvious on account of his powerfully angry prose, his strident defense of the value of protest fiction, and his profound concern with inequality and injustice in the Jim Crow South and across the globe. But I would submit that alongside such concerns, it is his hunger for modernity that we should examine—a hunger that at once leads him to the Global South in the wake of the deracination of Jim Crow and the break with the Communist Party, but also only allows him to articulate an ambivalent kinship. These ambivalences are important in a moment when appeals to transnational solidarities have become routine and movements for racial justice across the world learn from each other. Wright reminds us of the difficulties that attend transnational kinship in a world where nation states remain powerful as arbiters of race and violence. Instead of viewing the current political moment as exceptional, we thus need to situate it within a longer history of attempted alliances, setbacks, fault lines, and misrecognitions. Such divisions and frictions are not mere failures of translation but index deep ideological differences that complicate the very notion of diaspora, national belonging, and racial identity at home and abroad. So, it is very likely that Floyd's family's appeal will never be met by the UN. But perhaps, as Wright foresaw, a hundred Bigger Thomases across the world will listen and recognize a similar homelessness in the world, which, to understand, they will have to engage with Wright.

REFERENCES

Anderson, Carol. 2003. *Eyes off the Prize: The United Nations and the African American Struggle for Human Rights, 1944–1955* (New York: Cambridge University Press).
Baldwin, Kate A. 2002. *Beyond the Color Line and the Iron Curtain: Reading Encounters between Black and Red, 1922–1963* (Durham, NC: Duke University Press).
Diawara, Manthia. 1998. *In Search of Africa* (Cambridge, MA: Harvard University Press).
Dickinson, Daniel. 2020. "I am my brother's keeper, Philonise Floyd tells UN rights body, in impassioned plea for racial justice," UN News, June 17, https://news.un.org/en/story/2020/06/1066542, accessed February 12, 2022.
Du Bois, W.E.B. 1995. *Dark Princess: A Romance* (Jackson, MS: University Press of Mississippi).
Edwards, Brent Hayes. 2001. "The Uses of Diaspora," *Social Text* 66.19.1: 45–73.
Ellison, Ralph. 1986. *Going to the Territory* (New York: Random House).
Fabre, Michel. 1993. *The Unfinished Quest of Richard Wright*, trans. Isabel Barzun (Chicago, IL: University of Illinois Press).
Fanon, Frantz. 1667. *The Wretched of the Earth*, trans. Constance Farrington (London: Penguin).

Gaines, Kevin. 2006. *American Africans in Ghana: Black Expatriates and the Civil Rights Era* (Chapel Hill, NC: University of North Carolina Press).
Gilroy, Paul. 1993. *The Black Atlantic: Modernity and Double Consciousness* (Cambridge, MA: Harvard University Press).
Griggs, Sutton. 1969. *Imperium in Imperio* (Miami, FL: Mnemosyne Publishers).
Hall, Stuart. 1980. "Race, Articulation, and Societies Structured in Dominance," in *Sociological Theories: Race and Colonialism* (Paris: UNESCO), 305–345.
Ho, Fred and Bill Mullen, eds. 2008. *Afro-Asia: Revolutionary Political and Cultural Connections between African Americans and Asian Americans* (Durham, NC: Duke University Press).
Kelley, Robin D.G. 2002. *Freedom Dreams: The Black Radical Imagination* (Boston, MA: Beacon Press).
Lee, Christopher J. ed. 2010. *Making a World after Empire: The Bandung Moment and Its Political Afterlives* (Athens: Ohio University Press).
Meriwether, James H. 2002. *Proudly We Can Be Africans: Black Americans and Africa, 1935–1961* (Chapel Hill, NC: University of North Carolina Press).
Plummer, Brenda Gayle. 1996. *Rising Wind: Black Americans and U.S. Foreign Affairs, 1935–60* (Chapel Hill, NC: University of North Carolina Press).
Rasberry, Vaughn. 2016. *Race and the Totalitarian Century: Geopolitics in the Black Literary Imagination* (Cambridge, MA: Harvard University Press).
Roberts, Brian Russell and Keith Foulcher, eds. 2016. *Indonesian Notebook: A Sourcebook on Richard Wright and the Bandung Conference* (Durham, NC: Duke University Press).
Robinson, Cedric. 2000. *Black Marxism: The Making of the Black Radical Tradition* (Chapel Hill, NC: University of North Carolina Press).
Schuyler, George. 1931. *Slaves Today: A Story of Liberia* (New York: Brewer, Warren, Putnam).
Thompson, Mark Christian. 2007. *Black Fascisms: African American Literature and Culture between the Wars* (Charlottesville, VA: University of Virginia Press).
Von Eschen, Penny M. 1997. *Race against Empire: Black Americans and Anticolonialism, 1937–1957* (Ithaca, NY: Cornell University Press).
Wright, Richard. 1987. "How Bigger Was Born," in *Native Son* (New York: Perennial), 43–462.
Wright, Richard. 1994 [1956]. *The Color Curtain: A Report on the Bandung Conference* (Jackson, Mississippi: Banner Books, University Press of Mississippi), 207–208.
Wright, Richard. 1995 [1954]. *Black Power: A Record of Reactions in a Land of Pathos* (New York: Harper Perennial).
Wright, Richard. 2008. *White Man, Listen!* [1957], *Black Power: Three Books From Exile: Black Power; The Color Curtain; and White Man, Listen!*, Intro. by Cornel West (New York: Harper Perennial).
X, Malcolm. 1965. *The Ballot or the Bullet* (North Hollywood, CA: Pacifica Foundation).
Young, Cynthia A. 2006. *Soul Power: Culture, Radicalism, and the Making of a U.S. Third World Left* (Durham, NC: Duke University Press).

CHAPTER 10

"WARM WITH TIPSY EMBRACES"

Allen Ginsberg, the US–China Writers' Conferences, and Queer Internationalism

HARILAOS STECOPOULOS

> Cultural diplomacy can enhance our national security in subtle, wide-ranging, and sustainable ways. Indeed, history may record that America's cultural riches played no less a role than military action in shaping our international leadership.
>
> The U.S. State Department, 2005

OFTEN considered "a euphemism for propaganda," US cultural diplomacy names the deployment by state and state-affiliated organizations of art, literature, and performance to improve the global reputation of the United States (Cull 2008: 498A). As a 2005 State Department advisory committee put it, "America's cultural riches" play a key role in "our international leadership." During the post-war era, government officials mainly exported modernist or middlebrow culture like the "Advancing American Art" painting exhibit (1946) or Hal Holbrook's Mark Twain show (1960–1961) to demonstrate "that the United States was not just a nation of cars, chewing gum, and Hollywood movies" (Menand 2005). Yet the popular arts and postmodernist culture also have played a role in US outreach initiatives, which have ranged from the famed global tours of Louis Armstrong (1955–1965) to an overseas junket by John Ashbery and Susan Sontag (1979). The government has drawn upon the full range of US culture in its attempts to win friends and influence people around the world. Aesthetically, no less than geographically, US cultural diplomacy always covers a lot of ground.

Increasingly, Americanists have recognized this rich archive as integral to understanding the American Century. Important work by Penny Von Eschen on jazz diplomacy, Deborah Cohn on hemispheric literary relations, Brian Edwards on *Shrek* in Iran, Greg Barnhisel on the magazine *Perspectives*, and Harris Feinsod on transnational American poetry has helped us gauge the myriad effects of the government's cultural diplomatic mission at home and abroad. As these examples should suggest, most scholarship on US cultural diplomacy tends to privilege questions of ideology and race. And for good reason. The importance of anti-communist discourse, civil rights activism, and anti-colonial resistance urges such a focus. Yet mapping the cultural Cold War also demands sensitivity to the politics of the sex/gender system. Kate Baldwin's work on "the cold war kitchen" at the American National Exhibition in Moscow (1959) (Baldwin 2016); Ann Blaschke's study of gender and sports diplomacy in the 1960s and 1970s (Blaschke 2016); and Victoria Philips's analysis of Martha Graham's work as a female cultural ambassador well illustrate how issues of embodiment, broadly defined, have an important place in Cold War studies. If US propaganda and, more broadly, US foreign relations have traditionally been examined from a top-down perspective that privileges policy, these scholars urge a lower-scale and affective understanding of state cultural outreach.

Various types of intimacy played a crucial role in the 1950s heyday of US cultural diplomacy. Witness Maya Angelou's moving embrace with a Yugoslavian family of Paul Robeson fans during the 1954 Porgy and Bess tour or, more disturbingly, the State Department's recognition that placing "several pretty young girls in the front two rows of any public appearance" would encourage William Faulkner "to keep his attention up" during the author's 1955 visit to Japan.[1] From hugs to gift-giving and drunken bonding, hospitality and camaraderie have often contributed crucially to the cultivation of bilateral good will. On occasion, though, the more intimate aspects of cultural diplomacy didn't so much shore up the state's goals as incite the unsettling, even subversive, expression of counter-hegemonic sentiments. And this is particularly germane to female and queer diplomats for whom questions of gender, sexuality, and embodiment are often a concern. However rare (given that US propaganda programs skew misogynistic and homophobic and are often racist), such ambassadors frequently respond to state imperatives in an oppositional manner. As much is the case with celebrated gay poet Allen Ginsberg, the focus of this chapter.

Ginsberg's participation in the US–China Writers' Conferences (1982–1988) inspired him to re-imagine Cold War literary exchange in affective and physical terms. Deeply hostile to the Reagan Administration (1981–1989) and wary of the Deng Xiaoping-run People's Republic of China (1978–1989), the two states whose cooperation enabled the conferences, Ginsberg nonetheless proved willing to work as a de facto US literary ambassador during these unprecedented events. The countercultural icon did so, however, in his own inimitable manner, finding in his frustrated attempts to connect with the Chinese public inspiration for a series of meta-diplomatic poems that dramatized his libidinal approach to cultural diplomacy. Rather than decry government power on both sides of the Pacific or, alternately, attempt to forge substantive geopolitical ties, Ginsberg imagined a literary exchange richly sensitive to bodies and pleasures. For him, the queer

---

[1] Angelou 1976: 216. The State Department guidelines for managing William Faulkner are cited in Barnhisel 2015.

value of cultural outreach "was predicated on an embodied pull toward otherness ... innocent of the intention to dominate, improve, or instrumentalize" (Goodlad 324).²

I begin by briefly describing the US–China Writer's conferences and then turn to how Ginsberg used his cultural diplomatic experience to find in literature an alternate perspective on the Cold War. Concentrating on Ginsberg's 1984 trip to the People's Republic of China (PRC), I argue that the writer found in the affective propagation of lyric poetry aesthetic and erotic energies that resisted authoritarian control. Drawing upon the examples of Walt Whitman, William Carlos Williams, and other poets, Ginsberg sought to bond with the Chinese through an embodied poetics that would exceed the control of either regime. The writing to emerge from Ginsberg's 1984 trip is replete with references to his sexuality and his desire to connect with Chinese men. Whether celebrating poetry with a Chinese male official at a farewell dinner or engaging in imagined intimacy with a Tang Dynasty writer, the US poet understood cultural diplomacy as an opportunity to publicly express same-sex desire across borders. Rather than affirm the emerging US–Chinese relationship, Ginsberg used his ambassadorial duties to forge a queer internationalism defiant of Cold War realpolitik.³

Organized by ex-*Saturday Review* editor and University of California, Los Angeles (UCLA) professor Norman Cousins, the four US–China Writers' conferences were scheduled biennially, alternating between the United States and the PRC.⁴ The first conference was staged in Los Angeles in 1982; the second in Beijing in 1984; the third in Los Angeles in 1986; and the fourth in Beijing and Leshan in 1988. Inspiring the conferences was Cousins' longstanding belief in literature's capacity to promote unity and peace. As he put it in a 1984 letter, "Writers more than any other group perhaps can help people transcend the tribalism that is such a morose characteristic of the modern world" (Cousins 1984). For this ardent internationalist, writers were the real ambassadors—visionaries whose aesthetic and moral capacities allowed them to see beyond political divisions to a future Parliament of Man. In keeping with his estimation of the literary, Cousins sought to define the conferences as distinct from state propaganda, then run by the conservative Reagan Administration. That the project depended most visibly on

---

[2] I take this phrase from Lauren Goodlad's important analysis of E. M. Forster and queer internationalism (2006). While Forster and Ginsberg are very different types of writers and thinkers, I think they would both agree that, in Goodlad's words, "queer internationalism is an ethical ideal in tension with the strong imperative to `change the world' which animates the politics of justice as they are variously articulated by liberals, Marxists, and social democrats" (330).

[3] I should emphasize that Ginsberg's queer cultural diplomacy does not resemble the homonationalist cultural diplomacy that J.Y. Chua identifies, for example, in Serbia's decision to enter a bisexual singer in the 2007 Eurovision contest. For all his unease with the PRC, Ginsberg had no interest in defining the Reagan administration or, indeed, the United States as liberal and inclusive. See Chua's fascinating essay, "Eurovision and the Making of Queer (Counter)Cultural Diplomacy" (2016). For a brilliant account of homonationalism, see Puar (2007).

[4] With the exception of Perry Link and Kenneth Lincoln, two UCLA literature professors affiliated with the project, scholars haven't written about the US–China Writers' Conferences. The bulk of my information comes from the Norman Cousins Papers at UCLA. For some first-person accounts, see Link (1985) and Lincoln (1999).

state or private supporters—UCLA, the Kettering Foundation, and the now defunct corporation Computerland—helped support his vision of nongovernmental literary exchange.

The list of participating writers indicates that Cousins had free rein in the selection process. During the early Cold War, US literary diplomacy had been dominated by such politically moderate or conservative figures as Saul Bellow, William Faulkner, Robert Frost, Allen Tate, and John Updike. Yet most of the writers in Cousins' conferences were liberal, if not leftwing, and openly antagonistic to the Reagan Administration's vision of the United States. The 1982 conference at UCLA included Ginsberg, Annie Dillard, John Hersey, Gary Snyder, and Kurt Vonnegut, while the 1984 entourage that traveled to China had an even more politically engaged roster of Ginsberg, Snyder, William Gass, Maxine Hong Kingston, Toni Morrison, and Lesley Marmon Silko. The conference of 1986, once again staged in Los Angeles, included Paula Gunn Allen, Rolando Hinjosa-Smith, Kingston, and Carolyn Kizer, and the final event also testified to a steady commitment to left writers, with Kingston, Alice Fulton, Larry Heinemann, Barry Lopez, Roberta Hill Whiteman, and Jay Wright traveling to China one year before the massacre at Tiananmen Square put an end to this unprecedented experiment in US–Chinese literary exchange. Thanks to Cousins' bold initiative, a bloc of leftist American writers had the opportunity to turn cultural diplomacy to their own ends, creating their own version of internationalism in the process.

That they enjoyed this opportunity during the Reagan Administration may seem surprising. Reagan's regime was notorious during the 1980s for attempting to censor left and liberal discourse in the United States, and this tendency extended to cultural diplomacy. In 1984, for example, the United States Information Agency (USIA), then directed by Reagan's Hollywood friend Charles Wick, labeled certain Americans ineligible for overseas assignments. Betty Friedan, Coretta Scott King, and Ralph Nader were on this blacklist but so were James Baldwin, Stanford English professors Albert and Barbara Gelpi, N. Scott Momaday, and Ginsberg (Brinkley 1984: 18).[5] Given the rightwing political climate in Washington, the fact that left white writers and left writers of color traveled to China as de facto US representatives seems nothing less than miraculous. Indeed, inasmuch as they constituted a veritable Heath anthology of contemporary literature, the conference rosters almost appeared designed to invite censure from the Reagan era State Department and USIA.

Yet the state form is never as monolithic as we think (even during Reagan's tenure), and it is important to recognize the role of the government in facilitating, even promoting, these unprecedented cultural diplomatic events. Early in the Administration, Reagan and his advisors decided to follow the example of the Carter Administration and maintain diplomatic relations with the PRC, if only to gain a potential new ally against the Soviet Union. And even as this unusual relationship had its difficulties, whether due to Reagan's refusal to accept a "one China" policy or due to his enthusiasm for Chinese

---

[5] Also see United States Advisory Commission on Public Diplomacy (1985: 44).

defectors, the President and his advisors tended to avoid demonizing the PRC as they did the Soviet Union and its satellite states. Reagan would even claim the Chinese weren't really Communists—thus giving the Asian nation perhaps the highest compliment he could imagine.[6] He maintained full diplomatic relations with the PRC and, more surprisingly still, visited Beijing in 1984, where he urged both nations to move beyond the differences that separated them and then signed a cultural exchange agreement. This compact sanctioned official cultural diplomacy but also promoted the unofficial cultural diplomacy central to Cousins' mission.[7]

Indeed, for all their purported nongovernmental status, the US–Chinese writers' conferences were never as autonomous as their US organizers believed. As Cousins' correspondence with state bureaucrats in Washington and Beijing makes abundantly clear, this supposedly unofficial program manifested ties to governments on both sides of the Pacific.[8] The American organizers relied on the US State Department for financial and logistical assistance, and they required the assent of the Chinese Writers' Association (CWA) in order to facilitate the exchanges. While the US writers clearly had more latitude than their Chinese counterparts, neither nation viewed this sort of literary exchange as innocuous; in both cases, some sort of oversight, if not outright control, seems to have been required. The totalitarian PRC determined which Chinese writers took part in the gatherings; and US State Department involvement meant that the American delegations, while selected by Cousins, had been vetted by the government. Not because the participating writers toed the Reagan Administration's ideological line (that was unlikely) but rather because savvy Cold War veterans in Washington recognized that the potential value of having Lesley Marmon Silko or Toni Morrison serve as cultural emissaries outweighed the potential danger of emboldening them as domestic political figures. That the US writers traveling abroad were as likely to indict the failures of the PRC as they were to comment on American social problems made such ideologically suspect selections all the more appealing.

That said, it is still somewhat remarkable that a figure like the gay and anti-war Ginsberg ever passed muster with an administration notorious for its homophobia and its militarism. After all, Ginsberg already had made public his rejection of US literary propaganda. In 1975, he published "T.S. Eliot Entered My Dreams," a poem in which his speaker asks the Nobel Prize winner to explain the relationship between the Cold War state and American literature by addressing the role of James Jesus Angleton, chief of the Central Intelligence Agency's (CIA's) counterintelligence staff, in coopting high

---

[6] Reagan referred to "this so-called Communist China" in a speech at the University of Alaska on May 2, 1984.

[7] Unlike Richard Arndt and Ien Eng, Yudhishthir Raj Isar, and Phillip Mar, I don't distinguish between cultural diplomacy as a governmental enterprise and cultural relations as a nongovernmental project. Virtually all US initiatives focused on cultural relations have depended on state support in one way or another, and it's something of an internationalist fantasy to suggest otherwise: see Arndt (2006) and Eng et al. (2015).

[8] I don't have space to cite and examine the correspondence in this article. For a much fuller account of the conferences focused largely on Maxine Hong Kingston, see Stecopoulos (forthcoming).

modernism for anti-communism. "What did you think of the domination of poetics by the C.I.A.?," queries Ginsberg's speaker. "After all, wasn't Angleton your friend? Didn't he tell you to revitalize the intellectual structure of the West against the ... Stalinists?" Eliot's response proves less than satisfying: "I did, yes, know Angleton's literary conspiracies, I thought they were petty—well meant but of no importance to literature" (Ginsberg 1978: 46). But that frustrating answer is precisely Ginsberg's point: in his view, the author of *The Wasteland* had little understanding of, or concern over, how modernism had been coopted for the anti-Communist cause by organizations like the Congress for Cultural Freedom. And for Ginsberg, this remarkably apathetic reaction rendered Eliot and his ilk complicit with repressive state forces eager to instrumentalize literature and culture for propaganda purposes.[9] In direct contrast with some of his modernist predecessors, Ginsberg refused to accept the notion that writers might either work with or tacitly support the CIA and its various cultural fronts. As he put it in a late interview, Americans should reject the "CIA invasion of the intellectual body politic ... Congress for Cultural Freedom, all those magazines; even the Pen Club," the latter most likely a reference to Secretary of State George Schulz's appearance at the 1986 PEN International Congress.[10] For Ginsberg, the Cold War state's interest in literary and intellectual life could only guarantee the degradation of American writing.

A refusal to countenance the state's cooptation of language and literature would play an increasingly important role in the poet's contemporary work. Few writers protested so vigorously the Reagan Administration's attempt to revive the containment culture of the early Cold War era. In "Industrial Waves" (1981), a poem written the same year as Reagan's inauguration, Ginsberg mocks the idea that freedom of expression exists in the United States, claiming that powerful interests have "Freedom to ban your verse in the high school library" and that only they have "Freedom to announce what you want to the Press" (1987: 3). The absence of free speech affects domestic life, and Ginsberg also recognizes that it impacts international cultural relations as well. At another point in "Industrial Waves," for example, he chides the Administration for refusing to endorse any cultural exchanges with left literary figures: "Freedom to ban Genius entering the Land/& slap Nobel Prize novelists on the hand" (4). This critique would grow more specific in the wonderfully titled poem "On the Conduct of the World Seeking Beauty against Government" (1986), when Ginsberg writes "40,000 names Doris Lessing too on National Automated Immigration Lookout System barred entering U.S.A." (1994: 41). Invoking the left-leaning British novelist as a symbol of the many world writers excluded from the United States under the Republican regime, Ginsberg

---

[9] To be sure, in 1945, Eliot made a similar point about the relationship of the state to literature when he worried about "the dangers" to which "men of letters would be exposed, if they became, in their professional capacity, servants of the State," but this comment was inspired more by a fear of left-liberal propaganda than it was by an incipient Cold War modernism: see Eliot (1945).

[10] Interview with Allen Ginsberg. August 11, 1996. National Security Archive, George Washington University, https://nsarchive2.gwu.edu//coldwar/interviews/episode-13/ginsberg1.html, accessed February 14, 2022.

highlights the Administration's regular use of the McCarran–Walter Act (1952) to safeguard the supposed sanctity of the nation.

And yet, even as he regularly protested the Reagan presidency, Ginsberg also expressed significant disagreement with Communist state governments. Beginning with his expulsion from Cuba for proclaiming gay rights (1965) and from Czechoslovakia for consorting with dissident youth (1965), the poet knew full well that the Communist bloc hardly constituted a utopia. In 1970, he sent a letter to New York politician Donald Manes stating that he saw "little difference between the armed and violent governments both communist and capitalist."[11] His awareness of Communist control only increased during the 1970s and 1980s, when a burgeoning Western human rights movement focused on the persecution of writers behind the Iron Curtain. In 1982, Ginsberg joined E.L. Doctorow, Susan Sontag, Kurt Vonnegut, and other countercultural icons at a meeting affirming the Polish workers' organization Solidarity.[12] Two years later, he traveled to Poland to meet with Akademia Ruchu (the Academy of Movement), a Situationist-like performance group that existed in the grey area between official approval and official condemnation (Ginsberg 2014). "I don't think the ruling elites [in the United States and the Soviet Union] hate each other as much as they hate their dissidents," Ginsberg would argue in a contemporaneous PEN International report. "They need each other in order to burgeon and prosper" (2001: 42).

Some of the more astute US diplomats understood that Ginsberg's willingness to identify with dissidents and critique Communist bloc policy rendered him a potentially valuable propaganda asset. While in Poland in 1986, for example, Ginsberg was hosted by John Brown, a Foreign Service officer at the US Consulate in Krakow. Brown, we may speculate, had no particular interest in the Beat poet, but he may have understood that, in Ginsberg's words, "the inspiration for the rebellion in Eastern Europe was very much the American counter culture." The consulate officer likely recognized that the United States would benefit from association with radical poets, rock music, and other signs of subversive youth.[13] But he ignored the fact that Ginsberg sought a writers' international that resisted Cold War militarism on both sides of the divide. As he and fellow poets Yevgeny Yevtushenko and Ernesto Cardenal would put it in a 1982 collective statement decrying the US treatment of Nicaragua, "if the writers of the world get together, their pens will be mightier than any sword of Damocles" (*Deliberate Prose* 52).[14] Here at his most idealistic, Ginsberg follows Cousins in viewing writers as global citizens capable of creating a peaceful universalism beyond state control. Little wonder, then, that the poet

---

[11] Quoted in Flood (2014).

[12] Ginsberg signed a public letter announcing the meeting: see Ginsberg (1982).

[13] Interview with Allen Ginsberg, August 11, 1996, National Security Archive, George Washington University, https://nsarchive2.gwu.edu//coldwar/interviews/episode-13/ginsberg1.html, accessed February 14, 2022.

[14] Michelle Hardesty offers a valuable analysis of this literary internationalist intervention in Hardesty (2012).

urges the reader to "stand up against governments" in "On the Conduct of the World Seeking Beauty against Government" in *Cosmopolitan Greetings* (1994: 42).

Despite his suspicion of both capitalist and communist governments, Ginsberg did his part for the US-China writers' conferences. Indeed, apart from Maxine Hong Kingston, he contributed more to Cousins' project than any other American participant. Ginsberg delivered a speech at the 1982 event in Los Angeles, expounding on how "art ... must annihilate the distance between subject and object" before scandalizing some of the Chinese writers by discussing his homosexuality and his usage of peyote and psilocybin.[15] A few days later, he assumed the role of helpful tour guide and helped lead the visitors around Disneyland. This first conference experience would, in turn, lead to Ginsberg's journey to China for the 1984 event. In 1986, he made a cameo appearance during the Los Angeles-based conference's New York side trip and walked the PRC contingent across the Brooklyn Bridge, in effect offering them a Beat instantiation of Whitman's "Crossing Brooklyn Ferry."[16] Journalist and conference stalwart Harrison Salisbury highlighted the poet's importance to the conferences when he referred to Ginsberg as something of an ambassadorial "star" in a letter to Cousins (Salisbury 1986). For all his countercultural brio and outrageous behavior, Ginsberg sometimes displayed the diplomatic skills one would expect of a figure who had from the 1960s defined himself as "a kind of literary and cultural ambassador ... appealing to people of all nationalities and ideologies" (Schumacher 1992: 678).

Of his three experiences with the US–China writers' project, Ginsberg's 1984 sojourn proved by far the most important because it offered him his first opportunity to visit China, a nation he had longed to visit ever since he had become a Buddhist in the 1960s.[17] As in the first conference, Ginsberg insisted on discussing his sexuality, scandalizing the Chinese writers and officials in attendance with a frank account of his same-sex desire. Rather than play the proper cultural diplomat and contribute to the budding US-China geopolitical relationship, Ginsberg sought to explore the PRC as a queer space. The conference had lighter moments as well. On October 30, 1984, in Suzhou, Gary Snyder captured in verse the image of Ginsberg "writing down his poem" on "the bridge arch." And this lyrical effort prompted UCLA professor Robert Rees, one of Cousins' lieutenants, to respond with his own lyric about how both Beat poets had responded poetically to the ancient scene (Rees 1984).[18] For Snyder and Rees, the cultural diplomatic mission constituted an opportunity to invoke relationships among the US writers as they collectively engaged with a foreign culture.

---

[15] Annie Dillard describes the Chinese reaction to Ginsberg's speech in Dillard (1984: 64).

[16] It is tempting to speculate that the nineteenth-century poet's line "The certainty of others, the life, love, sight, hearing of others" resonated powerfully for Ginsberg in this cross-cultural context: Whitman 1856.

[17] For an important account of Ginsberg's interest in Chinese history and culture, see his 1990 correspondence with Chinese poet Zhang Ziqing (Ginsberg 2017a). I have also learned a great deal about Ginsberg's relationship to China from the following works: Schumacher (1992), Hui (2012), and Fazzino (2016).

[18] Rees also cites the short Snyder lyric.

Ginsberg didn't adopt this approach, however. The work inspired by his trip to China refrains from mentioning any of his fellow literary ambassadors. Ginsberg may have enjoyed traveling with a group of fellow American writers, yet he understood this cultural diplomatic mission to a totalitarian China in individual terms, focusing in his contemporary writing on his experiences after the conference. Indeed, it sometimes seems as though the enforced collectivity of the PRC required him to emphasize his point of view all the more. This was in many ways an almost stereotypically American approach to travel; as always, the maverick American goes it alone. Yet in other respects, Ginsberg's insistence on a unilateral encounter implies that this trip was for him an opportunity to experience China in highly personal terms, particularly when it came to questions of embodied experience. His attempt to express a queer internationalism demanded a certain distance from the other American literary ambassadors and, as we shall see, a marked refusal to endorse the idea that literary exchange should contribute to a new United States–China geopolitical relationship.

His one journalistic account of the journey suggests as much. Foregrounding the poet's individual perception and largely ignoring the diplomatic mission of which he was a part, "China Trip," (1985), first published in the *San Jose Mercury News*, forthrightly acknowledges the censorship and oppression omnipresent in China and provides a fairly conventional Cold War perspective on the east Asian nation. Ginsberg begins the piece by foregrounding his desire to take the measure of the "real" China in the post-Cultural Revolution era and then admits that this proved difficult. Few Chinese felt comfortable talking to an official guest in groups, particularly when the conversation turned to sensitive topics:

> I went through China asking everybody I met what they really thought—and found the general atmosphere is one of opening up, of reform and new breath. In individual conversations, the Chinese are completely clear and Mozartean-minded, very friendly, and tell you everything they can about themselves. But you can only have a subtle, real, frank conversation on a one-to-one level.
>
> If you talk with three people, they'll be somewhat inhibited because it is considered anti-state activity to criticize Deng Xiaoping, China's paramount leader, or the socialist basis of the state, or say anything funny about China's occupation of Tibet.
>
> (Ginsberg 2000: 53)

In this passage, Ginsberg doesn't so much wear the mantle of the maverick poet as adopt the persona of a relatively ordinary American visiting a totalitarian society for the first time. The poet notes how Chinese students work hard to avoid "standing out as too individualistic" because that sort of behavior might attract attention and "be noted" in their file (53). He deplores what he perceives as the Chinese people's absence of "real emotion and frankness and feeling" at a time when "the excesses of the Cultural Revolution are still very much a part of their lives" (54): "If a student is caught just making out," writes the poet in a tone of disbelief, "it could mean a mark in his dossier" (54). "Frankness and feeling" and physical pleasure seem strictly controlled in Deng Xiaoping's regime.

To be sure, Ginsberg also notes wryly that the prudishness of the totalitarian society made it seem as though "the Moral Majority is running China" (54) and he indicts "the dog-eat-dog time when the European nations' free market—including Western nations peddling opium—dominated Chinese politics" (56). But these left critiques of the United States and Europe are almost an afterthought in an essay that, for the most part, portrays the writer as a Westerner trying, with mixed results, to understand a deeply authoritarian society that bans individualism and intimacy in equal measure. As in his earlier experiences in the Soviet Union and Czechoslovakia, the poet seems uncannily American when confronting the oppressive reality of the totalitarian East.

This attitude extends to Ginsberg's comments on censorship in the literary realm. Writing for a mass-market newspaper audience, Ginsberg refrains from his usual impulse to critique the contemporary United States and its repressive tendencies. The indictment of Reagan-era censorship pivotal to "Industrial Waves" and any number of other contemporary poems makes no appearance in "China Trip." On the contrary, he indicates that the official presence of American writers provided a brief respite from the totalitarian oppression because party officials feel compelled to allow some freedom of speech at such cultural exchanges. He thus points out that "The Source of Inspiration," the official theme of the conference, was "designed to dodge the doctrine of art as revolutionary propaganda and give Chinese and American writers a chance to talk about individual sources of inspiration and for them to air their ideas of liberty of expression" (54). Even as neither Ginsberg nor the other American writers proselytize for their nation, their Americanness enables a certain sort of literary, cultural, and political conversation that would typically be impossible under Deng Xiaoping's regime. Ginsberg points out that "Chinese students laughed or tittered whenever I said something outrageous. American teachers in China are allowed to say anything they want" (57). His countercultural identity ensures his freedom of expression even more. Ginsberg recognizes that he benefits from the Chinese estimation of the Beat Generation "as a literary movement in rebellion against capitalism, or American imperialism" (57).[19]

Yet, if Ginsberg runs the risk of becoming an inadvertent US propagandist by critiquing the PRC, his assertion of a queer perspective anathema to the Reagan Administration necessarily complicates matters. The poet signals his refusal to accede to Cold War homophobia in the conclusion of "China Trip," when he swerves away from overt political and cultural commentary to pair a pedagogic discussion of William Carlos Williams's poem "Dance Russe" (1916) with a Chinese official's recitation of a passage from Mao's poem "Snow" (1936). Ginsberg explains to the *San Jose Mercury* readers that he used the Williams poem as a way to challenge Chinese students' notions of "American conformity" and demonstrate that even "the American businessman" has feelings of loneliness and anomie (57). But this explanation of how he teaches "Dance Russe" hardly exhausts the poem's function in the essay "China Trip." In the closing

---

[19] It is worth noting here that Wen Chu-An's pioneering, book-length translation of Ginsberg's poetry into Mandarin wouldn't appear until 2000.

scene, Ginsberg's invocation of this lyric anatomy of American capitalist identity—as Williams puts it, "I am lonely, lonely/I was born to be lonely"–sits cheek by jowl with his Chinese companion's citation of such Mao lyrics as "The mountains are dancing silver serpents,/The hills on the plain are shining elephants/I desire to compare our height with the skies." Ginsberg explains that the Chinese cadre member performed this portion of Mao's poem because "we were Americans, we were going away and he wanted to manifest his great feeling for China" (58). Yet even as the essay recognizes the power of nationalism in its penultimate moment, the last sentence affirms the desire to cross borders. "Our farewell was warm with tipsy embraces," the poet concludes in a homoerotic vein. Rather than confirm Chinese jingoism, the cadre member expresses "great feeling" for an American. (58). And poetry facilitates this surprising bond. The bold linkage of Williams to Mao subtends the "warm … tipsy embraces" of the two men; in effect, the newspaper article concludes with two male couples united through poetry. In this last moment of "China Trip," Ginsberg indicates that he hopes to do more than facilitate better US–China relations in the usual cultural diplomatic fashion. He has come to the Asian nation to foster a cultural exchange that demonstrates the queer potential of literary connection.

The ten poems Ginsberg produced during the trip to China tend to foreground this affective conception of cultural exchange even as his lyrics sometimes also concede the inescapability of bureaucratic power and control in a totalitarian state. In "I Love Old Whitman So," Ginsberg seizes upon the work of the Good Gray Poet to re-imagine cultural diplomacy as intimate pedagogy. Published in the volume *White Shroud*, the poem speaks powerfully of how teaching *Leaves of Grass* at Baoding University provided Ginsberg with something of an allegory of how cultural exchange might bring Americans and Chinese together. "I Love Old Whitman So" first emphasizes how teaching the Chinese students has reminded Ginsberg of his deep affection for Whitman: "I skim Leaves beginning to end, this year in the Middle Kingdom," writes Ginsberg, "touched by his desperado farewell, 'Who touches this book touches/a man'" (Ginsberg 1987: 58). But this isn't only a personal reflection on Ginsberg's passionate connection with an esteemed national predecessor as evinced by the poem "A Supermarket in California" (1956). It is also an implicit commentary on the desire to share that passion with a foreign public, despite considerable obstacles. Hoping to give the class the gift of *Leaves of Grass*, Ginsberg explains how he "read aloud to those few Chinese/boys & girls/who know enough American tongue to ear his hand" (58). Implicitly yoking Whitman's famous lines, "who touches this book touches/a man," to his own phrase "to ear his hand," Ginsberg makes clear that he not only hopes to share with the Chinese the brilliance of the nineteenth-century poet but also seeks in Whitman's intimate aesthetic a model for cultural exchange itself. If Ginsberg hoped to define cultural exchange as physical interaction rather than state propaganda, Whitman's greatest poem helps him instantiate that vision. The nineteenth-century writer's lyric invocation of tactile connection, initially directed at an American audience, now signifies as Ginsberg's attempt to connect with a foreign public.. For all their difficulty reading *Leaves*, the Chinese students will, through their engagement with Whitman, extend intimacy across the Pacific in a gesture of affective internationalism not unlike the "embraces" Ginsberg shares with the cadre member in "China Trip." In the poet's view, we might say, Whitman's embodied expansiveness ("I contain multitudes") extends beyond the United States to tenderly encompass distant nationalities.

As the Whitmanian "catalog" poem "One Morning I Took a Walk in China" makes evident, the Beat poet would pursue a similarly expansive strategy during his six-week visit to China, not only through his pedagogic interaction with students at Hebei University but also through his exploration of streets, businesses, and everyday life. Consider "One Morning's" litany of polychromatic goods in the Baoding market: "mandarin Tangerines, yellow round pears ... apples yellow red-pinked, short bananas half-black'd green (61). One thinks again of "A Supermarket in California," a poem whose speaker also dreams "of ... enumerations," as he catalogs the various foodstuffs for sale in a very different sort of marketplace. And while "One Morning" doesn't name queer desire explicitly (no one eyes "grocery boys" here, as in "Supermarket"), the poem still provides a hint of Ginsberg's sexuality. Witness the attention paid to the "students" dancing "with wooden silvered swords," and the fascination with a "student" in the barber chair, "black hair clipped at ears straight across the back of/his neck" (61). If the queer embodiment so palpable in "I Love Old Whitman So" doesn't obtain here, it's only because the alterity of the Baoding market has supplanted the speaker's usual object of desire. In this exotic catalog, the "strange" pears, bananas, and other goods of a Chinese market prove as distracting as the male students performing with their swords.

To be sure, Ginsberg's experience of literary exchange didn't always lend itself to the pleasures of touch. Even as he attempted to find in cultural diplomacy a much-needed corrective to the cold and brutal forces he decried in "Industrial Waves," Ginsberg also confronted the power of the state in structuring and delimiting his cultural diplomatic experience. Other poems written on the trip make evident how his quest for the real China repeatedly clashed with the omnipresence of government officials and minders. One senses as much in an untitled 1984 poem in which Ginsberg, pleased to be on his own after the scheduled conference activities had concluded, has yet to escape the Chinese state: "omnipresent kindly Chinese/Bureaucracy meets me at airports & boats ... I'm/trying to figure a way out" (Ginsberg 2017b: 185). Eager to connect to the Chinese in a personal manner, Ginsberg instead finds himself bound to the impersonal "Bureaucracy"; the irreverent beatnik who had so often confronted power at home now finds himself stymied by the "kindly" but "omnipresent" Communist state.

Such experiences were part and parcel of literary ambassadorship during the cultural Cold War. Yet even as the poet acknowledged the realities of state power in restricting his access to the Chinese people, he refused to jettison an intimate model of cultural diplomacy, and in "Reading Bai Juyi," the finest poem to emerge to from the visit, he balances these competing pressures to great effect. A poem celebrating the Tang Dynasty writer, much of "Reading Bai Juyi" highlights Ginsberg's distance from ordinary Chinese citizens as he enjoys the comfortable privacy afforded an important guest by the inescapable Communist state. The poem opens by stressing that the poet's extensive travels throughout the Asian nation haven't minimized this gap—"I'm a traveler in a strange country China and I've been to many cities"—but have instead left him alone in a new metropolis: "Now I'm back in Shanghai, days under warm covers in a room." For all his sensitivity to the alterity of China, Ginsberg soon makes clear that his fame has resulted in state hospitality more alien to him than the Asian nation itself. His privileged position as an American literary ambassador is indisputably "strange" when contrasted with the disadvantaged lives of the "hundreds of millions" who "shiver." And Ginsberg emphasizes this unsettling fact by repeatedly contrasting his own easy travels in China with the demanding work of students, workmen, fruit sellers, rowers, porters. He doesn't "have to push … boat oars … in the Yangtze/gorges, or pole … downstream/ … through yellow industrial scum." While the Chinese work hard and contend with environmental pollution, Ginsberg sleeps "late" and enjoys his cigarettes in a warm bed (Ginsberg 1987: 63).

Not that the American poet ignores the broader political implications of the situation. "Reading Bai Juyi" emphasizes that the distance between Ginsberg and the Chinese workers reflects the enormous gulf between a prosperous United States and an impoverished China still recovering from the Cultural Revolution. In an account of being ill while on tour, the poet implies that these larger political issues necessarily determine the meaning of his cultural diplomatic initiative:

> I woke to find I was a sick guest in a vast poor kingdom
> A famous visitor honored with a heated room,
> medicines, special foods and learned visitors
> inquiring when I'd be well enough to lecture my hosts
> on the music and poets of the wealthy
> Nation I had come from half way round the world
>
> (66).

It is hard to overstate the irony at work here. Riffing on the rhetoric of hospitality that so often informs cultural diplomacy, Ginsberg portrays himself as "a sick guest" of considerable means who unworriedly consumes all his "poor" "hosts" have to offer. He stresses how the Chinese have provided him with modern comforts—"heated room,/medicines, special foods"—so that he might recover and "lecture" them "on the music and poets of the wealthy/Nation." In these darkly comic lines, the success of the poet's cultural diplomatic mission does not depend on his capacity to cultivate close relations with Chinese people but rather on the Communist state's capacity to nurse a famous American back to health. The American literary ambassador has become a ward of Chinese officialdom, and if he experiences any bond at all, it is not with the workers in the street but with the anonymous bureaucrats and "learned visitors" who contribute to his recovery in expectation he will inform them about US literature and culture. Ginsberg unwittingly becomes one with the very governmentality he usually decried.

But even as he deplores the difficulty of fulfilling his intimate conception of US–Chinese exchange in the face of state interpellation, "Reading Bai Juyi" also makes evident that Ginsberg finds in Chinese literature another means of achieving the personal bond he desires. He may argue "about boys making love with a student," as he puts it in the second section of the poem, but he can also devise a less "contentious" means of expressing his desire through a transhistorical literary connection (64). The very title of the poem suggests the importance of engaging with ancient Chinese lyric, and Ginsberg repeatedly describes himself reading Bai in various stanzas. Early on, the poet informs us he'll "stay in bed again & and read old Chinese poets," and this personal comment looks toward a more emotional moment when he confesses, "Something Bai said makes me press my finger/to my eyes and weep—maybe his love/for an old poet friend" (63, 65). The Tang Dynasty's "love/ for an old poet friend" inspires a lachrymal response on Ginsberg's part as he lies in bed connecting with his Chinese predecessor.[20] The Beat's synchronic attempt to connect intimately with the Chinese people takes on atemporal dimensions as what Carolyn Dinshaw would call "queer historical touches" link the two poets (2007).[21] Indeed, a disjunctive approach to literary history may offer Ginsberg the "way out" denied him by the Chinese authorities.

The end of "Reading Bai Juyi" makes clear the appeal of connecting with the poets of the past, as Ginsberg bonds with Bai through a revisionary stanza entitled "Transformation of Bai's 'A Night in Xingyang.'"[22] More of an homage than an appropriation, "Transformation" makes evident the Beat poet's desire to embrace and inhabit one of Bai's poems, retaining its structure and feel as he substitutes American experiences and modern memories for the ancient material of the original. Thus, even as Ginsberg replaces Xingyang with Paterson, New Jersey, highlights his teenage "fears" instead of retaining Bai's emphasis on childhood "fun," and adds details on parental death, the American poet still follows his predecessor's lyrical meditation on change and loss. Both poems mourn the destruction of "old houses" (Bai) and "childhood houses" (Ginsberg); both emphasize "buildings and roads are different" (Bai) and "New buildings rise on that street" (Ginsberg); both highlight the transformation of urban environments. And both works end by invoking the ceaseless and reliable movement of a familiar river as a counterpoint to the melancholic subject matter. "The Rivers Zhen and Wei" cited in Bai's work find their echo in "the Passaic river" of New Jersey; the waterways link past and present in an autobiographical register even as they also symbolize the conduit between a late-twentieth-century poet and his eighth-century Chinese predecessor.[23]

---

[20] It is not clear how much Ginsberg knew about the tradition of intense male–male friendship during the Tang Dynasty, but Bai Juyi's much-celebrated relationship with fellow poet Yuan Zhen no doubt resonated with the US writer. For an important commentary on Bai Juyi and Chinese male homosocial and homoerotic connections, see Hinsch (1990).

[21] For a fuller account of Dinshaw's argument, see Dinshaw (1999).

[22] Ginsberg cites Rewi Alley's translation as the source to which he responds. As Ginsberg puts it in *White Shroud*, 68: "After Rewi Alley's Bai *Juyi*, 200 Selected Poems (Beijing: New World Press, 1983), p.303." However, Alley's translation isn't completely reliable. As David S. Wills has argued, the Bai Juyi poem central to Ginsberg's revision is most likely "Stopping the Night at Rong-Yang," as translated by Arthur Waley. For the Waley version, see Waley (2012). For Zhang Dandan and Wills's more Ginsbergian translation of the same poem, see Dandan and Wills (2018).

[23] See *Poems of Bai Juyi*, 303 (Ginsberg1994: 68).

Intertwining his lyric with the work of a Tang Dynasty poet constitutes Ginsberg's attempt at establishing a bond denied by geopolitical divisions. If he invoked Whitman's famous line "Who touches this book touches a man" as an emphatically proximate way to imagine cultural exchange, he demonstrates through his gentle rewriting of Bai's poem that the engagement with historical distance can, paradoxically enough, lead to equally intimate results.

In certain ways, the last stanza of "Reading Bai Juyi" may seem to link Ginsberg to Orientalist predecessors like Ezra Pound. From this perspective, the author of *Howl* appears less the maverick culture hero, the activist who led the levitation of the Pentagon, than a canonical white modernist. Ginsberg comes to resemble the very writers he scorned as coopted by the Cold War state. Yet, this is where his investment in a queer and embodied cultural diplomacy proves significant. By demonstrating that literary exchange only succeeds through personal contact ("tipsy embraces," male–male poetic identification, etc.), Ginsberg implicitly rejects upper-scale cultural relations designed to promote major transnational bonds. The ties between Ginsberg and the party cadre official and the Baoding students are intense and memorable, but they are not productive of new US–PRC relations, literary or otherwise. For Ginsberg, we may speculate, only global poetic exchange that challenges conventional geopolitical ambitions has value. Literary diplomacy matters to him to the degree that it forgoes grand political aims for short-term intimacy—for, in Nan Z. Da's words, "the pleasures … of apprehending the lightness of contact in a very close world" (Da: 11). Coopting cultural diplomacy in the name of his own desire, Ginsberg propagates poetry to assert a queer internationalism defiant of national or political belonging.

References

Angelou, Maya. 1976. *Singin' and Swingin' and Gettin' Merry Like Christmas* (New York: Random House).

Arndt, Richard. 2006. *The First Resort of Kings: American Cultural Diplomacy in the Twentieth Century* (Washington, DC: Potomac Books).

Baldwin, Kate. 2016. *The Racial Imaginary of the Cold War Kitchen: From Sokol'niki to Chicago's South Side* (Hanover, NE: Dartmouth College Press).

Barnhisel, Greg. 2015. "'Put Someone in Charge of His Liquor' and Other Foreign-Service Rules for Handling William Faulkner," *Slate*, February 26, https://slate.com/human-interest/2015/02/william-faulkner-biography-the-writer-s-overseas-tour-during-the-cold-war.html, accessed February 14, 2022.

Blaschke, Anne M. 2016. "Running the Cold War: Gender, Race, and Track in Cultural Diplomacy, 1955–1975," *Diplomatic History* 40.5 (November): 826–844.

Brinkley, Joel. 1984. "U.S.I.A.'S BLACKLIST," *New York Times*, March 15, 18.

Chua, J.Y. 2016. "Eurovision and the Making of Queer (Counter)Cultural Diplomacy," *Yale Review of International Studies*, http://yris.yira.org/essays/1650, accessed February 14, 2022.

Cousins, Norman. 1984. Letter to the Second US–China Writers' Conference, October 16, UCLA Special Collections. Box 964, Folder 1.

Cull, Nicholas. 2008. *The Cold War and The United States Information Agency* (New York: Oxford University Press).

Da, Nan Z. 2018. *Intransitive Encounter: Sino-U.S. Literatures and the Limits of Exchange* (New York: Columbia University Press).

Dandan, Zhang, and David S. Wills. 2018. "The Mystery of Allen Ginsberg's 'Reading Bai Juyi,'" March 16, www.beatdom.com/mystery-allens-ginsbergs-reading-bai-juyi, accessed February 14, 2022.

Dillard, Annie. 1984. *Encounters with Chinese Writers* (Middletown, CT: Wesleyan University Press), 64.

Dinshaw, Carolyn. 1999. *Getting Medieval: Sexualities and Communities, Pre- and Postmodern* (Durham, NC: Duke University Press).

Dinshaw, Carolyn. 2007. "Theorizing Queer Temporalities: A Roundtable Discussion," *GLQ* 13.2–3 (June): 178.

Eliot, T.S. 1945. "The Man of Letters and the Future of Europe," *The Sewanee Review* 53.3 (Summer): 341.

Eng, Ien, Isar, Yudhishthir Raj, and Mar, Phillip. 2015. "Cultural Diplomacy: Beyond the National Interest?," *International Journal of Cultural Policy* 21.4: 365–381.

Fazzino, Jimmy. 2016. *World Beats: Beat Generation Writing and the Worlding of U.S. Literature* (Hanover, NE: University Press of New England).

Flood, Alison. 2014. "Allen Ginsberg postcard condemns 'Red Lands' of eastern Europe," *The Guardian*, April 24.

Ginsberg, Allen. 1978. "T. S. Eliot Entered My Dreams," in *Poems All Over the Place, Mainly Seventies* (Cherry Valley, CA: Cherry Valley Editions), 46.

Ginsberg, Allen. 1982. "Solidarity Meeting," *New York Review of Books*, February 18, www.nybooks.com/articles/1982/02/18/solidarity-meeting, accessed February 14, 2022.

Ginsberg, Allen. 1987. *White Shroud: Poems, 1980–1985* (New York: Harper Perennial).

Ginsberg, Allen. 1994. *Cosmopolitan Greetings: Poems, 1986–1992* (New York: Harper Collins).

Ginsberg, Allen. 2000. "China Trip," in *Deliberate Prose: Selected Essays, 1952–1995* (New York: Harper Collins).

Ginsberg, Allen. 2000. *Deliberate Prose: Selected Essays, 1952–1995* (New York: Harper Perennial).

Ginsberg, Allen. 2014. "Allen Ginsberg in Poland," *The Allen Ginsberg Project*, September 11, https://allenginsberg.org/2014/09/allen-ginsberg-in-poland, accessed February 14, 2022.

Ginsberg, Allen. 2017a. "Ginsberg and China," *The Allen Ginsberg Project*, September 10, https://allenginsberg.org/2017/09/ginsberg-china-2, accessed February 14, 2022.

Ginsberg, Allen. 2017b. *Wait Till I'm Dead: Uncollected Poems* (New York: Grove).

Ginsberg, Allen. 2018. *Intransitive Encounters: Sino–U.S. Literatures and the Limits of Exchange* (New York: Columbia University Press).

Goodlad, Lauren M.E. 2006. "Where Liberals Fear to Tread: E. M. Forster's Queer Internationalism and the Ethics of Care," *Novel: A Forum on Fiction* 39.3 (Summer): 307-336.

Hardesty, Michelle. 2012. "'If the Writers of the World Get Together': Allen Ginsberg, Lawrence Ferlinghetti, and Literary Solidarity in Sandinista Nicaragua," in Nancy M. Grace and Jenny Skerl, eds, *The Transnational Beat Generation* (New York: Springer): 115–128.

Hinsch, Bret. 1990. *Passions of the Cut Sleeve: The Male Homosexual Tradition in China* (Berkeley, CA: University of California Press).

Hui, Su. 2012. "Allen Ginsberg's 'China,'" in Zhang Yuejun and Stuart Christie, eds, *American Modernist Poetry and the Chinese Encounter* (Berlin: Spring Link), 123–132.

Lincoln, Kenneth. 1999. *A Writer's China: Bridges East and West* (Santa Barbara, CA: Capa Press).

Link, Perry. 1985. "US–China Second Writers' Conference," *Modern Chinese Literature* 1.2 (Spring): 271–278.

Menand, Louis. 2005. "Unpopular Front: American Art and the Cold War," *The New Yorker*, October 9, www.newyorker.com/magazine/2005/10/17/unpopular-front, accessed February 13, 2022.

Phillips, Victoria. 2019. *Martha Graham's Cold War: The Dance of American Diplomacy* (New York: Oxford University Press), 132–164.

Puar, Jasbir K. 2007. *Terrorist Assemblages: Homonationalism in Queer Times* (Durham, NC: Duke University Press).

Rees, Robert. 1984. "A Day of Poetry at the Han Shan Temple," http://robert-rees.org/wp-content/uploads/2013/04/A-Day-of-Poetry-at-Han-Shan-Temple.pdf, accessed February 14, 2022.

Salisbury, Harrison. 1986. Letter to Norman Cousins, June 5, UCLA Special Collections, Box 964, Folder 2.

Schumacher, Michael. 1992. *Dharma Lion: A Biography of Allen Ginsberg* (New York: St Martins Press).

Stecopoulos, Haralaos. Forthcoming. *Telling America's Story to the World: Literature, Internationalism, Cultural Diplomacy* (Oxford: Oxford University Press).

United States Advisory Commission on Public Diplomacy. 1985. *United States Advisory Commission on Public Diplomacy: 1985 Report* (Washington, DC: State Department).

US Department of State. 2005. "Cultural Diplomacy: The Linchpin of Public Diplomacy," Report of the Advisory Committee on Cultural Diplomacy, September.

Waley, Arthur. 2012. *Waiting for the Moon: Poems of Bo Juyi* (Edinburg, VA: Axios Press).

Whitman, Walt. 1856. "Crossing Brooklyn Ferry," *The Poetry Foundation*, www.poetryfoundation.org/poems/45470/crossing-brooklyn-ferry, accessed February 14, 2022.

PART 3
ATTACHMENTS

CHAPTER 11

THE LAST PURITAN IN SHANGHAI

The Faded Romance of China Trade Finance and the Queerly Transnational Melancholy of Emily Hahn's Wartime Opium Smoking

KENDALL JOHNSON

> John Jacob Astor; a name which, I admit, I love to repeat, for it hath a rounded and orbicular sound to it, and rings like unto bullion.
>
> narrator, "Bartleby, the Scrivener: a Story of Wall-Street,"
>
> Melville (1856: 33)

IN 1936, the author and journalist Emily "Mickey" Hahn (1905–1997) reviewed George Santayana's *The Last Puritan: A Memoir in the Form of a Novel* (1935) for the English-language monthly *T'ien Hsia* while living in Shanghai (Hahn 1936).[1] Santayana's memoir and Hahn's situated response open twentieth-century American literature to the cultural legacy of the China Trade that the nineteenth-century *mercantile biography* presented as a national romance of globally extensive free trade.[2] This allegorical *bildungsroman*

---

[1] *The Last Puritan* (1935) was first published by Constable Publishers in London. The following year, Charles Scribner's and Sons published it in New York. Citations are from the MIT edition (Santayana 1994 [1935]), which includes a listing of all the editions (575).

[2] The phrase "mercantile biography" comes from *Hunt's Merchants' Magazine* in 1840; examples include those of Samuel Shaw, Stephen Girard, Thomas H. Perkins, John Jacob Astor, and others (see Johnson 2020). For an extensive account of the interwoven family relations of the US China Trade, see Downs (1997).

charted the rise of a heroic commercial patriarch who ventured to China on a quest to secure a capital foundation for his family in New England. The linear narrative development of this individual character straightened the complexity of global finance capital, inaugurating patrilineal vectors of China Trade fortune that promised national free trade futurity.

Even as the Bretton Woods Agreement (1944) set post-War terms of US financial hegemony, Hahn and Santayana were strikingly out of step with the previous century's aspirational romance of commercial patriarchy (Arrighi 2007: 384). Their autobiographical writings evoke melancholic social alienation in reaction to the abstracted terms of transoceanic commercial speculation, an affective vacuum of inter-imperial "financialization" that "[permitted] money to be used to make more money" through "instruments that [exploited] the role of money in credit, speculation, and investment"(Appadurai 2016: 2).

The literary and cultural scholar Elizabeth Freeman has considered how *queer* senses of time imply intimacies of situated affection and social consciousness that are beside and outside (rather than confined within) the hetero-normative cultural geography of national progress and commodity capitalism (Freeman 2019: 9).[3] The queerness of Hahn and Santayana's *chronotopes* help explain the very different ways that their melancholic retrospections evoke global scales of national alienation in the affective shadow of the China Trade's inter-imperial financial system.[4] The chronotope of Santayana's autobiographical character queers patriarchic ambition by setting an Archimedean point of philosophical retrospection on life experience that his autobiographical text monumentalizes as a ruin of mortally frustrated affective potential. In contrast, Hahn queers commercial romance by revising autobiographical pacts with readers over decades of multi-generic publication.[5] Her chronotopes express the vulnerability of refusing protective governance of national patriarchy in affiliation with women struggling to claim their affective powers at transnational sites of potentially mortal sexual exploitation.

The semi-colonial treaty port of Shanghai was a canny site for Hahn to write the review because an inherited China Trade fortune features prominently in Santayana's life and memoir. Both *The Last Puritan* and his subsequent three-volume autobiography *Persons and Places* (1944; 1945; 1953) consider the slide of a "Great Merchant" family of New England into cultural stagnation that counterpoises self-righteously genteel

---

[3] In using the term *queer*, I borrow from Halberstan (2005: 5). I also draw on the work of Luciano (2007) and Rifkin (2017).

[4] Bakhtin defines "chronotope" as the "the intrinsic connectedness of temporal and spatial relationships that are artistically expressed in literature" ("Forms of Time and of the Chronotope in the Novel" in Bakhtin 1981: 84).

[5] Lejeune describes the autobiography's validity as a provisional pact between an author and a reader that depends on the reader trusting the author to represent senses of their experience; for the basic definition on which Lejeune and subsequent scholars ruminate, see Lejeune (1989: 4).

provincialism and sensualist opium addiction.⁶ *The Last Puritan* draws on Santayana's youth in Boston as an ancestrally alienated member of the Sturgis family whose Great Merchant forefathers were icons of "raw energy" and masters of the "material concerns" that drive the "line of history" (Trilling 1980 [1956]: 168). *Persons and Places* subverts this epic legacy by typifying his uncle Russell Sturgis, Jr (1805–1887; Figure 11.1) as the *last* Great Merchant and then relishing "the melancholy pleasure of watching" his descendants (Santayana's half-siblings and cousins) "in their gradual obscuration, dispersion, and decline" into irrelevant "sensualists" or (worst of all) self-righteous moralists of the leisured genteel class.⁷

Despite his family connections, Santayana presents himself as categorically beyond the anti-romance of what he had derided as the "Genteel Tradition."⁸ Santayana introduced the phrase in a 1911 lecture at the University of California, Berkeley, where he appreciated the experiential thrill of immersive frontier imperialism in contrast to the comforts of New England, where the "beliefs and standards of the [nation's] fathers" had fallen out of step with the striving "instincts, practice, and discoveries of the younger generation."⁹ Although Santayana deemed Calvinist orthodoxy to be a vestigial delusion, he respected "Puritan" forefathers for living an "expression of the agonized conscience," accepting the futility of their actions in sustained conviction that "it is beautiful that sin should exist to be punished" (Santayana 2009: 5). He did not respect latter-day New Englanders, whose genteel propriety was propped up by inherited fortune rather than spiritual dread.

In quest adventures, whether to China or the continental frontier, Santayana appreciated the naïvely vibrant masculinity of American imperialism. As Lionel Trilling wrote, Santayana was generally uncomfortable in the United States but "had a tolerance and affection" for the "young and barbaric" "America" with its "raw energy" and "material concerns," as evident in the satirical lyric "Young Sammy's First Wild Oats" (1900) and "Spain in America" (1901) (Trilling 1980 [1956]: 168).¹⁰ Despite the appropriation of Santayana's phrase the "Genteel Tradition" by scholars who valorized literature for its democratic implications, Santayana's philosophical world view was determinedly amoral.¹¹ Hence, in *Persons and Places* he pokes fun at William James and his Aunt Sarah Blake Sturgis Shaw for their morally romantic egotism in condemning US conquest of Spain and the Philippines. From Santayana's perspective, mortality undercuts

---

⁶ *Persons and Places* is in three volumes: *The Background of My Life* (1944), *The Middle Span* (1945), and *My Host the World* (1953), all published by Charles Scribner's Sons (New York). Citations here are from the edition by William G. Holzberger and Herman J. Saatkamp, Jr (Santayana 1987).

⁷ *The Background of My Life* (1944) (Santayana 1987: 57, 73).

⁸ Santayana delivered "The Genteel Tradition in American Philosophy" before the Philosophical Union and it was reprinted in Santayana (1911); all citations are from the Seaton edition (Santayana 2009).

⁹ For discussion of the event, see McCormick 2003: 206–208.

¹⁰ Both of Santayana's essays are in Santayana (1901).

¹¹ In "'That Smile of Parmenides Made Me Think'" (Trilling 1980 [1956]), Trilling noted that it would be "impossible to imagine" "what the academic historian of American culture would do without Santayana's phrase" (168). The highbrow–lowbrow opposition gained currency in relation to potential for populist democracy through the work of Van Wyck Brooks, Harold Sterns, Malcolm Cowley, and others, who embraced democracy as an antidote to the elite (McClay 1982).

FIGURE 11.1 "Russell Sturgis" from a painting by George Richmond. From *Some Merchants and Sea Captains of Old Boston* (1918), p. viii

> One of the best known merchants of his time. He was partner of Russell & Sturgis and of Russell, Sturgis & Co., of Russell & Co. after the consolidation of the two latter firms. He was later partner and, finally head, of Baring Brothers of London.

morality in the long course of imperial history. Each human being faced nature's infinite abyss from a mortal perch and, normatively speaking, ought not be "suffered to criticize or reform"; it was more honorable to cultivate a philosophical stoicism, accepting that "what you can do avails little materially and in the end nothing" (Santayana 2009: 19). Santayana's autobiographies model a personal economy of philosophical detachment from the will either to exercise imperial power or to judge imperialists on a moral basis; both ambitions are opiates that distract from exercising Reason to apprehend and accept the materialist amorality of life. Santayana thus divests himself from any romance of American free trade or literature by situating himself philosophically beyond the allure of nationally exceptional aspiration.

It is more than trivial that Hahn reviewed the novel while addicted to "old fashioned" smoking opium that she recounted decades later in "The Big Smoke" (1969), a melancholic *New Yorker* article and a central chapter of her final autobiography *Times and Places*: A Memoir* (Hahn 1970: 227).[12] Like Santayana, she resisted the heroism of nineteenth-century "Great Merchant" patriarchy and self-righteous New England gentility, but she also criticized the masculine autonomy of Santayana's fatalistic philosophical materialism.[13] Across her long international career, she challenged the "allegorical force" of genteel feminine types related to the American Girl and the American Woman, which Martha Banta defines generally as "visual and literary form[s]" of "abstract eternal verities" governing the domestic propriety of intimacies, paradoxically reconfigured amidst the "fears of and desires of its citizens" (Banta 1987: xxxii).[14] In recounting her opium addiction, Hahn highlights her vulnerability as a woman *and* her relative privilege as a white American professional journalist. Her ritual of smoking the drug generates queer senses of place and time and so does her representation of it, especially as she situates herself at the crossroads of inter-imperial crisis in wartime Shanghai. She recalls enigmatic temporal disjunctions in scenes of smoking with a group of Shanghainese and international literati—scenes ambivalently charged with degrees of intimacy and alienation born from the social context of the war. Across her career, as Hahn revisits her time in Shanghai, she celebrates Chinese women who endured the sexual violence of Japanese occupation. She also depicts expatriated women who struggled to survive exploitative circulation in trans-imperial economies of sexual and emotional service to men. In highlighting these struggles Hahn pushes readers to reject genteel senses of sexual purity and conventions of American Girlhood. Hahn's chronotopes excite powers of female sexuality as her characters see hope in the postwar horizon—hope springing from transnational intimacies that exceed the patriarchic hero of mercantile biography and its national terms of allegory.

Born to Jewish immigrant parents in St Louis, Hahn grew up in Chicago before attending the University of Wisconsin, where she was the first woman to earn a degree in mining engineering that equipped her to track down oil claims and diamond

---

[12] "The Big Smoke" first appeared in Hahn (1969).
[13] The key biographies of Hahn are Cuthbertson (1998) and Grescoe (2016).
[14] See Stoler (2006: 3–6).

deposits. Instead, she travelled and published as a "metropolitan newspaperwoman" who deployed her body as a "conduit for news" to attract and hold audiences in the spirit of Nelly Bly (Lutes 2006: 2).[15] Initially Hahn travelled to China inspired by an "American Orientalism" as she used "gender as a narrative tool and analytical category" to establish authority in the United States as well as around the world (Yoshihara 2003: 6).[16] She arrived in Shanghai from Japan in 1935 on what was supposed to be a circuitous route back to what was then the Belgian Congo, where she had spent two years and then published the travelogue *Congo Solo* (1933) and the novel *With Naked Foot* (1934). She stayed on in the "Paris of the East" (Shanghai) to report on its vibrant nightlife for the *North-China Daily News* after befriending Sir Victor Sassoon, the Jewish British financier and third Baronet of Bombay whose company owned the Cathay Hotel and other real estate throughout the zones of French Concession and International Settlement (Hahn 1944a: 23).

Hahn first smoked opium with the noted Chinese poet, essayist, and publisher Shao Xunmei (Zau Sinmay 邵洵美; 1906-68) in 1935.[17] Soon after they became literary collaborators and lovers, despite Shao having a wife and children. When Japan invaded in 1937, Hahn and Shao married to shield his printing press from confiscation with her citizenship. In the early stages of smoking opium, Hahn was highly productive, teaching English at university, reporting, editing magazines, and writing essays for the *New Yorker*.[18] Her flat on Kiangsi Road in the International Concession area resembled a salon, attracting visits from "poets, artists, teachers and intellectuals," including Mao Zedong and Zhou Enlai (Cuthbertson 1998: 146). Through Shao, she met Wen Yuan-ning, who edited *T'ien Hsia*, founded by Sun Fo (the son of Sun Yat-sen) to foster "mutual understanding between West and East by means of literature" (Hahn 1944a: 16).[19] Joining its roster of luminary contributors (such as Lin Yutang, John Wu, Hu Shi, and Louis Cha), she reviewed novels by Nobel Prize winner Pearl S. Buck, Lawrence Durrell, Sinclair Lewis, Margaret Mitchell, Virginia Woolf, Santayana, and others.

Her residence in China undoubtedly helped her "[gain] material and affective power" in relation to American audiences curious about "Asian subjects," whom she

---

[15] In Hahn's young adult biography of Elizabeth Cochrane Seaman (Hahn 1959a), she considers how Bly's international career as "newspaper girl" (145) defied the propriety regarding what it meant to be an "American girl" and "American woman" (14, 33, 87, 128, 168).

[16] On the varieties of "American Orientalism" in the early national period, see Schueller (1998), Eperjesi (2005), Huang (2008), Egan (2011), Frank (2011), and Lowe (2015).

[17] This chapter renders 邵洵美 in standard Chinese as Shào Xùnméi. However, as Hutt (2010) explains, Shao was known as "Zau Sinmay" according to the Shanghainese (Hu language 滬語) pronunciation. In his 2010, Hutt uses "Zau" in the title at the request of Zau's daughter Shao Xiaohong and then switches to using "Shao Xunmei" in the body of the essay in order to avoid confusion of scholarly reference. Grescoe explains his use of "Zau" in *Shanghai Grand* (2016: 3). On Shao's importance to Shanghai urban modernity and to Chinese literary culture of the twentieth century, see Lee's influential chapter (1999).

[18] This included *Candid Comment*, which lasted six months (September 1938–March 1939) during Japan's invasion, and the bilingual *Vox*, which lasted three months in late 1935 (Grescoe 2016: 190).

[19] See Shen (2009: 59–93).

represented in fashioning her professional image (Yoshihara 2003: 6).[20] But her residence was not a shallow exercise in sensationalizing the exotic or braving exposure to racist depictions of vice. Her reflection on the thrill and disappointment of the residence opened her to literary projects in Indonesia, India, Malaysia, Singapore, the Philippines, Ireland, Taiwan, the United Kingdom, and across post-colonial nations of Central and South Africa. Looking back across history she paid attention to women surviving at sites of trans-imperial colonial conflict, imagining the eponymous heroine of her 1951 novel, *Aprha Behn*, making the declaration, "I'd rather be whore than wife, if marriage means a lifetime like my aunt's or my mother's," before escaping London for Holland and then Suriname, where she raged against slavery (Hahn 1951: 27). Her historically prescient novel *Indo* (1963a) was an inter-racial romance of Indonesian independence in Japanese-occupied Java.[21] Her biography of Mabel Dodge Luhan celebrated the thrill of sexuality and friendship beyond conventions of heterosexuality or racist segregation.[22] When she died in 1997, she had published over 180 articles for *The New Yorker* and more than fifty books of biography, history, novels, and children and young adult literature.

This chapter next turns to nineteenth-century mercantile biography to give an overview of the China Trade and to show how its allegory of free trade rationalized financial imperialism in a quest narrative of New England commercial patriarchy. From there, the chapter delves into Santayana's autobiographical divestment from the American romance of free trade and the complementary allegory of opium addiction in *The Last Puritan*. The chapter concludes by contrasting Hahn's autobiographical accounts of opium smoking in Shanghai. She not only refuted Santayana's affective fatalism but also pursued a "queer hypersociality" of literary concern with women struggling for agency in transnational sexual economies, maintaining hope in "connectivity" and "conjunction" outside the idealization of national family (Freeman 2019: 15).

THE MERCANTILE BIOGRAPHY AND THE ROMANCE OF THE CHINA TRADE

Hahn and Santayana both depict opium consumption as confusing senses of *time*, *place*, and *person*—a confusion that disrupts the ideal alignment of personal, familial,

---

[20] In specific regard to Hong Kong, see Ford (2011). Hahn was part of a constellation of American women wartime journalists who deserve more attention, including Agnes Smedley and Anna Louise Strong.

[21] The young heroine of *Indo* is the orphaned Julie de Jong, a mixed-race child raised in a Dutch orphanage. Julie arrives to Dutch-controlled Batavia before the Second World War. By the novel's end, as Indonesian nationalist forces wrestle control from Japanese occupiers in anticipation of rebelling against colonial Dutch retrenchment, Julie rejects a marriage proposal from an American, trading a married life in California to partner with a charismatic Indonesian revolutionary who is already married.

[22] See *Love Conquers Nothing: A New Look at Old Romances* (1959b [1952]); *Romantic Rebels: An Informal History of Bohemianism in America* (1967); *Once Upon a Pedestal: The Fascinating and Informal Chronicle of the American Woman's Struggle to Stand on Her Own Two Feet* (1974); and, *Mabel: A Biography of Mabel Dodge Luhan* (1977).

and national types evinced in the mercantile biography. This allegory of "patrician Orientalism" featured a commercial patriarch who aspired to traffic opium rather than consume it (Tchen 1999: xx). The *bildungsroman* modeled a personal economy of self-disciplined temperance enabling Eastern ventures that generated capital subsequently consolidated as family fortune in New England. The merchant prince's rise from humble obscurity to a state of affluence and cultural influence implied that profits in the China Trade were meritocratic reward for young men with the courage and discipline to realize high familial status within the nation by speculating beyond it. But opium was more than a lucrative material commodity connecting voyages from New England to Canton on the basis of supply meeting demand. It was a powerful tool in coordinating the associative references of notional value in systems of credit related to the movement of commodities across geographies of inter-imperial contest.

Five years after the First Opium War (1839–1842), the influential early national biographer and former Harvard University president Josiah Quincy published *The Journals of Major Samuel Shaw, the First American Consul at Canton, with a Life of the Author* (1847). In 1784, Shaw was a threadbare Revolutionary War officer when he became the supercargo on the first US voyage to Canton by the *Empress of China*. He went on to make three more voyages but never made a fortune. However, his nephew Robert Gould Shaw did and passed his uncle's writings to Quincy. Robert Gould Shaw also married Susan Parkman, the sister-in-law of the merchant Nathaniel Russell Sturgis, who was the father of Santayana's step-uncle Russell Sturgis (pictured in Figure 11.1) (Downs 1997: 368).[23]

Quincy delivered a typical mercantile biography that discerned in past commercial uncertainty the emergence of a heroic *character* that was a trustworthy representative type portending the nation's intergenerational free trade futurity. Quincy begins by attesting that he had never known "an individual [Shaw] of a character more elevated and chivalric, acting to a purer standard of morals with a higher honor, and uniting more intimately the qualities of the gentleman, soldier, the scholar, and the Christian" (Quincy 1847: iii–iv). The righteous traits that Quincy ascribes to Shaw signify an exceptional personal integrity (*character*) on the basis of which Shaw exemplifies *character types* (soldier, Christian, etc.) for readers who ought to respect and emulate Shaw as a model American.

In setting this foundational character of national commerce, Quincy overlooks Shaw's frustration with the financial challenge of transoceanic speculation. Instead, he recounts Shaw's diplomatic and nautical accomplishments on a national chronotope of global trade adventure after the American Revolution. The ship *Empress of China* had managed to cross the Indian Ocean, move through the straits of Southeast Asia, and anchor outside the Portuguese-controlled port of Macao at the mouth of the Pearl River, winning recognition from Dutch, French, and Portuguese authorities along the way. Shaw had then followed the Qing regulations of the Canton System that licensed

---

[23] Quincy, Russell Sturgis, and Emerson were also classmates at Harvard; see Sturgis (n.d. [1893]: 76).

procession up the river to the island of Whampoa and factory residence of Canton, outside the walled city of Guangzhou, where foreign traders were quarantined during the trade season as they negotiated with a designated Hong merchant of the Cohong guild.[24] More daunting were the Qing requirements forbidding the sale of opium and stipulating that foreign traders settle all transactions in silver specie (Hao 1986: 29–137).[25]

On his second voyage, Shaw took notice of opium as a financial hurdle to profiting in the China Trade. On an excursion to Calcutta, Shaw describes how the monopoly of the British East India Company (EIC) controlled the drug, overseeing cultivation in colonial Bengal and restricting sale at auction to private British "country traders" who then trafficked it to Canton where it became a contraband medium of exchange that circumvented silver requirements.[26] Because opium brokered trade with Chinese merchants of the Cohong guilds in Canton, it helped Britain open up restricted trade through the Straits Settlements (Trocki 2000: 79–104). It also sustained notational value in densely referential fields of finance that the EIC and banking institutions, such as Baring Brothers, organized, administered, and insured. For example, bills-of-exchange, which functioned on discount as a form of currency, promised to the bearer the future delivery of silver in London in order to underwrite the purchase of opium at auction in Bengal for subsequent sale in China (Poovey 2008: 36–42).[27] Opium's systematic financial functions, as contraband currency and a form of notional value in credit economies, coordinated credit-based speculation that linked inter-imperial commerce across oceans from the Far East to the Far West.[28] Opium became even more important after revolutions across the Americas disrupted the global supply of silver during the Napoleonic Wars (1803–1815).[29]

Quincy's biography of Shaw derived representative national character from the financial complexity of the China Trade, demonstrating the overlap of financial and literary signifying practices related to printed *type*. In *Specters of the Atlantic* (2005), Ian Baucom charts this discursive overlap across the longue durée of circum-Atlantic slave trade. He contends that representational powers of printed type enabled both readers of literature and commercial investors to recognize reality as a notional form in a "system-wide determination to credit the exercise of imaginary values" (Baucom 2005: 17, 37). The powers of printed type also helped focus a sense of reality in the face of financial activity that was become referentially complex in structuring speculative investment across horizons of space and time. The representative logic of such complex speculative finance moved across terms of metaphor, allegory, and into nested senses of allegory that defy

---

[24] On the Cohong merchants, see Van Dyke (2011) and Wong (2016).

[25] For an overview of the Canton System, see Van Dyke (2005). On early American involvement in the trade, see Aldridge (1993), Downs (1997), Tchen (1999), and Haddad (2008; 2013), Fichter (2010), and Johnson (2017).

[26] Also see Trocki (1999), Brook and Wakabayashi (2000), and Lin (2007).

[27] See also Fichter (2010: 107–108) and Haddad (2013: 77–80).

[28] For work recognizing the importance of the Pacific in the global scale of national literature, labor contracts, and imperial commerce, see Lowe (2015) and Burnham (2019).

[29] On the importance of silver as capital and currency, see Fichter (2010: 5, 33, 113).

a clear organizing character type of individual hero or nation. Baucom describes how the exchange of commodities and use of currency (money) operates through a logic metaphor, whereby real estate (which had formerly grounded property as wealth in a place and time of hereditary status) became a mobile form of transferable property to be bought and sold among all other commodities of the marketplace (Baucom 2005: 23).[30] The *marketplace* was an allegorical concept that framed metaphorical operations of commodity exchange in a system of value equivalence indexed by the function of money. Credit dynamics of "speculative discourse" introduced another degree of representational complication, conjuring hyper-allegorical signification of notional value across many marketplaces through bills-of-exchange and actuarial contracts that hedged the risk of capital losses by promising reimbursement of a commodity's value if it were to be destroyed (Baucom 2005: 17). Ironically Shaw's commentary on his first voyages shows how ignorant he was of the contingencies at play in the inter-imperial financial dynamics of the China Trade.

The systematic force of opium's powers of financial reference resonates in the phrase "free trade imperialism," broadening conceptions of *British* imperialism beyond explicit military prowess on land and sea (Gallagher and Robinson 1953: 1). This dissonant juxtaposition of "free trade" and "imperialism" stressed the coercive powers of financial services, backed up by maritime force, in governing the "biopolitical circulation of goods and people" in "the vast, dense, and shifting networks of the British opium and coolie trade" (Lowe 2015: 132). In *Limits of Capital* (1982) and *The New Imperialism* (2003), David Harvey lays out the informal governing powers of financial imperialism in describing the global credit network as a "spatio-temporal 'fix' " that redirects capital pooled within the empire's borders to outward channels of extraterritorial investment in dispossessive extraction (Harvey 2003: 115).[31] In the financial regimes of global trade, credit was like a valve that relieved the social crises of labor stagnation within the empire by directing accumulated capital to extractive horizons beyond it, *fixing* the "temporal deferral" of capital investments across expansive geographical networks (Harvey 2003: 115). The establishment and maintenance of opium's financial powers played out in an inter-imperial (primarily Portuguese, Spanish, Dutch, French, British) competition for maritime and financial hegemony that Giovani Arrighi tracks over longue durées in *The Long Twentieth Century: Money, Power and the Origin of Our Times* (2010 [1994]). After losing the American Revolutionary War, Britain was able to use opium to govern *spaces-of-flow* in global circuitries that extracted capital from India and China for accumulation in the empire's sovereign *space-of-place* (81–83). US ventures to Canton and Calcutta developed as a related orientalist exercise in "free trade imperialism"

---

[30] On the rise of mobile property and development to credit-based speculation, see Pocock (1985: 103–123).

[31] Also see Harvey (1982: 426–427). I am echoing application of Harvey's description from Arrighi (2007: 216–217) and Hsu (2010: 11–12).

conducted by ambitious merchant traders on the margins of Britain's hegemonic spatio-temporal fix.[32]

In the literary context of "financial culture" that Baucom describes, the mercantile biography would be a national form of "theoretical realism," projecting the future success of American commercial "character" as it transcends the imperial history of global finance underpinning the China Trade.[33] The mercantile biography personified or typified an emblematic patriarch to inspire confidence that Americans could master the complex referential contingencies of the global credit economy—a confidence that Herman Melville mocks when the narrator of "Bartleby" professes his love of repeating the name "John Jacob Astor" because it "rings" "orbicular," "like until bullion" (Melville 1856: 33). Ironically, mercantile biographies did not feature in literature canonized in the American Renaissance through the genre of Romance.[34] In the ideology of culturally rooted Romanticist genius, dealing and brokering wasted imaginative powers and residence in China was a state of culturally errant deracination. The figurative capacity of opium as a commodity, currency, and financial instrument of credit was beyond the literary pale of national allegory. As for consumption of the drug, it continued to supplant literary creativity rather than to supplement it (as it would for Coleridge and De Quincey).[35]

Exploiting the dramatic effect of the United States' post-revolutionary financial disadvantage, Quincy fixed Shaw as a foundational American character of anti-monopolistic "free trade." In this national chronotope of global commerce, the American David faced the imperially tyrannical goliaths of both Britain and the Qing Dynasty. On a rhetorical level, the phrase "free trade" straightened the hyper-allegorical dynamics of financial abstraction into a national romance, personifying the state-charted family firms in Shaw, John Jacob Astor, Stephen Girard, Thomas H. Perkins, Samuel Russell, Russell Sturgis, and other commercial patriarchs who managed to trade in Canton without exclusive

---

[32] For an account of successful US merchant activity in Canton and Calcutta in the decade after Shaw's death, see Fitcher (2010: 107–108, 181–192, 195).

[33] Baucom contrasts the "theoretical realism" of speculative financial practices with the "melancholy realism" of speculative literary practices that solicit "readerly sympathy" by typifying trauma (a singularity that defies typification) as an opportunity for the reader to experience a melancholy identification with the "dying and dead"; in this melancholic reflection on representation of past trauma, the reader is both an ideal sympathetic spectator of the ideal liberal marketplace in a double sense of taking interest in the suffering of others through a form of representation of that suffering that proves the reader's sympathetic capacity, transforming melancholy into an act of mourning that reconnects the reader to liberal marketplace futurity (2005: 276–282). I read Santayana as explicitly resisting this mode of liberal sentiment. Hahn is a better fit, although her melancholy does not court readers' appreciation of her sympathetic powers to validate national hegemony of free trade imperialism. Her writing idealizes a United Nations marketplace that is progressively anti-colonial and dedicated to transnationally confederative uplift of women as individuals whose rights are realized and affirmed in communitarian association not reducible to the conventional heteronormative family.

[34] For examples in which the configuration (and reconfiguration) of generic Romance is key to American literary canonization, see Matthiessen (1941), Lewis (1955), and Chase (1957).

[35] For an account of how opium use burnished the reputations of Coleridge, De Quincey, Crabbe, and Francis Thompson, see Abrahm (1971 [1934]).

federal privileges comparable to those of the EIC monopoly (Downs 1997). However, most US firms (with a few important exceptions) were no less imperialistic than private British "country traders" in regard to harnessing the financial powers of opium.[36] Their investments permeated a globally speculative circuit of credit sustained through the financial instruments of circum-Atlantic slave trade, bills-of-exchange in Calcutta, Spanish galleon trade in Mexican and Peruvian silver dollars, and the Northwest Pacific fur trade (Wilson and Dissanayake 1996; Frank 1998; Grandin 2014; Matsuda 2012). Their transoceanic investments in Canton folded into collateral speculation in land and railway across the continental West, enabled by Federal Indian Law that justified wars of Indian Removal, the basis of settler colonialism that literary scholars have highlighted in eviscerating idealization of the United States as anti-imperial in the early national period (Cheyfitz 1997 [1991]; Kaplan and Pease 1993; Rowe 2000; Kaplan 2005).

Furthermore, the goal of harnessing opium's complex financial powers of representation was to extract resources from the Qing (Trocki 1999; Lin 2007). Before the expiration of the EIC monopoly in 1833, American merchants sourced opium from Turkey, transshipped it for private British merchants, and brokered trade related to it through Manila. By the mid-1830s, American merchants were able to take keen advantage of credit lines from Barings Brothers, whose directors had backed US merchants trading parallel with the EIC and with subsequent powerful members of Russell & Company (Canton-based) and Russell, Sturgis, & Company (Manila-based) after the EIC lost its monopoly control in 1834 (Haddad 2013: 27–80; Sturgis n.d. [c.1893]: 209–212, 223). The British defeat of China in the First Opium War (1839–1842) resulted in "unequal treaties," beginning with Treaty of Nanjing (1842) that opened additional "treaty ports," including Shanghai. The smuggling of opium continued to expand despite the Taiping Rebellion (1850–1864) and the Second Opium War (1856–1860), which opened even more ports.[37] In 1859, Karl Marx averred in the *New York Tribune* that the dramatic increase in lucrative opium smuggling into China had stymied general market development.[38]

On the one hand, the twentieth-century portrait of Santayana's uncle Russell Sturgis (Figure 11.1) nostalgically epitomizes the mercantile biography's allegorical fix of character that portrayed the individual and the family company as an iconic New England merchant prince of the China Trade. On the other, the portrait's caption suggests the precariousness of any nationally allegorical fix of global finance capital's hyper-allegorical references. After retiring briefly to Boston from Canton and Manila in 1844, Sturgis relocated to London to join Barings Brothers, of which he later became the head. During the Civil War, he sympathized with the South, despite opposing slavery,

---

[36] See He (2012). Russell Sturgis notes that almost every "foreign" firm was involved in opium in the 1830s; see Sturgis (n.d. [c.1893]: 223). The exceptions among US merchants were D. W. C. Olyphant, Charles W. King, and Nathan Dunn (a Quaker), who adamantly decried the smuggling of opium; see Haddad (2013: 118–121).

[37] On the expansion of the opium trade leading to the Second Opium War, see Wong (1998), Trocki (1999), and Lin (2007).

[38] "Trade with China" (3 December 1859) in Marx (2007: 43). Wong (1998) dives deeply into the records and registers the inter-imperial tensions of the numbers. Also see Wong (2000: 200).

and never returned to the United States before his death in 1887.[39] The firms Russell, Sturgis, & Company and Russell & Company went bankrupt in 1875 and 1891, respectively (Downs 1997).[40]

Profits from the China Trade diminished for US merchants as the US diplomat Anson Burlingame pursued cooperative strategies that supported the Qing Self-Strengthening Movement and as steam technologies and telegraphy restructured the spatial-temporal terms of fixing credit across the globe and into China's treaty ports (Blue 2000: 31–54).[41] In the 1870s, Chinese companies gained control over the steamship schedules moving inland, opium production developed on farms in Southeast Asia and in the "poppy-growing interior" of China, and various Chinese merchants competed to control the opium monopolies in Hong Kong and Singapore (2000: 13).[42] In the late 1890s, the US Open Door Policy adapted to the outright land grabs in China, for example after the First Sino–Japanese War (1894–1895) by annexing Hawaii and Guam and envisioning Manila as an "American Hong Kong": a "commercial *entrepôt* to the China market and a center of American military power" (McCormick 1963: 159).[43] As for opium, in 1906 the Qing introduced regulatory reforms that gained traction through the next decade of Republican revolution, leading to "international illegalization" of importation in late 1917 (Blue 2000: 14).[44] Opium continued to be a major source of revenue until the end of the Second World War, as "Chinese warlords, criminals, the Guomindang [Nationalists]," "the Chinese Communist Party," and Japanese companies and the Japanese government wrestled to control the revenues of traditional paste and industrially refined heroin and morphine (Blue 2000: 23).

Hahn and Santayana's melancholy bowers of opium smoking are thematic tangles of romantic errand and error that queer the chronotope of the mercantile biography and defy idealization of China Trade fortunes as anti-imperial Romance of exceptional national history.[45] However the catastrophic consequences of opium's financialization for Shanghai and China register in Hahn writings but not in Santayana's. He represents the China Trade's global spaces-of-flow as a wasteland of the Great American Merchant's

---

[39] On his sympathies for the South, see Sturgis (n.d. [c.1893]: 83–84).

[40] Also see Sturgis (n.d. [c.1893]: 82).

[41] Russell & Company sold their steam fleet to the Chinese Navigation Company in 1877; see Liu (1959: 440). On Burlingame, see Johnson (2017: 247–251).

[42] In regard to the ascendance and diminution of Chinese merchant control of the British monopoly in Hong Kong, see Munn (2000).

[43] In her history of the Philippines entitled *The Islands* (1981), Hahn writes of Manila's strategic commercial importance for the China Trade and the continuing importance of silver into the twentieth century (73–74, 123). Merchants anticipated profits in the "China Trade" but were disappointed in the so-called "Open Door Era": see McCormick (1967) and Eperjesi (2001: 210–215).

[44] See also Wong (2000: 200) and Baumler (2000).

[45] Rather than a genre, scholars have described *romance* as a pervasive theme that has crossed genres for centuries (Fuchs 2004). In relation to US literatures, see Baym (1984) and Fluck (2009), who consider how debates over the generic characteristics of the Romance reflected insecurity about the distinctiveness of US culture and its status as exceptional.

exhausted imperial will, the fading national legacy of which he memorialized on the grounds of New England's stagnant Genteel Tradition.

THE CHINA TRADE AND THE GENTEEL TRADITION

In *Person and Places*, Santayana presents a character of affective contraction, recounting the recession of past relationships into a vortex of grief. The title *Persons and Places* echoes a melancholy philosophical contentment that defies mourning by tracking progressive affective detachment from "Persons" who "yielded in interest to places."[46] Christopher Lane offers a strong interpretation of Santayana's philosophical method of addressing "passion's ontological difficulty" (1999a: xvii). As Santayana sought "a redemptive and desexualizing power" in philosophy, the "relations among art, desire, and object-choice become troubled, even antagonistic" (1999b: 212). Extending Lane's analysis by considering the historical context of this antagonism, I read Santayana's conflation of "persons and things" and places as a strategy of restructuring a sense of family ancestry to dodge any implicit moral responsibility of inheriting and living on a fortune secured through the China Trade. As Santayana looks back on his life, personal friendships, family attachments, national affiliation, and the China Trade, all become remnants of mortal futility in the ongoing courses of empire.

Santayana calls his primal grief event a *metonia*, occasioned in 1893 by the unexpected death of a beloved student named Warwick Potter, whom Santayana calls "my *last* real friend."[47] Afterward, Santayana felt as though "the whole world was retreating to a greater distance and taking on a new, more delicate coloring, as if by aerial perspective."[48] The loss of Potter, followed by the deaths of Santayana's father and then his favorite half-sister, leads him to conclude: "A perfect love is founded on despair."[49] He dedicates himself to cultivating a "psyche" that has "learned to vibrate harmoniously to many things at once in a peace which is an orchestration of transcended sorrows."[50]

The "philosophical *metonia*" leads Santayana to "*disintoxicate* [his] mind" in renouncing "the world as Will while retaining it as Idea."[51] It is worth noting that his autobiographies are self-conscious characterizations of selfhood rather than recollections of the actual affections that he maintained and enjoyed with his relatives and fellow "bachelor expatriates," including his "inimitable friend and quasi-cousin"

---

[46] *The Middle Span* (1945) (Santayana 1987: 352).
[47] *My Host the World* (1953) (Santayana 1987: 423).
[48] *The Middle Span* (1945) (Santayana 1987: 350).
[49] *My Host the World* (1953) (Santayana 1987: 428).
[50] *My Host the World* (1953) (Santayana 1987: 419).
[51] *My Host the World* (1953) (Santayana 1987: 423, 426).

Howard Sturgis and Henry James.[52] Inspired by Lucretius and Spinoza, Santayana's five-volume *The Life of Reason: The Phases of Human Progress* (1904–1905) criticized German romantic philosophy (Kant and Hegel) for idealizing the ego as a progressive point for viewing and shaping the line of history. He lamented the immature romantic sensibility of subjective "psychologism" that followed in the nineteenth century, including Emerson's transcendentalist optimism, for the "conceited notion that man, or human reason, of the human distinction between good and evil, is the center and pivot of the universe" (Santayana 2009: 19). Reflecting on the teleology of his philosophical *metonia*, he concludes that "Materially I might be the most insignificant of worms; spiritually I should be the spectator of all time and all existence."[53] This experience culminates with him writing *Persons and Places* "under drastic restrictions" in the Second World War, while "in the clinic of the Blue Sisters upon the Caelius" of Rome, "happy in solitude and confinement" and content that "the furious factions into which the world is divided" could not "inspire hatred" of any party "in my heart."[54]

From this Archimedean point of philosophical detachment, he looks back on his youth to discern affective limits, rendering his family and friends as interesting character types that evince the failure of the affective Will. The opening chapter "Place, Time, Ancestry" fractures the mercantile biography's heroic frame by splitting the name "George Santayana" across reference to the two marriages of his Spanish mother Dona Josefina Borrás: first to *George* Sturgis, of the "great [American] merchant" family and second to Santayana's father, Don Agustín Ruiz de *Santayana*, a "colonial official," whose career coincided with the last phase of Spanish control over the Philippines. Josephina and George Sturgis met in Manila, where Sturgis & Company was headquartered and where she accompanied her father on his diplomat duty. Because she was Catholic and George was Unitarian, their wedding took place on the deck of a "British man-of-war at anchor in Manila Bay."[55] Eight years later, George suddenly died "in the midst of [a] disastrous commercial venture."[56] The Sturgis family signed over his inheritance to Josephina and provided for her three surviving children.[57]

---

[52] Santayana's reference to Howard Sturgis is from the Preface to *The Last Puritan*, (1994 [1935]: 11). John McCormick notes that Santayana seems to have "maintained a close lifelong connection" and a pride of association "heavily and perhaps unfairly concealed by irony in his autobiography" (2017: 14). Santayana's autobiographies also conceal the camaraderie that Ross Posnock discerns as Santayana's "fastidious, immaculate asexuality," which found queer fellowship with "androgynous" "bachelor expatriates," including Henry James and Howard Sturgis, in *Trial of Curiosity* (1991: 194, 196). Lane (1999) agrees with McCormick that Santayana "sought in art a redemptive and desexualizing power" (212) but also senses in Santayana's early works *Sonnets and Other Verses* (1894) and *The Sense of Beauty* (1896) signs of Santayana's intimate friendship and sexual passion for specific male friends (1894; 1896: 221).

[53] *My Host the World* (1953) (Santayana 1987: 442).
[54] *My Host the World* (1953) (Santayana 1987: 422).
[55] *The Background of My Life* (1944) (Santayana 1987: 40).
[56] *The Background of My Life* (1944) (Santayana 1987: 50–51).
[57] *The Background of My Life* (1944) (Santayana 1987: 51).

The widowed Josefina then married Santayana's father, whom she had also met in Manila. His Spanish Catholicism becomes a point of "Ancestral" identification for Santayana, segregating him categorically from his Sturgis relatives and US culture on the basis of the "initial diversities of race, country, religion, and career."[58] Jorge (George) Agustín Nicolás Ruiz de Santayana y Borrás was born in Madrid in 1863 and spent his early childhood with his father in Avila, Spain before joining his mother and his Sturgis half-brothers and half-sister in Boston at No. 302 Beacon Street, where their neighbors included Emerson, Dr Oliver Wendell Holmes, and the previously mentioned Aunt Sarah Blake Sturgis Shaw, the sister of George and Russell Sturgis, the wife of the son of the previously mentioned Robert Gould Shaw (Samuel Shaw's nephew), after whom she named her son Robert Gould Shaw, Jr, who died in the Civil War as a colonel in the "coloured regiment" of the 54th Massachusetts Volunteer Infantry.[59] Santayana attended Boston Latin School and then Harvard College, where he was a student of William James and eventually James's colleague as a professor of philosophy. When his mother died in 1912, Santayana inherited her portion of the Sturgis trust and left the United States forever.

Written after the Second World War, the epilogue of the final volume of *Persons and Places: My Host The World* (1953) sums up the philosophical undercurrent of the three volumes' family saga with the retrospective declaration: "we were a blue-sea family: our world was that of colonial officials and great merchants."[60] The "blue-sea" is not a setting for a romantic comedy of cross-cultural futurity or an epic of rising US hegemony. It is sublime mortality that outpaces the worldly reference of allegory and hyper-allegory, a philosophical apprehension of Time as a concept that engulfs the aspirations, affections, and desires of all individuals, families, and empires in the world.

This "blue-sea" sense of human mortality subsumes the power of the merchant prince, foreshadowing the dissipation of the Sturgis family and of the United States. Santayana recalls feeling as a boy that the Sturgis family seemed an "aristocracy of commerce" with Uncle Russell Sturgis as the icon of Great Merchant accomplishment.[61] Uncle Russell had started his career "in the East, in Manila and China; but somehow from there he passed to England" and eventually became a "senior partner, of Baring Brothers in London."[62] Due in great part to her brother-in-law's generosity, Santayana's mother regarded Sturgis as "virtue personified."[63] George's Spanish father concurred, regarding him as "the perfection of manhood, as exalted as he was kind, a center of dazzling wealth and exquisite benefactions."[64]

---

[58] *The Middle Span* (1945) (Santayana 1987: 351).
[59] *The Background of My Life* (1944) (Santayana 1987: 168).
[60] *My Host the World* (1953) (Santayana 1987: 538).
[61] *The Background of My Life* (1944) (Santayana 1987: 57).
[62] *The Background of My Life* (1944) (Santayana 1987: 57).
[63] *The Background of My Life* (1944) (Santayana 1987: 57).
[64] *The Background of My Life* (1944) (Santayana 1987: 57).

To exemplify the mortal limit of such romantic idealization, Santayana recalls his failed attempt to meet his benefactor, who was then succumbing to dementia in London. While on break from studies at Oxford in the 1880s, Santayana knocked on Uncle Russell's door, but a servant politely turned him away. Santayana then typifies "Uncle Russell" as a spectral force of dissipated commercial masculinity: his heroism was an abiding ideal to which subsequent Sturgis sons failed to live up. The *lack* of "Uncle Russell's" portrait conveys a primal impotence resonating at levels of individual, family, and empire that Santayana explains:

> But I can give a name, in lieu of a portrait, and will call [Russell Sturgis] and his generation the Great Merchants: a type that in America has since been replaced by that of great business men or millionaires, building up their fortunes at home; whereas it was part of the romance and tragedy of those Great Merchants that they amassed their fortunes abroad, in a poetic blue-water phase of commercial development that passed away with them, and made their careers and virtues impossible for their children.
>
> *The Background of My Life* (1944) (Santayana 1987: 58–59)

Notice how Santayana evokes the representative force of the mercantile biography's hero but mobilizes and sustains melancholy to snuff out optimism of speculative futurity. Santayana's "Uncle Russell" is a monumental ruin of "Great Merchant" virility, conjuring spectral ambition that haunts rather than inspires. The reputation of his personal accomplishment was *merely* a "phase," the diminution of which Santayana regards as inevitable in the world historical course of international and intra-national antagonisms. In divesting from national speculation on the past and futures of free trade imperialism, Santayana arrests the referential powers of finance, equating the "poetic blue-water phase of commercial development" with Russell Sturgis's naïve seafaring heroism. He merely mentions Sturgis's long financial career with Barings before fixing him in the demise of his expatriated London isolation.

Having typified the fall of the Great Merchant, Santayana turns to the dissonant intergenerational fade of the Sturgis descendants. Despite the rising phase of United States imperialism, manifested in the defeat of Spain to take control of the Philippines, his half-siblings proved to be wayward and genteel weaklings, and Santayana speculates that: "being grandsons dominated their characters and their whole lives. In other words, they illustrated the decline of an age—the age of the great merchants."[65] They represent "a failure of nerve, the sense of spent momentum, of being sons of Great Merchants, but without either need or opportunity for enterprise, and without money enough to be important men about town. Superfluous persons who felt themselves superfluous: dry branches on the green family tree."[66] The most "pathetic victim" of this spectral legacy is his cousin Howard Sturgis, the youngest son of "Uncle Russell," whom Santayana typifies

---

[65] *My Host the World* (1953) (Santayana 1987: 348).
[66] *The Background of My Life* (1944) (Santayana 1987: 74).

as "a perfect young lady of Victorian type" and memorializes in "a beautiful china cup" from which Howard's surviving lover Babe (William Haynes-Smith), grown old and pathetically lonely, drinks tea, in a scene of alienation which Santayana describes as epitomizing the "cyclical character of all my friendships."[67]

Persons and Places is a monument standing on the ruin of the China Trade that had set the foundation of Sturgis patriarchy. Santayana's ascetic exercise in affective diminution abstracts specific persons into cultural types that convey naiveite and enervation. His demeaning characterization of his cousin Howard does more than refuse the mercantile biography's national commercial patriarchy and idealization of free trade imperialism. Santayana's autobiography rejects affective or erotic potential by fixing all desire—heteronormative or otherwise—as tragically comical or comically tragic in a philosophical frame of negation (his philosophical *metonia*) that undercuts the affective trap of social ephemera. By rendering and ruminating on character types of his life, Santayana models abstention from literal opiate pleasures and the figurative ones of material wealth, religious superstition, and the ancestral heroism of national free trade imperialism. A decade earlier, *The Last Puritan* had similarly typified the Great Merchant family, stranding its leisured sons in degenerate bowers of sensuous opium addiction and the stagnant backwaters of the Genteel Tradition's anemic "agonized conscience" (Santayana 2009: 5).

The Last Puritan in Shanghai

The Last Puritan begins with a Preface in which Santayana explains that the novel's "characters," including the narrator, compose "a stage-presentation of myself" (Santayana 1994 [1935]: 3).[68] In the subsequent Prologue, the narrator recalls deciding to write the novel after happening to reconnect with a younger male friend while living on the Left Bank of Paris after the First World War. They reminisce about pleasant summer afternoons before the war, spent among a "swarm of friends and relations" in the leisured Windsor garden of Howard Sturgis, "host and hostess in one"(Santayana 1994 [1935]: 11). The post-war conversations inevitably turn to those killed or traumatized into blank existence, leading the narrator to pursue the "sad tale" of their mutual friend Oliver Alden, whom he deems "THE LAST PURITAN" (Santayana 1994 [1935]: 14, 17).[69]

Reviewing *The Last Puritan* for *T'ien Hsia* in November 1936, Hahn criticizes "the Novel" as a punitive allegory with character types incapable of expressing affection or feeling erotic desire. She resisted the amoral rationale of this affective doom by pointing out that Santayana predicates his protagonist's constitutional crisis on biological

---

[67] *My Host the World* (1953) (Santayana 1987: 513, 514).
[68] The Preface was not included until Charles Scribner's Triton Edition in 1937, so Hahn would not have read it before writing her review.
[69] Capitalized emphasis in the original.

masculinity, the premise of his moral determination, and his inheriting an imperial fortune (Hahn 1936: 418, 420). Her review counters the novel's austere moral economy by invoking Santayana's earlier philosophical work in which he had charged the affective energy of sensual pursuits with potentially oracular, albeit primitive, significance—an affective energy that Hahn pursued in her accounts of falling into and surviving opium addiction in Shanghai.

In *The Last Puritan*, opium is a fatal vice that renders Oliver's father Peter Alden incapable of either perpetuating his ancestors' imperial will or rehearsing the genteel script of his guardian and older brother Nathan, whom Oliver grows to idolize. *The Last Puritan* is not a *bildungsroman*. Its chronotope invokes an aesthetically classicist sense of Fate that parodies religious predestination by treating moral determination as a tragic flaw. In the Preface and Prologue, we are told that Oliver is born with a "sovereign" and "absolutist conscience" that makes him immune to his father's wayward receptivity and any romance of imperial will (Santayana 1994 [1935]: 8, 17). Oliver does not develop; he defends unto death, with an "inner blind fortitude," a primal sense of moral purity that the narrator derides as a "purification of puritanism" (17). This "puritanism" is "deep and speculative" rather than "fanatical" (14). Oliver's infatuations with men and women repeatedly culminate in his disaffected pity of them for lacking comparable moral conviction. The reader follows Oliver's foreshortened errands in curiosity down a spiraling path of ostensible benevolence that compounds his puritanical alienation, culminating in a photographic portrait of Oliver's eerily peaceful corpse.

The allegory of Great Merchant dissipation begins before Oliver's birth with his father Peter's rambunctious childhood in the Back Bay of Boston, where the austere and disapproving older brother Nathaniel, immune to the lore of blue-sea adventures, manages rents from inherited family properties. In the genteel cove of his "back-parlour," Nathaniel sits with an "iron strongbox filled with old letters and documents," which have become "meaningless" and a "bronze crocodile" "paper-weight" that as a child he had "associated with Satan" (39). This mundane paperweight contrasts starkly with the crocodiles that De Quincey had charged with sublime geographical promiscuity in recounting his "oriental dreams" as an opium eater.[70] Santayana does not imbue the Alden brothers with De Quincey's dramatically expressive literary powers or his acute racist distress over the geo-historical integrity of imperial order. However, as a boy Peter does upset Nathaniel by consorting with low-class Irish Catholics. He forbids Peter to spend summers in the port city of Newport, where his mind might be "poisoned with that strange and false fascination, which the notion of sea-faring exerts on some boys" and sends him instead to a Wyoming boy's camp in the "Wild West" run by a former Episcopalian missionary to India (Santayana 1994 [1935]: 41). This move fails to muffle the sirens' call of the East when Peter befriends "the son of an Indian Rajah" (43,

---

[70] De Quincey's *Confessions of an Opium-Eater* (1890) presents the crocodiles as a totem of Asian antiquity's terrifying geographical promiscuity: "I was kissed, with cancerous kisses, by crocodiles, and was laid, confounded with all unutterable abortions, amongst the reeds and Nilotic [of the Nile River] mud" (443).

46). Peter soon ends up in the "East" when forced to escape Harvard after accidently killing a night watchman during a hazing prank in his first year.

Peter's licentious romp in the "East" is a parody of the mercantile biography's global circuitry of abstinent commercial ambition and accumulation (56). His "long wanderings" begin in Japan, where he sows some wild oats, "temporarily [marrying], a little Japanese lady" before "dissolving" the "mock marriage" and heading to China, where he charters a junk and sails "up those great rivers far into the interior" (57). He then heads to India and Muscat, growing serially disillusioned; on first glance, the "curious tenets and practices" of exotic people draw him in, but "after the romance of novelty had worn off" they seemed "unspeakably tiresome and foolish" (58). He spends money on objects that he plans "to bring home for the Museum of Fine Arts"—objects that later decorate his opium bower (58). Homeward bound, he begins medical studies in Vienna and Paris that he finishes at Harvard to become a doctor. He marries Harriet Bumstead, who evinces her shallow gentility in dispassionate assessment of Peter as her potential husband: "He's a bit rickety in body and mind; there have been times when he has drunk too much, and indulged in a little cocaine or opium or both; but he's *not* to be regarded as a reformed dipsomaniac or victim of a drug-habit" (63). When Oliver is born, Uncle Nathaniel predicts that he will follow his father's wayward course.

After Peter marries, opium lingers in his mind and he insists "on a Chinese room" for himself when designing the family's Connecticut home (67). He later abandons the family residence for life on a yacht that he fashions into a "faddish refuge for debility, a pleasure-dome decree for burning incense-sticks, a polite imitation of an opium den" (170). In opposite corners of this inner sanctum sit "Two gilded Buddhas" with "perpetual smiles" that oversee a dining table on which stands "a Chinese lantern" that "cast[s] a thousand coloured reflections" on his private collection (145, 159). To perform services as a captain and valet, Peter hires Jim Darnley, a happy-go-lucky philanderer who has been expelled from the Royal Navy. Peter nicknames him "Lord Jim." Hoping to eke out a living from the Alden fortune, Lord Jim dresses in "picturesque" "Oriental garments," cheerfully facilitating Peter's addiction" (159). To divert Oliver's attention from Peter's long naps and absences from dinners, Lord Jim entertains with anecdotes of the rigorous physicality and passionate friendships of life at sea (159). Oliver is initially infatuated by Lord Jim but disconcerted to see him speaking to his father "soothingly, as you would a baby" while administering "sleeping-draughts" (165).

The yacht is the setting for Oliver's dawning pity of his father, whose "comatose condition" he deems "a wretched parody of Nirvana, produced by black arts and destined to be ephemeral" (170). Contemplating the "moral dimensions" of the addiction, Oliver concludes: "*Dope* was the very denial of courage, of determination to face the facts, a betrayal of responsibility. *Dope* was a cowardly means of escape, of hiding one's head like an ostrich, and choosing not to know, or to act or to think" (170). Peter wastes progressively away before finally committing suicide after learning that Oliver has summoned his mother to take care of him despite their years of estrangement. "Too weak to drive to the India docks" for a ship to "India or China," Peter chooses "to go to sleep and never wake up" (311, 319).

After his father's death, Oliver rededicates to a transcendent moral conviction ironically suffused with "romantic sympathies," concentrating his egotistic autonomy by restricting the potential of his affection for others (308). He is perceptive enough to intuit that the "very sense of freedom and infinity which threatens [his] self-esteem [was] itself a symptom of [his] youthful energy" but reacts by "demand[ing] some absolute and special sanction for his natural preferences" (308). At first, Oliver idealizes Lord Jim's experience at sea, but Lord Jim's promiscuity troubles him. Instead of surrendering to the "blue-sea" of erotic marine adventure, Oliver attends Williams College, where he strives to be an impressive athlete (172). Determined to protect his conscience from the taint of affective sociality, Oliver never falls in love. Protection of his purity precludes ambition to become a merchant, financier, or an industrial capitalist. He never tries opium. Before he can settle into the genteel cove of Boston's Back Bay, his path takes him to the warfront.

The *Last Puritan* ends with Oliver's repeated attempts to idealize the First World War as morally worth his self-sacrifice. After losing his nerve in a disillusioning stint as an ambulance driver in France, Oliver enlists in the army after the US entrance to the War resets, on national terms, the implications of potential self-sacrifice. He recalls university football competition as a "mock war" that has prepared him for "the greatest excitement, the greatest adventure in human life" (517). His mother was never "so cheerful as now when he took up the duty of service" because he seemed to be "discarding at last that fatal proclivity to waste his life abroad, as his father had done" and might yet disprove his uncle Nathaniel's "ill-natured prophecy" that "he was destined to *Peter out*" (517–518).[71]

Oliver's moral egotism survives the war but not the peace. As life at the front frustrates football field heroics, he ponders a potentially unfulfilled debt born of youthful infatuation with Lord Jim's sister Rose, whom he has grown to pity. On leave, he undertakes a "last pilgrimage" and proposes marriage; Rose rejects him in no uncertain terms: "Can't you see that I would rather die than marry you?" (550). Likening himself to his Uncle Nathaniel, who kept his "thoughts inviolate" and did not "allow the world to override," Oliver self-allegorizes his return to the front as all the more pure for being untainted by irrational passion of love or desire: "I am walking out into the night, into my true life, into the inexorable humdrum punctual company of real things" (551). Oliver is finally killed in an auto accident after the armistice. The narrator's brevity punctuates Oliver's self-absorbed moral determination: "He was played out" (557). His last will dispenses his fortune to the Boston Art Museum, a hospital for the insane, Williams College, and those whom he had pitied, including Rose. With her family, she contemplates a post-mortem photographic portrait of genteel self-sacrifice in which

---

[71] Italics in the original.

Oliver's corpse, relieved of an agonized conscience, appears to sleep peacefully like a child.

Hahn did not consider *The Last Puritan* a masterful play of classicist aesthetics but rather an unrelenting and perverse exercise in frustrating readers' affective concern with Oliver. To protest the genteel legacy of puritanism, Santayana had reduced the First World War to a punitive *force majeure* in the demise of Oliver—"the least sympathetic protagonist who has for many years appeared in fiction"—who "fades away into the grey landscape," "A gaunt, fleshless soldier in ugly canvas clothing" (Hahn 1936: 418, 420). With sarcastically shaded irony, she appreciates Santayana's "thoughtful, kindly scholar's brain" for being "admirably and coolly detached" and not at "war with his heart" in a "common cause against the Fate which cruelly warped Oliver" (418). As a reader, she had grown "angry with his Creator, whether that be God or Mr. Santayana, for the merciless judgment which works out [Oliver's] destiny so inevitably" (418).

Hahn ties the novel's affective austerity to a fundamentalist sense of masculinity that compounds into tragedy Oliver's dual inheritance of cold spiritual determination and a vast China Trade fortune. From Oliver's "first breath" he was not only a "young millionaire" filled with the "bitter, dry self-questionings" of "some Roundhead ancestor" (419 but also *a man* because "his little organism, long before birth, had put aside the soft and drowsy temptation to be female" (419).[72] The privileged terms by which Oliver maintains his "absolutist conscience" seals the Fate of the Alden line in a vortex of cultural annihilation that inverts the nineteenth-century mercantile biography's straight chronotope of patriarchic ambition and resulting familial providence (Santayana 1994 [1935]: 17). Peter had queered his millions in his transatlantic opium bower, but far more disconcerting to Hahn is the determined abstinence with which Oliver uses his fortune to fantasize exercising powers of moral oversight. "Grave and priggish, [Oliver] looked upon his money as a 'great responsibility,' and gave away portions of it in careful, just doses" to anyone "who came within his orbit" (Hahn 1936: 419–420). In this economy, Oliver is both a dealer and an addict. In dispensing "just" doses, he condescends to satiate the material needs of those whom he pities and subordinates as morally inferior. In turn, Oliver sustains his moral high, all the while descending "deeper into the icy subterranean caves of himself" (420). Hahn concludes the review by breaking this circuitry of affective doom, citing Santayana's earlier appreciation of libertines who succumb to sensualist thrill with a primitively visceral self-abandon. Facing the tragic-comedy of human mortality, Santayana had then averred that, aesthetically speaking, it was "easier to make a saint out of a libertine" than out of a genteel "prig" whose "worldly mind" lacks any "human pathos" (420).

In pursuit of his philosophical *metonia*, Santayana would have likely relegated Hahn's writings about opium smoking to pathetically "loose whimsies and passions" that he had likened to a libertine's "ill-bred children"(420).[73] But her melancholy reflections do

---

[72] Quoting *The Last Puritan*.
[73] Quoting Santayana.

more than flout the priggishness of the Last Puritan's agonized conscience by fostering senses of transnational erotic power beyond the genteel legacy of national commercial patriarchy.

Hahn's Transnational Confessions of an Opium Smoker

Reflecting on her opium addiction, Hahn recounts the initial thrill of realizing in Shanghai immersive powers of intimacy that transgressed the national propriety of American feminine type. The eventual limits of this intimacy coincided with the end of her affair with Shao Xinmei and her recognition of the devastating consequence of opium's financial power in imperial violence that Japan justified as an anti-colonial pursuit of a Greater East Asia Co-Prosperity Sphere.[74]

In 1939, Hahn got clear of opium in order to spend extended time interviewing Madame Chiang Kai-shek in the Nationalist wartime capital of Chongqing. After braving bombing raids, which she describes in *The Soong Sisters* (1941), Hahn settled in Hong Kong and had a daughter with the British intelligence officer Charles Boxer, who became a prominent historian of Portuguese and Dutch colonialism in Southeast Asia after the war. When Japan invaded Hong Kong in 1941, Hahn avoided internment by using her marriage to Shao to be classified as "Asiatic" instead of "American" or "Jewish" (Hahn 1944a: 310). Two years later, she was evacuated and repatriated to the United States with her daughter, forced to leave Boxer in a prison camp. After his release, they married and lived together for a few years in England before splitting their residences across the Atlantic, with Hahn in New York. Hahn and Shao met for the last time in 1948, when he visited the United States. After the establishment of the People's Republic of China, he struggled to earn money by translating Percy Shelley, Mark Twain, and Rabindranath Tagore. In 1958, he was arrested when authorities intercepted a letter to Hahn that he had signed with her pseudonym for him: "Heh-ven Pan." After being released from detention in a weakened state, he lived three more years until May 1968 (Grescoe 2016: 349–350).

The following year, Hahn wrote publicly about their affair and her wartime addiction to opium in the article "The Big Smoke" (1969). Hahn recalls that smoking opium made her feel as though "Time" was "something that lost its grip" on her (Hahn 1970: 228). The article begins by recollecting childhood curiosity about opium that defied the feminine propriety she would later challenge as an adult writer: "Though I always wanted to be an opium addict, I can't claim that as the reason I went to China" (220). In 1936, she grew careful not to depict herself explicitly as an opium smoker after a Shanghai newspaper

---

[74] See Hahn (1963a) for a fascinating inter-racial romance of Indonesian independence.

rejected one of her articles.[75] She never mentions using opium in articles featuring Shao as "Heh-ven Pan" for the *New Yorker* that became the book *Mr. Pan* (1944). She deflected opium smoking into drinking in her post-war autobiographies *China to Me: A Partial Autobiography* (1944) and *Hong Kong Holiday* (1946a), on the cover of which appears the Chinese name Shao had given to her: "Sha Mei-Lee" or 項美麗 (Xiàng měilì) (Grescoe 2016). Her novels are a better "partial autobiography" of her opium smoking. *Steps of the Sun* (1940) relates an opium-infused affair in Shanghai between a young American writer (Dorothy Pilgrim) and a well-known Chinese literary figure (Sun Yuin-loong). *Miss Jill* (1947), considered below, avoids American characters in depicting how opium related to sex work and survival in wartime Shanghai and Hong Kong. Hahn's subsequent non-fictional works (biographies, histories) adopt a transnational frame of reference for the diplomatic, economic, and political history of the drug, including its function as a currency in the nineteenth century China Trade.[76]

In "The Big Smoke," Hahn describes the temporal aura of opium smoking as seeming "old-fashioned" in several senses related to the changing inter-imperial economy of its traffic and consumption.[77] In the 1930s, Japan waged financial war through the industrial manufacture of heroin and morphine, designated as "white drugs" for their color. From the occupied territories of Manchuria and later Liaodong, Japan produced and distributed vast quantities in order to undercut Chinese commercial networks, incapacitate the Chinese banking system, and circumvent international currency sanctions (Alcott 1943: 221). At one-third the cost of opium, the "poor man's drug" pulled in approximately USD 20,000,000 worth of Chinese and foreign currencies every month, thereby funding about one-tenth of "Tokyo's annual war budget" and amassing a US dollar denominated war chest of credit (USD 150,000,000) that enabled the purchase of oil and iron as the Chinese yuan depreciated (225). White drugs were also more lethal. Those who chewed, drank, or smoked opium could lead functional lives, with serious users such as Hahn facing debilitation after six years. In contrast, two years on heroin either turned "a strong man or woman into a complete wreck" or killed them (221).

In designating opium smoking as "old-fashioned," Hahn also suggests the cultural, literary, and social boundaries that she crossed in using it. She initially reported

---

[75] The autobiographical essay was the "Price of Poppies"; on the sensitivity of the publisher that rejected it, see Grescoe (2016: 265).

[76] She first wrote on the drug in an article about it trafficking into New York City where she lived in the late 1920s (*Sunday New York World*; see Cuthbertson [1998: 65]). Her historical work *China Only Yesterday: 1850–1860, A Century of Change* (1963b) reaches back to the China Trade in describing it as a "troublesome commodity" that Chinese people had long taken more "a medicine" than "for pleasure," before "traders" (assumably both Western and Chinese) "found it a convenient medium of exchange" to circumvent imperial regulations that restricted foreigners purchases to silver, which became especially difficult to obtain "After revolutions in South and Central America disrupted the supply" (9). In *The Picture Story of China* (1946b), one of Hahn's two illustrated children's books on China, she notes China's resentment of "English importation of opium" and Britain's declaration of war after China's destruction of 20,000 chests (un-paginated, 39). Hahn also published *Cooking in China: The Cooking of China* (1968).

[77] See Bob Tadashi Wakabayashi, "From Peril to Profit: Opium in Late-Edo to Meiji Eyes," 71–73 and Kobayashi (2000: 152–166).

FIGURE 11.2 "項美麗"
"Sha Mei-Lee" (Xiàng Měi-lì)," Shao Sinmay's name for Emily Hahn
From the cover of Emily Hahn, *Hong Kong Holiday* (New York: Doubleday & Company, 1946).

on the expatriate bubble of cocktail parties and horse races in which hard alcohol was the modern thrill. But smoking opium opened the door to Shao and his circle of influential literary friends whose social standing reflected other senses in which opium seemed "old-fashioned." In the context of 1930s Shanghai, "Opium was decadent" because it conjured the leisured privilege and waning influence of merchant and imperial "grandfathers" whose fortunes had faded after the Republican revolution (1911) (Hahn

1970: 228).[78] Because Shao's grandfather had been a Qing envoy to Tsarist Russia, Shao grew up enjoying the prestige of being the oldest son in one of the "city's best families" (Hutt 2001: 119). In the 1920s, he seemed "blessed with the unique ability to transcend factional boundaries," consorting with "left-wing dramatists," "apolitical humorists," Nationalist powerbrokers, and Francophiles (111). Across these factions, Shao's opium smoking struck a privileged cosmopolitan chord of *fin de siècle* European literary decadence. In 1923, he had studied political economy at Cambridge University and spent time in Paris at the École des Beaux Arts, reveling in Sappho, Swinburne, the Pre-Raphaelites, Baudelaire, and Verlaine. Returning to Shanghai in 1926, he "made a sensational debut with the publication of his decadence-infused poetry collection" and an aesthetic manifesto.[79] By marrying his cousin Sheng Peiyu, the daughter of one of the city's wealthiest men, he consolidated his social standing.

When describing her admission into Shao's circle of Shanghai intellectuals and literati in "The Big Smoke," Hahn imbues his home with an ethnographically gothic allure that conveys the naiveté of her initial curiosity about his "domestic habits" as a *Chinese* literary figure (Hahn 1970: 222). The trite bohemian thrill of venturing beyond the International Concession area and into his "old Victorian" home presumes a complacency out of which she is jolted after becoming the object of curiosity. Heh-ven's wife, mother, and "four of five children scampering and giggling in whispers" all "gawk" at Hahn as her "Western eyes" adjust to a stark and bare interior (222). The thrill to unconventional association returns as Heh-ven prepares opium paste in a bedroom, with fellow guests lounging on couches in anticipation. The first pipes that Hahn smokes disappoint her until Heh-ven points out that she has not moved from the couch during the entire night of conversation. He tells her: "We call it Ta Yen, the Big Smoke" (225). This first smoking experience arrested a sense of time's passing, sweeping away her sensational orientalist anticipation of carnal pleasures while promising more immersive intimacies: "Gone were the old romantic notions of wild drug orgies and heavily flavored dreams, but I didn't regret them, because the truth was much better" (225).

Heh-ven's translation of *Ta Yen* into *Big Smoke* is densely allusive, conjuring the erotic charge of a "little death" that portends the rise and fall of Hahn and Shao's sexual relationship and professional collaboration, Hahn's eventual sense of guilt for being Shao's mistress, and her blunted awareness of escalating wartime violence. The pseudonym "Pan Heh-ven" ironically fixes on the initial pleasure of an all-encompassing (Pan) heavenly bliss (Heh-ven): "To lie in a quiet room talking and smoking—or, to put things in proper order, smoking and talking—was delightfully restful and pleasant" (227). More ominously "the Big Smoke" suggests Raymond Chandler's noir phrase "The Big Sleep" in adapted allusion to addicts' risk of suffocation as increased tolerance matched chronic

---

[78] On the implicit senses of "class distinction" (181) implied in the stylistic valences of smoking the drug, see Des Forges (2000: 181). On the Nationalist's attempts to govern opium revenue, see Slack (2000).

[79] The collection *Paradise and May* (Tiāntáng yú wǔ yuè; 天堂與五月) (Zau 1927) and the manifesto "Fire and Flesh" (Huǒ yǔ ròu; 火與肉) (1928).

malnutrition. Sustaining life often depended on enduring the agony of withdrawal. Hahn and those in Shao's circle of smokers mulled over the stages of dependency. One of Heh-ven's friends (Hua-ching) professed that he could avoid addiction by varying the "time pattern" of dosages (229). Ironically, such fixation on self-administering doses often implied the deepening social isolation of progressive dependency. Hahn's intensifying addiction dimmed her awareness of the war and she remembers that even as "Shells fell all around … our little island of safety" the "war didn't bother me too much" except that "Opium went up in price—that was all that mattered" (231).

Hahn represents a chronotope of opium addiction that dissolves senses of time and place in a solipsistic routine that makes social relations feel vague and confused. She "stopped caring" who knew about her addiction and was even pleased to "feel detached" from her friends' concerns, just like many opium addicts who ceased to feel "troubled with unpleasant emotions" (228, 231). Such alienation echoes Peter Alden's viscerally isolated transatlantic bower of orientalist hedonism but with a difference. As an American woman addicted to opium in Shanghai, Hahn was potentially beyond the secular pale of scarlet letter redemption. As an addict, she continued to write with a Prynne-like determination to hold power in transgressively errant erotic experience. In the decades that followed, Hahn forged queerly transnational senses of feminine community born of having witnessed patriarchic regimes of inter-imperial violence in Shanghai and Hong Kong.

Personal disappointment, political exigency, and professional ambition overlapped in her decision to quit opium, the account of which concludes "The Big Smoke." She felt disillusionment with Shao and increasingly uncomfortable around Shao's wife and family. She was also determined to continue circulating in the political economy of wartime China as a writer. Hahn had first joined Shao's "old-fashioned" circle of patriarchal Chinese literati as a white American woman author with a charismatic personality and influential expatriate connections. But her opium addiction also grew to suggest uncomfortable terms of subordination to Shao. She conveys unease in an anecdote of Shao's amusement over an "oil smudge on [her] finger" that "came from testing opium pellets as they cooled," and "wouldn't easily wash off" (231). Heh-ven "used to call attention of friends to it. 'Look,' he would say, 'have you ever before seen a white girl with that mark on her finger?'" (231). Hahn is further taken aback when Shao's wife Sheng Peiyu chastises him in front of her for having turned her into an addict.

Hahn does not portray detox as an escape from Shao but as a long goodbye tracing the affective limit of their mutual affair that coincided with her vexed reclamation of literary agency. This reclamation required passing through patriarchic psychiatric intervention premised on another drug economy. Hahn arranged for treatment after a "German refugee" doctor and friend (Bobby) warned her that she would be risking her life traveling to Chongqing as an addict (232). Shao refused to join, unwilling to submit to a regime of barbiturate-induced hypnosis followed by days of excruciating abstinence in a sanitarium.[80] After Hahn had regained a measure of physiological

---

[80] She continued to cope with a morphine habit, the withdrawal from which in the late 1940s was excruciating (Cuthbertson 1998: 303).

composure, no longer sweating profusely and vomiting, Shao came to visit. She recalled that, at first, she felt as though she had "almost forgotten" him (Hahn 1970: 239). In her clean state, his eyes appeared cloudy, his teeth dirty, and he "sounded and looked like a stranger" (232). On the one hand, these comments evince Hahn's privilege as she addressing audiences in the United States (as a white woman) to elevate her "discursive status" by exhibiting her authority over "Asian men" (Yoshihara 2003: 194). On the other, the scene is a retrospective memorial of Shao as his inherited privilege faded during Japanese occupation and the Chinese Revolution fixed him in insurmountable debt and eventually prison.

Hahn does not present the German refugee doctor (Bobby) as a white knight of redemption. On the contrary, when admitting her to his clinic, he first drugs her and then presses her to undergo psychoanalysis (Hahn 1970: 232). Hahn recalls mumbling consent as she goes under but stipulates that he must later reveal what she has divulged. He never does. Each time she presses him to tell, he repeats: "Oh, yes, that. Very interesting" and asks her to spread word about the efficacy of his treatment (240). Although she shrugs off his refusal as an unresolved riddle in the ordeal of kicking addiction, her situational vulnerability to patriarchic governance of her body, mind, and writing resonates in the subsequent attention that she pays to women who used opium to cope with life in subordinated states of sexual service in Shanghai and Hong Kong.

Hahn's smudged white fingers, about which Shao joked with his friends, reflect her concern with women struggling with material deprivation and the moral governance of female sexuality. In writing on Shanghai's nightlife, Hahn echoed scandalous reports of American sex workers that had filled newspapers a generation previous. The historian Eileen Scully explains that in *fin de siècle* "colonial discourse," the phrase "American Girls" had designated an "aristocracy of labor in the hierarchy of Asian colonial prostitution" (Scully 1998: 876). At the top of this hierarchy were the "American Girls" "from the United States" and "Europe west of Germany," who enjoyed "privilege and success" relative "to the presumed depravity and destitution of 'Asiatics' and 'White Russians'" (857). In the early twentieth century, a "vigorous campaign, extending from the US Consulate to the White House" tried to "restrict" activities of American "women in Shanghai and Hong Kong" (Ford 2011: 51). By the time Hahn arrived in the 1935, most '"American girls' were of Russian birth" and only "a tiny minority of women were able to sustain the élite status formerly conveyed by the phrase" (Scully 1998: 857, 875).[81] During the war, Hahn also felt vulnerable as a woman of Jewish heritage.[82] Initially, being Jewish helped her form a friendship with Sir Victor Sassoon, whom she called "our local millionaire" (Hahn 1944a: 8). As more Jewish refugees from Germany arrived there, she regarded

---

[81] Also see Ford (2011: 46–55).

[82] Her father was "the son of a German Jew" and her mother (Hannah Schoen) was the daughter of "conservative Jews from Bavaria" (Grescoe 2016: 63). On Hahn, see also Messmer (2012: 70–78). In the 1950s, she wrote the historical novel for young adults *Aboab: The First Rabbi of the Americas* (1959c), published by the Jewish Publication Society.

them with a "strange mix of sympathy and condescension" (Grescoe 2016: 251).[83] This attitude changed in Hong Kong, where Hahn feared that Japan would introduce German-style "Concentration camps" "for special classes, such as 'Jews,' 'criminals,' and Chungking patriots" (Hahn 1944a: 300). Hahn's ambivalence starkly contrasts with what Santayana's biographer describes as his "inexplicable venom and vituperation against Jews" and his coolly detached indifference to German and Italian policies of genocidal extermination while writing in retreat in Rome (McCormick 2017: xiii).[84]

Hahn's postwar novel *Miss Jill* (1947) delivers a remarkable appreciation of a woman's will to survive the inter-imperial intersections of sex traffic and drug addiction in wartime Shanghai and Hong Kong.[85] Rejecting the austere moral chronotopes of *The Last Puritan* and the mercantile biography, Hahn presents a white Australian woman named Jill who is groomed from girlhood to be the mistress of a married wealthy Tokyo businessman. After a scandal erupts, she flees Japan for Shanghai, where another man seduces her into sex work that he oversees. She begins to take opium pills to cope with long nights of dancing at a casino where she secures clients. Jill reflects: "The work itself? After a few weeks she was able to think of it as a part of normal life, sometimes unpleasant, as normal life is at times, but more often completely mechanical, and neither pleasant nor unpleasant" (Hahn 1947: 81). From the casino she moves to a brothel managed by a Canadian madame who warns her to avoid "all drugs together": "meddling with that stuff is the easiest way in the world to lose your looks." [...] "I've seen plenty of the Harbin girls once they got started on heroin. There's no turning back with that stuff" (87). However, Jill's favorite Chinese client (B.W. Liu) and his friends advise her that "Eating it is bad" but "Smoking it is all right if you do not overdo it" (87).

As the war intensifies, Jill escapes to Hong Kong, where she ends up being interned for four years in the Japanese prison camp of Stanley. Ironically, she feels relatively safe there, free from hunger, and befriends a supportive Catholic priest named Father Sullivan. Hahn does not end the novel with Jill's renunciation of sex work or redemption into redemption into national matrimony. On the contrary, her first name becomes honorific as Hahn imbues *Miss* Jill with a utilitarian perspective on her past sexual experience, alleviating her former shame as she anticipates life in the post-war "jungle" (271). When Jill attempts to confess to Father Sullivan that imagining life outside the camp she might "do anything to get a pretty outfit" (272), the priest replies that survival in the "jungle" is better than confinement in a "zoo," thwarting her confession with a sympathetic recognition of human solidarity in a phrase that Hahn repeats to close the novel: "it's not only you" (272). In the final scene, Jill watches the British navy fleet as it arrives in Hong Kong. Standing among the former "waiting, jostling prisoners," she feels as though she "understood each one of them and recognized their hearts as replicas

---

[83] In *China to Me*, Hahn reflects: "I can't remember how many times [Hitler] instituted drives to purge his land of Jews, but we in Shanghai watched them" arrive "with a special interest" (1944a: 77).

[84] See also "Chapter 25: Moral Dogmatism: Santayana as Anti-Semite" (352–367).

[85] Retitled *Miss Jill from Shanghai* in the "specially revised and edited" paperback edition by New York's Avon Publishing in 1947.

of her own" (272). Suddenly, she recalls lines from the poet Conrad Aiken that allay her apprehension: "There are roses to kiss, and mouths to kiss, and the sharp-pained shadow of death" (272). This recognition of death's shared inevitability relieves the moral pressure of equating the value of her life with the genteel determination to be chaste outside of marriage. Hahn opens a panorama of sympathetic hope as Jill gazes over the sea and is emboldened by the potential power of her sexuality. In choir-like affirmation of this hope, the "blue sky, the little waves near the sand, and the massive benevolence of those ships" amplify the priest's earlier reassurance in the novel's final line: "'Not only you,' sang the ships" (273). Hahn's appreciation of Miss Jill's sense of erotic power and the narrative's orchestral swell of affective potential in the face of death's certainty emphatically counter Santayana's cold vision of Oliver Alden "[fading] away into the grey landscape" of the First World War with clear and cold conscience (Hahn 1936: 420). The intertextual dialogue with *The Last Puritan* was not coincidental; Aiken was one of Santayana's final students at Harvard (Aiken 1922: 40).

There is not room here to delve into Hahn's first-hand descriptions of bombing raids in Shanghai, Chongqing, and Hong Kong and her commentary on the brutalizing rape of Chinese women in Nanjing and elsewhere following the invasion of Japanese forces. Prefacing her reflections on her own survival in *China and Me*, Hahn admits that after having been "locked up in a Japanese concentration camp on a huge scale" in Shanghai and later in Hong Kong, she remained "reluctant to come to grips with the Japanese" (Hahn 1944a: 42). Recalling the vulnerability that she experienced, she qualifies it by counting herself lucky, despite some close calls, because so "many Chinese women were raped" and "suffered a lot more than we [expatriates] did" (289). She remembers reassuring herself that: "If I am raped I won't care. It won't be my fault. It will mean nothing; it is like being wounded" (286). Admitting the futility of offering this conviction as "practical" comfort to women wounded in the war, she ventures that in order to "alleviate the misery caused by war rape" it is important to "lift the guilt burden from the minds of the victims" and to avoid perpetuating the gendered premise of vulnerability by continuing to "scare" "girls deliberately" with warnings that make them feel powerless (288). Citing the murderous violence of lynching African American men in the United States, she laments imperial masculinity for projecting sexual aggression on categorical enemies and typifying white women as innately vulnerable to this enemy unless protected by the national hero (287–288). Three decades later, the wartime violence of Shanghai and Hong Kong haunted the final chapter of *Time and Places**, entitled "The Scream." She relates the lingering inadequacy that she felt as a mother when trying to comfort her young daughter Carola, who is distraught after failing to stop the family cat from killing a baby rabbit in family's yard. As Carola quietly sobs, Hahn strokes her hair, hoping to be honest yet comforting, even as she herself felt "small and weak in our small house" surrounded by "the endless outside—the earth with hunters prowling on it, the sky from which things fall" (Hahn 1970: 304).

In "The Big Smoke," Hahn opens her expatriate journalistic ambition to ironically old-fashioned leisured addiction that belied the catastrophic legacy of opium's financialization to which she stood witness in her writing on China. She refuses the patriarchic fix of hyper-allegorical financial abstraction promulgated by the mercantile biography and post-Bretton Woods hegemony. She also refuses the ruins of Santayana's philosophical fatalism. Her melancholic reflections on using and quitting opium evoke senses of a world that credit women's survival amidst the "informal" and "blatant forms of conquest and colonization" by the United States "in other parts of Asia-Pacific, such as the Philippines, Guam, and Hawai'i" (Yoshihara 2003: 7). Looking beyond the nation, she pursues a literary "modality of cosmopolitanism" that mourns lost relations to places and persons in order to "*open* to the emergence" of sociality born of women's capacity to govern their sexuality (Cheah 2016: 19). At her best, Hahn moved beyond orientalist type-casting in fostering transnational respect for women refugees of Russia, Europe, Australia, China, and other parts of Asia who used opiates not only to survive but also to maintain a hope in their post-war futures.

References

Abrams, Meyer H. 1971 [1934]. *The Milk of Paradise: The Effect of Opium Visions on the Works of De Quincey, Crabbe, Francis Thompson, and Coleridge* (New York: Octagon Books).
Aiken, Conrad. 1922. *The Charnel Rose Senlin: A Biography and Other Poems* (Boston, MA: The Four Seas Co.).
Alcott, Carroll. 1943. *My War With Japan* (New York: Henry Holt and Co.).
Aldridge, Alfred Owen. 1993. *Dragon and the Eagle: The Presence of China in the American Enlightenment* (Detroit, MI: Wayne State University Press).
Appadurai, Arjun. 2016. *Banking on Words: The Failure of Language in the Age of Derivative Finance* (Chicago, IL: University of Chicago Press).
Arrighi, Giovanni. 2007. *Adam Smith in Beijing: Lineages of the Twenty-First Century* (London: Verso).
Arrighi, Giovanni. 2010 [1994]. *The Long Twentieth Century: Money, Power and the Origins of our Times*, expanded edn (London: Verso).
Bakhtin, Mikhail. 1981. *The Dialogic Imagination: Four Essays*, trans. Caryl Emerson and Michael Holquist (Austin, TX: University of Texas Press).
Banta, Martha. 1987. *Imaging American Woman: Idea and Ideals in Cultural History* (New York: Columbia University Press).
Baucom, Ian. 2005. *Specters of the Atlantic: Finance Capital, Slavery, and the Philosophy of History* (Durham, NC: Duke University Press).
Baumler, Alan. 2000. "Opium Control versus Suppression," in Timothy Brook and Bob Tadashi Wakabayashi, eds, *Opium Regimes: China, Britain, and Japan, 1839–1952* (Berkeley, CA: University of California Press), 270–291.
Baym, Nina. 1984. "Concept of Romance in Hawthorne's America," *Nineteenth-Century Fiction* 38.4 (March): 426–443.
Blue, Gregory. 2000. "Opium for China: The British Connection," in Timothy Brook and Bob Tadashi Wakabayashi, eds, *Opium Regimes: China, Britain, and Japan, 1839–1952* (Berkeley, CA: University of California Press), 31–54.
Brook, Timothy and Bob Tadashi Wakabayashi, eds. 2000. *Opium Regimes: China, Britain, and Japan, 1839–1952*. (Berkeley, CA: University of California Press).
Burnham, Michelle. 2019. *Transoceanic America: Risk, Writing, and Revolution in the Global Pacific* (New York: Oxford University Press).
Chase, Richard. 1957. *The American Novel and Its Tradition* (New York: Doubleday Anchor).

Cheah, Pheng. 2016. *What is a World?: On Postcolonial Literature as World Literature* (Durham, NC: Duke University Press).

Cheyfitz, Eric. 1997 [1991]. *The Poetics of Imperialism: Translation and Colonization from The Tempest to Tarzan*, expanded edn (Philadelphia, PA: University of Pennsylvania Press).

Cuthbertson, Ken. 1998. *Nobody Said Not to Go: The Life, Loves, and Adventures of Emily Hahn* (New York: Faber and Faber, Inc.).

De Quincey, Thomas. 1890. "Confessions of an Opium-Eater," in David Masson, ed., *The Collected Writings of Thomas De Quincey*, Vol. 3 (Edinburgh: Adam and Charles Black), 207–449.

Des Forges, Alexander. 2000. "Opium/Leisure/Shanghai: Urban Economies of Consumption," in Timothy Brook and Bob Tadashi Wakabayashi, eds, *Opium Regimes: China, Britain, and Japan, 1839–1952* (Berkeley, CA: University of California Press), 167–185.

Downs, Jacques M. 1997. *The Golden Ghetto: The American Commercial Community at Canton and the Shaping of American China Policy, 1784–1844* (Bethlehem, PA: Lehigh University Press).

Eperjesi, John R. 2001. "The American Asiatic Association and the Imperialist Imaginary of the American Pacific," *boundary 2* 28.1 (Spring): 195–219.

Eperjesi, John R. 2005. *The Imperialist Imaginary: Visions of Asia and the Pacific in American Culture* (Hanover, NH: Dartmouth College Press).

Egan, James. 2011. *Oriental Shadows: The Presence of the East in Early American Literature* (Columbus, OH: Ohio State University Press).

Fichter, James R. 2010. *So Great a Proffit: How the East Indies Trade Transformed Anglo-American Capitalism* (Cambridge, MA: Harvard University Press).

Forbes, Allan, ed. 1918. *Some Merchants and Sea Captains of Old Boston: Being a Collection of Sketches of Notable Men and Mercantile Houses Prominent During the Early Half of the Nineteenth Century in the Commerce and Shipping of Boston* (Boston, MA: Walton Advertising & Printing Co., printed for the State Street Trust Co.).

Fluck, Winfried. 2009. "American Literary History and the Romance with America," *American Literary History* 21.1 (Spring): 1–18.

Ford, Stacilee. 2011. *Troubling American Woman: Narratives of Gender and Nation in Hong Kong* (Hong Kong: Hong Kong University Press).

Frank, Andre Gunder. 1998. *ReOrient: Global Economy in the Asian Age* (Berkeley, CA: University of California Press).

Freeman, Elizabeth. 2019. *Beside You in Time: Sense Methods and Queer Sociabilities in the American Nineteenth Century* (Durham, NC: Duke University Press).

Fuchs, Barbara. 2004. *Romance* (New York and London: Routledge).

Gallagher, John and Ronald Robinson. 1953. "The Imperialism of Free Trade," *Economic History Review* (2nd series) 6.1: 1–15.

Grandin, Greg. 2014. *The Empire of Necessity: Slavery, Freedom, and Deception* (New York: Henry Holt).

Grescoe, Taras. 2016. *Shanghai Grand: Forbidden Love and International Intrigue in a Doomed World* (New York: St Martin's Press).

Haddad, John Rogers. 2008. *The Romance of China: Excursions to China in U.S. Culture: 1776–1876* (New York: Columbia University Press).

Haddad, John Rogers. 2013. *America's First Adventure in China: Trade, Treaties, Opium and Salvation* (Philadelphia, PA: Temple University Press).

Halberstam, Judith. 2005. *In a Queer Time and Place: Transgender Bodies, Subcultural Lives* (New York: Columbia University Press).

Hahn, Emily. 1930. *Seductio ad Absurdum: The Principles and Practices of Seduction—A Beginner's Handbook* (New York: Brewer & Warren).

Hahn, Emily. 1931. *Beginner's Luck* (New York: Brewer, Warren, and Putnam).

Hahn, Emily. 1933. *Congo Solo: Misadventures Two Degrees North* (Indianapolis, IN: Bobbs-Merrill Co.).

Hahn, Emily. 1934. *With Naked Foot* (Indianapolis, IN and New York: Bobbs-Merrill Co.).

Hahn, Emily. 1935. *Affair* (Indianapolis, IN: Bobbs-Merrill Co.).

Hahn, Emily. 1936. "Review of *The Last Puritan*. By George Santayana," *T'ien Hsia Monthly* 4.3 (November): 417–420.

Hahn, Emily. 1940. *Steps of the Sun* (New York: Dial Press).

Hahn, Emily. 1941. *The Soong Sisters* (London: Robert Hale Ltd).

Hahn, Emily. 1944a. *China to Me: A Partial Autobiography* (Philadelphia, PA: Blakiston Co.).

Hahn, Emily. 1944b. *Mr. Pan* (London: Museum Press Limited).

Hahn, Emily. 1946a. *Hong Kong Holiday* (Garden City, NY: Doubleday and Co.).

Hahn, Emily. 1946b. *The Picture Story of China* (New York: Reynal & Hitchcock).

Hahn, Emily. 1946c. *China: A to Z* (New York: Franklin Watts).

Hahn, Emily. 1946d. *Raffles of Singapore: A Biography* (Garden City, NY: Doubleday & Co.).

Hahn, Emily. 1947. *Miss Jill* (Garden City, NY: Doubleday & Co.); also republished as 1958. *House in Shanghai* (Greenwich, Connecticut: Fawcett Crest).

Hahn, Emily. 1950a. *A Degree of Prudery: A Biography of Fanny Burney* (Garden City, New York: Doubleday); also published as 1950. *Purple Passage: A Novel about a Lady both Famous and Fantastic* (Garden City, New York: Doubleday).

Hahn, Emily. 1950b. *England to Me* (London: Jonathan Cape).

Hahn, Emily. 1951. *Aphra Behn* (London: Jonathan Cape). Also published as 1950. *Purple Passage: A Novel about a Lady Both Famous and Fantastic* (New York: Doubleday & Co.).

Hahn, Emily. 1953. *James Brooke of Sarawak: A Biography of Sir James Brooke* (London: Arthur Barker).

Hahn, Emily. 1955. *Chiang Kai-shek: An Unauthorized Biography* (Garden City, NY: Doubleday and Co.).

Hahn, Emily. 1956. *Diamond* (London: Weidenfeld and Nicolson).

Hahn, Emily. 1959a. *Around the World with Nelly Bly* (Boston, MA: Houghton Mifflin Co.).

Hahn, Emily. 1959b [1952]. *Love Conquers Nothing: A New Look at Old Romances* (London: Dennis Dobson).

Hahn, Emily. 1959c. *Aboab: First Rabbi of the Americas* (New York: Farrar, Straus and Cudahy).

Hahn, Emily. 1960. *Africa to Me: Person to Person* (London: Secker & Warburg).

Hahn, Emily. 1963a. *Indo* (New York: Doubleday and Co.).

Hahn, Emily. 1963b. *China Only Yesterday: 1850–1950: A Century of Change* (London: Weidenfeld and Nicolson).

Hahn, Emily. 1968. *The Cooking of China* (New York: Time Life).

Hahn, Emily. 1969. "The Big Smoke," *New Yorker* (15 February): 35–43.

Hahn, Emily. 1970. *Times and Places*: A Memoir* (New York: Thomas Y. Crowell).

Hahn, Emily. 1974. *Once Upon a Pedestal: The Fascinating and Informal Chronicle of the American Woman's Struggle to Stand on Her Own Two Feet* (New York: Thomas Y. Crowell).

Hahn, Emily. 1977. *Mabel: A Biography of Mabel Dodge Luhan* (Boston, MA: Houghton Mifflin Co.).

Hahn, Emily. 1981. *The Islands: America's Imperial Adventure in the Philippines* (New York: Coward, McCann & Geoghegan).

Hao, Yen-p'ing. 1986. *The Commercial Revolution in Nineteenth-Century China: The Rise of Sino-Eastern Mercantile Capitalism* (Berkeley, CA: University of California Press).

Harvey, David. 1982. *The Limits to Capital* (Chicago, IL: University of Chicago Press).

Harvey, David. 2003. *The New Imperialism* (Oxford: Oxford University Press).

He, Sibing. 2012. "Russell and Company and the Imperialism of Anglo-American Free Trade," in Kendall Johnson, ed., *Narratives of Free Trade: The Commercial Powers of Early US–China Relations* (Hong Kong: Hong Kong University Press): 83–98.

Hershatter, Gail. 1989. "The Hierarchy of Shanghai Prostitution, 1870–1949," *Modern China* 15.4 (October): 463–498.

Hsu, Hsuan. 2010. *Geography and the Production of Space in Nineteenth-Century American Literature* (New York: Cambridge University Press).

Huang, Yunte. 2008. *Transpacific Imaginations: History, Literature, Counterpoetics* (Cambridge, MA: Harvard University Press).

Hutt, Jonathan. 2001. "*La Maison d'Or*—the Sumptuous World of Shao Xunmei," *East Asian History* (Australian National University) 21 (June): 111–142.

Hutt, Jonathan. 2010. "Monstre Sacré: The Decadent World Sinmay Zau 邵洵美," *China Heritage Quarterly* 22 (June), www.chinaheritagequarterly.org/features.php?searchterm=022_monstre.inc&issue=022, accessed February 16, 2022.

Jackson, Stanley. 1968. *The Sassoons* (London: Heinemann).

Johnson, Kendall A. 2017. *The New Middle Kingdom: China and the Early American Romance of Free Trade* (Baltimore, MD: Johns Hopkins University Press).

Johnson, Kendall A. 2020. "Once Upon a Time in 1784: American Mercantile Biographies and the Romance of Free Trade Imperialism," in *Tribute and Trade: China and Global Modernity, 1784–1935*, edited by William Christie, Angela Dunstan, and Q.S. Tong (Sydney: Sydney University Press), 109–145.

Kaplan, Amy. 2005. *The Anarchy of Empire in the Making of U.S. Culture* (Cambridge, MA: Harvard University Press).

Kaplan, Amy and Donald E. Pease, eds. 1993. *Cultures of U.S. Imperialism* (Durham, NC: Duke University Press).

Kobayashi, Motohiro. 2000. "Drug Operations by Resident Japanese in Tianjin," in Timothy Brook and Bob Tadashi Wakabayashi, eds, *Opium Regimes: China, Britain, and Japan, 1839–1952* (Berkeley, CA: University of California Press), 152–166.

Lane, Christopher. 1999a. *The Burdens of Intimacy: Psychoanalysis and Victorian Masculinity* (Chicago, IL: University of Chicago Press).

Lane, Christopher. 1999b. "George Santayana and the Beauty of Friendship," in Richard Dellamora, ed., *Victorian Sexual Dissidence* (Chicago, IL: University of Chicago Press), 211–233.

Lee, Ou-fan Lee. 1999. *Shanghai Modern: The Flowering of a New Urban Culture in China, 1930–1945* (Cambridge: Harvard University Press).

Lejuene, Philippe. 1989. *On Autobiography*, ed. Paul John Eakin; trans. Katherine Leary (Minneapolis, MN: University of Minnesota Press).

Lewis, Richard. W. B. 1955. *The American Adam: Innocence, Tragedy, and Tradition in the Nineteenth Century* (Chicago, IL: University of Chicago Press, 1955).

Lin, Man-houng. 2007. *China Upside Down: Currency, Society, and Ideologies, 1808–1856* (Cambridge, MA: Harvard University Press).

Liu, Kwang-Ching. 1959. "Steamship Enterprise in Nineteenth-Century China," *Journal of Asian Studies* 18.4 (August): 435–455.

Lowe, Lisa. 2015. *The Intimacies of Four Continents* (Durham, NC: Duke University Press).

Luciano, Dana. 2007. *Arranging Grief: Sacred Time and the Body in Nineteenth-Century America* (New York: New York University Press).

Lutes, Jean Marie. 2006. *Front Page Girls: Women Journalists in American Culture and Fiction, 1880–1930* (Ithaca, NY: Cornell University Press).

Marx, Karl. 2007. *Dispatches for the New York Tribune: Selected Journalism of Karl Marx*, ed. James Ledbetter (New York: Penguin).

Matsuda, Matt K. 2012. *Pacific Worlds: A History of Seas, Peoples, and Cultures* (New York: Cambridge University Press).

Matthiessen. Francis O. 1941. *American Renaissance: Art and Expression in the Art of Emerson and Whitman* (London: Oxford University Press).

McClay, Wilfred M. 1982. "Two Versions of the Genteel Tradition: Santayana and Brooks," *New England Quarterly* 55.3 (September): 368–391.

McCormick, John. 2003. *George Santayana: A Biography* (London: Routledge).

McCormick, Thomas J. 1963. "Insular Imperialism and the Open Door: The China Market and the Spanish–American War," *Pacific Historical Review* 32.2 (May): 155–159.

McCormick, Thomas J. 1967. *China Market: America's Quest for Informal Empire, 1895–1901* (Chicago, IL: Quadrangle Books).

Melville, Herman. 1856. *The Piazza Tales* (New York: Dix & Edwards).

Messmer, Matthias. 2012. *Jewish Wayfarers in Modern China: Tragedy and Splendor* (Lanham, MD: Lexington Books).

Munn, Christopher. 2000. "The Hong Kong Opium Revenue, 1845–1885," in Timothy Brook and Bob Tadashi Wakabayashi, eds, *Opium Regimes: China, Britain, and Japan, 1839–1952* (Berkeley, CA: University of California Press), 105–126.

Pocock, John G.A. 1985. *Virtue, Commerce, and History* (Cambridge: Cambridge University Press, 1985).

Poovey, Mary. 2008. *Genres of the Credit Economy: Mediating Value in Eighteenth- and Nineteenth-Century Britain* (Chicago, IL: University of Chicago Press).

Posnock, Ross. 1991. *The Trial of Curiosity: Henry James, William James, and the Challenge of Modernity* (New York: Oxford University Press).

Quincy, Josiah. 1847. *The Journals of Major Samuel Shaw, the First American Consul at Canton, with a Life of the Author* (Boston, MA: Wm. Crosby and H. P. Nichols).

Rifkin, Mark. 2017. *Beyond Settler Time: Temporal Sovereignty and Indigenous Sel-Determination* (Durham, NC: Duke University Press).

Rowe, John Carlos. 2000. *Literary Culture and U.S. Imperialism: From the Revolution to World War II* (New York: Oxford University Press).

Santayana, George. 1894. *Sonnets and Other Verses* (Cambridge, MA and Chicago, IL: Stone and Kimball, 1894).

Santayana, George. 1896. *The Sense of Beauty: Being the Outline of Aesthetic Theory* (New York: Charles Scribner's Sons).

Santayana, George. 1901. *A Hermit of Carmel and Other Poems* (New York: Charles Scribner's Sons).

Santayana, George. 1905-1906. *The Life Of Reason: The Phases of Human Progress.* 5 volumes (New York: Charles Scribner's Sons).

Santayana, George. 1911. "The Genteel Tradition in American Philosophy," *University of California Chronicle* (Berkeley, CA: University of California Press) 13.4 (October): 357–380.

Santayana, George. 1987. *Persons and Places: Fragments of Autobiography*, ed. William G. Holzberger and Herman J. Saatkamp, Jr (Cambridge, MA: MIT Press) (includes: *The Background of My Life* (1944); *The Middle Span* (1945); and the posthumous *My Host the World* (1953), all published by Scribner's Sons, New York).

Santayana, George. 1994 [1935]. *The Last Puritan: A Memoir in the Form of a Novel*, ed. William G. Holzberger and Herman J. Saatkamp, Jr (Cambridge, MA: MIT Press).

Santayana, George. 1998 [1922]. "Marginal Notes on Civilization in the United States," in Douglas L. Wilson, ed., *The Genteel Tradition: Nine Essays by George Santayana* (Lincoln, NE: University of Nebraska Press), 131–152.

Santayana, George. 2009. *The Genteel Tradition in American Philosophy and Character and Opinion in the United States*, ed. James Seaton (New Haven, CT: Yale University Press).

Schueller, Malini Johar. 1998. *U.S. Orientalisms: Race, Nation, and Gender in Literature 1790–1890* (Ann Arbor, MI: University of Michigan).

Scully, Eileen P. 1995. "Taking the Low Road to Sino–American Relations: 'Open Door' Expansionists and the Two China Markets," *Journal of American History* 82.1 (June): 62–83.

Scully, Eileen P. 1998. "Prostitution as Privilege: The 'American Girl' of Treaty Port Shanghai, 1860–1937," *International History Review* 20:4: 855–833.

Semmel, Bernard. 1970. *The Rise of Free Trade Imperialism: Classical Political Economy, the Empire of Free Trade and Imperialism, 1750–1850* (Cambridge: Cambridge University Press).

Shen, Shuang. 2009. *Cosmopolitan Publics: Anglophone Print Culture in Semi-Colonial Shanghai* (New Brunswick, NJ: Rutgers University Press).

Slack, Edward R., Jr. 2000. "The National Anti-Opium Association and the Guomingdang State, 1924–1927," in Timothy Brook and Bob Tadashi Wakabayashi, eds, *Opium Regimes: China, Britain, and Japan, 1839–1952* (Berkeley, CA: University of California Press), 258–269.

Smith, Logan Pearsall. 1920. *Little Essays Drawn from the Writings of George Santayana, with Collaboration of the Author* (London: Constable and Co.).

Stoler, Ann Laura. 2006. "Intimidations of Empire: Predicaments of the Tactile and Unseen," in Ann Laura Stoler, ed., *Haunted by Empire: Geographies of Intimacy in North American History* (Durham, NC: Duke University Press), 1–22.

Sturgis, Julian. n.d. [1893]. *From Books and Papers of Russell Sturgis* (Oxford: Oxford University Press).

Tchen, John Kuo Wei. 1999. *New York before Chinatown: Orientalism and the Shaping of American Culture, 1776–1882* (Baltimore, MD: Johns Hopkins University Press).

Trilling, Lionel. 1980 [1956]. "'That Smile of Parmenides Made Me Think,'" in *A Gathering of Fugitives* (New York: Oxford University Press), 164–179.

Trocki, Carl A. 1999. *Opium, Empire and the Global Political Economy: A Study of the Asian Opium Trade* (London and New York: Routledge).

Trocki, Carl A. 2000. "Drugs, Taxes, and Chinese Capitalism in Southeast Asia," in Timothy Brook and Bob Tadashi Wakabayashi, eds, *Opium Regimes: China, Britain, and Japan, 1839–1952* (Berkeley, CA: University of California Press), 79–104.

Van Dyke, Paul A. 2005. *The Canton Trade: Life and Enterprise on the China Coast, 1700–1845* (Hong Kong: Hong Kong University Press).

Van Dyke, Paul A. 2011. *The Merchants of Canton and Macao: Politics and Strategies of the Eighteenth-Century Chinese Trade* (Hong Kong: Hong Kong University Press).

Wakabayashi, Bob Tadashi. 2000. "From Peril to Profit: Opium in Late-Edo to Meiji Eyes," in *Opium Regimes: China, Britain, and Japan, 1839–1952* (Berkeley: University of California Press), 55–75.

Wilson, Rob and Wimal Dissanayake, eds. 1996. *Global Local: Cultural Production and the Transnational Imaginary* (Durham, NC: Duke University Press).

Wong, John D. 2016. *Global Trade in the Nineteenth Century: The House of Houqua and the Canton System* (Cambridge: Cambridge University Press).

Wong, J.Y. 1998. *Deadly Dreams: Opium Imperialism, and the Arrow War (1856–1860) in China* (Cambridge: Cambridge University Press).

Wong, Roy Bin. 2000. "Opium and Modern Chinese State-Making," in Timothy Brook and Bob Tadashi Wakabayashi, eds, *Opium Regimes: China, Britain, and Japan, 1839–1952* (Berkeley, CA: University of California Press), 189–211.

Yoshihara, Mari. 2003. *Embracing the East: White Women and American Orientalism* (New York: Oxford University Press).

Zau, Sinmay. 1927. *Paradise and May* (*Tiāntáng yú wǔ yuè*; 天堂與五月) (Shanghai: Guanghua Bookstore).

Zau, Sinmay. 1928. "Fire and Flesh," (Huǒ yǔ ròu; 火與肉) (Shanghai: Golden House Bookstore).

CHAPTER 12

MODERNISM'S CARES
Reading For and With

RACHEL ADAMS

NEAR the end of *Let Us Now Praise Famous Men*, James Agee describes an incident of uncomfortable intimacy. As night falls, his car gets a flat tire, forcing him back to the house of his informants, a family of Alabama sharecroppers living in abject poverty. They rouse themselves to care for their guest according to their gendered roles. Mrs Gudger, half asleep, toils over a simple but enormous meal, while her husband makes conversation and wakes the children to make room for the unexpected visitor. Agee finds himself awash in conflicting sensations of gratitude, compassion, and regret for inconveniencing people who are so generous, despite having so little of their own. He feels guilt at his inability to lessen their misery and a deep sense of kinship arising from their shared humanity. But no matter how fervently he throbs with empathic recognition, his body recoils in disgust at the unappetizing dinner and squalid environs of the poor (Agee and Evans 1988). He chokes on their food and his skin crawls at their flimsy, bedbug-ridden mattress. Throughout the book, he struggles mightily with the affordances of his chosen medium—the literary—to capture this ambivalent fusion of identification and repulsion, while maintaining the dignity of his subjects. In this way, *Famous Men* is an extended meditation on human interdependency, the universal obligation to care it entails, and the gaping asymmetries in resources, status, and ability that divide persons and communities.[1] How modernist literature sought innovative narrative forms to represent the inherently uneven social and affective dynamics of care is the subject of this chapter.

Modernity had a transformative impact on the social organization of dependency and the nature of care work, and modernist literature explores the contradictory effects of such changes on vulnerable persons and those who sustain them. This may seem a surprising way to describe a movement known for embracing youth, vigor, and newness.

---

[1] As the collaboration of a writer and a photographer, *Let Us Now Praise Famous Men* is also a meditation on interdependency at the level of form since the work's meaning arises from the sometimes complementary and sometimes tense interaction of written and visual media.

However, relations of care—and associated conditions of dependency, frailty, and toil—remain strikingly central to modernist aesthetic and social commitments, overlapping the more familiar preoccupations with subjectivity, relatedness, collaboration, and temporality. Care is also an evident, if seldom acknowledged, dynamic in modernist literary treatments of family, aging, motherhood, child rearing, domestic work, and disability, all of which have been the subject of recent scholarly analysis (Herring 2022; Martell 2019; Phillips 2016; Reed 2004; Rosner 2020; Wilson 2004).

Care is work, an attitude, and an ethical ideal. Although the need for care is universal among human animals, history and culture shape who counts as dependent, what kind of care they receive, and how caregivers are compensated for their work. In what follows, I briefly sketch out the evolution of institutions, policies, and social organization of care as a context to reconsider the narrative concerns and aesthetic experimentation of American literary modernism. I treat the history of care as a contextual frame but also take care as a critical method for reading literary texts with attention to relatedness, intimacy, emotion, and the uneven distribution of vulnerability among persons and environments. It also allows consideration of form by asking how the dynamics of interdependency inspire modernist innovation at the level of narrative structure, pacing, and choices about inclusion and exclusion. I begin with a more extended account of the ethical principles and social history of care, which intersect with modernist literary concerns at a moment when the caregiving role of an emerging welfare state, the presumably instinctual obligations of maternal care, and the work of paid domestic servants were entangled with newfound intensity. I then turn to two celebrated modernist works—Gertrude Stein's *Three Lives* (1973) and William Faulkner's *The Sound and the Fury* (1946)—as examples of how interdependency and care can serve as a critical lens for reading literary texts, illuminating overlooked characters and themes and offering new insight about their experiments with form. While Stein's *Three Lives* has been recognized for its unusual focus on working-class women, my reading concentrates the centrality of care to the work (paid and unpaid) that her protagonists do and how the asymmetrical interdependencies that structure care relations motivate the pacing and emphases of Stein's narrative form. I then turn to the very different case of Faulkner, whose decisions about narrative perspective make visible the uneven distribution of care work within a family: white men who are the subjects of care are also entitled to first-person narrative, while the women who care for them are narrated from without. For the novel's Black characters in particular, the absence of first-person perspective is a sign of subordination but also of expertise, knowledge, and relationships that remain inaccessible to their white employers.

Care, Modernity, Modernism

I define care as the intimate and necessary labor, paid and unpaid, required to sustain those who are in a position of dependency. Immediate relations of care involving direct contact between individual persons do not take place in isolation but rather are embedded in broad and often fragile webs of interdependency. My attention to narrative representations is informed by care ethics, particularly as developed by feminist scholars. In place of the abstract universals favored by moral philosophers, the ethics of care focuses on the local and specific, on relatedness rather than discrete, bounded individuals. It eschews the philosopher's traditional claim to objectivity, attending to emotion, partiality, and embodied particularity. And instead of defining selfhood in terms of capacity for reason, philosophers of care claim that persons are bound together by shared vulnerability and interdependence (Held 2006; Kittay 1999; Ruddick, 1989; Tronto 1993). Dependency is a universal human condition, but it is unevenly distributed among persons and groups, as is the work of caring for those who are dependent. These basic principles are the bedrock for attitudes and practices that vary widely across cultures and historical periods.

All human animals require care at some stage of life, but perceptions of dependency and care are socially constructed (Boris and Klein 2012; Fineman 2005; Fraser and Gordon 1994; Glenn 2010; Tronto 2013). In the monarchial societies of Europe, ordinary people were subjects, rather than citizens, and dependence was the norm. The public submission of monarchial subjects was replicated within individual households, where wives, children, and servants were socially and legally subordinate to the family patriarch. Each class of person was assigned a place and corresponding duties in a hierarchy believed to be dictated by natural law and structured to sustain the well-being of family and community (Fraser and Gordon 1994: 312–314). The radical innovation of the American Revolution was to make independence the foundation of national identity. Where formerly independence meant the possession of land or wealth, it was redefined as the capacity to work and ownership of one's labor. Independence was a status extended to all white men regardless of whether they owned property, guaranteeing them an avenue to rights and political representation. Dependence was no longer the norm but a status identity assigned to subordinate classes. These included children but also women, enslaved persons, and Native Americans, who were understood to be inherently weaker, more vulnerable, and childlike (Fraser and Gordon 1994: 313). Denied direct representation in the public sphere, dependent persons would be represented by white male citizens who recognized their needs and spoke on their behalf.

Modernity reshaped the definition of dependency and obligations of care. Families became smaller, generations that once cared for one another dispersed, and children were newly inspired to make their own way in the world. Diverse populations of strangers lived crowded together in growing cities, proximity giving new visibility to disparities in health, income, and social stature. The arrival of industrialization sharpened divisions within existing social hierarchies, reinforcing the separation and gendering of public and private, work and domestic life, care and labor. Wage labor was valorized over domestic activities, making the time-consuming, physically taxing activities of caring for the home, and dependent family members, increasingly invisible as work. Historians Nancy Fraser and Linda Gordon note that, under capitalism, working men were designated as "independent"—meaning possessed of the capacity to work and freedom to engage in contractual relationships with an employer—even as they were subordinated within the system of wage labor. This understanding of independence obscured the conditions of their exploitation, while narrowing the definition of "dependency" to economically marginalized groups such as paupers, women, and non-white people (Fraser and Gordon 1994: 315–319). It was during the period of industrialization that disability was reconceived as the inability to work (Rose 2017). This definition persists into the present, where being "on disability" means being unemployed because of a physical or mental impairment that precludes "any substantial gainful activity" (Social Security Administration 2020). Dependency became an increasingly pejorative term linking economic need to moral qualities of weakness, inability, and poor character, and caregiving activities were increasingly separated from understandings of meaningful work.

New divisions also emerged within the private sphere, separating the moral and spiritual aspects of domesticity from the physical labor of running a household. Women responsible for presiding over the home and maintaining domestic virtues were elevated above those who did the manual work of care (Glenn 2010: 42–87). The availability of appliances, consumer goods, and mass entertainment put greater emphasis on the housewife as a consumer of merchandise and leisure activities than as a producer who contributed to the household economy (Cowan 1983). Although the use of household servants had declined somewhat by the early twentieth century, Mary Wilson notes that they remained a common enough feature of domestic life to make regular appearances in modernist literature (Wilson 2016).[2] Poverty and overwork hampered the ability of servants to care for their own families according to the ideals established by more affluent households. Those unable to meet new standards of cleanliness, nutrition, and emotional labor were seen as inadequate mothers and caregivers. Their perceived failures gave rise to social reforms targeted toward improving domestic and maternal caregiving skills among the poor, assimilating immigrant women and children, and uplifting Native American children by removing them to residential schools (Fraser and Gordon 1994: 317–318; Glenn 2010: 42–87). As the state became increasingly involved in such projects, it assumed a contradictory role, at once newly committed to caring for those most in need and imposing new forms of dependency.

In the early twentieth century, the United States followed many European countries in developing nationwide social welfare programs to care for the poor, sick, and disabled who once would have relied on their families or local charities (Garland 2016). In official language, the stigmatized "pauper" was replaced by the term "dependent" to describe recipients of government aid, such as children and single mothers (Fraser and Gordon 1994: 319–323). Yet, despite the name change, the moral judgments associated with poverty persisted, branding dependent adults as burdensome, lazy, and unproductive. These connotations were reinforced by New Deal era programs divided between "entitlements" for the elderly and unemployed—understood to deserve the support of a system to

---

[2] On servants in nineteenth-century literature, see Bruce Robbins' excellent *The Servant's Hand: English Fiction from Below* (1993).

which they had contributed—and "aid" for the dependent poor—seen as getting something for nothing. When poor women needed to care for children or disabled relatives, their labor was not seen as work and they were described as dependent on state aid. By contrast, those who received social security were called "claimants," sustained by benefits that aimed "to prevent old-age dependency" (Mandell 2010: 17, 24). This language held up "dependency" as the stigma that deserved government entitlements were designed to forestall. Where dependency had once been a neutral description of a social relation, by the mid-twentieth century it had become firmly associated with such flaws as weakness, laziness, low intelligence, and lack of motivation. As more people of color qualified for benefits, dependency was increasingly racialized and Welfare came to be seen as a program that served (often undeserving) Black women (Fraser and Gordon 1994: 319–325; Glenn 2010: 161–174, 191–192).

In the first decades of the twentieth century, modernist authors and artists prided themselves on living in bohemian opposition to many of the bourgeois values that would soon be crystallized in policies of the welfare state (Gluck 2005; Stansell 2000). Where state programs addressed the vulnerability of women and children, modernist women were proud of their independence and autonomy, and some defied the feminine imperative to marry and reproduce (Miller 2017). Modernists replaced the wholesome, precious children of Victorian literature with feeble degenerates and broke apart the image of the family as a site of warm, nurturing activity idealized by domestic fiction of the nineteenth century (Rosner 2020: ch. 5). Where Welfare addressed the dire financial needs of dependent persons, modernist artists often romanticized poverty, refused or disparaged wage labor, and subverted the capitalist economy with barter and gift giving. Instead of defining personal worth through the ownership of property, they experimented with alternative communal living arrangements.[3] And where modernity valued standardization, efficiency, and productivity, modernist artists embraced unreason, disorder, and asymmetry (Jones 2004; Rosner 2020).

As they sought alternatives to the priorities and values of modern society, modernists recognized the social importance of caring relations and, perhaps more surprisingly, found them an unexpected source for aesthetic inspiration (Davidson 2019; Sanchez 2016). Many saw interdependency—reciprocal relationships that acknowledged the mutual dependency of all parties—as an opportunity for creative potential that had been obscured by the narrow individualism of modern work and social organization. Where romanticism celebrated the artist as an individual genius, some modernists explored the forms of creativity that arise when artists work collectively. Collaboration and mutual inspiration were all the rage in modernist salons, communes, and group households, publishing collectives like the Bloomsbury group, group art forms like manifestos, murals, or the surrealists' exquisite corpse, inter-art projects like *Famous Men*, and celebrated couples like Virginia and Leonard Woolf, Frida Kahlo and Diego Rivera, Georgia O'Keefe and Alfred Steiglitz (Curkpatrick 2020; Gluck 2005; Pontellier

---

[3] On modernist attitudes toward class and poverty, see Joseph Entin (2007).

2019; Potter 2012).[4] The same intimate entanglements that might lead to generative productivity could also devolve into more burdensome codependency, as was famously true of the Woolfs, F. Scott and Zelda Fitzgerald, or T.S. and Vivian Eliot.[5] Complex interdependencies, both generative and debilitating, were a lifestyle and a creative method but also a topic of modernist literary works such as Djuna Barnes's *Nightwood*, Samuel Beckett's *Waiting for Godot*, *Endgame*, and *Mercier and Camier*, or Gertrude Stein's *Autobiography of Alice B. Toklas*. In literary representation, as in life, these relationships could be inspiring, but they also involved the daily work of caring for another. When vulnerability is unevenly distributed, the maintenance of dignity and personhood is an ongoing negotiation. The ebb and flow of dominance and submission, ability and need, are part of any long-term caring relationship. The readings to come show how such imbalances find their aesthetic analogue in the modernist concern with asymmetry and telling variations in narrative perspective.

Another point of intersection between modernist creativity and care is a shared skepticism about the temporalities of modern life. Modernity ushered in an era of routines, schedules, and fixed trajectories for human development. Standardization of time was key to such modern developments as factory labor, mass transit, and international commerce. New imperatives to efficiency and order governed modern institutions of care like hospitals, schools, and residential facilities for the disabled and elderly. But modernists balked at the notion that human life should be organized around clock time or that temporal experience could be measured out in predictable units (Christian 2011; Felski 2000; James 2016; Levenson 2011; Olsen 2009; Rancière 2014; Randall 2007; Rosner 2020; Schwarz 2010). They were inspired by Albert Einstein's discovery that time and motion were relative to the observer and, influenced by philosopher Henri Bergson, they sought to depict time as it is experienced and remembered rather than as measured by a clock (Gontarski and Ardoin 2013). Authors like Dorothy Richardson, Virginia Woolf, T. S. Eliot and Marcel Proust experimented with the slowing down or speeding up of remembered time and sought forms to capture how memory is measured out in the accumulation of qualitative impressions. Modernists recognized care as an activity that exemplified their own commitments to temporal plasticity. Compassion cannot be documented on a time sheet, measured in units of effort, or quantified with any of the typical gages used to record and compensate labor. And care had no regard for whether the future is bright; indeed, it is often most necessary and intense when there is no future except immanent loss and death.[6] These points of connection among the awareness of

---

[4] Scott Herring's chapter on the less well-known late-life partnership of Henri Ford and Intrad Tamang makes a fascinating addition to the scholarship on modernist collaboration and interdependency.

[5] Thanks to Victoria Rosner for suggesting this detail.

[6] For further reading on the relationship between care and time, see my forthcoming book, *Critical: Care, Narrative, and the Art of Interdependency*. My argument draws on writing about temporality in queer theory and disability studies by Lee Edelman (2004), Jack Halberstam (2011), Kathryn Bond Stockton (2009), Alison Kafer (2013), Robert McRuer (2018), and Ellen Samuels (2017).

human interdependency, performance of care, and modernist aesthetics are the basis for the readings that follow, as well as a model for further readings of modernist literature and beyond.

The romantic partnership of Gertrude Stein and Alice B. Toklas was premised on an interdependency so profound that Stein felt herself capable of writing Toklas's autobiography (even as she laid solitary claim to the genius emerging from Alice's caring ministrations). Where Stein's *Autobiography of Alice B. Toklas* depicts Gertrude and Alice caring for each other, each according to her capacities, her earlier novella, *Three Lives*, makes the dynamics of interdependency and care a narrative focus and the ordinary experiences and inner lives of working-class women its subjects (Stein 1990; 1973). Although its title promises to capture the totality of particular lives, each of the three narratives skips over the dependencies of infancy and childhood to begin with the stage of maturity when working-class women are burdened with the care of others, following its protagonist through the inevitable onset of illness, advancing age, and then death. All three stories take interdependency as a structuring principle, centering on a woman's intimate relationships with romantic partners, employers, and friends. As with all prolonged relationships, these interdependencies are dynamic and shifting. The roles of caregiver and recipient evolve over time or on a daily basis. Those who provide care also need it; their bodies tire, age, weaken, and experience debilities of their own, while those who require care reciprocate by exuding welcome and gratitude or sometimes resistance and denial. For example, in the first story, Anna's employer, Miss Matilda, enjoys having a servant who allows her to be "always without care," a claim immediately modified by the observation that Miss Matilda finds it "a burden to endure" Anna's prodding and managing (Stein 1973: 22). This sentence captures the intimate relatedness and subtle asymmetries of power involved in care work. Within the overarching power dynamic of domestic service are more subtle negotiations in which the employer benefits from a servant, but must also reciprocate, however unevenly, by accommodating the servant's needs and temperament. Where often this side of the equation goes unmentioned, Stein builds it into the description of the mistress and her domestic helper.

Each story in *Three Lives* follows the linear chronology of a life, but they develop according to the temporalities of affiliation rather than the measured clock time of modernity. In place of predictable work routines or phases of individual development, time in *Three Lives* moves in accordance with the ebbs and flows of interconnection among lives. The narrative eddies around conversations and emotionally fraught interactions, then flows quickly over large periods where relationships remain relatively stable. Stein is particularly interested in the temporalities of chosen relationships of friendship or romance rather than those sanctioned by custom or biology. Her concern with the arc of interdependency is aptly captured in this reflection on the changing dynamics of an intimate female friendship:

> In friendship, power always has its downward curve. One's strength to manage rises always higher until there comes a time one does not win, and though one may not

really lose, still from the time that victory is not sure, one's power slowly ceases to be strong. It is only in a close tie such as marriage, that influence can mount and grow always stronger with the years and never meet with a decline. It can only happen so when there is no way to escape.

(Stein 1973: 54)

In contrast to marriage, unromantically described as a bond with "no way to escape," friendship evolves, along with relative degrees of power and influence over another. The changing tides of relationships that absorb long stretches of narrative attention contrast starkly with this abrupt account of Anna's middle age: "So Anna's serving and her giving life went on, each with its varied pleasures and pains" (Stein 1973: 52). A single, unadorned sentence captures the life's work of a woman devoted to "serving" and "giving." A similar rhythm characterizes the middle story, "Melanctha," which takes up the bulk of *Three Lives*. The most extended episodes follow the redundant give-and-take between the protagonist and her lover, Jeff Campbell, as their need and desire for one another waxes and wanes. Much of the remaining narrative recounts the shifting balance of dominance and submission within Melanctha's female friendships. All three lives unfold without dramatic emphasis on conflict, extreme tragedy, or notable achievement; instead, each narrative dwells on the mundane and repetitive patterns of care entailed by women's toil, obligations, and relationships.

Three Lives recognizes the gendering of care work, acknowledging its unavoidable prominence in women's experience while also seeking to dismantle the view that women are naturally predisposed to nurture and compassion. Stein's commitment to denaturalizing care is striking, given that she engages in various other kinds of essentialism, most notably connecting Black people with spontaneity, emotion, and humor but also depicting the immigrant Lena as "simple and human, with the earth patience of the working, gentle, german woman" (Stein 1973: 241). While Stein willingly attributes some aspects of temperament and character to her protagonists' ancestral origins, she refuses to associate women's biological role in reproduction and childbirth with an ingrained proclivity for mothering activity. It isn't that her three protagonists are incapable of forming warm, caring intimacies, which they enjoy with friends, lovers, employers, and even pets, but none extends these sentiments to children. Melanctha is a daughter but has no children of her own; "Anna had no strong natural feeling to love children" (Stein 1973: 25) and she maintains only an obligatory, but cool, acquaintance to her biological family. Lena is the only one of the three protagonists to become a mother, and the epithet in her story's title "The Gentle Lena," suggests qualities of a more promising caregiver. But despite being a biological mother, she has no feelings of attachment toward her own children. Instead, motherhood seems to bring on a permanent state of depression in which she "dragged around and was careless with her clothes and all lifeless, and she acted always and lived on just as if she had no feeling (Stein 1973: 276). Where Lena is lethargic and uninterested in her children and domestic responsibilities, her husband, Herman, is more genuinely inclined to mothering. After Lena dies, Herman cares for the children of their loveless marriage with devotion and joy. Their family attests to the fallacy of assuming that gender predetermines who will be the more willing or capable caregiver.

Three Lives was published some thirty years before the emergence of a welfare state in the United States, and its characters suffer from the absence of a government-sponsored safety net to care for the dependent poor. In youth, all three women are vigorously capable of caring for themselves and others. But with time they encounter the inevitable frailties of advancing age, combined with the draining effects of worry and sacrifice. In a time before Social Security or Medicare, former employers seem to feel no sense of obligation to care for their debilitated servants. The wearing away of the working poor is particularly evident for the once robust Anna, who

> worked, and thought, and saved, and scolded, and took care of all the boarders, and of [the dogs] Peter and of Rags, and all the others. There was never any end to Anna's effort and she grew always more tired, and more pale yellow, and in her face more thin and worn and worried.
>
> (Stein 1973: 80)

Not only is Anna's body depleted by physical and emotional toil, but also she is constantly spending money to care for needy members of her community with no hope of repayment. Moreover, Anna has no children of her own to care for her in old age. Consistent with a life where she "could never take a rest" (Stein 1973: 81), she dies abruptly during a surgery.

Care, for Stein's three protagonists, is a social obligation as well as an assumed proclivity of their status as women. All women are somebody's daughter, but immigrants like Anna and Lena have left behind parents and other relatives who might need their care, while the American-born Melanctha fulfills the obligations assigned to daughters despite feeling no love for her biological parents. The difference between Melanctha's fate and that of her mother bespeaks the transition from more traditional modes of nursing the ill to the impersonal, bureaucratic systems of modern health care. Melanctha's mother remains at home through a long illness because she has the attentive care of her daughter, overseen by visits from the doctor, Jeff Campbell. At the turn of the twentieth century, home care for the frail elderly was still the norm for those lucky enough to have capable female relatives, while hospitals were reserved for more involved medical procedures and containment of infectious disease. Charitable hospitals, associated with suffering, contamination, and immanent death, were a last resort for the poor and destitute (Risse 1999; Starr 1982). When she gets sick, Melanctha endures the grim fate of an African American woman with no financial means or family attachments. There is no return on the time and effort she expended in caring for her mother; absent a daughter or other female relative, Melanctha dies alone, her last days captured in two simple sentences:

> Melanctha went back to the hospital, and there the Doctor told her she had the consumption, and before long she would surely die. They sent her where she could

be taken care of, a home for poor consumptives, and there Melanctha stayed until she died.

(Stein 1973: 236)

The impersonality of Melanctha's plight is captured by an anonymous "they" that sends her away. The doctor's pronouncement that "she would surely die" is a judgment of his patient's physical condition, but also a prescription for diminished care. At a "home for poor consumptives" her well-being and comfort is by no means guaranteed since such facilities were notorious for overcrowding and squalor. The next sentence concludes by succinctly fulfilling the doctor's deterministic pronouncement with the conjunction, "until she died." In this way, Melanctha's story reflects the decoupling of medicine from care that occurs under modernity. The professionalization and technological sophistication of health sciences meant that doctors (almost always male) would be increasingly occupied by diagnosing, ordering treatment, and performing surgery, leaving care to nurses (almost always female), who were lower in salary and status. Where more prestigious medical procedures would be conducted in hospitals, care for a Black woman like Melanctha, who suffers from an incurable illness, would be outsourced to charitable homes.

Three Lives captures the weathering effect of a lifetime devoted to caring for others, effort that cannot be explained away as effortless or instinctual. It attends to the affective, as well as material, costs of modern life on family and community at a time before the safety net provided by the Welfare State. And it employs a narrative form that attempts to measure out a woman's life in terms of the work she does, both paid and unpaid, and the imperfect net of interdependencies that embeds her, instead of the usual milestones like marriage and motherhood. The three lives of Stein's protagonists are storied through the give-and-take of interdependency, each woman's position shifting, with the passage of time, through positions of dominance and submission, generosity and neediness, provider and vulnerable dependent.

Care is equally relevant to my second example, William Faulkner's modernist novel, *The Sound and the Fury*, although it could not be more different from *Three Lives* in style, setting, or plot. Both works employ a kind of literary cubism, an interest in depicting multiple points of view of a similar subject; however, in Faulkner's novel each section is part of a larger story, a device that attests to the interdependency of its characters' lives and how differently the same events can be experienced and interpreted. Critics have been particularly interested in the novel's opening chapter, narrated in first person by a non-verbal intellectually disabled character, Benjy Compson. Benjy has long been seen as a symbolic figure for vulnerability, innocence, or unreason or as a device to experiment with atypical minds, as modernists also did in adopting the perspectives of children, primitives, and mentally ill people (Cecil 1970; Minter 2001; Lester 1995; Parker 1996; Waid 2013). More recent critics have brought attention to Benjy's condition as a disability since it is rare to find intellectually disabled narrators in American literature. Michael Bérubé, for example, observes that Benjy is the moral center of the novel, a character whose intellectual difference also "enables a potential democratization of narrative representation" (Bérubé 2005; Garland-Thomson 2005; Oswald 2016).

Because Benjy's section comes first, it conditions the reader to proceed with patience and attention to difference as well as establishing moral standards to judge later sections narrated by Benjy's brothers, Jason and Quentin. Taking Benjy's difference more seriously as a disability invites attention to its social and historical meanings as well as its symbolic resonance. Reading with care in mind, it also might prompt questions about the circumstances that left him so utterly dependent, the support he receives, and how caregiving responsibilities are delegated within the Compson household. Through Benjy's disjointed narrative, we see that his helplessness is learned through never being taught or invited to care for himself, that his male relatives speak about but not to him, that Dilsey and Caddy are the only people who offer him affection, and that the physical work of his care is performed entirely by the family's Black servants. The Appendix discloses that, after his mother's death, Benjy will suffer a dehumanizing fate: castration and confinement to an institution. This tragic outcome bespeaks the costs of a modern society that equates personhood with productivity, reason, and self-sufficiency. Assumed incompetent, a person like Benjy is relegated to a lifetime of dependency simply by virtue of the diagnostic label "idiot."

The Sound and the Fury is equally notable for the voices it excludes: women and African Americans who play important roles in the plot are narrated only through the perspectives of white, male characters. It is as if Faulkner, even as he gave voice to a nonverbal person, found himself unable to imagine the voices of these gender and racial others—except as they are heard by white men—but also unable to write about domestic life without putting them squarely in the center of the action. These asymmetrical social relations motivate the form of *The Sound and the Fury*, a novel that makes domestic work a focus of narrative interest *and* draws attention to the processes of marginalization that deprive women and people of color, particularly those engaged in care work, the capacity to tell their own stories. Denying certain persons control over their own narratives is thus both a structuring principle of the society inhabited by Faulkner's characters and of the novel he crafts about them.

Faulkner's Yoknapatawpha novels and short stories chart the degeneracy of the Compson family. Their decline is due, in part, to a complete failure to do the physical or emotional work required for social reproduction, meaning that each generation suffers more greatly and is more damaged by a surfeit of care. Only in the Appendix to *The Sound and the Fury* does the reader learn the full details of the Compson family history prior to the events that unfold in the novel: that the family patriarch, Jason III, presides over a shabby and diminished household, selling his ancestral land to pay for his daughter's wedding and his son's first year at Harvard; that his sickly and neurotic wife, Caroline, spends most of her time in bed, feebly issuing orders for others to care for her children and household; and that the four Compson children are reared almost entirely by the housekeeper, Dilsey, who reminds them of this burden at every possible opportunity.

Each descendant's character flaws can be seen to stem directly from a failure of care. Quentin (the elder) is depressed, self-centered, and incestuously drawn to his own sister, committing suicide after his first semester at Harvard. His younger brother Jason is cruel, dishonest, and fiercely independent, embittered by being denied the resources offered to his older siblings, Quentin and Caddy, and the burden of supporting his dependent relatives. Benjy spends his days mourning the loss of his sister, Caddy, the one person who cared for him, his tragedy described as a perpetual inability to "remember his sister but only the loss of her" (Faulkner 1946: 424). Caddy, the only female sibling, does not get to speak for herself. Depending on who is describing her, she may appear as the one person who genuinely understands and cares for her disabled brother or as a fallen woman who cares only for herself. Speaking to the gendered distribution of labor within the family, Caddy's mother (overheard by Benjy, the narrator) tells her, at the age of seven, that she will inherit responsibility for Benjy: "Someday I'll be gone and you'll have to think for him" (Faulkner 1946: 8). In this context, the duty to "think for him" is a weighty burden that means anticipating the needs and best interests of a person considered worthless, incapable of self-representation, and utterly dependent.

While Caroline bequeaths the work of thinking for Benjy to his sister, the people who actually take on those duties are the African American servants, Dilsey and her family. Although Dilsey does not get her own narrative section, her contribution to the well-being of the household and the Compson family is evident throughout the novel. She is constantly in motion with the work of raising all four Compson children, as well as Caddy's daughter, Quentin, cooking, cleaning, and overseeing the other domestic help. The novel's final section, narrated in third person, describes Dilsey repeatedly hauling her body—heavy and aching from a lifetime of domestic service—up and down the stairs to tend the needs of the bedridden Mrs Compson and other family members. Dilsey's son, Versh, and grandson, Luster, are charged with caring for Benjy but under her direction and regular interventions to check the quality and constancy of their attention. She does all the emotional work of comfort and empathy. When Versh or Luster are neglectful or unkind, Dilsey steps in to soothe and care for Benjy. When Benjy is disturbing someone else in the family, Dilsey takes responsibility for figuring out how to calm or remove him. Her laboring body pauses only to quiet Benjy with rocking and gentle sounds.

Given Dilsey's centrality to the novel's action, her absence as a narrator draws attention to the limits of what can be known about her. In addition to the uneven distribution of resources and power between a domestic and her employer, paid care work involves an epistemic asymmetry, where the provider must know the intimate details of a recipient's body and daily life without disclosing many aspects of her own life experiences and embodied condition.[7] Dilsey is a constant and enduring presence within the Compson household; she is completely immersed in the lives of her employers, while they have only partial access to hers. This unevenness is captured formally when the narrative recounts dialogue and action among servants that will never be known by the Compsons. It is further underscored in the Appendix, which provides

---

[7] I discuss the concept of epistemic asymmetry in more detail in my forthcoming book, *Critical: Care, Narrative, and the Art of Interdependency*.

almost twenty-five pages of biographical information about the Compsons, ending with Quentin, Caddy's illegitimate runaway daughter, and less than half a page on Dilsey and her family. The final paragraphs begin with a sentence that sounds like an ending: "And that was all," positioning what follows in a lower margin almost completely out of view of the narrative proper. "These others were not Compson," the narrative continues, "They were black." It provides abrupt accounts of Dilsey's children and grandson, TP, Frony, and Luster, saying of Dilsey, simply, "They endured" (Faulkner 1946: 427). With this ending, Faulkner's novel perfectly captures the imbalance between a family whose fate is recorded in history largely because it is white and one that—because "they were black"—is destined to the anonymous work of maintaining their white employers. Equally striking is that Dilsey's fate is described with the plural "they," as if to capture how the life story and subjectivity of a Black servant is absorbed by those she has cared for.

With such devices, *The Sound and the Fury* emphasizes that Dilsey's work is not only physical but also what Arlie Hothschild calls "emotional labor" (Hothschild 2003). She is the affective center of the book, constantly aware of, evaluating, and responding to the feelings of others. She provides Benjy with the tenderness required to calm his outbursts of distress and, under her management, her family develops skills to supplement that care. They understand the circumstances that make Benjy agitated and give him comfort: watching the fire, an old slipper of Caddy's, going for a ride in the carriage. Their attunement to Benjy makes them aware of his unacknowledged intelligence: "'He know lot more than folks thinks,' Roskus said," speculating on Benjy's dog-like ability to sense impending death, "'He knowed they time was coming, like that pointer done. He could tell you when hisn coming, if he could talk. Or yours. Or mine'" (Faulkner 1946: 37). While it is unlikely that Benjy has the kind of clairvoyance Roskus describes, Roskus recognizes that Benjy has knowledge and understanding far beyond his capacity for expressive language. Dilsey's grandson Luster is often impatient but also feeds Benjy "with skill and detachment" (Faulkner 1946: 345) born of extensive experience as well as an underlying empathy. Luster's brief mention in the Appendix centers on his competence at caring for Benjy. Only after the narrative ends does the reader learn that he is only fourteen—an age when a young man is especially unlikely to be patient and nurturing—before describing him as "capable of the complete care and security of an idiot twice his age and three times his size, but could keep him entertained." Calling Luster a "man" emphasizes that a person of his race and class is typically required to bypass youthful self-absorption and freedom from responsibility. Sociologists call this premature burdening of Black youth "adultification bias," meaning they are more likely to be judged by adult standards than are their white peers (Epstein et al. 2017). Moreover, the brevity of Luster's biography underscores the imbalance between the deep and expert knowledge he is required to have of his charge and what is considered worth knowing about him.

Having established a pattern of epistemic asymmetry that prioritizes detailed knowledge about the Compsons, it is notable that the Appendix gestures to a future when Dilsey's family will part ways with her employers. Having devoted herself to knowing the intimate details of the Compsons' life and the physical and emotional work of sustaining them, Dilsey is eventually worn out, subject to the same weathering forces as the protagonists of Stein's *Three Lives*. When the town librarian thinks she recognizes a photo of Caddy in a gossip magazine, she seeks out Dilsey for confirmation. She finds the aged former servant in Memphis, living in a "neat yet cluttered bedroom" in the household of her daughter, Frony. Her body attests to the wearing effect of caring for the Compson family. Once "a big woman," Dilsey is now shrunken and nearly blind. Her literal inability to see the photo also suggests a more symbolic unwillingness to care about Caddy's fate. Yet, despite the debilities caused by age and physical strain, Dilsey enjoys one of the most peaceful endings in all of Faulkner's fiction. She has succeeded in raising her own children alongside the Compson siblings and the Appendix finds her resting and enjoying the care of her daughter.

What would Dilsey say if she had a story of her own? Dilsey is certainly not voiceless. Her voice is heard frequently throughout *The Sound and the Fury*, her scolding, bossing, and comforting a soundtrack to daily life in the Compson household. But it is always filtered through the perspective of others, whether Benjy, Quentin, Jason Compson, or the third-person narrator of the novel's final section. What would Dilsey say in the privacy of her cabin or her daughter's home? How might she address the contradictory demands of paid care work and emotional labor inherent in her position as a servant, a Black woman, and a mother? Alice Childress offers one set of possibilities in her brilliant and overlooked 1956 novel, *Like One of the Family*, a series of vignettes told by Mildred, a Black domestic worker. Her spirited, biting monologues respond to the microaggressions, blatant insults, injustice, and acts of courage that take place behind the closed doors of the affluent homes where she works. In the novel's eponymous chapter, Mildred describes chiding her employer for treating her like an animal:

> In the first place, you do not love me; you may be fond of me, but that is all.... In the second place, I am not just like one of the family at all! The family eats in the dining room and I eat in the kitchen. Your mama borrows your lace table-cloth for her company and your son entertains his friends in your parlor, your daughter takes her afternoon nap on the living room couch and the puppy sleeps on your satin spread ... and whenever your husband gets tired of something you are talkin' about he says, 'Oh, for Pete's sake, forget it....' So you can see I am not just like one of the family.
>
> (Childress 1956: 2)

Narrated retrospectively in the first person, this passage must be read as washed with wishful thinking, since few domestic workers are in a position to speak so frankly to their employers. It is nonetheless a powerful rendition of unspoken fantasy, addressed more to an imagined white reader than the mistress in the story itself. As such, it is a reminder of the uneasy intimacies of employers and domestic servants and the agency of care workers to perceive, if not to act out on, injustice in their work environments.

And what would Agee and Evans's sharecroppers say? Although they were allowed no direct speech in the massive book about their lives, some eventually had an opportunity to talk back. Between 1986 and 1988, journalists Dale Maharidge and Michael Williamson retraced the steps of Agee and Evans's journey, publishing a follow-up to *Famous Men* called *And Their Children After Them* (1989). It describes what happened to many of Agee and Evans's informants, their memories of the visiting journalists, and reaction to seeing themselves depicted in *Famous Men*. One particularly damning revelation concerns Clair Bell Ricketts, who had an accident that left her in a coma during the journalists' visit. In *Famous Men*, Agree predicts she would not survive for long, while Evans's bleak photograph shows the body of a young child lying on the porch, her face and upper body covered by a thin cloth. While the vision of Clair Bell's vulnerability fit well with the story told by *Famous Men*, a different version emerges in Maharidge and Williamson's follow-up. They interview fifty-four-year-old Clair Bell, who reveals that one of the visiting journalists caused her injury during an episode of rough play. Clair Bell further reports that when Agee revisited the families in 1937, he found her alive and well but did not revise his grim story. Obviously, it made better drama to depict Clair Bell's life as short and fragile and the journalists as anguished onlookers, instead of complicit participants.

These dissenting voices add welcome complexity to the stories told by literary modernism, but they are not required for the method I describe as reading for and with care. More often, the voices of the most vulnerable dependents and the caregivers who maintain their homes, bodies, and emotional well-being go unrecorded. But reading care fully and reading carefully means approaching modernist literature with attention to aspects of form, theme, and historical context that might otherwise be overlooked. As in life, literary representations of care often take place at the margins or off the page altogether, but we can read for them even when the voices of care workers or dependents are not represented and even when care is not an overt narrative topic. Returning to these works at a moment when income inequality and antipathy to state-sponsored welfare is taking a particularly devastating toll in the United States, we can see the modernist era—and the contradictions among care as an obligation of government, a form of paid work, and an affective bond that its notable authors sought to represent—as an instructive historical mirror. In it, we see that dependency and the need for care are universal human conditions even as their meaning is shaped by modern preoccupations with individualism, productivity, and growth, and reshaped anew as modernist authors respond to their historical circumstances. For readers in the present, modernism's inventive narrative forms illuminate how past inequities are shaped by historical forces but perhaps also give us license to imagine a future that is otherwise. This recognition can be the starting point for rereading an established canon and keeping it dynamic by adding new works with care in mind and body.

References

Adams, Rachel. Forthcoming. *Critical: Care, Narrative, and the Art of Interdependency*.
Agee, James and Walker Evans. 1988. *Let Us Now Praise Famous Men: Three Tenant Families* (Boston, MA: Houghton Mifflin Co.).

Bérubé, Michael. 2005. "Disability and Narrative," *Publications of the Modern Language Association* 120.2: 568–576.

Boris, Eileen and Jennifer Klein. 2012. *Caring for America: Home Health Workers in The Shadow of The Welfare State* (New York: Oxford University Press).

Cecil, L. Moffitt. 1970. "A Rhetoric for Benjy," *Southern Literary Journal* 3.1: 32–46.

Childress, Alice. 1956. *Like One of The Family: Conversations from A Domestic's Life* (Brooklyn, NY: Independence Publishers).

Christian, David. 2011. *Maps of Time: An Introduction to Big History* (Berkeley,CA: University of California Press).

Cowan, Ruth Schwartz. 1983. *More Work for Mother: The Ironies of Household Technology from The Open Hearth to The Microwave* (New York: Basic Books).

Curkpatrick, Samuel. 2020. *Singing Bones: Ancestral Creativity and Collaboration* (Sydney: Sydney University Press).

Davidson, Michael. 2019. *Invalid Modernism: Disability and the Missing Body of the Aesthetic* (Oxford and New York: Oxford University Press).

Edelman, Lee. 2004. *No Future: Queer Theory and The Death Drive* (Durham, NC: Duke University Press).

Entin, Joseph. 2007. *Sensational Modernism: Experimental Fiction and Photography in Thirties America* (Chapel Hill, NC: University of North Carolina Press).

Epstein, Rebecca, Jamilia J. Blake, and Thalia Gonzalez. 2017. *Girlhood Interrupted: The Erasure of Black Girls' Childhood* (Washington, DC: Georgetown Law Center on Poverty and Inequality).

Faulkner, William. 1946. *The Sound and the Fury* (New York: Random House Vintage).

Felski, Rita. 2000. *Doing Time: Feminist Theory and Postmodern Culture* (New York: New York University Press).

Fineman, Martha. 2005. *The Autonomy Myth: A Theory of Dependency* (New York: The New Press).

Fraser, Nancy. 2016. "'Capitalism's Crisis of Care,' Interview by Sarah Leonard," *Dissent Magazine*, Fall, www.dissentmagazine.org/article/nancy-fraser-interview-capitalism-crisis-of-care, accessed February 21, 2022.

Fraser, Nancy and Linda Gordon. 1994. "A Genealogy of Dependency: Tracing a Keyword of the U.S. Welfare State," *Signs: Journal of Women in Culture and Society* 19.2: 309–336.

Garland, David. 2016. *The Welfare State: A Very Short Introduction* (Oxford: Oxford University Press).

Garland-Thomson, Rosemarie. 2005. "Disability and Representation," *Publications of the Modern Language Association* 120.2: 522–527.

Glenn, Evelyn Nakano. 2010. *Forced to Care: Coercion and Caregiving in America* (Cambridge, MA: Harvard University Press).

Gluck, Mary. 2005. *Popular Bohemia: Modernism and the Urban Culture in Nineteenth-Century Paris* (Cambridge, MA: Harvard Uni.versity Press).

Gontarski, S. E., Laci Mattison, and Paul Ardoin, eds. 2013. *Understanding Bergson, Understanding Modernism* (New York: Bloomsbury).

Halberstam, Jack. 2011. *The Queer Art of Failure* (Durham, NC: Duke University Press).

Held, Virginia. 2006. *The Ethics of Care: Personal, Political, and Global* (Oxford; New York: Oxford University Press).

Herring, Scott. 2022. *Aging American Moderns* (New York: Columbia University Press).

Hochschild, Arlie Russell. 2003. *The Managed Heart: Commercialization of Human Feeling* (Berkeley, CA: University of California Press).

James, David. 2016. "Modern/Altermodern," in Joel Burges and Amy Elias, eds, *Time: A Vocabulary of the Present* (New York: New York University Press), 66–81.

Jones, Amelia. 2004. *Irrational Modernism* (Cambridge, MA: The MIT Press).

Kafer, Alison. 2013. *Feminist, Queer, Crip* (Bloomington, IN: Indiana University Press).

Kittay, Eva Feder. 1999. *Love's Labor: Essays on Women, Equality, and Dependency* (New York and London: Routledge).

Lester, Cheryl. 1995. "Racial Awareness and Arrested Development: *The Sound and the Fury* and The Great Migration (1915–1928)," in Philip M. Weinstein, ed., *The Cambridge Compaion to William Faulkner* (Cambridge and New York: Cambridge University Press), 123–145.

Levenson, Michael. 2011, *Modernism* (New Haven, CT: Yale University Press).

Maharidge, Dale and Michael Williamson. 1989. *And Their Children After Them: The Legacy of Let Us Now Praise Famous Men, James Agee, Walker Evans, and The rise and Fall of Cotton in the South* (New York: Pantheon Books).

Mandell, Betty Reid. 2010. *The Crisis of Caregiving: Social Welfare Policy in the United States* (New York: Palgrave Macmillan).

Martell, James. 2019. *Modernism, Self Creation, and the Maternal* (New York: Routledge).

McRuer, Robert. 2018. *Crip Times: Disability, Globalization, and Resistance* (New York: New York University Press).

Miller, Christanne. 2017. "The "New Women" of Modernism," in Vincent Sherry, ed., *The Cambridge History of Modernism* (New York and Cambridge: Cambridge University Press), 457–477.

Minter, David L. 2001. *Faulkner's Questioning Narratives: Fiction of His Major Phase, 1929–1942* (Urbana, IL: University of Illinois).

Olson, Liesl. 2009. *Modernism and the Ordinary* (Oxford and New York: Oxford University Press).

Oswald, David. 2016. "Otherwise Undisclosed: Blood, Species, and Benjy Compson's Idiocy," *Journal of Literary and Cultural Disability Studies* 10.3: 287–304.

Parker, Robert Dale. 1996. "'Through the Fence, between the Curling Flower Spaces': Teaching the First Section of *The Sound and the Fury*," in Stephen Hahn and Arthur F. Kinney, eds, *Approaches to Teaching Faulkner's The Sound and the Fury* (New York: Modern Language Association of America), 27–37.

Phillips, Michelle. 2016. *Representations of Childhood in American Modernism* (New York: Palgrave).

Pollentier, Sarah Wilson. 2019. *Modernist Communities across Cultures and Media* (Jacksonville, FL: University Press of Florida).

Potter, Rachel. 2012. *Modernist Literature* (Edinburgh: Edinburg University Press).

Rancière, Jacques. 2014. "Rethinking Modernity," *Diacritics* 42.3: 6–20.

Randall, Bryony. 2007. *Modernism, Daily Time, and Everyday Life* (Cambridge: Cambridge University Press).

Reed, Christopher. 2004. *Bloomsbury Rooms: Modernism, Subculture, and Domesticity* (New Haven, CT: Yale University Press).

Risse, Guenter B. 1999. *Mending Bodies, Saving Souls: A History of Hospitals* (New York: Oxford University Press).

Robbins, Bruce. 1993. *The Servant's Hand: English Fiction from Below* (Durham, NC: Duke University Press).

Rose, Sarah F. 2017. *No Right to Be Idle: The Invention of Disability, 1840s–1930s* (Chapel Hill, NC: University of North Carolina Press).

Rosner, Victoria. 2020. *Machines for Living: Modernism and Domestic Life* (Oxford: Oxford University Press).

Ruddick, Sara. 1989. *Maternal Thinking: Toward a Politics of Peace* (Boston, MA: Beacon Press).

Samuels, Ellen. 2017. "Six Ways of Looking at Crip Time," *Disability Studies Quarterly* 37.3: https://dsq-sds.org/article/view/5824/4684, accessed February 21, 2022.

Sanchez, Rebecca. 2016. ""Perfect Interindependency": Representing Crip Futurity in Beckett's *Mercier and Camier*," *Journal for Cultural and Religious Theory* 15.2: 59–70.

Schwartz, Bill. 2010. *Memory: Histories, Theories, Debates* (New York: Fordham University Press).

Social Security Administration. 2020. *"Red Book," A Summary Guide to Employment Supports for Persons with Disabilities under the Social Security Disability Insurance (SSDI) and Supplemental Security Income (SSI) Programs*, www.ssa.gov/redbook/index.html, accessed February 21, 2022.

Stansell, Christine. 2000. *American Moderns: Bohemian New York and the Creation of A New Century* (New York: H. Holt).

Starr, Paul. 1982. *The Social Transformation of American Medicine* (New York: Basic Books).

Stein, Gertrude. 1990. *The Autobiography of Alice B. Toklas* (New York: Vintage).

Stein, Gertrude. 1973. *3 Lives* (New York: Vintage Mass Market).

Stockton, Kathryn Bond. 2009. *The Queer Child, or Growing Sideways in The Twentieth Century* (Durham, NC: Duke University Press).

Tronto, Joan C. 1993. *Moral Boundaries: A Political Argument for An Ethic of Care* (New York and London: Routledge).

Tronto, Joan C. 2013. *Caring Democracy: Markets, Equality, and Justice* (New York: New York University Press).

Waid, Candace. 2013. *The Signifying Eye: Seeing Faulkner's Art* (Athens: University of Georgia Press).

Wilson, Mary. 2016. *The Labors of Modernism: Domesticity, Servants, and Authorship in Modernist Fiction* (New York: Routledge).

CHAPTER 13

BLACK LITERARY HISTORY AND THE PROBLEM OF IDENTIFICATION IN ISHMAEL REED'S *MUMBO JUMBO*

AIDA LEVY-HUSSEN

Most of the narrative action in Ishmael Reed's 1972 novel, *Mumbo Jumbo*, unfolds against the backdrop of a fantastically defamiliarized Harlem Renaissance. But in the epilogue, Reed flashes forward to a university classroom at the time of his writing. At the invitation of an unnamed "Black professor," our protagonist-hero, the Harlemite voodoo priest PaPa LaBas, appears as a now-centenarian guest speaker, recounting to an audience of young Black students his involvement with the storied "Negro Awakening." The class receives PaPa LaBas as an elder: they see in him both the endearing eccentricity of anachronism and a living link to "those golden times" of their collective, creative past. LaBas, for his part, returns their imprecise gesture of recognition. Here, he thinks approvingly, is "a classroom that knew what he was talking about .... The 20s were back again. Better" (Reed 2017 [1972]: 214, 217, 218).

Thus, the epilogue asserts a relation of continuity and identification (but also of succession and non-identicality) between two crucial moments in Black literary history. The 1970s, a time of remarkable artistic productivity for Black writers and the decade in which the scholarly enterprise of Black Studies belatedly gained footing in the American academy, finds its lineage and an uncanny mirror in the creative flourishing of the Harlem Renaissance—that original and "transformative period in African American life and culture ... marked by vigorous debates about the relationship between race and art" (Sherrard-Johnson 2015). Bridging past and present in a shared narrative frame, Reed lays claim to something like a tradition: a resonant, intergenerational *sense* of Black literature as a collective and sustained, yet also, protean and irreducible, endeavor.

Reed's project of delineating an African American literary tradition—of consecrating, through a pedagogical scene, his vision for that tradition's parameters, its assumptions, and its "fundamental syntax"—should be read as a timely intervention into literary, scholarly, and activist discourses of the 1970s, when Black Studies began to assume its contemporary, institutionalized shape (Pease 1990).[1] The novel, in other words, aims to supply something like a usable origin myth and a corresponding "program" for an emergent scholarly undertaking.[2] Retrospective readers will appreciate Reed's prescience, for *Mumbo Jumbo* anticipates a number of critical reorientations that would come to figure prominently in subsequent decades of African Americanist study. Renewed interest in the Harlem Renaissance, the diasporic turn in Black literary studies, the elevation of the vernacular, and emphasis on "signifyin(g)" as a distinctive Black cultural practice and expressive form all find voice in the novel's plot and in the lesson of PaPa LaBas's concluding lecture.[3]

In the pages that follow, I read *Mumbo Jumbo* as a prospective field manifesto, equally remarkable to the twenty-first-century reader for its foreknowing and its defamiliarization of today's Black literary studies. I identify and elaborate on the revisionist literary historical account that undergirds Reed's vision for the field—an account that begins long before the Harlem Renaissance with the spontaneous, irrepressible utterance of racial authenticity, and proceeds toward the "working out of an autonomous, self-authorizing [artistic] sensibility" in the late-twentieth-century academy (Warren 2011: 78). But, what interests me most is *Mumbo Jumbo*'s pronounced ambivalence toward this posture.

For even as the novel explicitly works to shore up an affirmative conceptualization of a Black literary tradition, much of its narrative action is propelled by the elusiveness of authentic racial meaning. Within the novel, the guarantor of such meaning is "the Book of Thoth"—an ancient ur-text of Black expressive culture that originates in the Egypt of Osiris and Isis but is stolen in the twelfth century by a stateless, Germanic "ruffian"-cum-librarian named Hinckle Von Vampton (Reed 2017 [1972]: 187). Once restored to its diasporic heirs, the Book promises to articulate the "relevance" of an ostensibly disparate and undisciplined Black art, the potency of which will unmake "Civilization As We Know It" (4). The Harlem Renaissance, according to *Mumbo Jumbo*, is a moment in

---

[1] Beginning in the late 1960s, Black Studies activists across the country staged sit-ins, marches, and other forms of collective protest to endorse a radical intellectual project that would not simply beg for inclusion into the extant academic curriculum but would remake the values, assumptions, and accessibility of scholarly thought. The range of demands put forth by the Black Studies movement included open admissions, accountability to proximate minority communities, and new curricula attuned to domestic and international power structures. On the origins *and* the constitutive limits of Black Studies, see Ferguson (2012); Rojas (2010); Rooks (2006).

[2] In a contemporaneous analysis of the novel, Neil Schlitz describes *Mumbo Jumbo* as "an ingenious dissertation on the nature of Afro–American art, a dissertation with a program for the revival of that art": Schlitz (1974: 136).

[3] Henry Louis Gates, Jr famously identifies "signifyin(g)" as the definitive trope of African American literature and indeed, of Black discourse more generally. By his definition, this "trope for repetition and revision" by way of "punning" works to amplify and repurpose the "ambiguities of language." In *Figures in Black*, he points to *Mumbo Jumbo* as exemplary of the signifyin(g) tradition: Gates (1987: 236).

which such repossession seems imminent. Yet, both the retrieval of the Book and the realization of its promise are steadfastly deferred beyond the final pages of the novel.

What kind of origin story is this? How should we interpret the idea of a Black literary ur-text that is at once the pure, incorruptible harbinger of a revolutionary Age of Black Art, and (at least for a time) the discovery and illicit possession of a rogue, European thief? And what kind of figure is this thief—this villain of cultural appropriation who sets the plot in motion but whose very existence curiously falls out of PaPa LaBas's summary lecture?

Despite his provocative characterization and centrality to the plot, *Mumbo Jumbo*'s chief antagonist remains curiously under-studied in the novel's surrounding criticism.[4] It is almost as though scholars, taking their cue from LaBas, have agreed to forget Von Vampton. Against this interpretive habit, I argue that Von Vampton must be reckoned with as an essential figure in Reed's formulation of African American literature's origins and development. For it is through Von Vampton that Reed at once emplots and unsettles the fantasy of an African American literature that thwarts the advances of white power and desire and, in so doing, confirms its autonomy.

Von Vampton, in other words, is the criminal outsider who reveals what (according to Reed) cannot be avowed by or assimilated into the Black literary tradition. But he is also a boundary-crosser—a thief, an interloper, and a desirous appropriator—whose prominent role in Reed's account of Black literature's origins and development troubles the notion of an uncontaminated Black aesthetic. The point, to be sure, is not that *Mumbo Jumbo* ultimately divests from its ideal of an ingenious and profound Black literary autonomy; rather, it is that the novel recognizes *both* the pursuit of this ideal and the complication of it by the material and psychological histories from which African American art has emerged. Von Vampton, I argue, is an interpretive key to this seemingly paradoxical premise. Although he is often dismissed as nothing more than a caricature of white depravity and greed, I will show how his characterization invites nuanced explorations of the role and status of cultural appropriation in Black literary history.

---

[4] By way of illustration, the following texts include thorough and compelling readings of the novel in which Von Vampton plays a notably minor role: Chaney (2003), Dubey (2003), Ingram (2012), Mason (1988), and Schlitz (1974). Gates is an exception in that he dedicates several pages to deciphering Von Vampton's plausible referents. He sees in the character not only Van Vechten but also the German engraver Knackfuss, whose Eurocentric image "appears in *Mumbo Jumbo* on page 155" (258). Even so, Gates's commentary on the novel's villain is, for the most part, treated as peripheral to his broader concern with how Reed's signification on a chain of Black literary pre-texts works to discredit the idea that Blackness exists as a transcendental signified. See Gates, "'The Blackness of Blackness': A Critique of the Sign and the Signifying Monkey," in Gates (1987: 235–277). For an intriguing, if brief, reading of Von Vampton, see Donofrio (2017). Donofrio suggestively posits that Reed's framing of LaBas and Von Vampton as polar opposites is, at least in part, a ruse. Not only are they both involved in the business of culture, but they also "share a knack for symbolic action. LaBas calls his potions and spells 'FITS FOR YOUR HEAD' (24), but the work of producing them, not to mention the work they do, might well be summed up in the phrase Hinckle uses to gloss his own editorial responsibilities—'setting heads' (60)" (113).

To do so, I employ a methodological approach that combines close attention to the text with literary historical contextualization and psychoanalytic theory. With regard to literary history, I turn in particular to Von Vampton's heavy-handed allusion to an actual Harlem Renaissance personality: Carl Van Vechten. Controversial in his time but subsequently much forgotten, Van Vechten—once "Harlem's most enthusiastic and ubiquitous Nordic"—was a close friend and benefactor to Langston Hughes, Zora Neale Hurston, James Weldon Johnson, and Nella Larsen, among many others (Lewis 1997 [1981]: 182). But he was also the author of the salacious and voyeuristic *Nigger Heaven* (1926), a novel whose title, publication, and commercial success provoked the ire and confirmed the distrust of many African American readers. A white writer whose stereotyped portrait of Black urban life became "by far, the best-selling novel of the Harlem Renaissance," Van Vechten is readily discernible in Reed's insidious and profiteering, yet tone-deaf, literary thief (Bernard 2012: 116).

What follows, however, is not a work of biographical criticism. My primary interest lies less with the fine details of Von Vampton's correspondence to Van Vechten than with Reed's broader, symbolic preoccupation with the figure of the white appropriator—not the slaveholder, not the segregationist—as Black art's most pernicious rival.[5] Explicit racist contempt has a place in the story, too, but it is Von Vampton's figuration of white proximity, emulation, and desire that provokes an anxious mood and generates *Mumbo Jumbo*'s sense of urgency to reclaim and defend a distinctive Black literary essence or identity. To interpret this charged relation between African American literature and Reed's take on its most salient antagonist-pursuer, I turn, in the latter part of this chapter, to psychoanalytic theories of identification.

The psychoanalysts Jean Laplanche and Jean-Bertand Pontalis define identification as the "psychological process whereby the subject assimilates an aspect, property, or attribute of the other and is transformed, wholly or partially, after the model the other provides. It is by means of a series of identifications that the personality is constituted and specified" (Laplanche and Pontalis 1973: 205). As such, identification is related—and prior—to public discourses of identity. Yet, because it is at least partly unconscious, it is never only a matter of self-affirming and voluntary affiliation. Identification is disorderly, at times embarrassing, and irreducible to the "instrumental and moralistic" demands of "political efficacy" (Cheng 2009). I will argue that Reed's ostensibly straightforward story of Black literary identity is in fact underwritten by a complex network of identifications and that by attending to their psychic logic, we can gain insight into how the figure of the white appropriator takes shape in the Black literary imagination.

***

[5] Reed's fixation on the figure of the cultural appropriator may have been intensified by his aversion to conceptions of African American literature that take the historical trauma of slavery to be the presumptive, originating, ineradicable trope. *Mumbo Jumbo* explicitly renounces this formulation through its humorous assertion that the titular term is "Mandingo" for "magician who makes the troubled spirits of ancestors go away" (7). In this respect (i.e. in his effort to steer Black literary studies away from the subject and attendant affects of the slave past), Reed has not proved prophetic.

But first, a few words on plot.

When the novel begins in 1920, the United States is witnessing the rapid spread of a "once dormant" "psychic epidemic" first observed in New Orleans but now making its way North toward Chicago and New York. The epidemic takes its name from the author, anthologist, composer, and statesman James Weldon Johnson's account of "the earliest Ragtime songs." "Like Topsy," Johnson wrote, in his landmark collection, *The Book of American Negro Poetry*, they "jes' grew" (Johnson 1922: 11). Reed's fictional Jes Grew is a contagious ecstasy that allegorizes the phenomenon of Black expressive culture emerging organically from Black life.

"Electric as life" and "lusting after relevance," Jes Grew initially manifests as uninhibited musicality, sensuality, and dance (6, 4). According to the afflicted, it feels like nothing short of liberated and authentic Blackness: like "deserting [one's] master," according to one testimonial; like "the gut heart and lungs of Africa's interior," according to another (5). The American ruling class—heirs to the Enlightenment tradition who control political power, the military, the police, news media, museums, and systems of formal education—regard Jes Grew as a plague and coordinate efforts to stamp it out. But armed with subversive insight derived from ancestral knowledge and a dedicated voodoo practice, our protagonist-hero, PaPa LaBas, rightly recognizes Jes Grew as the "anti-plague" (25). His ambition, supported by a loosely knit group of diasporic Black occultists, is to help Jes Grew thrive. If "dark" and "light" powers are at conspicuous cross-purposes, then what they agree upon is this: Jes Grew's potential to supplant governing ideologies of Western culture depends upon its ability to come into textual representation. More precisely, what Jes Grew seeks is its articulation *as African American literature*, the imminence of which portends a revolutionary reversal of the existing world order.

Crucially, we learn, Jes Grew's corresponding text is both old and new, a repetition and an original; that is, Jes Grew is not only a psycho-spiritual and artistic current taking hold of the nation during the first historical period in which "the black influence on American culture became a widely recognized fact" (Taylor 2019: 4) but also an iteration of a recurrent creative force, whose essence was first transcribed in ancient Egypt in the aforementioned, mystical Book of Thoth. After a centuries-long disappearance, the Book of Thoth has recently resurfaced in Harlem by way of the swindling Hinckle Von Vampton.

Much of the novel's narrative action tracks the ensuing, largely covert war for possession and control of the Text. LaBas and the Black occultists wish to reunite the Book of Thoth with its spiritual source, Jes Grew, now thriving in the bodies and minds of African Americans. By doing so, they promise to reclaim an ancient legacy of Black letters for modern use. The defenders of Western Civilization (known in *Mumbo Jumbo* by their secret society name, the Atonist Path) wish to destroy the Book in order to maintain their power. Von Vampton, a disgraced Atonist, seeks to redeem his status among the Eurocentric elite by trading on his illicit possession of the Text.

***

Von Vampton, as I have noted, draws inspiration from the historical persona of the author, photographer, collector, and Harlem Renaissance patron, Carl Van Vechten. Like his referent, the fictional Von Vampton is distinguished by his curation of library collections; his eccentric, near-reverential fascination with cats; and his penchant for expensive, ostentatious fashion. Amplifying into grotesque caricature Van Vechten's reputation as an unwholesome aficionado of Black culture, Von Vampton is further depicted as a pretender of a "Negrophile," whose true appetites are ghastly and perverse. He feasts on "tiny non-poisonous snakes, crocodile eggs" and "weeds gathered at the grave site of a recently dead infant" (Reed 2017 [1972]: 78)! (The homophobia underlying Reed's characterization of Von Vampton is pervasive and unsubtle.)[6]

Once a key figure and lightning rod within Black literary circles, Van Vechten's influence faded in subsequent decades, and by the 1940s, as Lawrence Jackson notes, many writers and critics came to remember his role as an avid and effective (if also self-important and exoticizing) promoter of the Harlem Renaissance as something of an embarrassment.[7] Jackson describes not only Van Vechten's reputational decline but also the critical dismissal of the Harlem Renaissance that characterized literary scholarship, Black and white, between the Great Depression and what is sometimes called the Second Renaissance of the late 'sixties and 'seventies. In *Mumbo Jumbo*, Reed joins late-twentieth-century efforts to restore esteem to the Harlem Renaissance. Renouncing scholarly accounts that would cast the movement as faddish, effete, aesthetically wanting, or politically compromised, Reed instead proffers a story of the Renaissance as "one of the classiest, noblest, artiest, brightest, most terrifically spiflicated, smartest, shook-up, and elegant moments of [the] Century" (Reed 1989: 258).

Seemingly essential to Reed's literary historical revision is his refusal to credit Van Vechten's contributions to the development of modern African American literature. Indeed, the fictional Von Vampton is not merely an unhelpful interloper; he is also a monstrosity who "resembles the 4th Horseman of the Apocalypse as depicted in a strange painting by William Blake" (55). In the world of the novel, where nothing is more revered than the Afrocentric life force of Jes Grew, Von Vampton's ancient European aura of death marks him as a repulsive and unsuitable custodian of Black culture. Although he absconds with the Book of Thoth, he never learns its deepest truths; although he ventriloquizes Black literary style, his efforts come across as "tasteless" and false (Reed 2017 [1972]: 116).

Von Vampton cites but also conspicuously exceeds the parameters of the historical Van Vechten. In addition to being a Jazz Age sensationalist and voyeur, Reed's Von

---

[6] Van Vechten's biographer, Emily Bernard, points out that homophobia has been a common, if often tacit, feature of anti-Van Vechten criticism, noteworthy in the written remarks of both early twentieth-century proponents of respectability politics like W.E.B. Du Bois and "subsequent generations" of African American critics for whom Van Vechten symbolized "what was wrong with the Harlem Renaissance," due to his "sexuality as much as race": Bernard (2012: 9).

[7] By the 1940s, Jackson writes, the idea of "a literary movement of blacks partly engineered by a [white,] bi-sexual playboy, one that left little evidence of confrontation or belligerent protest, seemed humiliating": Jackson (2007: 240).

Vampton is a death-cheating, thousand-year-old librarian who accidentally finds the Book of Thoth in a secret room of his masonic library.[8] At once an ancient thief and a modern possessor of the Black literary ur-text, he alludes to familiar histories of modernist Negrophilia and centuries of racial plunder and unites them in a single, criminal body. Von Vampton, we might say, is less the historical than the *synecdochal* Van Vechten: he is Van Vechten-the-appropriator as a stand-in for an expansively imagined phenomenon of timeless, infinite white greed.

What makes Von Vampton an interesting literary character—irreducible to the one-dimensional bogeyman he initially seems to be—is Reed's curious, paradoxical representation of his power. On the one hand, Von Vampton must be apprehended as a commanding presence, for his subplot is meant to convey that the appropriation of Black culture by whites is a devastating crime warranting punishment. On the other hand, Reed resists any positive acknowledgment of his villain's strength. As we will see, Von Vampton's procurement of the Text involves neither talent nor chosen-ness nor proper contest. He has it but only in the manner of a passive, second-hand thief. He errs and fumbles in his attempts to make it his own. Von Vampton's characterization thus encodes and struggles to resolve Reed's warring desires: to indict and to dismiss the harm done by appropriation.

Von Vampton's narrative arc unfolds as follows. Upon discovering the Book of Thoth, he quickly recognizes its mystical potency and, seeking to possess it, he defies both the Atonist censure of its dark power and the Book's own resistance to ownership by him. (The Book resists by perverting its magic.) Von Vampton carries the book with him as an illicit, stolen treasure through centuries of exile and persecution at the hands of the dominant Atonist subgroups. At the end of the nineteenth century, he flees to America, whereupon the dynamic shifts. The Book, which had long been separated from its intended readers, senses its compatibility with the spirit of Jes Grew that is beginning to thrive among African Americans. In kind, the "symptoms of Jes Grew"—joy, creativity, dance—"[begin] to rise" and travel toward New York, where Von Vampton is stationed, in pursuit of "a potential coming together with the Text" (189).

But Von Vampton does not facilitate the triumphant renaissance of Jes Grew in the way that Van Vechten, according to his champions, promoted and advanced the Harlem Renaissance. Instead, he forestalls the reunion of spirit and Text to seize a personal opportunity. Cannily predicting that the Atonists will seek out the Text to destroy it, Von Vampton splits it into pieces and hires a staff of fourteen Jes Grew Carriers—"janitors, Pullman porters, shoeshine boys, dropouts from Harvard, [and] jazz musicians"—"to send the Text around to each other in a chain, each time changing the covering so that the authorities wouldn't get suspicious" (69, 189). Since only he knows the secret routes it travels, Von Vampton explains to the Atonist leader, "only I can call it in and anthologize it" (69). Von Vampton, in effect, asserts his importance as a usurping proprietor

---

[8] The fictional Von Vampton belongs to the masonic order of the Knights Templar, as did the father of the historical Van Vechten: see White (2014: 13).

of African American literature's "field-*materiality*."⁹ Although he is shut out from the authentic emotional circuitries that emanate from the Book, it is his prerogative to withhold or deliver Black creative genius in the cohesive and readable form of the anthology.¹⁰

But in spite of his declaration of singular power, Von Vampton's plan is thwarted twice. First, it is thwarted by the disloyalty of the Jes Grew Carriers, who leak serialized sections of the Book to the proto-Nation of Islam leader, Abdul Hamid.¹¹ In a state of awe and reverence, Hamid reconstitutes the Book and translates it from its original hieroglyphics, but he later burns it when ideological zealotry leads him to suspect the Book of unholiness. Second, Von Vampton's plan is thwarted by PaPa LaBas and his colleague Black Herman,¹² who, with assistance from Hamid, uncover the details of Von Vampton's misdeeds and, as punishment, deliver him to his fate: he is to be sacrificed to a Haitian voodoo spirit.

Thus, the plot posits, but ultimately seems to neutralize and defeat, the notion that an immortal white antagonist wields a singular and insidious power over African American literature. Although Reed elaborates at length on Von Vampton's theft of the Book and his sinister intentions, in the end, it is not him but Abdul Hamid who consolidates *and* destroys the Book of Thoth. Perhaps Von Vampton's power, we are encouraged to consider, was illusory all along.

To an extent, such a reading is defensible: Von Vampton is shown to be pathetic, miscalculating, and ineffectual; his threats fail to materialize. But *Mumbo Jumbo*'s eagerness to discount its villain is belied by its narrative structure, which derives definition, movement, and stakes from the assumption that Von Vampton is a consequential agent of malice and danger. His charlatanism shores up the novel's investment in an ethic of Black cultural authenticity. His deviousness confers moral authority on those who would return the Book to its rightful source. The long arc of his protracted crime and his eventual defeat occasion *Mumbo Jumbo*'s central account of Black letters as a heroic drama of self-definition and self-defense. Von Vampton, I mean to say, is narratively indispensable—not because he creates African American literature nor because he destroys it but because he clarifies the parameters of Black culture (according to Reed)

---

⁹ Thanks to Russ Castronovo for this crucial insight, and for giving language to the concept of the "field-materiality."

¹⁰ My phrasing here borrows from James Weldon Johnson, who described his own pathbreaking anthology as a catalog of "the undeniable creative genius of the Negro": (Johnson 1922: xlvii).

¹¹ The character Abdul Hamid takes his name and certain telling characteristics—his extraordinary self-invention, his adopted faith, and his rigid and censorious moralism—from the outlandish, early twentieth-century Harlem orator and economic organizer, Sufi Abdul Hamid (née Eugene Brown): see Russell (2009). But in addition to his namesake, the fictional Hamid draws inspiration from the biography of a later, still more influential Black nationalist and convert to Islam: Malcolm X. Suggestively, Reed's Abdul Hamid is an ex-convict and autodidact who learns to "read omnivorously" "in the clink" and prophecies the coming of a red-haired "conjure man" who will earn the respect of "the people" with the authenticity and accessibility of his message (Reed 2017 [1972]: 37–39).

¹² As Gerald Early has shown, Reed's Black Herman appears to be loosely based on a Harlem Renaissance-era magician, astrologer, and herbalist of the same name (Early 1994).

by laying bare what is outside of and against it. The plot *requires* his appearance and his repeated, covetous approach, for it is the steadfast repudiation of the white appropriator that secures the novel's vision of African American literature as a righteous tradition of vitality, endurance, and authenticity.

Nowhere is this maligned yet constitutive relation more apparent than in a scene just preceding Von Vampton's sacrifice to "a very mean and high-powered loa" (a voodoo spirit). Prior to the sacrifice, the loa requests the recitation of numerous accounts, only slightly varied, of Von Vampton's "crimes." One by one, a series of "sensible hardworking" Black artists oblige the loa, approaching a Dictaphone through which they "record and feed" it their reminiscences of how they were "propositioned" but unswayed—indeed, repelled—by Von Vampton's advances. Through this collective, reiterated refusal, a second, purifying "anthology" of sorts, they lay the foundation for Von Vampton's death and concomitant erasure from the scene of Black cultural production. At the same time, through the same gesture, they secure their own belonging to a fraternity (inexplicably, they are all men) of authentic Black creativity: each, in return for his contribution, is given "an honorary houngan [voodoo priest] license" (151).

But if, as the scene so explicitly lays out, the ritualized eschewal and effacement of the white villain underwrites the confirmation of Black literature's heroic identity, then it also bears noticing that the ritual's off-stage culmination consists in a specific mode of aggression against Von Vampton. In the end, Von Vampton is not to be incinerated, dismembered, or thrown into an abyss (i.e. unmade, gotten rid of). He is to be eaten—literally, incorporated into the body of the Afro-Haitian spirit. Through this deft and provocative figuration, the repudiation of Von Vampton is revealed to be at once constitutive and impossible.

***

Digestion is a common psychoanalytic figure for *identification*—that continuous, often unconscious process through which the self is (re)made in the image of others. I intend to argue that the loa's consumption of Von Vampton signals Reed's implicit acknowledgement of Black literature's discordant, yet unshakeable, identification with him. But what can it mean to say that Reed *identifies* Black literature with its antagonist?

I am not suggesting that the Black artists who seem to despise Von Vampton have secretly adored him all along. Nor do I mean to say that Von Vampton has a true claim to the energy and Text of Jes Grew. Rather, my contention is that the very category of the "true claim" loses something of its authoritative meaning within the realm of the psyche. To put this another way, *Mumbo Jumbo* posits, and has often been received as, a story of confrontation between intractable cultural opposites: on one side, whiteness, connoting rationality, discipline, and order; on the other side, Blackness, attached to nature, "ebullience," and freedom (6). Yet, the novel's depiction of this confrontation as in large part a psychic one slyly undercuts the fiction of a cleanly divisible dualism.[13] For,

---

[13] To be clear, *Mumbo Jumbo*'s depiction of the Harlem Renaissance's psychic underpinnings makes few claims to reveal the inner lives of New Negro luminaries. On the contrary, a key feature of Reed's trademark style is the shedding of what he calls "tedious character descriptions" (Ishmael Reed in Dick

psychoanalytically speaking, there can be no rivalry or struggle for power without intimacy, desire, and identification.

Reconsider, through this lens, Von Vampton's appropriation of Black culture. It is a given—perhaps the novel's most obvious truth—that Von Vampton is a thief, in possession of a precious material object not rightly his own. Carrying the Book across continents and centuries, exploiting it for personal gain, he calls to mind histories of slavery and empire and the attendant ledgers of the Euro–American plunder of Africa. But crucially, Von Vampton does more than steal a thing. What he steals—appropriates, and also *preserves* when he takes it as his own—is the object form of an infectious psychic energy, through which he comes to reorder his own subjectivity and desire. He takes on properties of Jes Grew (its swampiness, its undisciplined sexuality); he becomes a student of Blackness (however ambivalent and ineffectual); and even his private expressions of desire are transformed. (Although Von Vampton purports to only "disguise" himself as a "Negrophile," his landlady catches him, in an unsuspecting moment, worshipfully "kissing some ugly nigger doll" [78, 55]). Having enmeshed his "self" with (a distorted version of) the Blackness he stole, there is no possibility of simply restoring rightful ownership and balancing the ledger.[14]

In the world of the novel, this identification unsettles everyone, Black and white. But what can be done? The Atonists try and convict Von Vampton for his misplaced attachments and illicit self-fashioning, only to discover that their juridical system holds little sway over the force and formations of his psychic life (67). Counter to the tenets of Atonist self-discipline and rational action, psychic life is inescapably unwieldy, irreverent, unbeholden to strict intellectual, ideological, or racial rationale. Diana Fuss puts it this way: "To the unconscious, there are no 'correct' or 'incorrect' identifications, no 'proper' or 'improper' desires. There are only identifications and desires that mold and shape the ego—which is why attempts to legislate the unconscious have always had rather mixed success" (Fuss : 49).

Equally unnerved, LaBas and Black Herman try a different tactic. Foregoing the police department and the official courts, they escort their criminal to the "Other Authorities"

---

and Singh [1995]). Rather than excavating the individual mind, Reed's interest lies with the psychic life of the *field* of African American literature. Downplaying the realist approaches of social history and institutional analysis that often characterize studies of the Harlem Renaissance, *Mumbo Jumbo* instead attributes the literary movement to a "psychic epidemic" and instructs its readers that empirical methods are inadequate to explain the movement's origins and arc (Reed 2017 [1972]: 5). Moreover, in the novel's epilogue, LaBas's lecture explicitly reframes the preceding text with the question of how Freud would have made sense of the Harlem Renaissance! He wouldn't have gotten it, LaBas decides, but his methods—a "compromise" between the Enlightenment and the occult—would come closer than many others to apprehending the cultural phenomenon (172).

[14] Although it is beyond the scope of the current chapter, there is also a psychoanalytic argument to be made about how the Book of Thoth operates as a fetish, not only for Von Vampton but also more generally in the novel's psychic economy. Among other things, such a reading would need to track *Mumbo Jumbo*'s engagement with non-identical conceptualizations of the fetish in psychoanalysis and Afro-Haitian voodoo. Indeed, here we find yet another occasion for exploring the dynamics of cross-racial appropriation.

of Haitian spiritual practice, under whose watch Von Vampton is to be consumed by the very culture he sought to consume. An early image of Von Vampton "licking his chops" in the presence of a Black man finds its answer in the image of a loa whetting its appetite on tales of Von Vampton's failed advances, and in this reversal, LaBas and Black Herman perceive the operations of "justice" (76, 197).

Presumably, they mean that justice has taken its ancient form as a reversal of power ("an eye for an eye"), as the spirit of black creativity renounces and reassigns its object status. But surely, the act of eating—of taking in, rather than casting out—unsettles the meaning and finality of such a formulation. What kind of justice is this? How should we understand a theory of redress in which the wronged party is not purified of the thief but rather, by eating him, made inextricable from him?[15]

I contend that the loa's vengeance does not amount to a portrait of justice or redress after all. Instead, it represents the impossibility of purification. To be sure, Reed maintains the novel's animating desire to destroy Von Vampton and, by doing so, to restore the prior order of a self-authorizing Black literary autonomy. But, by expressing this desire through the imagery of digestion, he insists that the vanquishment is also an incorporation: the wish to be rid of the white appropriator is hopelessly (con)fused with a notion of Black literary identity that hungers for, and indeed remakes itself through, the internalization of its foe. There can be no return to Black culture before Von Vampton stole the Book; histories of appropriation and embattlement leave their marks on both dominant and minority subjects; and what is altered by these histories is not only the rightful distribution of resources and prestige but also the very constitution of subjectivity and desire. By simultaneously avowing and thwarting its fantasy of Black literature's redeemed autonomy, *Mumbo Jumbo* brings into view the discomfiting messiness of modern racial consciousness in relation to the production and circulation of Black art.

***

Rather than dwelling in the scene of Von Vampton's punishment, Reed pivots away from its revelation. LaBas and Black Herman deposit the criminal into the hands of their Haitian allies, only to turn their backs on the culminating scene. They "leave the ship" and "walk toward their cars," never to see Von Vampton again (198). The plot progression thus approaches but ultimately retreats from the question of how the crime of the appropriator affects the self-constituting, identificatory processes of Black culture. And indeed, Reed's anti-climactic refusal to represent the loa's digestive entanglement with its antagonist is in keeping with many preceding scenes in which the novel implies but declines to explore Black culture's susceptibility to white power. In one such scene, the Book of Thoth itself, though it is possessed by Von Vampton alone for some 800 years, "refuses to be [his] whore" and "[saves] all of its love" for its rightful culture bearers (188)!

---

[15] Freudian readers will detect an allusion to the political creation myth of *Totem and Taboo* in Reed's re-imagining of an act of cannibalism that transfers power from the solitary grasp of an envied and hated father, to an egalitarian fraternity.

But in the very defensiveness of such formulations, in the hyperbole of their refusal, one detects a psychic logic that Judith Butler would later make famous: "what at first [appears] as a refused identification" is "more accurately ... termed a disavowed one—an identification that has already been made and denied in the unconscious."[16] The novel's repudiation of Von Vampton, I mean to suggest, is belied by a *prior* identification with him—or, more precisely, with the despised text to which his character alludes: Van Vechten's *Nigger Heaven*. Before Von Vampton is devoured by the loa, before Von Vampton even appears on the scene, *Mumbo Jumbo* has incorporated and disavowed *Nigger Heaven* within its very premise. The refusal of this association gains force and coherence—it takes shape as a plot of heroic and self-possessed Black literary *identity*—through its compulsive, reiterative opposition to the contradictory, embarrassing *identification*.

It is worth underscoring once more that psychoanalytic identification does not connote affinity or admiration. It is not a profession of sympathy or fellow feeling (though such sentiments may accompany it) but a phenomenon of psychic aggression in which one's unfaithful, self-serving citation of the other consolidates the illusion of the undivided, individuated self. Consider in this light how *Mumbo Jumbo*'s central quest, to redeem and enshrine African American literature as a heroic drama of self-possession, absorbs and appropriates *Nigger Heaven*'s most memorable warning: that if "young Negro intellectuals" don't rise to the task of telling their stories, then "a new crop of Nordics ... will exploit this material before the Negro gets around to it" (Van Vechten 2000 [1926]: 223).

The warning—issued by a Menckenesque[17] editor to an aspiring Black novelist suffering from writer's block—has been read as a metafictional nod to Van Vechten's own literary intervention, and surely such a reading is intended: Van Vechten himself was a "Nordic" author "[exploiting]" the "material" of Black life, to unprecedented commercial success. Within the novelistic scene, however, the emphasis falls not on the identity of the white appropriator but on the editor's characterization of the Harlem Renaissance as a moment of Black creative frustration. Harlem, he declares, is "overrun with fresh, unused material," but its richness remains untapped, as Black writers "continue to employ all the old clichés and formulas" (222, 223). Such is the view of Van Vechten's novel

---

[16] Diana Fuss uses this language to paraphrase a central argument of Butler's *Gender Trouble* (7).

[17] A close friend of Van Vechten's since 1916, H.L. Mencken was an iconoclastic editor, essayist, cultural critic, and scholar, who exerted extraordinary influence over American literature in the 1920s. *American Mercury*, the magazine he started in 1923 with George Jean Nathan and Alfred Knopf, devoted considerable energies to staging a multifaceted conversation about "the role of race and racism in American culture." Toward this end, *American Mercury* "solicited more works by black writers than all the major white-owned journals of the time combined"(Hutchinson 1995; Franklin 1987). Mencken's considerable support of African American letters and Black social causes, however, was not without complication. In his introduction to Mencken's notorious, long-sealed diary, Charles A. Fecher notes that Mencken's "attitude toward black people was a curious mingling of total egalitarianism on the one hand and patronizing superiority on the other": Fecher 1989: xxii. For more on Mencken's relationship to the Harlem Renaissance, see Hutchinson (1995) and Scruggs (1984).

more generally. Its exciting urban milieu is mediated by a repressed librarian in the role of protagonist-heroine and her paramour, a bright but uninspired "pseudo-literary fake" (227).

In Reed's retelling, the editor's warning is amplified into a threat which *Mumbo Jumbo*'s plot is designed to forefend. The story of the encroaching, acquisitive "Nordic" is contained and suppressed by the story of Black culture's ascendance toward self-possession. Yet, even as Von Vampton is vigorously rejected, the initiated reader readily perceives how *Mumbo Jumbo* takes in and constitutes itself through the central narrative elements of *Nigger Heaven*: Black creative potential and the longing for its realization, the backdrop of Harlem in the 1920s, the specter of a white appropriator, even the major role afforded to the librarian.

An early, seemingly superfluous scene further underscores this point and particularizes *Mumbo Jumbo*'s connection to its source text and shadow other. As PaPa LaBas and his driver, T Malice, discuss the insidious strategies of white supremacy, T Malice makes a derisive reference to "these fagingy-fagades." LaBas, a studious collector of black linguistic innovation, asks, "Fagingy-fagade? What's that?" T Malice explains that the term refers to "white people .... Ofays," and LaBas dutifully records the word and its definition in "his black notebook" (49). What on the surface reads as a witty, periodizing digression, whose time-stamped linguistic code places us at the scene of the Harlem Renaissance, should not be mistaken for that alone. Reed's portrayal of Black men cataloguing Black culture is also an explicit rewriting of *Nigger Heaven*'s cheeky glossary, through which Van Vechten, nearly fifty years earlier, introduced a voyeuristic, mostly white audience to this specific, esoteric word (Van Vechten's definition: "a white person. This word and the corresponding word for Negro are theatrical hog Latin" [285]).

Reed's rewriting of the record-keeping gesture returns authority over Black language and culture to its originators, but it does so by citing—by taking in rather than casting out—Van Vechten's appropriative offense. In this sense, LaBas's "black notebook," which absorbs but obfuscates Van Vechten, may be said to anticipate the loa, who devours and renounces Von Vampton. But rather than resolving the problem of cultural theft, these reclamations generate a new set of questions. What happens next? What becomes of African American literature after its transformative encounter with the white appropriator?

Although La Bas and Black Herman turn their backs on such questions, the novel itself may be understood as an extended response to its climactic provocation. Reed's novel, I mean to say, is itself the visionary emplotment of a post-Harlem Renaissance African American literature that feeds on, yet suppresses, its foundational entanglement with white power and desire. Published to great acclaim at a crucial moment in Black literary history—as the enterprise of Black Studies began to enter and change university culture—*Mumbo Jumbo* inscribes a heroic origin story *and* a constitutive, ineradicable ambivalence at the heart of the field imaginary.

***

With its joyful turn to a scene of creative exchange in an early-seventies classroom, *Mumbo Jumbo*'s epilogue appears to welcome the rise of Black Studies as a development commensurate with the novel's own, metafictional fulfillment of its organizing quest to realize Black artistic potential. As I argued at the beginning of this chapter, LaBas's lecture—the epilogue's central event—consolidates the foregoing text as an origin story and guiding vision, while the new setting of the Black professor's classroom gestures toward the coming institutional legitimization of African American literature.

Yet, it would be a mistake to regard the epilogue as an uncomplicated endorsement of the field's late-twentieth-century institutional turn. After all, the main text of the novel expends considerable energy to depict institutions and institutionalization as instruments of discipline and power, inimical to the life force of art.[18] And, although the "Black professor" invites and celebrates LaBas (a pointed reversal of an earlier scene in which a college professor speaks "as if he didn't know [people of color] were in the room"), LaBas remains stubbornly peripheral to the contemporary academic scene (89). His presence in the classroom is explicitly occasional and extracurricular; he appears before his young audience less as an artist or scholarly authority than as a relic and primary source, whose lengthy speech prompts the professor to interrupt him and "some of the students [to leave] the hall" (212). Reed, it seems, is at once enthused by the prospect of an academy "reborn from the protests and agitation of the sixties and seventies" and skeptical about the academy's will and capacity to "make good on its promise to minorities" (Ferguson 2012: 4).

Von Vampton's name is all but erased from the epilogue, appearing just once in a subordinate clause. Indeed, reading the epilogue as a postscript to the loa's consumption of Von Vampton, we might say that the celebratory classroom scene, in which a Black artist addresses a Black audience under the authorization of a Black professor, is *premised upon* the triumphant removal of the appropriative white villain. At last, the antagonist Von Vampton is diminished and dismissed, clearing a path for a self-authored and self-authorizing Black creative tradition! But, alongside the optimistic scene of cultural repossession, there remains the stubborn possibility that Von Vampton is not removed at all so much as he is internalized and disguised. Surely, it is no coincidence that the plot's sudden and largely incongruous will to institutionalization chronologically follows Black culture's ingestion of the calculating, acquisitive, renegade librarian to the West.

Indeed, Reed's final, thematic turn to the institutionalization of African American literature may be read as a tacit reference to the broad arc of Van Vechten's career in Black letters. Although the publication of *Nigger Heaven* remains the most notorious iteration

---

[18] E.g. its central villain is a librarian and an archivist; it depicts academic discourse as a white supremacist endeavor, disingenuously fixated on formal conformity; it wryly renames museums "Centers of Art Detention"; it romanticizes autodidacts and turns a nostalgic eye toward a mythic past when "every man was an artist and every artist a priest"; and it summarily dismisses the Enlightenment legacy as "2,000 years of probing classifying attempting to make an 'orderly' world so that when company came they would know the household's nature and would be careful about dropping ashes on the rug" (57, 50, 42, 164, 153)!

of his "passionate attachment to blackness," Van Vechten spent much of the 1920s promoting Black writers and facilitating connections between them and the American literary establishment. Furthermore, after his friend James Weldon Johnson died in a car accident in 1938, a bereaved Van Vechten devoted over a decade to "establishing a proper memorial to Johnson's life," which ultimately took shape as the James Weldon Johnson Collection of Negro Arts and Letters, founded by Carl Van Vechten. This sprawling, extraordinary repository—which includes the entirety of Van Vechten's trove of "Negro books, manuscripts, letters, photographs, phonograph records, and music," along with donated materials from Langston Hughes, W.E.B. Du Bois, Walter White, and others— became the first major archive of African American literature and culture at a predominantly white university when it opened at Yale in 1950 (Bernard 2012: 23, 214, 228). A tribute to Van Vechten's late friend, whose wide-ranging achievements included an abundance of original writing, professorships in literature and creative writing at Fisk and New York Universities, and pioneering work as an early anthologist of African American poetry, the Collection anticipated and aimed to expedite the widespread institutional legitimization of Black literary and cultural studies.[19]

It is striking to observe how *Mumbo Jumbo* takes in and reformulates (which is to say, identifies with) not only *Nigger Heaven* but also Van Vechten's work on the James Weldon Johnson Collection. The elevation of Johnson as an exemplar and forefather of Black expressive culture, the prized notion of consolidating the foundational texts of the tradition,[20] and the will to academic institutionalization are all features of Van Vechten's enterprise that recur as central premises of Reed's novel. Indeed, even Reed's subordination of the white appropriator's name and role is anticipated by Van Vechten himself, whose choice to foreground Johnson's name derived in part from his fear that "some people would not be willing to donate materials if the collection bore his [Van Vechten's] name" (Bernard 2012: 228). Thus, even when the novel moves to erase Von Vampton from its final inscription of African American literature's field imaginary, Reed ironically, inescapably, cites Van Vechten.

To end like this—affirming African American literature's rich citational imbrication with a disavowed custodian—may strike some as discomfiting or even out of bounds, at odds with the story that Reed, through LaBas, asks us to remember and recite. But I would argue that such a move is precisely in keeping with the novel's most essential impulse: to revivify and explore the affective histories of desire that inspirit Black expressive culture in their dynamic complexity. What might we learn by restoring Van Vechten's visibility within genealogies of African American literature and its institutionalization?

---

[19] Bernard quotes from a 1941 letter to Langston Hughes, in which Van Vechten "enthused ... about his vision for the collection: 'I have a DEFINITE FEELING that in LESS than five years Yale will have a chair of Negro life and culture and whoever sits in that chair will have the best source material in the country to guide him'" (2012: 231).

[20] It is ironic that Reed associates Von Vampton with the willful and destructive division of the Book of Thoth, when in fact, a condition of Van Vechten's donation to Yale was that "above all, the collection must be preserved as an entity. The material was not to be divided across the university under any circumstances" (Bernard 2012: 229).

What becomes of the ungovernable array of identifications and desires that Black art inspires in its heterogeneous audiences? What does the self-mythologizing psychology of field formation illumine and obscure about the forces that drive and shape literary history? By constructing a narrative in which questions like these come with the territory of his triumphalist fantasy, Reed advances a capacious conceptualization of African American literature as an open site at which history's unfixed and unwieldy psychic effects may be continuously interpreted, negotiated, and remade.

References

Bernard, Emily. 2012. *Carl Van Vechten and the Harlem Renaissance: A Portrait in Black and White* (New Haven, CT: Yale University Press).
Chaney, Michael. 2003. "Slave Cyborgs and the Black Infovirus: Ishmael Reed's Cybernetic Aesthetics," *Modern Fiction Studies* 49.2 (Summer): 261–283.
Cheng, Anne Anlin. 2009. "Psychoanalysis without Symptoms," *differences* 20.1: 87–101.
Donofrio, Nick. 2017. "Multiculturalism, Inc.: Regulating and Deregulating the Culture Industries with Ishmael Reed," *American Literary History* 29.1 (Spring): 100–128.
Dick, Bruce and Amritjit Singh, eds. 1995. *Conversations with Ishmael Reed* (Jackson, MI: University Press of Mississippi).
Dubey, Madhu. 2003. *Signs and Cities: Black Literary Postmodernism* (Chicago, IL: University of Chicago Press).
Early, Gerald. 1994. "'Black Herman Comes through Only Once Every Seven Years': Black Magic, White Magic, and American Culture," in Werner Sollors and Maria Diedrich eds, *The Black Columbiad: Defining Moments in African American Literature and Culture* (Cambridge, MA: Harvard University Press), 234–243.
Fecher, Charles A. 1989. *The Diary of H. L. Mencken* (New York: Knopf).
Ferguson, Roderick. 2012. *The Reorder of Things: The University and its Pedagogies of Minority Difference* (Minneapolis, MN: University of Minnesota Press).
Franklin, Ben A. 1987. "Mencken show rebuts racism charge," *New York Times*, February 10: C13.
Fuss, Diana. 1995. *Identification Papers: Readings on Psychoanalysis, Sexuality, and Culture* (New York: Routledge).
Gates, Henry Louis. 1987. *Figures in Black: Words, Signs, and the "Racial" Self* (New York: Oxford University Press).
Hutchinson, George. 1995. "'Superior Intellectual Vaudeville': American Mercury," in *The Harlem Renaissance in Black and White* (Cambridge, MA: Harvard University Press), 313–341.
Ingram, Shelley. 2012. "'To Ask Again': Folklore, *Mumbo Jumbo*, and the Question of Ethnographic Metafictions," *African American Review* 45.1–2 (Spring–Summer): 183–196.
Jackson, Lawrence. 2007. "'The Aftermath': The Reputation of the Harlem Renaissance Twenty Years Later," in George Hutchinson ed., *The Cambridge Companion to the Harlem Renaissance* (New York: Cambridge University Press), 239–253.
Johnson, James Weldon. 1922. *The Book of American Negro Poetry* (New York: Harcourt Brace).
Laplanche, Jean and Jean-Bertrand Pontalis. 1973. *The Language of Psycho-Analysis*, trans. Donald Nicholson-Smith (New York: Norton).

Lewis, David Levering. 1997 [1981]. *When Harlem Was In Vogue* (New York: Penguin).
Mason, Jr, Theodore O. 1988. "Performance, History, and Myth: The Problem of Ishmael Reed's *Mumbo Jumbo*," *Modern Fiction Studies* 34.1 (Spring): 97–109.
Pease, Donald E. 1990. "New Americanists: Revisionist Interventions into the Canon," *boundary 2* 17.1 (Spring): 1–37.
Reed, Ishmael. 1989. "Harlem Renaissance Day," in *Shrovetide in Old New Orleans* (New York: Atheneum), 258.
Reed, Ishmael. 2017 [1972]. *Mumbo Jumbo* (New York: Penguin).
Rojas, Fabio. 2010. *From Black Power to Black Studies: How a Radical Social Movement Became an Academic Discipline* (Baltimore, MD: Johns Hopkins University Press).
Rooks, Noliwe. 2006. *White Money/Black Power: The Surprising History of African American Studies and the Crisis of Race and Higher Education* (Boston, MA: Beacon).
Russell, Thaddeus. 2009. "Sufi Abdul Hamid," in Henry Louis Gates, Jr, ed., *Harlem Renaissance Lives from the African American National Biography* (New York: Oxford University Press), 235–237.
Schmitz, Neil. 1974. "Neo-HooDoo: The Experimental Fiction of Ishmael Reed," *Twentieth Century Literature* 20.2 (April): 126–40.
Scruggs, Charles. 1984. *The Sage in Harlem: H. L. Mencken and the Black Writers of the 1920s* (Baltimore, MD: Johns Hopkins University Press).
Sherrard-Johnson, Cherene. 2015. "Introduction: Harlem as Shorthand: The Persistent Value of the Harlem Renaissance," in Cherene Sherrard-Johnson, ed., *A Companion to the Harlem Renaissance* (Malden, MA: Wiley Blackwell), 1–14.
Taylor, Yuval. 2019. *Langston and Zora: A Story of Friendship and Betrayal* (New York: Norton).
Van, Vechten, Carl. 2000 [1926]. *Nigger Heaven* (Urbana, IL: University of Illinois Press).
Warren, Kenneth W. 2011. *What Was African American Literature?* (Cambridge, MA: Harvard University Press).
White, Edward. 2014. *The Tastemaker: Carl Van Vechten and the Birth of Modern America* (New York: Farrar, Straus, and Giroux).

CHAPTER 14

ANDREA LEE'S EUROPE

Race, Interracial Desire, and Transnationalism

MELISSA DANIELS-RAUTERKUS

Introduction

In an interview with Jennifer D. Williams, Andrea Lee candidly discusses her signature theme: affluent African American women who live or travel abroad, who are married to white/European men, and who have to negotiate their race, class, and gender beyond the borders of the United States. Having suddenly realized that she had spent more time outside the United States, living in Europe and other locales than she had inside it, Lee describes herself as an "unwilling expatriate" (quoted in Williams 2017: 508). Suggesting that she did not make a conscious decision to leave the United States. as much as she just ended up living overseas, Lee admits that after almost thirty years of living in Italy with her Italian husband and their two children, she still does not feel completely at home in her adopted country. As it turns out, "home" is, for Lee, an elusive concept. Occupying an interstitial space, she describes a different kind of double consciousness: "Always when I'm here, I have a feeling that I'm looking over there, then when I'm there, I have a feeling of always peering across the sea to the rest of the world. You're always divided" (Lee quoted in Williams 2017: 509).

This dividedness that Lee speaks of is crucial to comprehending her work, and that work, as I argue in this chapter, provides a critical corrective to how we think about race, interracial desire, and African American literature. My readings of Lee's award-winning, but critically neglected, travel memoir, *Russian Journal* (1981), and her more well-known semi-autobiographical novel, *Sarah Phillips* (1984), address the subject of her dividedness, demonstrating that she does not inhabit a fragmented self as much as she formulates an unfixed positionality that produces a fluid subjectivity that flows beyond national borders. Taking up residence in a transnational liminality that exists betwixt and between the United States and Europe, Lee contests the arbitrariness of American racial divisions and challenges the political assumptions made about Black female/white male couplings. In this way, Lee calls into question the oversimplification of race in the United States, jettisoning binary thinking about racial consciousness for something messier and more complicated—that is, "in-betweenness" and "negotiation." Presenting these concepts as powerful modalities for comprehending contemporary Black life, Lee provides us with a paradigm of Black being and feeling that is profoundly ambivalent about the promises of racial collectivity and nationality. Moving beyond overt anger and rage as the predominant affects by which we can assess Black racialized experience, Lee unveils the sense of alienation, grief, and uncertainty that attends Blackness in the late twentieth century. As I will show, reading *Russian Journal* and *Sarah Phillips* through the lens of transnationalism can be a transformative experience that not only articulates how physical place may create new possibilities for how we identify and theorize our emotional and sexual attachments but also opens up new ways of talking about race, interracial desire, and African American literature and criticism as a whole.

In foregrounding the transnational, my intention is not to position it as some kind of utopian or post-racial alternative to the racially divided and unequal America that produced Lee but rather to underscore its ability to reorder the sequence of identifiers that organize and give meaning to Black identity. In America, race trumps nationality, meaning that you are your race first and everything else is subordinate to it. Outside of America, you are your nationality first and everything else is of lesser importance. For an African American author like Lee, the allure of the transnational provides an escape hatch out of the pigeonhole of the label "Black writer." But there are also limits to the transnational and what it can really offer *anyone* in terms of running away from so-called domestic political baggage. As the adage says, "Wherever you go, there you are." More to the point, though, the transnational is not a panacea for the pitfalls of nationalism as ideas about racial, cultural, and national identity—like people, culture, commodities, and currency—circulate throughout the world, and in multidirectional ways no less, that are always changing how we feel and think about ourselves and the world at large. In this way, the transnational is not just a matter of geography, but it is also what Raymond Williams has called a "structure of feeling"—that is, a heuristic for comprehending how aesthetic, cultural, and political practices and processes create new ways of thinking and feeling.[1] What this means with regard to Lee is that the Europe she inhabits in *Russian Journal* and *Sarah Phillips* is as much a region in her imagination and in her heart as it is a geopolitical reality. All of this raises very interesting questions for scholars about how we categorize her work and how we delineate the boundaries of African American literature.

Scholarship on Lee's writing tends to focus on its refusal to conform to the aesthetic and political conventions of African American literature (especially Black women's literature) and, perhaps more problematically, what some critics see as Lee's seeming disregard for racial history and a blasé attitude towards ongoing racial oppression. It's easy

---

[1] See Williams and Orrom's *Preface to Film* (1954).

to understand why critics have negatively responded to her work when we consider the politicized context within which African American literature emerged and developed. Because of its origins in the Black Power movement, as Gene Andrew Jarrett has observed, African American literature has traditionally and consistently been valued for its ability to accurately represent the race and stage resistance to the white power structure. Historically, this has meant that in order for the literature to be considered *properly* Black, it had to meet the "tripartite standard of racial authenticity: It had to be by, about, and for African Americans. More intricately, the literature had to emphasize such issues as African American empowerment, political self-determination, racial solidarity, and a shared history of racial oppression" (Jarrett 2011). For Black women writers, meeting this standard of authenticity also entailed de-emphasizing sexuality; embracing motherhood, martyrdom, and redemptive victimization; and rejecting whiteness.[2] Although Lee throughout her career has been fascinated with identity (particularly in terms of race, class, and gender) and what she describes as the "concept of exoticism, foreignness, and by the theme of encounters between strangers," critics have failed to properly appreciate the complexity with which she writes about these topics as well as the nuance and elasticity by which she broadens and stretches our understanding of such phenomena (quoted in Treisman 2019).

For many critics, Lee's reluctance to perform a certain kind of angry Black woman persona or participate in any recognizable form of resistance is troubling—to say nothing of her predilection for white/European men. As a case in point, Mary Helen Washington wrote a scathing review of *Sarah Phillips*, in which she rebukes the novel on the grounds that, "there is no solidarity or friendship or even conversation between Sarah and other [B]lacks. Nowhere is there anger at the racism that causes her to feel alienated from her racial identity. Lee's narrator retreats into a permanent ambiguity in which she can only report a vague feeling of loss" (1985: 3). Similarly, in her foreword to the 1993 reprinting of the text by Northeastern University Press, Valerie Smith criticizes the novel for similar reasons, underscoring Sarah's "nonchalance about her privilege, gratuitous rebelliousness, ambivalence about her familial and cultural roots, confusion about the direction her life should take, and uncertainty about where to place her loyalties" (1993: x). Playing the respectability card, Smith also censures Sarah for her sexual choices and behavior, observing that, "Despite the history of [B]lack women's sexual exploitation at the hands of white men, she confesses to a 'lively appetite for white boys' (Lee, *Sarah Phillips* 4), and at least appears to revel in being fetishized as an erotic, exotic other by Henri, Alain, and Roger" (xiii).

That Sarah does not have any racial hang-ups about white men and that she transgresses conservative ideas about sex and gender would appear to be too problematic for Smith. While Smith grants that the novel's reluctance to "conform to conventions of representing '[B]lackness' and '[B]lack womanhood' raises for the reader challenging

---

[2] For more on the aesthetic and political conventions of Black women's literature, see McDowell (1995).

questions," (x), rather than attempt to work through these questions she settles for lamenting "the difficulty one has situating this text in relation to a progressive political agenda" (xx). Suspicious of Lee's politics, and perhaps to a larger extent *Sarah Phillips*'s ambiguous stance on race, Smith concludes her reading in an equally ambiguous way. She grants that the novel is deserving of critical attention but speculates that one of the reasons why it might not be more popular with readers may have something to do with how its "protagonist and narrator alike negotiate ideologies of race and class" (xxii).[3] Of course, I would add gender to this configuration as I imagine that, for some readers, what Smith describes as Sarah's "irreverence and iconoclasm" is all the more offensive because she is a woman—a Black middle-class woman at that (xiii). In the final analysis, Smith skirts the question of how to interpret Sarah's negotiations by suggesting that this issue remains a problem for future generations of scholars, like myself, to ultimately resolve.

Readings like those of Washington and Smith are very telling—not for what they reveal about Lee's writing but for what they reveal about the assumptions and expectations that scholars and general readers often have of African American literature. The problem with their readings is that they proceed from a foundational binary opposition that divides African American literature into two competing categories: "authentic" and "inauthentic." As Frances Smith Foster and Kim D. Green have elucidated, "'Authentic' African American literature deplores slavery, resists racism, and genuflects to the gods of ancient Africa," whereas "'Inauthentic' literature, so the theory goes, portrays racial ambivalence, Anglophilic aspirations, and insufficient subversion or protest of values routinely attributed to American mainstream culture" (2013: 47). Such a narrow, binary view unsurprisingly results in a narrow, binary account of African American literature. In actuality, African American literature is far more complex, diverse, and incoherent than what Lee's critics have generally recognized. Indeed, readings like Washington's and Smith's fail to appreciate the aesthetic and political tensions that lie at the heart of the African American literary project. Moreover, the schematic, either/or approach to assessing, categorizing, and valuing the literature cannot adequately address the manifold ways in which this literature challenges the very structures of difference upon which such interpretations stand.

What I want to examine in this chapter is what happens when we open up this rigidified schema. How does moving away from the United States and the Black/white racial binary create the conceptual space to reimagine how we think about race, interracial desire, and African American literature? Acknowledging that this latter enterprise is organized around linguistic, social, aesthetic, and political structures of

---

[3] Here, Smith responds to Mary Helen Washington's review of the book, in which she situates *Sarah Phillips* within the conservative political environment of the Reagan–Bush era and speculates that "a novel by a [B]lack writer which exalts class privilege and ignores racism, is bound to find wide acceptance" (1985: 4). Smith disagrees with this reading and points to the novel's unpopularity as evidence that it has been met with disapproval, theorizing that this may have something to do with Sarah's unconventional choices (Smith 1993: xxii).

difference, I propose that we attend to the in-between, in a transnational framework, so as to make visible and unsettle the binaries that limit our understanding of this literature and how it calls into question the arbitrariness of geographical borders, racial categories, and notions of nationality and racial feeling. In this way, I am suggesting that the in-between and the transnational are analogous frameworks that function as crucial analytics of place and affect. Here, I am reminded of Shelley Fisher Fishkin's Presidential Address at the 2004 American Studies Association's annual meeting, "Crossroads of Culture: The Transnational Turn in American Studies" (2005). As Fishkin elucidated, putting the transnational at the center of American studies means that not only should we pay attention to physical borders, but we should also consider the "pain that they inflict, ... the harsh realities of internal colonization, ... and ... the challenges and delights of embracing multiple psychic locations" (17).[4]

In doing so, we gain an important opportunity to engage with the continuums that, in actuality, stretch between seemingly natural polarities like Black/white, oppressor/oppressed, and America/Europe. Departing from the dominant foci in critical conversations about Lee's writing, which tends to concern itself with the question of whether or not her work adheres to a progressive or regressive political agenda or discussions of the attitudes and behaviors of the post-civil rights Black middle class, I foreground negotiation as a method of reading that mobilizes the spaces in between seemingly fixed referents and elucidates how Lee looks to Europe—both as a geographical reality and as a region in her imagination—to disrupt and trouble the narrow binaries that structure American conversations about race, interracial desire, and African American literature. Additionally, negotiation opens up the affective registers with which we can engage the less obvious and less theorized affects, such as ambivalence or grief, that are also a key part of contemporary African American experience. In this way, we might be able to achieve some measure of what I call "affective restorative justice"—a kind of emotional reparation for the harm that *has been and still is* inflicted upon Black people by marginalizing modes of critique that focus on blatant displays of anger and rage to the exclusion of other emotions, flattening how we conceive of Black subjectivity and, perhaps more problematically, denying us the emotional range and depth of full humanity.

In casting negotiation as an approach towards reading, then, I seek to illuminate how a focus on method produces certain strategies for rethinking not only the texts under study here (and to a greater extent Lee's larger corpus) but also how we approach the field of African American literary studies. As I will show, in *Russian Journal* and *Sarah Phillips*, Lee negotiates certain American expectations of race and racial feeling as well as literary expectations of subject matter, theme, and genre. Neither fully aligning with or against these expectations, Lee instead transforms them so as to exercise greater personal and artistic autonomy. By highlighting the ways in which she navigates and upsets

---

[4] Fishkin made these remarks about the late Gloria Anzaldúa, to whom Fishkin dedicated her address, commemorating her work as one of the most significant theorists of borders—literal and figurative—in American and Chicana Studies as well as cultural, feminist, and queer theories.

readers' expectations, we gain an appreciation for the novelty and complexity of her work and its cultural and political value in expanding the canon of African American literature in the twentieth century.

Of course, the risk of such an approach is its potential to further marginalize an already marginalized writer, drawing greater attention to the ways in which she does not conveniently fit into neat and tidy aesthetic or political categories within African American literature. Inevitably, in tracking how an African American female writer resists conforming to certain longstanding conventions governing Black women's literature, one unwittingly reifies those conventions by acknowledging their taxonomic logic and force. But, as I will illustrate, Lee's refusal to conform to these standards is precisely what gives her writing its aesthetic and political power. As Aida Levy-Hussen has observed, Lee's work can be located "within an extra-canonical counter-tradition—a missing archive—of contemporary African American literature" (2016: 95). Making sense of this undertheorized and underappreciated body of writing is an important part of the project of telling a new and different story about African American literature and literary culture.

In order to challenge a false narrative about aesthetic unity and political coherence that persists in spite of our best efforts, we must attend to the fractures and tensions that characterize the literature. Not to reinforce these divisions or binary oppositions but to show the range and diversity of Black experiences that give rise to this literature so that we have a fuller portrait of Black life and African American literature. Hence, I believe any risk involved in assessing Lee's negotiations of race, interracial desire, and the expectations of African American literature is worth the reward. The pay-off of such an approach is twofold: (a) it gives us a newer, more cosmopolitan model for theorizing race and interracial desire; and (b) it gives us an expanded sense of what counts as African American literature, where we can locate it (in terms of physical and emotional landscapes) and what its enduring value is to us as twenty-first-century readers of twentieth-century texts.

Russian Journal

Despite having won the 1984 Jean Stein Award from the National Academy of Arts and Letters and being nominated for a National Book Award, *Russian Journal* is not a very popular book. While book critics have published reviews of the travel memoir, there are hardly any scholarly assessments of its intrinsic merits or its literary and cultural value.[5] Considering that with *Russian Journal*, Lee, in Jennifer D. Williams's words, "joined a select few [B]lack women writers and intellectuals, like Audre Lorde and Angela Davis,

---

[5] At the time of writing, the only published scholarly analysis of *Russian Journal* that I have come across is Shaundra Meyers's essay, "Black Anaesthetics: *The New Yorker* and Andrea Lee's *Russian Journal*" (2019).

in Cold War deliberations about life under communism," the book's descent into academic obscurity is all the more bizarre (Williams 2017: 507). Based on Lee's ten-month stay in the Soviet Union with her then husband, a doctoral student in Russian history, the book chronicles Lee's various interactions with students with KGB ties, *babushki* (old women) on the metro, *fartsovchitsa* (Black marketeers), and members of the tourist and diplomat communities. Comprised of thirty-six dated, self-contained entries, the journal foregrounds Lee's perceptions of her environment and the people she meets, relegating the details about her own identity to the background. To the frustration of some readers, Lee's relative silence about the fact that she is African American registers as a fatal flaw of the book, a deliberately deceptive narrative choice that downplays the significance of race.[6]

For insight into Lee's thinking about race, we might turn to her own words. In her introduction to the 2006 Random House paperback reissue of *Russian Journal*, Lee addresses the race question head on. Not only does she talk about her first marriage (also to a white man), but she also responds to criticism about the book's racial evasiveness—that is, its refusal to capitulate to the "rules of racial representation" in African American literature—and her feelings about her racial identity. By rules of racial representation, I mean what Jarrett has described as the set of aesthetic features and narrative strategies that have always governed depictions of Black identity or experience. These rules demand that Black writers announce their Blackness and render it legible for a predominately white readership, usually, by way of dialect, racial stereotypes, and Black themes like oppression, resistance, and racial uplift.[7] She begins by telling the reader that the "creation of *Russian Journal* is inextricably linked not only with [her] first marriage, but also with [her] first professional work as a writer" (Lee 2006c: ix). This is crucial information as it crystallizes for the reader the interconnectedness of these issues—making the book's context also its subject. To bring this into greater relief, Lee gives us the backstory from which her journal emerges:

> Toasts in Russian and raunchy nuptial references to Moscow nights abounded at my wedding to Tom Fallows, my first husband, [then] a brilliant third-year Harvard graduate student of Russian history who had won an IREX research grant to Moscow and Leningrad that included—fatefully for me—provisions for a spouse: we were leaving almost immediately after the ceremony for the Soviet Union, and the trip that inspired my book also would be a honeymoon.
>
> (ix)

In this subtle way, Lee positions her interracial marriage as a key component of the book's para-text, suggesting that it is as much a part of her account of a foreign culture

---

[6] See Peter Osnos's review of *Russian Journal*, in which he writes: "Discovering that Andrea Lee is [B]lack gave me the feeling that, for all of its candor, *Russian Journal* is holding some things back" (1981: 10).

[7] For more on this, see the Introduction of Jarrett's *Deans and Truants* (2007).

as it is a part of her own subjective experience of being an African American woman in Soviet Russia—even if that experience is not explicitly marked as "Black."[8] This is to say that, like her Blackness, Lee's marriage to Tom Fallows is an important filter through which she views Russian life. Given that American attitudes towards mixed marriages were still fairly conservative during the late 1970s, this detail is not insignificant. In attaching the backstory about her wedding and the pretext of the trip to the new introduction of the reissue, Lee separates a much longer history of slavery, rape, and sexual exploitation from the book's present. What emerges from this break is a contemporary narrative about an affluent African American woman sojourning in Soviet Russia with her white husband. In terms of temporality and methodology, this reframing of the narrative provides a more modern, progressive way to think about race and interracial desire.

Of course, the irony is that Lee's Blackness is *not* a significant feature of *Russian Journal*. As Susan Jacoby put it in her *New York Times* review, there is one "regrettable omission" to the book: "Miss Lee is a [B]lack American—a fact that even an alert reader might miss, because it is mentioned only once, in an oblique reference late in the book" (1981: 122). One might expect the logic of transnationalism to modify such a pronouncement, either positioning Lee as a tourist or a member of the diplomat community, or by making more of the fact that Lee is "American" as opposed to "African American," but here Jacoby's remarks point to the limits of the transnational, showing the fixity of national and racial designations for Black Americans when they are outside the United States. Of course, Jacoby is an American, so we have to consider her remarks within this context as it betrays the obsession Americans have with race. But notwithstanding her concern with Lee's racial identity, Jacoby rightfully acknowledges the longstanding presumption that Black writers must always write from an overtly, recognizable Black perspective and the attending racism of a literary marketplace that pigeonholes Black authors. Indeed, Jacoby is generous and perceptive enough to read Lee's omission as a "conscious decision not to use her race as one of the prisms for reflecting Russian life." This determination stems from an understanding that this "choice may have been motivated by an understandable fear that her book would be merchandised as an ethnic curio piece" (122).

---

[8] Lee acknowledges that her impressions of Russia are not objective or free from bias as they are filtered through her own subjectivity. In this way, *Russian Journal* is not just a work of travel writing but also a work of imagination and memoir. In the introduction to the 2006 paperback reissue, she discusses a trip she made to Russia with her daughter in 2005 and how she saw the ghost of her younger self on the street and saluted her, realizing that "what I had chronicled in *Russian Journal* was actually two extinct countries—Soviet Russia, and a territory of my own life as a very young adult, a time that has vanished as completely as if it had been erased from a map" (2006c: xiv). In the foreword of the 1981 edition she makes a similar point, offering: "If, as sometimes happens, the separate parts of *Russian Journal* combine in the imagination of the reader to give an impression of a broader scene, it is important to realize that this is still largely a personal landscape—my own and my husband's. The Russia of other sojourners might be quite different" (2006b: xvii).

Despite the fascinating implications of Jacoby's hypothesis (and its critical bearing on how we might approach Lee's work), Lee herself has challenged this reading, most recently from the distance of twenty-five years since *Russian Journal* was first published, offering a much more complex, transnational view of the racial, cultural, and political environment in which she wrote the book:

> Looking back now, I can only feel that, like everything in *Russian Journal*, it was not a conscious decision, but had to do with extreme youth. It is important to remember that I was swept away by my new experiences, and that because my skin is not dark, my ethnic background was not much of a social issue for the Russians I met. Except for an occasional facetious inquiry as to whether I was a Cuban comrade, my new friends and acquaintances made much more of the fact that I was Western, capitalist, and American.
>
> (Lee 2006c: xi–xii)[9]

Although Lee's response to a valid criticism of her work is somewhat of a cop-out, attributing a significant oversight like authorial racial identity to youth, the much more interesting part of her explanation troubles how we think about race in America.

In the simplest of terms, Lee supplants a binary view of race with a broader conception of the word. For a start, she challenges the ocular logic of racial legibility that assumes one can tell what another person's race is just by looking at them. But by acknowledging the fact that Black people come in all shades and hues and that some people who identify as Black have racially ambiguous features, Lee undermines the saliency of this cultural fiction. Secondly, she pushes past the narrow Black/white racial binary that tends to, regrettably, overdetermine any and all conversations about race in the United States. By mentioning that she was occasionally mistaken for a "Cuban comrade," Lee renders visible an often unseen, intermediary category that scholars working in race and ethnicity studies have termed the "racially in between"—a grouping that has historically consisted of certain immigrant, Indigenous, Latinx, Asian, and Indian peoples. What is more, she backgrounds a uniquely American/domestic preoccupation with racial identity to foreground international political concerns, so as to frame her book as a broader, transnational critique of the West/East, capitalist/communist, and American/Soviet divides that dominated political discourse during the Cold War. In this context, we should not underestimate the aesthetic and political significance of Lee's choice to downplay her Blackness. In a literary marketplace where the demand for what Jarrett has called "racial realism" has always driven the publishing and marketing decisions surrounding Black literary and cultural production, Lee's finessing of this standard should be viewed as a

---

[9] As Shaundra Myers has revealed, back in 1990, during a speech at the New York Public Library, Lee contradicted this statement, saying that she "consciously decided" not to mention her Blackness and that she "adopted this policy partly as a tease and partly with the quite serious idea that any book of the kind written by someone describing herself as a [B]lack American would be viewed by some myopic literary people as 'a [B]lack look at Russia'" (Lee 1991: 71). Also see Myers (2019: 53–54).

type of negotiation that enables her to engage in a kind of large-scale, socio-political critique that is seldom made available to Black writers—especially to Black women writers.[10]

This is precisely the kind of global critique that Lee gives us in the section of the book where she mentions in passing that she is African American. In the entry entitled, "Ibrahim," Lee introduces the eponymous subject of the chapter—a "young man in his late twenties, with a huge mass of frizzy hair, brown cheeks ... and the beautiful linear features of the saints in ancient Ethiopian church frescoes" (2006a [1981]: 147). In a self-referential manner, Lee writes: "Toward me he showed the absolute lack of interest with which many Africans greet American [B]lacks" (147). While this observation may seem like a throwaway line, in actuality, it precipitates a transnational critique of anti-Blackness and points to the limitations of the transnational as it illustrates the persistence of national affiliation (over other kinds) and the dangerous consequences of the Cold War political chess games that the Soviet Union played with its satellite states and adversaries. We learn that Ibrahim is a student at Patrice Lumumba University (which now goes by its original name of the Peoples' Friendship University of Russia), an institution in southwest Moscow named after the African nationalist and first prime minister of the Democratic Republic of the Congo, who appealed to the Soviet Union for assistance in suppressing the Belgian-backed Katangese revolt after the United States and the United Nations failed to help and was later assassinated by Katangese officials in 1961 (Gerard and Kuklick 2015).

As Lee explains, the university was created to educate "'Third World' students in advanced technology and Communist ideology," but the education that it gives its African students is a lesson in racism and the repercussions of Cold War antagonisms (2006a [1981]: 147). When Lee asks Ibrahim how he likes the Soviet Union, he laughs and says:

> It would take me a long time really to answer that question. Most of my African classmates hate it here because of the climate, because we live here under miserable conditions, and because the Russian *narod*, the masses, call us [B]lack devils and spit at us in the street. One African hated it here so much that he went home and wrote a book called *Seven Years in Prison*. I've suffered here, but that doesn't concern me now. What I'm most full of worry and bitterness about is my own political situation.
>
> (147)

Of course, the political situation that Ibrahim is in is that he is not really Ethiopian at all but Eritrean, a crucial distinction. At the time of the book's writing, Eritrea was engaged in a conflict with Ethiopia, as Eritrean separatists—supported by the United States— fought to break away from Ethiopian rule. Ibrahim arrived in Moscow when the Soviets were still supporting Eritrea, but when the U.S.S.R. switched sides and started backing

---

[10] "Racial realism" refers to literature created to offer authentic accounts of Black experience to offset or counter anti-Blackness and satisfy white curiosity about Black life: see Jarrett (2007).

Ethiopia, Ibrahim was no longer welcome in Moscow. Ibrahim's story is important because it illustrates that anti-Black racism is a problem in Russia too and that the notion of African nationality is fraught with many problems surrounding cultural identity, political allegiances, and alliances. It also troubles our tendency to think of political conflicts in terms of "us" versus "them" or the "domestic" and the "foreign" as the Cold War was not just a dispute between two superpowers—the United States and the U.S.S.R.—but an international conflict that involved many other nations as well.

What is more, Lee's interaction with him, albeit brief, invites us to consider how nationality beats out other forms of identification and affiliation such as race, global citizenship, or diasporic Blackness. Indeed, in some ways, this exchange registers a moment of transnational identification and affiliation gone awry. What I mean is that Ibrahim and Lee could have acknowledged their kinship as members of the international/global community or as Black people with origins in Africa and a shared history of slavery and oppression. In other words, they could have bonded over their shared identifications and mutual affiliations. But regrettably, this mutual recognition does not happen. As Lee indicates, Ibrahim is not remotely interested in her because he can only see her through the lens of nationality. As far as he is concerned, Lee is first and foremost an African American. She is not his fellow traveler or his "sister." This attitude reinforces a nationalist paradigm that compels us to compare their different political situations. Ibrahim's situation is as Lee describes it, "precarious and dangerous," whereas her situation—as a light-skinned, affluent African American woman married to an affluent white American man—is secure and privileged. While Lee does not explicitly make this comparison, it is implicitly a part of the chapter's subtext. Taking a broader view, we would do well to also weigh her situation against the political situation facing most African Americans in the United States in the 1970s, a period marked by white flight in urban centers, divestment in Black communities, deindustrialization, stagnating wages, rising crime, gang violence, an intensifying War on Drugs, race riots, and police brutality. This missing domestic backdrop offsets Lee's foregrounding of the international stage.

Lee's relationship to Ibrahim prompts another key consideration and that is the subject of her own racial identity. In the 2006 introduction to *Russian Journal*, Lee candidly discusses how she racially identifies, and, in the process, establishes a crucial link between her first book and her second, *Sarah Phillips*, making a compelling argument for why they should be read in tandem. In a lengthy passage worth quoting in full, Lee writes:

> My complicated background—which includes West African, Danish, English, Irish, and Native American blood—as well as my suburban middle-class family, who sent me to integrated schools in the days of the civil rights struggle, was something that, in my twenties, I had yet to sort out for myself. I felt then, and I think rightly, that any approach to my own identity was so momentous as to require another book in itself—and it is no coincidence that in my Lenin Library hours, when I was not writing about my Russian friends or refreshing myself with "A Sportsman's Sketches," I was already jotting down descriptive passages about my childhood in Philadelphia

and experimenting with plots for the autobiographical short stories that would be published first in *The New Yorker* and then collected as chapters in the novel *Sarah Phillips*.... So *Sarah Phillips*—conceived at the same time—represents the background not expressed in *Russian Journal*.

(2006c: xii)

Lee here posits a more fluid conception of race, acknowledging that it is possible to both identify as Black/African American and claim a mixed-race ancestry. In fact, we might say that she was at the forefront of what would become by the 1980s the widely accepted view, in academic circles at least, that race is socially constructed. According to this view, then, race is not a binary construct as much as it is a multifaceted and malleable system that people negotiate. In this way, racial identity is more about how we negotiate existing rubrics of identification than it is about fitting into arbitrary racial categories. Adding greater complexity to her comments about race, Lee also addresses the fraught issue of class. In recognizing her class privilege, she nuances our view of Blackness, owning up to the fact that her particular Black experience was not, and remains not, the norm for most African Americans in the United States, who continue to be disproportionately poor, sick, under-employed or unemployed because of structural racism and disparities in our institutions. If *Russian Journal* leaves readers feeling unsatisfied about its author's personal perceptions and family history, then *Sarah Phillips* fills in these gaps and omissions.

Sarah Phillips

Like *Russian Journal*, the chapters that comprise *Sarah Phillips* were also first published in *The New Yorker*, and in this way, they too challenge traditional notions about readership, genre, and subject matter in African American literature. Of course, it goes without saying (but I'm saying it anyway) that *The New Yorker* was then, as it is now, a white, upper-middle-brow magazine. As Shaundra Myers has observed, when the magazine hired Lee in 1979, she was "only its third [B]lack regular staff writer" (2019: 47), and as an up-and-coming author, she had to have viewed the opportunity to be published in *The New Yorker* as "an invitation to join an elite group of writers, among them John Cheever, John Updike, [James] Baldwin, [Jamaica] Kincaid, and Ann Beattie" (54). In its glossy pages, a mostly white, upper-middle-class, left-of-center readership found content that was in line with their cultural, social, economic, and political affiliations and preoccupations. For the most part, the fiction featured in the magazine reflected white life, its institutions and values, focusing on themes like internal alienation and domestic turmoil (marital conflict and infidelity) and was set in various villages in New England. If African American literature has historically been defined as literature written by, for, and about Black people, featuring themes of oppression, racial solidarity, and resistance, then it would appear that *Sarah Phillips*, with its focus on the cloistered world of the

Black bourgeoisie and their suburban prosperity, has more in common with the world of *The New Yorker* than with a literary tradition obsessed with slavery and historical trauma.

The very plot of *Sarah Phillips* rejects this standard. Set in the 1960s and '70s, the book traces its narrator and protagonist's coming of age in a middle-class African American family in suburban Philadelphia, Pennsylvania. The daughter of a well-respected Baptist minister father and a schoolteacher mother, Sarah (Lee's alter ego) is the privileged beneficiary of her parent's hard-won fight for civil rights. As a card-carrying member of the "post-soul generation" (the group of African Americans who grew up in the aftermath of the Civil Rights movement), Sarah embodies the cultural and racial fluidity and sense of alienation from the protest and resistance politics that characterized her parents' Black experience. Like her white counterparts, Sarah attends exclusive private schools and summer camps, eventually graduating from Harvard and making the obligatory rite-of-passage trip to Europe after college.

The portrait that emerges across the novel is one of a privileged African American girl, desperately trying to make sense of her identity, while also feeling ambivalent about her familial and racial history. Unconventionally, the novel begins where it ends, in 1974, in the wake of her father's death, when Sarah is twenty-one, and spending a year in Switzerland to study literature in Lausanne. But in actuality, she is trying to distract herself from the grief she feels over the loss of her dad and to sever ties with her family and past. In this way, the novel opens up the possibility of theorizing Black experience and racial feeling beyond the usual manifestations of anger and rage. Decoupling Blackness from these emotions produces new and different pathways for comprehending how contemporary narratives of Black life engage with the legacies of the slave past and what that past signifies in the present. Of course, Sarah's privilege complicates any discussion of how she *should* relate to that history. Because her affluence affords her greater social mobility, she can adopt a more fluid transnational subject position that enables her to reimagine, at least initially, her physical and emotional proximity to a history of slavery the reality of ongoing racial oppression. As the chapters in between the first and the last proceed chronologically, we not only witness Sarah's transition from childhood to young adulthood, but we also gain greater awareness of how she was socialized and how that might necessitate a more elastic account of what it meant to be African American then and what it means now and in relationship to African American literature.

A key scene from the novel's opening chapter, entitled "In France," vividly illustrates Sarah's ambivalence about her family, the racial history she has inherited, and how she identifies with that past. While having lunch with her French boyfriend, Henri Durier, at the Cercle d'Or near Rouen, Sarah has a racist encounter with her lover. Three months into their relationship, the mutual fascination with each other having waned, Henry takes several jabs at Sarah. He grabs her ponytail, calls her a "savage from the shores of the Mississippi!" and then proceeds to tell what he describes as "a very American tale" about her pedigree (1993 [1984]: 11). He says that she is the offspring of a half-Jewish, half-Irish mother and a monkey father. He goes on to say: "one day this *Irlandaise* was walking through the jungle near New Orleans, when she was raped by a jazz musician as big and [B]lack as King Kong, with sexual equipment to match. And from this agreeable encounter was born our little Sarah, *notre Négresse pasteurisée*" (11). Immediately after making these appallingly racist remarks, Henry eagerly searches Sarah's face for proof of injury, "as if he were waiting for a reward" (11). After a brief silence, Sarah calls him "stupid" and walks off to the women's restroom. Once inside, she sits down on the toilet lid and crouches into the fetal position, "breathing soberly and carefully" as she tries to "control the blood pounding in my head" (12).

For most of the novel's critics, this scene reads as an inevitable racial confrontation, one in which Sarah is more of a victim of her own racial naïveté than she is a victim of her boyfriend's racism. After all, only a silly child would think that she could "cast off kin and convention in a foreign tongue" and discard her Blackness by running away to Europe (4). That she fails to get properly angry, in critics' minds, and stand up for herself seems to be sufficient proof of her passivity and complicity in bringing about her own racial alienation and victimization. In her review, Mary Helen Washington asks, "Why isn't Sarah angry at this insult? Why does the narrator offer intellectual explanations and refuse to identify her feelings?" (1985: 3). W. Lawrence Hogue reads Sarah as a type of failed modernist heroine, someone who neglects "to realize that coming to grips with her existential freedom means not repressing, but confronting and accepting one's past" (1994: 88). Similarly, Adrienne McCormick has argued that the scene illustrates Sarah's "inability to interpret how her class, gender, and race intersect in her subjugation" (2004: 809) and that although she is "not angered by Henri's racism, his remarks make Sarah realize she must return to the States" (816). Despite their different concerns, what all of these critics seem to agree on is that Sarah's inaction or lack of knowledge is a kind of resignation or failure, one in which the real tragedy of the situation is that she does not seem to resist or challenge the racial status quo.[11]

But rather than find fault with Sarah, what if we shifted the blame to critics who have mostly failed to properly read and understand the scene? That Sarah's retreat into the murky recesses of her mind results in internal intellectualizing rather than something more external, proactive, and quantifiable has compelled many critics to argue that Sarah suffers from the debilitating effects of racial alienation and that her real problem is that she does not seem to understand her place in racial history. But what if they are wrong? What if the real failure lies in critics' inability to approach the scene with a wider range of emotional expression? Although Sarah "*is* angry," as Aida Levy-Hussen has rightfully observed (2016: 94), challenging the dominant critical view, I am much more

---

[11] Other critics depart from this view, offering more reparative readings that endow Sarah/the novel with greater complexity and/or agency. See Murray's "The Time of Breach" (2010) where he argues that Lee "crafts the novel as a means to interrogate the premise that the black bourgeoisie's interests are synonymous with those of the working poor" and contends that this "warrants critical analysis rather than moral indignation"—an obvious allusion to Mary Helen Washington's and Valerie Smith's critiques of the novel (13); Williams's "Black American Girls" (2015), where she argues that "the refusal of closure in *Sarah Phillips* enables Sarah to maintain a mobile subjectivity whose liberation hangs in the balance" (248); and Ohito and Khoja-Moolji (2016) on Sarah's subversive reclaiming of an objectified sexuality and her sexual pleasure as a means beyond victimization.

interested in asking the basic question of *why do Black women always have to be angry?* And why does that anger have to conform to a certain stereotype about Black women being confrontational and ill-tempered in order to be legible?

Levy-Hussen has pried open new ways of reading the novel, asking: "Might we approach *Sarah Phillips*, not as a novella about the emotional bereftness that attends racial alienation, but as a text that boldly insists upon an index other than intergenerational trauma for measuring contemporary [B]lack experiences of racial formation and discrimination?" (95). I see my argument as building on her work in that I am offering in-betweenness and negotiation as alternative metrics by which we can assess twentieth- and twenty-first-century Black experience. It is far too reductive and pathologizing to restrict contemporary conversations about Black subjectivity to intergenerational trauma. While the legacies of slavery continue to affect the lives of African Americans today, not all African Americans experience this evenly or with the same intensity due to differences in socio-economic status and mobility. And neither should we reify anger and rage are the primary affective lenses through which to view Black racialized experience. (Doing so glorifies resistance to the white power structure as if this were the only way to be properly Black.) More than anything, what Sarah feels is deep ambivalence about her familial and racial heritage. She also feels tremendous grief about her father's sudden death—a grief that she cannot really access until Henri's racist joke forces her to acknowledge it. Ultimately, any failure that we might be tempted to attribute to Sarah (or to Lee, for that matter) really deserves to be placed on critics who have failed to endow Sarah with greater self-awareness, complexity, and humanity.

In fact, if for most critics Sarah's reaction to Henri's racist joke illustrates her ignorance about and estrangement from her racial history, I would argue that it actually reflects her sudden comprehension of where she stands in relationship to that past. On this point, Sarah's bathroom epiphany is key. In her internal dialogue, she discloses that she is not upset by the racism of what Henri had said, as "[n]asty remarks about race and class were part of our special brand of humor" (1993 [1984]: 12). But she acknowledges that his stupid joke had done something far worse than hurt her: "it had somehow—perhaps in its unexpected extravagance—illuminated for me with blinding clarity the hopeless presumption of trying to discard my portion of America." Sarah realizes that the joke "had summed me up with weird accuracy" and that she felt "furious and betrayed by the intensity of nameless emotion it had called forth in me" (12).

This "nameless emotion" is in a word, grief. Henri's horrifyingly racist joke pierces Sarah's frozen grief about her father's death, which, in turn, forces her to finally acknowledge her sadness and accept her familial and racial inheritance. In this way, her father functions as a kind of emotional catalyst that triggers a sober realization about the futility of trying to outrun history and the limits of the transnational—that is, the ways in which nationalist and racial associations continue to follow the Black subject beyond the borders of the United States. As is true of real life, reckoning with the past does not always result in catharsis, a more coherent self, or decisive action. Sarah's sudden recognition of her grief, or what Sianne Ngai would call her "ugly feelings," does not result in any tangible net gain; rather, it is followed by what Ngai has described as a state of "obstructed agency" or passivity (2005: 3). Almost as if to wake herself up from a stupor, Sarah gently bites herself on the knee, stands up, and brushes her hair before returning to her friends. There is no confrontation with Henri. She doesn't give him a piece of her mind in the belligerent manner we might stereotypically expect from a Black woman. In fact, Sarah doesn't say anything. Instead, she withdraws inward and muses about the "slanting sunlight" and the "mysterious empty quality" of the village, comparing it to "Edward Hopper's paintings" and "think[ing] of loss" (1993 [1984]: 13). To Sarah's surprise, Henri apologizes, but he doesn't show any remorse or sincerity. As Lee puts it, he somehow manages to turn "'I'm sorry' into another form of bullying," admonishing Sarah to "Don't sulk" (13).

In the end, there is no satisfying resolution or anything in the way of "affective restorative justice." In fact, later that night, Sarah and Henri even have sex. After they finish, Sarah falls asleep and has a dream that she is wrestling with one of the old, Black Philadelphia churchwomen who used to babysit her. It is with this image in mind that she comes to the conclusion that her days in France are numbered and she resolves to go back home. But before going back to sleep she says to herself: "I can stay here longer, but I have to leave by spring" (15). While this final statement might read like a capitulation for some critics, I would argue that it is an act of agency and autonomous decision-making. Instead of going home with her proverbial tail tucked in between her legs, Sarah refuses to give Henri the satisfaction of thinking that he wounded her enough to make her run away. Defiantly, she decides to leave on her own terms. That she decides to stay until the spring is not a form of back-peddling as much as it is her striking the middle ground between staying indefinitely and leaving right away. This decision is Sarah's way of adopting the in-between position and negotiating the details of her departure from a real and imagined Europe that provided a much-desired buffer between her and her family. In this manner, she bargains with herself that she can stay a little longer before making the "complicated return" to America (15).

With its focus on in-betweenness and negotiation, then, *Sarah Phillips*—like much of Lee's writing to a greater extent—provides new ways of thinking about race, interracial desire, and African American literature. By disrupting the foundational binary opposition upon which so much of African American literature is structured, Lee transforms our ideas about "who" and "what" African American literature must depict, "where" it must take place, and questions "why" anger and rage must always be the indices by which we measure the literature's aesthetic, affective, and political value. In looking to Europe as a means of moving beyond the Black/white racial binary (and to a larger extent the limiting expectations of what African American literature in the twentieth century does), Lee does not find an idealized loophole of racial retreat. But vis-à-vis the transnational, she finds a way to add greater elasticity to how we view race, so as to complicate and trouble the uncomplicated assumptions that we often have about identification, racial affect, and Black literary and cultural production. What emerges from her shift away from the American scene is a new kind of consciousness, a modality of being and expression that permits for greater negotiation of how we relate to the racial past and the present of racial oppression. In terms of methodology, this geographical and conceptual shift also opens up new possibilities for how we organize and interpret texts in African American literary studies.

It is high past time for us to discard our narrow and stereotypical ideas about what constitutes African American literature. As so many African American writers and critics have illustrated in their work, there is no singular Black experience. Implicit in much of twentieth-century African American literature, like *Russian Journal* and *Sarah Phillips*, is a fundamental understanding that Blackness is fluid, dynamic, and that it is as diverse as the people who identify as such. That said, we need a new African American literary studies—one with new vocabularies, new rubrics, and new methodologies for assessing the aesthetic and political value of an ever-changing and evolving literary tradition. Most urgently for me, we need an African American literary studies that is big enough to make room for alternative portraits of Blackness and that can meditate on interracial desire, especially between a Black woman and a white man, beyond the historical context of slavery and outside the discourses of victimization and sexual exploitation. For inspiration, we might look to contemporary television. Long before Shonda Rhimes gave us Olivia Pope in *Scandal* and Annalise Keating in *How To Get Away with Murder*, Andrea Lee gave us herself.

References

Fishkin, Shelley Fisher. 2005. "Crossroads of Cultures: The Transnational Turn in American Studies—Presidential Address to the American Studies Association," *American Quarterly* 57.1 (March): 17–57.

Foster, Frances Smith and Kim D. Green. 2013. "Ports of Call, Pulpits of Consultation: Rethinking the Origins of African American Literature," in Gene Andrew Jarrett, ed., *A Companion to African American Literature* (Chichester, U.K.: Wiley-Blackwell), 45–58.

Gerard, Emmanuel and Bruce Kuklick. 2015. *Death in the Congo: Murdering Patrice Lumumba* (Cambridge, MA: Harvard University Press).

Hogue, Lawrence W. 1994. "The Limits of Modernity: Andrea Lee's Sarah Phillips," *MELUS* 19.4 (Winter): 75–90.

Jacoby, Susan. 1981. "One Year in Moscow," *The New York Times*, 25 October, www.nytimes.com/1981/10/25/books/one-year-in-moscow.html, accessed November 4, 2021.

Jarrett, Gene Andrew. 2011. "African-American Literature Lives On, Even as Black Politics Expire," *The Chronicle of Higher Education*, 27 March, www.chronicle.com/article/African-American-Literature/126867, accessed February 17, 2022.

Jarrett, Gene Andrew. 2007. *Deans and Truants: Race and Realism in African American Literature* (Philadelphia, PA: University of Pennsylvania Press).

Lee, Andrea. 1991. "Double Lives," in William Zinsser, ed., *They Went: The Art and Craft of Travel Writing* (Boston, MA: Houghton Mifflin Co.), 55–74.

Lee, Andrea. 2006a [1981]. *Russian Journal* (New York, NY: Random House).

Lee, Andrea. 2006b. "Foreword," in *Russian Journal* (New York, NY: Random House), xv–xvii.

Lee, Andrea. 2006c. "Introduction," in *Russian Journal* (New York, NY: Random House), ix–xiv.

Lee, Andrea. 1993 [1984]. *Sarah Phillips* (Lebanon, NH: Northeastern University Press).

Levy-Hussen, Aida. 2016. *How to Read African American Literature: Post-Civil Rights Fiction and the Task of Interpretation* (New York: New York University Press).

McCormick, Adrienne. 2004. "Is This Resistance? African American Postmodernism in 'Sarah Phillips,'" *Callaloo* 27.3 (Summer): 808–828.

McDowell, Deborah E. 1995. *"The Changing Same": Black Women's Literature, Criticism, and Theory* (Bloomington, IN: Indiana University Press).

Murray, Rolland. 2010. "The Time of Breach: Class Division and the Contemporary African American Novel," *NOVEL: A Forum on Fiction* 43.1 (Spring): 11–17.

Myers, Shaundra. 2019. "Black Anaesthetics: *The New Yorker* and Andrea Lee's *Russian Journal*," *American Literary History* 31.1 (January): 47–73.

Ngai, Sianne. 2005. *Ugly Feelings* (Cambridge, MA: Harvard University Press).

Ohito, Esther O. and Shenila Khoja-Moolji. 2016. "Reparative Readings: Re-Claiming Black Feminized Bodies as Sites of Somatic Pleasures and Possibilities," *Gender and Education* 30.3 (August): 277–294.

Osnos, Peter. 1981. "Blue Jeans in Red Square: An American in Moscow." Review of *Russian Journal*, by Andrea Lee," *Washington Post*, 25 October, 10.

Smith, Valerie. 1993. "Foreword," in Andrea Lee, *Sarah Phillips* (Lebanon, NH: Northeastern University Press), ix–xxiv.

Treisman, Deborah. 2019. "Andrea Lee on Cross-Cultural Encounters," *The New Yorker*, 3 June, www.newyorker.com/books/this-week-in-fiction/andrea-lee-06-10-19, accessed February 17, 2022.

Washington, Mary Helen. 1985. "Young, Gifted, and Black." Review of Sarah Phillips, by Andrea Lee," *Women's Review of Books* 2.6 (March): 3–4.

Williams, Jennifer D. 2015. "Black American Girls in Paris: Sex, Race, and Cosmopolitanism in Andrea Lee's *Sarah Phillips* and Shay Youngblood's *Black Girl in Paris*," *Contemporary Women's Writing* 9.2 (July): 238–256.

Williams, Jennifer D. 2017. "An Interesting Woman: A Conversation with Andrea Lee," *Meridians: Feminism, Race, Transnationalism* 15.2: 507–517.

Williams, Raymond and Michael Orrom. 1954. *Preface to Film* (London, U.K.: Film Drama).

CHAPTER 15

WHERE BORDER MEETS NARRATIVE, WHERE BODY MEETS WORD

The Animality of Border Subjectivity

BERNADINE HERNÁNDEZ

THE border narrative is a genre of literature that is not foreign to Chicanx identity. Chicanx writers Tomás Rivera, Rolando Hinojosa, Gloria Anzaldúa, and Ana Castillo all give us nuanced border narratives that move among spaces, bodies, identities, and customs. In her foundational work *Borderlands/La Frontera: The New Mestiza*, Chicana scholar Gloria Anzaldúa states, "The US–Mexican border es una herida abierta where the Third World grates against the first and bleeds. And before a scab forms it hemorrhages again, the lifeblood of two worlds merging to form a third country—a border culture" (Anzaldúa 1987: 3). This border culture maps on to the border text itself through multiple narrative forms. This "open wound" allows for profuse bleeding of different narrative and literary strategies in the border text. Whether it is fragmented characterization, non-linear plotlines, stream of consciousness language, or magical realist literary elements, the border narrative looks like an entropic compilation of unrelated literary landscapes.

Within the US–Mexico context, the actual border, or as Anzaldúa deems it, *la frontera*, is a 1954-mile international border separating Mexico and the United States. It extends from the Pacific Ocean to the west of the Gulf of Mexico and traverses vastly different terrains. Formed in 1848 and 1853 after the Treaty of Guadalupe Hidalgo and the Gadsden Purchase were signed at the end of the Mexican–American War, the southern border of the United States has been a site of contestation, violence, celebration, migration, and militarization. It is a space where two worlds collide and create transnational encounters as well as a borderlands identity that migrates with bodies all over the world. José Saldívar reminds us that the US-Mexico border is a cultural space that should never be viewed as a static and homogenous phenomenon (Saldívar 1997: 20). In his study, he critically interrogates how US cultural production is increasingly becoming a form of border narrative. This argument, while bold, is attempting to think about how many new works in literature, music, and the arts are "hybridized" forms of their original conventional form. Along with this, Saldívar links border narrative and art with a reframing of cosmopolitanism that cultural theorists take up in their own work. The border matters for Saldívar. But as Mary Pat Brady warns us, the border has become a focal point for a variety of "theoretical labors" that despatializes and universalizes its material space (Brady 2000). Brady explains that the "border" is a term that describes a "personality disorder ("borderline"), the effect of navigating multiple subjectivities, the liminal space between binary categories, or the potential complexities of relationships where difference is central to the narrative of those relationships" (2000: 172).

Borderlands scholarship is defined as the historical and theoretical work that lies at the interstices between empires and nations. In 1921, Herbert Eugene Bolton coined the phrase "Spanish Borderlands" (Bolton 1996). Bolton's mission was huge: to forge a history of the United States to highlight the Spanish "origins of territories only later claimed by the United States" (Hernández 2011). However, as Kelly Lyttle Hernandez later states, "Bolton did little to alter the prevailing architecture of American history ... it would take future generations of borderlands scholars to expand Bolton's critique of the "original thirteen colonies" theory of U.S. history (2011: 325). With the rise of social history and cultural studies, Borderland Studies has become enriched with the histories of contested power relations, cultural exchanges, processes of racialization, and resistance to differential power relations.[1] There are two arguments that have shaped Borderlands Studies. One has "wanted to imagine or to create the nation-state as a culturally homogeneous unit [that has] accordingly sought to eradicate local identities and to erase or to subordinate regional loyalties in the name of a greater motherland" (Guitiérrez and Young 2010: 29). The other camp of scholars has

> been more realistic about the ways in which local understandings of personhood and seemingly primordial notions of belonging resist change [and] have focused their studies on the ways in which state borders and boundaries fail—how they fail to contain, to constrain, to delimit, or to fully define how humans live their lives.
>
> (2010: 362)

Anzaldúa conceptualized "the borderlands" as a metaphor that marks the body through different genders, sexualities, and nations. *Borderlands/La Frontera* was first published in 1987 and embodies the borderlands through the different forms it utilizes and the new consciousness that replaces the mind/body split of Western thought. Her creation of a new *mestiza* consciousness works to dislodge nation-state boundaries but is not without problems. Josie Saldaña Portillo observes that while the term *mestiza* claims to jointly

---

[1] For a historiography of borderlands scholarship, see Aron (2004), Gutiérrez and Young (2010), Johnson and Graybill (2010), Truett and Young (2004), Weber (2000), Weber (1986), and Weber (2005).

synthesize Spanish and Indigenous cultures, more often than not "the erasure of the indigenous is interior to the logic of mestizaje" (Saldaña-Portillo 2001: 407). Yet at the same time, "Indian identity ... does not disappear with mestizaje. Rather, mestizaje depends on it for its self-definition" (2001: 409). This essay riffs off of Anzaldúa and thinks of the borderlands as something violent yet unfixed. For the purposes of this chapter, the borderlands is not only a geopolitical space from Northern California to Colorado down to Houston, Texas, but also an ideological construction of the racialization of people who live and thrive in this place.

How can we reconcile the metaphorzing of the border with the material realities of the border in narrative form? Where do border narratives open up a space for alternative stories that take us beyond words? While the border narrative is well established in American literary history, this chapter is most concerned with where this literary tradition has taken us in to the contemporary moment. What does the written border narrative open for us? What aesthetics of border narrative allows for a continuation of border crossing through the ephemera of movement and performance? This chapter thus makes multiple moves. First, it maps out the material and metaphoric histories of the border in relation to gender and sexuality. Second, it examines the history and aesthetics of Chicanx literary border narratives. Finally, the chapter examines and interrogates what the written border narrative offers Chicanx performers from the border region and the alternative narratives enabled by bodies in performance art. Where the written border narrative focuses on the fragmented subjectivity of the marginal border-crosser and their journeys, Chicanx performance art has built on this fragmented subjectivity and pushed it beyond the boundaries of the human.

Gloría Anzaldúa's *Borderlands/La Frontera: The New Mestiza* and Ana Castillo's *Give It To Me* represent a subset of American literature, the border narrative, which can be taken up in other cultural forms, such as performance art. Performance artists such as Naomi Rincón Gallardo, Xandra Ibarra, also known as La Chica Boom, and Rafael Esparza, all utilize the border narrative aesthetics in their works and push against it to ask "Where is border subjectivity?" These three Latinx performance artists extend the border narrative to include the body as text, while connecting to a lineage that traces back to the streets of East Los Angeles in the 1960s with a dynamic history connected in part to civil rights activism and political upheaval among Chicanos and, by extension, Latinx communities, over issues related to inequality and matters of race, gender, class, education, and the Vietnam War. Leticia Alvarado reminds us that Chicanx performance artists illuminate the limits of inclusion and respectability, which ultimately highlights alternatives to border-crossing narratives (Alvardo 2018: 3). The border narrative is one of the first cultural forms we see that links hybridity, nation, and movement together, as well as "circulations, resistances, and negotiations" (Saldívar 1997: 3). The goal of this chapter is to think about how these negotiations and movements are mapped on to bodies in Latinx performance art that considers the species border among animal, thing, and human. The "brownness" of the Latinx performer or even the border narrative subject is evoked in the liminality of their subjectivity. José Esteban Muñoz grounds brownness in his oeuvre of writing, suggesting that "queerness is on the horizon, forward dawning and not-yet-here .... Brownness is already here. Brownness is vast, present, and vital" (Muñoz 2020: xii). Brownness for Muñoz chronicles a certain ethics of the self that is utilized and deployed by Latinx subjects who don't feel quite right within the protocols of normative affect and comportment. Naomi Rincón Gallardo, Xandra Ibarra, and Rafael Esparza all have taken up the marginality of the "human" and focused on the subhuman, the animal, and/or the object through "brownness." This chapter focuses on the subhuman in relation to the Chicanx body on the border and how the enunciation of it as tied to the animal species marks a blurring of lines between animal species being and the human Anthropocene. The performance artists I examine in this chapter explode traditional border narratives with their bodies and tell a story of what is next for the Chicanx subject, imagining a new future of possibility.

The Gendered and Sexual History of the Borderlands

If we are going to define the US–Mexico border, we must first look at how it became a named space in the first place. During the mid-nineteenth century, many Anglo-Americans coveted the natural landscape of the Mexican northwest. In 1845, President James Polk (1845–1849) annexed Texas for the United States after Texans successfully fought a war for independence in 1836. President Polk pressed for more territory through the American discourse of "Manifest Destiny"; the doctrine of expansion throughout the Americas was both justified, inevitable, and a god-given right of Anglo settlers. In 1846, Polk sent troops into Mexico to dispute territory in Northern Mexico and by 1848, United States forces occupied Mexico City and declared victory in the US–Mexico War of 1846–1848 (Hernández 2010: 21). Mexico was forced to cede most of its northern territory and the new US–Mexico border was drawn along the Rio Grande between the Gulf of Mexico and El Paso, Texas and pushed west across the deserts and mountains to the Pacific Ocean (22). The Treaty of Guadalupe Hidalgo of 1848 was the beginning of the violence that has haunted the US–Mexico border for decades, a space of rich culture and tradition yet influenced by this history of division.

The border, immigration policy, race, gender, and sexuality all combined in explosive ways immediately when the US–Mexico border was created. On July 12, 1891, "the Bureau of Immigration began operation in the Department of the Treasury, twenty-four border inspection stations were set up, and a system of medical inspection was implemented" (Luibhéid 2002: 8–9). This selective immigration process modified the Immigration Act of 1882, which "banned all lunatics, idiots, convicts, and those liable to become public charges, and those suffering from contagious disease."[2] This act defined

---

[2] Immigration Act of 1882, 47th Congress, 1st session (18 *Stat.* 477), March 3, 1875. See also Hernández (2010) and Luibhéid (2002).

the concept of deportation and excluded the sexually aberrant, such as persons with charges against them for adultery, bigamy, rape, sodomy, and polygamy. The earliest immigration laws were concerned with banning immigration from Asia and curbing immigration from eastern and southern Europe, as well as denying entry to "prostitutes, illiterates, criminals, contract laborers, unaccompanied children, idiots, epileptics, the insane, paupers, the diseased and defective, alcoholics, beggars, polygamists, [and] anarchists," among others (Hernández 2010: 27).

The Page Act of 1875 thus foreshadowed the next 100 years of immigration law and beyond by solidifying the interchangeability between xenophobic national projects and the sexuality of women of color. Passed in 1875, the Page Act, which prohibited the first-time entry of convicts, contract laborers, and Asian women coming to work in prostitution, targeted all Asian women "even when other women of other nationalities were significantly involved in prostitution work too," according to Eithne Luibhéid (2002: 31). The threat to white supremacy, the heteronormative family, and respectable white femininity intersected with the ways that race and sex/sexuality influenced immigration law; however, Mexican women were not viewed as being at the forefront of the threat at first. While prostitutes have always been excluded from entering the United States based on their non-normative sexuality, it was at the turn of the century and through Progressive Era politics that the sexual racialization of Mexican women living on the border became tied to who they were *not*: proper, white, feminized victims of male sexual exploitation.

The Page Act foreshadowed the Immigration Act of 1903,[3] which continued to solidify the bridge between morals and immigration by prohibiting immigrant women and girls from engaging in prostitution and stipulating that anyone who kept or supported prostitutes faced felony charges. The act explicitly referenced sex workers; if found guilty, the defendant faced felony charges, between one and five years in jail, and a fine not exceeding 5,000 dollars.[4] When looking at the evolution of immigration law in relation to race, gender, sex, and surveillance, it becomes clear that the United States was attempting to mask how it associated foreigners with the cleansing of a nation. Four years later, the Immigration Act of 1907 strengthened these restrictions and required all immigrants entering the United States to pass through an official port of entry, submit themselves to inspection, and receive official authorization.

Conflating the voluntary practice of prostitution (or any reason for the voluntary entry of sex work, i.e. single parenthood, divorce, abandonment) with the involuntary sex trafficking of moral white women and girls, the Mann Act in 1910 made it a crime to

---

[3] This chapter cannot possibly contend with all the nuances of Asian female sexuality (particularly Chinese and Japanese) and the interchangeability of xenophobic national projects and the sexuality of Mexican and Asian women. Without going into great detail, the intersection of patriarchy (family, social, and government structures) with American capitalism and racism enunciate the ways in which Asian female migrants and Mexican female migrants become part of an overarching structure to pathologize them outside of proper white femininity. For more on Chinese and Japanese women and their sexuality as tied to American Empire, please see Young (1986), Hirata (1979), and Glenn (1986).

[4] Ch. 1012, section 3, 32 Stat. 1213, 1214 (1903).

"transport women and girls across international and interstate lines to prostitute them, to have sex with them, or to cohabitate with them" (Delgado 2012: 177). Not until 1924 with the National Origins Act did Mexican migrants become viewed by nativists as racially inferior and undesired, and by the beginning of the 1930s Border Patrol began policing Mexicans nationally (Hernández 2010: 63). On May 28, 1924, the US Border Patrol was officially established.

Meanwhile, the conflation of mental health pathology and sexuality began in 1917, when "constitutional psychotic inferiors," including those with "abnormal sexual instincts," became excludable.[5] However, the passage of the 1952 McCarran–Walter Act was originally supposed to have a clause that stated, "Classes of mental defectives [who are excludable] should be enlarged to include homosexuals and other sex perverts"[6] but the final wording of the McCarran–Walter Act did not explicitly mention homosexuals but instead became rolled up in the clause that barred entry by "psychopathic personalities."[7] In 1965, lesbian and gay exclusion was reinterpreted under a provision barring entry by "sexual deviants" (Luibhéid 2002: 78). The inextricable links between the border, racialization, migration, gender, and sexuality is historically apparent in the policies and laws at the border.

Traditional border narratives examine mobility and migration at the turn of the twentieth century while mixing form and genre in order to speak to the consciousness of living between two spaces but also the gendered nature of migration. After the Immigration Act of 1917 was passed, immigration was restricted rather than merely regulated, marking a turn towards nativism. During the Mexican Revolution, which forced many Mexicans to migrate, there were more than 1 million border crossings. By 1942, the Bracero Program had been rolled out to meet the demand for manual labor in the United States as a result of the Second World War and the economic situation in Mexico. Male farmworkers were allowed to give their labor to the United States but were not allowed to apply for citizenship. These laws and policies changed how the material relations of the border inform the border narrative.

The Narrative of Borders

The fissures among these histories, movements, and subjectivities are central to border narratives of the Chicana/o movement. The literary border narrative stages and represents the contested zones that we see reflected in immigration history. The long history of immigration policy is reflected in the literary genre of the border narrative. Whether by setting the narrative within the context of the immigration history that affected brown bodies or by bridging the immigration history to the hybridization of

---

[5] Cited in 1965. *Matter of LaRochelle*, 11 I&N Dec. 436 (BIA).
[6] Senate Report 1515, 81st Cong., 2nd Sess., 345 (1950).
[7] See Senate Report 1515, 82nd Cong., 2nd Sess., 46–48 (1952).

border narrative literary techniques, there is a rather long tradition of thinking about both sides of the US–Mexico border.

One of the earliest border narratives was published by Los Angeles' Spanish-language daily newspaper *El heraldo de México* in 1928 and is titled "The Adventures of Don Chipote, or, When Parrots Breast Feed" by Daniel Venegas, republished by Arte Publico Press in 2000. The novel is about poor rural farmer Don Chipote de Jesus Maria Dominguez, who naively leaves behind his wife and children in Mexico to seek riches in the United States where, he is assured, one can sweep up gold dust from the streets and suck the nectar from the tree of life. This novel is set during the Immigration Act of 1917, when the United States aimed to restrict immigration by imposing literacy tests and hygiene rules, as we see with the "stringent bathing, disinfection, and delousing protocols Venegas recounts with Don Chipote's border crossing were instated" (Bracken 2018). Not only do the hygiene rules further enforce gender binaries and gender inspection that is seeped in the discourse of proper sexuality through immigration policies, but also the novel elucidates its repressed sexuality through the close relationship Don Chipote has with Policarpo, where he approaches him "como pollo que esta enamorado y no ha visto a su gallina por algunas dias" (Venegas 1999: 94).[8] The border narrative of *Don Chipote* exemplifies how sexuality informs migration through its repressed logic of the gender binary and the homosocial relationship that accompanies migration.

A border narrative that deals directly with sexuality in the Chicano community published three years before *Borderlands/La Frontera* is Arturo Islas's *The Rain God*. Set in the fictional small town on the Texas–Mexico border, this narrative tells the story of Miguel Chico and the aesthetic representation of his "break" with the Chicano movement, his border family, and his sense of isolation as a border subject. The opening movement of the text evokes Miguel Chico's separation as he looks at a photograph of him and his grandmother, Mama Chona, "in the early years of World War II by an old Mexican photographer who wandered up and down the border town's main street on the American side" (Islas 1984: 3). The camera catches them in flight to the next world all the while Miguel Chico is transitioning into a new world. He stares at the photograph from his deathbed at a university hospital after having been away for twelve years. He is separated from his family, but he still has a deep connection to his community and has a very vexed border positionality. The entire narrative is plotted out by Miguel Chico's alienation from himself, his body, and his family. In this multifaceted border narrative, Frederick Aldama reminds us:

> Islas carved out a new storytelling voice as he hybridized the many genres and styles found in literature on both sides of the U.S./Mexico border and beyond. He used this voice to chart the many symbolic and real borderlands (cultural, linguistic, racial, and sexual) that threatened to destroy but also create new life forms: Chicana/as struggling to inhabit a threatening and living-giving borderland world.
>
> (Aldama 2004: 48)

---

[8] Translation: Like a lovesick rooster who hasn't seen his hen for days.

The narrative technique Islas utilizes in *The Rain God* consistently butts up against his own subjectivity as a border subject. For example, in a novella-like technique after Miguel Chico takes up his dysfunctional Mexican family and the ways in which he escaped it, we see Miguel Chico at the end of the novel wrestling with his alienation from his very own body. He dreams of a monster colored in greys, blacks, and dark browns like his Mama Chona used to wear. The monster comes up behind him and whispers,

> "I am the manipulator and the manipulated." It put its velvet paw in Miguel Chico's hand and forced him to hold it tightly against his gut right below the appliance at his side. "I am the victim and slayer," the creature continued, "I am what you believe and what you don't believe, I am the loved and the unloved. I approve and turn away, I am judge and advocate."
>
> (Islas 1984: 159)

Miguel Chico remembers the monster's breath smelled of fresh blood and feces. Firstly, the either/or construction paints an image of someone who is not wholly human, but both human and monster. This in-between state is standard for border narratives. However, what becomes more intriguing is the in-between place Miguel Chico is within his sexual journey. Finally confronting freedom from family and the Chicano movement in general, Miguel Chico is rendered "monstrous" as he carries a colostomy bag next to him for his survival and is not able to fully become free. Paired with Mama Chona's death by the "monster between her legs" (her uterus), Miguel Chico is ironically mapped on to her monstrosity through his father Miguel, Mama Chona's offspring (177). In a turn of language, Miguel Chico is not only a hybridized border subject but also alienated from himself.

These early border narratives set the foundation for how migration and sexuality were inextricably inseparable from each other; however, they took a perspective that attempted to undo the masculine perspective of border culture. Adding on to this, Gloría Anzaldúa and Ana Castillo interrogate masculinity while centering the feminine body in their work. Anzaldúa is known for co-editing the volume *This Bridge Called My Back: Writings by Radical Women of Color* with Cherríe Moraga in 1981, and for her groundbreaking work in *Borderlands* in 1987. She uses her own position as a queer Chicana on the South Texas border to disrupt Anglocentric nationalist histories, while also questioning the Chicano nationalist agenda through a feminist lens. Anzaldúa's *mestizaje* represents a consciousness that breaks down the subject–object duality that keeps the Chicana a prisoner. Anzaldúa uses two terms to theorize border consciousness and subjectivity: *mestizaje* and *nepantla*. For Anzaldúa, *nepantla* is not only being in between two worlds but also it signifies the spiritual dimensions of experience for *la mestiza*. *Neplantilism* is an Aztec word meaning "torn between two ways," while *nepantla* is Nahuatl for "in the middle of it" or "middle." *La mestiza* is a product of the transfer of the cultural and spiritual values of one group to another. Considering how the land has shifted five countries for Anzaldúa (Spain, Mexico, the Republic of Texas, the Confederacy, and the United States), mental *neplantilism* creates a new border consciousness.

Conceptualizing her identity through the border, Anzaldúa engages a narrative form that is also hybrid. She utilizes the corrido, poetry, and prose in *Borderlands*, while switching between Tex-Mex, Spanish, English, and caló. Her *neplantilism* directly correlates to the broken tongues and fractures of her historical positionality and the fractures within the text. Readers encounter a text that refuses to conform to hegemonic standards in terms of form and language. Anzaldúa begins her text with the use of the violent history of the border, her own family history, and a corrido, which is the epitome of folk border culture. She states, "In the 1800s, Anglos migrated illegally into Texas, which was then part of Mexico, in greater and greater numbers and gradually drove the *tejanos* (native Texans of Mexican descent) from their lands, committing all manner of atrocities against them" (Anzaldúa 1987: 6). She follows up this history with excerpts from the Mexican corrido "Del Peligro de la Intervención." After mixing personal border history with more conventional border history, Anzaldúa visits the wound of the *india-mestiza*, which is a result of colonization and the construction of the US–Mexico border. The hybrid identities that Anzaldúa constructs through history are mapped on to her text and the multiple literary strategies and genres she uses. Continuing her goal of fusing the Chicana and the *mestiza*, she gives a history of Our Lady of Guadalupe, emphasizing the figure's Indigenous ancestry: "La Virgen de Guadalupe's Indian name is Coatlalopeuh. She is the central deity connecting us to our Indian ancestor" (1987: 27). Anzaldúa rejects Catholic "traditions" by attempting to distance Chicanas from the constraints of the regional cultures, which allows for the condition of possibility for Chicana/o nostalgia over our Indigenous subjectivity as a rarefaction of Indigenous peoples as past (Saldaña-Portillo 2001). Simultaneously, she is caught between various colonial languages and dialects; her form reflects the "neither español ni inglés, but both" (Anzaldúa 1987: 77). Anzaldúa's border narrative is about a subjectivity fractured not only by colonialism but also by Chicano cultural norms like heteronormativity and Catholic orthodox doctrine, which emphasize homophobia, sexism, and Chicano nationalism. She speaks to her sexuality and lesbianism as something she chooses for herself, a type of border where she continually "slips in and out and the white, the Catholic, the Mexican, the indigenous, the instincts" (1987: 19). She experiences fear of going home because of her sexuality, indicative of a more general fear of crossing over the border to the unknown. The border narrative captures all these different positionalities for Anzaldúa.

A very different border writer from Anzaldúa, Ana Castillo utilizes the border as a character in her novels. Castillo has long been praised for her Chicana feminist agenda coupled with her expansive writings on the border and borderlands. Critics have said that her narratives promote social justice and are written about communities that are underrepresented. Her prose is simple yet rhythmic. Castillo captivates audiences with her outrageous characters but also aims to tell a larger story. Published in 1993 and skyrocketing her to mainstream fame, Castillo's novel *So Far From God* utilizes a "conscienticized poetics" that interrogates racialized and gendered violence while simultaneously blending and breaking genre form. With many writings in between, Castillo's 2007 novel *The Guardians* is a quintessential border narrative based on the

Juárez border towns of Cabuche and El Paso, where people live in constant danger and crossing the border results in disappearance or murder, in gendered violence and femicide. However, it is Castillo's 2014 novel *Give It to Me* that gives us an alternative view of excessive Chicana bodies and their (non)function on the borderlands within the US nation state. *Give It To Me* rejects a tidy plotline and follows its forty-three-year-old Chicana protagonist, Palma, on over twenty sexual escapades. Palma, a bisexual Chicana, grows up in Chicago, where she lives with her seemingly judgmental grandmother after her parents leave her to work on the migrant trail. Palma's Chicana sexuality is elaborated through her exploration of multiethnic forms of belonging and desire; she interacts (sexually and not) with characters who do not see her as a whore figure. Traditional Chicano norms are no longer operating among her friends but continue in society. Palma is a border subject who traverses many borders and attempts to place herself outside of her race, barrio, culture, and restrictive norms, but the novel establishes her racialized sexuality by, and through, her disavowal of her race and culture.

Palma's empty attitude towards life, relationships, and sex allows readers to mark her as promiscuous or liberated, but it is in between these two poles that we can read her sexual excesses. The novel begins with incest. Palma attempts to have sex with her cousin, Pepito, but right before they begin to have intercourse he abruptly walks out. Palma finds out by the end of the novel that Pepito is not her cousin, but the taboo of incest runs throughout the narrative as a border between normative sexuality and deviance. She immediately leaves Chicago, disappointed, and goes back to her home in Albuquerque to continue her sexual affair with her "on again, off again" girlfriend Ursula. When Ursula gets to her house, she tells Palma she will be moving back to Houston to finish nursing school, where she has family. "Palma got caught up. She kissed her mouth, moved down her neck and then each nipple. Her lover had large areolas. They showered together and made love ... Palma knew that when she was gone she would not love her anymore" (Castillo 2014: 25–26). Within these two polarities, one can argue that her lack of emotion makes her a unique border character. In an attempt to make sense of her moment, Palma evacuates understandings of historical influence and refuses traditional forms of understanding in the narrative. Her split subjectivity is the very condition of conquered and colonized Westerners who utilized survival skills under previous cultural eras and is not particular to the postmodern condition (Sandoval 2000: 32–33). We could read Palma as a nihilistic character that engages in sexual activities that have no meaning or we can read her as a product of structures of violence and power against women of color that remove her from her community and political entanglements, while simultaneously confronting the reality of her border subjectivity. In the context of her Chicana border subjectivity, Palma's refusal to become invested in anything but her sexual life gestures to a performative undoing that challenges the status quo of modern production and clearly overexaggerates her position as a sexual Chicana; it is a position that tends to be hidden or flaunted but is here tragically displayed.

Performance Art and the Body of the Border: An Animalistic Turn

While the border narratives within Chicano/a/x cultural production have given readers a vision of what life on the US–Mexico border and on the borderlands is like for Latinx and Chicanx people, this chapter asks the question: how do these written words open up space for alternative border narratives? Chicanx and Latinx performance artists juxtapose the traditional literary border narratives that I have explored above using their own bodies as a border. *En Cuatro Patas*, part of the *Pacific Standard Time Festival: Live Art LA/LA (PST LA/LA)* led by the Getty Museum in 2018 and translated as "On All Fours," redefines the boundaries of the human through the animalistic, arthropod, and subhuman. Artists Nao Bustamante and Xandra Ibarra, known as La Chica Boom, utilize inter-corporeal performance aesthetics that test the border and boundaries of what is properly human and what is not. They very specifically curated the performances to explore and embody the limits of the human in relation to the Chicanx/Latinx body, which pushes up against, and beyond, borders by evoking the animal as a site of expression for how Chicanx/Latinx subjects come to deal with negative stereotypes and violence enacted on their bodies. *En Cuatro Patas* obliterates the concept of the human and the ways in which Chicanx literary history centralizes border narrative, migration, gender, and sexuality. These performance artists examine the ways in which racialized bodies have been rendered nonhuman through programs like the Bracero Program, which metaphorized the body part as a stand-in for the whole (the representational figure being the arm [*bracero*] of the farm worker). They likewise consider the ways in which Chicanx/Latinx bodies are mapped as animalistic, transhuman, or subhuman through the transnational locations of migration and movement. *En Cuatro Patas* examines how brownness conditions the very ways in which the human is constructed and how "the question of race's reality has and continues to bear directly on hierarchies of knowledge pertaining to the nature of reality itself" (Jackson 2015).

The four-part program begins with Naomi Rincón Gallardo's *The Formaldehyde Trip*,[9] which practices what Eva Hayward and Jami Weinstein theorize as the prefixial nature of trans: "Across, into, and through: a prepositional force—further [transfigured

---

[9] The second performance installation blends the ugly, wild, and uncomfortable with the corporeal Latinx body through choreographed movements of (re)gaining uncivility in Uruguayan Brooklyn-based choreographer Luciana Achugar's piece, *FEELingpleasuresatisfactioncelebrationholyFORM*. This piece pairs well with the rest of the second installation, which includes music by Mexican Los Angeles-based experimental vocalist Carmina Escobar and videos by Amapola Prada, Joiri Minaya, Xandra Ibarra, also Rob Fatal, Julie Tolentino, and Abigail Severance, and Mickey Negron. The third and fourth part of the program featured performances by Deborah Castillo (*Slapping Power*), Oscar David Alvarez ("*Band Shirts*"), Nadia Granados (*Spilled,*) Gina Osterloh (*Shadow Woman*), and Nao Bustamante (*Entregados al Deseo [Given Over to Want]*).

by] the animal turn" as a "threshold on emergence" (Hayward and Weinstein 2015). Rincón Gallardo, an artist practicing in Mexico City, fuses together songs and videos dedicated to murdered Mixtec activist Alberta "Bety" Cariño, who was killed in 2010 in a paramilitary ambush on a humanitarian caravan in San Juan Copala, Oaxaca, and mixes vernacular ideas of speculative fiction with a journey through the underworld. The performance lies at the interstices of form and genre in its portrayal of a transtemporal journey where she finds companions with intersexed animals and deities who guide her toward a rebirth ceremony. The cycle of song and video coupled with the ornate animal species costume weaves Mexican B-side sci-fi films of the 1960s and 1970s with Mesoamerican cosmologies, feminist and Indigenous activisms, and the Latinx corporeal body. The Latinx body is always already becoming in this performance piece, which gives the audience the space to imagine what possibilities are ahead for the liminal body that is turned into different animals and deities throughout the performance. What we get is the subhuman through the inhuman. The Latinx subhuman is "always becoming" through the construction of the excessive Latinx human. The axolotl (Mexican salamander) narrates the trip and begins the show by stating, "On behalf of a denied wretched majority of speechless and paperless others from the so-called Third World, and other endemic species, I welcome you aboard my Formaldehyde Trip."[10] The friction the narrator/salamander poses in the performance functions not only through the dual capacity talking animal species pose through their anthropomorphic qualities but also through the symbolic meaning of these near extinct amphibians: stunted by neoteny (delaying of physiological development) but also able to regenerate limbs by some sort of fantastical elements, a fitting metaphor for the Latinx body, one that in public discourse is stunted yet excessive and thriving. I should mention that the title of this performance piece, *The Formaldehyde Trip,* references the very substance that is used to preserve animals as lab specimens. The motility of the axolotl is in direct contrast with the stasis of a specimen held in formaldehyde, which allows viewers to question if the axolotl is actually real reality. *The Formaldehyde Trip* asks the audience to imagine what a new subjectivity looks like apart from the human that is constructed through liberal subjectivity and continental philosophy. In a journey toward collaborative social struggle that does not deal with a liberal framework of the immigrant success story, this piece fuses rock music with the "it" of Hayward and Weinstein's project of an abstract space that can only be embodied by particular objects, "a process through which thingness or beingness are constituted".[11] That thingness exists in the tension not only between the peripheral Chicanx/Latinx subject and imperialism, white supremacy, and capital but also between the Chicanx/Latinx and the Indigenous subject. The tension between these is foundational to the fissures of subjectivity: the Chicanx/Latinx subject has been racially made-over from their Indigenous roots and cannot claim indigeneity.

---

[10] Naomi Rincón Gallardo's *The Formaldehyde Trip.*
[11] Ibid, 196.

In a song toward the end of the show, a punk melody plays while a video with different "humans" in animal species costumes roll around to a chorus that sings:

> Shoulder to shoulder
> mud, mud, mud
> elbow to elbow
> mud, mud, mud
> bones to ashes.

The lyrics represent a process of mutation, of change, and of rebirth. The mud is the maker of something new in between the body parts that it covers. In the end, this performance piece helps a new subject to emerge from the murder of Cariño and asks the audience to consider what it means when an artist sets out to value different Chicanx/Latinx aesthetics focused on irreverence, degradation, and pleasure.

On the other side of the border, Oakland-based performance artist from the border of El Paso/Juarez, Xandra Ibarra, also known as La Chica Boom, works across performance, video, and sculpture to address abjection and joy and the borders between proper and improper racial, gendered, and queer Chicanx subjects. Ibarra also profoundly focuses on the boundaries of the human on the border through the animalistic. Whereas written border narratives create a space of in-betweenness while simultaneously utilizing the border narrative to explicate a positionality on the margins, Ibarra's performances of border narratives turn the genre on its head by explicitly evoking the animalistic in relation to Chicanx border subjects. Ibarra's short film *F*ck My Life (FML)*, coproduced with Rob Fatal in 2012, runs three minutes and forty-five seconds long and begins with Ibarra in a blackened room, lying in bed with a vibrator, cucaracha tasseled pasties on her nipples. Her makeup is smudged and La Lupe's "Esta Es Mi Vida" plays in the background. Guadalupe Yoli Raymond, or "La Lupe" as she was famously called, was born in Santiago de Cuba in 1936 and rose to fame performing in small nightclubs in Havana. Her performance style is described as "screaming, disorderly and disrespectful" and mirrors Ibarra's performance style in multiple ways (Rondón 1980: 46). The lyrics of La Lupe's "Este Es Mi Vida," which translates to "This is My Life," alludes to the story of Ibarra's failed burlesque persona as "her life." In addition, this failure that we see Ibarra living through in *F*ck My Life (FML)* alludes to the rumors surrounding the death of Hollywood's "Mexican Spitfire" actress Lupe Velez, who died by suicide. According to one account, she died with her head in the toilet after taking 75 seconal pills and a glass of brandy. The two Lupes in this silent short film haunt Ibarra and she embodies their excessive, dark, sexual voice and personas as we see her dragging herself through the everyday motions of life.

As Ibarra gets out of bed in her cucaracha nipple tassels and underwear, La Lupe's track plays in the background singing, "What good is my life?".[12] Ibarra's room has blackout curtains and is strewn with bottles of pills and alcohol. She takes a deep breath

---

[12] La Lupe, "Esta Es Mi Vida" ("This is My Life"), Tico Records/Concord Records, 1977.

and drags herself out of bed as she puts on a beautiful black robe. The next shot captures Ibarra shaking on the toilet as she brushes her teeth, rinses with whiskey, and spits the remains of the toothpaste into the toilet. Ibarra walks down the hallway and opens the room where a bright orange light shines through. As she walks up to her vanity, the audience can see she has a huge coin on top of her mirror that says "token" along with a sewing machine and burlesque costuming adornments all around. As Ibarra looks at her self sadly in the vanity mirror, she begins to put on her makeup, not in a precise way but in a desperate, flailing manner. This is when her transformation begins. As she begins to put on her cucaracha attire, the lighting in the film dims. Ibarra emerges out of her house, a cucaracha carrying a suitcase. She looks both ways before she gathers herself on to the sidewalk and begins walking away from the camera and La Lupe belts out "This is my life." We see the back of the cucaracha thorax and antennas bouncing up and down and Ibarra walks down the cement sidewalk, with her suitcase and her stiletto heels.

This "death" of La Chica Boom, the burlesque persona of Ibarra, takes the form of the reanimation of her body as an insect. And not just any insect. The insect she becomes is a cucaracha, the symbolic of filth; they infest homes and built spaces and can reproduce at a rapid rate, living in the filthiest of conditions. A symbol of the Mexican people in the popular national imaginary, they also symbolize hefty regeneration. As José Esteban Muñoz theorizes about brown bodies, Ibarra's lesson in becoming animal-like transcends the "identitarian and nationalist ideologies" that render Chicanidad a singular subjectivity (Muñoz 2020: 79). Where border narratives open up the space for marginal subjectivity to be seen and reckoned with, Ibarra takes what seems to be the traditional narrative of border subjectivity in the face of US multiculturalism and undermines the Mexiphobic gaze. Through her transformation into an insect, Ibarra embraces all the stereotypes we think about Mexicans and embodies the cucaracha figure as the most basic symbol of survival. Her transformation is the not literal "becoming" of the insect itself but everything that she can literally embody that falls outside of normative stereotypes and history. Muñoz reminds us, "Metonymically linking a population with the specter of animality is primarily about dehumanization of life itself and specific groups in particular" (82). However, her film isn't about racist humor. It is about the in-between space of the border narrative opening possibilities of becoming. We see Ibarra walking away from the camera. We don't know what happens to her or where she ends up. She goes on to live forever as the symbolic cucaracha in society.

Similar to *F*ck My Life (FML)*, Ibarra shows the false promise of metamorphosis in her photo series "Spic Ecdysis," which traces Ibarra's molting like that of a cucaracha. Ibarra uses the word "ecdysis" in this photo series because it comes from the Ancient Green term "Ekduo," which means, "to take off, strip off." A collection of six photographs, the first one is of Ibarra directly next to her cucaracha costume in a pool of water. The cucaracha costume is face down and she is face up with her hands placed on her head. She is topless and wears only underwear and tassels to cover her nipples. The second photograph in the series is the Lady of Guadalupe costume Ibarra donned when she was performing as La Chica Boom. It is left on the US–Mexico border, along a chain-link fence. The third photograph is of Ibarra laying next to another of her burlesque costumes. However, in this photograph, she is lying down next to a finely crafted backyard with cement, tables, chairs, and greenery all around. The remaining photographs are of Ibarra lying again next to the cucaracha costume, but this time the pool of the first photograph is empty and we see the stark contrast between its white cement and her brown skin. Christina León states:

> the depiction of the roach focuses on its bodily transformation through ecdysis, an invertebrate's sloughing off of an old cuticle and generation of a new shell—a heightened reminder that all of our cells, through skin and skein, are always already in the process of exposure, deadening, sloughing off, and regenerating.
>
> (León 2017)

Ibarra's performance of border narrative and construction of Chicanx animality doesn't allow for anything certain. In her photo series, she lies next to the cucaracha skin, not a new Chicana by any means, but instead a formation of brownness that is not legible in the narrative of beginning, climax, resolution, or ending.

Finally, Ibarra's *Nude Laughing* (2014) is a live performance where she walks around naked and laughing, just as the title suggests. However, she has exaggerated prosthetic breasts at the beginning of the performance and she drags around a nylon stocking filled with "womanhood"—wig, pearls, and heels. Drawing from John Currin's 1998 painting "Laughing Nude," Ibarra performs racialized nude laughing, where femininity goes awry. In the final moments of her performance, she lies in the middle of the floor, kicks off her heels, and inserts her body in to the cocoon of womanhood she has been carrying around. No longer an insect, she becomes a "thing," a knot of a cocoon in all her racial glory. The heels, the wig, the pearls: none of that can save Ibarra. She remains "becoming" in the context of the border narrative. She embodies what Cherríe Moraga calls *theory in the flesh*, "where the physical realities of our lives—our skin color, the land or concrete we grew up on, our sexual longings—all fuse to create a politic born out of necessity."[13]

Ibarra plays with the construction of the human in relation to the animal or insect in many of her pieces. Her art practice is rooted in conventional "failure" through the discourses of proper femininity. Where she focuses on the metaphor of undesirable people, Rafael Esparza weaves migration, queerness, and brownness through his performance of inanimate objects. Born in Los Angeles, California, Esparza utilizes live performance as his main form of inquiry into borders, colonization, brownness, sexuality, and violence. His art is also grounded in laboring with land and adobe making, a skill learned from his father, Ramón Esparza, an immigrant from Durango, Mexico. A border subject firmly rooted in Los Angeles, Esparza doesn't necessarily perform the animal species in relation to the Chicanx body on the border as does Ibarra, but he

---

[13] Cherríe Moraga and Gloría Anzaldúa. 1981. *This Bridge Called My Back: Writings by Radical Women of Color.* New York: Kitchen Table: Women of Color Press, 23.

enacts a performance of the inanimate. Esparza pushes up against the discourse of the Western subject, examining its ontology; Achille Mbembe warns against the dangers of being seduced by the aesthetic (European) mythologizing of the world and the violent history (Mbembe: 2003: 201). While Mbembe argues that colonial Africans' transgressive animality stalks the "origins" of "the human," I read Esparaz's border performance narrative as transgressive inanimacy that stalks the "origins" of "the human" (201).

Pulling aspects of Chicano performance art's past into the present, Esparza builds on the contradictions within the long history of Chicano culture. In *Corpo Ranfla*, a piece he created for the *Pacific Standard Time Festival: Live Art LA/LA (PST LA/LA)* led by the Getty Museum, he performed in the Mayan Theatre, a club in a storied old cinema in downtown Los Angeles stylized with pre-Columbian iconography. The use of a club normally populated by a heavily straight and male-dominated dancing scene reinforces the connections of his art to the traditional rituals of sex and gender roles as his cis-gendered male body exhibits queerness in that space. For *Corpo Ranfla*, Esparza and collaborator Sebastian Hernández stood at the entrance of the Mayan Theatre on a black platform separated from the public by a red velvet rope, on display as figures in a human zoo. The duo changed poses every few minutes but never looked directly at anyone entering the space. Esparza was painted neon pink with matching pink underwear and adorned with a gold chrome neck placard that read "Brown Persuasion." This first performance by Esparza takes cues from Guillermo Gomez Peña and Coco Fusco's traveling performance, "The Couple in the Cage," which satirically represents both as caged Amerindians from an imaginary island. While originally made to be a satire, many viewers believed that the two were savages. Esparza is building off this tradition of the spectacle and utilizing the viewer to become embedded in the performance.

The second part of the performance took the form of the early twentieth-century vaudeville shows known as varidades presented by Mexican performers in Los Angeles. Esparza took the stage to Kid Frost's 1990 hip-hop hit "La Raza" with lyrics boasting, "Chicano and I'm brown and I'm proud." Blue lights beamed down as a large disco ball hung from above. Esparza began by posing "low" or crouched down, evoking the pose gang members used for pictures but also mimicking the appearance of the low-rider car seen cruising and—pointedly, politically—slowing traffic on Whittier Boulevard since the '60s, just as Chicano performers such as Cyclona and Asco had all those decades ago.[14] As tough as Esparza appeared, the elements of femininity (pink body, lace-up heels, jewelry) paired with his masculine stare are inextricably linked with *carnalismo*

---

[14] Robert Legorreta, aka Cyclona, was one of the first Chicano performance artists to make an impression in Los Angeles. In the mid-'60s, he would don women's clothing he sewed himself from curtains, put on makeup and false breasts, and walk up and down Whittier Boulevard in East Los Angeles. His performances in what he called "semi-drag"—identifiable as such thanks in part to his beard—often met with harassment and assault. Working with the reactions he provoked, Legorreta took such daily hostilities and transformed them into materials to craft his art through his body. His first collaborative performance was *Caca-Roaches Have No Friends* (1969), a dialogue-free play featuring performers in the role of huge lips. He often times collaborated with ASCO, a performance group in Los Angeles that performed in the streets from 1972 to 1987.

(brotherhood) in low-rider culture. This particular work subverts low-rider culture, art, and music. The main aisle of the Mayan Theater gave way to queer poses and prancing to magnificent effect. More importantly, Esparza became the very low-rider car he was mimicking in the ways he was crouching down on stage as an inanimate object. In a sweeping move that embodies the inanimate object while simultaneously moving between conventional gender roles, Esparaza utilizes Chicanx culture to shift subjectivity between human and inanimate object. The performance artists of the '60s and '70s were confronting the freedom of expression through avant-garde embodied art practices and with Esparza's performance, the elements of drag in the piece brought to the fore how the body as a "thing" (similar to a car itself) can represent both the masculine and the feminine. The curator of the *Variadades* show, Marcus Kuiland-Nazario, put together the show with all Los Angeles performers with the intent to counter the myth that Chicanx performance was always rooted in folk forms. While the low-rider culture is a tradition that Chicanx and Latinx subject participate in, Esparza disengages the culture from its conventional form of masculinity. Esparza, Ibarra, and Rincón Gallardo all take up border folk forms and push them to their limits.

Conclusion

If Anzaldúa situates border identity as fragmentation, performance artists in the contemporary moment carry this theme into their performances by deploying the X in their practice. Becoming popular with Latino millennials in the late 2000s, the X in Chicanx refers to whose subjectivity cannot be verbalized within the naming Chicana/o, highlighting diversity. Antonio Viego states that the X is the general indeterminacy that marks the moment with respect to conceptualization of the human subject. It also refers to a person of Latin American origin or descent that uses a gender-neutral or non-binary alternative to Chicana or Chicano. Where Anzaldúa is firmly rooted in her Chicana identity, these performance artists interfere with the genealogy of Chicana feminism to unsettle the "human" in general and shift border narratives from celebrating fragmentation to a critique of the Mexiphobic subhuman.

This chapter has shown how the material and metaphoric histories of the border in relation to gender and sexuality show up in not only border narratives of the early 1980s but also in performance pieces that build upon the literary tradition. Chicanx and Latinx performers from the border region map out alternative narratives enabled by bodies in performance art and interrogate the limits of marginal subjectivity through the examination of the nonhuman, subhuman, and the animal. The conception of the border is rendered historically continuous with criminalizing migration and sexuality, thereby devaluing brown bodies as being less than animal. Where the written border narrative focuses on the fragmented subjectivity of the marginal border-crosser and their journeys, Chicanx and Latinx performance art has built on this fragmented subjectivity and pushed it beyond the boundaries of the human.

As in literary border narratives, Chicanx and Latinx performance art stages the disobedient, abject, degraded, and excessive politicized Chicanx/Latinx body to explore what type of desire, enjoyment, pleasure, hope, and future we can find through the nonhuman, or subhuman. In an interview, I once asked Ibarra how exploring the politicized, abject, bestial, and nonhuman nature of the body is linked to Chicanx and Latinx border narratives. She responded:

> Our curation makes a mess of, celebrates, and toys with the predictable humanist construction of the animal as a contaminating threat to humanity through crossing. It asks Latinx artists to show us how the animal—on all fours, hairy, maybe with breasts dangling, bound, pregnant, and maybe undisciplined—manages to transgress or bind what divides the human from animal or Latinx from human.
>
> (Interview with Ibarra)

I would say she has thoroughly succeeded.

References

Aldama, Frederick. 2004. *Dancing with Ghosts: A Critical Biography of Arturo Islas* (Berkeley, CA: University of California Press).

Alvardo, Leticia. 2018. *Abject Performances: Aesthetic Strategies in Latino Cultural Production* (Durham, NC: Duke University Press).

Anzaldúa, Gloría. 1987. *Borderlands La Frontera: The New Mestiza* (San Francisco, CA: Aunt Lute Press).

Aron, Stephen. 2004. "The Making of the First American West and the Unmaking of Other Realms," in William Deverell, ed., *A Companion to the American West*. Wiley: Blackwell, (Malden, MA), 5–24.

Bolton, Herbert Eugene. 1996. *The Spanish Borderlands: A Chronicle of Old Florida and the Southwest* (Albuquerque, NM: University of New Mexico Press).

Bracken, Rachel Conrad. 2018. "Borderland Biopolitics Public Health and Border Enforcement in Early Twentieth-Century Latinx Fiction," *English Language Notes*. 56.2 (October): 31.

Brady, Mary Pat. 2000. "The Fungibility of Borders," *Nepantla: Views from South* 1.1: 172.

Castillo, Ana. 2014. *Give It To Me* (New York: The Feminist Press).

Delgado, Grace Peña. 2012. "Border Control and Sexual Policing: White Slavery and Prostitution along the U.S.–Mexico Borderlands, 1903–1910," *Western Quarterly* 43.2 (Summer): 177.

Glenn, Evelyn Nakano. 1986. *Issei, Nisei, War Bride: Three Generations of Japanese American Women in Domestic Service* (Philadelphia, PA: Temple University Press).

Gutiérrez, Ramón A. and Elliott Young. 2010. "Transnationalizing Borderlands History," *Western Historical Quarterly* 41.2 (Spring 2): 27–53.

Hayward, Eva, and Jami Weinstein. 2015. "Introduction: Tranimalities in the Age of Trans* Life," *TSQ* 2.2: 200.

Hernández, Kelly Lyttle. 2010. *Migra!: A History of the U.S. Border Patrol* (Berkeley, CA: University of California Press).

Hernández, Kelly Lyttle. 2011. "Borderlands and the Future History of the American West," *Western Historical Quarterly* 42 (Autumn): 325.

Hirata, Lucy Cheng. 1979. "Chinese Women Immigrants in Nineteenth Century California," in Carol Ruth Berkin and Mary Beth Norton, eds, *Women of America* (Boston, MA: Houghton Mifflin Co.), 223–244.

Islas, Arturo. 1984. *The Rain God* New York: (Harper Collins Publisher).

Jackson, Zakiyyah Iman. 2015. "Theorizing Queer Inhumanisms: OuterWorlds: The Persistence of Race in Movement 'Beyond the Human,'" *GLQ* 21.2–3: 216.

Johnson, Benjamin H. and Andrew R. Graybill. 2010. "Borders and Their Historians in North America," in Benjamin H. Johnson and Andrew R. Graybill, eds, *Bridging National Borders in North America: Transnational and Comparative Histories* (Durham, NC: Duke University Press), 1–29.

León, Christina A. 2017. "Forms of Opacity: Roaches, Blood, and Being Stuck in Xandra Ibarra's Corpus," *ASAP/Journal* 2.2 (May): 381.

Luibhéid, Eithne. 2002. *Entry Denied: Controlling Sexuality at the Border* (Minneapolis: University of Minnesota Press).

Mbembe, Achille. 2010. *Sortir de la grande nuit: Essai sur l'Afrique décolonisée* (Paris: La Découverte).

Moraga, Cherríe and Gloria Anzaldúa, eds. 1981. *This Bridge Called My Back: Writings by Radical Women of Color* (New York: Kitchen Table: Women of Color Press).

Muñoz, José Esteban. 2006. "Feeling Brown, Feeling Down: Latina Affect, the Performativity of Race, and the Depressive Position," *Signs* 31.3: 675–688.

Muñoz, José Esteban. 2020. *The Sense of Brown* (Durham, NC: Duke University Press).

Rondón, Cesar Miguel. 1980. *El libro de la salsa: cróninca de la música del caribe urbano* (Caracas: Editorial Arte).

Saldaña-Portillo, Josefina. 2001. "Who's The Indian In Aztlán?" in Ileana Rodríguez, ed., *The Latin American Subaltern Studies Reader* (Durham, NC: Duke University Press) 402–423.

Saldivar, José. 1997. *Border Matters: Remapping American Cultural Studies* (Berkeley, CA: University of California Press).

Sandoval, Chela. 2000. *Methodology of the Oppressed* (Minneapolis, MN: University of Minnesota Press).

Truett, Samuel and Elliott Young. 2004. "Introduction," in Samuel Truett and Elliott Young, eds, *Continental Crossroads: Remapping U.S.-Mexico Borderlands History* (Durham, NC: Duke University Press), 1–32.

Weber, David J. 1986. "Turner, the Boltonians, and the Borderlands," *American Historical Review* 91 (February): 66–81.

Weber, David J. 2000. "The Spanish Borderlands of North America: A Historiography," *OAH Magazine of History* 14 (Summer): 5–11.

Weber, David J. 2005. "The Spanish Borderlands, A Historiography Redux," *History Teacher* 39 (November): 43–56.

Venegas, Daniel. 1999. *Las Aventuras de Don Chipote* (Houston, TX: Arte Publico Press).

Yung, Judy. 1986. *Chinese Women of America: A Pictorial History* (Seattle, WA: University of Washington Press).

PART 4
IMAGINARIES

CHAPTER 16

OF CANONS AND CABINETS

Indigenous Bodies, Epistemological Spectacle, and an Unusual Indian in the Cupboard

BECCA GERCKEN

The truth about stories is that that's all we are.

Thomas King (2003)

SCHOLARS of American Indian literature have been moderately successful in decolonizing the canon, meaning that we have made space for Indigenous texts. We have not, however, been as successful in decolonizing our reading strategies. As Chad Allen points out in *Trans-Indigenous*, although the academy is several decades into having access to Indigenous methodologies, our reading strategies remain largely unchanged. Perhaps it is not surprising, then, that many of the Indigenous books that make their way into the canon are those that reward traditional literary readings and are seen as reinforcing or echoing the voices of non-Indigenous authors and/or their plots, characters, themes, and assumptions. And although we do have a growing body of Indigenous research methodologies that offer us new ways into a text (Red Readings, trans-Indigenous readings, decolonized readings), some of these methodological approaches require restricted cultural knowledge few may hold or can (or should) gain access to.[1]

There are many explanations for the slow adoption of Indigenous research methodologies. One is that because much of the theory is grounded in the social sciences, it requires some maneuvering to apply it as a close reading strategy. Another

---

[1] See, e.g. Womack (1999), Weaver et al. (2005), Allen (2012), and Smith (1999).

is the cultural divide between Indigenous and Western academic understandings of the value of knowledge. Yet another is the call for community-based research. The two explanations that most interest me are the call for activist, community-centered research in American Indian Studies and the invented, culturally coded notion of "rigor" in the academy. Let us start with the notion of activist, community-centered research, a necessary corrective to early research strategies and an important reflection of Indigenous cultural values. Part of this call for activism is that research should benefit the community it studies. Although this call makes sense, especially in a social science or medical science context, it is a less comfortable fit in literary studies. Complicating this issue is the fact, noted above, that many of the Indigenous methodological approaches that are available do not apply in easy or smooth ways to literary analysis as they are grounded in education, psychology, or sociology. And while I would like to think that members of the Turtle Mountain community would appreciate my respectful and culturally informed readings of Heid Erdrich's poetry, I do not think my research can have the kind of impact on that community that, say, a study of diabetes or land tenure documents would have.

Thus, I think our energy in the humanities might be better spent in another type of activism: fostering different ways to establish and engage with the canon—our cabinet of literary treasures—that we have worked so hard to transform. This activism means first constructing a more varied canon and then developing syllabi and assignments that ask students to interact with the canon in ways that better reflect the origins of its texts. For me, one crucial way to do that, in addition to assigning Indigenous theories and methodologies regardless of whether or not they are a natural or obvious fit with literary analysis, is to choose literary texts that foreground the tension between Western and Indigenous readings and offer active resistance to Western ways of knowing and representing Indigenous bodies. I would extend this argument to say that there is also value in choosing texts that resist a singular Red Reading. Jace Weaver, Craig Womack, and Robert Warrior asked questions that led to the rise of literary nationalism, the so-called Red Readings that call for Indigenous literature to be read within the context of the nation that produced it. In *American Indian Literary Nationalism*, they write:

> We believe that being a nationalist is a legitimate perspective from which to approach Native American literature and criticism. We believe that such a methodology is not only feasible but that it is also crucial to supporting Native national sovereignty and self-determination, which we see as an important goal of Native American Studies generally. At the same time, however, we do *not* believe that it is the only possible approach to Native literature, and the nationalism we advance herein is not exclusionary.[2]
>
> (2005: xxi; italics in original)

---

[2] When Weaver, Womack, and Warrior write that the nationalism they advance is not "exclusionary," they are specifically referencing the fact that they welcome nationalist readings produced by non-Native scholars of Native American literature.

Through this political or, one might argue, sovereign methodology that foregrounds focus and outcome rather than theory or abstraction, Stephen Graham Jones's *Ledfeather* (2008) would be read through the lens of Blackfoot culture, while LeAnne Howe's *Shell Shaker* (2001) would be read through a Choctaw lens. Such readings are important and necessary, but, as with a Western reading, they alone should not provide the framework for textual analysis. Have not the Blackfoot people and the Choctaw shared colonized experience via the reservation system, the Bureau of Indian Affairs (BIA), and Indian Residential schools? And have these nations—and their authors—not interacted with American society and other nations more broadly?[3] The alternative to Western readings that validate Indigenous texts only or primarily as they align with Western values and literary tropes must not—or at least must not *only*—be Red Readings that place Indigenous texts within a cultural bubble that does not reflect the complex and often trans-Indigenous realities of Native people's lives. Nor do such restrictive Red Readings make space for the influence of other authors—many undoubtedly Ameripean—on Native stories and storytelling.[4] It is important to note that those who first called for Red Readings, as noted above, made clear that they "do *not* believe that it is the only possible approach to Native literature" (Weaver et al. 2005: xxi; italics in original), a sentiment Womack shares in *Red on Red* when he calls for a conversation that is "more suggestive than prescriptive" (1999: 1).[5] In spite of the clear evidence that the framers of Red Readings did not want them to be restrictive or exclusionary, that is how the methodology is all too often understood and applied. Sean Teuton's approach to nation-based readings is both more nuanced and contextualized—in a historic sense—than many. In "Cities of Refuge: Indigenous Cosmopolitan Writers and the International Imaginary," Teuton reminds readers that "scholars often employ theories of racial and cultural hybridity as the primary means of understanding Indigenous–European action" while "overlooking the Indian nation in the American colonial narrative" (2013: 42). Teuton also calls out Red Readings that lack appropriate nuance and context as being "uncritical" (42). He shares the warnings of Arnold Krupat and Elvira Pulitano, who "rightly

---

[3] Womack himself makes this point in *Red on Red*, writing:

One of the obvious areas of inquiry in Native studies in the future will have to the effect of pan-tribalism on Native cultures, from boarding schools to the urban demography of Native populations, to the powwow circuit, to beginning global alliances and awareness among indigenous populations worldwide, to name a few examples (not that these phenomenon mark the beginning and ending of pan-tribalism, but they seem like cogent ones).

Womack (1999: 18–19)

[4] Carter Revard, a poet and medieval scholar of Osage, Ponca, and European-American descent, created the word "ameropean" to describe Americans of European descent. My use of Ameripean has the same definition, although, unlike Revard, I capitalize the term (as I would European, American, Cherokee, etc.) and offer a slight spelling variation with an I rather than an O (Revard 1982: 305–318).

[5] A further indication of Weaver, Womack, and Warrior's desire to have Red Readings be *an* option, not *the* option, and to create a more inclusive conversation can be found in the shift in title language from the "separatism" of Womack's 1999 *Red on Red: Native American Literary Separatism* to the "nationalism" of Weaver, Womack, and Warrior's 2006 *American Indian Literary Nationalism*.

warn that crude nationalism leads to political repression and border patrolling" (42) and in his conclusion notes the irony that "nationalism among scholars of indigenous studies today often grows more retrograde in its isolationist desires than theories of the nation from the nineteenth century, when Native nations were more critically under attack" (51).

Rather than shifting our reading paradigm from the pole of Western validation to the pole of cultural authentication, I suggest that our pedagogical goal should be somewhere in the middle, informed by both but limited to neither. As we think about the canon and the work we ask our students to do with it, we should not be asking students to produce a Western validation reading (methodology A) or a Red Reading (methodology B) but rather methodology C, a reading positionality with awareness of both A and B operating together to understand a text. This borderland methodology, inspired by Gloria Anzaldúa's *Borderlands—La Frontera: The New Mestiza* (1987), allows us to think about Native American literature not in terms of content but in terms of approach. In her discussion of the US–Mexican border and the people who cross it and live on both or either side, Anzaldúa calls on space to be imagined not as a line of demarcation that one can neatly jump, occupying only one space or the other, but rather as a border space born of the two sides: "A border is a dividing line, a narrow strip along a steep edge. A borderland is a vague and undetermined place created by the emotional residue of an unnatural boundary. It is in a constant state of transition" (3).

Readings grounded solely in the Western literary tradition do not recognize the "constant state of transition" Anzaldúa's methodology offers and thus serve only to reify Ameripean literary norms. Moreover, they risk romanticizing Indigenous peoples via colonial nostalgia, a desire to represent Indians as at best static and at worst existing only in the past. Womack asks in *Red on Red*, "Does the Native American literary renaissance, in addition to its many positive qualities, also play, in troubling ways, into the vanishing notion [of Indians] by allowing Native people to be fictional but not real?" (1999: 11). My response is that any such issues are not a reflection of the texts themselves but rather the result of what is canonized and what reading methodologies are encouraged or even allowed.

Red Readings, while providing a necessary check on Western reading strategies of Native texts, offer their own pitfalls, with scholars producing an anthropological reading that is very much about identifying so-called "tribal elements" while ignoring or failing to understand that some cultural knowledge can only be shared with certain people or at certain times. Such readings can also elide nuances of the historical and contemporary implications of any individual tribe, band, or pueblo's interaction with the assimilating forces of the federal government. Finally, Red Readings may lead to texts that valorize a certain type of Native story such as the homing plot narrative that focuses on the protagonist's return to traditional homelands.[6]

---

[6] Clearly, Native American authors are interested in narratives of the return home, a narrative trope that came to be known as the "homing plot." But the fact that such stories have historically been so heavily canonized over stories of urban Natives suggests Western academic bias towards such stories.

The readings that follow offer a map for new canonical and pedagogical approaches through Indigenous texts that are ill suited for either Western validation readings or Red Readings due to their nationally Indigenous, even trans-Indigenous subject matter and their rendering of the consequences of Western colonialism and Indigenous cultural loss for Native bodies. All of the texts actively resist Western readings in some way through critiques of science or settler-colonial curation—represented in the actual bodies of Indigenous people in cupboards. Similarly, they resist Red Readings through their hemispheric rendering of Indigeneity in the case of Erdrich, Turcotte, and Alexie, and through Kiowa cultural loss in Momaday. All of the texts analyzed here call for an Indigenous understanding—tribal, national, transnational—of Indigenous bodies. In doing so, they challenge the tradition of Native spectacle articulated by the trope of the "Indian in the Cupboard."

Indians in cabinets or cupboards is a layered allusion with curatorial and literary foundations. Curiosity cabinets, originally rooms that housed treasures, objects of wonder, and oddities, have been documented as far back as the sixteenth century. The literary *Indian in the Cupboard* topos first appeared in 1980 with the publication of Lynne Reid Banks's children's book of the same name. The objects and bodies in cabinets have value or, in the case of the Banks's Haudenosuanee Chief Little Bear, existence through white curation and containment that marks them as quaint and segregates them. In literary studies, we have our own curiosity cabinet—the canon. And while that cupboard has become increasingly diverse, the methods of interpreting the treasures within has not. Curation is not only about selection but also about interpretation. My analysis of the four Indigenous texts in this chapter reveals authors overtly challenging Western and Red Readings through their portrayal of Indigenous bodies in cabinets in ways that resist any singular framework of interpretation.

***

The notion of brown bodies on display for white eyes is not new in American Indian literature (nor, more broadly, in any post settler-colonial literature), but a handful of Native authors offer an interesting turn on the notion. Heid Erdrich, Mark Turcotte, Sherman Alexie, and N. Scott Momaday have each written about Indians in cabinets. Each author repeatedly emphasizes encasement: their Indians are enclosed. Sometimes that enclosure represents safety and endurance, but it more often signifies intrusion and spectacle. And while the authors' personas offer some recognition of an Indigenous gaze upon these bodies, greater emphasis is placed on how they are seen or understood by the non-Indigenous eyes that see them or imagine them, with that emphasis being created through the disconnect between Indigenous and non-Indigenous ways of knowing the body. Perspective is vital in each rendering, the literal perspective of how the bodies can or cannot be seen and the epistemological perspective of how the bodies are understood. Reading these cabinet images, which appear in different genres and across

William Beavis describes the so-called "homing plot" in comparison with European plots, which, he argues, are grounded in leaving. In contrast, he argues, Native American novels are grounded in "coming home ... [This return] is not only the primary story, it is a primary mode of knowledge and a primary good" (Beavis 1987: 582).

several decades, can help us understand how world views inform the representations of and responses to the spectacle of Indigenous bodies. There are no magic Indians in cupboards brought to life or given meaning through an Ameripean gaze here; there are instead Indians who offer specular lessons in survivance.[7] In the Erdrich, Turcotte, and Alexie poems, Indigenous bodies are encased and on display for white eyes, made spectacle. In contrast, the Indian in the cabinet in Momaday is unseen, at least in a literal sense, by white or Indigenous eyes. I am interested in reading these works for signs of disruption and resistance as well as for what they can teach us about our literary "cabinet"—the canon. As viewers gaze on Indigenous corporeal spectacle, or its absence, what do their literal and metaphorical perspectives reveal about Ameripean Indigenous epistemologies? And how might we translate that knowledge into rethinking the American literary canon?

In "Girl of Lightning" from *National Monuments*, Heid Erdrich begins by describing the Indigenous enclosure of one of three Incan children discovered in Argentina in 1999; her focus is on the child she calls "the girl of lightning."[8] Erdrich writes that the girl has been "shelter[ed] for five centuries" (2008: 13) during which the girl "huddled, red-painted / wreathed in feathers" (14–15). The thunder "loves" (1) her and "mumbles charms to warm" (2) her "folded cold body" (3) while lightning "licks a kiss" (5). These images show the girl protected and honored by both the landscape that enfolds her and the people who placed her there. The natural world speaks to her through thunder and lightning, while the mountain shields her from discovery that would interrupt a ceremony in process for 500 years even though the Gods are "long gone or gone underground" (11).

But that ceremony is disrupted as the mountain's "girl of lightning" now finds herself in a glass cabinet, rendered readable to modern viewers by science in a way that violates her meaning to Indigenous peoples, both those that placed her in the mountain and those who see her or read of her now. No longer protected by her landscape, the girl of lightning is "cased in plastic, cased in glass" (31). She is displayed, framed by a narrative that reifies settler-colonial scientific practices while denying and demonizing Indigenous spiritual practices, a framework that reminds readers of the god-like status often given to modern science in Ameripean culture. Erdrich writes that the girl was sent "up the mountain" (22) with her mother's hair, which was meant to be "an introduction to the Gods" (24). The stanza break here suggests that the girl's community sent her on this ceremonial journey with a sign that could be read and understood by their gods. However, the next stanza opens with "of Science" (25), and thus readers are jarred into

---

[7] I am using Vizenor's definition of survivance here: "Native survivance is an active sense of presence over absence ... survivance is the continuance of stories .... Survivance stories are renunciations of dominance, detractions, obtrusions, the unbearable sentiments of tragedy, and the legacy of victimry" (2008: 1).

[8] In her opening commentary to selected poems from *National Monuments* published in *Museum Anthropology*, Erdrich notes that the collection "began first as a response to monuments of literature that use indigenous figures as a metaphor" (2010: 249). In the context of my argument here, one might think of the canon as the monument in question.

realizing that the gods now receiving the introduction are scientists who use the hair's DNA "to determine who you / were related to when human" (26–27).

Erdrich argues that when framed by science as a sacrifice, the girl of lightning justifies settler-colonial narratives about Indigenous people both past and present. She describes viewers responding to the girl of lightning display with self-righteous horror: "*see what they did—child sacrifice, / fattened 'em up, drugged 'em*" (33–34; italics in original). Rather than seeing a spiritual ceremony, non-Indigenous viewers conclude that "Spanish violence, Christian influence, / border fences, all deserved because of her" (35–36). The new discovery does not lead to new knowledge; it instead solidifies settler-colonial convictions of the "savage" nature of Indigenous peoples and settlers' own superiority. Only one white voice, represented in an introductory quote beneath the title, seems to speak of the girl of lightning and her companions with compassion: "'the bodies seemed so much like sleeping children that working with them felt 'almost more like a kidnapping than archeological work,' Dr. Miermont said. *New York Times*, September 11, 2007" (67). Yet even this discomfort, this awareness of the girl of lightning as a person rather than an archeological or anthropological artifact is not enough to stop the scientific analysis; indeed, it is not even enough to have that analysis offer a new narrative of Indigenous people.[9] It simply reinforces the settler-colonial narratives of savage Indigeneity and civilized settler-colonialism.

And yet the girl of lightning persists, with some viewers understanding her original purpose. Even "cased in plastic, cased in glass," (31) the natural world remembers her and tries to reach her: "Thunder won't forget you, hums / a generator's song in cooler vents" (44–46). Although the persona voices concern for the girl of lightning's fate in the hands of science and almost closes the poem with the distressing notion that the girl's "six years plus five centuries / come to this: *doom, doom, doom*" (47–48; italics in original), the persona precedes the threat of doom with the thunder still reaching the girl and ends the poem with the assertion that "Lightning still sighs: *release, release, release* (49; italics in original). Erdrich thus suggests not only that the natural world still understands and accepts the girl's ceremony but also that if she were to be released from this new scientific display, rendered more damaging by Erdrich than any notion of

---

[9] Karen Poremski's commentary on Erdrich's *National Monuments* and the inclusion of some of the collection's poems in *Museum Anthropology* is helpful here. She argues that

> Erdrich engages in a mode of storytelling that makes it possible for her readers to understand that things—bones and sacred objects—can be imbued with life. By doing so, she makes the first step in a process that change museum policy, public policy, and more widely, human attitudes about American Indian remains and artifacts.
>
> (2015: 3)

She goes on to write that "the poems from Erdrich's *National Monuments* in *Museum Anthropology* give voice to remains and objects and speak out against the colonialist practices of collection and study" (4). I have discussed *National Monuments* with Erdrich on multiple occasions and she often talks about academics, saying "that's who I wrote it for" (personal communication with author). With Erdrich's comment in mind, we should extend Poremski's argument to include literary scholars, who I suggest here need a change in policy when it comes to constructing the canon.

"sacrifice" imagined by non-Indigenous viewers, the girl of lightning will once again be a positive messenger for her people. For American Indian literature to avoid the voyeuristic, even violent reading that Western science gives the girl of lightning, we must expand the ways we give readers to approach literary texts.

Like Erdrich, Turcotte opens his poem about an Indigenous girl in a cabinet—"Now We Sleep"—by emphasizing the dominant culture's efforts to frame our understanding of her body. Under the title and distanced from the first stanza, Turcotte writes "INCA MAIDEN DEBUTS—headline, *USA Today*, 22 May 1996, 57." Each stanza is dedicated primarily to the West's understanding of the "Inca Maiden," with Indigenous people's understanding rendered almost exclusively through parenthetical commentary. However, rather than having the usual rhetorical effect of signaling non-vital information, the parentheses here function as heightening signifiers. The poem reads as if the persona is carrying on one conversation with the dominant culture—"you"—while telling the "real story" to Indigenous people—"we," "us," in the parenthetical comments, even when those remarks are addressed to the dominant culture. They function as theatrical asides intended only for the Indigenous audience. The poem's form further emphasizes this point by indenting, setting these parenthetical remarks apart and in opposition to the Western scientific understanding of the bodies.

The asides, taken separately from the rest of the poem, form a rebuke of the Western arrogance that disturbs the Inca Maiden through the application of Western epistemologies. They remind readers that "(she was not lost)" (2002: 3), "(she was given")" (11), "(you did not hear her whisper)" (18), and "(we must name her La Molestada)" (26). The progression of pronouns here serves to heighten the opposing understandings of the young girl. The persona spends the first two stanzas highlighting the personhood—not the spectacle—of the girl by twice opening the parenthetical comments with "she." This emphasis is amplified by the opening stanza's focus on the Western "discovery" of the young woman, which is in opposition to the insurgent parenthetical commentary:

> Now that you have found
> our little southern sister
> (she was not lost),
> at twenty thousand feet
> upon a steep Peruvian slope,
> frozen and crouching
> to her knees.
>
> (1–7)

This notion of discovery is interrupted, however, by the parenthetical observation in line 3 that the girl "(was not lost)." The persona continues to disrupt the Western narrative in the second stanza by countering the imputation of "sacrifice" with the assertion that "(she was given)" (11).

The persona again directly rebukes the Western reading of this Indigenous body in the third stanza, noting that even though

> you have counted
> all of her beautiful teeth
> (you did not hear her whisper).
>
> (16–18)

Here, science, the pre-eminent form of Western knowledge, does not—or will not—hear the girl's voice. Science is too busy counting her teeth to hear what she might have to say. Western scientific epistemologies cannot hear Indigenous epistemologies and thus cannot fully understand the meaning of the girl or her gift. The demand for such an Indigenous understanding comes in the penultimate stanza, in which the persona's parenthetical voice changes to first person plural: "(we must name her La Molestada)" (26). The plural here is important—the poem asks us to understand Indigenous people in hemispheric terms, unified by their colonized experience—as is the auxiliary verb "must." Indigenous people are compelled to push back against Western science's reading of this body; they cannot let the West's reading of this body stand uncontested.[10] The Indigenous naming of the girl—La Molestada, the bothered or disturbed—highlights the irony of the West's chosen name, Juanita, god's gift. Here, the aside functions as dramatic irony with the Indigenous audience being more likely to understand tension between the meaning of Juanita and their name, La Molestada, which signifies Western science's inability or unwillingness to understand that the girl was a gift for the creator(s).

The painful irony of the penultimate stanza cannot be missed. "La Molestada" has been taken from her resting place:

> as you seal her inside your glass
> refrigerated case, to place
> her forever on display
> to presidents and kings.
>
> (27–30)

While failing to recognize the Indigenous cultural meaning of this girl, anthropologists and curators make a spectacle of her body, encased in glass on the altar of Western science, for "presidents and kings" (30). Turcotte's poem ends on a less hopeful note than Erdrich's, whose maiden can still feel the love of thunder and lightning and thus has a connection to the Indigenous world. In contrast, Turcotte's Indigenous people seem trapped, just as the maiden is in the "glass / refrigerated case" (27–28):

> Now we curl up, so civilized,
> to join her

---

[10] Lee Schweninger writes in his analysis of *Exploding Chippewas* that Turcotte "asks probing questions about authenticity, rejecting the process ... through which authenticity is granted" (2010: 77). Schweninger makes these comments in his discussion of the "Back When" poems, but they are also appropriate for "And Now We Sleep."

> in the terrible dream
> she has been given by you.
>
> (32–35)

The titular line that closes each stanza but the last, "now we sleep," at first seems harmless, almost peaceful, but the last stanza reveals otherwise. All Indigenous people now "join" the maiden, who is no longer at rest but instead on display, misrepresented, and misunderstood. Thus, they will not experience rest but rather "terrible dream[s]" (34). This ominous final image of Indigeneity—invoked by La Molestada, the disturbed—unsettles the viewer with its message that Indigenous people continue to suffer at the hands of colonizers. The shared experience described here evokes the historical and intergenerational trauma that marks the lives of many Indigenous people.

Sherman Alexie's Indians face a living nightmare that reads as a logical extension of the experiences of Turcotte and Erdrich's encased Indians. Alexie offers a dark and irreverent take on Indians in cabinets through the poems "Evolution" and "Pawn Shop" from his first poetry collection, *The Business of Fancydancing* (1992). "Evolution" at first does not seem concerned with the notion of Indians in cabinets. While there is a focus on collection of Indian artifacts by Ameripeans, represented here by the original creator of Indigenous spectacle for non-Indigenous entertainment, Buffalo Bill, the poem begins by describing a pawn shop as the "cabinet" that will contain these artifacts. The pawn shop, which is "right across the border from the liquor store" (1992: 2) and "open 24 hours a day, 7 days a week" (3) sees its Indian customers "come running in with jewelry / television sets, a VCR" (4–5). These items seem harmless, devoid of cultural patrimony, and, because the business is a pawn shop, suggest a paradigm that recognizes Indian agency and also the chance for Indian reclamation. But as the poem progresses, the dangers of the pawn shop emerge. First, the shop holds a valuable cultural item, "a full-length beaded buckskin outfit / it took Inez Muse 12 years to finish" (5–6). While this pawned item reads as more tragic than the TVs and VCRs, it could still be reclaimed and is a product of Indigeneity rather than Indigeneity itself. But then, in stanza 3, Buffalo Bill "takes everything the Indians have to offer" (7) and, sounding more like a curator than a pawn shop owner, "catalogued and filed [it] in a storage room" (8). And then the real carnage begins:

> … The Indians
> pawn their hands, saving the thumbs for last, they pawn
> their skeletons, falling endlessly from the skin.
>
> (8–10)

With the loss of their thumbs, the Indians lose their ability to hang on to things; they even lose their bones and are left with only their "skins," a racially charged word, as their remaining value. Once he is satisfied with his collection, Buffalo Bill "closes up the pawn shop, paints a new sign over the old" (13) and "calls his venture THE MUSEUM OF NATIVE AMERICAN CULTURES" (14). Readers are left wondering, with Buffalo

Bill charging "five bucks a head" for Indians to enter, if this entry fee is for Indians only because the "museum" is housed on the reservation and thus Indians are the most likely audience or if this line implies that this spectacle will be free to white viewers.

In spite of this bleak transition from pawn shop to museum, readers might find a brief glimmer of hope in stanza 4, when the persona observes that "the last Indian has pawned everything / but his heart" (11–12); these lines suggest that Indians have been able to hang on to the most important part of themselves and keep themselves alive. But the rest of the stanza tells us that "Buffalo Bill takes [the heart] for twenty bucks" (12) and the penultimate poem in the collection, "Pawn Shop," confirms that any hope was foolish.

"Pawn Shop" offers the most violent image of Indians in cabinets seen thus far. It does so in spite of its lack of a confirmed white colonial presence—the bartender may be white, but we cannot be sure—and its focus on absence:

> I walk into a bar, after being gone for a while, it's empty.
> The Bartender tells me all the Indians are gone, do I know where
> they went? I tell him I don't know, and I don't know, so he gives
> me a beer just for being Indian, small favors, and I wonder where
> all the Skins disappeared to, and after a while I leave, searching
>   the streets, searching storefronts, until I walk into a pawn shop, find a single
>   heart beating under glass, and I know who it used to belong
> to, I know all of them.

While it may not at first be clear that this pawn shop is the one referenced earlier in "Evolution" (understandable since that pawn shop transitioned to being THE MUSEUM OF NATIVE AMERICAN CULTURES and was located on the rez), the relationship between these two poems is confirmed when the persona observes the "single heart beating under glass" (7), the last item pawned before the pawn shop transitioned to the "museum."

Other readers might infer, as I do, that the bartender is white because he assumes that the Indian persona has knowledge of Indians that he does not have; it can also be inferred in the persona's insistence that he really does not know the Indians' location and is not just refusing to tell the bartender. Perhaps most tellingly, the inference can be found in the persona's aside that actions such as giving the "beer just for being Indian" (4) are "small favors" (4)—a beer for the consequences of settler colonialism? The displacement effected by settler colonialism is represented here in the location of the pawn shop—it was once on the reservation but is now described as being on urban streets amidst storefronts. Whether one assumes land loss or relocation here, both describe processes devastating to Indigenous communities. But even this reference to settler colonialism is not the real violence of the poem. It is not that Ameripean settlers have taken Indigenous lands; it is that they have taken Indigenous hearts. As with the young women in Erdrich's and Turcotte's poems, these bodily remains are displayed in a glass cabinet, spectacle for any wandering eye. While there is only one heart here, as there is only one girl with Erdrich and Turcotte, the poem makes clear that these remains represent Indigenous multitudes. The persona sees only a "single heart beating under glass" (7) and first says that "I know who *it* used to belong to" (7; italics added) but then ends the poem with the statement that "I know *all of them*" (8; italics added). The persona's recognition, combined with the bartender's observation that "all the Indians are gone" suggests that while one heart can be seen, encased in glass as a spectacle of loss and available for purchase, it represents the loss of Indians in the broadest possible sense.

Erdrich, Turcotte, and Alexie describe the outcomes of Western curatorial containment of brown bodies; in contrast, Momaday's Indian in a cabinet is more about the possibility of lost Indigenous readings and the implied danger of Western misreadings of a Kiowa body. Much of N. Scott Momaday's *Way to Rainy Mountain* (1969) is preoccupied with what is visible and what is not as well as the importance of perspective—as much geographic as cultural—in what is seen and not seen. In the book's final section, "The Closing In," Momaday writes the following in what he describes as "the voice of my father, the ancestral voice, and the voice of the Kiowa oral tradition" (2001 [1969]: ix):

> East of my grandmother's house, south of the pecan grove, there is buried a woman in a beautiful dress. Mammedaty used to know where she is buried, but now no one knows. If you stand on the front porch of the house and look eastward toward Carnegie, you know that the woman is buried somewhere within the range of your vision. But her grave is unmarked. She was buried in a cabinet, and she wore a beautiful dress. How beautiful it was! It was one of those fine buckskin dresses, and it was decorated with elk's teeth and beadwork. That dress is still there, under the ground.
>
> (82)

The brown body Momaday describes, unlike those depicted in Erdrich, Turcotte, and Alexie, is not on display and in fact may never be on display because specific knowledge of her is lost. What is compelling here, however, is not what is lost, but what knowledge remains to be "seen." Momaday begins by creating ambiguity regarding the woman in the cabinet through his diction, telling readers that "East of my grandmother's house, south of the pecan grove, there is buried a woman in a beautiful dress" (82). There is no question here, only a statement of fact. But the next sentence introduces the loss of factual information: "Mammedaty used to know where she is buried, but now no one knows" (82). The phrasing here complicates the issue in its suggestion that the knowledge is gone not simply because Mammedaty is gone but because he lost the knowledge while he was still alive. Momaday raises interesting questions about how we are to respond to the image of the woman in the cabinet and what she represents to Momaday specifically and the Kiowa more generally. Is the phrasing of "Mammedaty used to know" rather than "Mammedaty knew" a reflection of the book's larger theme of cultural loss? Or does it instead reflect cultural survivance because the knowledge of the woman persists even without the specifics that a grave marker provides? The additional information Momaday provides suggests the latter and, in its assertion that the past is still vibrant and present, highlights Kiowa temporality and epistemology.

Momaday's description of the Kiowa woman focuses on the material cultural aspects that remain. He writes of her dress—"how beautiful it was!" (82)—and explains that "it was one of those fine buckskin dresses, and it was decorated with elk's teeth and beadwork" (82). It is clear that Momaday culturally sees the dress; it exists in his mind in great detail because of his Kiowa cultural knowledge. And his focus remains on the cultural expression that marked the woman's burial—he tells readers that "the dress is still there, under the ground" but does not mention the cabinet in which the woman was buried, which is surely there as well. But the cabinet is not part of Kiowa cultural practices, so Momaday gives it only brief mention in his "viewing" of the woman's grave.

There are several key distinctions between the woman Momaday sees and Erdrich's girl of lightning, Turcotte's La Molestada, and Alexie's pawn shop Indians, all of whom, while visible, seemed more imagined than real as their personas push back against white, curated readings of the bodies with Indigenous cultural readings and understandings. Momaday's focus remains on the cultural expression associated with the woman's grave rather than the woman's body: he notes only that the dress persists. In contrast, for the girl of lightning and La Molestada, their remains literally *remain*, pulled from the safety of the mountain and subjected to the gaze of museumgoers, while Alexie's museum pawn shop Indians are displayed in bits and pieces. The contrast between these burials and the ongoing knowledge associated with them is telling. Momaday's story, grounded in Kiowa epistemology and ontology, teaches us that we do not need to see to understand. Moreover, the persistence of Kiowa culture in the face of the loss that the woman represents suggests that spectacle—of brown bodies, of Indigenous material culture—erodes while it claims to preserve. We see this erosion in the brown bodies of Erdrich's, Turcotte's, and Alexie's poems whose Indians have lost their cultural protection and much of the cultural context needed to understand their ceremonial bodies.

Momaday's conclusions about his Indian in a cabinet is in one sense more hopeful than the conclusions of Erdrich, Turcotte, and Alexie. First, the remains of the woman are on Kiowa land with Kiowa people and are, therefore, protected from white containment and curation. However, Momaday's story simultaneously reveals implicit threats to these Kiowa remains.[11] The specific community knowledge of the woman has faded, lost even in Momaday's grandfather's lifetime, and only a general sense of the woman's whereabouts endures, with the knowledge of her cultural dress persisting even as knowledge of her exact location fades. As that knowledge leaves the community, the probability of white curation of her remains, should they be discovered, looms ominously, especially when this story is understood in the larger context of cultural loss that permeates Momaday's memoir.

***

[11] Michael Tavel Clarke's comments on Momaday's text capture the ambiguity of Momaday's rendering of the woman in the cabinet and the narrator's knowledge of her: "Momaday's *Way to Rainy Mountain* inherits the complexities of modernist anthropology. The text is neither a simple postmodernist rejection of modernism nor a straightforward postcolonial (or anticolonial) critique of anthropology. Instead, *The Way to Rainy Mountain* perpetuates the modernist project and its long-standing anthropological preoccupations, simultaneously supporting and challenging both" (2017: 387).

The texts I discuss here offer overtly literal renderings of the trope of the colonial gaze, explicitly mapping colonial disruptions of Indigenous narratives represented by the Western curation of Indigenous bodies and the cultural loss that Indigenous people experience as a result of colonization. The emphasis on perspective and relationships to Indigenous spectacle informs and transforms who is on display for whom because in crafting their narratives, Erdrich, Turcotte, Alexie, and Momaday have encased the colonial narrative in an Indigenous one, telling a story of survivance as their Indians in cabinets transcend the notion of spectacle. Erdrich, Turcotte, and Alexie all speak of the problematic curation of Indigenous bodies and the knowledge they hold, while Momaday invokes the potential threat of such curation.

In literary studies, the canon is our curated cabinet and texts are the bodies within. How should we decide what that cabinet contains? And, once that decision is made, how should we curate our cabinet? What signage do we post for readers? In what paradigms do we place the work? I have asked elsewhere "What happens if we keep reading canonical texts the same way? What happens if we read new texts using existing methodologies rather than seeing how the texts might shape a new methodology or pedagogical approach?" (Gercken 2016: 188).[12] I originally asked these questions in the context of a trans-Indigenous analysis of Native American and Maori literature. I ask them now with the addition of questioning the formulation of the canon itself, which risks the inability to more fully understand Indigenous texts if it does not diversify its methodologies. If we rely on such narrow parameters to establish the canon of Native American literature or simply turn 180 degrees and shift to texts that reward Red Readings, what might be lost—or missed entirely?[13]

The ways in which Erdrich, Turcotte, and Alexie engage with problematic Western (mis)readings of Indigenous bodies and Momaday's warning of the potential to misread offer us a way forward as we work to establish canonical parameters and reading strategies that will not only transform the content of the American literary canon but also the ways that we engage with that content. Moreover, Momaday reminds us of the potential limitations to being able to construct a Red Reading with the indication that a Kiowa-specific reading of the Indigenous body he describes is made challenging by the cultural loss he narrates in *The Way to Rainy Mountain*.

With this reading of "Indians in Cabinets," I hope to have demonstrated that by thinking differently about what enters the canon and by approaching existing canonical texts in new ways, we can stimulate new readings, new pedagogical strategies, and perhaps even new methodologies. At the very least, we can expand the canon. As members of the academy, we do not want to be Alexie's Buffalo Bill, choosing fetishized bits of

---

[12] Renato Rosaldo's description of an "elegiac mode of perception" (1989: 107) affecting one's research methodology is useful here not only for its evocation of epistemology but also for its emphasis on nostalgia—colonial nostalgia in this case—to prefer to perceive things as they once were. Such "elegiac postures" (109) also resonate with the concept of curiosity cabinets.

[13] Winter counts and ledger narratives are two important examples of Native story that are too often overlooked in academic literary conversations.

Indigenous stories and placing them in THE CANON OF AMERICAN LITERATURE because of how they reflect Western literary values or a colonial nostalgia for Indians of yesteryear. Nor do we want to produce a separatist category of Native American literature that best serves Red Reading practices and thus emphasizes a vital but not exclusive aspect of Indigenous literary texts.

In *Trans-Indigenous*, Chadwick Allen reminds us that transforming Native American literary scholarship is not a matter of "which writers and texts" we choose "but rather how to train ourselves—and how to train the generation behind us—for the Indigenous scholarship of the future' (2012: *xxxiii*). However, in the broader context of what the academy recognizes and validates as American literature, the question of "which writers" and "which texts" remain. Thus, while I agree that much of the answer to the question of what our critical approach should be lies in the methodologies we adopt, we must first ask ourselves what we are encouraging our students to read—and it must go beyond Indigenous texts that reify Western literary traditions, romanticize our conceptions of Indigenous peoples, or understand them only in a tribal context.

References

Alexie, Sherman. 1992. *The Business of Fancydancing* (Brooklyn, NY: Hanging Loose).
Allen, Chadwick. 2012. *Trans-Indigenous: Methodologies for Global Native Literary Studies* (Minneapolis, MN: University of Minnesota Press).
Anzaldúa, Gloria. 1987. *Borderlands/La Frontera: The New Mestiza* (San Francisco, CA: Aunt Lute Books).
Beavis, William. 1987. "Native American Novels: Homing In," in Brian Swann and Arnold Krupat, eds, *Recovering the Word: Essays on Native American Literature* (Berkeley, CA: University of California Press), 580–620.
Erdrich, Heid. 2008. *National Monuments* (East Lancing, MI: Michigan State University Press).
Erdrich, Heid. 2010. "Poems. *National Monuments*," *Museum Anthropology* 33.2: 249–251.
Gercken, Becca. 2016. "World of Water, World of Sand: Teaching Silko's *Gardens in the Dunes* and Sullivan's *Star Waka*," in David L. Moore, ed., *Leslie Marmon Silko: Ceremony, Almanac of the Dead, Gardens in the Dunes* (London: Bloomsbury), 177–190.
King, Thomas. 2003. *The Truth About Stories* (Minneapolis, MN: University of Minnesota Press).
Momaday, N. Scott. 2001 [1969]. *The Way to Rainy Mountain* (Albuquerque, NM: University of New Mexico Press).
Poremski, Karen M. 2015. "Voicing the Bones: Heid Erdrich's Poetry and the Discourse of NAGPRA," *Studies in American Indian Literatures* 27.1: 1–32.
Revard, Carter. 1982. "Report to the Nation: Claiming Europe," *American Indian Quarterly* 6. 3/4: 305–318.
Rosaldo, Renato. 1989. "Imperialist Nostalgia," *Representations* 26: 107–122.
Schweninger, Lee. 2010. " 'Back When I Used to Be Indian': Native American Authenticity and Postcolonial Discourse," in Deborah L. Madsen, ed., *Native Authenticity: Transnational Perspective on Native American Literary Studies* (New York: State University of New York Press), 69–86.

Smith, Linda Tuhawai. 1999. *Decolonizing Methodologies: Research and Indigenous Peoples* (Dunedin: University of Otago Press).

Tavel Clarke, Michael. 2017. "The New Modernist Studies, Anthropology, and N. Scott Momaday's *The Way to Rainy Mountain*," *Texas Studies in Literature and Language* 59.3: 385–420.

Teuton, Sean Kicummah. 2013. "Cities of Refuge: Indigenous Cosmopolitan Writers and the International Imaginary," *American Literary History* 25.1: 33–53.

Turcotte, Mark. 2002. *Exploding Chippewas* (Evanston, IL: TriQuarterly).

Vizenor, Gerald. 2008. "Aesthetics of Survivance: Literary Theory and Practice," in Gerald Vizenor, ed., *Survivance: Narratives of Native Presence* (Lincoln, NE: University of Nebraska Press), 1–23.

Weaver, Jace, Craig S. Womack, and Robert Warrior. 2005. *American Indian Literary Nationalism* (Albuquerque, NM: University of New Mexico Press).

Womack, Craig S. 1999. *Red on Red: Native American Literary Separatism* (Minneapolis, MN: University of Minnesota Press).

CHAPTER 17

THE LIBERAL IMAGINATION REVISITED

Saul Bellow, Ralph Ellison, and the Crisis of Democracy

JOHANNES VOELZ

LITERATURE and politics, Lionel Trilling claimed in the preface to his best-selling essay collection *The Liberal Imagination* (1950), shared a connection that was "inevitabl[y] intimate, if not always obvious" (2008 [1950]: xviii). While even very good literary critics tended to resist the connection, creative writers, Trilling claimed, embraced it "with enthusiasm" (xviii). Indeed, "the very large majority [of literary writers] have in one way or another turned their passions, their adverse, critical, and very intense passions, upon the condition of the polity" (xviii). The claim that modern literature since about 1800 focused on the political, Trilling insisted, was in no way contradicted by its focus on exploring the self and reviving "concepts of religion" (xviii). These interests, Trilling suggested, "rather support the statement about [literature's] essential commitment to politics" (xviii).

Trilling's insistence on literature's "commitment to politics" may surprise the contemporary reader. After all, throughout the seventy years since the publication of *The Liberal Imagination*, Trilling has come to be seen as the embodiment of the kind of liberalism that stood in the way of an adequately political literary criticism. Trilling's very title— *The Liberal Imagination*—itself pointed to his own critique of an earlier kind of liberalism, that of 1930s progressivism. Trilling rejected it for an alternative kind of liberalism that focused on moral complexity, ambiguity, and dialectics, and that thus repudiated the moral certitude allegedly characteristic of the "red decade." No wonder, then, that the revisionist critics who came after Trilling and took him to task for what could be interpreted as political evasiveness insisted that what he called "political" was in truth a conservative ideology. Its function was to support the Cold War state by elevating the individual to an anti-totalitarian force. The individual envisaged by Trilling's Cold War liberalism, his critics have suggested, could be claimed to be political only by virtue of being apolitical: turning to the moral complexities and difficulties of life at the expense of action, Trilling's ideal self was in truth committed to political passivity and, in remaining passive, embodied a kind of citizen that could be mounted against totalitarian states in which everyone had to act according to the party's master plan.¹

Today, these critiques of Trilling's Cold War liberalism are revealed as having their own history. Expressed most forcefully by critics writing in the 1980s and 1990s, they are the product of a period in which the United States had perfected the use of the Cold War to its own advantage, building a global empire on the scaffolding of the bipolar world order. The faltering of the Soviet bloc, from the perspective of these critics, offered little reason for joy. It suggested, rather, that the United States, as the only remaining super power, would now install its empire—capitalist, militaristic, racist, and hostile to any other form of political organization—on a worldwide scale, with no checks remaining, no alternative imaginable. The rapid embrace of unshackled capitalism in much of the Eastern bloc during the 1990s initially seemed to prove them right.

What has happened since, however, is something the critics of Trilling's liberal imagination did not, and ccould not, foresee. No longer is liberal democracy the political order that the United States unequivocally touts as the way to freedom and urges the rest of the world to adopt. Forces of authoritarian illiberalism that had been simmering for a long time but were generally overlooked now have a firm footing in the global political landscape. And not only at what in the language of the Cold War would have been called the periphery—Brazil, India, Hungary, Poland, etc.—but also at the center of the liberal hegemon. Even while occupying the White House, Donald Trump tested liberal democracy, aimed to dismantle the liberal state as well as the international system once known as the "Washington consensus," and captivated his base by flouting democratic norms. And in a country divided more starkly than at any point since the Civil War, nearly half of the voters supported his politics and political style. They heeded the populist call that promised to take revenge on the cultural, political, and economic establishment in the name of "real" Americans and that openly announced xenophobia, racism, and misogyny as pillars of its platform.²

Partisanship in the United States has been strikingly asymmetrical since its gradual emergence from the late 1960s onwards: it is the right that has increasingly radicalized its own positions, strategically branded political opponents as enemies, and turned political conflict into a culture war (Rosenfeld 2017). Yet, liberal politicians and elites, and a good part of their constituencies, have played their part in turning up the gauges of hyper-partisanship. In the 2010s, they emulated the right's political obstructionism and promoted "negative partisanship" as a way of papering over the cracks in the Democratic Party between a neoliberal establishment and a progressive faction rediscovering class

---

¹ In his New Americanist manifesto "The New Americanists: Revisionist Interventions into the Canon," Donald E. Pease (1990) articulated perhaps the most forceful critique of Trilling along these lines. Other readers of Trilling who brought forth similar critiques are Russell Reising (1993) and Daniel T. O'Hara (1988) and, to some extent, also Cornel West (1989).

² On the connections between authoritarian populism and polarization, see Levitsky and Ziblatt (2018).

politics.³ In political rhetoric, they celebrated themselves for "going high" as others "go low." And night after night, liberal late-night television hosts served as drill masters of their audience. By way of jokes, they inculcated the message of moral superiority ad nauseam.⁴

In the language of the liberal imagination (not just that of Trilling, but of liberal democracy more broadly), it is not an overstatement to say that Trumpism marked the point at which the divisions that had been deepening in the United States since the late 1960s finally led to a fundamental crisis of liberal democracy. US society continues to be politically highly animated (the crisis of democracy is not one of political apathy), but its animation takes the form of animosity. The country has all but lost a functioning civil society in which people engage one another on the basis of their differences. Differences are now treated as differences of identity rather than political position.⁵ While the former cannot be altered but demand respect, the latter are open to revision and transformation through discourse. Liberalism's critics often ridicule the idea of a civil society and the claim that it has deteriorated as a nostalgic dream of a society in which everyone agrees, in which common sense rules, in short: in which people simply get along. But this caricature misrecognizes the crucial idea of what constitutes a liberal-democratic civil society: it is one in which people with a plurality of viewpoints interact with one another and accept the responsibility to respond to those from whom they differ. That responsibility consists of the willingness to reconsider one's own convictions in the face of someone else's views, to hone the "ability to think the limits of [one's] own thought."

This last phrase is Louis Menand's. It is his description, in his preface to a 2008 edition of *The Liberal Imagination*, of Lionel Trilling's intellectual legacy (Menand 2008 [1950]: xiv). "Rethinking the limits of one's own thought" is an ethos, skill, and aspiration. It is endlessly difficult to achieve, and if it has any political dimension, it is a way of engagement that is indirect since it at best contributes to the well-being of a democratic political culture rather than to the attainment of a predetermined political goal. But in times of democratic crisis, in which the ability to engage with those of different persuasions meets structural impediments, it has a vital political function. If, for Trilling, literature was the field in which "essential commitment to politics" could take

---

³ The term "negative partisanship" was popularized—in a critical spirit—by political scientists Alan Abramowitz and Steven Webster. See Abramowitz and Webster (2016), as well as Abramowitz (2018). For a brazen espousal of negative partisanship on the part of liberal elites, as a necessary means to electoral power, see the political writings of novelist Joseph O'Neill in *The New York Review of Books*, particularly "Save the Party, Save the World" (2020).

⁴ In "Toward an Aesthetics of Populism, Part II: The Aesthetics of Polarization," Tom Freischläger and I have offered an analysis of the different cultural and aesthetic strategies of the polarizing right and left (2019). We argue that aesthetic repertoires on the right build on the affect of resentment while those on the left build on that of indignation. From such a bird's eye view, polarization is a process shaping a large-scale cultural formation. At the same time, polarization is strikingly asymmetrical. Resentment and indignation are qualitatively different for only the latter holds up the values from which might be generated a revitalized liberal political culture.

⁵ Several political scientists working on polarization have developed this point. For a particularly useful account, see Mason (2018).

the form of doing "research into the self" (2008 [1950]: xviii), something similar can be claimed from today's perspective. Literature (and literary criticism) may be a field particularly fertile for exploring the possibilities, limitations, and drawbacks of fostering a civil society by putting the self in question, by rethinking the limits of one's own thought. The novel, indeed, may be regarded as an artistic form that is committed to the dialogism—the responsibility to respond—that is the prerequisite for liberal civil society. It is in this sense that Lionel Trilling's insistence on the intimate relation between literature—by which he essentially meant the novel—and liberal democracy remains an urgent concern today.

In this light, this chapter revisits the liberal imagination of two mid-century novels—Saul Bellow's *The Adventures of Augie March* (1953) and Ralph Ellison's *Invisible Man* (1952)—using an expressly presentist method. The aim is not to prove that Cold War liberals were right after all nor to reconstruct their world view, aesthetics, and political context as accurately and comprehensively as possible. Rather, the idea is to plough the literature and literary criticism of the Cold War liberal imagination in search of a "usable past" (to use a phrase coined by Van Wyck Brooks in 1918), to re-read its concerns against our present democratic predicament. It is a form of strategic presentism that is not mindless of history but revisits and revisions history to change the terms and ideological parameters of present-day discourse. Put differently, presentist criticism of this kind uses the past to reconfigure the present. Its starting point is a conviction that Trilling's generation shared with the critics who came to subject them to ideological critique: the problems of American politics are problems of American literature. Not only were literary writers concerned with the polity and the state (and continue to be), but also literary fictions (and other fictional media) have ramifications for whether and how the problems beleaguering American democracy can be confronted. I suggest that this is because democracy is more than a system of government. It is, as Sidney Hook once put it (1939), a "way of life." And while democracy as a way of life is put into practice in the everyday, it is reflected upon, criticized, and reimagined, in fiction.

AUGIE MARCH'S PICARO SOCIETY

In the eyes of many Cold War literary critics, Saul Bellow's third novel, *The Adventures of Augie March*, from 1953, along with Ralph Ellison's *Invisible Man*, published shortly before, in 1952, opened a new chapter of American literary history. "Saul Bellow's new novel is a new kind of book," wrote Delmore Schwartz in his review in *Partisan Review* (1954: 112). In the case of both *Augie* and *Invisible Man*, that alleged newness had much to do with what was *not* new about them: both novels recognizably inscribed themselves into the American literary tradition yet did so with an ethnic and racial difference. Following what Lawrence Buell calls the "Up-From" script that (as he has shown in a magisterial study) makes for one of the major variants of the Great American Novel (2014: 170), Bellow's eponymous protagonist grows up in a poor Jewish and Catholic neighborhood of Chicago but quickly outgrows his humble beginnings. His path leads him to such places as Mexico and Paris, and in between he returns to the place and social setting of his childhood. "A widening spiral," Bellow called the form of his plot, "that begins in the parish, ghetto, slum and spreads into the greater world" (2010: 102). In Buell's apt words, the novel "extravagantly hybridized the ethnic bildungsroman template" (2014: 170), but to get the point just right, the emphasis needs to be placed on hybridization: the novel is neither a classic *bildungsroman* nor a mythical tale of upward mobility. As the allusion of the novel's title to Mark Twain's *The Adventures of Huckleberry Finn* suggests, *The Adventures of Augie March* is more deeply indebted to the picaro tradition. In surprising twists and turns, it details its hero's string of experiences, encounters, leave-takings, and inhabitations of ever new scenes and scenarios, without any clear sense of direction, purpose, or determination. Augie is not out to get rich, make it in the world, become famous, or find recognition by others in any discernible way. He is out for the experience itself, engulfed in sheer immanence. In this respect, there is no qualitative difference between his shenanigans with his pool hall friends in his Chicago neighborhood, his stay with Mrs Renling at a rich people's resort at Benton Harbor, Michigan, his attempt (with his femme fatale girlfriend Thea) to train a bald eagle to hunt iguanas in Mexico, or his shady post-war business deals in Paris. Nor do the other two series of his life—the women he dates and the various jobs he takes on— have any discernible trajectory or even recognizable hierarchy of importance. The focus of the novel, then, is experience itself, a single life lived by one individual who happens to be endowed with extraordinary resources of energy, an usual degree of vivacity, and an insatiable desire for sensory intake and verbal output.

Both Augie March and his creator came to be seen as the embodiment of an idea that lay at the heart of the liberal imagination: that the literary exploration of life, of what it means to be human, must take place in a universal register; that the specificity of circumstance, of social conditioning, is not to be neglected but in no way should be taken as the confining limits of what it means to be human. Trilling, in a short review written for the book club he directed at the time (reprinted as the introduction to the novel's 1965 Modern Library edition), praised Bellow for depicting sordid social conditions, not for the purpose of social critique but to show "that people who live in 'conditions' really do live" (1965: ix). Having created, in Augie, a character who transcended his social situatedness into universal significance, Bellow managed to have the same achievement conferred unto himself. Leslie Fiedler, in a 1957 essay on Bellow occasioned by the publication of *Seize the Day*, the novella that followed *Augie March*, announced Bellow's "appearance as the first Jewish-American novelist to stand at the center of American literature" (1999 [1957]: 110), a feat that, according to Fiedler, wasn't merely Bellow's personal accomplishment but in line with the larger move of American Jews from the margins to the center of US culture.

In the mind of Cold War critics, Bellow's achievement of having universalized the marginal—as Menand notes laconically, this is what "Nobels are awarded" for (2015: 76); Bellow got his in 1976—rested on his novel's individualist outlook, its focus on the eponymous hero's continuous flight from any encumbrance. Echoing earlier critics, Menand wrote in 2015 that "The subject of *Augie March* is the same as the subject of [his previous two novels] *Dangling Man* and *The Victim*: the danger of becoming trapped in other people's definition of you" (76). The novel itself shouts out this interpretation, especially in light of Augie's romantic life. Augie, strikingly good-looking, seldom finds himself in the role of pursuer, though he does try, unsuccessfully, to conquer his first crush, Hilda Novinson, as well as Esther Fenchel, the woman he is most deeply infatuated with. For the most part, however, it is women who are out to conquer him. Most audaciously, Esther's sister Thea, in full awareness that Augie has fallen for Esther, sets up her mind to pursue him until he will obey her. She eventually succeeds but—crucially—only temporarily. As Thea prophesies in one of the couple's many fights, Augie repeats this pattern over and over: it is he who gives in to whoever pursues him until the arrival of the next pursuer. The pattern even extends to women who must grudgingly accept that their proper role in Augie's life is that of mother rather than wife. Mrs Renling, the wife of Augie's employer in Evanston, comes close to casting Augie in the role of male escort, only to propose to adopt him. As Augie muses, he has the personality—"pliable and grateful-seeming" (1996 [1953]: 151)—that invites such friendly takeovers. "Something about me suggested adoption," he notes (151). But whether it is Mrs Renling, Thea, or anybody else, Augie will not be held back. "Just when Mrs. Renling's construction around me was nearly complete I shoved off" (151).

As much as contemporaneous critics praised Bellow for capturing his protagonist's vitality, Augie's perennial shoving off became a bone of contention. Trilling, at the end of his overwhelmingly positive review, rejected Bellow's controlling idea that "whatever fixes life and specializes and limits a person to a function ... endangers [the] wholeness of life" (Trilling 1965: x). "I resist [the novel's] propaganda," Trilling ended his review in a sudden switch of tone, "holding an opinion the direct opposite of Mr. Bellow's, that without function it is very difficult to be a person and have a fate" (xiii). Bellow and Trilling extended the debate in an exchange of letters. Bellow insisted, "It isn't that Augie resists every function—that would make him a tramp," and further explained that Trilling, in imputing propaganda to the book, had overlooked the Emersonianism of Augie that redefined social aloofness as spiritual integrity. Quoting from Emerson's "The Transcendentalist," Bellow wrote, "Your virtuous projects, so called, do not cheer me. If I cannot work at least I need not lie" (2010: 122). Trilling, for his part, doubled down, suggesting that the Emerson reference amounted to an evasion of the novel's problematic moral import:

> I had the sense, which before I had never had, that there was an issue between us. A really very important one, and maybe someday we will join it! You mustn't underestimate the doctrinal intention of your book—I mean its cultural, characterological, moral point, whether or not it was consciously made. It's there, and it's important.
>
> (2018: 227)

The alternatives of Bellow's and Trilling's debate—an unencumbered individualism associated with the name of Emerson versus a non-reductive humanism committed to moral and social duty—were characteristic of Cold War liberalism's discursive universe. They are, incidentally, the very terms Ralph Ellison employed in his essay "Twentieth-Century Fiction and the Black Mask of Humanity," published in 1953 (the year of Bellow's and Trilling's exchange) in order to identify "the two major conflicting drives operating in nineteenth-century America." "Humanism," wrote Ellison, "is man's basic attitude toward a social order which he accepts, and individualism his basic attitude toward one he rejects" (2003: 89–90). If this was no longer the basic conflict in the twentieth century, it was because individualism had won out, suggested Ellison. Trilling's position, for Ellison, was démodé but nonetheless present as something America had lost.

There is no reason, however, to stay beholden to the Cold War liberals' terms of the debate, and, in fact, a strategically presentist reading ought to revise the terms of the past in order to generate new ones for the present. Regarding Bellow's novel in this light means exploring whether Augie March's perennial shoving off might be interpreted quite differently from the way Cold War critics like Trilling, and at times even Bellow himself, had suggested. For it is not necessary to interpret Augie as a self that breaks loose from any and all encumbrances, no matter whether one approves of it, in the Emersonian spirit, as a sign of incorruptible self-reliance, or rejects it as an ultimately asocial form of irresponsibility. Indeed, Augie's picaro career can be understood precisely as a kind of responsibility, understood quite literally as dialogical responsiveness.

The phrase "dialogical responsiveness" requires a quick detour, given that references to the dialogical necessarily invoke the name of Mikhail Bakhtin. It should be noted that a broad array of thinkers during the first half of the twentieth century committed themselves to theorizing the dialogical.[6] But in the late twentieth century, it was Bakhtin, more than anyone else, who captivated the interest of American literary critics exploring the ramifications of dialogue. Ken Hirschkop, in an influential study of Bakhtin's dialogism, has taken American liberal readers of Bakhtin to task for their inadequate understanding of what is involved in Bakhtin's concept of dialogism. Hirschkop's critique, insofar as it concerns American liberals' investment in the idea of dialogue, is relevant in the present context, although the argument I am developing here does not directly build on Bakhtin. In Hirschkop's telling, American readers typically conflate dialogism with actual dialogue and then elevate dialogue to an ideal image of liberal democracy. In the case of literary criticism, this misreading leads to the argument that literary representations of dialogue become charged with political (i.e. democratic) promise. As Hirschkop states:

> American interpreters derive models of social life from supposedly unadorned linguistic reality so effortlessly because in their context "dialogue" is already freighted with social and political meaning. In American public life dialogue stands for that

---

[6] Michael Theunissen (1986) has provided a philosophical genealogy of the concept of dialogue within the continental tradition. Among American thinkers, Kenneth Burke's (1953 [1931]) concept of "counter-statement" may be the most salient.

scene of negotiative give-and-take, of debate aimed at compromise, so central to the identity of liberal democracy.

(1999: 8)

For Hirschkop, a fuller understanding of dialogism as worked out by Bakhtin distinguishes actual dialogue from the dialogical understood as genre—a much larger, historically specific, communicative formation. The genre that concerned Bakhtin more than any other as the proper realm of dialogism was the novel, not because the novel provided space for the literary representation of dialogue, though some novels—*Augie March* among them—do, but because novels create a dialogue between and among different languages. Bakhtin referred to this as "heteroglossia," defined by Hirschkop as "the 'internal stratification of a unified national language' into a multiplicity of linguistic styles, jargons, and dialects, differentiated by various social pressures and contexts" (22; quote in single quotation marks from Bakhtin 1982).

To understand how the dialogical responsiveness of Augie March—protagonist and novel—can serve as a resource for revisiting the liberal imagination, Hirschkop's critique of American liberal interpretations of dialogism needs to be taken seriously, if not quite on its own terms. To say that dialogism is not to be confused with dialogue is a crucial point—I will come back to it—but to effectively exclude dialogue from dialogism, as Hirschkop suggests, is unproductive. For *Augie March* is a case in which dialogue is a building block of dialogism.

Dialogical responsiveness is a key to reinterpreting Augie's habitual leave-taking because Augie's adventures take him from one social and communicative situation to the next. Readings that emphasize the fact that he leaves each situation—or that the situations leave him—create the false idea that Augie is a lone individual: uncommitted, self-concerned, obsessively autonomous. The tale Bellow tells—which is presented, explicitly, as the tale that Augie tells—couldn't differ more strikingly from such a portrayal, not least because each episode is one in which people tell Augie their story. "I was a listener by upbringing," he himself points out (1996 [1953]: 72).

Augie March is not only episodic in that it strings together adventures but also in that it serializes the telling of episodes, shared among characters. This, in fact, is how Bellow manages to cram the many characters, each with their own story, into his book. And it is their actions, related in their own words or those of yet other characters, that provide the substance of what becomes legible as "the adventures of Augie March." As a more or less random example, one can point to the closing of the novel. Here, in a final, directionless turn, Augie accompanies his and Stella's Paris housemaid, Jacqueline, to Bruges. Jacqueline is an ordinary woman, and she does not take up any special place in Augie's life nor in the narrative logic of the novel. Yet, the reader gets to witness her *en route* conversation with Augie: she asks him to sing a song; he can only think of "La Cucaracha" and, upon learning that the song is Mexican, she exclaims that it has always been her dream go to Mexico; he is struck by a fit of laughter, at the absurdity of her dream as much as at the absurdity of life. Save for the ensuing philosophical reflection on laughter that provides the novel's landing point, the episode is insignificant so long as the characters are viewed as separate entities. Its significance resides in the characters' communicative interaction. It is, to be sure, just another conversation. But, like all the other interactions that make up the book, it creates, if only briefly, a scene made unique and memorable by way of the characters' interaction. The novel's picaresque episodes, in other words, are communicative situations that give rise to shared realities. For the reader, this episodic structure has the effect of traveling from one world to the next, each of these worlds arising from a dialogical encounter.

Augie March is a novel of witnessing, listening, following, of becoming part of ever new scenes. It only makes sense that Augie lets himself drift along, becoming a metaphorical adoptee. In a letter written shortly after his exchange with Trilling, Bellow himself goes even further and interprets Augie's passiveness in terms of servitude, thus flipping around the charge that his hero shirks duty:

> People have accused me of asociality, and Trilling asserts Augie is "wrong" i.e. unprincipled. To me Augie is the embodiment of willingness to serve, who says "For God's sake, make use of me, only do not use me to no purpose. Use me."
>
> (2010: 126)

What appears as curious, and even magical, is that in all his passiveness and obedience Augie is so attractive to others. But this is only curious because we perceive the world through Augie's eyes and thus adopt his outlook onto the world, an outlook whose sensory apparatus is oriented to observing others and ill suited to perceive how, in the shadow of his own perceptions, he also acts. Taking his perspective, the reader becomes as blind as Augie is to the ways in which he helps shape his world. From a dialogical perspective, on the other hand, it is not surprising that he who knows how to listen leads a popular life, stocked with a wide variety of characters with whom he co-creates a social world. Far from being an unencumbered individual who evades social responsibility and "function," he is embedded in life made vibrant by his own ability to listen. Put differently, behind Augie's alleged unencumbered individualism emerges a particular social form of mixture that becomes more readily discernible if we focus on the novel's non-individualist features such as the crowded *dramatis personae* characteristic of the picaro novel. Crucially, however, this social form is presented under the guise of individualism—a new, capacious individualism that is starting to include ethnic minorities who have not been heard from before.

Indeed, Bellow's Cold War critics employed individualist terms—such as energy, vitality, exuberance—to capture a quality Augie seems to be endowed with by some mysterious force. What these critics failed to see is that these qualities don't belong so much to Augie as they emerge from the social life into which he inserted himself "by upbringing." A similar individualist bias is noticeable in the critical response to the novel's striking language. While Cold War critics praised the innovative vitality of Bellow's (and by extension Augie's) language and celebrated it as uniquely American, that vitality is the result of a dialogic force field that is reminiscent of what Bakthin meant by heteroglossia. Here, it becomes apparent that, at least in the case of *Augie March*, dialogism cannot be understood outside of dialogue since a good deal of the novel's "strange mélange of ornate locutions, Chicago patois, Joycean portmanteaus, and Yiddish cadences" (Menand 2015: 76) depends on character speech.

But the novel's dialogism extends beyond "the multiplicity of linguistic styles, jargons, and dialects" to "the various social pressures and contexts," to recall Hischkop (1999: 22). "Bellow's supple style," notes Steven Kellman, "accommodates not only the varied languages Augie hears, but also varied registers of the English language, from the vernacular to the inkhorn" (2017: 37). Having absorbed languages, dialects, and styles of the world around him, he becomes an oratory machine that mixes high and low, ethnic margin and cultural center. In short, the novel and its protagonist refuse to accept any social limits of language.

Necessary for such a fiction of linguistic democracy is the conceit that Augie is an autodidactic scholar of the canon, someone who can quote freely from Montesquieu, Plotinus, Tolstoy, Chaucer, and, of course, the Bible without displaying the least trace of an academic habitus. He is, as Kellman puts it pointedly, "a child of Chicago's mean streets, but he actually reads the books he is commissioned to steal" (37). He has also come into possession, through Einhorn, his one-time boss, teacher, and figurative adoptive father, of a "damaged set of Dr. Eliot's Five-Foot Shelf" (187), from which he reads extensively (including the works of Helmholtz). The allusion is clearly to the fifty-two-volume Chicago "Great Books of the Western World," on which Bellow had worked, under the direction of Mortimer Adler, from 1943 to 1945 at the University of Chicago, and which had just appeared in 1952. If the education gained from these books allowed Augie to fuse high and low in his speech and thus sound out a notion of democracy centered on the idea of dehierarchization, the Great Books project could itself be understood as a democratic endeavor built on the idea of timeless human equality (though a more chastened perspective trained by ideology critique would, of course, be quick to point out the exclusions that are effected by canonization). As Mark Greif explains in *The Age of the Crisis of Man*, "The Chicago Great Books idea, of course, required as its essence that men were the same in all ages, and the 'human spirit' the same—that was why the same canon of books could be read with profit by all" (2015: 194).

Augie's performance of heteroglossia thus balances his own speech—a dehierarchized tumbling of the social structure become language—with that of his myriad interlocutors, who are likewise spread across the social space. The novel creates the utopian scenario of a world in which everyone can talk, and listen, to everyone else, and, even better, it promises how such a vision come true would feel: not frightening, unnerving, or sense-numbing, but outright exhilarating. And to drive home the aesthetic effect, Bellow directs his protagonist's speech at the reader, involving them in a dizzying exchange. At times, Augie sounds as if he were writing the reader a postcard: "Stella and I are in Europe now and have been since the end of the war" (1996 [1953]: 516). The next moment, Bellow has Augie sound as if he were talking to a friend over late-night beers, except that the only one there to listen is the reader: "She wanted to come for professional reasons, and I'm in a kind of business I'll soon tell about. Anyway, I was in Florence; I travel all over; a few days before I had been in Sicily where it was warm" (516). Augie, the meandering democrat, addresses the reader directly at his most colloquial. In *Augie March*, the dehierachizing force of heteroglossia pushes informality to the point where it becomes a form of intimacy.

Reading Bellow in a presentist spirit, in short, allows us to reconsider *Augie March* as a novelist's rumination on the sensory reality of a civil society in which people may not be primarily concerned with politics but, in part for that reason, can engage one another with desire, sympathy, cunning, and above all, mutual fascination. But there are also less obvious dimensions to this reconceived version of Bellow's liberal imagination. The novel rather subtly insists that Augie's Heraclitean flux depends on agents and agencies of stability. Most immediately, this dependency is made clear by Augie's frequent returns to Chicago, his old friends, his mother, and his brothers.

Moreover, it is the book's myriad institutions, some of which belong to the welfare state, some of which are private, that stabilize Augie's path of impermanence. The attitude toward them, however, is seldom appreciative. Welfare institutions are there to be taken advantage of. Right from the start, Grandma Lausch, the March family's boarder who has come to dominate the household, instructs young Augie to lie to people at the free dispensary where his mother hopes to get her glasses. "The idea was that Mama wasn't keen enough to do it right. That maybe one didn't need to be keen didn't occur to us; it was a contest" (4). Towards the end of the novel, after having surgery at Chicago's County Hospital, Augie reflects on "how of all our family, including old Grandma, Simon was the only one who had managed to stay out of an institution" (488). His mentally challenged brother Georgie, Grandma Lausch, his mother: all have been institutionalized. This is what has allowed Augie and his brother Simon to pursue their paths.

While, in the world of *Augie March*, the very idea of relying on institutions evokes mixed emotions of shame, resentment, and the desire to outsmart them, at crucial points there is also a very different valuation of social organization. One of Augie's jobs, after all, is to organize workers as a Congress of Industrial Organizations (CIO) operative. It is a job that stays with him after he has left it. Indeed, being a union organizer becomes part of Augie's identity, though it should be noted that for Augie, identity, in order to lose its constricting force, must be put into the retrospective mode: "I, the ex-organizer, didn't say anything," Augie relates as he observes Thea's chaotic home (315).

Most crucial for the revaluation of institutions is Augie's plan for the future: he wants to build and run an orphanage in the countryside, a pastoral community of love, care, and bliss:

> I'd fix up a shop for woodwork. Maybe I'd even learn how to repair my own car. My brother George could be the shoemaking instructor. Maybe I'd study languages so I could teach them. My mother could sit on the porch and the animals would come around her, by her shoes, the roosters and the cats. Maybe we could start a tree nursery.
>
> (457)

It is the only scheme for the future Augie ever develops, and it is clear that he doesn't have the wherewithal to make it work. But its sheer existence nonetheless underlines that *Augie March* can be read as a thought experiment of a liberal imagination that is democratic not in its universal individualism but in its overcoming of individualism. More precisely, Bellow's novel reconceives individual liberty as a form of social embeddedness that retains individualism's fluidity, mobility, and impermanence. The diagnostic (and, one might add, literary) strength of the novel is that it moreover points to the limits of that vision. *Augie March* registers its vision's dependence on social formations of permanence, stability, and care, but it also recognizes that such forms of collective being can be reconciled with the ideal of the democratized picaro society only by a dreamy stretch of the imagination. The two worlds will have to coexist, but in actual fact, they will do so in a mood of mutual begrudging.

INVISIBLE MAN'S BLUES INTERVAL

Both *Augie March* and Ellison's *Invisible Man* are novels that feature famous first sentences (or, in the case of *Augie*, half-sentences). Indeed, they sound like echoes of one another. "I am an American, Chicago born," asserts Augie (1996 [1953]: 3). Ellison's protagonist offers an equally emphatic self-definition—"I am an invisible man" (1995 [1952]: 3)—but what he claims is something like the inversion of Augie's proclamation. Technically, Augie was born into a Jewish American community and has spiraled out of this world into ever wider orbits. But the opening line, in denying that there is a difference between the narrating and the narrated self, insists that he has always already transcended the limitations of being an American Jew, that he has always already embodied national, even universal, subjectivity. To Ellison's unnamed protagonist, no such transcendence is available. And yet, in defining himself as an invisible man, he, too, rejects the particular (in this case, racial) category that society ascribes to him. Instead, he defines himself as misrecognized: his identity lies in the interval of a racist classification imposed upon him and an individuality transcending social conditions. This gap demarcates the identity space of not being seen.

Invisible Man's identity space thus works like a musical interval: it can only be perceived and identified if, to the inner ear, two notes sound together. Because of this simultaneity, it becomes a matter of perspective whether *Invisible Man* discloses that the liberal fiction of a colorblind, universal subject is a lie or whether Invisible Man (the character) becomes an embodiment of the liberal subject because of his insistence on human complexity in the face of dominant racial stereotypes.

This ambiguity lies at the heart of Ellison's novel, and it marks the crucial difference to Bellow's. Instead of arranging, in the manner of *Augie March*, the particular and the universal as a progressively outward spiraling sequence, *Invisible Man* puts them side by side. The result is an imagination that is liberal and that at the same time registers, even puts center stage, the fact of persistent racist exclusion that cannot be squared with the principles of liberalism. For Ellison's protagonist, this duality leads to a split of self and world: "I've come a long way from those days when, full of illusion, I lived a public life and attempted to function under the assumption that the world was solid and all the relationships therein," Invisible Man muses in the epilogue. "Now I know men are different and that all life is divided and that only in division is there true health" (576).

Not all readers heard the two notes of *Invisible Man*'s interval. Indeed, the novel's universalist appeal and its affirmation of the ideals of American democracy—what Invisible Man, in the epilogue, calls "the principle on which the country was built" (574)—garnered Ellison recognition among Cold War liberals. Bellow, in his review of *Invisible Man* for *Commentary*, published in June 1952, praised Ellison for speaking for humanity. "Mr. Ellison has not adopted a minority tone. If he had done so, he would have failed to establish a true middle-of-consciousness for everyone" (2015: 62). In pointing to Ellison's tone, Bellow makes a point about Ellison's modernist aesthetic. Like many contemporaneous critics, Bellow took Ellison's recognizably artistic writing style as a claim to universality. By the same token, Bellow imagined that the style itself had something to do with the consciousness represented. If what went on in Invisible Man's consciousness could be expressed in these terms, then clearly it was a book that addressed not any specific experience (say, racism) but concerns "that we can all recognize, burn at, weep over" (61).

Ellison and James Baldwin, in rejecting Richard Wright as guide for their own literary aesthetics, found keen listeners in the likes of Lionel Trilling. For when Trilling, in "Reality in America," the first part of which was originally published in *Partisan Review* in 1940 and later featured as the opening essay to *The Liberal Imagination* (1950), takes down Theodore Dreiser and the entire naturalist tradition and praises Henry James instead, he spells out a set of concerns that share common ground with Ellison and Baldwin. As Michael Nowlin argues:

> "[P]ostwar liberalism," peculiarly harnessed to a modernist canon, got one of its most influential elaborations in Lionel Trilling's *The Liberal Imagination* (1950), which, though devoid of a single reference to an African American writer, helped establish the terms for debunking Richard Wright...
>
> (2004: 118)

Indeed, in "Reality in America" (in the version published in *The Liberal Imagination*) Trilling opposed "Dreiser's vulgar materialism" (2008 [1950]: 20) to James's "awareness of tragic, irony, and multitudinous distinctions" (11). The question of literary aesthetics—Dreiser's naturalism versus James's modernism—was a question of the political imagination. Much more was at stake in the espousal of James's (proto-)modernism than a matter of aesthetic judgment. "Dreiser and James: with that juxtaposition we are immediately at the dark and bloody crossroads where literature and politics meet," Trilling wrote in a voice of urgency (11).

Baldwin and Ellison made their case against Wright in terms that rhyme with Trilling's, and they published it in the same venues. Baldwin placed "Everybody's Protest

Novel" (1949) and the follow-up piece "Many Thousands Gone" (1951) in *Partisan Review*, the leading publication of anticommunist liberalism. In the latter essay, he charged that Wright had "attempted to redeem a symbolical monster in social terms" (1998: 26) instead of taking on the true task of the black novelist: "To tell his story [i.e. Bigger Thomas's, and by extension, any Black man's living under racist conditions] is to begin to liberate us from his image and it is, for the first time, to clothe this phantom with flesh and blood, to deepen, by our understanding of him and his relationship to us, our understanding of us and of all men" (34). Baldwin draws an immediate connection between battling racist stereotypes and illuminating the human condition and ends up on a point not unlike Bellow's: great Black writing speaks to what concerns "all men."

Ellison, for his part, was more even-handed in appraising Wright and, in "Richard Wright's Blues," published in *Antioch Review* in 1945 and later included in Ellison's first collection of essays, *Shadow and Act* (1964), found much positive to report about the outlook of Wright's autobiographical novel *Black Boy*. "Wright knows perfectly well that Negro life is a by-product of Western civilization, and that in it, if only one possesses the humanity and humility to see, are to be discovered all those impulses, tendencies, life and cultural forms to be found elsewhere in Western society" (Ellison 2003: 143). But in "That Same Pain," a 1961 interview with Richard Stern that was also included in *Shadow and Act*, he echoed Baldwin's critique, adopting cold war liberalism's rejection of "determinism" and "ideology" in favor of "imagination," "the individual," and "humanity":

> I felt that Wright was overcommitted to ideology—even though I, too, wanted many of the same things for our people. You might say that I was much less a social determinist. But I suppose that basically it comes down to a difference in our concepts of the individual. I, for instance, found it disturbing that Bigger Thomas had none of the finer qualities of Richard Wright, none of the imagination, none of the sense of poetry, none of the gaiety. And I preferred Richard Wright to Bigger Thomas. Do you see? Which gets you ... back to his conception of the quality of Negro humanity.
>
> (2003: 74; ellipses added)[7]

The echoes between Ellison and Baldwin, on the one hand, and Trilling and Bellow, on the other, are revealing for an historical understanding of how Ellison and Baldwin succeeded in writing themselves into the center of mid-twentieth-century American literature. Yet, such contextualization threatens to hide as much as it reveals. What it can easily obscure is, indeed, the characteristics of the peculiar identity space of invisibility. In the liberal imagination, as expressed by Trilling and Bellow, the particular must be made to coincide with the universally human and ultimately become fully synthesized

---

[7] *Shadow and Act* is a rich repository for studying Ellison's evolving perception of Wright. Also included in this collection is "The World and the Jug," in which Ellison revisits his earlier assessment of *Black Boy* in "Richard Wright's Blues." Indeed, Ellison's turn against Wright takes place in a reading of a passage that had already featured, on opposite terms, in the earlier essays. I thank Stephan Kuhl for pointing this out to me. For an instructive account of Ellison's relation to Wright, see Kuhl (2021).

in a dialectical *Aufhebung*. In *Invisible Man*, on the other hand, the particular and universal exist as interval: they sound out together without becoming one.

Spelling out the substance of the interval takes the form of negativity: *Invisible Man* is not a novel about racism in America, yet it is never not about racism in America. The very vocabulary of invisibility—understood, in Ellison's sense, as the onlooker's incapacity to see another person on individual terms—has long played a significant role in theories of modernity that focus on the conflict between conformity and individuality. It also resonates with philosophical ideas of intersubjectivity and particularly with Hegelian theories of recognition.[8] A novel centered on invisibility thus invites readings in a philosophical, and hence universal, key. Yet, at the same time, *Invisible Man* is not a work of philosophy but a novel. And as Ellison put it in his essay "Change the Joke and Slip the Yoke," "novels are time-haunted. Novels achieve timelessness through time. If the symbols appearing in a novel link up with those of universal myth they do so by virtue of their emergence from the specific texture of a specific form of social reality" (2003: 111). Replace "myth" with "philosophy" and you have *Invisible Man*'s specific double-voicedness: it is at once an exploration of a specific social reality and of a generalizable drama of social philosophy.

If Bellow's protagonist eschews the reifying effects of social ascription by immersing himself in ever new social interactions, Invisible Man must undergo a process of learning—a mythical descent into the underground and a subsequent rebirth—in order to develop a sense of self in a world set against the people of his race. Both protagonists are picaro figures, but their trajectories differ significantly.[9] Scene after scene, setting after setting, from the Battle Royal to the disastrous chauffeuring of Mr Norton, and on to the betrayal by Jack and the leadership of the Brotherhood, Ellison's hero must learn painfully that in such a world, the hope of becoming recognized, in colorblind fashion, simply for what he is—a human being, an individual—is futile. To remain pledged to this hope requires appealing to recognition from whites who, limited by their privileged position, their fear of losing status, and their unwillingness to confront their own guilt, are incapable of recognizing him.

By the time of the prologue and epilogue, as he is composing his notes from the underground, Invisible Man has come to understand that invisibility is not a characteristic of his own but rather a deficiency in others: "That invisibility to which I refer occurs because of a peculiar disposition of the eyes of those with whom I come in contact. A matter of the construction of their *inner* eyes, those eyes with which they look through their physical eyes upon reality" (1995 [1952]: 3). Entailed in this hard-won insight about the white world's unseeing reality construction is a radical shift of attitude: no longer does Invisible Man hope to build up an identity from the recognition of others; from now on, his identity is based on his ability to see that the other cannot see him.

---

[8] Among several literary critics, Mark Greif (2015) has used the Hegelian dialectic as an approach to the novel. Among philosophers, Axel Honneth (2001) stands out.

[9] I thank Andrew Gross for convincing me to regard both protagonists as picaro figures.

But having put insight in place of recognition, a further crucial question emerges: what are the conclusions to be drawn from the knowledge of white people's limitations? One option would be to cynically accept one's fate: to know that one will remain invisible, to accept the inescapability of racist stereotypes and yet to hold on, by way of skillful power analysis, to a sense of self that hopefully can remain undetermined by the symbolic power of whiteness. Another response is to say No! in thunder and mobilize as much counterforce as is available to strike out against white power. Invisible Man opts for a third way: he adopts the stance of ironist and commits to the world view of the comic.

As Bryan Crable has shown in greatest detail, Ellison's understanding of the comic was crucially shaped through his exchanges with Kenneth Burke, and a good many key terms and phrases of *Invisible Man* are the result of Ellison's adaptation of ideas Burke had spelled out in *Attitudes Toward History* (Crable 2012: 88). For Burke, at the root of what he called "the comic frame" was an impulse toward enlightenment that consisted in "picturing people not as vicious, but as mistaken" (Burke 1984: 41, quoted in Crable 2012: 93–94). As Crable explains:

> Because human action relies upon symbolic structures that are necessarily partial, error—or "blindness"—is an inevitable result. The comic frame calls us not to vengeance against those whose perspectives differ, but to the ironic appreciation of our common symbolic finitude, and a cooperative attitude toward the amelioration of conflict.
>
> (94)

From such a perspective, a world without blindness, without invisibility, is indeed unthinkable. But because invisibility is an inevitable result of symbolic action, a necessary mistake rather than a viciousness born into the fabric of those who misrecognize others, fatalism and pessimism are temptations to be resisted. In *Invisible Man*, the fact that there will always be blindness—that not only those in power but also even the oppressed are prone to the failure of vision—becomes the ground for holding on to the hope that the vision of structurally blind white people can at least partially be restored. Blindness, on this view, cannot be gotten rid of as it is a corollary of seeing; but structural blindness can.

Ellison himself favored this interpretation in his introduction to the novel's thirtieth-anniversary edition. "I decided," writes Ellison, "that [the narrator] would be one who had been forged in the underground of American experience and yet managed to emerge less angry than ironic. That he would be a blues-toned laugher-at-wounds who included himself in his indictment of the human condition" (2003: 481). In this move toward the "human condition" and the ironic inclusion of himself in the indictment of human folly (i.e. of blindness) resounds the liberal language of universalism, and it is in this voice that Ellison—to the chagrin of many of his readers—ended his novel, concluding on a sentence that has the dubious distinction of being more famous than the novel's opening line: "Who knows but that, on the lower frequencies, I speak for you?" (1995 [1952]: 581).

Interpreting this sentence as a depoliticizing gesture that sells out to (white) Cold War liberals[10] misrecognizes how consistently Ellison, throughout his novel, vamps on the blues man's interval, the space in between the notes of racist ascription and universal individuality. In fact, the infamous final sentence enacts a claim that is fundamental to *Invisible Man*, namely that no matter how entrenched and inescapable racism in America may appear, it cannot, and must not, blot out the fact of human equality. Indeed, it is the stubborn insistence on equality, on the capability of Invisible Man to speak for his white readership, that grounds the decidedly political character of his analysis of America's racist structures.

Ellison's brand of the liberal imagination rests on the idea that effective political change must involve altering the way people perceive the world. As in Hegel's master-slave dialectic, in which the slave ends up developing a greater competence of survival than the master, in Ellison's view it is those placed in a structural position of power who must learn to see; the oppressed have already had to develop the keenest awareness of the powerful in order to survive. Changing racist structures, on this view, cannot be effected through institutions, laws, and regulations alone. American citizens—particularly whites—must adopt ways of behaving, speaking, thinking, and feeling that are grounded in the conviction of equality. In this sense, Ellison's novel of invisibility paves the way for the idea, so prominent in the emerging new Civil Rights movement growing out of #Black Lives Matter, that America's racist structures can be transformed only if white people learn to confront their racial bias.

But the need for awareness of structures of invisibility notwithstanding, Ellison's attachment to "a blues-toned laugher-at-wounds who ... includes himself in his indictment of the human condition" expresses a hope for something more encompassing than white people coming to terms with their racist bias. That hope lies in a movement against racial and other injustice, a movement whose criterion of participation is radically at odds with the categories that prop up the injustice in the first place. Its sole criterion is commitment to the fact of equality—including equality of fallibility. At the very end, Invisible Man, charged with the power of 1,369 light bulbs, comes to the decision that "the hibernation is over. I must shake off the old skin and come up for breath" (1995 [1952]: 580). Like Augie March, he is an "ex-organizer," and he is ready to organize once again, this time a movement of equals. This decision requires a giant leap of faith, namely that those who follow him have truly embraced equality and have mastered the two-note interval, "say[ing] no and say[ing] yes, say[ing] yes and say[ing] no" (579). It is a risky step, the stakes of which are existential: "There's a stench in the air, which, from this distance underground, might be the smell either of death or of spring—I hope of spring" (580).

Invisible Man asks "you" to come along—he is willing to speak for you—on the path past the old exclusions hidden beneath the universalism of the liberal imagination. It is a path that leads ever deeper into the blues-toned interval, into a social space of saying yes

---

[10] For an influential, and cogently argued, version of this critique, see Schaub (1991).

and saying no, into a collective that is egalitarian, non-identitarian, democratic. It is on these terms that Invisible Man seeks to define and inhabit a new kind of invisibility, to be made use of in our time.

References

Abramowitz, Alan I. 2018. *The Great Alignment: Race, Party Transformation, and the Rise of Donald Trump* (New Haven, CT: Yale University Press).
Abramowitz, Alan I. and Steven Webster. 2016. "The Rise of Negative Partisanship and the Nationalization of U.S. Elections in the 21st Century," *Electoral Studies* 41: 12–22.
Bakhtin, Mikhail. 1982. "Discourse in the Novel," in Michael Holquist, ed., *The Dialogic Imagination* (Austin, TX: University of Texas Press), 259–422.
Baldwin, James. 1998. *Collected Essays*, ed. Toni Morrison (New York: Library of America).
Bellow, Saul. 1996 [1953]. *The Adventures of Augie March* (New York: Penguin).
Bellow, Saul. 2010. *Letters*, ed. Benjamin Taylor (New York: Viking).
Bellow, Saul. 2015. "Man Underground: On Ralph Ellison," in Benjamin Taylor, ed., *There Is Simply Too Much to Think About: Collected Nonfiction* (New York: Penguin), 60–64.
Brooks, Van Wyck. 1918. "On Creating a Usable Past," *The Dial* LXIV (April 11): 337–341.
Buell, Lawrence. 2014. *The Dream of the Great American Novel* (Cambridge, MA: The Belknap Press of Harvard University Press).
Burke, Kenneth. 1953 [1931]. *Counter-Statement* (Los Altos, CA: Hermes).
Burke, Kenneth. 1984. *Attitudes Toward History*, 3rd edn (Berkeley, CA: University of California Press).
Crable, Bryan. 2012. *Ralph Ellison and Kenneth Burke: At the Roots of the Racial Divide* (Charlottesville, VA: University of Virginia Press).
Ellison, Ralph. 1995 [1952]. *Invisible Man* (New York: Vintage).
Ellison, Ralph. 2003. *The Collected Essays of Ralph Ellison*, rev. and updated edn, ed. John F. Callahan (New York: Modern Library).
Fiedler, Leslie. 1999 [1957]. "Saul Bellow," in *A New Fiedler Reader* (New York: Prometheus Books) 108–116.
Greif, Mark. 2015. *The Age of the Crisis of Man: Thought and Fiction in America, 1933–1973* (Princeton, NJ: Princeton University Press).
Hirschkop, Ken. 1999. *Mikhail Bakhtin: An Aesthetic For Democracy* (New York: Oxford University Press).
Honneth, Axel. 2001. "Invisibility: On the Epistemology of 'Recognition,'" *Aristotelian Society Supplementary Volume* 75.1 (1 July): 111–126.
Hook, Sidney. 1939. "Democracy as a Way of Life," in John N. Andrews and Carl A. Marsden, eds, *Tomorrow in the Making* (New York: Whittlesey House), 31–46.
Kellman, Steven G. 2017. "Bellow's Breakthrough: *The Adventures of Augie March* and the Novel of Voice," in Victoria Aarons, ed., *The Cambridge Companion to Saul Bellow* (New York: Cambridge University Press), 32–42.
Kuhl, Stephan. 2021. "The Wright School," in Paul Devlin, ed., *Ralph Ellison in Context* (New York: Cambridge University Press).
Levitsky, Steven and Daniel Ziblatt. 2018. *How Democracies Die* (New York: Crown).
Mason, Lilliana. 2018. *Uncivil Agreement: How Politics Became Our Identity* (Chicago, IL: University of Chicago Press).

Menand, Louis. 2008 [1950]. "Introduction to Lionel Trilling," in *The Liberal Imagination: Essays on Literature and Society* (New York: New York Review Books), vii–xiv.

Menand, Louis. 2015. "Young Saul: The Subject of Bellow's Fiction," *The New Yorker* (May 11): 71–77.

Nowlin, Michael. 2004. "Ralph Ellison, James Baldwin, and the Liberal Imagination," *Arizona Quarterly* 60.2 (Summer): 117–140.

O'Hara, Daniel T. 1988. *Lionel Trilling: The Work of Liberation* (Madison, WI: University of Wisconsin Press).

O'Neill, Joseph. 2020. "Save the Party, Save the World," *New York Review of Books*, August 20, www.nybooks.com/articles/2020/08/...-the-party-save-the-world , accessed February 18, 2022.

Pease, Donald E. 1990. "New Americanists: Revisionist Interventions into the Canon," *boundary 2* 17.1 (Spring): 1–37.

Reising, Russell. 1993. "Lionel Trilling, The Liberal Imagination, and the Emergence of the Cultural Discourse of Anti-Stalinism," *boundary 2* 20.1 (Spring): 94–124.

Rosenfeld, Sam. 2017. *The Polarizers: Postwar Architects of Our Partisan Era* (Chicago, IL: University of Chicago Press).

Schaub, Thomas H. 1991. "From Ranter to Writer: Ellison's Invisible Man and the New Liberalism," in *American Fiction in the Cold War* (Madison, WI: University of Wisconsin Press), 91–115.

Schwartz, Delmore. 1954. "Review of *The Adventures of Augie March*," *Partisan Review* 21.1, 112–115.

Theunissen, Michael. 1986. *The Other: Studies in the Social Ontology of Husserl, Heidegger, Sartre, and Buber*, trans. Christopher Macann (Cambridge, MA: MIT Press).

Trilling, Lionel. 1965. "Introduction," in Saul Bellow, ed., *The Adventures of Augie March* (New York: Modern Library), vii–xiii.

Trilling, Lionel. 2008 [1950]. *The Liberal Imagination: Essays on Literature and Society* (New York: New York Review Books).

Trilling, Lionel. 2018. *Life in Culture: Selected Letters of Lionel Trilling*, ed. Adam Kirsch (New York: Farrar, Straus and Giroux).

Voelz, Johannes (with Tom Freischläger). 2019. "Toward an Aesthetics of Populism, Part II: The Aesthetics of Polarization," *Yearbook of Research in English and American Literature* (REAL) 35: 261–286.

West, Cornel. 1989. *The American Evasion of Philosophy: A Genealogy of Pragmatism* (Madison, WI: University of Wisconsin Press).

CHAPTER 18

CONSTRUCTING WHITENESS
Faulkner, Ferber, and the American Racial Imagination

HEIDI KIM

THE constitution of the American racial imagination in the mid-twentieth century owed a great deal to politics, shifting internal and transnational migration patterns and policies, and the upheaval of wars. But it was also refracted and redirected by fiction and film, which in the culture industry of that era had a much wider saturation than in today's more varied marketplace. Two of the most prominent writers of their day, William Faulkner and Edna Ferber, used both historical and contemporary settings to examine the anxiety of whiteness in response to the racial and gendered prerequisites and effects of socioeconomic mobility. Their epic works created a comprehensive portrait of these contradictions in American society, Ferber by utilizing a breadth of settings around the country and Faulkner by the depth and detail of his imagined Mississippi microcosm. Across their fictional output from the 1920s to the 1950s, they respond to shifting economic anxieties and definitions of race, often placing their contemporaneous concerns in historical settings to trace the evolution of a family. Their bestselling works, along with Ferber's better remembered film and musical adaptations, illustrated US racial strife, indicting mainstream white society and leaving few characters (and, by extension, readers) unscathed.

Ferber and Faulkner serve as an ideal pairing for the examination of the mainstream racial imagination because of their nearly parallel high-profile careers and their common interests, as well as their common struggle to follow up their greatest and most renowned works after their soaring successes in the 1930s (and even earlier for Ferber). Their dominant concern with the fragility of whiteness and its imbrication in economic exploitation crumbles into confusion against the legal indeterminacy of race, which shifted rapidly over the course of their careers. During the accumulation of Jim Crow laws in the 1920s and early 1930s, Ferber and Faulkner, as newly emerging literary stars, witnessed and critiqued the hollow construction of white supremacy in the legal arena. Their portrayal of whiteness is further rooted in the economic anxieties of the Great Depression, which finally lifted during the Second World War—crises of white masculine economic opportunity and domestic preeminence exacerbated by rising labor organizing among communities of color and increased employment among white women. Post-war, the authors confronted a new world order of US dominance abroad and a social consensus that obscured massive economic and racial shifts at home, including legal desegregation. By this time, Faulkner and Ferber were past what was already considered their literary prime, though Faulkner, in particular, was at the height of his national and international fame, thanks to his receipt of the Nobel Prize for Literature in 1949. They, like so many of their peers, were greatly concerned by the boom of consumerism, suburbanization, and uniformity that has dominated the popular image of the 1950s. Their later novels correspondingly take aim primarily at stultified, over-civilized white societies that have moved away from the pioneering, idealistic spirit, chiefly through critiques of white masculinity, though also reflecting on the circumscribed roles of white women.[1]

Faulkner and Ferber's divergent reputations and literary styles have granted them equally disparate places in literary history. It seems almost unnecessary to summarize Faulkner's literary stature and celebrity; critically acclaimed, Nobel-decorated, and, in later years, best selling during his lifetime, his innovative uses of literary form as well as his searing vision of the South lifted him to national and international prominence. Ferber's more straightforward and picturesque writing and automatic best-seller status, as well as the adaptation of her work to cinema, classified her as a writer of the popular, perhaps even a women's writer. Elyse Vigiletti has vividly described the rise of Ferber's popularity simultaneous with a severely qualified critical lauding of her fiction; her hit plays, all but forgotten today, were hardly held up as groundbreaking theatre even when they opened (Vigiletti 2016).

In putting Faulkner and Ferber into conversation here, I offer a broadly historicist comparison of their works, starting with their common attempt to fill in the terrible blankness of whiteness as they seek to define it against consideration of the Black–white color line and to examine the intersections of whiteness, gender, and economic power from the Jim Crow era to the decade of post-war economic expansion and desegregation. I do so with multiple goals in mind. One is undoubtedly to blur the lines between the literary and the popular, particularly in literary works that struggle with the imagination of race and ethnicity; a number of cultural studies critics have done so not only in looking at the "middlebrow" but also at various other genres such as pulp fiction, children's literature, and other media. Such criticism better helps us to understand the cultural currents about race and racialization which were so critical in this period when the definition of race was rapidly shifting. Another goal is to suggest that the study of Faulkner can benefit from a wider comparative dialogue with his contemporaries. Comparison of Faulkner and the popular has chiefly focused in recent years on his screenwriting, as in Mark Goble's chapter in this volume, a fresh and important archive

---

[1] Unsurprisingly, this is the period in which the paradigm of the male hero in the wilderness as the American literary form *par excellence* also appears, showing a common concern with the loss of this ideal. The most famous and focused exponent of this idea is Lewis (1955).

to explore both form and theme. The consideration of Faulkner in conversation with popular literature has been somewhat limited, mostly on his early novel *Sanctuary*. Such comparative examinations of Faulkner, as well as the attention paid to his speeches and essays, can serve to illuminate his participation in the larger cultural and literary conversations of his late career, which were long swept aside by the media image of the hermit farmer-sage of Rowan Oak and his towering literary reputation. In the classroom, likewise, such approaches serve to deepen thematic conversations and to point up the more innovative formal qualities of Faulkner's writing and modernist/postmodern writing as a whole.[2]

Though both writers could certainly be used to help teach other literary movements, such as regionalism, I do not focus on the consideration of regionalism here because I think it is a red herring when it comes to the criticism of Ferber and perhaps Faulkner as well; Ferber's Midwestern works—her home region—are not her best, aside for some well-drawn short stories, and she is not a regionalist so much as an irrepressible regional dabbler, seeking for particularities and contrasts to define the white American experience. Her work, however, offers us other insights into the literary history of the twentieth century. The strengths of her writing are all in the areas traditionally written off as feminine; her food writing offers an insight into the period in a manner often underappreciated or demeaned as sociological or local color—so, too, does her other descriptive writing, which vividly depicts social scenes and milieus. Ferber is not a formally intricate writer, and theoretical or close reading approaches have often passed her by. Her understanding of history, though it comprises erasure, forgetting, and violence, is more simplistic than that of Faulkner. However, her outstanding ability to capture a sense of difference and celebration when depicting various subcultures around the United States and to tap into the zeitgeist with contemporary topics and realist details of everyday life, particularly in her focus on women's lives, make the resurrection of her work highly useful in expanding our understanding of the racial imagination in this era and, in terms of literary history, enlarging the male-dominated literary industry of the twentieth century. In critiquing her work in a historicist fashion, I attempt to do justice as well to these aspects of her precise writing, though a full accounting of her oeuvre—some of which she disclaimed as old-fashioned during her career—is beyond the reach of this chapter.

One salient difference between critical approaches to these two authors—inasmuch as Ferber has been critically approached at all—is the marked difference in the biographical strands of criticism. The examination of Faulkner's biography is considerable and its use in criticism over the decades has been correspondingly voluminous, multifaceted, and contentious. Even proportionally, the use of Ferber's biography has been much less, perhaps stymied by two lengthy autobiographies, her unclear and undocumented sexuality, her Jewish identity, which she only openly explores in memoirs and

---

[2] Among such considerations, Greg Fortner (2000) considers *Sanctuary* as a crime novel, and Ben Railton (2003) notably compares Quentin Compson with white gentleman characters in *Gone with the Wind*, noting their shared remembrance of the South as a site of white gallantry and burning houses.

the semi-autobiographical novel *Fanny Herself*, and the fame of her "Algonquin Table" literary circle. Yet, there are areas in which the study of Ferber's career still would have much to offer in conversation with Faulkner and others. For example, in recent years, as examination of authors' cooperation (or complicity) with the government during the Cold War has grown, works such as Greg Barnhisel's *Cold War Modernists* have naturally looked at Faulkner's work in this area, which was relatively sparse. But scholars have importantly shown the cultural work that these government-sanctioned or enabled trips by authors both major and minor did in publicly representing nation, race, and artistic accomplishment abroad. Ferber's considerable travels, some governmental, some private, all over Europe and the United States and also to Israel constitute an archive worth investigating, as does the international circulation and wide translation of her work, though again, it is beyond my reach here. (Barnhisel 2015).

I hope this chapter may further open up some critical spaces into which the study of Faulkner may be expanded; conversely, I submit that the study of Ferber and other popular authors should be considered seriously in dialogue with the well-studied and theorized authors of twentieth-century US literature. Ferber's seemingly simpler and more sentimental works did at least as much to forward the discussion of race in the United States as Faulkner's more celebrated works and likely more, as the critical appraisal of Faulkner so rarely rested on his treatment of race, while Ferber's value was explicitly thought to be in her documentation of different subcultures.

Because of their wide readership and cultural influence, Faulkner's and Ferber's works were key attempts to define whiteness for a readership that, over time, was coming more and more into contact with other races through domestic and international migration, war, new media, and a changing global order. From early in his career, Faulkner examined all the shades of white in Yoknapatawpha, not just the all-important color line; if Ferber never forgot her love of racial or ethnic intermarriage as a metaphor for America, neither did she ever lose her true interest in whiteness and white ethnic subcultures, from the Dutch farmers of her first hit, *So Big*, to her final, Alaska-set novel, *Ice Palace*. Her focus on detailed description of the everyday adds an important valence to the semiotics of race as she minutely describes physical cues, clothing, food, and social performance by which white readers, as well as her white characters, navigate their expectations of Blackness and other non-white races.

Beyond simply reflecting culture, Faulkner's and Ferber's respective engagement with intertwined contemporary economic, social, and racial anxieties crystallizes readers' understandings of the creation and preservation of whiteness during a slow but seismic shift in racial definitions and relations in the United States. In examining these concerns, my goal is not to reify or recentralize whiteness but to examine the struggles of these authors to narrativize the foundations upon which an anxious but monumental American whiteness was built. Their creation of Black characters and other characters of color, as well as the white protagonists who reflect upon them with both sympathy and revulsion, grants us access, once again, to the ongoing construction of whiteness in the American literary imagination (Morrison 1993). As white protagonists navigate these intimate relationships, the anxiety and oppression of whiteness can be most clearly seen. At the start of their careers, the legal strictures of Jim Crow seem to give both authors traction to forcefully point out the hypocrisies and difficulties of racial definitions in realms ranging from law to science. As their careers continued, however, the diminishment of these laws (first in public discussion and then by federal desegregation) left them both negotiating the definition and distinctions of race in the more nuanced area of social norms. Their later works show deep ambivalence about the project of whiteness and white economic and social dominance, when we see Blackness and otherness used to address the development of what we might today call white fragility, but which, in this period, I call simply anxiety about whiteness.

Troubling the Color Line

Faulkner and Ferber's most famous works reflect their origins in the era of Jim Crow and nativism during which, as scholars have long argued, different European ethnicities gradually moved into the white racial category while the legal apparatus of racial definition continued to grow. For both authors, the one-drop rule of blood by which a seemingly pure whiteness was legally and socially preserved was the chief absurdity of racial definition. However, they diverge most in this early period in their treatment of race. Certainly, their critique of one-drop logic is defined by its impact upon whiteness, but Faulkner more urgently conveys the imperilment of whiteness. His work directly contravenes the logic of the one-drop rule that protected not only white bodies but also white property by excluding mixed-race heirs, instead displaying the intimate reliance upon Black bodies and labor (Pascoe 2009: 11, 104). In Faulkner's *Absalom, Absalom!*, Thomas Sutpen's rise depends on his ability to leverage whiteness, his chief asset, within the plantation economy of Mississippi, but his downfall comes from misunderstanding the fluidity of whiteness as it travels through Haiti, New Orleans, and other parts of the plantation South. *Show Boat*'s use of the one-drop rule is a small part of a white heroine's coming of age, and because of this superficial treatment, it demonstrates the vulnerability of a mixed-race woman, Julie, to economic replacement and cultural appropriation as her livelihood is taken by a heroine with dark enough hair to look a little indeterminate; whiteness is difficult to define but exploits Blackness more successfully than in *Absalom*. Both authors convey anxiety about white labor as a product of the contemporaneous scrutiny of race in law and performance, particularly as the reliance upon black labor blurs both racial and gender roles. *Show Boat* and *Absalom* commence chronologically decades before the time of their composition, dramatizing both authors' contemporaneous concerns in a narrative that extends a single family's cross-racial dependencies up to the present.

The economic valences of Sutpen's rise and fall reflect upon the legal transformation of children into chattels and the financial status necessary to perform whiteness

(Godden 1997; Duvall 2011).³ *Absalom* is a classic tale of the fall of a potentially great American house, starting from a pioneering poor man whose fairytale rise is undone by his fatal flaw and his children. Historically, it is also a reflection on the Great Depression, a legacy of greatness undone by greed and conflict and lived out in poverty—chiefly a public concern with *white* poverty and emasculation in straitened economic times. Sutpen's rise to slaveholder is shown in stark terms of financial profit and the attempted abandonment of his shadow family. However, the novel's deeper examination of the vulnerability of whiteness lies in the description of Charles Bon, the cast-off mixed-race son of Sutpen's first marriage, whose reappearance out of a different cultural economy turns him, as Richard Godden puts it, into a bond that has come due. As the Compsons, father and son, seek to explain Charles Bon's otherness in legal terms, they avoid the unspeakable possibility of their own inability to define whiteness (Godden 1997).

Show Boat is now chiefly remembered thanks to its musical and filmic adaptations, one of which (featuring Paul Robeson) was released in 1936, putting it into recirculation alongside *Absalom*. The memory of the films' blackface controversies and the striking representation of the one-drop rule has framed *Show Boat* as a work about segregation, but such is not the case when the novel is viewed as a whole. In *Show Boat*, Ferber deliberately seeks to document a fading economy of riverboat entertainment which served white and Black audiences in an era of segregation, but it is also the tale of the rise of a woman-dominated white dynasty of an industry that profits from Black culture and audiences. The heroine Magnolia, who grows up on the show boat, leaves for urban settings and returns at last, standing "eternal and unconquerable" as she floats out of sight and into history to close the novel (Ferber 2014: 299). But the story of Julie, the tragic mulatta figure who briefly stars in the shows of Magnolia's childhood, is forgotten. The deceptively episodic quality of the novel, stitched together by atmospheric description delivered in short phrases, creates a decisive historiography that pushes everything except Magnolia out of sight as her ill-fated marriage to a gambler takes her away on a roller coaster of economic lavishness and deprivation. A decade later, when Magnolia finds Julie working as a secretary-companion in an exclusive Chicago brothel, in an otherwise very finely drawn scene of class confrontation, all she has to do to reassert her racial and class status in a public space is to enter a downtown department store and redo her toilette so she can feel better and forget Julie forever.⁴

---

³ John Duvall (2011) interprets Faulkner's outcast characters as doing whiteness "wrong," by being too sexually active, or inappropriately active, or otherwise not adhering to the segregated and heteronormative social laws of Yoknapatawpha, Bon being a key example.

⁴ This pushing of Julie out of sight, except for the songs that Magnolia can sing, is mirrored by the anecdote which opens the novel, in which Magnolia's daughter serves "ham a la Queenie" at her fancy New York parties, appropriating the name and food culture of the show boat's African American cook for her entertainment. In a fine irony, the filmic adaptations are likewise remembered for pushing Black women out of performance opportunities as Ava Gardner famously played Julie in a slightly darker pancake makeup, rather than Lena Horne. The 1936 film also features a blackface minstrel performance by Irene Dunne as Magnolia. Likewise, the films shift attention away from white *female* independence and economic rise by ending with the reunion of the married couple.

In both works, the legalities critique the inability of these segregated, all-white societies (wildly different in location and class) to see or articulate racial difference, which inevitably renders them vulnerable to infiltration by mixed-race people. Neither novel relies on the underlying logic of race law at the time. The rapidly expanding category of white was bookended in the Supreme Court cases of *Ozawa* and *Thind*, which famously relied on science only when it confirmed the justices' desire to understand race as a clear and easily perceived difference (see Haney López 2006: 65–67). Both novels early confront the reader with the one-drop rule or hypodescent, known at that time by the euphemism of "racial integrity laws," noting the seemingly redundant legalities ruling a society divided by race and class and, by virtue of that redundancy, highlighting the anxiety of defining whiteness. *Show Boat* famously literalized the one-drop rule when Julie's white husband cuts her finger and sucks the blood so that everyone present may honestly swear to the local sheriff that he "got more than a drop of—[n—] blood in [him]" (Ferber 2014: 109). Ferber here most pointedly critiques the absurdity of the color line and anti-miscegenation law, but not by claiming whiteness or equality for Julie. Rather, she demonstrates how easily whiteness can be taken away and how artificial its legal and social privilege is. Even Julie's body is an insufficient boundary for the color line as her Blackness bleeds outwards to threaten the entire show boat with closure. Her husband's literalization of "drop" as descent for a drop of blood in this scene gestures subtly to a critique of eugenics and racial pseudoscience. Yet, Ferber's novel as a whole depicts the triumph of whiteness so firmly as to uphold it altogether, a subsuming of her critiques that lasted throughout her career. Julie's departure, though symbolized by a last embrace with Magnolia in which her black dress mingles with Magnolia's white frock, closes the discussion of the one-drop law firmly in favor of Magnolia's life story.

Absalom's society is more lastingly troubled through the defiant actions of men—not women—who flout or embrace the one-drop rule through their legal and public actions. Mr Compson imagines for Bon a shared white racial identity dependent upon law, blood, and the othering of mixed-race women, in particular: "we—the thousand, the white men—made them, created and produced them; we even made the laws which declare that one eighth of a specified kind of blood shall outweigh seven eighths of another kind" (Faulkner 1990: 91). It is Bon's imagined willingness to say "we," to put himself on the white side of this fictitious line, that identifies him, even as his other words critique the artificiality of law. Yet this flash of critique must be thoroughly undermined as Mr Compson then imagines Bon both undercutting the attraction of these women—one of them his own mistress and mother of his son—and rhetorically rejecting them, throwing the n-word at Henry and asking if he has forgotten the dehumanization of an African American woman and child, "You … of Mississippi?" (94). Bon's son similarly embraces the dehumanizing implications of the one-drop rule and refuses to pass as a white Sutpen, instead deliberately marrying the darkest-skinned (and, in Faulkner's extreme description, most animalistic) Black woman he can find, returning to fling not only his wife but also his marriage certificate at his white aunt. This mingling of law and performance ruins all hopes of economic and racial redemption via the passing of the shadow family, setting the stage for the Sutpens' final immolation.

Both novels also critique these specious legalities by showing the indeterminacy of race in embodiment and performance. It is through Bon that shades of white come to the fore in the novel. Bon's appearance at university supposedly dazzles Henry with his difference, which is one not only of attitudinal difference but also a performance of difference in his dressing gowns and his urban, foreign ways, as his Blackness is clearly not legible on his body nor in his wealth.[5] Bon is both Southerner and foreigner, masculine and feminine, and—in one of Compson's flights of fancy—barbarian and civilized but also fully white. Bon has a "Scythian glitter" and also a "sardonic and indolent detachment like that of a youthful Roman consul ... among the barbarian hordes," both a Roman (not an Anglo-Saxon) aristocrat and the nomads that he conquers, nomads who have a foreshadowing tinge of darkness or Asiatic otherness (Faulkner 1990: 74). In himself, then, Bon troubles the easy definition of race by blood because so much of his difference seems deliberate and performative. His ambiguity then retrospectively frames his father's determination to create his whiteness as a matter of class rather than blood, as Thomas Sutpen's story later tells of discovering that "there was a difference between white men and white men" in wealth and social status (Faulkner 1990: 183), and he sets out on a fatal trajectory of using Blackness to uplift himself to the higher echelons of whiteness. Likewise, Bon's own family, his octoroon mistress and their son, trouble local notions of Blackness and whiteness in their confusing mixture of class, linguistic difference, and not least, their light skin.

Ferber also largely eschews pseudoscientific definition while using ambiguous bodily signifiers symbolically. She undermines the stability of physically evidentiary distinctions of race by describing Julie and Magnolia in extremely similar language, both dark-haired, "sallow" in skin tone (a coded word for the trope of the "tragic mulatta" reaching back to antebellum literature) and yet with such differing social positions and possibilities marked in their speech and clothing instead. When Magnolia is deserted by her husband and has to go on the stage to make a living, she takes on the voices and mannerisms of all the African Americans she has known throughout her life, auditioning with her childhood songs and "manag[ing] to get into her voice that soft and husky Negro quality" (Ferber 2014: 271). In this moment, race becomes culture, performed but then rapidly written onto the body to the point that, to her mortification, Magnolia's whiteness is questioned and further undermined by her unfeminine need to make money. *Show Boat* and *Absalom* expose the destabilization of whiteness along multiple lines—economic, cultural, and bodily.

The Jim Crow era thus opens the careers of both authors with a critique of the legal absoluteness of whiteness as they expose both its exploitative privilege and its vulnerability developed over the past several decades. In *Show Boat*, whiteness still triumphs economically, allowing for a nostalgic final tableau of white social and economic rise built on African American labor and even culture. However, Ferber's novel clearly questions

---

[5] I have written elsewhere about the valences of foreignness that Faulkner deploys in *Light in August* and other works, which question and undercut whiteness (Kim 2016).

the modern values of mainstream white culture, positioning Magnolia as an appealingly hybrid figure which is passing away into history. It thus makes a sentimental appeal for the value of Black culture while not assigning the same value to Black lives. *Absalom*'s famous ending, in which yet another mixed-race Sutpen burns down the house with herself and the last white Sutpen inside, refuses an easy supremacy, leaving two young, white male narrators who are not Sutpens contemplating their racial vulnerability even as they sit in privilege on their snowy white college campus. At the same time, Faulkner implies that Blackness and ruin go hand in hand as the sole Sutpen descendent, a mixed-race man described in animalistic terms, howls in the ruins of the plantation. If there is no security in whiteness, there is likewise none anywhere else.

THE PRE-WAR ECONOMIC ERA

The Great Depression fueled concerns about white masculinity that lasted until the Second World War as high levels of unemployment did not end until the advent of wartime production. Organized labor protested and highlighted the abuses of a swelling capitalist system. Ferber and Faulkner's novels published just before the war turn to the untrammeled, immoral economic schemes of white male protagonists, paired with female protagonists whose sexuality poses a potential threat to whiteness. The pre-war era serves as a useful time point in these authors' careers because of their fame and productivity during a period of extreme economic uncertainty and continuing racial strife. Jim Crow laws held the South, in particular, in a crushing grip, with the anti-miscegenation laws described in the previous section still firmly in place along with disenfranchisement, commercial discrimination, and social segregation. Perhaps in reaction to such a fiercely legally divided society, both authors turned to a new treatment of race that blended a flagrant, almost defiant depiction of interracial contact with desperate economic ambition, once again setting the action of their novels in the past and tracing the development of a modern-day white supremacy based on ruthless economic warfare. In *Saratoga Trunk* (1941), which looks back at the unregulated era of railroad expansion, Ferber treats Blackness solely as performance and local color that can fuel economic schemes; her mixed-race heroine passes, joining her white Texan beau in triumphing over Saratoga Springs millionaires. Faulkner's *The Hamlet* (1940), which stitched together several short stories with new material, describes the decades-long attack of the white Snopes family on the more established, well-to-do families around them. The rural society of the novel is full of publicly accepted interracial interactions, from the sexual to the economic, and African Americans and upper-class white locals alike fall prey to the Snopes's schemes. Both novels attempt to subordinate the treatment of race to a focus on white economic rise, but the imaginative importance of Blackness endures as the authors employ scenes of racial confrontation to dramatize their strongest critiques of the socioeconomic structure.

In a rare move for this time period, Ferber's *Saratoga Trunk* features a mixed-race heroine, Clio Dulaine, the vengeful daughter of a white New Orleans man and his octoroon mistress, exiled to France after her father's scandalous death. Clio inhabits a Creole identity in the first half of the novel and then passes as a French countess to marry money when she heads North. It is likely that Ferber was inspired by the case of Antoinette Monks in California in 1939, who was accused of posing as a French countess to marry a wealthy white man and ultimately denied her inheritance on the grounds that her marriage was a fraud (Pascoe 2009: 127– 128). It may also have been a response to the passing novels of the earlier twentieth century.[6] But *Saratoga Trunk* unevenly treats Clio's racial identity and ironically ignores the legalities of mixed marriage or the possible threat of any marriage Clio should contract with her various white romantic interests. Instead, the novel highlights financial legalities and illegalities committed by the white elite, from Clio and her mother's dispossession to violent railroad takeovers. Likewise, it turns to social scenes, where clashes arise at the confluence of racial, national, gendered, regional, and class difference. Ferber's keen eye for food writing leads her to a prescient observation of the performativity of everyday rituals such as public eating, which Clio repeatedly uses to boldly flout the social rigidity of New Orleans and Saratoga Springs, two wildly different societies. The predictable dilemma of the novel is not whether she can infiltrate white society, but how: will she marry the impoverished but masculine Texan Clint Maroon or one of the scions of the wealthy white families of Saratoga Springs? Though Ferber fails to fully dramatize the passing aspect, Clio's Blackness almost bursts out of her at key moments, a further illustration of the intertwined hierarchies that she sets out to climb. However, the novel opens and ends in the contemporaneous moment, suggesting that Clio's story, including her forgotten Blackness, has created the society in which Ferber writes and her reader consumes—one of triumphant, conventional whiteness.

The Hamlet similarly overleaps the legal definitions of race, portraying a society legally segregated yet intimately linked. Law and order seem deeply embedded in this society, but Flem Snopes's machinations are so diabolically clever that he eludes lawsuits, law enforcement, and even the shrewdness of Ratliff, his foil. It is all the more notable, then, that the legalities around segregation or racial definition so completely drop out of consideration. Instead, the close relationship between the white protagonists and the unusually prevalent (for Faulkner) African American laborers, mistresses, and other supporting characters ultimately point out the imperfect separation of law. The white characters, including Ratliff, will in the end share their status as Flem Snopes's victims and prey, with none of the usual protection given by race and class. As Ratliff says, Cassandra-like, Flem starts by "working the top and the bottom both at the same time. At that rate it will be a while yet before he has to fall back on you ordinary white folks in the middle" (Faulkner 1959: 71–72).

---

[6] The national newspaper references I found to this case did not mention that Monks had posed as a countess, so it is not clear that Ferber was directly inspired. *Saratoga Trunk* might be viewed as part of a wave of white responses to the passing novel, such as Sinclair Lewis's *Kingsblood Royal* (1947).

The Snopeses work their way through the rural society of Frenchman's Bend, breaking the rules of this intimately tied interracial society as they exploit all available weaknesses, whether the poverty and illiteracy of the Black sharecroppers or the out-of-wedlock pregnancy of Eula Varner, the most powerful man's daughter, a figure of over-whiteness in her privilege and the goddess-like beauty that drives white men mad. The racial implications of Flem's rise are immediately presented to us, as "[Billy] Varner and Snopes resembled the white trader and his native parrot-taught headman in an African outpost" (61), but then Flem takes over fully, symbolically rising to full whiteness. The physical intimacy of the Black–white economic relationship is seen in so many of the pairings offered in the novel: the Black man who must carry the lazy Eula to school with her legs sexily dangling down his back or the Black male companion who Hoake McCarron pays to endure his beatings. Labor and sexuality are inseparable, uniting economics and racial mixing, and the Black supporting characters, unnamed but specifically enumerated, serve alternately or simultaneously as cook, mistress, groom, partners in financial schemes, insurance customers, and more. The Black presence drops out during one elaborate scheme that Flem pulls off, a sale of untamable horses, perhaps partly because it was drawn from an earlier short story for which Faulkner had not yet fleshed out a full society (Faulkner 1931).[7] But even the juxtaposition of the story of white men being bilked and cheated and the matter-of-fact African American exploitation reveals an uneasy cross-racial identification as Flem upsets the racial hierarchy with equal-opportunity exploitation.

Clio's economic scheme in *Saratoga Trunk* is necessarily different as she herself represents both the presence and the suppression of Blackness within the novel. She conceives of a scheme to lift herself, an orphaned mixed-race woman, out of the power of wealthy white men and to prey on them instead. She goes to New Orleans deliberately, embarrassing her father's white family into paying her to leave so she will not ruin her half-sister's debut. Indeed, the initial plot set-up, created to play out between daughters rather than sons, promises a female drama to rival that of *Absalom*, except that Ferber endows Clio with a ruthless practicality that takes her to greener pastures all too soon. Her Blackness is also curiously malleable, sometimes marked on her body and temperament but at other times clearly a matter of performance, aided by two Black servants. Clio's physical vitality—language which Ferber uses to chastely mask her obvious sexuality—serves as Ferber's contradictory metaphorical and, unusually for her, pseudoscientific basis for extolling the children of mixed marriage, a "hybrid vigor" argument common to other sentimental liberal authors at this time such as Pearl Buck.[8] Clio serenely critiques her sickly white half-sister, and Ferber delicately hints that besides her jewels and clothes, Clio "had been bequeathed other valuables of courtesanship less tangible but equally important" (Ferber 1941: 90). Her racialized sexuality, like Eula's fecundity, positions her as an object of desire and a commodity in the sexual economy

---

[7] Faulkner had drafted this story years earlier.

[8] The term and concept of hybrid vigor was popularized around this time in genetic science: see "heterosis, n." and "hybrid vigour, n." (*Oxford English Dictionary Online* 2019).

of New Orleans. She explicitly rejects this status when she goes North seeking marriage, saying that she will not share the fate of her female relatives as the property of white men, and yet, even posing as a wealthy white woman, she needs a white man to forward her masquerade and, ultimately, to make the money. Nobody in the North seems aware of her racial identity in the least, but that does not necessarily remove the reader's sense of the threat of passing. Ferber tries to lighten this tandem journey of racial passing and economic escape into a general adventuress identity. "[W]hat I say I am—that I am," (Ferber 1941:45) Clio ambiguously declares, a proclamation of liberation but also an implicit threat if her racial identity is held in mind.

Though both novels interweave the Black presence into their societies so deftly and without legal concern, they each set up a confrontation with an overdetermined Blackness as a metaphor for the imperilment of whiteness by economic schemes. Faulkner self-reflexively employs a white narrator metaphorizing economics to illustrate the precarity of white male economic dominance at the end of the long Great Depression. At the opening of the section entitled "The Long Summer," a season during which the newly married Flem and Eula are gone to Texas and the locals deal instead with the scandals of the other Snopeses, Ratliff cynically opines that they are all far from done with the indignities and extractions from Flem. He compares Varner, the highest of the white, to the lowest of the Black because he has succumbed to Flem by giving him Eula and her dowry. He embarks on an astonishing extended metaphor about a nameless woman who "has done already went around behind the counter and laid down on the floor because maybe she thinks by now that's what you have to do ... to get out of that door again." Yet even as she is lying beneath Flem in exchange for her last purchase, she looks up at the cans "every time his head would get out of the way long enough, and says, 'Mr Snopes, whut you ax fer dem sardines?'" (Faulkner 1959:166). Unperturbed by her own exploitation, it seems, this hypothetical Black working-class woman, now clearly racialized by Faulkner's characterization of her speech, gets drawn in by Flem's tempting offerings and enmeshes herself further in this system. Ratliff is not far enough removed from concerns about his own whiteness and status to be truly concerned with the exploitation of African Americans. Instead, this metaphorical anecdote is meant to try to awaken the white men around him to a sense of their own danger.

The virulence of Ratliff's description of this hypothetical woman also forcefully demeans Will Varner and also all the other white men who have accepted Flem's financial dominion. At first, she is merely uneducated and therefore easy to cheat, "not knowing no more about what he wrote in that book and why than she does how that ere lard got into that tin bucket," something she shares with many of Flem's other customers and victims. But as Ratliff finishes his speech, he denigrates her further to "this here black brute from the field with the field sweat still drying on her that she dont know it's sweat she smells because she aint never smelled nothing else, just like a mule dont know it's a mule for the same reason" (Faulkner 1959: 166).[9] As his previous comparison of

---

[9] Because Flem is stated in *The Town* to be impotent, we may look back on this with even more conviction of its metaphorical quality. This *Hamlet* episode is little read, even among the relatively few

Flem's victims across the racial divide has not been heard, Ratliff seeks to shock his audience with this extreme and animalistic description. As the reader either knows or is in the process of figuring out, the current Snopes scandal is a peep show in which the mentally disabled Isaac Snopes has sex with a cow, exploited for gain by yet another ruthless Snopes cousin. Most of the men in the area have already seen it. Ratliff's suggestion of bestiality in Flem's financial dealings thus tries to reach their sense of shame even beyond feminization and Blackness, articulating their abject position by pushing them across the species divide as well as the color line. Yet, as far as we can tell, Ratliff's warnings make no difference to white men, even to himself, as he falls for Flem's new scheme in the last section of the novel.

Ferber similarly draws upon the extremes of racial stereotype to shock and critique a white society's economic corruption although, as with Faulkner, the effect of the critique is transient, allowing the episode to also function as racist titillation. When Clio sickens of pretense, she horrifies the white upper class of Saratoga Springs by appearing at a lavish masquerade in blackface that takes up not only physical stereotype but also labor as markers of difference. "[T]he faces of the satellite dowagers were masks of horror as they beheld the shuffling, slapping feet, the heaving rump, the rolling eye, the insolent grin," as she sings and pretends to sell pralines (Ferber 1941:339). There is no indication that the audience understands that this is a racial declaration rather than Clio's ancestry; the dowagers are simply horrified by what they think is a minstrel performance. However, as with Ratliff's speech, Clio's performance is most meaningful as part of her own characterization, having little impact on the audience but evincing her own recognition of the resistance of the white elite even to her otherness as a potato chip-eating French countess. She demonstrates this in her choice of a Black persona that represents the most stereotypical and readily understood socioeconomic role rather than her own elite Black Creole identity that she flamboyantly performed in New Orleans and—as Faulkner had meditated on in *Absalom* as well—that was often illegible to outsiders.

The regulation of the railroads becomes the regulation of race in *Saratoga Trunk*. Ferber's historical framing device undermines the rebellion and anger of Clio's youth. In her old age, which opens and closes the novel, Clio turns into an icon of white gentility as not only rumor of her Blackness but also the historical scene which produced her mixed-race status and her married wealth have vanished from society. Clio and Clint hold a press conference to announce the charitable gift of their millions and their retirement to a small house. They are apparently childless, so Clio's Blackness conveniently

---

critiques of *The Hamlet*. John T. Matthews offers a softened summary of it (2009a: 131–132). He largely reads the episode as an illustration of Flem's rapacity.

There is another episode in the novel of slipping self-identification onto a black body. Labove, the teacher whose growing obsession with Eula culminates in a clumsy and humiliating grope that she fends off with complete contempt, believes that he is about to be shot by her protective brother. Suddenly, he remembers seeing a Black man shot on a train and the slow peeling away of the man's clothes and dignity as he died on the platform, gawked at by spectators. In his sexual humiliation, Labove suddenly finds a common degradation with this Black man and his ragged clothes, showing his understanding of the intertwined nature of race, economic status, and masculinity.

dies with her, ensuring that there will be no Jim Bonds to disturb modern society. Ferber most frequently reflected on the dwindling of families' vigor and morality across her works, so the *termination* of a family is quite singular among her works and should be interpreted in the light of this unusual but invisible interracial pairing. Blinded by decades of wealth and respectability, the reporters see only Clio's beauty, not her telltale "delicate brown hand" (Ferber 1941:7). They refuse to believe Clint's outpouring of the truth of their backgrounds, including Clio's mother's status as a "placee," a euphemism that they cannot even understand. Ferber merges the wild days of railroad expansion and the sexual slavery of mixed-race women into one forgotten economic history, whitened by wealth.

Together, Clio and Clint's regional and outsider identities offer a critique of the effete white aristocracy of the Northeast, but the framing device of modern obsolescence encapsulates their rise as an old-fashioned adventure, a romance of Depression escapism, not the establishment of a more vital, egalitarian, or mixed-race new America. *The Hamlet* ends on an entirely different note, with Flem looking down expressionlessly at the pathetic wreck of the white man, an "ordinary white man in the middle," whom he has driven insane by cleverly defrauding him over and over. Flem is on his way out of the Bend with his family, on to greener pastures where, as we shall see, his depredations take a new form. Faulkner's bleak ending thus sees no future safe from Flem, with no economic regulatory era at hand. Though these endings seem so radically different in their economic visions, both employ a vision of a triumphant white couple, more or less admirable, surrounded by deceived white men. If we are not able to remember the continued debt of white supremacy to Black labor and subjugation, Ferber and Faulkner insist on at least staging its erasure for us.

Post-war Supremacy without Superiority

In the 1950s, Ferber and Faulkner found themselves in a changed world, one of the oft-proclaimed Cold War consensus and the commencement of social desegregation with the decision in *Brown v. Board of Education* (1954). Amid these changes, both pulled away from their confrontation with the Black–white binary in favor of examining the crisis caused by whiteness confronting itself. Their last major novels featured white men climbing the socioeconomic ladder, enabled by the technological and lifestyle changes of the post-war era in the United States. Metaphorizing the national scene through family clans, these novels attack the faults and the hidebound ways of established white social structures, which had perpetuated so many abuses and yet flattened out to a whiteness without distinction or merit during the postwar era. Ferber's Jett Rink (immortalized in cinematic fame with James Dean's last performance in the 1956 film *Giant*) and Faulkner's Flem Snopes, sullen, unsympathetic white men climbing up from low-class obscurity against all odds, testify to the promise and the hollowness of white supremacy. Their rise is furiously contested by the established elite, who cannot stand this new dialectic of old and new moneyed whiteness instead of the racial superiority on which they long depended (and still do, in the background of these novels). Both authors undermine this nostalgia for a previous order, offering an ambivalent psychological portrait of a furious internecine strife that critiques both the established and emerging sides of the white power structure. So fragile is whiteness, increasingly dependent on an imagined classification rather than one in law, culture, or body, that even white social mobility threatens its definition.

Both novels dramatize the exclusions and inequities inherent in the booming economy of the 1950s as Faulkner's emphasis on the local bank reminds us of financial expansion and Ferber's oil, airplanes, and shopping sprees show us both infrastructural shifts and consumer lifestyle changes. The rise and fall of Flem, who critics quickly labeled a prime example of capitalism,[10] and the rise and inconsequence of Rink to the wealthy central family's sense of self are illustrated by both authors with a realist scrutiny of social mores and practices. Faulkner's language dwindles from the demonic imagery of Sutpen riding into history to a small-town world of bouquets, cars, and ice-cream sundaes. Ferber likewise has to push herself into a new scene, describing politics and finances to the best of her ability, often lapsing from the realistic into the impressionistic (missing the semiotics of Blackness that she deployed so freely to describe Julie, Clio, and even Magnolia). And within the plot, this white, male-dominated world can be critiqued but not changed by people of color—as both authors look more broadly at racial difference, not exclusively at the Black–white color line—or by white women, whose power is contained within marriage. But though their plotlines do not evoke change, what they bring to our understanding of Faulkner and Ferber's imagination of race is their overt commentary on the structures and defensiveness of whiteness, especially its psychological dependence on a reliable subjugation of people of color. The search for stability familiarly leads both authors back to encapsulating or killing off any possible outbreaks by characters of color, but not without some sly possible critiques of a whiteness so fragile that it cannot bear even white outsiders.

In the late 1950s, Faulkner finally returned to the characters of *The Hamlet*, adding *The Town* (1957) and *The Mansion* (1959) in quick succession to fully dramatize the rise of a new order in the South through the inescapable Snopeses, whose far-flung and diverse clan is still headed by the quietly ruthless Flem. In *The Town*, trading on Eula's beauty and an exterior of respectability, Flem works his way up from anonymity to become the bank president of Jefferson, buying the mansion of the aristocratic Manfred De Spain, whom he managed to chase out of town. The old-fashioned Gavin Stevens, with his symbolic white hair, bitterly critiques and contests them throughout, while the other two narrators, Charles Mallison (Stevens' nephew) and Ratliff, try to interpret Flem and Stevens' actions for the reader, as they clash first over Eula and, later, over her equally

---

[10] See, e.g. Brooks (1966).

magnetic daughter. Flem falls prey to his own extended family in *The Mansion* when his rise seems to be undone. But when Linda, Flem's stepdaughter, tries to give the mansion back to the De Spain family to undo Flem's legacy, she cannot find him. There is no way to refound the original De Spain dynasty; nor, in *The Mansion*, is there any way to restore the Compsons, who, in Faulkner's ultimate act of destruction, have burned down their house.[11] There is a deliberate uncertainty in the trilogy's end as power does not revert to the older white families, nor does it remain with Flem, though it will remain in white hands, sympathetic or not.

Ferber likewise meditates on the uncertain future of all-white dynasties, this time in Texas, with the advent of technology and new wealth, which the novel presents as the chief forces of change, while both the characters and the larger shape of Ferber's narrative refuse to address racial change. The novel begins and ends with a clear focus on Leslie Benedict, a repurposed version of Magnolia—slight, dark, yet unimpeachably white, and with a more liberal, sentimental attachment to people of other races than the characters surrounding her. She provides the hopeful ending of *Giant*, as she suggests to her hidebound husband, Bick, that their more moral and principled grandchildren, some mixed-race, will make "the Benedict family … a real success at last" (Ferber 2019: 402). However, *Giant*'s structure strangely undercuts this hope: at beginning and end, the Benedicts have flown in to attend the extravagant party of Jett Rink, once an insolent and racist ranch hand and now a vulgar oil tycoon, with some reluctance. Amid the rich and powerful of Texas, their son, Jordy, rushes in to fight Rink over the insult to his wife, Juana, who has been refused service at Rink's hotel because she is Mexican. When Jordy is beaten and humiliated, Leslie says to Bick, "You see. It's caught up with you, it's caught up with us. It always does." What this "it" is we must wait to find out until the end of the novel when Leslie and Bick argue about doing things against their own vague "feelings and principles" about social hypocrisy, bigotry, or the humane management of the ranch and the Mexican workers' livelihoods. But this passive "catching up" of racial inequity that may take down the dynasty takes a back seat to Ferber's much more vivid description of change wrought in Texas by the big money that floods in with oil, creating a new white power.

In Jefferson and Benedict, these two scenes of white-dominated economic and social competition, the reader's understanding is constrained by the insights of the supposedly powerless white narrators. Ratliff is a traveling commercial salesman who represents an older economic age. His dry and philosophical attitude toward the Snopeses is the reverse of Gavin Stevens' fury, but both are ineffectual. In *Giant*, Leslie (not a first-person narrator but the focal lens for the readers' discovery of Texas) is somewhere in between these two, her barbed critiques occasionally hitting a vulnerable spot but never causing

---

[11] Linda can only find a distant relative in Los Angeles. Faulkner may be wryly commenting with the location of the De Spain relative on the cultural shift of power to a hollow Los Angeles (as critics have investigated his ambivalent relationship with the film industry in, e.g. Faulkner (2017). In *The Mansion*, of course, we discover that Benjy Compson burned down the family house, and Jason Compson falls prey to Flem Snopes when attempting to outwit him on the sale of the family land.

action. She stands apart from Bick's economic and political actions just as Stevens (furiously) and Ratliff (cynically) deny implication in Flem's rise. Her critiques of racial and economic inequality combine with her complaints about the confined roles of women in upper-class Texas society to position her as a slight outsider herself, yet reaping the rewards of whiteness and wealth. Ratliff already possesses a finely honed sense of Flem's techniques and explains to the reader the machinations of the business side of his schemes, which Stevens, a Harvard-educated lawyer and member of the upper class of Jefferson, never fully understands. (Leslie has a kind of Ratliff of her own, the more liberal but patronizing uncle of the Benedict clan.) But these insider–outsider characters are unable to advocate for or effect meaningful change, which leaves both plots to unroll with an air of inevitability and also leaves us with a gendered critique of the ineffectual white masculinity of the old guard, which for Leslie skews more to an overt critique of women's lack of power and for Stevens results in constant attacks on his own masculinity. What is there to protect or differentiate from the brash white newcomers, the authors seem to ask?

The deepest betrayal of Faulkner and Ferber's uncertainty about the flattening of whiteness arises in the destabilizing characters of color of *The Town* and *Giant*.[12] In small, encapsulated episodes, both authors offer characters who refuse to conform to the racial and economic systems of their societies. Angel Obregon, born on the Benedict ranch into a family of Benedict workers, is raised as a girl because his hair is vowed as an offering for his safe birth. He grows into a figure of change, rejecting work on the Benedict ranch, wearing tight clothes, and speaking "a bastard dialect made up of Mexican jargon, American slang, Spanish patois" (Ferber 2019: 347). Reflecting his family's comment on his aping of whiteness by working in a town at a hotel, he bursts not only the boundaries of race and gender but also of the rancher/laborer economic structure that Ferber describes as baked into the Texas heat of tradition and custom, suggesting their intertwined nature in upholding the white status quo.

In *The Town*, Faulkner unusually offers briefly appearing African American characters narrative power as their avenue of escape from "Snopesishness," one that is impossible for those, like Stevens or even the ingenue-like Linda Snopes, who are so imbricated in their own whiteness and status. Tom Tom and Turl, the two African American workers at the water tank who Flem Snopes pits against each other in the scheme that opens *The Town*, are the only ones who ever outwit him. Incited to fight each other, they sit down to confer and eventually turn the tables on Flem by throwing his ill-gotten gains into the tank and confronting him together, wielding wits and words against him as Stevens rarely does. Tom Tom and Turl disappear from the novel after the first chapter not only because Faulkner's chief interest is in whiteness but also because white economic and social rise has to be marked by lifting Flem beyond the need to deal

---

[12] *The Mansion* also has some minor African American characters, but they are not, to my eye, used as critically as in *The Town*.

with African Americans.[13] It is a mere flash of possibility, an unappealing idea of Black triumph even though Flem's rise is so despised.

The singularity of these characters within the text must also be considered at least partly as relics of the novel's patchwork construction as it incorporates two earlier short stories: "Centaur in Brass" (1932) and "Mule in the Yard" (1934).[14] The rest of *The Town* suggests that Faulkner was very little concerned with a discussion of race relations only a year after his controversial public pronouncements on desegregation. However, this opening episode situates Blackness as a site of resistance to the negative effects of a conformist, over-civilized white society, if only because Tom Tom and Turl are already so disenfranchised and segregated that a white man scheming for respectability can scarcely hurt them further. It must be stressed that this critique is deeply romanticized, but it is still a drastic turnaround from the shared position of all as prey for Flem or the degrading metaphor of Flem's Black customer in *The Hamlet*. It sets whiteness at a further remove from Blackness yet suggests that rather than succeeding first in legal and now in social separation, it may lose its meaning.

Obregon's embodied critique of the racial order in *Giant*, told as if disconnected from Rink's repulsive rise, is also enclosed and then foreclosed. Ferber takes a characteristically abrupt narrative way out of the dilemma of Obregon's future. His gender, racial, and class nonconformity are first covered over with an army uniform, which Ferber plays with imaginatively as a social setting where Obregon would be included in all-white regiments, since he serves before the desegregation of the military in 1948. More decisively, Obregon is promptly killed in the Pacific. Even his body cannot return to Benedict, where there is no suitable desegregated graveyard, but rests instead in Arlington Cemetery, securely contained in the service of the state. (The 1956 film took a different approach to containing Obregon, removing his gender play and class disruptions.)[15] Ferber was unable to imagine a future for Obregon, at least in a world focused on the Benedicts' attempted retention of privilege and power.

The racial inequity of economic opportunity in *Giant*, though linked to the Benedicts' ranching empire and the Texan economic boom, filters primarily through Leslie's biases, reminding the reader of the continuing debt of white supremacy to the labor of people of color. But these relations must be traditional and legible to be acceptable even to the liberal Leslie. Leslie sporadically plays the Lady Bountiful in the miserable Mexican laborers' villages nearby, mirroring her comfort with the post-slavery racial order of her native Virginia. But she collapses into hysterical fear when she encounters a starving

---

[13] Flem's preying upon African Americans here seems to be a relic of the 1930s, when the story was originally written. Faulkner emplots this inconsistency; he accounts for it by having Ratliff muse that Flem must be ashamed of having tried such an amateur trick and that he will never do so again.

[14] Tom Tom and Turl appear in "Centaur in Brass," while "Mule in the Yard" features another Black character, Old Het, discussed below.

[15] This was not the only time that Ferber took an expedient way out of a narrative problem. In *Come and Get It*, her tale of Midwestern lumber kings, at the point of maximum conflict between the elder and younger generation the elder's boat explodes on Lake Michigan. Even Ferber later wrote of regretting this choice, not least because it killed off (in my opinion) the only interesting character in the novel.

Mexican boy who has crossed the Rio Grande. The twofold economic and forcible migratory flow in the post-war period of Mexican men (primarily) to fill agricultural labor needs in what was called the *bracero* project, and the loosely corresponding deportation project dubbed Operation Wetback set up what many contemporary critics have deemed a contested racial, classed, and gendered borderland in which national belonging was constantly redefined by competing interests. Ferber describes the *bracero* project and Operation Wetback in complacent terms that enshrine them almost as historical inevitabilities, as a Benedict uncle contrasts the "wetbacks" with the "regular Mexican labor lot" (Ferber 2019: 288). Despite this attempt to normalize the boy's presence, Leslie's inability to confront the brutal racial system except in the most general affecting terms, as well as the novel's extremely brief treatment of it, leaves her liberal Southern whiteness intact and resilient. The novel opts instead for a perfunctory sentimental reconciliation via the more familiar form of Jordy's interracial marriage and his choice to work in a clinic serving Mexican Americans. Tellingly, his choice of occupation drives far more family conflict than does his marriage, because the novel's focus is so heavily on white economic dominance and his choice is less sentimentally legible than an interracial romance.

Faulkner offers one more explicit but comedically diffused episode in *The Town* to comment slyly on the importance of liberal economic patronization of people of color in stabilizing whiteness. Old Het, a fascinatingly verbose character, aids a white woman in an "automatic compact of female with female against the world of mules and men," overcoming one long-running Snopes scheme, though in the process, they serve Flem's purpose of ridding himself of his relatives, who are not interested in respectability. Old Het issues an ostensibly comic but deeply critical observation of the white charity that sustains her:

> I serves Jefferson too. If it's more blessed to give than to receive like the Book say, this town is blessed to a fare-you-well because it's steady full of folks willing to give anything from a nickel up to a old hat. But I'm the onliest one I knows that steady receives. (Faulkner 2011: 256)

Old Het ironically claims her place as someone who is not outside the white socioeconomic order as a beggar but an essential part of it. The social system depends on exclusion and poverty, particularly the exclusion of African Americans, and Old Het's satirical use of a Biblical framework lances the pretensions of the town aristocracy, whose cast-offs mark their history on her body.

Both novels so determinedly focus on the warfare of whiteness that the critique offered by these small portraits seems perfunctory, not worthy of notice. Indeed, in this sense, the novels serve to further show the obtuseness of the white upper class to the slow surge of immigration and civil rights happening outside their immediate sphere. But the characters of color accepted by white society, like Old Het or the well-behaved Mexican laborers, exist in counterpoint to the ability of despised white men to grasp the full privilege of whiteness, forcing a complacent elite to realize the shakiness of racial superiority. The upwardly mobile white men are motivated by personal benefit in the replication of predominantly white institutions, not systemic change. Flem Snopes wants ascendancy, not revolution, and, more than anyone else, tries to keep the town static and safe even from his own relatives. Rink serves not as a reformer but as a new, corrupt millionaire outspending and out-abusing the old corrupt millionaires; he hates the Benedicts and their Mexican workers alike, a white man in an intermediate and hopeless place in this feudal system. (In this, he bears some resemblance to Sutpen.)

The hostility toward these social climbers only demonstrates the weaknesses already extant within whiteness. The unsympathetic narrators view the social climbers as grotesque despite their white identities; Flem is always negatively portrayed, and although Rink does not suffer a violent death, as far as the novel is concerned, he is a nonentity once he becomes rich and successful, a monstrous figure who appears chiefly through others' anecdotes of his corruption and abuse. *The Town* once again showcases Flem's ability to use extralegal means to achieve his ends, but his ends have drastically shifted in the decades since the composition of *The Hamlet*. As with Sutpen, his white racial status seems the one thing needful as, for all of Stevens' bitter complaints, Flem clearly is suitable and able to rise. He wants "respectability" and "there aint nothing he wont do to get it and then keep it," a biting critique of the middle-class mores of the 1950s, which he ponderously imitates in his clothing, furniture, and strategic ignoring of his wife's adultery (Faulkner 2011: 270–271). He shores up his whiteness, at least outwardly, by marrying Eula and accepting her child as his own, hiding his impotence and taking a suitable place as a family man. He even allies with an unwilling Stevens to end the unsavory business enterprises of his cousin Montgomery Ward's pornographic slide show, a sly commentary on the unsavoriness not only of the show but also of the aggressive business practices of the retailer Montgomery Ward; Ferber openly deplored the rapacity of mail-order businesses and department stores in some of her small-town stories and novels. Stevens, himself a relic of an older age of feudal chivalric ideals, denigrates Flem's economic understanding, saying that "[h]is idea and concept of a bank was that of the Elizabethan tavern or a frontier inn" (274). But Flem's understanding, as recounted by Ratliff, is a pragmatic and modern one, leveraging voting stock and public pressure to get himself elected vice president of the bank, and eventually he performs a similar feat, using private threats and fear of scandal to force his purchase of more bank stock and become president—the pinnacle of his worldly aspirations. Parallel with his rise, however, are Stevens' ridiculous and even predatory attempts to "save" Eula and Linda from Flem, in which he violates social taboos, his own dignity, and the truth. Flem's rise shows the hollowness of whiteness as respectability, so easily achieved by socioeconomic means and entirely without the kind of essential difference that Stevens seeks to enforce.

Leslie exemplifies the recently much-discussed political position of white heteronormative middle and upper-class women in her proximity to power; her superficial sympathy for Mexicans is paired with an instinctive revulsion to Rink and unhappiness with her son's interracial marriage. At what, then, are her critiques truly aimed? The system she dislikes is a socioeconomic novelty to her; the Benedicts' Texas "institution" and "closed corporation" are reminiscent of the system Flem quietly takes over

(209). Like Stevens, she initially represents the values of a more old-fashioned world; the trains and perilous car rides around Texas quickly open her eyes to a different world. "You want everything prettified up, that's what's the matter with you," Jett Rink charges early on, and responding to the challenge, she asks him to take her to Nopal, the Benedicts' Mexican worker town, implicitly situating ugliness and harsh reality with people of color. She comments on the corruption inherent in the white intergenerational wealth she enjoys, from the Spanish colonial land grants to the depreciation exemption on oil. "Absolute power corrupts absolutely," she quotes to her husband, but he sleeps right through her warning and, to the end of the novel, persists in his course (284). The changes she can make are all personal or familial, rather than structural, suggesting the weakness of women within this power structure and that whiteness is inimical to sentimental reform from the inside. But her critiques do serve to puncture the moral superiority of the Benedicts, at least to the reader. Even though she despises Rink as well, she has shown that they are all cut from the same Texan cloth.

Both novels end with a confrontation over race relations, but curiously anticlimactic and distanced ones that draw our attention back to the white protagonists. *The Town* ends with the intrusion of mixed-race Snopeses who annoy but cannot destroy Flem's climb. Across multiple novels, Faulkner consistently describes the English and Scottish and Welsh heritage of people in the backcountry, making the Snopeses who are more unimpeachably white and almost an animalistic part of the landscape at times, while the older, more established families with aristocratic foreign names like "De Spain" start to look more artificial and tenuous, threatened by this Indigenized white presence. When Flem's cousin sends his four half-Apache children to Jefferson in a coda to the main plot, the entire town is staggered by their seeming savagery, inability to speak English, and gender indeterminacy, all of which position these children as an exaggerated version of Flem's threat to the identity and order of their town. Flem sends them away to hide his own savagery, though we have already seen the full extent of his ruthlessness. The children's racial identity provides a legible and more comfortable framing for the viciousness that is already inherent in the Snopes family, a savagery that could also postulate them as more American, more part of Yoknapatawpha and its original inhabitants (of whom Faulkner periodically speaks). These contradictions undercut still more of the traditional distinctions of race and remind us that Flem's whiteness, more than blood or family, is a willingness to adhere to an entirely artificial façade of respectability.[16]

Neither Faulkner nor Ferber is quite able to imagine a system in which racial outsiders can be fully integrated in the post-war era, as the vibrant possibilities of Obregon or Old Het are narratively subsumed in the uncontrolled expansion of white dominance. Even more bleakly, they posit the resistance to social mobility as an unneeded effort

---

[16] Matthews suggests that the little half-Apache Snopeses who are shipped into Jefferson by a distant cousin at the end of *The Town* signify the waves of dark migrants that threaten the United States in this era, such as the *braceros*, with their uncivilized behavior and their foreign language. This reading naturally aligns them closer to *Giant*, but I have chosen to emphasize their explicit racial positioning here because of its identification with animality (Matthews 2009b: 17).

by an entrenched elite. Not only does Flem expel the half-Apache Snopeses but also Flem's limited difference is ended by his violent death at the hands of his own cousin in *The Mansion*. On top of that, his funeral, attended by "not just the town but the county," is the moment when Gavin Stevens—admittedly never a reliable judge of these things—realizes that the Snopeses are really "not alien at all" but identical to the townsfolk, removing even the faint air of foreignness with which they are tinged in *The Town* and substituting a parodical white conformity that renders useless Stevens' decades of opposing Snopesism (Faulkner: 1036–1037).[17] Even *Giant*, though it has an unsettling moment for Leslie when she is refused service because she is thought to be a Mexican woman with her daughter-in-law and grandson, ends with a cinematic close-up on Leslie's hopeful and happy face, depositing us right where we started.

The society of these novels constructs whiteness as a state of insular racial and socioeconomic privilege that, thanks to the intrusion of the Rinks and the Snopeses, now loses even a sense of traditional superiority. The novels of the 1950s do not lead anyone to question Snopes's or Rink's blood or race; instead, characters scrutinize their class, their education, their morals, and their sources of wealth—while the authors turn those hypocritical queries on the already existing white establishment. Relegating characters of color to the sidelines, Faulkner and Ferber's post-war era ushers in a chaotic, over-moneyed, whites-only socioeconomic scene that both authors strongly deplore but cannot write their way out of—a token, perhaps, of pessimism about the post-war' era's false promise or simply an unwillingness to keep burning down the house.

Conclusion

The focus on white social mobility and a consequent imaginative loss of a sense of moral and cultural superiority married with race in the 1950s grows out of Ferber and Faulkner's initial interest in the indeterminacy of race and its definition along class lines as well as bodily, cultural, and scientific ones. Both authors clearly observe the intertwined nature of these categories, as well as the confinement of gender roles, and consistently depict a society in which white masculinity is the key to mobility, whether it is Flem's unimpeachable Anglo-Saxon roots or Clio's successful passing scheme, which requires a man's aid and wealth. Their novels thus indict the narrative of post-war economic prosperity and comfort for all. And yet, while so ready to critique the insecurity and the hypocrisy of whiteness, Ferber and Faulkner find themselves stymied in replacing it, even imaginatively. Their novels often reconfirm the hierarchy whose constructedness they reveal, with the possible exception of *Absalom*, which nonetheless fails to imagine a new order that can rise out of the ashes.

---

[17] I write about alienness and *The Town* in *Invisible Subjects* (2016).

Because of their rootedness in the changing definitions of race, however, Ferber and Faulkner are also able to deepen our understanding of the ceaseless defensiveness and anxiety of whiteness. The considerations of race law and "one-drop" characters diminish (but never disappear) over the decades, as Faulkner and Ferber focus on the socioeconomic as the primary battleground of whiteness, the site where privileged white characters' expectations, rather than legal strictures, hold sway. Looking back at the works of the 1920s and 1930s, we can see how Ferber and Faulkner already saw the establishment of white comfort and triumph as irretrievably dependent on Black bodies and labor and the erasure of Black presence and humanity to an extent which ensnares and ruins Sutpen's dynastic design. They still warn in the era of legal desegregation that the presence of racial Others may only be contained and ignored temporarily, part of a larger pattern of white blindness to a racial debt.

As Faulkner and Ferber's careers reached their conclusions post-war, the critical assessment of both authors had already been set on tracks which have rarely, if ever, intersected. Undoubtedly, however, judging from their own narrative struggles, their greatest common concern was also their greatest common failure—to slay the great white whale of racial hierarchy. But their work represents, at the very least, a lasting commitment to holding a mirror up to their predominantly white readership. Ironically, I would even argue that the greatest differences in their writing, Faulkner's experimental forms and Ferber's rich and romantic description, which have led them to such different places in literary history, work similarly to gild their critiques of whiteness for their contemporaneous audience. As Charles Mallison puts it in *The Town*, "[They] were looking at exactly the same thing: they were just standing in different places" (Faulkner 2011:176).

Acknowledgements

Thanks to my colleagues Lynn Itagaki, Jinah Kim, Jeehyun Lim, and Vinh Nguyen for their workshopping of this piece.

References

Barnhisel, Greg. 2015. *Cold War Modernists: Art, Literature, and American Cultural Diplomacy* (New York: Columbia University Press).
Brooks, Cleanth. 1966. *William Faulkner: The Yoknapatawpha Country* (New Haven, CT: Yale University Press).
Duvall, John. 2011. "Faulkner and the Minstrel Performance of Whiteness." In *Faulkner and Whiteness*, ed. Jay Watson (Jackson: University of Mississippi): 92–106.
Faulkner, William. 1990 reprint. *Absalom, Absalom!* (New York: Vintage International).
Faulkner, William. 1931. "Spotted Horses," *Scribner's Magazine* (June): 165–183.
Faulkner, William. 1959 [1940] reprint. *The Hamlet* (New York: Vintage).
Faulkner, William. 2011 reprint. *The Town* (New York: Vintage).

Faulkner, William. 2017. *William Faulkner at Twentieth-Century Fox: The Annotated Screenplays*, ed. Sarah Gleeson-White (New York: Oxford University Press).

Faulkner, William. *The Mansion* in *The Snopes Trilogy* (New York: Random House Publishing Group, Kindle edn).

Ferber, Edna. 2019 reprint. *Giant* (New York: Perennial Classics).

Ferber, Edna. 1941. *Saratoga Trunk* (Garden City, NY: Doubleday, Doran, & Co.).

Ferber, Edna. 2014 reprint. *Show Boat* (New York: Knopf Doubleday).

Forter, Greg. 2000. *Murdering Masculinities: Fantasies of Gender and Violence in the American Crime Novel* (New York: New York University Press).

Godden, Richard. 1997. *Fictions of Labor: William Faulkner and the South's Long Revolution* (Cambridge: Cambridge University Press).

Haney López, Ian. 2006. *White by Law: The Legal Construction of Race* (New York: New York University Press).

Kim, Heidi. 2016. *Invisible Subjects: Asian America in Postwar Literature* (Oxford: Oxford University Press).

Lewis, R.W.B. 1955. *The American Adam: Innocence, Tragedy, and Tradition in the Nineteenth Century* (Chicago, IL: The University of Chicago Press).

Matthews, John T. 2009a. *William Faulkner: Seeing through the South* (Malden, MA: Wiley-Blackwell).

Matthews, John T. 2009b. "Many Mansions: Faulkner's Cold War Conflicts," in *Global Faulkner: Faulkner and Yoknapatawpha, 2006*, ed. Annette Trefzer and Ann J. Abadie (Jackson, MS: University Press of Mississippi), 17.

Morrison, Toni. 1993. *Playing in the Dark: Whiteness and the Literary Imagination* (New York: Vintage Books).

Pascoe, Peggy. 2009. *What Comes Naturally: Miscegenation Law and the Making of Race in America* (Oxford: Oxford University Press).

Railton, Ben. 2003. "'What Else Could a Southern Gentleman Do?': Quentin Compson, Rhett Butler, and Miscegenation," *Southern Literary Journal* 35.2: 41–63.

Vigiletti, Elyse. 2016. "Edna Ferber and the Problems of the Middlebrow," *Studies in the Novel* 48.1 (Spring): 65–85.

CHAPTER 19

UNIDENTIFIED FLYING OBJECTS

Conceptualism, Interpretation, and Adrian Piper

RACHEL JANE CARROLL

Undisciplining Scholarly Objects

In the 1960s, conceptual art emerged amidst intense friction between modernist notions of art's distinctness—the idea that an art object is self-contained and separate from the social and political world—and leftist skepticism of aesthetic autonomy. Ideological differences crystallized in the writings of Michael Fried and Clement Greenberg and in social and political movements: anti-war movements, the New Left, the Women's Movement, queer movements, and anti-racist movements such as the Black Power, Asian American, Chicano, and American Indian movements. The demands issued from these latter groups required a radical re-examination of how context, history, and norms shape the conditions of daily life—including the operations of the art world and its institutions.[1]

This chapter reads the social and political promise of conceptualism via the Black radical tradition as conceived by Cedric J. Robinson. While Black radicalism and conceptualism are not often discussed in the same breath, I argue that conceptualism's process-based proceduralism can deepen our understanding of forms of racialization. Moreover, the Black radical tradition's freedom-seeking experiments historicized within the development of modern racism and anti-Blackness helps us to understand the liberatory possibilities of abstraction. In exploring these connections, I read Adrian

---

[1] For more on radical politics and conceptual art, see Nizan (2017).

Piper's works from the 1970s as forms of conceptualist abstraction which are also, potentially, tools of freedom-seeking.[2]

Born in Manhattan in 1948, the only child in a middle-class African American family, Piper is one of the leading conceptual artists of the twentieth and twenty-first centuries.[3] She is also a philosopher specializing in the work of Immanuel Kant, teaching at institutions such as Wellesley College, until she moved to Berlin in 2005.[4] Examining Piper's transformational work from the early 1970s, this chapter argues that Piper experimented in a literature of art objecthood. I offer a reading which aims to expand the relevance of conceptualism for literary studies, while also demonstrating the centrality of Black radicalism to the history of conceptualism.

But Piper is primarily known as an artist and a philosopher, so what role does her work have to do with the discipline of literary studies? Conceptualism is strongly associated with the visual arts; however, this chapter focuses on what I regard as the literary aspects of Piper's textual works. Text-based conceptualism challenges the separateness of literature and literary reading from other modes of reading and writing. It embraces the contradictions and ambiguities of reading practices that won't stay in their place, challenging the ways that reading can keep people in their place.

Following disciplinary critiques by Kandice Chuh, I argue that a restrictive notion of discipline restrains critical inquiry and the liberatory work that the study of literature might perform (Chuh 2019). For those who see their work as part of a communal project of "critiquing normativities and the violence of the status quo" and "working toward and for alternatives," it follows that methodologies must become undisciplined (4). As my readings of Piper's work suggest, the impropriety of objects can generate exciting shifts in interpretation. I advocate for an openness to undisciplined reading methodologies in part because conceptualism demands "promiscuous" reading and also because methods of interpretation, including those which espouse disciplinary fidelity, can mistake dominant thinking for rigor (4). In this chapter, I examine Piper's *Talking to Myself: The Autobiography of an Art Object* (1974) and the *Mythic Being* series (1973–1975) using literary studies methods, illustrating how questions of literary style, voice, and address can be useful tools for analyzing artworks that live amid the textual, performative, and visual. I approach these pieces using conceptualism as a critical lens, in which the idea behind the work of art is regarded as more important than the art object itself, focusing on characteristics such as self-reflexivity, the dematerialization of

---

[2] I wish to thank the archivist at the Adrian Piper Research Archive (APRA) for their fact-checking of this essay and generally illuminating consultation. Out of respect for APRA's high standards for critical clarity, I will often use phrases such as "I read" or "I argue" to eliminate any ambiguity that my interpretations of Piper's work might by be shared by Piper (unless quoted directly).

[3] In the Adrian Piper Research Archive Foundation's biography of Piper, she is described as "a first-generation Conceptual artist and analytic philosopher" (Adrian Piper Research Archive Foundation).

[4] Piper left the United States permanently after discovering that her name had been added to the "Suspicious Travelers Watch List." This was the final straw for Piper after struggling for years as the first tenured African American woman in the department of Philosophy at Wellesley College. For more on Piper's "escape" to Berlin, consult her memoir (Piper 2018).

the art object, and a critical stance toward traditional definitions of art (Alberro and Stimson 1999: xvi–xvii). I argue that the critical and analytical modes embedded in conceptual aesthetics can be understood as consonant with what Cedric Robinson, the eminent scholar of Black studies, named the Black radical tradition. In this chapter, I am interested in investigating a sympathy that I locate between conceptualism and radical politics as both encourage us to critically regard our perspectives and assumptions about the world. What new practices of reading might be developed out of this aesthetic and political companionship?

In the 1960s and 1970s, many artists began rethinking their relationships to the commercial art world and institutions, including the culpability of art institutions in state violence. Artist activist groups formed quickly and with intensity. Notable examples in New York City in the late 1960s and early 1970s include the 1970 New York Art Strike against Racism, War, and Repression and the Art Workers Coalition (AWC), whose members included an eclectic group of conceptual and non-conceptual artists including Vassilakis Takis, Hans Haake, Lucy Lippard, Tom Lloyd, and Wen-Ying Tsai, among many others.[5]

Stylistically, conceptual art aimed to critique the elitism of the art world by embedding analytical and critical perspectives into the work of art itself. In this vein, artists pursued systematic, process-oriented methods exploring how organizational structures and even the idea of information itself are produced and experienced subjectively. Often as a form of anti-capitalist critique, many artists pursued nonvisual forms, using performance, text, or sound as medium, attempting to dematerialize the art object so that it would not be limited by its commodification. Theoretically, through dematerialization, art could be democratized. Art markets and institutions, having no precious object to buy and sell, would have less influence over the production, distribution, and valuation of art and artists. This control would be ceded to artists and expanded art audiences.

As critique became the subject of artworks and the importance of the visual receded, language and text came to play a crucial role in conceptualism. Language has a privileged relationship with communication, information, and procedure. However, language also has the capacity to exceed its intended meaning and functionality. Conceptualism's interest in democratizing art and wresting its production and distribution away from the art establishment made text an important tool. When text is the medium, artists do not need an elite education, special tools, galleries, museums, or technical skill to make art. Anyone can be an artist.

Language also facilitated conceptualism's exploration of 'neutral' systems and the sorting of information. For example, there is Piper's piece *Here and Now* (1968), a book of sixty-four unbound sheets of graph paper filled with eight-by-eight grids (sixty-four squares total). Encountering *Here and Now*, the reader registers the paradoxes of passing time, as *Here and Now* progressively marks one square of the grid per sheet with text that describes the square's location within the grid, for example:

---

[5] For more on art activism in this period, see Bryan-Wilson (2010) and Hockley and Morris (2017).

> HERE: the sq
> uare area in
> top row, righ
> t corner of
> page.

Traditionally, conceptualism values the concept behind the work over the object produced. Thus, I read *Here* and *Now* as utilizing conceptualist proceduralism—tediously inscribing where "here" is within each square of the grid as the book progresses—creating a system to execute a concept. A literary reading of *Here and Now* reveals a meditative poesis emerging in the aggregation of each stanza-like cube of text. The enjambment forced by the literal constraint of the graphic square causes the reader to take a breath mid-word, a small gasp or stutter that adds musicality to the terse, informational diction. The reader may linger in what Piper calls the "indexical present," what is happening "here and now" (Piper 1996). In *Here and Now*, I interpret the poetic text not as a way of expressing feelings or revealing truths but as a device to refer the reader back to their own embodied consciousness. In this reading, the seemingly neutral systems ordering our world (the grid) are relational. The reader expands the 'here' of each square as she reads it, allowing her world to fill the airy spaces of the work.[6]

A literary reading of the affectively flat writing in text-based conceptualism from the late 1960s, such as *Here and Now*, reveals that no writing is neutral. It always has a position, a history, a context, a mode of expression—a location in the grid. By undisciplining reading, we can bring literary studies methods to texts that decline literariness with interesting results. As Jacquelyn Ardam puts it, "Conceptual art and conceptual writing demand more of their viewers and readers; both movements ask us to read more expansively, not less, and the question of how to interpret these works is part and parcel of the works themselves" (Price 2015). Thus, one of the benefits of reading conceptualist texts is that they awaken us to different approaches to, and contexts of, interpretation, reading between and across administrative, instructional, visual, performance, and literary modes.

Unidentified Flying Object

In Adrian Piper's 1994 poem entitled "My Nose Cone," the speaker imagines not what it is like to fly *in* a rocket ship but what it's like to fly *as* a rocket ship. The speaker imagines her body transformed into a spaceship, hurtling through the cosmos. Beginning on line 34:

---

[6] For more on the modernist grid, see Krauss (1979).

> My nose cone,
> a shiny silvery pointy number
> makes me look like the Tin Man
> I don't mind
> it's cute
> it glows
> it hurtles through everything
> plumbs deep space
> and deep truths
> goes where no nose cone has ever gone before
>
> Piper (2018: 23), © Adrian Piper
Research Archive Foundation Berlin

While early in the poem, the speaker enjoys her object-body, its cuteness and shininess which makes her "look like the Tin Man," at the end of the poem, this metallic body is shed, a tool no longer needed. A few lines later, the speaker describes:

> my nose cone shattering,
> opening up to let it all in
> my head burning cool blue flame
> drenching me in white light
> I disperse
> into the vast and ancient timeless night
> waiting and humming beneath us
> yawning everything and anything in.
> 'Bye!
>
> (2018: 25)[7]

Now the speaker experiences flight, not indirectly through the reflection of the shiny nose cone, but immediately through her dispersion "into the vast and ancient timeless night / waiting and humming beneath us / yawning everything and anything in." As I read the poem, the speaker's rocket body is a pleasurable vehicle for transformation, but the goal is to jettison objecthood for something else.

I read the idea of "flight" in this poem as a metaphor for freedom through abstraction, aesthetic abstraction being a rejection of inherited and fixed aesthetic forms in favor of experimental, unstable, and open-ended forms. Reading "My Nose Cone," the dual and overlapping meanings of flight—to ascend and to escape—come into focus. In these musings on abstraction as flight and flight as freedom, the reader might also hear the resonances of fugitivity, *marronage*, Afro-futurism, and freedom by self-abscondence theorized and practiced in the long history of the Black radical tradition. In a 1987 catalogue essay titled "Flying," wherein Piper states both that "Abstraction is flying"

---

[7] This is an excerpt and not the full poem. The poem continues.

and "Abstraction is also flight," Piper propounds that "Abstraction is freedom from the socially prescribed and consensually accepted; freedom to violate in imagination the constraints of public practice, to play with conventions, or to indulge them" (Piper 1987).[8] Reading these words in conversation with "My Nose Cone" (1994), I understand abstraction-as-flight as a method, seeking freedom *from* the limitations of both objecthood and subjecthood and freedom *to* become something beyond these social forms.[9]

As I will argue in my readings of Piper's work, self-objectification can be interpreted as a conceptualist tool used toward the transcendence of subjecthood and objecthood in pursuit of freedom. As in "My Nose Cone," self-objectification can be read as a method for the radical re-imagination of the self. Throughout this chapter, I identify procedures of highly stylized aesthetic objectification (exemplified by the shiny nose cone), which I argue are aesthetic processes working toward an unscripted mode of being ("'Bye!'"). In the early 1970s, these acts of self-objectification often took the form of performances. For example, in *Untitled Performance at Max's Kansas City* (1970), Piper wore a blindfold, nose clip, ear plugs, and long evening gloves as she stumbled unguided through the New York nightclub and restaurant. Piper's act was part of a program of performances, featuring contemporaries like Vito Acconci, in a spot frequented by ultra-hip artists like Andy Warhol. As Piper reflected back on this piece, writing in 1981:

> I didn't want to be absorbed as a collaborator, because that would mean having my own consciousness co-opted and modified by that of others: It would mean allowing my consciousness to be influenced by their perceptions of art, and exposing my perceptions of art to their consciousness, and I didn't want that. I have always had a very strong individualistic streak. My solution was to privatize my own consciousness as much as possible, by depriving it of sensory input from that environment; to isolate it from all tactile, aural, and visual feedback. In doing so I presented myself as a silent, secret, passive object, seemingly ready to be absorbed into their consciousness as an object. But I learned that complete absorption was impossible, because my *voluntary* objectlike passivity implied aggressive activity and choice, an independent presence confronting the Art-Conscious environment with its autonomy. My objecthood became my subjecthood.
>
> Piper (1996: 27)

Fred Moten might call this the "resistance of the object," a work of theatrical self-objectification as a means of preserving the self against the violence of anti-Blackness (Moten 2003: 234). Uri McMillan calls this "performing objecthood," a "performance-based method that disrupts presumptive knowledges of black subjectivity" using the aesthetic to develop forms of being that preserve what anti-Blackness and heteropatriarchy seek to destroy while also creating something new (McMillan 2015: 9).

---

[8] For more on abstraction in African American expressive culture, see Harper (2015).
[9] For more on freedom in Piper's work, see Cervenek (2014).

However, as many scholars have noted, such methods raise questions about the risks of immanent critique and the history of Black women's objectification within the afterlives of slavery. For some scholars, such as John Bowles, Cherise Smith, and Kobena Mercer, Piper's investigation of objecthood yields fruitful ruminations on representation, stereotype, and identity (Bowles 2011; Smith 2011; Mercer 2008). Others, including McMillan, Moten, and Tavia Nyong'o, are oriented toward Black studies and performance studies, focusing on questions related to Black radicalism, performance, and Black ontology (McMillan 2015; Moten 2018; Nyong'o 2018). Via this latter group, we might situate Piper's work within what Cedric Robinson named the Black radical tradition, an ongoing "revolutionary consciousness that proceeded from the whole historical experience of Black people and not merely from the social formations of capitalist slavery or the relations of production of colonialism" (Robinson 2000: 169). As Erica Edwards summarizes, "If racial regimes are fabrications of Western order, the Black Radical Tradition is the history of 'a whole other way of being,'" which Robinson writes grants "supremacy to metaphysics, not the material" (Edwards 2016: xix; Robinson 2000: 169).[10] The performative assertion of freedom through self-objectification may seem oppositional to Black radical consciousness and its collectivism. The perceived explorations of art objecthood are charged as they recall the commodification of Black people-as-objects under slavery and in its afterlives. Yet, however unexpectedly, I interpret the procedure of self-objectification as a strategy for undoing the object–subject logics of racial capitalism. As Uri McMillan presents it, "To Piper, abstraction was flight," and yet, "her flight was continually grounded by the political upheavals of the 1970s and the affective responses of others to her embodiment as a black woman (most especially in the hallowed halls of academia), both of which trapped her back in her subjectivity" (McMillan 2015: 102). In my reading of Piper's work, objecthood and subjecthood are not direct opposites mapping onto unfreedom and freedom. Subjecthood is also an enclosure that may be opened through abstraction. Art objecthood can be read as such an aesthetic strategy (102). Following McMillan, I read the procedural abstractionism of conceptualist aesthetics as a rejection of identity-based interpretations of Piper's work, interpretations in which the conclusions are always already formed, departing from an ahistorical or asocial notion of freedom, artistic and otherwise.

It is important to note that Black radicalism and Black artists are infrequently linked to the history of conceptualism.[11] Conceptual art in the 1960s and 1970s has been strongly associated with whiteness and white men in particular. For years, Piper was effectively the only artist of African American descent, regardless of gender, whose name appeared on the regular lists of conceptualist pathbreakers alongside Sol LeWitt, Joseph Kosuth, John Baldessari, George Maciunas, and other mostly white and male peers.[12]

---

[10] For more on the culture and aesthetics of the Black radical tradition, see Kelley (2002).

[11] For more on Black conceptualism and art history, see Wilson (2019) and Adkins (2005).

[12] Piper has expressed a complex position on how race and gender are relevant to understanding her work. Since the early 1970s, Piper's art has been regularly interpreted as exploring racial and gender identity, as in works such as *The Mythic Being (1973–1975)*, the *Political Self-Portraits* series (1978–1980), *Self-Portrait Exaggerating My Negroid Features* (1981), or *Cornered* (1988). In 1990, Piper wrote "The

Recently, scholars and curators have come to recognize that artists of color working in the same period, such as David Hammons, Maren Hassinger, Shigeko Kubota, Senga Nengudi, Yoko Ono, Nam June Paik, or Benjamin Patterson, also demand our attention as early and impactful contributors to conceptualism. I would like to argue that abstraction offers resistance to fixed frameworks of interpretation, pre-formed by racial and gendered meaning.

Autobiographical Objects

Around 1970, Adrian Piper experienced a political awakening. As Piper tells it, as a child she was generally protected from an awareness of the world's constitutive racism:

> I was an only child in a family of four adults devoted to creating for me an environment in which my essential worth and competence never came into question. I used to think my parents sheltered me in this way because they believed, idealistically, that my education and achievements would then protect me from the effects of racism. I now know that they did so to provide me with an invincible armor of self-worth with which to fight it. It almost worked. I grew up not quite grasping the fact that my racial identity was a disadvantage. This lent heat to my emerging political conviction that of course it shouldn't be a disadvantage, for me or anyone else, and finally fueled my resolution not to allow it to be a disadvantage if I had anything at all to say about it.[13]
>
> Piper (1992: 9)

At the end of the 1960s, the realities of anti-Blackness, gender oppression, and imperialism became impossible not to see. In 1969, Black and Puerto Rican students led a large-scale strike and occupation of the City College of New York, where Piper took classes, shutting down the university for two weeks to successfully demand anti-racist institutional changes. In the spring of 1970, the United States invaded Cambodia. In May, students were massacred by National Guard and police at Kent State and Jackson State universities. That same year, Piper joined the AWC (Adrian Piper Research Archive Foundation).[14] As previously mentioned, the art world was hardly a welcoming place for women or artists of color during the 1960s. In this period, Piper began making

---

Triple Negation of Colored Women Artists," critiquing the art world's tendency to offer stereotyped readings of art by women of color that discounted its aesthetic particularity and value, fixating on the artist rather than the art. However, Piper declines the framing of "Black woman artist" and objects to her inclusion in exhibits exclusively comprised of Black artists, i.e. her 2013 request that her work be removed from *Radical Presence: Black Performance in Contemporary Art* curated by Valerie Cassel Oliver. In September 2012, on her sixty-fourth birthday, she "retired from being black" (Piper 2010; 2012).

[13] See also Piper (2018: 57).
[14] See also McMillan (2015: 108–109).

performance-based pieces, taking place in public non-art-world spaces for unsuspecting audiences. These engaged her emerging questions about the relationship between the self and the social, including the degree to which art might intervene in oppression and violence.

Talking to Myself: the Autobiography of an Art Object is a key text in this transformative period in Piper's work. I argue that it continues to experiment with the aesthetic of neutral objectivity that we see in Piper's earlier text-based art from the 1960s, like *Here and Now*, but also builds upon this previous work by adding narrative elements and invoking the genre of autobiography. In calling herself an "art object," I argue that Piper makes a double move, seeming to strip away agency through self-objectification yet also bestowing upon herself the authority of critical distance. By identifying an object (her self) which can be described and analyzed, Piper also creates a subject whose authority is crafted through the critical practices of description and analysis.

Talking to Myself makes exemplary use of an objective voice and, for this reason, scholars tend to read it as documentation of Piper's *Catalysis* series, rather than as a literary object. Yet, *Talking to Myself* existed independently of the performances as a unique, stand-alone text. The text is organized into seven dated chronological sections written between August 1970 and November 1972, as well as a preface, dated January 1973. It was translated and printed in two separate editions: an English–French edition published in 1974 and an English–Italian edition published in 1975. The content of *Talking to Myself* mostly reflects upon Piper's *Catalysis* series, a performance-based work that I read as an early exploration of "xenophobia," or the rejection of difference and perceived intrusion of an alien other, and "xenophilia," an attraction to difference, topics that Piper wrote about in her later philosophical work.[15] I read *Talking to Myself* as more than a record of events; like many works of life writing, I interpret it as cannily navigating choices of style and address to give readers a sense of privileged access to the truth. Meanwhile, the text's conceptualism complicates the narrative's transparency.

In *Catalysis*, I argue, Piper seeks to understand and critique responses to an alien other by turning her body into an art object, appearing in public in bizarre, even abject, ways. For example:

> *Catalysis IV*, in which I dressed very conservatively but stuffed a large white bath towel into the sides of my mouth until my cheeks bulged to about twice their normal size, letting the rest of it hang down my front and riding the bus, subway, and Empire State Building elevator; *Catalysis VI* in which I attached helium-filled Mickey Mouse balloons from each of my ears, under my nose, to my two front teeth, and from thin strands of my hair, then walked through Central Park and the lobby of the Plaza Hotel, and rode the subway during morning rush hour.
>
> Piper (1996: 43)

---

[15] For information on Piper's understanding of xenophobia and xenophilia, see Piper (1997). For another scholarly perspective on the relevance of xenophobia to Piper's conceptual and performance art, see Costello (2018).

Other iterations involved covering herself in substances like oil, rotten food, or wet paint, or breaking out in a dance to Aretha Franklin's "Respect," which Piper had memorized and played silently in her head.

The main conflict in the autobiographical narrative of *Talking to Myself*, the piece of grit which becomes a pearl by the end, is Piper's sense that her private world has been infiltrated by outside influences. In the past, Piper feels she could consider aesthetic questions separately from social and political questions. This illusion has been shattered by recent events. When Piper feels the strangeness of her interrelationship with others, she experiments with new ways of provoking strangers' consciousness of difference. I believe that this marks not only Piper's awareness of her connection to issues like American imperialism, the militarized suppression of student protest, or institutional racism but also her own position within a racist and sexist society. In later philosophical work, Piper defines xenophobia "as a special case of a more general cognitive phenomenon, namely the disposition to resist the intrusion of anomalous data of any kind into a conceptual scheme whose internal rational coherence is necessary for preserving a unified and rationally integrated self" (Piper 1997: 23). When one's sense of self is grounded in the misconception that whiteness, masculinity, heterosexuality, able-bodiedness, and so on, are fundamental to personhood, then Blackness, disability, femininity, and queerness can be perceived as "anomalous data," dangerous threats to the unity of the self.

In my reading, *Catalysis* uses conceptualist procedures to produce abstraction, singular methods for exploring embodied difference that do not refer directly to any one identity. The illegibility of her self-objectification serves a self-preservative function similar to the Max's performance. Even as Piper puts her body at risk in a public space, her undecipherability resists stereotypes and pre-formed interpretations. Applying her terms, she becomes "anomalous data." Through self-objectification, she attempts to avoid being sorted, to generate new forms of personhood. And yet, these interpretive frameworks reassert themselves. We can read Piper's abstractions as nevertheless prompting racialized, classed, or ableist social disqualifications: an other who smells strange, disrupts social norms, appears psychologically and socially deviant.[16]

I want to emphasize that *Catalysis* does not simply stage audience repulsion, violence, or willful blindness in response to difference. It also has the potential to provoke xenophilic responses—an expansion of the human upon exposure to difference.[17] Moreover, these experiments have as much to do with *Piper's* experience as the audience's. Piper is working through her own questions about the coherence of the self, its potential for violation, and her engagements with difference.[18] If we view performances like *Catalysis* through the lens of the Black radical tradition, then we can

---

[16] See McMillan (2015) for more on how Piper's identity may have affected these performances.
[17] On 'xenophilia,' see Piper (1997).
[18] Piper wrote later, looking back from the perspective of 1987:

> I experimented with my own object-hood, transforming it sculpturally as I had other objects, took it into the street, confronted others with the end products, and watched the effects on my

recognize the movements to both preserve and expand the self within the historical conditions of anti-Blackness, catalyzing a new ethical imaginary. I read in *Catalysis* a refusal of the violent misreadings and an experiment with radical forms of being.

Talking to Myself unfolds as a philosophical narrative of artistic maturity—a kind of autobiographical *kunstlerroman*. Yet stylistically, *Talking to Myself* does not bear many of the expressive markers that we associate with autobiography, even as the genre is invoked in its title. Piper projects an objective, distant tone, writing about herself and her work from a position of universal authority. For example, the opening of *Talking to Myself* reads more like a treatise on artmaking than a memoir:

> One reason for making and exhibiting a work is to induce a reaction or change in the viewer. The stronger the work, the stronger its impact and the more total (physiological, psychological, intellectual, etc.) the reaction of the viewer. The work is a catalytic agent, in that it promotes a change in another entity (the viewer) without undergoing any permanent change itself.
>
> Piper (1996: 32)

I believe that Piper's conceptualism should push us to probe the "neutrality" of her pedantic non-style. In her preface to volume I of her selected writings, *Out of Order, Out of Sight*, where *Talking to Myself* is republished, Piper humorously refers to this objective persona as her 'sense of entitlement' which she cultivated as "an upper-middle-class heterosexual WASP male, the pampered only son of doting parents" (1996 xxxiii). In this wry performed identification with white cishet masculinity, I argue that perceived literary objectivity is inseparable from historically situated formations of racialization, gendering, class relations, and other systems of power which are entangled with literary forms.[19] Piper acknowledges that

> Many of the early chapters in these volumes express my white male's sense of entitlement unconsciously. These chapters are written in the objective voice. They are reasonable, tolerant, modest, and dogmatic. They are touchingly naïve in their unspoken assumption that the world of art ideas is there to be mined and ordered by my intellect. They express the undifferentiated and prereflective abstract consciousness of the infant whose world is a nipple available on demand. This is the voice of objective universality. It is the voice of innocent, humble authority.
>
> Piper (1996: xxxiv)

In my reading, to write like an upper-middle-class straight white man is not to identify a set of characteristics as essentially belonging to a particular identity but to claim the

> social relations (the *Catalysis* series). I traumatized myself, burned out, and began to withdraw from the artworld into the external world.
>
> Piper (1987: 28)

---

[19] On the racialization of rationality, see Da Silva (2007), McKittrick (2015), and Wynter (2003).

privilege of objectivity which has been coded as white, male, straight, and elite. Piper wittily presents this authoritative voice as a specific literary style ("reasonable, tolerant, modest, and dogmatic"), which I argue are qualities inseparable from the unremarkable structures of domination. The apparent *lack* of style is what allows its association with power to appear natural and reasonable. Those who are objective are also without style, style being a marker of identity and historical embeddedness. This is consonant with the mistaken assumption that whiteness itself has no content but is a universal form of the human. I see here a playful critique of fragile claims to objective authority ("touchingly naïve") as well as authority's puerile violence—god forbid the infant is denied the nipple. While the cerebral affect suggests no style at all, in my reading, the non-style of imagined objectivity is a literary formalism quite important to conceptual writing.

Through her objective tone, Piper performs critical distance in relation to her work and her own body. However, *Talking to Myself* is not just a collection of personal notes or a purely philosophical exegesis. It narrates a clear progression from an initial point of confusion and conflict—Piper's disillusionment and her search for a new art ideology—and ends with an artistic breakthrough. This is fitting as the text marks a major transition in Piper's practice as the result of her emergent political consciousness.

In *Talking to Myself*, Piper presents her sense of self as something that once felt sealed and sovereign. However, she has since experienced "an invasion by the 'outside world' of my aesthetic isolation" (31). As the sensorial intensity (for both performer and audience) of *Catalysis* suggests, becoming self-conscious is not a smooth, harmonious experience, but transgressive. Thus, the hermeticism of "talking to oneself" performs a kind of repair, resealing the self rent by racism and sexism through a closed conversation with the self. The poetics of address that structure "talking to oneself" are recursive. One often resorts to "talking to oneself" to work through a concept or a problem or to voice a feeling or idea that has little hope of being affirmed by another. Talking to oneself is a feedback loop that can accrue incredible affective and intellectual density. Whole worlds can be built in the back and forth of a conversation with oneself. In this way, talking to oneself resembles the process of writing. Although writing often includes the introjection of "outside" voices, in the form of editors or readers, writers must still play the role of their own audience, talking to themselves along the way. This suggests a continued interest in self-preservation which echoes the performative radicalism of the *Max's Kansas City* performance. Similarly, *Talking to Myself*, can be read as an attempt to write toward freedom, composing a world of the self via art objecthood.

Piper is indeed talking to herself—describing, reflecting upon, and contextualizing her art, analyzing and evaluating its effects, offering herself suggestions on where her project should go next, and integrating her own feedback. But she also performs a double mode of address through publication. The reader experiences a sense of "overhearing" or peering into the private world of Piper's artmaking as she talks herself through it.[20] "Overhearing" is a kind of reading that we often associate with lyric poetry but that

---

[20] On lyric address, see Culler (2015) and Jackson and Prins (2014).

appears also in life writing genres like diaries and collections of letters. I argue that in talking to herself in front of readers, *Talking to Myself* stages how the poetics of address both produce and undo a composed self; autonomy is negotiated in an inescapably relational world. As Judith Butler has written, the poetics of address affirm the validity of our existence and contribute to our sense that we can affect change in the world (Butler 2004: 130). The text attempts to prevent racism's and sexism's misreadings, their failure of address, by folding interpretation and reception into the work itself.

Unfortunately, social categories of interpretation like race and gender are never fully displaced, only complicated. As *Talking to Myself* closes, Piper increasingly performs the work without an audience in the privacy of her apartment or deserted locations. By the end of *Talking to Myself*, Piper asserts that an external audience for *Catalysis* has become unnecessary because she has internalized them into her consciousness:

> When I do a work in private, I perceive myself (1) through the eyes of the general audience, that is, the world in general, for whom an art object—myself—exists; (2) through the eyes of an informed but limited art audience, for whom the art is worthwhile, and who perceives the work as having aesthetic merit.... Because I see myself objectively in this sense, it just doesn't matter whether there is an actual audience there or not. I have assimilated its double vision into my own consciousness.
>
> Piper (1996: 53)

It is difficult not to hear echoes of W. E. B. Du Bois's "double consciousness" in Piper's claims to "double vision," which she has "assimilated" into her consciousness—as Du Bois famously put it, a "sense of always looking at one's self through the eyes of others, of measuring one's soul by the tape of a world that looks on in amused contempt and pity" (Du Bois 1999: 11). However, Piper's tone is markedly different from that of Du Bois, portraying a capacity for "double vision" as the cultivated apex of an artistic practice, a practice which has become so complete that it no longer requires an external audience. The effect for readers is that Piper seems to have achieved the goal of becoming "an independent presence confronting the Art-Conscious environment with its autonomy" (Piper 1996: 27), as she writes in 1981 reflecting on the *Max's Kansas City* performance. In writing *Talking to Myself*, Piper externalizes her "double vision" as both art object and "art perceiver" into an elegantly composed portrait, wresting interpretive control of her "art-object life," dispensing with the need for an audience to validate that life (53).[21] In claiming roles of both art perceiver and art object, readers can interpret a strategy of asserting subjecthood, which is common within identity-based aesthetic and social movements, as well as a simultaneous departure from this strategy through the textual performance of a conceptualist defamiliarization of the self. In doing so, we can read a complication of the assumed continuity between subjecthood and freedom.

---

[21] We might read Piper within a history of Black women's autobiographical self-fashioning: Zora Neale Hurston, Maya Angelou, Assata Shakur, Audre Lorde, Janet Mock, and many more.

Speaking Objects

The *Mythic Being*, initially referred to as "dispersion," continues Piper's experiments in art objecthood.[22] *Mythic Being* followed *Catalysis* and *Talking to Myself* and was executed in street performances, photographs, and ads placed in the *Village Voice* gallery pages. In *Mythic Being*, Piper plays the character of her "seeming opposite" "a third-world, working-class, overtly hostile male" (Piper 1996: 147). As the Mythic Being, she wore an afro wig, mustache, sunglasses, smoked a cigar, and assumed a masculine demeanor, sometimes engaging in acts of stereotypically raced and gendered behavior, including cruising white women and a staged mugging. In short, *Mythic Being* appropriates objectifying forms of race, class, gender, and sexuality. Piper writes, "A 'mythic being' is a fictitious or abstract personality that is generally part of a story or folktale used to explain or sanctify social or legal institutions or natural phenomena" (108). Yet, a potential reading of *Mythic Being* as straightforward satire is complicated by other aspects of the work. As the Mythic Being, Piper would memorize lines from her teenage diaries and repeat them as mantras. For example, "No matter how much I ask my mother to stop buying crackers, cookies, and things, she does anyway, and says it's for her, even if I always eat it. So I've decided to fast" (110). Or "Today was the first day of school. The only decent boys in my class are Robbie and Clyde. I think I like Clyde" (109). These diary fragments were also used in the photographic *Village Voice* ads, where Piper posed as the Mythic Being and then used an oil crayon to draw thought and speech bubbles containing her diary fragments directly onto the photograph.

As others have pointed out, *Mythic Being* uses direct address to shift the work of ethical relations from the artist to the audience.[23] For example, in *I Embody*, Piper poses as the Mythic Being in a tight close-up photograph, his face emerging from oil crayon shadows. The Mythic Being casually smokes his cigar and looks directly at the viewer. The speech bubble reads, "I EMBODY EVERYTHING YOU MOST HATE AND FEAR." In her visual and verbal use of direct address, Piper develops new ways of anticipating responses but forces the audience to bear the ethical weight rather than attempting to contain them though narrative self-fashioning, as I argued in my reading of *Talking to Myself*. While the objective voice may seem to naturalize its relationship to power and sublimate racial and gendered meaning into a non-style, one might consider how the Mythic Being performatively pushes the audience to reevaluate the racialization and gendering of style, marking an apparent change in aesthetic approach.

In the *Mythic Being*, I also read a performance of literary "overhearing," which we encountered in *Talking to Myself* in the context of life writing but which is associated with the lyric as well. As fragments, the mantras resemble poetic lines. They allude to a complex life history, but we receive only a glimpse into this life, expressed by an intimate,

---

[22] This early title is mentioned in Tavia Nyong'o's chapter "Brer Soul and the Mythic Being" (2019: 84).
[23] See Bowles (2011) and Lamm (2018).

distinct voice, reminiscent of a lyric speaker. Like the conventional lyric speaker whose expressive voice is "overheard" by the reader, the Mythic Being refused to acknowledge impromptu audiences in street performances, focusing intently on his mantra recitation, seemingly unaware that anyone was listening. In the *Village Voice* ads, Piper visualized the Mythic Being's interiority in comic-book-style thought bubbles rather than speech bubbles.

Kamran Javadizadeh argues that the lyric is not a universal form but "a literary form of white innocence" (Javadizadeh 2019: 476). Much like Piper's portrayal of the objective voice as a kind of white male naiveté, the lyric's evocation of unmediated expression "resonates with whiteness's implicit claims to universality and unmediated identity, whereby to be white in the United States is to be, apparently, without race and without a role in the erasure of whiteness's racialized others" (476). As Javadizadeh argues in reference to the lyric and I argue in my reading of the objective voice, neutrality is an aesthetic fantasy of power. I read Piper's use of objective voice in *Talking to Myself* and lyric address in *Mythic Being* experiment with transparency as a stylized aesthetic effect, showing how conceptualism can help us to perceive apparent lack of style as a style in itself. The *Mythic Being*, like the lyric, can be a lens for understanding "racism's role in the circulation of the self in public life" (475).

As I have argued thus far, Piper's 1981 reflections on the performance at *Max's Kansas City* attempt to preserve and forge subjecthood through aggressively passive objecthood by severing audience input. In *Talking to Myself*, aesthetic objectification also functions as a tool to restore agency. However, rather than disconnecting from an audience, as in the Max's example, in *Talking to Myself* Piper assimilates a representation of the audience into the work of art in an act of narrative containment. *Mythic Being* exemplifies aesthetic objectification as a procedure for refusing imposed limitations on the self. This is a double objectification, first through costuming as a racial, gendered, and classed type and second in the conversion of personal diary entries into art objects. In the *Mythic Being*, we can see resonances with less obvious identity play in the persona of an "upper-middle-class heterosexual WASP male." However, here, the emphasis on subjecthood through aggressive passivity or critical distance falls away.

Piper writes that she treats each diary excerpt as

> an object of meditation. I repeat it, reexperience it, examine and analyze it, infuse myself with it until I have wrung it of personal meaning and significance. It becomes an object for me to contemplate and simultaneously loses its status as an element in my own personality or subjecthood. As my subjecthood weakens, the meaning of the object thus weakens, and vice versa.
>
> (Piper 1996: 117)

When the Mythic Being fasts in order to avoid nibbling on cookies or weighs the benefits of dating Clyde over Robbie, the audience encounters expressions of fragility, desire, and anxiety that are not typically associated with straight, working class Black masculinity but more frequently associated with social narratives of bourgeois girlhood.

While Piper calls the Mythic Being "hostile," referring implicitly to stereotypes, these mantras can evoke a tender queerness and gentle complexity for the audience, especially as the mantras often circulate around the need to be desired by and connected to others. It is not just that we can read the *Mythic Being* as demonstrating the stereotype's fictionality—though I think it does this. But, more complexly, the performance of seemingly contradictory expressions of race, class, gender, and sexuality gestures toward ways of being that are unrecognizable within racial scripts of either heterosexual girlhood or masculinity. Thus, I read the *Mythic Being* as prompting a different ethics of relation and interpretation beyond these categorical modes.

Mythic Being critiques interpretation's management of difference, difference's reduction to fictions of the essential or biological, and the naturalization of xenophobia. In my reading of the *Mythic Being*, difference becomes irreducible to social categories. The character can also be read as providing a way to release the grip of deterministic narratives of gender and class. Presenting diary entries as aesthetic objects mediated by a fiction can be read as an abstractionist aesthetic process that turns away from the scriptedness of identity. I read this as a methodological departure from the kind of literary objectivity modeled in *Talking to Myself*. Rather than assume the position of authorial entitlement in "objective" non-style-as-style, the *Mythic Being* makes available the racialized abundance of style as an abstractionist tool.

Abstraction through objectification does not deny the ways that social categories shape experience but attempts to transcend them through the generation of new, open-ended forms. It is a method toward the unscripted, a mode of self-address re-imagining the terms of the social. My reading of these experiments interprets Piper's practice through the lens of the Black radical tradition and its experiments in fugitive modes of being, creating spaces of radical life, structured, but not defined, by anti-Blackness, while reaching for the transcendence of it.

In encountering Piper's work, I am moved by the sense that it imaginatively strives to understand how to be a person in the world—not this one, a world you would have to fly to. The mode of transportation is "cute / it glows / it hurtles through everything / plumbs deep space / and deep truths / goes where no nose cone has ever gone before" (Piper 2018: 23). I read Piper's work from the 1970s, an historical period of radical political consciousness on a mass scale, as presenting a practice of becoming unrecognizable.

In this chapter, I have argued that conceptualism's procedures of self-objectification urge readers and audiences to expand their practices of interpretation through encounters with difference, challenging the racialized and gendered authority of dominant ideas about objectivity and universality. The texts present the self as a mutable form, refusing the clarity of the subject. Provocations to authority and interpretation also reflect back upon the critic and their claims to knowledge. I hope that my understanding of Piper's work has deepened through my sustained reading, but I also believe that these readings are happily non-definitive. Any project of interpretation exists in anticipation of the difference that will unfinish it. The undisciplined reading that conceptualism demands helps us to recognize that while conceptualism has been understood as a white-dominated aesthetic practice, in fact, its most profound ideals owe a debt to Black radicalism, its refusals of misreading, and experiments in freedom-making.

References

Adkins, Terry, Valerie Cassel Oliver, Franklin Sirmans, Charles Gaines, and Adrian Piper. 2005. *Double Consciousness: Black Conceptual Art Since 1970* (Houston, TX: Contemporary Arts Museum Houston).

Adrian Piper Research Archive Foundation. "Adrian Piper: Personal Chronology," www.adrianpiper.com/personal_chrono.shtml, accessed February 18, 2022.

Adrian Piper Research Archive Foundation. "Biography," http://adrianpiper.com/biography.shtml, accessed February 18, 2022.

Alberro, Alexander and Blake Stimson, eds. 1999. *Conceptual Art: A Critical Anthology* (Cambridge, MA: The MIT Press).

Bowles, John. 2011. *Adrian Piper: Race, Gender, and Embodiment* (Durham, NC: Duke University Press).

Bryan-Wilson, Julia. 2010. *Art Workers: Radical Practice in the Vietnam War Era* (Berkeley, CA: University of California Press).

Butler, Judith. 2004. *Precarious Life: The Powers of Mourning and Violence* (New York: Verso Books).

Cervenek, Sarah Jane. 2014. *Wandering: Philosophical Performances of Racial and Sexual Freedom* (Durham, NC: Duke University Press).

Cherix, Christophe and Cornelia Butler, eds. 2018. *Adrian Piper: A Synthesis of Intuitions, 1965–2016* (New York: The Museum of Modern Art).

Chuh, Kandice. 2019. *The Difference Aesthetics Makes: On the Humanities "After Man"* (Durham, NC: Duke University Press).

Costello, Diarmud. 2018. "Xenophobia, Stereotypes, and Empirical Acculturation: Neo-Kantianism in Adrian Piper's Performance-Based Conceptual Art," in Cornelia H. Butler and David Platzker, eds, *Adrian Piper: A Reader* (New York: Museum of Modern Art), 166–215.

Culler, Jonathan. 2015. *The Theory of the Lyric* (Cambridge, MA: Harvard University Press).

Da Silva, Denise Ferreira. 2007. *Toward a Global Idea of Race* (Minneapolis, MN: University of Minnesota Press).

Du Bois, W.E.B. 1999. *The Souls of Black Folk* (New York: W. W. Norton & Company).

Edwards, Erica R. 2016. "Foreword," in Cedric J. Robinson, *The Terms of Order: Political Science and the Myth of Leadership* (Chapel Hill, NC: University of North Carolina Press), ix–xxviii.

Harper, Phillip Brian. 2015. *Abstractionist Aesthetics: Artistic Form and Social Critique in African American Culture* (New York: New York University Press).

Hockley, Rujeko and Catherine Morris, eds. 2017. *We Wanted a Revolution: Black Radical Women, 1965–1985: A Sourcebook* (Brooklyn, NY: Brooklyn Museum).

Jackson, Virginia and Yopie Prins, eds. 2014. *The Lyric Theory Reader: A Critical Anthology* (Baltimore, MD: John Hopkins University Press).

Javadizadeh, Kamran. 2019. "The Atlantic Ocean Breaking on Our Heads: Claudia Rankine, Robert Lowell, and the Whiteness of the Lyric Subject," *Journal of the Modern Language Association of America* 134.3: 475–490.

Kelley, Robin D.G. 2002. *Freedom Dreams: The Black Radical Imagination* (Boston, MA: Beacon Press).

Krauss, Rosalind. 1979. "Grids," *October* 9, 50–64.

Lamm, Kimberly. 2018. *Addressing the Other Woman: Textual Correspondences in Feminist Art and Writing* (Manchester: Manchester University Press).

McKittrick, Katherine, ed. 2015. *Sylvia Wynter: On Being Human as Praxis* (Durham, NC: Duke University Press).

McMillan, Uri. 2015. *Embodied Avatars: Genealogies of Black Feminist Art and Performance* (New York: New York University Press).

Mercer, Kobena, ed. 2008. "Adrian Piper, 1970–1975: Exiled on Main Street," in *Annotating Art's Histories: Exiles, Diasporas & Strangers* (Cambridge, MA: The MIT Press), 146–165.

Moten, Fred. 2003. *In the Break: The Aesthetics of the Black Radical Tradition* (Minneapolis, MN: University of Minnesota Press).

Moten, Fred. 2018. *The Universal Machine* (Durham, NC: Duke University Press).

Nizan, Shaked. 2017. *The Synthetic Proposition: Conceptualism and the Political Referent in Contemporary Art* (Manchester: Manchester University Press).

Nyong'o, Tavia. 2018. *Afro-Fabulations: The Queer Drama of Black Life* (New York: New York University Press).

Piper, Adrian. 1987. "Flying," in Jane Farver, ed., *Reflections: 1967–1987* (New York: Alternative Museum), 25–26.

Piper, Adrian. 1992. "Passing for White, Passing for Black," *Transition* 58: 4–32.

Piper, Adrian. 1996. *Out of Order, Out of Sight. Volume I: Selected Writings in Meta-Art 1968–1992* (Cambridge, MA: The MIT Press).

Piper, Adrian. 1997. "Xenophobia and Kantian Rationalism," in Mary Schott, ed., *Feminist Interpretations of Immanuel Kant* (University Park, PA: Pennsylvania State University Press), 21–73.

Piper, Adrian. 2010. "The Triple Negation of Colored Women Artists," in Amelia Jones, ed., *The Feminism and Visual Culture Reader* (New York: Routledge), 239–248.

Piper, Adrian. 2012. "News: September 2012," *Adrian Piper Research Archive Foundation*, www.adrianpiper.com/news_sep_2012.shtml, accessed February 18, 2022.

Piper, Adrian. 2018. *Escape to Berlin: A Travel Memoir* (Berlin: APRA Foundation).

Price, Katie L. 2015. "What is the Relationship between Conceptual Art and Conceptual Writing?," *Jacket2*, January 19, https://jacket2.org/commentary/what-relationship-between-conceptual-art-and-conceptual-writing, accessed February 18, 2022.

Robinson, Cedric. 2000. *Black Marxism: The Making of the Black Radical Tradition* (Chapel Hill, NC: The University of North Carolina Press).

Shaked, Nizan. 2017. *The Synthetic Proposition: Conceptualism and the Political Referent in Contemporary Art* (Manchester: Manchester University Press).

Smith, Cherise. 2011. *Enacting Others: Politics of Identity in Eleanor Antin, Nikki S. Lee, Adrian Piper, and Anna Deavere Smith* (Durham, NC: Duke University Press).

Wilson, Leslie. 2019. "'Can You Get to That': The Funk of 'Conceptual-Type Art,'" in Eddie Chambers, ed., *The Routledge Companion to African American Art History* (Abingdon: Taylor & Francis Group), 369–381.

Wynter, Sylvia. 2003. "Unsettling the Coloniality of Being/Power/Truth/Freedom: Towards the Human, After Man, Its Overrepresentation—An Argument," *CR: The New Centennial Review* 3.3 (Fall): 257–337.

CHAPTER 20

CULTURAL MEMORY STUDIES AND THE *BELOVED* PARADIGM

From Rememory to Abolition in the Afterlives of Slavery

MICHAEL ROTHBERG

Toni Morrison's 1987 novel *Beloved* is one of the most quickly and definitively canonized literary works of the twentieth century. A winner of the 1988 Pulitzer Prize, *Beloved* was also one of the novels mentioned by the Nobel Prize committee when Morrison won that award in 1993. Yet even those distinguished prizes do not quite capture *Beloved*'s extensive influence. We can get a more complete sense of the novel's impact by considering its importance for scholars and teachers as well as its place in library collections. Google Scholar lists 19,200 entries that refer to Morrison's 1987 novel in the thirty-three years since its publication. While absolute numbers cannot speak for themselves, a comparative search confirms *Beloved*'s status as *the* canonical work of recent times. *Beloved* far outpaces Morrison's other work: a search for the 1977 novel *Song of Solomon*, for instance, returns 7,430 entries and novels such as *The Bluest Eye* and *Sula* receive somewhat fewer. Even more tellingly, other prominent novels of the period also fall far behind *Beloved*. Margaret Atwood's influential *The Handmaid's Tale* (1985) receives 7,020. Don DeLillo's *White Noise* (1985), a signature text of the "postmodern" 1980s, receives 5,320 citations; his *Libra* (1988), *Mao II* (1991), and *Underworld* (1997) have received far fewer. The surprisingly incomplete Modern Language Association International Bibliography lists only 418 entries for *Beloved* but that is still far more than those for the other texts mentioned here. Combining data from Google Scholar, JSTOR, and leading American literature journals, the website *Metacanon* ranks *Beloved* as the most canonical work of twentieth-century American literature. The novel also occupies a prominent place in the classroom: Open Syllabus Explorer has recorded 2,743 appearances of *Beloved* on

English literature syllabi. That makes *Beloved* the twenty-eighth most frequently taught work in English-language literature courses across periods, but that list also includes numerous writing and style handbooks along with works of poetry and drama. Although it falls beyond the purview of this chapter, *Beloved*'s prominent status is without doubt global: WorldCat's Identities feature lists over 500 editions of the novel in 24 languages, which are held by over 13,000 libraries.[1]

Crowned by prizes, cited by legions of critics, and taught in thousands of high-school and college classrooms, *Beloved* is also much more than a novel. Indeed, as Stephen Best argues in an influential article, *Beloved* became a "paradigm" that "shape[d] the way a generation of scholars conceived of its ethical relationship to the past" (2012: 461, 459). In so doing, the novel extended the reach of literary influence far beyond the usual limits: "For a distinctive if not singular moment in the history of the interpretive disciplines, a novel set the terms of the political and historiographical agenda" (459). Those terms, which Best glosses in a skeptical vein, involve a "melancholic historicism" that collapses past and present and an "unassailable" assertion that "the slave past provides a ready prism for apprehending the black political present" (460, 453). In order to illustrate this melancholic paradigm, Best quotes an interview in which Morrison describes her goal in the novel as an attempt to make readers "yearn for [the] company" of the devastated families she depicts in order that they may "know what slavery did." For Best, this affective component of Morrison's novel turns her melancholic historicism into a vector for the production of collective memory: "'To know what slavery did,' to make it not simply an object of experience or epistemology but the grounds of memory, Morrison resists a view of loss as the property of an immediate circle of kin and encourages us to claim that loss for ourselves" (460). Through this transformation of history into collective memory or what Morrison calls "rememory," "the traumatic events of slavery and the middle passage ... suffuse the vastness of the Atlantic itself as a general historical framework and condition" (458).

Best's diagnosis of *Beloved*'s oceanic influence was meant critically. Against what he characterizes as the straitjacket of slavery's hauntings, he calls for a shift in the conversation about race and African American culture toward "a more baffled, cut-off, foreclosed position with regard to the slave past" (472)—a position he finds in Morrison's 2008 novel *A Mercy*. Yet, despite Best's attempt to wrest a different, less determinate relation between race and slavery from Morrison's late work, the *Beloved* paradigm has, if anything, intensified in the years since his essay appeared. In particular, the increased visibility of white supremacy, police violence against African Americans and other people of color, and the carceral state has brought with it a more widespread sense that present-day concerns grow out of unresolved injustices dating back to the nation's foundational

---

[1] On Google Scholar, I used the suggested search phrase "Author Title 'Criticism'": see also https://metacanon.org (accessed February 21, 2022) and https://opensyllabus.org/result/title?id=7516192773636 (accessed March 2, 2022). Taken individually, all of these pieces of evidence are flawed. Taken together, they confirm what many of us already believe is *Beloved*'s unusual status among twentieth-century American novels.

system of slavery. The #Black Lives Matter movement, which emerged in 2013 (the year after Best's essay appeared), the increasingly prominent calls for reparations, and the rise of Afropessimist thought in and beyond the academy illustrate how those foundational injustices continue to shape (without fully determining) prominent conceptualizations of the Black political present.

For the purposes of this chapter, the point is not to adjudicate the question of slavery's relation to the present but to recognize and attempt to understand the work of memory performed by Morrison's novel. Against the backdrop of *Beloved*'s outsized influence, I propose to read the novel as a lens through which to reflect on the relationship of literature to cultural memory studies.[2] The emergent interdisciplinary field of cultural memory studies offers a conceptual framework that helps explain the cultural work Morrison's novel does as well as the reasons it has resonated so powerfully across the late twentieth- and early twenty-first centuries. Memory studies as it is currently configured emerges primarily out of European thought and remains at its most robust in European academic networks and civil society organizations engaged with the memory of the Second World War and the Soviet bloc. Yet, increased attention in the United States to the memory of slavery and the Civil War as well as the relation of that memory to ongoing structures of white supremacy has brought questions of cultural memory to the fore in the public sphere in recent years. American literary and cultural studies thus have much to gain from engagement with the conceptual toolbox of memory studies. At the same time, the example of *Beloved* has much to contribute to the development of memory studies, which as a field has until recently neither sufficiently engaged questions of race nor adequately interrogated its European origins. Reading *Beloved* through memory studies and memory studies through *Beloved* may help open up what I have called a "multidirectional" vision for American literary studies.

The emergence of memory as a matter of both scholarly and public concern corresponds to an important shift in the status of history over recent decades. As literary critic and memory scholar Ann Rigney argues, the growing prominence of memory-based approaches in the humanities since the 1980s has accompanied the historical discipline's loss of a monopoly on interpretive authority about the past: films, works of literature, popular television documentaries, museums, memorials, and other cultural productions now compete with disciplinary history over the image of the past. In Rigney's words, "a society's dealings with the past can no longer be happily divided into 'history proper,' identified with the work of professional historians, and 'nonhistory' or 'improper history,' identified with all the rest" (2004: 364). Rigney's description of this transformation in historical culture helps contextualize Best's description of the *Beloved* paradigm as a moment in which a novel began to set the agenda for grappling with the past. If Morrison's 1987 novel—and its central category of "rememory"—resonates

---

[2] I provide a brief genealogy of cultural memory studies below. Cognitive, psychological, and neuroscientific approaches to memory also abound, but my focus remains limited to approaches found in the humanities and interpretive social sciences that have the greatest purchase among literary scholars of memory.

most powerfully as an evocation of what Saidiya Hartman and others have called the "afterlives of slavery," an approach grounded in memory studies can help connect the specificity of *Beloved*'s intervention with broader cultural currents inside and outside the academy. A memory studies approach helps us understand Morrison's novel as a *noeud de mémoire*, a knot of memory that serves as both outcome and conduit for multiple historical narratives (see Rothberg et al. 2010). Exploring *Beloved*'s canonicity as a problem of cultural memory also provides a new angle on twentieth-century US literary history: it allows us to situate that history within a more encompassing framework in which literary texts both "remember" the haunting past and subsequently become objects of remembrance in the unfinished struggles of the present.

CULTURAL MEMORY STUDIES: A VERY SHORT INTRODUCTION

As a topic of reflection, memory is both ancient and new. Exploration of the individual human capacity to recall the past extends back to Plato and Aristotle and accompanies the history of European philosophy (see Ricoeur 2004). For our purposes, however, a key turning point occurs in the early twentieth century. Not only was this a moment when individual memory was again at the forefront of investigation in thought and culture through the writings of Freud, Bergson, Proust, and others. It was also the moment when the insight emerged that memory is not simply a cornerstone of individual identity but also a building block of collectives—and, indeed, that individual memory is itself beholden to collectives. In a book published in 1925, the French sociologist Maurice Halbwachs coined the term "collective memory" [*la mémoire collective*] to describe the binding force of remembrance in the context of groups of all sizes—from the family to the nation to the great religious traditions—but his focus was especially on small-scale assemblages. For Halbwachs, a student of Emile Durkheim, individuals only remember because they possess "social frameworks" [*les cadres sociaux*] that allow them to retain and make sense of experiences. If the individual remains the carrier of memory, that memory only emerges in determining social contexts that provide the "language" or schemata for articulating the past in the present. According to Halbwachs, we possess multiple memories because we belong to multiple groups at a variety of scales; yet, each group remains relatively homogenous in his account.

Halbwachs's work—now considered the "first stage" of modern memory studies—became influential when it was picked up and developed starting in the 1980s.[3] Memory studies as a contemporary intellectual formation dates to this "second stage," not least to

---

[3] For an account of the three stages of modern memory studies, see Erll's influential "Traveling Memory" (2011a). For a complete survey of the field, including a chapter on "Literature as a Medium of Cultural Memory," see Erll's *Memory in Culture* (2011b).

the agenda-setting work of the French historian Pierre Nora on what he calls "les lieux de mémoire" (sites of memory). Published in three enormous collective volumes between 1984 and 1992, Nora's *Les Lieux de Mémoire* surveys various "sites"—material and symbolic—in which cornerstones of French identity coalesce. Ironically, Nora's project, which stimulated the contemporary efflorescence of memory studies, is premised on the notion that "We speak so much of memory because there is so little of it left" (1989: 7); that is, for Nora, "true" memory only takes place in the small-scale groups that were the primary focus of Halbwachs's approach to collective memory and that Nora calls "*milieux de mémoire*, real environments of memory" (7). Sites of memory, in contrast, are compromise formations that simulate memory at the national scale and at the moment when modernization is destroying the foundations of communal "milieus" of remembrance. Despite the critical perspective on contemporary formations of memory Nora set out to offer, he came to realize that his work actually fueled an expansion of the mnemonic imperative. For the US context, it was indeed the 1989 translation of Nora's introduction to the volume, "Between Memory and History"—two years after the appearance of *Beloved*—that catalyzed academic interest in cultural memory. Nora's work also found fertile ground in a post-Vietnam America that was grappling with questions of trauma and in which remembrance of the Holocaust was becoming a significant feature of public culture. Indeed, the field of memory studies in the United States would evolve in close connection to the early 1990s efflorescence of both trauma theory and Holocaust studies (a point to which I will return).

Particularly relevant for a consideration of the relation of literary studies to memory studies—and to the particular case of *Beloved*—are the subsequent interventions of two German scholars: Jan Assmann and Aleida Assmann, an Egyptologist and a literary scholar, respectively. In work that began in the 1980s and continues until today, the Assmanns explicitly take up Halbwachs's notion of "collective memory," but they argue that there are two fundamentally different forms of collective memory: "communicative memory" and "cultural memory" (J. Assmann 2008). For the Assmanns, communicative memory names the small group remembrance at the center of Halbwachs's thought, which was also described by Nora as originating in "milieux de mémoire." Communicative memories are transmitted primarily in face-to-face contexts, such as families, and have a lifespan of approximately three generations or 80–100 years. The Assmanns' notion of cultural memory [*das kulturelle Gedächtnis*] describes the institutionalization of remembrance, its ritualization, materialization, and textualization, which clearly echoes Nora's concept of sites of memory. Once given material form and consecrated as cultural memory, figures of memory can span hundreds, even thousands of years, as illustrated by religious symbols such as the Christian cross recalling the crucifixion or rituals such as the Passover Seder recalling the ancient Israelites' delivery from bondage. Communicative and cultural memory do not succeed each other historically as forms—as in Nora's linear schema of milieus giving way to sites of memory—but rather coexist and even feed into each other. The Assmanns' distinction thus avoids the teleological, pessimistic narrative of modernity embedded in Nora's project and permits a more dynamic account of the relations between different modes of remembrance. Yet, embodied, communicative memory *of particular events* must eventually pass into an institutionalized form of cultural memory or it will recede into oblivion. It is precisely this transition from communicative to cultural memory that motivates many of the contemporary discussions of Holocaust remembrance and that also has relevance for the memories of slavery that haunt contemporary Black life, as I will demonstrate.

An influential essay by Aleida Assmann offers a further distinction within cultural memory between the archive and the canon that likewise has implications for the remembrance of slavery offered by *Beloved*. The archive, a repository of potential cultural memory, gathers together the traces of cultures and civilizations but does not circulate them. It represents a "passive" form of cultural memory. The canon, in contrast, results from a process of selection that activates and circulates such material traces and establishes them as privileged reference points for cultures, nations, and religions. As Assmann summarizes this distinction:

> Cultural memory, then, is based on two separate functions: the presentation of a narrow selection of sacred texts, artistic masterpieces, or historic key events in a timeless framework; the storing of documents and artifacts of the past that do not at all meet these standards but are nevertheless deemed interesting or important enough to not let them vanish on the highway to total oblivion.
> (A. Assmann 2008: 101)

As the case of Morrison's canonical novel will demonstrate, an important aspect of the work of cultural memory involves the reframing of the archive through the resuscitation of marginal traces, voices, and narratives.

In the most recent, "third stage" of memory studies, which dates from the first decade of the twenty-first century, scholars put even greater emphasis on the dynamics of memory: on the interplay between communicative and cultural forms, canons and archives, the central and the marginal, and different media. Indeed, in recent work, cultural memory has lost the strict association with the canon found in the Assmanns' work and has come to take on the more heterogeneous notion of culture associated with work in cultural studies. For Rigney, "'cultural remembrance' ... designate[s] the complex set of mnemonic practices through which collective views of the past are continuously being shaped, circulated, reproduced, and (un)critically transformed with the help of media" (2009: 6). Literature plays a particular, but not unique role in Rigney's account; that is, it has particular affordances—imaginative narrative structures, possibilities for the cultivation of identification and empathy, etc.—that lend it power in performing the work of remembrance, but it should also be understood as one node in a broader network of mnemonic practices. For Rigney, literature is not a mere product; its meaning- and memory-making potentials are always in process and embedded in larger social processes of circulation and reception. She identifies "five interrelated roles played by literature in the performance of cultural memory" (2008: 350). Literary works function as: "*relay stations*" that "build on or recycle earlier forms of remembrance"; "*stabilizers*" that "provide a cultural frame for later recollections" by virtue of their "sticking power";

"*catalysts*" that draw attention to 'new' topics or ones hitherto neglected"; "*objects of recollection*" that are themselves remembered; and "*calibrators*" or "canonical literary 'monuments'" that are subject to revision and rewriting, as in the postcolonial practice of "writing back" (350-352).

Along with her frequent collaborator Astrid Erll, Rigney emphasizes that the roles literature plays in the performance of cultural memory function most powerfully because of their placement within intermedial networks. In other words, memories have staying power "in the public arena and *become* collective" because they pass through multiple media forms (Erll and Rigney 2009: 2). To give a not entirely arbitrary example, newspaper articles may serve as the source for novels, novels may become films or graphic novels, and so forth. Here, Erll and Rigney adapt Jay David Bolter and Richard Grusin's concept of "remediation," which describes the way all media forms reconfigure and revise other media forms (e.g. websites mimic newspapers; films mimic television formats [see Bolter and Grusin]). Erll and Rigney thus argue that "just as there is no cultural memory prior to mediation there is no mediation without remediation: all representations of the past draw on available media technologies, on existent media products, on patterns of representation and medial aesthetics" (4).

The categories offered by the Assmanns, Rigney, and Erll provide useful tools for understanding the memory work of *Beloved* and the prominence it has achieved as a paradigm-defining text. Morrison's novel stages the move from archive to canon, the passage from communicative to cultural memory, and it is itself embedded in the dynamics of remediation. Furthermore, the novel's status as a "hyper-canonical" text—a concept developed by Jonathan Arac in a discussion of *Huckleberry Finn* (1997)—derives, at least in part, from its remarkable performance of all the roles Rigney identifies in addition to its obvious literary virtuosity. Indeed, like Proust's *In Search of Lost Time*, with its discourse on voluntary and involuntary memory, *Beloved* performs an additional role that does not quite fit into Rigney's catalogue: it offers a theorization of memory as "rememory" that has influenced scholars as well as other writers.

From the Archive to the Poetics of Cultural Memory

Beloved's work of memory takes place on multiple levels—within the text, at its paratextual margins, and beyond its pages. If we can locate an origin to the novel's contribution, however, it would reside in its movement from archive to canon—an almost literal enactment of Aleida Assmann's account of the two primary components of cultural memory and one that also casts light on Morrison's institutional role as an agent of public remembrance. From 1967 to 1983, Morrison served as an editor at Random House, a role she used to bring visibility to numerous Black writers. In the course of her tenure there, she also helped publish *The Black Book*, a documentary collection traversing nearly 350 years of the "black experience in America," as the publishers put it. Produced by amateur historians and collectors, *The Black Book* is an example of the kind of "improper history" to which Rigney refers in describing how professional historians have lost their monopoly on narrating the past. Devoid of a table of contents or index, the work serves more as a sourcebook for cultural memory than as a work of historiography—though it certainly intervenes in dominant perceptions of US history. And indeed, Morrison treats the work as an archive for her mnemonic imagination.

While Morrison alludes to a Gwendolyn Brooks poem included in *The Black Book* in her earlier novel *Song of Solomon* (1977), the collection proves essential to *Beloved* and key to understanding its work of memory (see Rambsy 2015). Appearing on p. 10 of the collection is the facsimile of an 1856 newspaper article from the *American Baptist* called "A Visit to the Slave Mother Who Killed Her Child" (Harris 2019: 10; cf. also Mobley 1993; Weisenburger 1998; Reinhardt 2010). "A Visit" recounts the story of Margaret Garner, a mother who had escaped from enslavement and who had killed her two-and-a-half-year-old daughter Mary so that she would not be returned to slavery.[4] Garner's story caused a sensation and led to vigorous debates about slavery and the Fugitive Slave Act, which lay behind the case. In the midst of the attention created by Garner's case, "many antislavery commentators believed that the woman who had triggered so substantial a dispute was assured a permanent and prominent place in American political memory" (Reinhardt 2010: x). Yet, as Mark Reinhardt points out in an extensive study of the case, "these observers were wrong: Margaret Garner did not become an enduring household name or even one of the nation's minor political icons. At least as a matter of public discourse, the case faded into obscurity soon after the Civil War" (Reinhardt 2010: x). Only Morrison's remediation of the newspaper article in the form of a novel brought Garner back to public consciousness. As Reinhardt documents, despite its inclusion in *The Black Book*, the "story remained largely forgotten until 1987" with the publication of *Beloved* (Reinhardt 2010: x; see also Weisenburger 1998: 10). Morrison's recasting of Garner's story—which she situates in an imaginative, fictional framework centered on the protagonist Sethe and her murdered daughter Beloved—thus illustrates powerfully Rigney's description of literary texts as "catalysts" that bring "new" stories (back) into public memory; and it does so precisely by mining the archive and recirculating that "passive" piece of evidence constituted by the 1856 newspaper article. In Mobley's words, "*Beloved* dramatizes the complex relationship between history and memory by shifting from lived experience as documented in *The Black Book* to remembered experience as represented in the novel" (1993: 357). We can measure the success of *Beloved*'s role as a memory catalyst—and indeed its assumption of hyper-canonical status—in part by the fact that Margaret Garner is now a household name, at least in certain realms of the university and public sphere.

Although drawing on a key historical source, and certainly enriched by deep historical understanding of nineteenth-century US history, *Beloved* is most definitely not a

---

[4] For extended accounts of the Margaret Garner story, see Weisenburger (1998) and Reinhardt (2010).

historical novel. When Morrison describes her motivation and method in relation to Garner's story, she typically emphasizes the limits of the archive as a source of living history. Not simply the newspaper account, but also the entire genre of the nineteenth-century slave narrative fails to provide the kind of subjective, emotional evidence that Morrison desires. As she writes in a 2004 preface appended to recent editions of the novel:

> The historical Margaret Garner is fascinating, but, to a novelist, confining. Too little imaginative space there for my purposes. So I would invent her thoughts, plumb them for a subtext that was historically true in essence, but not strictly factual in order to relate her history to contemporary issues about freedom, responsibility, and women's "place."
>
> (2004: xvii)

Because of Morrison's commitment to linking history with the contemporary and with subjective experience, I would categorize *Beloved* not as a historical novel but rather as a "memory novel."[5] We know this not just because of what Morrison says outside the text but primarily because of the way she retells Garner's story—not in a strictly realist, historicist mode but rather in the gothic genre of the ghost story and through the lens of multiple characters who look back at slavery from the novel's 1873 present. *Beloved* is less the story of Margaret Garner than the story of our haunting by her story—or perhaps, better, by the way we *should* be haunted by her story but have not yet been. The return of the murdered child Beloved, first as a spectral but aggressive presence in Sethe and Denver's house and then as an embodied character who resides with them, allegorizes the return of Garner's story in the novel as "remembered experience" (Mobley 1993) and as the "grounds of memory" (Best 2012)—in short, as cultural memory and not as history. The figure of the ghost lies at the center of Morrison's poetics of memory—her textual staging of varieties of remembrance and forgetting—and, especially, her conceptualization of memory as rememory.

"Rememory" emerges from Sethe's vernacular language of remembrance but serves as a key for understanding the novel's poetics and has subsequently entered into the theoretical lexicon of memory studies. Although rememory is associated with Sethe, it is introduced in a chapter focalized through her daughter Denver, who was literally born on the border between slave-holding and free states and whose experience of enslavement derives entirely from the stories she has been told by her elders. Indeed, the section leading to Sethe's "theory" of rememory begins when Denver perceives a ghost: looking through the window of their haunted house, Denver

> saw her mother on her knees in prayer, which was not unusual. What was unusual (even for a girl who had lived all her life in a house peopled by the living activity of

---

[5] On the historical novel, see Lukács (1963) and Anderson (2011). "Memory novel" is my own term and has not been used extensively to my knowledge.

the dead) was that a white dress knelt down next to her mother and had its sleeve around her mother's waist.

(Morrison 2004: 35)

The vision triggers a memory for Denver—that of her own birth—which she knows through her mother's narration, but which she knows so intensely that she is able to "ste[p] into the told story" (36), a story that then unfolds as if the reader were witnessing it in the present (36–42). When the birth narrative ends and we return to the novel's present, Denver enters the house and tells Sethe about her vision of the white dress. At this point, Sethe explains what she was thinking as she knelt next to the ghost:

> I was thinking about time. It's so hard for me to believe in it. Some things go. Pass on. Some things just stay. I used to think it was my rememory. You know. Some things you forget. Other things you never do. But it's not. Places, places are still there. If a house burns down, it is gone, but the place—the picture of it—stays, and not just in my rememory but out there, in the world. What I remember is a picture floating out there outside my head. I mean, even if I don't think it, even if I die, the picture of what I did, or knew, or saw is still out there. Right in the place where it happened.
>
> (2004: 43)

A rememory, in Sethe's account, is not personal property, but rather collective memory: anyone can

> bump into a rememory that belongs to somebody else.... The picture is still there and what's more, if you go there—you who never was there—if you go there and stand in the place where it was, it will happen again; it will be there for you, waiting for you.
>
> (43–44)

Drawing out the consequences, Denver replies, "If it's still there, waiting, that must mean that nothing ever dies" (44). Sethe—or Morrison—may seem to literalize Nora's contemporaneous notion of *lieux de mémoire* in this passage, but in fact the novel's conception goes beyond his binary framework. Rather than polarizing history and memory or "true" and artificial forms of remembrance, the notion of rememory brings together milieus and sites of memory, personal and collective remembrance, and communicative and cultural memory in an amalgam that has since become central to the "third stage" of memory studies. In particular, *Beloved* resonates with recent interest in transgenerational memory and in what Alison Landsberg calls "prosthetic memories," memories that are adopted by someone who, in Sethe's terms, "never was there" (see Hirsch 2012; Landsberg 2004; for a critique, see Michaels 1996).

The power of memory to disrupt the present—figured both in the ghost and in the externalized force of rememory as something you can "bump into"—also explains why forgetting is a powerful force in the novel. Sethe tries "keeping the past at bay" (Morrison 2004: 51), while Paul D attempts to lock it up "in a tobacco tin buried in his chest" (86). And yet, despite these efforts at forgetting, the temptation to "[t]rust things and remember things" (21) is also strong, as is the involuntary recall of frequently traumatic content. Sweet Home, the plantation from which Sethe and Paul D escaped, appears "suddenly ... rolling, rolling, rolling out before [Sethe's] eyes"—a vision of "shameless beauty," of "[b]oys hanging from the most beautiful sycamores in the world" (7). Later, Sethe "remember[s] something she had forgotten she knew. Something privately shameful that had seeped into a slit in her mind": her mother's commission of infanticide (71). Likewise, an intimate encounter with Beloved erodes Paul D's tobacco tin lid (136). The novel's commitment to rewriting nineteenth-century accounts of enslavement from a subject-centered, presentist perspective does not, in other words, entail a simple valuation of memory or of the direct continuity between past and present that Best finds in the *Beloved* paradigm. Rather, it seems to imply that ongoing, traumatic racial histories are too complex to fit neatly into the opposition between continuity and discontinuity.

Ultimately, this unstable oscillation between remembrance and forgetting may constitute the "content" of the novel. In its famous coda, the novel focalizes through a collective perspective, the subject of which is "everybody" in the community and by extension the community of readers. The coda unfolds a series of paradoxes or performative contradictions, culminating in the repeated declarations "It was not a story to pass on .... This is not a story to pass on" (323–324)—a double-coded sentence that implies both the need to forget and the need to remember. In a sense, the novel closes by returning to the problem of its beginnings: the relationship between archive and canon. The ghost of Beloved has been exorcised and has disappeared; with her has gone the memory of the margins of the history of slavery and the Middle Passage, which Morrison hints at throughout in opaque references and passages. Yet, paradoxically, in intoning a discourse of forgetting in the coda—and indeed throughout the novel—Morrison also places the "disremembered" at the heart of an emergent cultural memory:

> By and by all trace is gone, and what is forgotten is not only the footprints but the water too and what is down there. The rest is weather. Not the breath of the disremembered and unaccounted for, but wind in the eaves, or spring ice thawing too quickly. Just weather. Certainly no clamor for a kiss.
>
> (324)

In a significant sense, traces of the dead—and especially the dead of the Middle Passage—may be irrecoverably lost, but *Beloved* brings us closer to the traumatic past than we were before and it does so, in part, by recovering and remediating the archival trace of Margaret Garner. At least at the textual level, the novel's hauntology challenges both the presence of the present and the absence of the past; the ghost and her disappearance leave us haunted but unsure of what remains of the slave past and of how to situate ourselves in its wake. By speaking of the "unaccounted," *Beloved* begins a necessary, non-redemptive process of accounting.

Beloved's Afterlives and the Discourse of Cultural Memory

Beloved is not just a brilliant novel about time and memory but a brilliant novel about memory that appeared at the right time. While the novel's textual discourse presents a rich and unsettling account of what is retained and what is lost from the past, its enunciation takes part in the wider turn toward cultural memory that Rigney associates with the unsettling of disciplinary history. This wider context helps explain and situate the paradigmatic nature of *Beloved*'s influence. The publication of the novel occurred at a significant moment in a global conversation about multiple (most often traumatic) pasts. In addition to appearing two years before Nora's work on *lieux de mémoire* was translated into English, *Beloved* appeared at a moment during which public memories of the Holocaust and other histories of violence were experiencing exponential growth. The year before *Beloved* appeared, Art Spiegelman published the first volume of his graphic, second-generation Holocaust memoir *Maus*. Plans were already well underway for the US Holocaust Memorial Museum, which would open in the nation's capital in 1993; Germany had just emerged from a major public debate about responsibility for the Nazi past (the *Historikerstreit*); South Africa was about to undergo its remarkable transition, which famously involved public accounting for past violence through the Truth and Reconciliation Commission; and the end of the Cold War would soon recalibrate memories of Europe's twentieth century—to name only a few relevant examples. Although the histories evoked here are heterogeneous, the moment of the late 1980s/early 1990s was precisely a time in which these histories resonated together and were perceived by some as components of a new "cosmopolitan memory" (cf. Levy and Sznaider 2005).

There are at least two different ways that *Beloved* intersects with this moment of transnational memory culture. First, Morrison seems to evoke memory of the Holocaust in the novel's powerful dedication: "Sixty Million/and more." While radically underdetermined in content, the particular number Morrison chooses—along with the implicit reference to the dead of the system of enslavement and the Middle Passage—has evoked for many a particular *lieu de mémoire*: the figure "6,000,000," the conventionally referenced number of Jewish victims of the Nazi genocide. While there may be an element of competitive upping of the ante in this dedicatory gesture, we can also read it as an attempt to place memory of slavery alongside memory of the Holocaust in a multidirectional juxtaposition of divergent histories at a moment when global memory cultures were increasingly coming into contact in public debate and culture (see Rothberg 2009).[6]

---

[6] The critic Stanley Crouch (1987) provided a less generous evaluation of this element of Beloved when he infamously described the text as a "blackface holocaust novel." Employing the precise vocabulary of competitive memory that I criticize in *Multidirectional Memory*, Crouch continues: "It

In addition to evoking the Holocaust at a moment when its memory was undergoing transformation and expansion, *Beloved* connects to larger transformations in memory culture and memory studies scholarship. In particular, it powerfully evokes issues of intergenerational transmission common to many traumatic histories. For the Holocaust, the 1980s was a moment when a discourse on the transition from living witnesses to future generations of secondary witnesses emerged as scholars and community organizations worried about what would happen when no more survivors were present to tell their stories. While transatlantic slavery ended decades before the Holocaust, it also—perhaps surprisingly—can be seen as lying on the cusp of transition from communicative to cultural memory. For instance, in *Lose Your Mother*, a text marked by *Beloved*'s influence, Saidiya Hartman recounts hearing about her great-great grandmother Ella, who was born in slavery, from her great-grandfather, although the details she garners remain sparse. As she writes, "The gaps and silences of my family were not unusual: slavery made the past a mystery, unknown and unspeakable" (2007: 13–14). What Hartman describes here might be understood as the outer limit of what Marianne Hirsch calls "postmemory," the partially and often indirectly evoked, but still affectively powerful versions of the past received by descendants of victims of traumatic violence. While Hirsch has generally, though not exclusively, focused on postmemories of the Holocaust, a fact shaped by autobiography as well as scholarly interest, she also recounts how "Toni Morrison's visit to Dartmouth and her public reading of the first chapter of *Beloved* a full year before the novel's publication" catalyzed her thinking on "the subject of memory and transmission." For Hirsch, Morrison's novel "dramatized the haunting, transgenerational reach of trauma, and it showed me that latency need not mean forgetting or oblivion. Generations after slavery, Morrison was able to convey its impacts and effects more powerfully than contemporary accounts." The concept of postmemory, developed in the wake of that moment in an essay on *Maus*, was, Hirsch remarks, "the story of Denver in the novel, as it is the story of Spiegelman's Artie. In some ways, I began to acknowledge, it is my story as well" (2012: 11). If Hirsch's response is highly personal, it also reveals how tightly *Beloved* fits into a larger paradigm not only of slavery's enduring presence but also of the transgenerational transmission of trauma *tout court*. That paradigm is, in turn, conceivable as part of a larger shift that brought memory culture into prominence and that Andreas Huyssen explains as an effect of a media- and globalization-driven transformation in "our ways of thinking and living temporality" (2003: 4).

The mass media and processes of remediation have certainly contributed to the canonization of *Beloved*—one thinks not only of the Oprah-produced film but also of Morrison's several appearances on Oprah's Book Club (though not for *Beloved*!). But I would wager that the clearest signals of the novel's influence have remained textual

---

seems to be written in order to enter American slavery into the big-time martyr ratings contest." While I do find Morrison's dedication pointed, the notion that the novel is a "blackface" rewriting of a Holocaust text strikes me as a gross exaggeration that misses precisely the overlapping traumas of these certainly very different histories.

and pedagogical—a fascinating testament to the ongoing presence of canonical textual culture in a post-literary world. In addition to its regular appearance on syllabi at the secondary and tertiary levels, *Beloved* appears regularly within a wide range of other literary texts. Intertextuality, that is, functions as a literary afterlife that parallels the ghostly return of Garner's story within the novel. Here, we turn from *Beloved*'s role as what Rigney calls "catalyzer" and "relay station" to the roles of "stabilizer," "object of recollection," and "calibrator."

We glimpse this intertextual afterlife in a range of texts; first of all, those that grapple with the legacies of chattel slavery in the Americas. When Hartman declares her family's past as "unknown and unspeakable," for example, we may hear an echo of another famous line from *Beloved* that introduces the most experimental portion of the novel, which consists of a series of monologues touching precisely on what remains "unknown and unspeakable" in slavery's traumatic legacies:

> When Sethe locked the door, the women inside were free at last to be what they liked, see whatever they saw and say whatever was on their minds.
> Almost. Mixed in with the voices surrounding the house, recognizable but undecipherable to Stamp Paid, were the thoughts of the women of 124, unspeakable thoughts, unspoken.
>
> (Morrison 2004: 235)

A significant strand of African American and Black diasporic writing since *Beloved* takes up this imperative to speak the unspoken, albeit in a way that, like Morrison's novel, continues to mark the gaps, silences, and traumatic ruptures transmitted into the present. In addition to Hartman's generically unclassifiable writings, a similar sensibility haunts Christina Sharpe's book-length essay *In the Wake* (2016). Sharpe makes frequent reference to *Beloved* and adapts one of its central categories—the "weather"—from the final passage of the novel, a demonstration that the conceptual tools offered by the novel are not limited to the notion of rememory. In fiction, we find *Beloved*'s influence in works of very different genres. Just in the last decade, we might point to N.K. Jemisin's speculative fiction *The Fifth Season* (2015), Yaa Gyasi's transnational, multigenerational family saga *Homegoing* (2017), and Jesmyn Ward's ghost-haunted, very contemporary *Sing, Unburied, Sing* (2017), in which the slave plantation is rewritten as Mississippi's infamous State Penitentiary, the Parchman Farm.

Beloved's afterlives do not end with their appearance in works treating American slavery and its impact nor, as the examples chosen so far indicate, do they stop at the genre boundary of the novel. This fact helps us see that the *Beloved* paradigm identified by Best does not limit itself to the presence of the slave past but actually emerges out of larger shifts of the sort tracked by scholars in memory studies. Viet Thanh Nguyen, for example, gave the title *Nothing Ever Dies* to his award-winning study of the Vietnamese and American memory of war in Vietnam (2016a). He thus makes direct reference to the "rememory" passage, a passage that also serves as an epigraph and which Nguyen discusses within the text as an example of a "memory that inflicts physical and psychic blows" (65). His novel *The Sympathizer*, a noir-ish spy thriller about a Vietnamese communist sleeper agent in southern California in the 1970s, does not much resemble *Beloved* formally, but, like Nguyen's scholarly study, it also makes reference to the fact that "[w]ars never die" (2016b: 235) and it includes a ghost that continually reminds the narrator of his participation in an act of deadly violence (otherwise very different from Sethe's).

As Nguyen's transnational study and novel suggest, the influence of *Beloved* does not stop at national borders either. Jennifer Gully and Lynn Mie Itagaki, for instance, find a reference to Morrison in Jenny Erpenbeck's best-selling 2015 novel about refugees in Germany *Gehen, Ging, Gegangen* (*Go, Went, Gone*). In the novel, a retired classics professor becomes more and more involved with a community of African refugees in Berlin. At one point, he reflects that:

> all the men he's gotten to know here ... could just as easily be lying at the bottom of the Mediterranean. And conversely all the Germans who were murdered during the so-called Third Reich still inhabit Germany as ghosts, sometimes he even imagines that all these missing people along with their unborn children and the children of their children are walking beside him on the street, on their way to work or to visit friends, they sit invisibly in the cafés, take walks, go shopping, visit parks and the theater.
>
> (221–222; cited in Gully and Itagaki 2020: 267)

Not only does Erpenbeck offer here a consummate example of multidirectional memory but she also, in Gully and Itagaki's reading, uses the figure of "living among ghosts of the dead" to allude to "Toni Morrison's concept of 'rememory.' ... Both African chattel slavery and current African migration to Europe have resulted in too many unmourned deaths and few, if any, permanent memorials" (2020: 268).[7] This "unspoken" link between unmourned refugee deaths in the Mediterranean and the unmourned dead of slavery and the Middle Passage becomes explicit in Sharpe's *In the Wake*, where it figures centrally as evidence of the ongoing structuring anti-Blackness of modernity.

As this small selection of heterogeneous examples begins to suggest, the *Beloved* paradigm has gone global in decades following its publication. The frequent reference to Morrison's novel in such heterogeneous contexts confirms Yogita Goyal's claim in an important study that Atlantic slavery has become a "defining template" that "frames a range of contemporary phenomena across the globe" (2019: 2). *Beloved* and the many neo-slave narratives Goyal discusses help us understand the central role that the afterlives of slavery play in the dynamics of contemporary memory and human rights cultures. Memory studies, in turn, helps us understand the dynamics of canonization

---

[7] Whether or not Gully and Itagaki are correct that this is a direct reference to "rememory," it remains a mark of *Beloved*'s influence in conceptualizations of memory that, for critics and readers alike, embodied, ghost-like memory now often calls up Morrison's internationally famous work.

that have helped transform a novel into a paradigm and it helps us place the questions Goyal considers within an even more encompassing global memory culture.

Conclusion

What conclusions can we draw from this account of a singular canonical—even hypercanonical—novel? The story told about *Beloved* here is not reproducible for all "memory novels," no less all works of twentieth-century American literature. Yet, the case does help illuminate general methodological tools for bringing literary studies and memory studies together. It also brings into view larger shifts in the experience of history and temporality that may be helpful for thinking about twentieth-century literary history in new ways. The field of memory studies orients us toward both textual and contextual features of literary meaning: both the way literary works help us conceptualize individual and collective memory and the way that the cultural dynamics of remembrance inflect our engagement with literary works. Although it can be challenging to practice in the classroom, Rigney's focus on the afterlives of literary works as vectors of cultural memory offers a methodology that emphasizes the social value of literary production and literary study.[8] Many aspects of this methodology are not unique to the field of memory studies, which shares concerns with broad currents in cultural studies, book history, media studies, and more. Yet, as the case of *Beloved*'s immense influence suggests, a focus on cultural memory is not simply an "add on." The dynamics of memory are a central feature of twentieth- and twenty-first-century national and transnational cultures.

The case of *Beloved* helps us see that if memory in both its individual and collective forms is a perennial topic of literature, it has also become an urgent matter of public concern in recent decades. As the worldwide toppling of monuments to racist and colonialist pasts demonstrates, the stakes of remembrance are social and political as well as cultural. #Black Lives Matter and contemporary abolitionist movements draw at least some of their energies from an implicit understanding of the *Beloved* paradigm. Seeking not reform but "abolition" ("the abolition of the carceral world, the abolition of capitalism"), these movements argue, in Hartman's terms, that "[w]hat is required is a remaking of the social order, and nothing short of that is going to make a difference" (Hartman 2020). The translation of the language of abolition into contemporary contexts demonstrates how activists and intellectuals set political memory in opposition to material continuities. Whether or not the connection to Morrison's work is conscious or explicit, the movement feeds on the temporal short-circuit that Best excavates (and criticizes): the connections presumed between, for instance, eighteenth- and

---

[8] For the fullest version of Rigney's method, see her study *The Afterlives of Walter Scott* (2012).

nineteenth-century slave patrols and the contemporary policing of communities of color.[9]

I would not argue that a memory-inflected literary studies should lead this conversation about abolition, but I believe it has something valuable to contribute. It might highlight the more complex logic of continuity and discontinuity that Morrison's novel actually depicts at the textual level (e.g. "This is not a story to pass on"), and it might bring into view the larger social frameworks (*les cadres sociaux*) that make claims for continuity and discontinuity legible. By illuminating these social frameworks (for instance, the prevalence of concerns about intergenerational transmission and the passage from communicative to cultural memory), the field of memory studies reveals how remembrance of slavery intersects with remembrance of the Holocaust, the US–Vietnam War, apartheid, and many other politically consequential traumatic histories.

Beloved does not simply reflect larger trends, however. As a catalyst and calibrator of memory, it has helped set the terms of public debate about the hold of the past on the present. A canonical late-twentieth-century novel that mines the archive of mid-nineteenth-century history, *Beloved*'s afterlives remain active in the twenty-first century. The unfinished project of abolition it narrates reminds us of the work that remains to be done.

References

Anderson, Perry. 2011. "From Progress to Catastrophe," *London Review of Books*, July 28, www.lrb.co.uk/v33/n15/perry-anderson/from-progress-to-catastrophe, accessed February 21, 2022.

Arac, Jonathan. 1997. *Huckleberry Finn as Idol and Target: The Functions of Criticism in Our Time* (Madison, WI: University of Wisconsin Press).

Assmann, Aleida. 2008. "Canon and Archive," in Astrid Erll and Ansgar Nunning, eds, *Cultural Memory Studies: An International and Interdisciplinary Handbook* (Berlin and New York: Walter De Gruyter), 97–107.

Assmann, Jan. 2008. "Communicative and Cultural Memory," in Astrid Erll and Ansgar Nunning, eds, *Cultural Memory Studies: An International and Interdisciplinary Handbook* (Berlin and New York: Walter De Gruyter), 109–118.

Best, Stephen. 2012. "On Failing to Make the Past Present," *Modern Language Quarterly* 73.3: 453–474.

Bolter Jay David and Richard Grusin. 2000. *Remediation: Understanding New Media* (Cambridge, MA: The MIT Press).

Browne, Simone. 2015. *Dark Matters: On the Surveillance of Blackness* (Durham, NC: Duke University Press).

Crouch, Stanley. 1987. "Literary Conjure Woman," *New Republic*, October 19, 38.

Erll, Astrid. 2011a. "Traveling Memory," *Parallax* 17.4: 4–18.

Erll, Astrid. 2011b. *Memory in Culture* (New York: Palgrave Macmillan).

---

[9] For a scholarly tracking of these continuities, see Browne (2015).

Erll, Astrid and Ann Rigney. 2009. "Introduction: Cultural Memory and Its Dynamics," in Astrid Erll and Ann Rigney, eds, *Mediation, Remediation, and the Dynamics of Cultural Memory* (Berlin and New York: Walter De Gruyter), 1–11.

Erpenbeck, Jenny. 2017. *Go, Went, Gone* trans. Susan Bernofsky (New York: New Directions).

Goyal, Yogita. 2019. *Runaway Genres: The Global Afterlives of Slavery* (New York: New York University Press).

Gully, Jennifer M. and Lynn Mie Itagaki. 2020. "The States of Memory: National Narratives of Belonging, the Refugee Novel, and Jenny Erpenbeck's *Go, Went, Gone*," *Modern Fiction Studies* 66.2: 260–280.

Gyassi, Yaa. 2017. *Homegoing* (New York: Vintage).

Halbwachs, Maurice. 1992. *On Collective Memory*, ed. and trans. Lewis A. Coser (Chicago, IL: University of Chicago Press).

Harris, Middleton A., ed. 2019, *The Black Book*, 35th Anniversary edn (New York: Random House).

Hartman, Saidiya. 2007. *Lose Your Mother: A Journey Along the Atlantic Slave Route* (New York: Farrar, Straus and Giroux).

Hartman, Saidiya. 2020. "Saidiya Hartman on Insurgent Histories and the Abolitionist Imaginary," *Artforum*, July 14, www.artforum.com/interviews/saidiya-hartman-on-insurgent-histories-and-the-abolitionist-imaginary-83579?fbclid=IwAR24FuXJvILNNlCh2m117LtquouZwQ9DNaYnQloV-CT6JvP5QhVcMrelmyY, accessed February 21, 2022.

Hirsch, Marianne. 2012. *The Generation of Postmemory: Writing and Visual Culture After the Holocaust* (New York: Columbia University Press).

Huyssen, Andreas. 2003. *Present Pasts: Urban Palimpsests and the Politics of Memory* (Stanford, CA: Stanford University Press).

Jemisin. N. K. 2015. *The Fifth Season* (New York: Orbit).

Landsberg, Alison. 2004. *Prosthetic Memory: The Transformation of American Remembrance in the Age of Mass Culture* (New York: Columbia University Press).

Levy, Daniel and Natan Sznaider. 2005. *The Holocaust and Memory in the Global Age* (Philadelphia, PA: Temple University Press).

Lukács, Georg. 1963. *The Historical Novel*, trans. Hannah and Stanley Mitchell (Boston, MA: Beacon).

Michaels, Walter Benn. 1996. "'You Who Never Was There': Slavery and the New Historicism, Deconstruction and the Holocaust," *Narrative* 4.1: 1–16.

Mobley, Marilyn Sanders. 1993. "A Different Remembering: Memory, History, and Meaning in *Beloved*," in Henry Louis Gates, Jr and Kwame Anthony Appiah, eds, *Toni Morrison: Critical Perspectives Past and Present* (New York: Amistad), 356–365.

Morrison, Toni. 2004. *Beloved* (New York: Vintage).

Nguyen, Viet Thanh. 2016a. *Nothing Ever Dies: Vietnam and the Memory of War* (Cambridge, MA: Harvard University Press).

Nguyen, Viet Thanh. 2016b. *The Sympathizer* (New York: Grove).

Nora, Pierre. 1989. "Between Memory and History: *Les Lieux de Mémoire*," *Representations* 26 (Spring): 7–24.

Rambsy, Howard. 2015. "Middleton A. Harris, Toni Morrison, and The Black Book," *Cultural Front* [blog], February 21, www.culturalfront.org/2015/02/middleton-harris-toni-morrison-and.html, accessed February 21, 2022.

Reinhardt, Mark. 2010. *Who Speaks for Margaret Garner?* (Minneapolis, MN: University of Minnesota Press).

Ricoeur, Paul. 2004. *Memory, History, Forgetting*, trans. Kathleen Blamey and David Pellauer (Chicago, CA: University of Chicago Press).

Rigney, Ann. 2004. "Portable Monuments: Literature, Cultural Memory, and the Case of Jeanie Deans," *Poetics Today* 25.2: 361–396.

Rigney, Ann. 2008. "The Dynamics of Remembrance: Texts between Monumentality and Morphing," in Astrid Erll and Ansgar Nunning, eds, *Cultural Memory Studies: An International and Interdisciplinary Handbook* (Berlin and New York: Walter De Gruyter), 345–353.

Rigney, Ann. 2009. "All This Happened, More or Less: What a Novelist Made of the Bombing of Dresden," *History and Theory* 48.2: 5–24.

Rigney, Ann. 2012. *The Afterlives of Walter Scott: Memory on the Move* (New York: Oxford University Press).

Rothberg, Michael. 2009. *Multidirectional Memory: Remembering the Holocaust in the Age of Decolonization* (Stanford, CA: Stanford University Press).

Rothberg, Michael, Debarati Sanyal, and Max Silverman, eds. 2010. *Noeuds de Mémoire: Multidirectional Memory in Postwar French and Francophone Culture*, a special double issue of *Yale French Studies*: 118/119.

Sharpe, Christina. 2016. *In the Wake: On Blackness and Being* (Durham, NC: Duke University Press).

Ward, Jesmyn. 2018. *Sing, Unburied, Sing* (New York: Scribner).

Weisenburger, Steven. 1998. *Modern Medea: A Family Story of Slavery and Child-Murder from the Old South* (New York: Hill and Wang).

Index

For the benefit of digital users, indexed terms that span two pages (e.g., 52–53) may, on occasion, appear on only one of those pages.

A

Adorno, Theodor, 1, 74
Adventures of Augie March, The (Bellow)
  civil society of, 347–48
  dialogical responsiveness of Augie March, 343–47
  opening line, 348
  the picaro tradition and, 340–41, 343, 344–45
  presentist reading, 343–47
  storyline, 340–41
  Trilling's review of, 341, 342–43, 345
  what it means to be human, 341–43
African American literature
  Andrea Lee's work within, 281–83, 284, 285–86, 296–97
  authentic/inauthentic binaries, 284, 285, 296–97
  definition of, 292–93
  rule of racial representation, 287, 288–89, 297
  transnationalist readings of, 284–85
African Americans *see also* race
  within the Indigenous nations (historical), 129–30
  justice and human rights, 171–72
  post-war radio programming for, 135–37, 144
  the relation between race and global politics, 172–73
Agee, James, 246, 259–60
Alberti, Rafael, 71–73, 74
Alexie, Sherman
  "Evolution," 330–31
  Indians in cabinets in the writings of, 325–26
  "Pawn Shop," 330, 331
  The Summer of Black Widows, 129–30
Allen, Paula Gunn, 119–20
American literature *see also* US literature
  cultural legacy of the China Trade, 209–10
  evolving genres of, 2
  interstitial approaches, 1–2, 3
  literary criticism, 2, 3–4
  relationship with radio, 136–37
  term, 3
  of the twentieth-century, 1
Anacaona, 124–25
Angelou, Maya, 174–75, 190
Anthropocene
  coloniality and, 41–42
  combustion in, 43, 44
  concept, 41
  genre writing, 48–49
  oil industry, 50–51, 52–54, 92
Anzaldúa, Gloria, 299–302, 306–7, 315, 324
Asian Americans *see also Crazy Rich Asians* (Kwan); *Mad Men, The* (Delany)
  excess and exaggeration in depictions of, 99, 100, 102–3, 107–8, 110–11
  in the labor market, 105–6
  model minority myth, 98–100, 102–3
  as transnational subjects, 99, 109
  in US literature, 99
Assman, Aleida, 402–3, 404–5
Assman, Jan, 402–3
Atwood, Margaret, 398–99

B

Bakhtin, Mikhail, 343
Baldwin, James, 174–75, 192, 292–93, 297, 349–51

Baraka, Amiri
  "the blues continuum," 144–45
  Blues People, 144–45
  "Coltrane Live at Birdland," 145–47, 150
  critical listening practice, 137–38, 142–43, 144–47
  "The Jazz Avant Garde," 144–45
  "In Memory of Radio," 135–37, 138, 143–44
  music criticism, 137–39, 144–47
  radio in the works of, 142–44, 147–51
  reversible flows of "love" and "evol," 135–36, 137–38, 150–51
  6 Persons, 142–43
  "Symphony Sid" (poem), 147–50
  "Symphony Sid" Torin and, 137–38, 142–45
  The System of Dante's Hell, 143–44
Barnett, Lauren, 34–37
Baucom, Ian, 217–18, 219
the Beats
  ambient listening, 141
  jazz music and, 138–42, 150–51
  radio in the works of, 139–40, 141
  "Symphony Sid" Torin and, 137–38, 140–42
Beckwourth, Jim, 129–30
Bellow, Saul, 349, *see also Adventures of Augie March, The* (Bellow)
Beloved (Morrison)
  The Black Book and, 405
  canonical status of, 398–99, 400–1, 403, 410–11, 414
  dynamics of remediation, 404, 405, 410–11
  historical sources, 405–6
  intersection with global memory cultures, 409
  intertextuality of, 410–13
  Margaret Garner's story, 405–6, 408
  melancholic paradigm, 399, 400–1
  memory work of, 399, 400–1, 404–5, 406, 413–14
  and the production of collective memory, 399, 400
  relations of race and slavery, 399–400, 405–6, 408, 410, 412–13
  remembrance and forgetting in, 407–8
  rememory in, 399, 400–1, 404, 406–7, 411–12

  speaking the unspoken, 411
  transgenerational transmission of memories, 407, 410
Bernstein, Robin, 17
Berryman, John, 59–60
Best, Stephen, 399–401
Black internationalism
  African American relations to anti-colonialism, 179
  internationalization of anti-Black racism struggles, 171–74
  literary studies and, 173–75
Black Power, 65–67, 179, 282–83
Black radical tradition
  Adrian Piper's work and, 386, 389–90
  conceptualism and, 380–82
  definition of, 386
  fugivity and abscondment, 384–85
Black Studies
  critical reorientations, 264–65
  emergence of, 264–65, 277
#BlackLivesMatter movement, 90–91, 399–400, 413–14
Blotner, Joseph, 156–57
bodies
  (mis)readings of Indigenous bodies, 325–34
  the body as an art object, 388–90
  brown bodies and performative subjectivities, 301–2, 309–15
  embodied cultural diplomacy, 199–203
  embodied forms of border narratives, 300–1
  Latinx subhuman bodies, 309–11
Bolton, Herbert Eugene, 300
border, the
  gendered and sexual history, 302–4
  as a geopolitical space, 299–300, 302, 307
  immigration policies, 302–4
border narratives
  the animalistic and border subjects, 311–14, 316
  brown bodies and performative subjectivities, 301–2, 309–15
  Chicana sexuality, 307–8, 315
  in Chicanx literature, 299–300, 304–5
  as a cultural space, 299–300
  embodied forms of, 300–1
  En Cuatro Patas, 309–11

exploration of the non-human, 301–2, 306, 309
feminist interrogations of, 306–8
history of immigration policy, 304–5
hybrid identities, 306–7, 315
in Indigenous literature, 131–32
Latinx subhuman bodies, 309–11
liminality of, 306
links between migration and sexuality, 305–6
mental *neplantilism*, 306–7
mestiza consciousness, 300–1
in performance art, 301–2, 309–15
Borderland Studies, 300–1, 324
Bourdieu, Pierre, 78–79
Braudel, Fernand, 168
Brodhead, Richard, 15–16, 19–20, 26
Brown, Margaret, 54
Brown, Margaret Wise, 18
Buell, Lawrence, 42–43, 340–41
Burke, Kenneth, 352
Bustamante, Nao, 309
Butler, Judith, 64, 391–92

C

capitalism *see also* precarious labor
   colonial capitalism, 41–43, 54, 55–56, 86–87, 88–90
   consumer capitalism and the food industry, 1, 41–42, 48–50
   gold extraction and speculation, 43–44, 51–53
   late-capitalism, 99
   male independence under, 248–49
   oil industry, 50–51, 52–53, 92
   pork and commodity capitalism, 45–48
   racial capitalism, 79–80, 87, 91, 92–93
   workers under, 80–81
   working-class movements, 85
care work
   affective dynamics, 246, 254, 255, 258
   care work by migrant women, 87, 89–90
   decoupling of medicine from care, 254–55
   definition of, 247–48
   by domestic servants, 247, 249, 252, 253, 257–59
   epistemic asymmetries, 257–59
   ethics of care, 247–48
   failures of care in *The Sound and the Fury* (Faulkner), 256–57
   historical and cultural contexts, 247–48
   of immigrant domestic workers, 87–90, 249
   in *Let Us Now Praise Famous Men* (Agee), 246, 259–60
   in *Like One of the Family* (Childress), 259
   maternal care, 247, 253–54
   modernist aesthetics of, 246–47, 250–52
   under modernity, 248–49
   precarious labor and gendered care work, 89–90, 92
   reading aloud as maternal care, 15–17, 19, 22–23, 25–26
   relations of dependency, 247–52
   social dynamics, 246–47
   social welfare programs, 249–50, 253–54
   in *The Sound and the Fury* (Faulkner), 247, 256–59
   of women, 87, 89–90, 92, 249, 252, 253–54
   of working class women in *Three Lives* (Stein), 247, 252–55
Castillo, Ana, 301–2, 306, 307–8
Chicanx literature
   "The Adventures of Don Chipote, or, When Parrots Breast Feed" (Venegas), 305
   border narratives in, 299–300, 304–5
   Borderlands/ La Frontera: The New Mestiza (Anzaldúa), 299–302, 306–7, 315, 324
   Give It To Me (Castillo), 307–8
   The Rain God (Islas), 305–6
Chicanx performance artists, 301–2, 309–15
children's books *see also* reading aloud
   alphabetization and phonics, 17, 19, 20–21, 22–29, 30–32
   On Beyond Zebra! ix, 30–33
   The Cat in the Hat, 28–29, 33
   The Cat in the Hat Comes Back, ix, 30
   Dr Seuss's nonsense literature, 27–36
   Goodnight, Moon, 18
   illustrations, 28–29
   learning instruction books, 28–29, 30
   nonsense literature, 27–28
   The Princess Bride, 26–27
   read aloud bedtime stories, 16–17
   resistance to, 17
   as scriptive things, 17
   Seussian alphabet, 30–36
Childress, Alice, 259

China, 190–91, 197–98, *see also* US–China Writers' Conferences
China Trade
 financialization of opium, 215–16, 217, 218–20, 221–22, 238–39
 the Genteel Tradition and, 222–26
 in mercantile biographies, 209–10, 215–22
Chuh, Kandice, 381–82
civil rights
 appeals to the United Nations, 171–73
 "The Ballot or the Bullet" (Malcom X), 172
 civil rights appeals to the United Nations, 171–73
 as distinct from human rights, 172
 trajectory of the achievements of, 173–74
Civil Rights movement, 62–63, 66–67, 138–39, 179
civil society, 337, 347–48
Clair, Rene, 159–60, 163–64
Clark, William, 129
climate change, 40–41
collective memory
 in *Beloved* (Morrison), 399, 400, 401–2
 "blood memory" in Native American literature, 119–24
 Indigenous monuments, 126–27
 memory and nostalgia, 72–73, 74
 recollections of Indigenous homelands, 115–17
 term, 401
colonialism *see also* decolonisation; settler-colonialism
 African American relations to anti-colonialism, 179
 colonial capitalism, 41–43, 54, 55–56, 86–87, 88–90
 in *Lucy* (Kincaid), 86–87, 88–90
 racist depersonalization, 182
coloniality
 the Anthropocene and, 41–42
 Asian colonial prostitution, 236–38
 in "To Build a Fire" (London), 43
 categories of humanity, 44–45
 colonial animal economies, 47–48
 concept, 41–42
 extractive economies, 43–44, 52–55
 of the food industry, 51

 in the materiality of industrial production and consumption, 41–43
 tobacco industry, 53–55
Color Curtain: A Report on the Bandung Conference, The (Wright)
 African and Asian writings about decolonization, 180–82
 on colonial violence, 182, 183–84
 criticism of Wright's readings, 176–77, 183–84, 186–87
 East/West binaries, 181, 184–85, 186–87
 transnationalism and, 173, 175, 180–81
 Wright's exploration of race and place, 177–79
 Wright's presence at the conference, 180
Coltrane, John, 145–47, 150
Comenius, Johann Amos, 20
conceptual art
 artists of color, 386–88
 emergence of, 380, 382
conceptualism *see also* Piper, Adrian
 the Black radical tradition and, 380–82
 text based conceptualism, 381, 382–83
 undisciplined reading methodologies, 381–82, 395–96
 and the visual arts, 380, 381
Congress for Cultural Freedom (CCF), 70, 180
Cousins, Norman, 191–92, 193, 195–96
Crain, Patricia, 15, 20, 22, 25–26, 30–31
Crazy Rich Asians (Kwan)
 Asian American characters in, 100
 Asian guest workers, 109
 authorial claims of fiction, 109–10
 class differences, 100, 106–7, 109, 111
 commercial success, 109
 excessive consumerism in Singapore, 107–8, 110–11
 portrayal of academia, 106–7
 racial difference, 109–10
 storyline, 106–7
Creeley, Robert, 145, 147–48
Cuban Missile Crisis, 69–70, 73–74
Cukor, George, 154–57, 156f, 163–64
cultural diplomacy *see also* US–China Writers' Conferences
 Congress for Cultural Freedom (CCF), 70, 180

Ginsberg's queer cultural outreach, 190–91, 196–97, 198–99, 200
  intimate perspectives on, 190–91
  under the Reagan administration, 191–95
  scholarship on, 189–90
  T'ien Hsia, 214
  by the US, 189–90
  US literary diplomacy, 190, 192, 193–94
cultural memory studies
  archive/canon distinction, 403, 404–5
  collective memory, 401
  communicative memory, 402–3
  cultural memory, 402–3
  disciplinary history and, 400–1, 404–5, 409
  the dynamics of memory, 403–4
  field of, 400, 401
  global memory cultures, 409
  the Holocaust, 179, 401–2, 403, 409, 410
  literary studies and, 401–4
  mediation/remediation, 404, 405, 410–11
  memory work of *Beloved*, 399, 400–1, 404–5, 406, 413–14
  postmemory, 410
  rememory in *Beloved*, 399, 400–1, 404, 406–7, 411–12
  sites of memory, 401–2, 407, 409
  transgenerational transmission of memories, 407, 410

D

Davis, Heather, 41–42
decolonisation
  African and Asian writings about decolonization, 180–82
  impact on African American politics, 173, 179
  in Richard Wright's thought, 184–87
Deepwater Horizon, 53, 92
Delany, Samuel R. *see also Mad Men, The* (Delany)
  personal life, 110
  Times Square Red, Times Square Blue, 100–1
DeLillo, Don, 398–99
Deloria, Philip, 118
Derrida, Jacques, 59, 63
dialogism, 343–44
diversity
  as an American brand, 1
  in the field of twentieth-century American literature, 1–2
Douglas, Susan, 138–39
Dr Seuss, 17
Du Bois, W.E.B., 172–73, 174–75, 179, 180, 277–78, 392

E

ecocriticism
  field, 42–43
  The Great Invisible (Brown), 54
  Waterworld (Reynolds), 53–54, 55
Eggers, Dave, 79–84, 95–96
Eliot, T.S., 27–28, 193–94, 250–52
Ellington, Duke, 149–50
Ellison, Ralph *see also Invisible Man* (Ellison)
  humanism vs individualism, 342–43, 345–46, 353
  rejection of Richard Wright's thought, 349–51
  "Richard Wright's Blues," 350
  submerged listening, 148, 150
  "Twentieth-Century Fiction and the Black Mask of Humanity," 342–43
Erdrich, Heid
  "Girl of Lightning," 326–28, 331–32
  Indians in cabinets in the writings of, 325–26
Erdrich, Louise, 117
Erll, Astrid, 404
Erpenbeck, Jenny, 412
Esparza, Rafael, 301–2, 313–14
Exxon Valdez, 53–54

F

Fanon, Frantz, 178–79, 182
Faulkner, William *see also Sound and the Fury, The* (Faulkner)
  Absalom, Absalom! 360–61, 362–64, 366–67
  biography, 358–59
  cinematic form and Faulkner's writing, 154–55
  destabilizing characters of color, 372–73, 374–75
  economics and critiques of white masculinity, 356–57, 364–69

Faulkner, William (*cont.*)
  exposure to slow motion techniques, 156–60, 163–64
  The Hamlet, 364, 365–66, 367–68, 369–71, 373, 375, 376
  intersections of whiteness, gender, and economic power, 357–58, 359–60
  the Jim Crow era and, 359–60, 363–64
  literary status of, 356–59
  manipulations of narrative time, 160–62, 166–68
  The Mansion, 168, 370–71, 376–77
  media studies and, 153–55, 157–58
  portrayals of whiteness, 356–57, 359, 360–64
  post-war socioeconomics, 356–57, 370, 375
  roles of white women, 356–57
  screenwriting career, 153–55, 156–57, 357–58
  temporalities in *Light in August*, 161–63, 164–66
  threat of female sexuality, 364, 366
  The Town, 370–71, 372–73, 374–75
  US literary diplomacy, 190, 192
  use of hypotaxis, 157–58, 162–63
  use of slow motion in *Light in August*, 154–55, 156–61, 162–64
  whiteness and post-war social change, 369–77
Ferber, Edna
  biography, 358–59
  destabilizing characters of color, 372, 373–75
  economics and critiques of white masculinity, 356–57, 364–69
  food writing, 358, 365
  Giant, 369–70, 371–72, 373–77
  intersections of whiteness, gender, and economic power, 357–58, 364–69
  the Jim Crow era and, 359–60, 363–64
  literary status of, 356–57, 358–59
  portrayals of whiteness, 356–57, 358, 359, 360–64
  post-war socioeconomics, 356–57, 370, 371–72, 375–76
  racialized sexuality, 366–68
  roles of white women, 356–57
  Saratoga Trunk, 364, 365, 367, 368–69
  Show Boat, 360–62, 363–64
  whiteness and post-war social change, 369–77

film
  cinematic form and Faulkner's writing, 154–55
  Entr'acte (Clair), 159–60, 163–64
  Faulkner's exposure to slow motion techniques, 156–60, 163–64
  "The Horse in Motion" (Muybridge), 163–66, 164*f*
  slow motion techniques, 156–60
  A Star is Born, 154–55
  temporalities and histories of technology, 164–66
  The Thief of Bagdad (Walsh), 159–60
  What Price Hollywood? 154–57, 156*f*, 163–64
Floyd, George, 171–72, 173–74
Floyd, Philonise, 171–72, 173–74
food
  canning processes, 48–50
  consumer capitalism and the food industry, 1, 41–42, 48
  Ferber's food writing, 358, 365
  meatpacking industry, 45–48
  "prepper" manuals, 48–49
  relationship with the petroleum_industrial complex, 50–51
  in the Yukon frontier, 48, 51
For the Union Dead (Lowell)
  cultural difference and cultural destruction, 68–69
  depictions of violence, 66–67
  dualistic logic of containment, 61, 69, 74–75
  expressions of memorialization, 62, 64–66
  images of Hiroshima, 62–63, 66–67
  "July in Washington," 68–69
  "The Lesson," 71, 72–73
  Lowell's borrowings from Alberti, 71, 72–73, 74
  memory and nostalgia, 72–73, 74
  mistranslation of the Shaw memorial dedication, 63–65, 66, 67–70
  as a nuclear poem, 61
  post-apocalyptic nuclear future, 62–63, 74–75
  racial readings of American history, 61–67, 69–70
  reading at the Shaw memorial, 61–62
  "Returning," 73, 74

revisionary rewriting, 61, 63–64, 69, 70–71
the Shaw memorial, 63–67
translation and transnationalism, 61, 63–64, 71–73, 74–75
"For the Union Dead," 61–67, 69–70
Ford, Phil, 141
Freeman, Elizabeth, 210

G

Gallardo, Rincón, 309–11
Garner, Margaret, 405–6, 408
Garvey, Marcus, 174–75
Geisel, Theodor, 27–36
gender *see also* queerness; sexuality
    and border migration, 302–4
    feminization of migration, 87
    gendered care work, 89–90, 92
    gendered expectations, 88–89
genre
    of the Anthropocene, 48–49
    in the field of twentieth_century American literature, 2
    nuclear criticism, 59–60
Gilroy, Paul, 175–76
Ginsberg, Allen
    "America," 48–49
    "China Trip," 197–99
    "On the Conduct of the World Seeking Beauty against Government," 194–96
    critiques of Communist state governments, 195–96
    embodied cultural diplomacy, 199–203
    global role of writers, 195–96
    "I Love Old Whitman So," 199–200
    "Industrial Waves," 194–95, 198, 200
    on literary censorship, 198
    queer cultural outreach, 190–91, 196–97, 198–99, 200
    radio in the works of, 139–40
    "Reading Bai Juyi," 200–3
    rejection of US literary propaganda, 193–95
    "A Supermarket in California," 48
    "Symphony Sid" Torin and, 137–38, 141–42
    at the US-China Writers' Conferences, 190–91, 192, 193–94, 196–97
Gitelman, Lisa, 3–4
Go the Fuck to Sleep, 18–19, 23, 25, 26, 27
Goldman, William, 26–27
Great Invisible, The (Brown), 54
Griggs, Sutton, 174–75
Gros Ventre, 117

H

Hahn, Emily "Mickey"
    affair with Shao Xunmei, 214, 231–36, 233*f*
    "The Big Smoke," 213, 231–32, 234–35, 238–39
    on female sexuality, 213, 235, 236–38
    journalism career, 213–14
    melancholic social alienation, 210
    Miss Jill, 237–38
    on opium and the China Trade, 221–22, 238–39
    opium consumption, 213, 214, 226–27, 232–34, 235–36
    queer chronotopes, 210, 213
    representation of "Asian subjects," 214
    review of Santayana's memoir, 209–11, 226–27, 230
    on war rape in Japanese camps, 238
    writings on opium, 213, 238–39
Halbwachs, Maurice, 401–2
Hall, Stuart, 180–81
Harjo, Joy, 117–18
Harlem Renaissance, 66, 264–65, 267, 269–70
Hartman, Saidiya, 410, 411, 413–14
Harvey, David, 218–19
Hemingway, Ernest, 2–3, 49–50, 55–56
Hernández Cruz, Victor, 142
Hersch Charles, 141–42
Hersey, John, 28–29
Hirsch, Marianne, 410
Hirschkop, Ken, 343–44, 346
history
    cultural memory studies and, 400–1, 404–5, 409
    Indigenous forms of historiography, 131–33
    Indigenous historical novel, 117–18
    Indigenous mythic history, 117–18, 131–32
    the *longue durée*, 168
    racial readings of American history, 61–67, 69–70
    Western historical evidence, 118
Holmes, John Clellon, 141
the Holocaust, 179, 401–2, 403, 409, 410

Horkheimer, Max, 1
human rights
  and the Civil Rights movement, 172, 179–80
  as distinct from civil rights, 172
  Third World solidarities, 172–73
Hunt, Peter, 26–27

I

Ibarra, Xandra (La Chica Boom)
  the animalistic and border subjects, 301–2, 316
  F*ck My Life (FML), 311–12
  Nude Laughing, 313
  "Spic Ecdysis," 312–13
identification
  definition of, 267
  digestion as a literary trope for, 272
  in Mumbo Jumbo (Reed), 272–74
identity see also transnationalism
  in Andrea Lee's work, 282–83
  African nationality, 290–91
  American Black identity, 281–82, 289–90, 296–97
  and racial history, 293–96
imagination
  identity space of invisibility in the liberal imagination, 340, 350–54
  in Trilling's thought, 337–38, 339–40, 349
imperialism
  financial imperialism, 215, 217–19
  imperialist nostalgia, 49–50
  the opium trade and, 218–20
  of the US in South America, 69–70
Indigenous peoples see also Native American literature; race
  (mis)readings of Indigenous bodies, 325–34
  African Americans within the communities, 129–30
  of the Columbus era, 124–26
  connection among Black, Brown, and Native communities, 129–33
  essentialist accounts of, 119–21, 122, 123
  Jefferson's stance on, 125–27
  monuments, 126–27
  murder of Indigenous peoples under Columbus, 124–25
  narration and cultural memory in literature, 116, 118
  oral tradition and world-building, 121–22
  Powhatan's speech, 125–26
  "real Indian" figure, 128–29
  recollections of Indigenous homelands, 115–17
internationalism, 200, see also cultural diplomacy; US–China Writers' Conferences
Invisible Man (Ellison)
  Bellow's review of, 349
  the comic in, 352
  critical reception, 340–41
  identity space of invisibility, 348–49, 350–54
  jazz music in, 147–48, 150
  the liberal imagination, 353–54
  liberal imagination alongside racial exclusion, 348–49, 350–51
  opening line, 348
Islas, Arturo, 305–6

J

Jacoby, Susan, 288–89
Jameson, Fredric, 99
Jarrett, Gene Andrew, 282–83, 287, 289–90
Javadizadeh, Kamran, 394
jazz music
  ambient listening and, 141, 147–48
  audile techniques, 141
  Baraka's music criticism, 144–47
  Beat literature and, 138–42, 150–51
  Ellington's arrangements of "In the Hall of the Mountain King," 149–50
  in Invisible Man (Ellison), 147–48, 150
  "Symphony Sid" Torin's shows, 140–41
Jefferson, Thomas, 126–27
Jim Crow era
  growing challenges to, 177
  laws, 178–79, 356–57, 359–60, 364
  monuments of, 163–64
  representations of the one-drop rule, 360–64
  Richard Wright's exile from, 174–75, 187
Jungle, The (Sinclair), 45–47, 48, 50–51

K

Kawin, Bruce, 153–54, 156–58
Kellman, Steven, 346

Kerouac, Jack
  audile techniques, 141
  childhood memories, 135–36
  food on the road, 50–51
  radio in the works of, 139–40, 141
  On the Road, 139–40
  "Symphony Sid" Torin and, 137–38, 140–41
Kincaid, Jamaica, 79–80, 86–90, 95–96, 292–93
Kittler, Friedrich, 19, 20, 21–23, 25–26, 29, 158–59
Koselleck, Reinhart, 166
Kubrick, Stanley, 62–63
Kwan, Kevin *see Crazy Rich Asians* (Kwan)

L

Languille, Julie, 48–49
Laplanche, Jean, 267
Latinx communities, 130–31, *see also* Chicanx literature
Lear, Edward, 27–28
Lee, Andrea *see also Russian Journal* (Lee); *Sarah Phillips* (Lee)
  within African American literature, 281–83, 284, 285–86, 296–97
  interracial desire, 281–82
  at *The New Yorker*, 292–93
  personal racial identification, 291–92
  scholarship on, 282–84
  transnational liminality, 281–82
  treatment of race, 281–82
LeMenager, Stephanie, 42–43, 50–51
Levy-Hussen, Aida, 294–95
liberalism *see also* neoliberalism
  crisis of in American politics, 338–39
  the liberal imagination, 337–38, 339–40, 349
  the liberal imagination in *Invisible Man* (Ellison), 340, 350–54
  the liberal imagination in *The Adventures of Augie March* (Bellow), 340–48
  literary criticism's engagement with, 337, 339–40
  Trilling's Cold War liberalism, 337–38, 339–40
London, Jack, 2–3, 52, *see also* "To Build a Fire" (London)
Love, Heather, 22–23

Lowell, Robert *see also For the Union Dead* (Lowell)
  affiliations with Cold War cultural institutions, 70–71
  description of Puerto Rican otherness, 67–68
  encounter with Alberti, 71
  nuclear anxiety, 73
  travels in South America, 70–71
Luce, Henry, 2

M

Mackey, Nathaniel, 144–45
Mad Men, The (Delany)
  Asian American characters in, 100
  authorial claims of fiction, 102–3, 110
  black queer intellectual practice, 101, 103
  Black–Korean relationality, 103–4
  Hasler's family history, 104–5
  Hasler's racialization as Asian American, 101–3
  the HIV/AIDS epidemic, 100–1
  storyline, 100
  value of the underclasses, 105–6
Malcom X, 172
Mallan, Lloyd, 71–72
Mamoulian, Rouben, 155–56, 163–64
Manguel, Alberto, 22–23
Martí, José, 3
Marx, Karl, 43–44, 51, 80–81, 88, 220
McCarthy, Cormac, 48–50, 55–56
McKay, Claude, 66
McNickle, D'Arcy, 131–32
meatpacking industry, 45–48
memory *see* collective memory; cultural memory studies
Menand, Louis, 339–40, 341–42
mercantile biographies
  commercial patriarchy, 210, 215–16
  financial and literary signification in, 217–20
  financial imperialism, 215, 217–19
  heroic patriarchal characters, 211–13, 216, 219, 220–21, 223, 224–26
  The Journals of Major Samuel Shaw, 216–18, 219–20
  The Last Puritan (Santayana), 209–13
  romance of the China Trade, 209–10, 215–22

Merritt, Stephin, 15
Mexico *see* border narratives
Mignolo, Walter, 41–42, 44, 50–51, 55–56
migration
    Asian guest workers, 109
    of the economic elite, 109
Milton, John, 131
model minority myth, 98–99, 102–3
modernism
    aesthetics of care, 246–47, 250–52
    collective working, 250–51
    the independent modernist woman, 250
    modernist narratives of care work, 246–47
    temporal plasticity, 251–52
modernity
    decoupling of medicine from care, 254–55
    standardization of time, 157–58, 251–52
Momaday, N. Scott
    House Made of Dawn, 115–17
    imagination and Native experience, 122–23
    Indians in cabinets in the writings of, 325–26
    Indigenous epistemology, 115–17
    ineligibility for cultural diplomatic assignments, 192
    Kiowa cultural loss, 332–33
    The Names, 116–17
    "In the Presence of the Sun: A Gathering of Shields," 119, 123
    use of the term "blood memory," 119, 120
    The Way to Rainy Mountain, 116–17, 122–23, 332–33
Moore, Jason, 47, 50–51, 52
Morrison, Toni *see also Beloved* (Morrison)
    The Black Book, 404–5
    Song of Solomon, 405
    at the US–China Writers' Conferences, 192, 193
Morse, Kathryn, 44, 48, 51
Moten, Fred, 147, 148–49, 385, 386
Moulton, Louise Chandler, 17–18
Mullikin, Melinda, 132
Mumbo Jumbo (Reed)
    Black literature's origins and development, 265–66, 267, 268, 270–72, 274
    the Harlem Renaissance, 264, 265–66, 275–76
    the institutionalization of African American literature, 277–79
    narrative arc, 264, 268, 270–72
    ongoing quest for Black literary authenticity, 274–76
    as an origin myth for Black Studies, 264–65, 277
    racial authenticity, 265–66
    in relationship to *Nigger Heaven* (Vechten), 267, 275–76, 277–78
    Von Vampton as the figure of white appropriation, 265–67, 268–72, 273
    Von Vampton's identification with Blackness, 272–74
Muñoz, José Esteban, 301–2, 312
Murray, Judith Sargent, 19–20
Muybridge, Eadweard, 163–66, 164f

N

Nadel, Alan, 60
narrative *see also* border narratives
    Faulkner's manipulations of narrative time, 160–62, 166–68
    Indigenous narration and cultural memory in literature, 116, 118
    modernist narratives of care work, 246–47
    narrative absences in *The Sound and the Fury* (Faulkner), 247, 256, 257–58
    settler colonial literature, 41–42, 45–46, 47–48, 50, 54, 327
    veracity claims of slave narratives, 129–30
National Association for the Advancement of Colored People (NAACP), 179
Native American literature *see also* Indigenous peoples; Momaday, N. Scott; Silko, Leslie Marmon
    (mis)readings of Indigenous bodies, 325–34
    activism and the canon, 321, 322, 325, 334–35
    activist, community-centered research, 321–22
    American literature in relation to, 124
    authenticity of Indigenous voices, 127–29
    blood memory in, 116–17, 118–19, 120
    borderland methodological readings, 324
    "Girl of Lightning" (Erdich), 326–28, 331–32
    the hidden voices of history, 118–19, 124–29
    imagination and Native experience, 122–23

Indian in the Cupboard trope, 325–32
Indigenous forms of historiography, 131–33
Indigenous futurity, 117–18
Kiowa cultural loss, 332–33
Life of Black Hawk, 127
"Now We Sleep" (Turcotte), 328–30, 331–32
reading strategies for, 321–22
recollections of Indigenous homelands, 115–17, 324
Red Readings, 322–24
the relationship to lands, 119–22
The Singing Bird (Milton), 131–32
use of the historical novel, 117–18
Western readings of, 321–22, 323–25, 327–29, 334
neoliberalism *see also* liberalism
destruction of organized labour under, 78–79
erosion of middle-class economic life, 81–82
literary figure of neoliberal angst, 81–82, 87
precarious labor, 78–80, 95
in US literature, 83, 95
New Yorker, The, 292–93
Nguyen, Viet Thanh, 411–12
Nigger Heaven (Vechten), 267, 275–76, 277–78
Nora, Pierre, 401–2, 407, 409
nostalgia
imperialist nostalgia, 49–50
memory and nostalgia, 72–73, 74
Nowlin, Michael, 349
nuclear criticism
genre, 59–60
institutional and ideological systems of power, 60
nuclear poetry *see also For the Union Dead* (Lowell)
Cold War anxieties, 60
containment ideology and policy, 60–61
genre, 59

O

oil industry, 50–51, 52–54, 92
opium
the China Trade and, 217, 218–20, 221–22
financialization of opium, 215–16, 217, 218–20, 221–22, 238–39
Hahn's consumption of, 213, 214, 226–27, 232–34, 235–36

Hahn's writings on, 213, 231–36, 238–39
Japanese produced white drugs and, 232
in *The Last Puritan* (Santayana), 227, 228–29
and literary creativity, 219
and sex work in *Miss Jill* (Hahn), 237
smoking and the distortion of time, 214, 215–16, 231–32, 235
Owens, Louis, 117

P

Patel, Raj, 47, 50–51, 52
performance art *see also* Ibarra, Xandra (La Chica Boom)
of border narratives, 301–2, 309–15
Catalysis series (Piper), 388–90, 391
Mythic Being series (Piper), 381–82, 393–95
Untitled Performance at Max's Kansas City (Piper), 385, 392, 394
petroleum culture, 50–51
Piper, Adrian
aesthetic objectification, 385, 390–92, 394–95
within the Black radical tradition, 386, 389–90
the body as an art object, 388–90
Catalysis series, 388–90, 391
conceptual art of, 380–81
the "double vision" of her artistic practice, 392
Here and Now, 382–83
literature of art objecthood, 381–82, 386
"My Nose Cone," 383–85
Mythic Being series, 381–82, 393–95
objective persona, 390–92, 393, 394–95
political awakening, 387–88, 389
self-objectification in the work of, 384–87, 388
Talking to Myself: The Autobiography of an Art Object, 381–82, 388, 389–92, 393–94
Untitled Performance at Max's Kansas City, 385, 392, 394
Plath, Sylvia, 59–60
poetry *see also* Baraka, Amiri; Ginsberg, Allen
"Evolution" (Alexie), 330–31
"Girl of Lightning" (Erdich), 326–28, 331–32
Indians in cabinets tropes, 325–31
"My Nose Cone" (Piper), 383–85
"Now We Sleep" (Turcotte), 328–30, 331–32
"Pawn Shop" (Alexie), 330, 331
The Summer of Black Widows (Alexie), 129–30

428 INDEX

Pokagon, Simon, 127–28
Pontalis, Jean Bertand, 267
postapocalyptic novels, 48–49
postmodernism, 99
Powhatan, 125–26
precarious labor
    competition/cooperation duality, 80–81, 82–83, 85–86, 87–88, 96
    gendered care work, 89–90, 92
    in *A Hologram for the King* (Eggers), 79–84, 95–96
    in *Lucy* (Kincaid), 79–80, 86–90, 95–96
    under neoliberalism, 78–80, 95
    penal labor as an extension of, 91–92, 93
    and the precariousness of Black lives, 91–92
    proletarian literary tradition, 94–95
    racial terror and violence in *Sing* (Ward), 90–94
    racialized workers, 79–80, 83–86
    in *Sing, Unburied, Sing* (Ward), 79–81, 90–94, 95–96
    term, 78–79
    in US literature, 79, 81
    in *… y no se lo tragó la tierra* (Rivera), 79–81, 83–86, 95–96
"prepper" manuals, 48–49

Q

queerness
    black queer intellectual practice, 101, 103
    Ginsberg's queer cultural outreach, 190–91, 196–97, 198–99, 200
    queer senses of time, 210
Quincy, Josiah, 215–18, 219–20

R

race
    Afro–Asian analogy, 180–81
    American Black identity and, 281–82, 289–90, 296–97
    in Andrea Lee's work, 281–82
    Black–Korean relationality, 103–4
    care work by migrant women, 87, 89–90
    connection among Black, Brown, and Native communities, 129–33
    interracial desire, 281–82, 283–84, 287–88
    Lowell's racial readings of American history, 61–67, 69–70
    the mid-century racial imagination, 356–58, 359–60
    model minority myth, 98–99, 102–3
    1955 Bandung conference, 180–81
    racial capitalism, 79–80, 87, 91, 92–93, 103–4
    racial terror and violence in *Sing* (Ward), 90–94
    racialized workers in precarious labor, 79–80, 83–86
    radio's post-war racial politics, 135–36, 144
    representations of the one-drop rule, 360–64
    in *Russian Journal* (Lee), 286–92
    temporalities of Black experience, 166–67
    whiteness of the golden age of radio, 135–36
radio *see also* "Symphony Sid" Torin (Sidney Tarnopol)
    audile techniques, 137
    in Baraka's works, 142–44, 147–51
    in Beat literature, 139–40, 141
    Black music on, 136, 140–42, 147–49
    Black radio stations, 136, 137, 138–39, 143–44
    figure of the disc jockey, 137–39, 142
    golden age, 135–37
    "In Memory of Radio" (Baraka), 135–37, 138, 143–44
    post-war racial politics of, 135–37, 144
    post-war transformation, 136
    relationship with literature, 136–37
    shift to music programs, 136–37, 138–39
    whiteness of, 135–36
radio ventriloquism, 143–44
reading
    failure of reading instruction, 28–29
    fostering a love of in children, 15–18
    maternalization of, 19–22, 23, 24–26, 29, 30, 36
    phonics, 20, 22–23, 24–25, 27, 28–29
    reading strategies for Indigenous texts, 321–22
    swallow alphabets, 22
reading aloud
    children's resistance to, 15–17, 23–24
    the coerced listener, 23–27

the coerced reader, 17–23
the Comenius alphabet, ix, 20–21
as a form of excision, 26–27
as a form of penetration, 26
Go the Fuck to Sleep, 18–19, 23, 25, 26, 27
as maternal care, 15–17, 19, 22–23, 25–26
multiple functions of, 17–18
read aloud bedtime stories, 16–18
sonic performativity, 20–23
Reed, Ishmael *see Mumbo Jumbo* (Reed)
Reid Banks, Lynne, 325
Reynolds, Kevin, 53–54, 55
Rigney, Ann, 400–1, 403–5, 409, 410–11, 413
Rincón Gallardo, Naomi, 301–2
Rivera, Tomás, 79, 83–86, 95–96
Road, The (McCarthy), 48–50
Robeson, Paul, 174–75, 179, 180, 190
Robinson, Cedric, 175–76, 177
Robinson, Cedric J., 380–82, 386
Rousseau, Jean Jacques, 19–20
Russian Journal (Lee)
American expectations of race and racial feeling, 285–86, 288–89
discussions of race in, 286–92
interracial desire, 287–88
Lee's personal racial identification, 291–92
links with *Sarah Phillips*, 291–92
scholarship on, 286–87
transnational views of race, 281–82, 288–89, 290–91

S

Saldívar, José, 299–300
Samuel, Shaw, 216–18, 219–20
Santayana, George
admiration for frontier imperialism, 210–13
decline of the Great Merchant family, 210–11, 224–26, 227–28
family background, 210–11, 223–24
"Genteel Tradition" phrase, 210–13, 221–22
Hahn's review of *The Last Puritan*, 209–11, 226–27, 230
The Last Puritan, 226–31
melancholic social alienation within global trade, 210
on opium and the China Trade, 221–22
opium in *The Last Puritan*, 227, 228–29
Persons and Places, 210–11, 222–26
philosophical *metonia*, 222–23, 226, 230–31
queer chronotope of *The Last Puritan: A Memoir in the Form of a Novel*, 209–10
Sarah Phillips (Lee)
in-betweenness and the Black experience, 295–97
American expectations of race and racial feeling, 285–86
Black women's anger and, 294–96
criticism of, 283–84
identity and racial history, 293–96
interracial desire, 283–84
the limits of the transnational, 281–82, 294–96
links with *Russian Journal*, 291–92
narrative arc, 293
Sarris, Greg, 130–31
Sartre, Jean-Paul, 167–68
settler-colonialism *see also* "To Build a Fire" (London)
extractive economies, 52–53, 54
Federal Indian Law, 220
food industry, 45–46, 47–48, 50–51
Indigenous bodies on display, 325–27, 331–32
industrial settler campaigns, 41–42, 50
settler colonial literature, 41–42, 45–46, 47–48, 50, 54, 327
sexuality *see also* gender; queerness; women
in border narratives, 305–8
Chicana sexuality, 307–8, 315
gendered and sexual histories of the border, 302–4
in Hahn's work, 213, 235, 236–38
links between migration and sexuality, 305–6
racialized sexuality, 366–68
Shao Xunmei, 214, 231–35, 233f
Sharpe, Christina, 166–67
Shaw, Samuel, 224
Silko, Leslie Marmon
Almanac of the Dead, 132–33
on "blood memory," 120
Ceremony, 130–31
oral tradition and world building, 121
Storyteller, 117–18
at the US–China Writers' Conferences, 192, 193

Sinclair, Upton, 45–47, 48, 50–51
slavery
    cultural memory studies and, 400
    intergenerational transmission of
        memories, 410
    intertextuality of *Beloved* (Morrison) and,
        412–13
    Margaret Garner, 405–6, 408
    penal labor as an extension of, 91–92, 93
    relations of race and slavery in *Beloved*
        (Morrison), 399
    veracity claims of slave narratives, 129–30
Smith, John, 125–26
Smith, Valerie, 283–84
Snyder, Gary, 192, 196
Sound and the Fury, The (Faulkner)
    domestic servants, 257–58
    epistemic asymmetry, 257–59
    failures of care, 256–57
    interdependency and care, 247
    narrative absences, 247, 256, 257–58
    narrative and distribution of care work, 247, 256
    slow motion and narrative time, 157–58,
        160–62, 167–68
Spaulding, William, 29
Spiegelman, Art, 409, 410
St Clair, Justin, 143–44
Stein, Gertrude
    relationship with Alice Toklas, 252
    working_class care work in *Three Lives*, 247,
        252–55
Sterne, Jonathan, 137
Steven, Mark, 157–58, 162–63
Stockton, Kathryn Bond, 26
Sturgis Jr, Russell, 210–11, 212f, 216, 219–21,
    224–25
"Symphony Sid" Torin (Sidney Tarnopol)
    appropriation of a Black idiom, 140–43
    impact on the Beat scene, 137–38, 140–42
    influence on Amiri Baraka, 142–45
    influence on Black and Latinx writers, 142
    radio shows of, 140–41
    "Symphony Sid" (Baraka), 147–50

T

Taylor, Jesse Oak, 41, 43, 44
Teuton, Sean, 323–24

Three Lives (Stein), 247, 252–55
time
    the aesthetic of slow motion, 162, 163–66
    cinematic and literary slow motion, 153–60
    Faulkner's manipulations of narrative time,
        160–62, 166–68
    Faulkner's use of slow motion in *Light in*
        August, 154–55, 156–61, 162–64
    Here and Now (Piper), 382–83
    "The Horse in Motion" (Muybridge), 163–66,
        164f
    and human mortality, 224
    the *longue durée*, 168
    media archaeology, 164–66
    modernism and speed, 166
    modernity's standardization of, 157–58,
        251–52
    opium consumption's distortion of, 214,
        215–16, 231–32, 235
    queer senses of time, 210
    slow motion in *The Sound and the Fury*
        (Faulkner), 161–62, 167–68
    temporalities of Black experience, 166–67
    in *Three Lives* (Stein), 252
"To Build a Fire" (London)
    the bacon sandwich, 42, 43, 45–46, 48, 51
    coloniality of, 43
    contemporary ecological conditions, 40–41
    deforestation of the Yukon, 44–45, 52
    denial of knowledge, 44–45, 54–55
    ecocritical reading, 42–43
    extractive economies, 52–53
    as a gold rush narrative, 43–44
    individual historical-planetary relations in,
        42, 55–56
    tobacco, 42, 43, 55–56
    use of animal power, 45–46
tobacco industry, 53–54
Todd, Zoe, 41–42
Toklas, Alice, 252
transnationalism *see also* Black
    internationalism
    in African American literature, 284–85
    American Black identity and, 281–82, 289–90,
        296–97
    Asian Americans as transnational subjects,
        99, 109

in *The Color Curtain: A Report on the Bandung Conference* (Wright), 173, 175, 180–81
Emily Hahn's feminine community, 235, 236–38
liminal experiences of, 281–82
of memory studies, 409
national identity and, 282, 290–91, 295–96
in *Russian Journal* (Lee), 281–82, 288–89, 290–91
in *Sarah Phillips* (Lee), 281–82, 294–96
and transnationalism in *For the Union Dead* (Lowell), 61, 63–64, 71–73, 74–75
of the US Mexico border, 299–300
views of race in *Russian Journal* (Lee), 288–89, 290–91
Trilling, Lionel
  on George Santayana, 211–13
  The Liberal Imagination, 337–38, 339–40
  "Reality in America," 349
  review of *The Adventures of Augie March* (Bellow), 341, 342–43, 345
Turcotte, Mark
  Indians in cabinets in the writings of, 325–26
  "Now We Sleep," 328–30, 331–32
Twain, Mark, 43–44

U

Ungaretti, Giuseppe, 73
United Nations, 171–72, 173–74
US literature *see also* American literature
  Asian Americans in, 99
  within global criticism, 4–5
  term, 3
US–China Writers' Conferences
  Ginsberg at, 190–91, 192, 193–94, 196–97
  Ginsberg's embodied cultural diplomacy, 199–203
  Ginsberg's queer cultural outreach, 190–91, 196–97, 198–99, 200
  Ginsberg's reflections on in "China Trip," 197–99
  governmental oversight of, 193, 200–1
  "I Love Old Whitman So" (Ginsberg), 199–200
  on literary censorship, 198

overview of, 191–93
"Reading Bai Juyi" (Ginsberg), 200–3

V

Vechten, Carl Van, 267, 269, 275–76, 277–79
Venegas, Daniel, 305
violence
  colonial violence, 182, 183–84
  racialized violence, 90–94
  in *For the Union Dead* (Lowell), 66–67
Von Eschen, Penny, 179–80, 189–90
Vorkapich, Slavko, 155–56

W

Walsh, Raoul, 159–60
Ward, Jesmyn, 79–80, 90–94, 95–96, 411
Warhol, Andy, 48–49
Warrior, Robert, 322
Washington, Mary Helen, 283, 284, 294
Waterworld (Reynolds), 53–54, 55
Weaver, Jace, 322
Welch, James, 117
Whitman, Walt, 191, 196, 199–200
Whyte, Kyle Powys, 41–42, 47–48, 56
Williams, Jennifer D., 281, 286–87
Williams, William Carlos, 1, 191, 198–99
Womack, Craig, 322, 324
women *see also* care work
  Asian colonial prostitution, 236–38
  the independent modernist woman, 250
  interracial desire, 281–82, 283–84, 287–88
  maternalization of reading, 19–22, 23, 24–26, 29, 30, 36
  mothers as educators, 19–21, 22
  prostitution and border immigration policies, 303–4
  reading aloud as maternal care, 15–17, 19, 22–23, 25–26
  war rapes during World War II, 238
Wright, Richard *see also Color Curtain: A Report on the Bandung Conference, The* (Wright)
  the 1955 Bandung conference, 173, 175, 176–77
  African and Asian writings about decolonization, 175–76, 180–82
  Black Boy, 350

Wright, Richard (*cont.*)
   Black Power, 174–75, 178–79, 182–83, 184, 185–86
   Congress for Cultural Freedom (CCF), 180
   Ellison and Baldwin's rejection of, 349–51
   literary criticism of his later writings, 174–76
   Native Son, 173, 174–75, 182–83, 185, 297
   notions of race and rootlessness, 173–74, 175–77, 183, 185
   The Outsider, 175–76
   the relation between race and global politics, 175
   on Western modernity, 173, 182–86, 187
Wynter, Sylvia, 44–45

Y

York, 129–30

Z

Zielinski, Siegfried, 164–66